Gender Inequality in Our Changing World

Gender Inequality in Our Changing World: A Comparative Approach focuses on the contemporary United States but places it in historical and global context. Written for sociology of gender courses, this textbook identifies conditions that encourage greater or lesser gender inequality, explains how gender and gender inequality change over time, and explores how gender intersects with other hierarchies, especially those related to race, social class, and sexual identity. The authors integrate historical and international materials as they help students to think both theoretically and empirically about the causes and consequences of gender inequality, both in their own lives and in the lives of others worldwide.

Lori Kenschaft is an independent scholar, teacher, and organizer with special interests in Islam, economic inequality, and reforming the criminal justice system. She has taught at Boston University and Harvard University and is the author of two previous books: *Lydia Maria Child: The Quest for Racial Justice* and *Reinventing Marriage: The Love and Work of Alice Freeman Palmer and George Herbert Palmer*. She holds a doctorate in American Studies from Boston University and a Masters in Theological Studies from the Harvard Divinity School.

Roger Clark is a professor in the Sociology Department of Rhode Island College and has taught gender using a cross-cultural/historical approach for twenty years. He is the coauthor, with Emily Stier Adler, of *An Invitation to Social Research: How It's Done*, currently in its fifth edition, and is the author or coauthor of more than 70 articles and book chapters, mostly on gender and gender inequality.

Desirée Ciambrone is a professor in the Sociology Department of Rhode Island College. She has taught courses titled "Unequal Sisters," which uses a multicultural feminist approach, and "Men, Women, and Bodies," which draws on her research in health care, aging, disability, HIV, and care-taking. She is the author of *Women's Experiences with HIV/AIDS: Mending Fractured Selves*.

Gender Inequality in Our Changing World

A Comparative Approach

Lori Kenschaft and Roger Clark, with Desirée Ciambrone

Routledge
Taylor & Francis Group

NEW YORK AND LONDON

First published 2016
by Routledge
711 Third Avenue, New York, NY 10017

and by Routledge
2 Park Square, Milton Park, Abingdon, Oxon, OX14 4RN

Routledge is an imprint of the Taylor & Francis Group, an informa business

Library of Congress Cataloging in Publication Data
Kenschaft, Lori J.
  Gender inequality in our changing world: a comparative approach /
  by Lori Kenschaft and Roger Clark, with Desirée Ciambrone.
  pages cm
  Includes bibliographical references and index.
  1. Women – Social conditions. 2. Women's rights. 3. Sex discrimination.
  4. Equality. I. Title.
  HQ1155.K46 2016
  305.4 – dc23
  2015000378

ISBN: 978-0-415-73310-6 (hbk)
ISBN: 978-0-415-73311-3 (pbk)
ISBN: 978-1-315-84864-8 (ebk)

Typeset in Stone Serif and Frutiger
by Florence Production Ltd, Stoodleigh, Devon, UK

CONTENTS

PREFACE

Gender Inequality in Our Changing World

This book is about what makes gender inequality change and what makes gender inequality resistant to change. We focus on the United States, since we expect that most of our readers will be in the United States and we believe it is particularly important to understand one's own country. We also believe, however, that people living in the twenty-first century need to have a global perspective. The world is increasingly interconnected as people and even more ideas regularly travel around the planet. About one in eight U.S. residents was born in another country, and many more will at some point travel, study, or work abroad. The forces of international trade, travel, migration, media, and the Internet affect nearly everyone worldwide. We believe we cannot really understand even the United States unless we examine its similarities and differences with other countries – the ways it partakes of larger patterns, and the ways it is distinctive. And just trying to understand the United States is not sufficient for navigating the global world we all live in.

Therefore, unlike most other text books about gender, we take a thoroughly comparative approach. Each chapter includes not just information about the United States and other countries, but also analyses that are informed by observations from around the world. International perspectives are not provided in separate sections or boxes, but instead integrated into the core of our arguments. We cannot, of course, provide in-depth information about every country and every topic, so instead we provide overviews of big patterns and a sense of recent changes. To some degree we focus on India and China (which together contain more than a third of the world's people), Muslim-majority countries, and sub-Saharan Africa. But we include the whole world in our scope, and most chapters include global maps that help students visualize worldwide patterns.

Our book is comparative in other ways too. We all have multiple identities, not just those of gender, and these other identities profoundly affect our experience and performance of gender. It is one thing to be a middle-aged wealthy white man on Wall Street, another to be a young poor black man in Detroit, and yet another to be an old Asian gay man living in rural California. Women's performances of femininity are similarly affected by their race, ethnicity, skin color, social class, age, geographic location, religion, sexual identities, physical ability, and many other factors. One of the emphases of this book, therefore, will be on the ways in which multiple intersecting identities shape people's experiences. Some books that say they are about gender are actually about women, but we intend to persuade readers that men and boys are just as gendered as women and girls. Understanding gender and gender inequality therefore requires looking at the world from many different perspectives.

Unlike other sociology of gender texts, ours is deeply historical, concerned with patterns and idiosyncrasies of change. We focus on change for three reasons. First, current patterns and practices often make a lot more sense if one understands how they evolved historically. Second, gender patterns have changed dramatically in the United States and many other places in the last two centuries, or even the last fifty years. Any language that suggests gender is static and unchanging is simply inaccurate. Finally, many people are intentionally trying to reduce gender inequality. Some of these people are motivated primarily by a sense of justice: they believe individuals' lives should not be constrained by gender. Others are motivated more by the growing awareness that increasing gender equality tends to have many other positive effects. Many specialists in international development, for example, now see gender inequality as a significant factor in keeping poor countries poor, as it deprives girls and women of the education, health care, and economic autonomy that will enable them to raise healthy children and contribute the most to their communities. If one wants to reduce gender inequality, it helps greatly to understand both how change has happened in the past and the impediments to change.

This book contains four sections. The introduction explores the concept of gender, offering seven different perspectives for students to consider. This chapter is relatively short so that it can be read during a half-week at the beginning of a semester. The next four chapters focus on four arenas that one might consider the crux of the issue in creating gender inequality: economics, family structures, violence, and the control of sexuality. Each of these chapters opens with an exploration of the key theories within each arena, making the case for its importance, and then discusses some specific issues within the United States and other countries. The sixth chapter stands alone, as it maps the consequences of gender inequality and other forms of inequality in terms of who lives and who dies. The second half of the book examines continuity and change within five important social institutions: education, politics, religion, media, and sports. We conclude with a final short chapter, suitable for the end of a semester, about three possible trajectories for the future of gender inequality.

Each chapter ends with a "Develop Your Position" section with questions that encourage students to engage with what they have read, connect it with their personal experience, and articulate and critique their own beliefs. Some questions are intended to help students ease into the material, while others are more challenging or may require some time for a small research project. These questions could be used as homework assignments and/or to stimulate classroom discussions.

In the end materials, a glossary provides short definitions of key ideas that may be unfamiliar to some readers. If a word is in the glossary, it appears in bold face the first time it is used in up to three chapters. The references section provides many options for additional reading and research.

A companion website, located at www.routledge.com/kenschaft, provides resources for both students and instructors. A list of films and video clips provides options for both classroom use and independent browsing. The website also includes color versions of the global maps contained in the book. We have found that collectively looking at and discussing the significance of these maps can be an excellent classroom activity, and we encourage instructors to consider projecting them on a classroom screen or wall. Instructors will also find, in the instructors' section, lists of potential topics for classroom discussions or essay assignments associated with each chapter.

The website also includes a selective list of organizations that are working to reduce gender inequality. No such list can begin to be comprehensive as there are probably millions of organizations, large and small, working on issues mentioned in this book. We realize, however, that some students can find it frustrating to just learn about problems without being offered any suggestions about how they can help. The "making a difference" section of the website therefore offers pointers to a few of the many organizations that are doing good work.

We are extremely grateful to our colleagues at other institutions for their generous comments on earlier drafts of the book:

Margo DeMello, Central New Mexico Community College

Ashley Vancil, University of Missouri

Jennifer Graves, Houston Community College

Danielle Hidalgo, Montana State University, Bozeman

Marybeth Stalp, University of Northern Iowa

Gregory Maddox, Southern Illinois University

Dana Dunn, University of Texas, Arlington

Amy Reynolds, Wheaton College

Zach Richer, University of Maryland

Donna King, University of North Carolina, Wilmington

Carol Caronna, Towson University

Danielle Giffort, University of Illinois at Chicago

Kristenne Robison, Westminster College

Elroi Windsor, Salem College

Ana Liberato, University of Kentucky

Amanda Moras, Sacred Heart University

Staci Newmahr, Buffalo State University

Nancy Sonleitner, University of Tennessee, Martin

LaDawn Prieto Johnson, Biola University

Bridget Seeley, Arizona State University, Tempe

Lisa Winters, Coastal Carolina University

We owe a debt of gratitude to Samantha Barbaro, our supportive and knowledgeable Routledge editor. We would also like to give special thanks to some of those who have given us their time, patience, inspiration, and support, including Bertha Clark, John Clark, Beverly Lyon Clark, Adam Clark, Wendy Clark, Patricia Kenschaft, Randy Smith, and Steve Kropper.

CHAPTER 1

Introduction
What Is Gender?

INTRODUCTION

If you had lived in 1900 nearly every aspect of your days would be shaped by **gender**, though the details of what that meant varied greatly from place to place. If you were a white woman living in an American city, for example, you might have a job for a few years before you married, but afterwards you were expected to stay home and raise children. If you were an American man you were expected to spend most of your waking hours working to support your family. Around the world, men had nearly all official authority: women were excluded from nearly all political and corporate positions, only men could vote in almost all elections, and most religious communities did not ordain women or allow them to speak during a worship service. Wives everywhere were expected to obey their husbands. People everywhere worked and socialized primarily with others of their own gender. Most colleges did not admit women, and those that did often segregated them in the classroom. In short, gender differences were strong and obvious, and most people took gender inequality for granted.

Today, gender is much less salient in the organization of the United States and many other countries. Women now work in almost every profession: they are politicians, executives, scientists, and clergy (though some religions still do not allow women to be clergy). Most American mothers work for pay, and growing numbers of men feel that being a good father means far more than just being a good provider. American men and women socialize freely, and many people have close cross-gender friendships that are not romantic. Nearly everyone has classmates or colleagues of the other gender.

Gender inequality still exists, however. Men still hold the large majority of high-income and high-power positions: most politicians, CEOs, investment bankers, celebrated athletes, and so on are male. American women persistently earn less than men, even if they work full-time in the same occupations with the same education. Mothers are widely seen as having ultimate responsibility for their children, and women still do most childcare and housework. The unequal division of parenting accounts for some of the income gap between women and men, but even young women without children earn less than similar men (BLS, 2012; Correll, 2013; Coontz, 2012).

Gender greatly affects patterns of violence. Around the world, men are much more likely than women to be perpetrators of violence, while women are more likely to be victims of sexual violence and violence by an intimate partner. Nearly one in five American women has been raped, compared to about one in 71 American men (Black *et al.*, 2011: 1). A quarter of American women report they have experienced serious physical violence from an intimate partner sometime in their lives, compared to an eighth of American men (Breiding *et al.*, 2014: 2). Men, however, are more likely to die from violence (WHO, 2011a). In the United States, white men are more than twice as likely as white women to be murdered, while black men are nearly six times as likely as black women to be murdered (FBI, 2010). As we will see later, violence against both women and men is often driven by gender.

Gender inequality varies greatly around the world, but in some places it is intense. In 15 countries a married woman may not take a job without her husband's permission, and in 25 countries she may not decide where to live. In five countries her husband exclusively owns and controls the household's money, land, and property – even if she earned the income (World Bank, 2013b: 16, 29). About 250 million women were married before the age of 15, nearly always in a marriage arranged by their families, often without their consent. More than a quarter of the women in India were married by the age of 15, as were nearly 40 percent in Bangladesh – and the percentage is rising in Iraq and other war-torn countries where parents feel they cannot feed their daughters or protect them from rape (UNICEF, 2014; Brown, 2014). Some of these girls have not even reached puberty before they are required to have sex with their husbands whenever he wishes (Ali *et al.*, 2010). A third of South African men and a quarter of Indian men admit that they have raped a woman or girl (Jewkes *et al.*, 2012; Barker *et al.*, 2011: 46). In China more than a million female fetuses were aborted in 2008 because the couple wanted a son (World Bank, 2011a: 15). In Chad one in 15 women dies in childbirth (WHO *et al.*, 2012: 32). In southern Asia only half of the adult women can read and write, compared with three-quarters of the men (UNESCO, 2010).

Trying to rank which countries have more or less gender inequality is a vexed venture. Figure 1.1, for example, is based on the United Nations' Gender Inequality Index, which makes Saudi Arabia and the United States look comparable. Saudi women tend to be better educated than Saudi men (partly because young women have few options other than studying), they are better represented in the Saudi Shura Council than the U.S. Congress (though Saudi Arabia is really ruled by the Saudi family), and their rates of teen pregnancy and death in childbirth are low (both good things). Together, these factors give Saudi Arabia a moderately good score. This index does not take into account numerous less measurable factors, such as social segregation of the genders or the requirement that every adult Saudi woman have a male guardian. No index can take into account the frequency and severity of

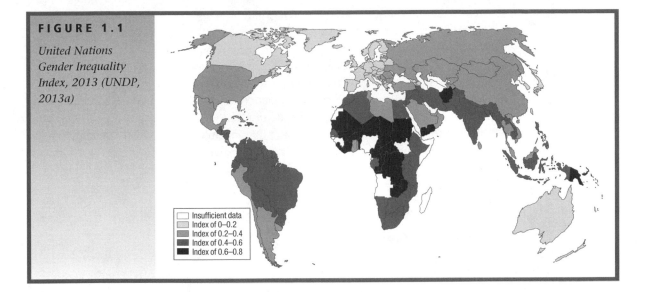

FIGURE 1.1

United Nations Gender Inequality Index, 2013 (UNDP, 2013a)

gender-related violence against women, as comparable international data simply do not exist. Any comparisons of gender inequality therefore need to be interpreted thoughtfully.

Many different observations suggest, however, that gender inequality tends to be highest in Africa, the Middle East, and southern Asia, and lowest in wealthy countries. Latin American countries historically had quite high levels of gender inequality, as well as other forms of inequality, but they have changed rapidly in recent decades and most are now more moderate. The Nordic countries (Denmark, Finland, Iceland, Norway, and Sweden) often come out at or near the top in measures of gender equality, but even there gender inequality persists. Only 6 percent of Norwegian companies, for example, have a female chief executive (*Economist*, 2014n).

The United States has more gender inequality than most wealthy countries, and ranks worse than many middle-income countries on a variety of measures. Men and women are more likely to receive the same pay for the same work, for example, in 64 other countries (WEF, 2014: 65). As of July 2014, 103 countries had a higher percentage of women in their national legislatures (Inter-Parliamentary Union, 2014). Women are five times as likely to die in childbirth in the United States as in Sweden, and 49 countries have lower maternal death rates (WHO *et al.*, 2012. 32–36). We will say more about these and many other topics later. For now, however, it is enough to point out that the United States is not an exemplar of gender equality.

The first four chapters of this book will offer several theories about the root causes of gender inequality. Some people believe that the origins of gender inequality are fundamentally economic: men's and women's different access to material resources and the power and respect that often accompany them. Other people believe the crux of the issue is family structures: how families regulate inheritance, marriage, childrearing, and so on. Other people believe that gendered violence is at the heart of all other forms of gender inequality. And other people believe that control of sexuality is the key issue. One simple definition of a **theory** is a way of thinking that identifies, explains, and predicts patterns in a wide range of observations, and all of these theories are supported by many observations made in many different contexts. We will not provide one unified "theory of gender inequality," because we have found the world more complicated than any one perspective can encompass. We therefore offer a variety of perspectives – you might think of them as mental tools – that we believe are helpful. We believe that all of these theories have merit and are worth your consideration.

WHAT IS GENDER? SEVEN PERSPECTIVES

First, though, we need to address an even more basic question: What is gender?

Social scientists typically use the term **sex** to refer to the reproductive biology that humans are born with – the organs, genetics, hormones, and secondary sex characteristics that enable new human beings to be born – while they use the term gender to describe how people understand the social and cultural significance of sex. Like many words, however, sex and gender have multiple meanings and connotations. Americans today may use one or more of at least seven different mental frameworks for understanding gender. We believe it is important to have a basic understanding of each of these seven frameworks, though you are likely to find some of them more plausible than others.

Essentialist Perspectives

Many traditional cultures, including the United States historically, saw sex and gender as a seamless whole. People believed that women and men had fundamentally different talents, tastes, desires, and destinies. These gender differences, they believed, were created by God and/or nature, and were simply part of reality. This perspective is often called **essentialism**, as it suggests that women and men are different in their essences – not just in their reproductive capacities, but also in their basic human natures. In this framework, sex and gender are considered synonyms, but people often prefer to use the word "gender" as a euphemism for the more earthy "sex."

The naive forms of essentialism have been widely discredited. Anyone who is reasonably well informed now acknowledges that gender varies in different cultures and changes over time, so gender is not an immutable creation of either God or nature. Many **feminists** look skeptically at any hint of essentialism, as essentialist arguments have often been used to justify existing practices and hierarchies. The idea that men are naturally inclined to rape, for example, has been used to argue that women should stay out of men's way rather than holding rapists accountable for their actions. Here and in many other examples, the belief that men and women are essentially different serves to perpetuate gender inequality.

One reason that essentialist arguments persist is that culture goes very deep into people's psyches. People often draw conclusions about differences between men and women by observing the people around them, but just because something is ubiquitous in one time and place does not mean it is universal. If you grow up inside a culture, the expectations of that culture will often seem intuitively obvious to you – like "second nature." Many American men, for example, feel uncomfortable if they travel to parts of Asia where men wear sulus, sarongs, or other garments that to American eyes look like skirts, especially if they try to dress like the local men. While their rational brains may tell them that clothing is a cultural phenomenon, their emotions may still insist that wearing a skirt is unnatural. Just because something is cultural does not mean it is easy, or even possible, to change at will – and just because a behavior feels natural does not mean that it is. In these cases, essentialist arguments give us important insights into people's subjective experiences, but not into the underlying nature of gender.

A subtler variant of essentialism, sometimes called evolutionary psychology, suggests that males and females have come under different evolutionary pressures because of their different roles in physical reproduction. In its rigid forms, evolutionary psychology can suggest that human behavior is static and predetermined, a belief that nearly all social scientists reject. In its more nuanced forms, however, it speaks of propensities and patterns. Take, for example, the easily measured physical characteristic of height. Men tend to be taller than women, on average, but we all know that some women are taller than some men. Height is also affected by non-genetic factors, such as nutrition. If you want to reach an item on a high shelf, it makes sense to ask the tallest person in the room, not the nearest man. And yet it is true that, on average, men tend to be taller than women. Some scholars argue that we should not ignore the possible role of biology in the rare gender patterns that seem to be universal, such as men's greater propensity toward violence. Using evolutionary history to explain human behavior is fraught with challenges, as people often develop theories that fit their pre-existing beliefs, but nor should we rule out the possibility that biology affects behavior and therefore culture.

Constructivist Perspectives

Most social scientists are **constructivists**, which means they believe gender is created by culture, not by God or nature. Every person is born into a particular **society**, or human community, each of which has its own **culture**, or characteristic ways of thinking, feeling, and behaving. By the age of three children are beginning to learn and follow (at least some of the time) the gendered codes of their culture. Social scientists (including the authors of this book) underline the distinction between sex and gender by using the terms male and female to refer to people's biological sex and **masculine** and **feminine** to refer to gender.

Many constructivists describe social life as an improvisational performance. Children learn the expectations of their society, but no one just follows those expectations. Indeed, it would be impossible to do so, as no society scripts word-for-word every possible scenario. Instead, we learn patterns of behavior that we draw upon as we go through our days and interact with other people. In a sense we are all actors, engaged in a performance both for other people and for ourselves. How we perform affects how others perform for us, and vice versa. Through these improvisational performances we create and re-create a shared world of meanings, symbols, and significance (Goffman, 1959).

Constructivists often refer to people as "performing gender" or "doing gender" to underline that gender is something that people continually create (e.g. West and Zimmerman, 1987; Butler, 1990). Women in many cultures, for example, are expected to keep their legs together and women often sit and stand in ways that minimize the space they occupy. Men, meanwhile, are expected to spread their legs and arms and take up an abundance of space. Such "gender displays" both indicate the individual's adherence to their community's norms and reinforce those norms (Goffman, 1979). Most people display their gender through their clothing, hairstyles, cosmetic use (or lack thereof), the timbres of their voices, the way they walk, and many other nuances of behavior. They thus assist each other in quick and easy gender categorizations.

Not everyone, of course, always follows the codes. Many people sometimes play with gender symbols in a spirit of humor. Some people regularly incorporate ways of being that are associated with the other gender into their own personal style. Although some communities tolerate, or even celebrate, individuals who flout gendered conventions, gender-nonconforming individuals may be subjected to social pressures that range from ridicule to ostracism, violence, and even murder. Most people therefore try to achieve a credible performance of the "correct" gender. Even the most gender-conforming individuals, however, do not always perform to type. Sometimes expectations are self-contradictory, and sometimes people enact behaviors associated with the other gender because they feel they are called for by the situation. The most macho police officer, for example, may display a tender "motherly" style when comforting a grieving child.

Most but not all feminists are constructivists. Many feminist achievements have been predicated on the belief that gender is a cultural category and therefore subject to change. In 1900, for example, women always wore skirts and no woman had ever served on the U.S. Supreme Court. Now, there are women on the Supreme Court who wear pants underneath their judicial robes and act very similarly to the men on the Court. Their presence is a profound challenge to the gender roles of a previous generation, and many people can remember a time when no women had ever served on the Court. (Sandra Day O'Connor, the first female Justice, was appointed by

Ronald Reagan in 1981.) But most women nowadays, when they wear pants or aspire to professional careers, see themselves not as wanting to be a man, but as a woman who wants to do things that men traditionally did. The belief that gender can change is thus rooted in the belief that gender is a cultural construct, not natural or God-given.

Not all constructivists, however, are feminists. Some theorists argue that gender performances are often a source of pleasure for the individuals involved, so feminists should not be so hasty to criticize them or try to eliminate them (Paglia, 1990). Feminists tend to focus on gender inequality, meaning hierarchies based on gender, and **male privilege**, the advantages that come to men simply by virtue of being men. Sometimes, though, gender codes are just a matter of difference: men's shirts button one way, women's another way, and we all get dressed just fine. Constructivists who focus on difference rather than inequality may feel that gender is something to enjoy, even celebrate, rather than challenge or critique.

Doubly Constructivist Perspectives

Some people argue that even the concept that there are two biological sexes is a cultural construction. Some individuals are born with genitalia that are ambiguous in appearance, or with various mismatches between their external appearance, internal organs, and genetics. These people may be called intersex or hermaphroditic, and they are more common than most people realize because many cultures require that every person be neatly categorized as male or female. When a baby is born with ambiguous genitalia, doctors often advise parents to choose surgery that will make the infant look more like one sex or the other – typically a female, as it is easier to cut away tissue than to add it. Some people argue that if sex sometimes needs to be assigned with a scalpel, nature does not really include only two sexes (Karkazis, 2008; Reis, 2009).

In the United States it is common to speak of just two sexes – male and female but some cultures recognize one, three, or more sexes (Roscoe, 2000; Nanda *et al.*, 2014). Until the eighteenth century most educated Europeans held that there is only one sex. The basic plan, physicians taught, had genitals outside the body, but if the fetus lacked sufficient energy the genitals did not descend during development. Women were thus defective men, which explained why they were intellectually inferior and needed to be kept under male rule (Laqueur, 1990). In India and Pakistan, people called *hijras* have been a culturally recognized (and often stigmatized) third sex for millennia. Today *hijras* are often called **transgendered**, but in traditional Indian culture they were seen as a distinctive third sex (Nanda, 1990). In 2014 India's Supreme Court ruled that government identity documents should include three sex/gender boxes, and that *hijras* should be considered an official minority and protected from discrimination (*New York Times* Editorial Board, 2014).

Some people argue that we should be wary of the terms "male" and "female," "men" and "women," because they reflect an unmerited assumption that these are meaningful categories. Sex as well as gender, they warn, is a cultural construction (Fausto-Sterling, 2000; Karkazis, 2008).

Other people argue that people's bodily experiences, while certainly interpreted by culture, are not just a cultural construction. Instead, they argue, sex-specific physical experiences can affect people's self-perceptions and relationships with others (e.g., Altman, 2001; Huber, 2007). For example, most women throughout most of human history spent most of their adult years pregnant or nursing, both of which are physically demanding experiences. Not all females can get pregnant, of course: some are too young or too old, and some are not fertile for any of wide range of other reasons, intentional or unintentional. But even today most women give birth at least once in their lives, and historically most women gave birth many times. Men did not. Having a body that is capable of becoming pregnant is, these gender-constructivists argue, a meaningful distinction that is not just a matter of cultural interpretation. Other sex-specific physical experiences, such as menstruation and erections, may also affect not just individuals' feelings, beliefs, and actions but also collective cultural forms. Although individuals always have their own personal experiences, the existence of individual variation does not invalidate the broader patterns sociologists call culture.

Genderqueer Perspectives

Some people argue that all of the conventional two-category divisions of sex (male and female), gender (masculine and feminine), and sexual orientation (heterosexual and homosexual) are part of a cultural system designed to control individual behavior (Butler, 1990; Valocchi, 2005). They use the term **heteronormativity** to refer to the cultural ideology that urges people to think of themselves as women or men, feminine or masculine, and heterosexual but not homosexual. When people engage in conventional performances, they argue, they reinforce the conventional boundaries and expectations. Although most people find these boundaries and expectations familiar and therefore comfortable, the price is human freedom not just for those who know they do not fit into the conventional categories, but also for those who have been unknowingly but successfully warped to match the prevailing norms (Wilchins, 2004).

Some people challenge the whole concept of gender assignment by mix-and-matching signifiers in ways that disrupt the cultural tendency to label people. They may adopt body language, vocal tones, clothing, and hairstyles that make it difficult for people to guess the shape of their genitalia, an ambiguity that many viewers find disconcerting. Sometimes these people call themselves androgynous, indicating that they partake of both masculine and feminine qualities, or **genderqueer**, indicating that they seek to break out of the boundaries of gender. Others refuse to identify themselves even that far, preferring to keep people guessing.

Genderqueer people seek to disrupt not just the aspects of gender that are associated with inequality, but all the little social signals and gender performances that suggest gender is an important category – that it is important to be able to identify an individual's gender, and presumably sex, quickly and reliably. Men's and women's hairstyles, for example, are sometimes (though certainly not always) equally comfortable and easy to maintain, but even when gender differences are inherently inconsequential their ubiquity sends the message that gender is important. Genderqueer people call into question the importance and reliability of the concepts of sex, gender, and sexual orientation (which is predicated on the assumption that people's identities are determined by the sex category of the people they are attracted to). The real goal, they suggest, is not just to treat all categories of people decently, but to break ourselves of the habit of categorizing people.

Transgender Perspectives

In many societies, both traditional and modern, some people describe themselves as having been born into a body of a different sex than the gender they feel comfortable performing. Traditional societies have a plethora of different names for these people, but in modern English they are often called transgendered or simply **trans.** People who identify as men after being assigned female at birth may be called **FTMs** (female to male), **trans men**, or men, whether or not they have had sex reassignment surgery. Similarly, people who identify as women after being assigned male at birth may be called **MTFs** (male to female), **trans women**, or women. People whose gender identity is in line with the sex assigned to them at birth may be called **cisgendered** (literally "same gendered").

Transgendered people suggest that gender identity is more basic and immutable than biological sex. Gender, they argue, is a deep and intrinsic part of one's personal identity, one's psychological structure. They thus see gender as not fundamentally a cultural construction. They acknowledge, of course, that how people exhibit gender varies in different times and places, but they feel that gender identity goes deeper than all such manifestations. Being forced to perform the other gender, they argue, is a violation of their nature (Boylan, 2003).

Sex, on the other hand, can be negotiated – with surgery, with hormones, or maybe with words on a birth certificate. Modern medical technology makes it possible for people to choose hormonal treatments and/or sex reassignment surgery to bring their bodies more into line with their gender identity. Some transgender people have gone to court to change their drivers' licenses and even birth certificates to match their gender identity, not their biological sex as assigned at birth. Such court cases underline that sex itself can be a social and legal construct, not something determined solely by nature.

People who are transgender, genderqueer, or otherwise gender-nonconforming may experience high levels of social stigma. They may be rejected by their families, discriminated against by schools and employers, unable to stay in homeless shelters or other facilities that sort people by gender, and subjected to verbal harassment and physical violence (Beam, 2007). One study found that trans people were more than twice as likely as other Californians to live below the poverty level. Although many had professional positions, almost a quarter reported that they had resorted to the "street economy" of prostitution and selling drugs to survive (Hartzell *et al.*, 2009: 7–8).

Trans women are especially at risk. In 2013, 13 trans women were murdered in hate crimes in the United States, 12 of them trans women of color. Most years there are no reports of hate-crime murders of trans men (NCAVP, 2014: 8). A study of transgendered people's experiences in the workplace found that many trans women experienced harassment, demotion, and termination, while trans men typically found they enjoyed more respect and authority, and sometimes even more pay (Schilt and Wiswall, 2008).

Today, growing numbers of both transgendered and cisgendered people believe that human liberation requires affirming transgender identities and life patterns. The transgender rights movement argues that transgender individuals should be accepted and affirmed, and that people who feel pulled toward gender-non-conforming behavior should be encouraged to explore the possibility that they are transgendered (Brill and Pepper, 2008; Erickson-Schroth, 2014).

Some feminists believe it is liberating for individuals to be able to choose their own gender, or even to change it day by day. Other feminists, however, are concerned that transgender activism represents a new form of gender essentialism. Millions of girls and women have sought to engage in activities traditionally considered masculine without calling into question their own sex. Transgender discourse can encourage people to interpret a gender-nonconforming girl as wanting to be a boy, rather than wanting to be a human being who is not limited by gender. On an individual level, the result may be hormone treatments and surgery, which can entail significant health risks. On a societal level, the result may be a retreat from the idea that gender is a cultural construction, not part of one's nature, and therefore open to change. Real human liberation, some feminists conclude, means not using gender to constrain individuals' self-images and aspirations (Jeffreys, 2014).

Institutionalist Perspectives

Some social scientists and feminists argue that focusing on the level of individual identity and behavior obscures most of how gender really functions. Instead, they believe, we need to look at **social institutions** – patterns of behavior that persist over the generations, embody lots of rules and assumptions, and govern a network of activities. An economic system, for example, is a social institution that organizes work and distributes money and other rewards. Families are institutions that organize intimate relationships and provide for the care of the young, old, and sick. What we usually call an "institution" – a particular school, college, church, synagogue, mosque, corporation, even a political party – is typically part of a much larger social institution that works through these smaller institutions but does not require the existence of any of them. Any given school can open or close, for example, without changing the institution of education.

Social institutions tend to have a lot of staying power. They are self-replicating: each generation is raised within their rules and assumptions and learns to take them for granted. They are also interconnected in ways that make them resilient. The formal and informal rules of the American economic system, for example, are supported by laws, schools, families, and the internalized assumptions of millions of people. A handful of rebels may be able to make a life for themselves off the grid, but it is very difficult to fundamentally change the system. Most people, furthermore, value the social institutions that shape their lives, as such institutions provide a degree of predictability and stability that most human beings appreciate. People often resist changes to social institutions simply because they prefer the familiar, even with its drawbacks, to the risks of the unknown.

Yet social institutions do change and evolve. This book will provide many examples of social institutions that have changed in recent decades and centuries, often but not always in the direction of increasing gender equality. Institutions may change in response to changed economic circumstances, new technologies, or political agitation (Acemoglu and Robinson, 2012). American families, for example, are now very different than they were in the 1950s, the 1850s, or the 1750s (Coontz, 1992). Institutions may also change in response to war, colonization, epidemics, or famine. Such shocks may shatter social institutions, as happened in Somalia in the 1990s and Syria in the 2010s. They may also leave social institutions so weakened that a society is vulnerable to the twin evils of chaos and authoritarian rule (Fukuyama, 2014). Institutions in sub-Saharan Africa, for example, did not recover from the massive disruptions caused by the slave trade and European colonization before they were hit by the massive disruptions caused by HIV/AIDS.

Institutional analysts argue that gender and gender inequality are located within these social institutions and the ways they are organized. For example, all known societies use gender, to one degree or another, to organize work. The details vary greatly, of course, but two things seem to be universal: women have primary responsibility for childrearing and other unpaid work within families, and women are paid less in the formal workforce even when they do the same work as men (WEF, 2014: 65). These facts are related. Many employers and professions, especially but not only those with high status and pay, assume that workers will focus their whole lives on their work responsibilities, with someone else, typically a wife, taking care of their needs and the needs of their families. Such job descriptions may seem gender neutral on the surface, but in reality they give men a huge advantage in pursuing high-status positions (Acker, 1990, 1998).

Some institutional analysts – often called **functionalists** – believe that institutions are generally beneficial to the societies in which they evolved. For example, many small-scale societies used gender as the primary division of labor: girls were taught some skills, boys were taught other skills, and once they became adults they were expected to form heterosexual marriages that brought together both sets of skills. These **gender roles** – or social expectations associated with each sex category – persisted because they increased the productivity and stability of both individual families and society as a whole. Early functionalists argued that gender roles in the United States were similarly beneficial, as they gave men and women complementary skills and aptitudes (men specialized in making money, women specialized in nurturing families) and linked them in a joint effort to maximize the wellbeing of their families and communities (Parsons, 1942, 1954).

At their weakest, functionalists have a hard time explaining social change: if everything is already as good as it could be, why would anything change? Feminists and other critics argued that functionalists extrapolated excessively from their own experiences, ignored the diversity that exists in any large-scale society, and obscured the ways in which gendered expectations damage both women and men. Today most writers about gender avoid the term "gender roles" because they see it as reflecting an overly static worldview.

At their best, however, functionalists offer helpful insights. Social expectations can indeed help a society function more smoothly. For example, when students and professors enter a classroom for the first time they have expectations about how each other will behave, based on their respective social roles. These expectations make it much more likely that students will learn than if everyone made it up as they went along. Similarly, people may accept or support existing gendered expectations not because they are misogynistic or brainwashed, but because they see benefits in those expectations to themselves and the people they care about. Three-quarters of Americans, for example, believe that the growing number of women working for pay outside the home has made it harder for parents to raise children well (Wang *et al.*, 2013: 6). Such concerns suggest that current social institutions may not adequately provide for the childrearing functions that Americans of previous generations (but not all societies) assigned to families.

When social institutions appear dysfunctional, functionalists may attribute the problem to **cultural lag** – the fact that different aspects of a culture can change at different speeds, so an institution that was functional at one time period may no longer be so under other circumstances. For example, most American schools dismiss children in the middle of the afternoon, a time when many American adults are expected to be at their jobs. Many parents rely on ad hoc after-school care, which varies greatly in quality, to fill the gap caused by the economy changing more quickly than the educational system.

Other institutional analysts, however, argue that institutional patterns are not usually created by benign attempts to make a society work as well as possible for everyone. Instead, they believe that different groups of people typically have different interests and typically pursue their own interests. For example, men in many societies – including the United States – have preferentially hired and promoted men because they felt more affiliation with other men than to women. White people, similarly, have preferentially hired and promoted white people because they felt more comfortable with people they perceived as "similar" rather than "different." The same basic argument can be made about many other groups in many other contexts. Around the world and through history, people have often considered it morally virtuous to be loyal to members of their own group (Niebuhr, 1932; Haidt, 2012).

Conflict perspectives therefore analyze how groups of people manipulate institutions to benefit themselves and disadvantage others. In this view, men are usually advantaged by institutions not because that happens to be how things worked out, but because men successfully shaped those institutions to benefit their own group.

Institutional analyses help explain why gender inequality can be so resilient among people who have egalitarian ideals. Just being of good will is not enough to end gender inequality if it is built into institutional systems. On the other hand, institutional analyses also help explain why gender patterns can change so quickly when institutions are changing due to other forces. For example, China's "one child" policies meant that many families had only daughters and could no longer favor their (nonexistent) sons. As parents realized that they would have to rely on their daughters in their old age, they invested in their daughters' education and employability. The Communist regime's desire to stabilize population size thus decreased gender inequality in families, schools, and workplaces.

Many institutions have changed and are changing because of **globalization**. The term "globalization" is used in many ways, and often loosely, but at its core is the growth in international travel of just about everything – money, trade goods, tourists, migrants, students, knowledge, ideas, media, and so on. Globalization has been occurring, with occasional temporary reversals, for centuries, and its effects have often been devastating. Both the Atlantic slave trade and the European colonization of North America, with its destruction of Native American cultures, were consequences of globalization. In the last few decades, though, globalization has begun to reduce global economic inequality, as many poor countries (most notably China) have used trade to improve their average standards of living. Economic inequality has simultaneously increased inside most individual countries, as global markets often help the rich get richer while less-skilled people fall behind. Although economic inequality has fallen in much of Latin America, long the most unequal continent, it has risen throughout most of Asia, Europe, and North America and in parts of Africa (*Economist*, 2012b). We will talk much more about the gendered implications of globalization throughout this book.

Intersectionality

Some people argue that gender never exists in isolation. Whether one looks at the personal or institutional level, how people experience gender is fundamentally shaped by a whole range of other social variables, including geographic location, age, race, ethnicity, nationality, skin color, religious affiliations, social class, sexual identities, levels of ability and disability, and many other factors. These factors are not simply additive, but instead interact with each other in ways that can be complex, powerful, and unpredictable. Some theorists therefore argue that any discussion of gender needs to focus on **intersectionality** – the connections between multiple coexisting differences, hierarchies, and systems of domination (Crenshaw, 1991; Collins, 1990). To understand the world, we need to look not just at who gets attention and who gets marginalized, but also at who gets to decide which perspectives are important (Enloe, 2013).

Around the world and over the millennia, people have demonstrated a tendency to form groups, categorize each other, and try to dominate other groups. The criteria for these groups have varied greatly and are sometimes called race, ethnicity, nationality, or religion. All of these words refer to cultural constructions that people have used to identify themselves and others. Each has been used to justify enslaving or otherwise subjugating another group, and each has been used to justify war and attempted genocide. Each has also been a positive source of personal and cultural identity. The meanings of these words are thus highly variable and context-dependent, and often highly politicized (Sussman, 2014; Hobbs, 2014).

In the United States, all of these categories have been used to establish and enforce hierarchies. The concept of race has been used to justify chattel slavery, social segregation, employment discrimination, differential laws and legal enforcement, rapes, whippings, killings, and many other practices. Numerous government policies have preferentially aided white families in accumulating wealth, security, and power. After World War II, for example, government-subsidized mortgages made homeownership newly possible for millions of families. Mortgage subsidies were unavailable, however, in areas with a high percentage of black residents, which were "red-lined" by the federal government. Black people could rarely purchase or rent housing outside majority black neighborhoods, sometimes because of racially restrictive covenants that were supported by the courts and sometimes because of widely practiced discrimination by sellers, landlords, and real estate agents. Black people therefore paid higher rents for worse housing, while they were excluded from the wealth-accumulating effects of homeownership during decades when house prices rose quickly. These patterns cascade through the generations, as parents who accumulate wealth are better prepared to send their children to college and into well-paid careers of their own. Although race is a cultural construction, it has had very real and material effects on people's lives (Lui *et al.*, 2006; Irving, 2014).

Ethnicity, nationality, and religion have similarly been grounds for discrimination and violence. Immigration laws have at times restricted or banned migration from countries that were not white and Christian, while the KKK targeted Catholics and Jews as well as black people (Baker, 2011). Religious bigotry became less acceptable after World War II, as many Americans were appalled by its consequences in Nazi-occupied Europe, and anti-racist movements have made it less acceptable to express prejudices based on ancestry and skin color. Many Muslim Americans can, however, attest that ethnic, national, and religious prejudices still exist (Bayoumi, 2008). While we consider race and ethnicity problematic ways to categorize people, we will use the conventional categories in this book – partly because these categories profoundly

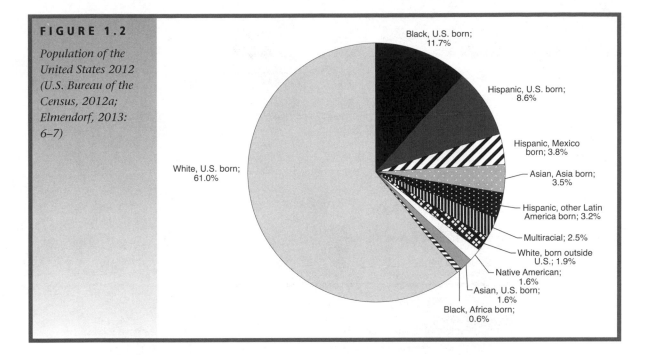

FIGURE 1.2

Population of the United States 2012 (U.S. Bureau of the Census, 2012a; Elmendorf, 2013: 6–7)

White, U.S. born; 61.0%

Black, U.S. born; 11.7%

Hispanic, U.S. born; 8.6%

Hispanic, Mexico born; 3.8%

Asian, Asia born; 3.5%

Hispanic, other Latin America born; 3.2%

Multiracial; 2.5%

White, born outside U.S.; 1.9%

Native American; 1.6%

Asian, U.S. born; 1.6%

Black, Africa born; 0.6%

affect people's lives, and partly because the sociological literature on which we draw uses the conventional categories and it would be very difficult to discuss diversity within the United States without using them.

Race and gender have always been intertwined. Back in the 1680s, the Virginia legislature encouraged the growth of slavery by, among other things, declaring white women tax-exempt if they did exclusively domestic work (Bruce, 1907: 101). These laws successfully discouraged plantation-owners from assigning white female indentured servants to fieldwork, which everyone at the time agreed was hard, unpleasant, and inappropriate for women. Instead, planters purchased black women as well as men to do fieldwork (Brown, 1996). Ever since then, black women have been largely excluded from the protections normatively (though patchily) extended to white women. "Women," in the ostensibly race-neutral formulation, have been portrayed as domestic, delicate, and needing and deserving protection. Black women, however, have been portrayed as strong, resilient, unattractive but sexually available, and capable of lots of hard work — and therefore unfeminine and undeserving of protection. The iconic "woman" is thus assumed to be white (Harris-Perry, 2011). Real black women have always been expected to do lots of hard work, either unpaid or poorly paid, often while raising children under challenging circumstances (Giddings, 2007). Some states even used to include the phrase "white woman" in their legal definitions of rape. A black woman could not, in the eyes of the law, be raped, as she did not have the race/gender status that allowed her to withhold sexual consent (Freedman, 2013: 28).

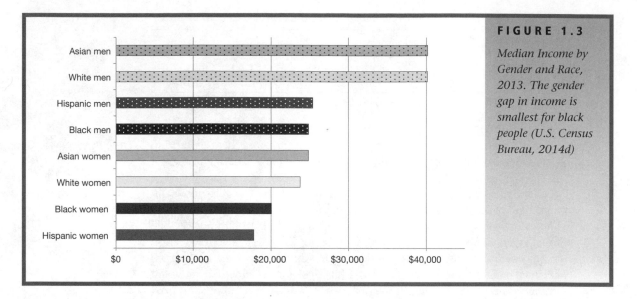

FIGURE 1.3

Median Income by Gender and Race, 2013. The gender gap in income is smallest for black people (U.S. Census Bureau, 2014d)

Being a "black man" is also quite different than being a "white man." Men, for example, are normatively supposed to be assertive and self-confident, and in white men these qualities are often seen as reflecting competence and leadership ability. In a black man, however, similar behavior may be seen as threatening, angry, or even criminal (Lopez, 2003; Ghandnoosh, 2014). Indeed, black men are as likely as black women and white women to report that they have experienced gender-related discrimination in hiring, pay, or promotion (Pew Research Center, 2013b: 50).

Generations of racial discrimination mean that race and social class are intertwined, though they are not identical. One important aspect of social class is financial – both incomes (how much a person or family earns) and wealth (what assets they have to fall back on in hard times or to mobilize for special projects, such as purchasing a house or a college education). Racial differences in wealth are even larger than racial differences in income. Nearly half of single black and Hispanic women have a negative net worth, meaning their debts exceed their assets (Insight, 2010).

According to government statistics, the poverty line for a single person in 2013 was an annual income of $11,490, and anyone above that level was officially not poor (Federal Register, 2013: 5183). Most people, however, recognize that earning $100 or even $1,000 over the poverty line does not change a person's circumstances very much and would still describe such a person as poor. In the United States, black, Hispanic, and Native American people generally earn less than white and Asian people, and they are much more likely to be poor – especially if they are children or women. There are, however, plenty of poor white people: about 19 million white Americans are officially poor, compared with 14 million Hispanic Americans and 11 million black Americans (U.S. Census Bureau, 2013b).

FIGURE 1.4

Median Wealth of Single Individuals, Ages 18–64, by Gender and Race, 2007. Gender gaps in wealth are smaller for white people than black or Hispanic people – but racial gaps dwarf gender gaps (Insight, 2010)

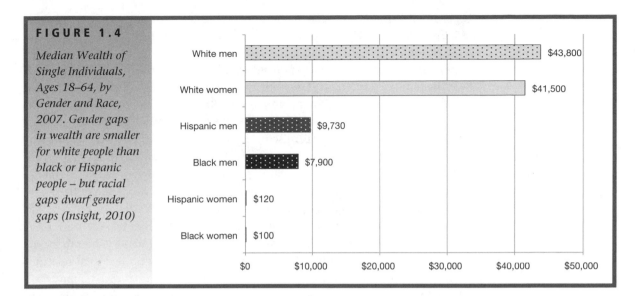

FIGURE 1.5

Poverty Rates by Gender, Race, and Age, 2011. More than a third of black, Native American, and Hispanic children lived in poverty in 2011, compared to 8 percent of white men (Entmacher et al., 2012: 13)

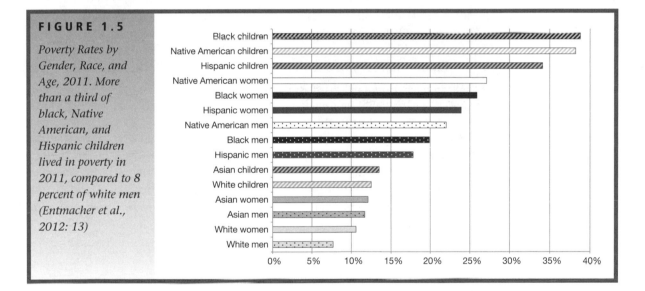

Social class is not just about money. When, for example, professional-class young adults go to college or graduate school their incomes may temporarily fall below the poverty line, but they remain part of the professional class because they and others continue to have professional-class expectations for their lives. Even more than income, then, social class is defined by status, expectations, assumptions, and behaviors – both how one sees oneself and how one is seen by others. Although the boundaries of social classes are blurry, class profoundly affects people's experiences at every stage of life (Sennett and Cobb, 1972; Larcau, 2003; Stuber,

2011; Leondar-Wright, 2014). Since there is no objective way to identify social class, especially for large numbers of people, sociologists typically use education or income as a proxy for class.

Another important hierarchy that intersects with all others is the appearance of heterosexuality. Most cultures have expected individuals to contract heterosexual marriages and conceive children, and many (but not all) have also expected individuals to refrain from expressing erotic desires for other people categorized as their own gender. As we will discuss at length in Chapter 5, these patterns have manifested in many different ways in different times and places. In every society, however, some people have not conformed to the heterosexual mandate. The language used to describe such people has varied greatly, but today they may identify themselves as lesbian, gay, bisexual, asexual, or a variety of other possibilities. Unlike other stigmatized groups, sexual minorities are usually minorities within their families as well, which can add to their isolation and vulnerability.

For most of the twentieth century, most Americans saw homosexual relationships as incompatible with acceptable masculinity or femininity. Indeed, many men felt that their masculinity required them to oppose homosexuality, a perception that fueled verbal, physical, and sexual attacks on men and women who were perceived as not heterosexual (Kimmel, 2006). In 2010, bisexual women were more than 50 percent more likely than lesbian or heterosexual women to report that they had experienced rape or sexual assault, while men's risk of sexual assault more than doubled if they were gay or bisexual (Walters *et al.*, 2013: 1). One study found that American teens who identify as lesbian, gay, or bisexual are roughly ten times as likely as teens who identify as heterosexual to make a suicide attempt that is serious enough to need medical treatment (Kann *et al.*, 2011).

Social acceptance of LGBT (lesbian, gay, bisexual, or transgender) people has increased significantly in the United States and many other countries in the last few decades, but hostility is increasing in some parts of the world (*Economist*, 2014k). A majority of Americans now believe that same-sex marriages and heterosexual marriages should be considered equally valid, including 78 percent of young adults between the ages of 18 and 29 (McCarthy, 2014). A recent large study suggests that approximately 3.4 percent of American adults currently identify as LGBT and people are significantly more likely to identify as LGBT if they are young, female, and/or black, Hispanic, or Asian. A third of LGBT people are not white, compared to just over a quarter of people who identify as heterosexual (Gates and Newport, 2013).

In short, no one performs gender just in the abstract, uninflected by other factors. It is a very different thing to be a young white man who works on Wall Street or a middle-aged white man who runs a ranch in Texas – a black businessman who owns a home in an affluent Atlanta suburb or a young black man who dropped out of high school and lives in inner-city Detroit – a Hasidic Jewish man who lives in Brooklyn or a young Mormon man who lives in Salt Lake City – a young gay man who lives in San Francisco or an elderly gay man who lives in rural Idaho.

Each of these men will perform masculinity, and if he does it well he will receive positive reinforcement and rewards from his community. If he were plopped down into any of the other communities, however, his way of performing masculinity could seem painfully inappropriate. There is no one "masculinity" to which all these men aspire.

Like other societies, however, the United States rewards some forms of masculinity and femininity much more than others. Sociologists use the terms **hegemonic masculinity** or **code masculinity** to refer to the ideal form of masculinity that is most valued and rewarded. We might describe today's ideal American man as white, heterosexual, cisgendered, a college graduate, native-born, tall, physically strong and coordinated, interested in athletics, handsome, Christian but not excessively devout, self-confident, assertive, fearless, dominant, and in a well-paid leadership position. The more a man fits this image, the more he can cloak himself in the aura of code masculinity and benefit from its power. Most men, of course, do not embody all of these characteristics, so they do not reap the full benefits of male advantage. Sometimes they even become the foil against which code masculinity asserts itself, as some men demonstrate their masculinity by defining other men as deviant (Kimmel, 2006).

The comparable terms for women are **rewarded femininity** or **code femininity**. The ideal woman is white, heterosexual, cisgendered, a college graduate, native-born, beautiful, nice, cooperative, warm but polite, sexy but faithful, family oriented, and loyal to a high-status man. Women who can embody these images may find that femininity works well for them, at least some of the time. Women who deviate from these norms – again, most women – are less likely to benefit from social approval. Even the most powerful women, however, do not have as much power as the most powerful men.

CONCLUSION

In this book we will look at gender and gender inequality from many different angles. We will explore how gender changes and how it is resistant to change. We will examine how individuals experience and perform gender and how institutions structure gender in ways that individuals living within those institutions often do not perceive. We will outline cultural norms and typical patterns and explore some of the multitude of ways in which people deviate from those norms and patterns. We will focus on gender but also analyze how gender intersects with other forms of inequality, especially race and class. We will explain how gender inequality can be lethal and show how it degrades the quality of life of men as well as women. We will focus on the United States but offer a worldwide perspective, looking both at countries with exceptionally high and exceptionally low levels of gender inequality. We will give special attention to China and India, which together contain more than a third of the world's people, but also lift up some interesting gender patterns in tiny countries like Sri Lanka and Fiji. Our fundamental goals are to pique your curiosity, help you understand this complex and endlessly changing world we live in, and encourage you to learn more about the topics and places that particularly interest you.

Develop Your Position

1   Which of the seven perspectives on gender outlined above seems most plausible and persuasive to you? Why? (It is fine to choose more than one, but not all seven.) Did reading this chapter change your answer to that question? If so, why? Which of the seven perspectives do you see most commonly used by people around you?

2   Take a moment to think about what you did yesterday – your appearance, action, and words. How did you "do" gender yesterday? Was your performance of gender mostly conventional? Can you see ways in which you performed gender unconventionally? Do any of the ways you do gender nowadays differ from how you did gender at some earlier point in your life? If yes, what are the differences and why did you change? If not, why do you think your performance of gender has remained so stable over time?

3   Take another look at the descriptions we offered above of the "ideal man" and the "ideal woman" – the masculine man and feminine woman that are, we suggest, most rewarded in the United States in the early twenty-first century. Do you agree that these images describe the type of man and woman that are most valued and celebrated in American society? If not, why not? If yes, are there any characteristics you would add to these descriptions? Any characteristics you would omit, or tweak a little bit?

4   Based on your own experiences, as well as anything you have read, make a list of at least five ways that gender inequality benefits men and at least five ways that gender inequality benefits women. Do you agree that, all in all, gender inequality benefits men more than women? Why or why not?

PART I

Four Core Issues

CHAPTER 2

Work and Its Rewards

INTRODUCTION

In every known society, gender affects both the work that individuals do and the rewards associated with different kinds of work. Even the most egalitarian societies display some degree of **gender segregation of occupations**, the tendency of men and women to do different kinds of work. In the United States, one gender holds more than 90 percent of the jobs in ten of the most common 35 occupations. Only 12 of the most common occupations are roughly gender balanced, with each gender holding at least 30 percent of the jobs (Coontz, 2012). The United States also has a significant gender **wage gap**, as women earn less than men at every age, educational level, and racial and ethnic group (BLS, 2012).

Many theories about the origins and mechanisms of gender inequality focus on differential access to work and its rewards, both material and intangible. The basic theory here is simple: the more a woman has to depend on men for food and shelter, security and status, the less power she has in her relationships with those men. Some societies do not allow women to own anything, perhaps with the exception of their clothes or cooking pots. In such societies, the fruits of women's labor are owned and controlled by their male relatives. Women generally receive food and other necessities, but men control land, wealth, and decision-making. In other societies, however, women can earn and control their own livelihoods, which enables them to have more egalitarian relationships with men.

Historians and anthropologists have identified strong, but not perfect, correlations between the economic foundations of a society and its degree of gender inequality in distributing the rewards of work (Blumberg, 2004). The first half of this chapter will outline these patterns, while the second half will explore how gender affects work in the contemporary United States. We will also briefly outline three of the most important theories about why gender segregation of occupations and income inequality continue today: work as gender performance, discrimination, and women's continuing primary responsibility for childrearing and other unpaid **care work**.

GENDER INEQUALITY IN DIFFERENT TYPES OF ECONOMIES

Hunting-Gathering Economies

People in **hunting-gathering** societies harvested food from their environments and regularly shared food and other resources. Each group had a familiar territory that it traveled over the course of a year or longer, but individual land ownership was meaningless and individuals could not accumulate more than they could carry. Since property acquisition was not one of their goals, these communities had a very low level of economic inequality.

Gender was the primary way in which these societies structured work. Anthropological studies suggest that women in food-scarce societies (as most were throughout history and pre-history) nursed their children frequently for several years. This intensive nursing maximized babies' chances of survival by providing nutrition and delaying the mother's next pregnancy until her current child was four or five and able to participate in the daily search for food rather than competing with the newcomer for milk. Most women spent most of their adult lives pregnant or breastfeeding, and their children's survival depended on their presence (Huber, 2007). Women therefore generally did work that was compatible with nursing a toddler, such as collecting plants or shellfish and processing raw foods into edible forms (grinding, cooking, etc.). Men did work that required more travel, upper-body strength, and/or willingness to risk physical harm, such as hunting animals or fighting with other tribes.

These were not universal divisions. In general, the more a society relied on hunting large game, the more it emphasized competition between men, the differences between men and women, and gender segregation of work (Sanday, 1981a: 76–90). Even here there were exceptions, as women hunted large game in about 7 percent of hunting-gathering societies, such as the Agta of the Philippines (Potts and Hayden, 2008: 55; Headland and Headland, 1997).

In most climates, women provided half or more of the calories and shared equitably in food distribution (Lee and Devore, 1968; Blumberg, 2004). Gender and the needs of young children thus loomed large in determining how people spent their time, but the gendered division of labor had relatively little impact on individuals' status and power.

Horticultural Economies

Gendered divisions of labor continued in **horticultural** societies, which used hoes and other light tools to cultivate their fields, but not plows or large domestic animals. Women continued to do work that was compatible with pregnancy and breastfeeding, which now included tending crops as well as making homes and more sophisticated tools and clothes. Indeed, many people suspect that women initially domesticated plants. Gathering women returned to productive locations year after year, observed what aided plants' fertility, and gradually intervened to create more reliable stands of grain, fruit, and vegetables. Over time, they invented basic tools and became horticultural women tending their gardens. Men, meanwhile, continued to do work that involved travel, upper-body strength, or danger, which now might include trade with other groups.

Many horticultural societies allowed an individual to choose which gender to occupy. A man might, for example, decide to wear women's clothes and do women's work, or vice versa (e.g., Amadiume, 1987; Roscoe, 2000). Such gender-crossing by individuals did not, however, disrupt the basic organization of work and life by gender.

Most horticultural societies gave each gender control over the products of their own work. Among the Igbo of southeastern Nigeria, for example, men grew yams and raised flocks while women grew a variety of other crops and made clothes and other handicrafts. Although men typically owned the land, women owned and traded the crops they cultivated and the objects they made. Each gender had its own area of activity, responsibility, and authority (Chuku, 2005).

Many traditional horticultural societies saw men's and women's responsibilities as complementary and equally important. Among the Iroquois of North America, for example, women owned the land and fields passed from mother to daughter. Women thus controlled the "village world" while men were in charge of the "forest world," including hunting and relations with other tribes. Chiefs were men, but they were selected by clan matrons who advised them on matters of war, peace, and other tribal concerns (Demos, 2000).

Not all Native American societies were this gender egalitarian. Some areas of the arid southwest required labor-intensive irrigation systems that were built and maintained by men, who then controlled the irrigated land (Demos, 2000). Men dominated in the Plains tribes, which relied on hunting buffalo rather than horticulture (Hoebel, 1960).

Crops grew easily, though, in the vast wooded areas of the east and west. In these regions, each gender had distinctive work and responsibilities, but they seem to have had more or less equal – though different – power and respect. Some historians see this balance of powers as gender egalitarian, while others are more skeptical of the claim that the genders can be highly differentiated but fundamentally equal. It seems, though, that women and men in many horticultural societies shared fairly equally in the material and non-material rewards of their work (Perdue, 1998; Demos, 2000).

Agricultural and Pastoral Economies

The invention of **agriculture** – which uses plows and domesticated animals (or, more recently, machinery) to cultivate fields – was accompanied by a rise in both gender inequality and inequality within each gender. Agriculture allowed more crops to be grown and more wealth to be accumulated, and thus put a new premium on the ownership of land. Nearly all agricultural societies assigned men ownership of both land and crops, giving women access to land and its products only through their family relationships with men (Blumberg, 1984). In addition, agricultural societies typically had high levels of inequality between men, with some men owning much land and others little or none. Landless men competed for the right to work on other men's land, while many agricultural societies developed race or caste systems that justified the subjugation of laborers (Lenski, 1966). **Pastoral** or herding societies, in which food comes primarily from larger animals such as cows or camels, sheep or goats, also tend to have high levels of gender inequality and other forms of inequality.

Men's monopolization of land and animal ownership had multiple roots. It probably began with the horticultural pattern of giving each gender control of the resources it produces. Guiding a plow and controlling large animals requires significant upper-body strength, so such work was assigned to men. Once men's work was necessary for preparing fields, there was a logic to assigning ownership of those fields to men. In pastoral societies, similarly, men and boys followed, protected, and laid claim to the livestock, which were the primary source of wealth and therefore power (Blumberg, 2004).

Over time men formed political and military alliances that protected their ownership of the land, typically excluding most men as well as nearly all women from wealth and political power (Lenski, 1966; Lerner, 1986). Huber (2007) argues that breastfeeding and women's resulting strong attachment to their children were the root causes of men's control of land, and therefore of everything else. Women avoided anything that separated them from their children, and especially violence that might leave their children motherless and likely to starve. Fighting and warfare were therefore male activities since the earliest days of humanity, which gave men a great advantage once there were significant resources to fight over.

Other theorists focus more on cultural ideas about gender and the relative value of women's and men's work (Sanday, 1981a; Collins *et al.*, 1993). In every type of society, women spend more time than men on what sociologists call **care work** or **reproductive work**, which includes bearing and raising children, food preparation, and all the other work that is required to keep a family going from day to day. Most agricultural societies deemed this care work less valuable or "indispensable" than the **productive work** (i.e., work that creates goods and/or generates income) typically done by men. Since men perceived women as playing only a minor role in agricultural production, they considered it fair that women receive fewer rewards for their work – not just less economic resources, but also less power and respect (Blumberg, 1984: 29).

Traditional agricultural and pastoral societies typically have **household economies**, also known as **family economies**, in which each household functions as an economic unit. Individuals in such societies generally cannot survive independently, as families control all resources and organize the time and skills of many people to create the necessities of life. These societies assign ownership of most or

PHOTO 2.1

In many agricultural and pastoral societies, men's greater ability to control large animals translated into greater economic and political power (Source: Thinkstock)

all material goods to the **head of household**, who is usually a man but in some societies may be a widow. The head of household is expected to direct the other members of his household as a well-functioning work team and is usually given a wide degree of latitude in telling them what to do and disciplining them if they disobey. Not all members of such households are necessarily related by blood or marriage, as more prosperous households may include servants, slaves, or other workers. These household members are often seen as part of the family (and therefore not free to leave), and like wives and children they are expected to obey and defer to the husband/father/master. Household economies thus produce multiple power gradients within each household, with men over women, the old over the young, and often those who have biological ties to the head of household over those who do not.

Subsistence-Oriented and Export-Oriented Agriculture

Not all agricultural societies were the same, of course. One important difference was whether people grew crops primarily for their own subsistence or for trade. Both types of societies existed in the British colonies that would later combine to become the United States. Colonial New England was a subsistence-oriented economy. People regularly traded with neighbors, and sometimes imported nails, books, and other products from England, but for the most part they grew crops for local consumption. The Chesapeake colonies, in contrast, were highly focused on trans-Atlantic trade. Their founders came in search of wealth and stayed because they discovered tobacco. A few wealthy families, known as planters, owned nearly all the fertile land and created plantations that grew crops for export. These different economic foundations profoundly affected gender relations in each region.

In New England, gender was the primary means of organizing work. Men cleared fields, plowed, and cultivated staple crops. Women tended gardens with vegetables, fruits, and herbs. Men ground grain or took it to a mill to be ground. Women baked bread, made butter and cheese and sausages, and cooked meals. Men cared for and slaughtered large animals. Women cared for and slaughtered chickens. Men chopped wood and made tools. Women tended fires and made soap and candles. Men built and maintained houses, barns, and fences. Women made and washed clothes. Men did long-distance errands. Women tended the sick and helped birth babies (Cowan, 1983: 26).

Many of these activities required skill and knowledge, and failure might mean that a family would perish. Girls and boys were therefore taught the skills appropriate for their gender from an early age. Mothers nursed their infants, but otherwise they were too busy for childcare. By the age of six, therefore, girls were running after toddlers and helping their mothers with other tasks. Young couples generally brought in a sister, niece, or cousin to help raise their first few babies until their oldest girl could take over. Boys similarly helped their fathers. Teenaged boys worked hard to acquire enough land and other resources to support a family of their own, while girls worked to assemble a trousseau of household furnishings and tools. When a couple married they brought together a complementary set of gender-coded skills, knowledge, and material resources that would, if all went well, enable them to support themselves and their children. If a spouse died, the remaining partner remedied the situation quickly by inviting an other-gender relative to move in, hiring a servant, or remarrying (Ulrich, 1982; Kessler-Harris, 1993).

These gendered expectations were very practical. Both men and women might do work assigned to the other gender if it was needed by their families, without any apparent threat to their gender identity or social status. Unlike in later generations, when people were concerned that a woman would become unfeminine if she did male-coded work, a woman could do any task as long as it furthered the good of her family and was approved by her husband (Ulrich, 1982: 38).

New England was far from gender egalitarian. Men owned nearly all land and other property, held all positions of public authority, and were the heads of their households. Women had few legal, political, or economic rights, and many widows lived in destitution. Work, however, gave women a path toward respect. Most women were "goodwives" – the title of respect given to a married woman who ran her own household. A woman was never the equal of a man, but the community valued a woman who was strong, diligent, and capable (Ulrich, 1982).

Most people in the early Chesapeake colonies were indentured servants who were bound to work for four to seven years in exchange for passage across the Atlantic. Life expectancies were short, and most servants died of disease, hunger, overwork, or violence before their terms were up. Planters preferred male servants since they were generally stronger and considered more appropriate for field labor. They also imported some women, some of whom did female-coded work while others worked in the fields. Maximizing exports, however, meant keeping domestic work and comforts to a minimum. In 1625 men were 74 percent of Virginia's population, women 10 percent, and children 16 percent (Taylor, 2001: 141).

The first enslaved Africans arrived in Virginia in 1619, but for several decades they were a rarity. English servants were a better investment than African slaves, who were more expensive but just as susceptible to dying (Taylor, 2001: 141). Race was not yet a major organizing feature in society: black and white people mingled socially, and some intermarried (Carr and Walsh, 1988).

Over time, however, the colonies became filled with landless men who could not marry and hated their poverty and powerlessness. In 1676 the rumble of resentment coalesced into an uprising known as Bacon's Rebellion, during which the capital of Virginia was burned to the ground. After that, planters preferentially imported Africans who could be enslaved forever, and tensions between white people eased as society placed all white people above all black people (Morgan, 1975; Webb, 1984). Planters withdrew white women from fieldwork, which they considered morally degrading when done by women, and instead assigned enslaved black women to work in the fields – and to carry the moral stigma that accompanied such work (Carr and Walsh, 1988; Brown, 1996).

Class and race thus loomed as large as gender in the organization of work and power. Land-owning men enjoyed a high degree of freedom and autonomy, while everyone else had few rights and many limitations. Most people remained poor in a society where a few families owned most of the productive land, most white people had few opportunities for advancement, and most black people were considered property (Morgan, 1975).

Not all export-oriented agricultural societies were, or are, as unequal as the colonial Chesapeake. By their nature, however, they create economic incentives that favor people or corporations that can acquire large amounts of land and control a large number of workers. An export market can make owning a plantation very profitable – but only if one has enough laborers and does not pay them too much. The result is often a large number of landless workers, women as well as men, who live near or sometimes below the subsistence level (Acemoglu and Robinson, 2012).

Colonization

One of the primary ways in which export-oriented agriculture spread throughout the world was **colonialism**, the practice of one country or society dominating another for economic gain. For at least five thousand years, since the birth of the ancient Egyptian dynasties and the Indus Valley civilization, relatively wealthy societies have tended to spread outwards in search of land, laborers, gold, and other resources. About six centuries ago Europeans invented ocean-worthy ships that ultimately enabled them to extend this search around the world. European colonialism has affected nearly every corner of the inhabited world, particularly if one includes the activities of the former European colonies now known as the United States (Getz and Streets-Salter, 2011; Reinhard, 2011).

Most colonial rulers and entrepreneurs sought to make a profit by exporting commodities, be they farmed, mined, or hunted. In each case, a profitable enterprise required controlling both land and people who would farm the soil, work the mines, or trap the animals. Most landowners preferentially hired or enslaved men for the hard and sometimes dangerous physical labor of producing, processing, and shipping commodities. Protecting land, wealth, and shipping routes required armies and navies, and nearly all soldiers and sailors were also men. Men therefore had better access to whatever wages were available. Many men, however, had to leave their families, temporarily or permanently, to obtain employment and they were more likely than women to be maimed or killed by their work. Women were often left to feed themselves and their children on whatever marginal land was available.

Colonizers typically created political and legal systems that favored men. They often instituted legal systems that assumed men would own all land, exercise all political power, and control their wives and other family members. They also sought to simplify ruling by identifying local leaders who could be counted on to keep the populace under control in exchange for money and other goods. These kings, judges, and other approved leaders were nearly always men. To some extent, colonizers were implementing their own ideas about gender and the proper roles of men and women. In many cases, though, they found willing allies among local men who saw the newcomers, with their wealth and weapons, as resources they could use to increase their own power.

Societies that were already highly male-dominated typically became even more so under colonial influences. The Masai of Kenya and Tanzania, for example, were a pastoral society with a high level of gender inequality. Although males were privileged in every realm, women had a certain degree of autonomy. Women owned the cattle they brought into a marriage, had a right to divorce, and typically went to market individually or in small groups, which indicates a certain level of trust and independence. British colonizers, however, treated older men as the only responsible adults. They taxed men on their cattle and wives, implying that men owned both. The traditional economy was based on barter, but the British introduced money and induced locals to use it by a combination of attractants (money could purchase new weapons, clothes, and other desirable goods) and threats (taxes had to be paid in money, not livestock). Men took complete control of family herds so they could sell cattle when they chose and pocket the cash. Women attempted to maintain their barter economy, with little success, and their lack of access to money greatly reinforced men's power (Hodgson, 1999, 2001; Flintan, 2008). Indeed, women sometimes described themselves as property to be bought and sold (Llewelyn-Davies, 1981: 341).

Colonization played out differently in societies that were originally horticultural and more gender egalitarian. In the Igbo regions of Nigeria, for example, the British established indirect rule in the 1880s, elevating a few men to a level of political authority that did not previously exist while excluding women and most men from political power (Korieh, 2001). Trading companies favored large palm oil plantations that displaced Igbo women's fields and their diverse crops. Companies also introduced new techniques for processing palm oil and cassava, which they taught nearly exclusively to men. Women were thus demoted to "unskilled labor," when previously they had passed huge amounts of horticultural knowledge from generation to generation (Chuku, 2005). In the short run, colonization clearly disadvantaged women more than men.

Today, however, the legacy of colonialism is more complex. Women were quite prominent in the anti-colonialist movements that led to Nigeria's independence in 1960. Chuku (2005) argues that men were more afraid of violent reprisals by colonial authorities, while women took advantage of their gender-based relative immunity to defy colonialist policies and practices. Some Igbo women have returned to horticulture, with all-female groups tending complex combinations of crops (Blumberg, 2004). Other women take advantage of new opportunities to engage in manufacturing and international trade, combining traditional skills with contemporary ideas and technology. Western-style education, urbanization, and war have all re-shaped Igbo society, with multiple contradictory effects on gender relations (Chuku, 2005).

Colonization similarly brought many generations of change to Native American societies and their gender dynamics. Early interactions with Europeans increased the salience of men's traditional work as hunters, traders, and warriors. Over time men lost their forest world to foreign conquest and plummeting animal populations, so women's horticultural work became more central. Yet later many Native American people were herded onto reservations in inhospitable locations that were not fit for growing crops. When women could not grow food they became more dependent on men who had better – but not good – access to U.S. labor markets and government programs. Since the 1970s Native American people have won increasing recognition of their right to cultural survival, and one result has been a reaffirmation of the importance of a balance of power between men and women (e.g., Perdue, 1998).

Most colonies in Asia, Africa, and Latin America gained political independence in the twentieth century. Weakened by world wars, the European powers could no longer withstand anti-colonial movements and nationalist ideologies. Some people argue, though, that "formal" colonialism has been replaced by "economic" colonialism, in which wealthy countries extract natural resources and labor from less-wealthy countries without taking any responsibility for the wellbeing of their people.

The **social institutions** created by colonial regimes have persisted and continue to favor elites and perpetuate poverty and gender inequality (Acemoglu and Robinson, 2012; Enloe, 2014). Many former colonies continue to be ruled by a small number of men who have much wealth and power. Plantations and mines continue to disproportionately hire men and pay them low wages for dangerous work. Women continue to have primary responsibility for feeding their children even though men have better access to land, money, and other resources. The economic, political, cultural, and environmental consequences of colonialism thus greatly affect the shape of the world today (Ansary, 2009).

Industrial Economies

The heart of **industrial** economies is the making of goods that are sold in the market. Most people gain most of their necessities and comforts not by growing and making them themselves, but by earning an income and purchasing them – or by sharing the income earned by other family members.

Industrialization increases men's power if cultural norms bar women from paid employment. Women in agricultural societies may not receive equal rewards for their work, but their work is clearly necessary and men without female relatives suffer real privations. Industrialization, however, allows well-paid men to purchase everything they need. If money is necessary for survival but women cannot earn money, women become dependent on their male relatives. Men are likely to resent women if they see them as economic parasites who contribute nothing to the family. In reality, most women in industrialized societies engage in large amounts of unpaid care work, including raising children, preparing food, and maintaining homes. The cultural idea that only paid work is real work, however, obscures these contributions, and even women who spend 12 hours or more a day doing physical labor are often described as "not working."

If, however, women have access to paid employment, then industrialization undermines household economies and men's power over women. If a woman can survive independently, families have less power not just over women who live on their own, but also over all women. The option of leaving affects family dynamics, and even women who do not earn enough to live independently tend to gain a greater say in family decisions. Young adults, especially women, who can support themselves have a degree of personal freedom and choice that is unimaginable in traditional societies with household economies.

Industrialization in the United States

In the United States, the early stages of industrialization benefited men more than women. In the eighteenth century, rapid population growth in the northeast meant that not everyone could make a living from agriculture and some people migrated into towns and cities in search of other livelihoods. Many men found work as artisans, making shoes and furniture and other handcrafted goods. Boys began as apprentices and many eventually set up shop as masters. Other boys became clerks and went into business as merchants and traders. Women were excluded from most of these opportunities. Men would not hire women in most occupations, most women did not have the money needed to set up their own business, and if a woman did manage to start an unconventional business most customers avoided her. Girls and women might earn meager wages as servants, boardinghouse keepers, sex workers, or men's assistants, but the better options were reserved for boys and men.

Inventors developed many new technologies in the early nineteenth century, and all of these new technologies were owned and controlled by men. Married women did not get the right to own property until the 1840s, and even then it was limited. They did not get the right to borrow money until the 1970s. Only men, therefore, had access to the land, loans, and human connections that were required to turn a good idea into a profitable business.

Industrialization decreased the work traditionally assigned to men. Commercial flour, for example, spared men the hard labor of hand-grinding grains or long trips to local mills. Coal mines relieved them of felling trees and splitting wood. As men's household duties declined, they were freer to look for other forms of employment.

Women's care work did not similarly decrease. Indeed, industrialization arguably increased women's work while improving everyone's quality of life. White flour, for example, allowed the baking of labor-intensive yeast breads and cakes, replacing the lumpy whole-grain quick-breads that had previously been the staff of life. Houses were warmer and better lit and furnished, diets more varied, clothes more abundant and washed much more frequently, and bodies cleaner, but women worked hard to achieve and maintain these comforts (Cowan, 1983: 40–68).

The result was that men's and women's lives became more separate, especially in more prosperous families. Men increasingly left the home to work and saw their primary role in the family as being a good **breadwinner** and providing financial support. Women stayed home, did lots of domestic work, and became primarily responsible for childrearing. Aspiring parents sent children to school so they could develop the complex social and intellectual skills needed (for the boys) to do the new high-status work or (for the girls) to attract a high-status husband. With children at school, yet more domestic work fell to their mothers.

Many affluent families embraced a new ideology of **separate spheres**: the idea that men and women, by their natures, live in different worlds. Men are strong, aggressive, rational, competitive, and suited to the world of industry and politics. Women are weak, nurturing, emotional, moral, and suited to the world of home and family. This ideology reinforced men's financial, political, and cultural power, and cast women into a narrow role of financial dependence and physical and emotional caretaking.

Most people, however, were not affluent and many suffered from hunger and cold. Women were typically paid half as much as men, or even less, and many male workers were terrified of being replaced by women. At best, they felt, female workers helped employers drive down men's wages. Men therefore did their best to exclude women from most occupations. If women did not undercut men by competing for jobs, many men argued, men would be able to bargain for a **family wage**, which would allow them to fulfill their breadwinner role by supporting a wife and children. Women then would not have to work, as the family wage debates assumed that every woman was attached to a man as part of a family.

Men were often hostile to women who tried to take what they considered men's jobs, and they used verbal, physical, and **sexual harassment**, and sometimes assault, to make such women's lives miserable. Because women were limited to a narrow range of occupations, competition for those jobs was intense, which drove down women's wages even further. Women were often paid just enough to stay alive, and sometimes less than that (Kessler-Harris, 2003).

Women could sometimes find their way into new occupations that did not yet have gender coding, such as typing or retail sales (Benson, 1988; Kessler-Harris, 2003). Many employers saw women as cheap, docile, and manually dexterous, so the early textile factories of the 1830s and 1840s hired primarily farmers' daughters. Thousands of rural women cherished this opportunity to live and earn money outside a family setting, but their freedom was temporary. Employers valued strength and dexterity, and most women were let go by their mid-twenties as their bodies began to wear out. Because so many women wanted so few jobs, employers sought to get more work for less money, and protests and strikes followed. By 1860 female factory workers were typically immigrants or their daughters, as many native-born women no longer considered these jobs desirable (Dublin, 1999: 20). Even as wages shrank, however, factory women had unprecedented control over their time and money. They received a paycheck and decided what to do with it, and their work was done when the bell rang at the end of the day – a novel luxury for women (Peiss, 1986).

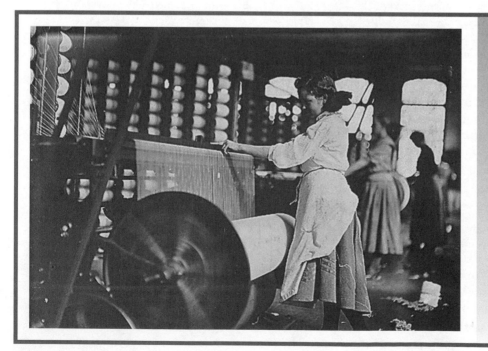

PHOTO 2.2

Young women in a mill. Mills were crowded, noisy, and full of dangerous cotton dust, and after a few years many workers had bad hearing or bad lungs. Many women, however, sought out these jobs as better than the alternatives (Source: National Archives, 1908)

By the turn of the twentieth century the economy was dominated by large corporations that mass-produced commodities and consumer goods. Many men found work as managers and executives, while even more men did heavy work: pumping oil, forging steel, and running the railroads. Most men worked long hours for their entire adult lives, from their teens until they literally could not work anymore. These men built much of their sense of identity around being workers and breadwinners (Rotundo, 1993).

For women, paid work was highly related to family and racial status. When families needed to supplement the father's income, they tried to send children, not wives, to work. One reason was ideology: the idea that "women should not work." A more practical reason was that running a nineteenth-century household was so labor-intensive that if a mother took on outside employment her children were more likely to die from disease or accidents. Day care was a rarity. Black children were often raised by their grandmothers, but many white working mothers were immigrants whose mothers were in their home countries. They were often forced to give their infants to wet nurses, who were typically overworked and malnourished, while children of age three or older were often unsupervised. Roughly one in five American children died before the age of five, and the children of working mothers were especially at risk (U.S. Bureau of the Census, 1975: 63; Addams, 1910).

Married women typically worked outside the home only if their incomes were essential for their families' survival – as they were for about one in three black families and one in fourteen white families in 1880 (Kerber, 1998: 66). For most white women paid work was a temporary phase of life before marriage, or sometimes an unfortunate necessity after widowhood or divorce. Many black women, however, worked as long as they physically could. According to the Census Bureau, nearly one in five American women (more than 5.3 million women) worked for pay in 1900 (U.S. Bureau of the Census, 1975: 128). This calculation does not include many women, disproportionately black, who worked as farm laborers or domestic servants but were not considered "working" by statisticians.

For many women, the image of finding a man who could support her and her children was a distant dream. Gender discrimination meant that many women worked long hours for meager and unstable pay, while racial discrimination meant that very few black men were paid a "family wage" capable of supporting a family. Black women faced the double discrimination of race and gender, and few could find employment other than backbreaking fieldwork or domestic service – which was characterized by long hours, low pay, intense supervision, little personal freedom, and often sexual harassment or assault (Wilkerson, 2010; Landry, 2000). Even white working women were often paid so little that they were chronically hungry, and many suffered the diseases of malnutrition and at least sometimes supplemented their incomes by more or less formally exchanging sexual favors for food or money (Stansell, 1982). The visible misery of many working women reinforced the idea that women should not work.

Industrialization Today

Many countries are currently experiencing industrialization, as **globalization** has made it possible to transport and sell manufactured goods all over the world. Many factories in poor countries with weak health and safety regulations are dangerous places, and workers are often exposed to toxic chemicals, machinery that can cut off a finger or limb, and exhaustingly long work hours that increase the risks of both accident and disease. Many female workers face the additional hazards of sexual harassment and rape by male bosses and coworkers (Larson, 2013). A series of factory fires and a factory collapse that killed 1,127 workers in Bangladesh, most of them women, drew comparisons with the Triangle Shirtwaist Factory fire in New York City in 1911, which killed 146 workers – most of them young immigrant women – and galvanized the American movement for worker safety and workplace regulation (Doyne *et al.*, 2011; Marshall, 2014). Unlike the Americans in 1911, however, the Bangladeshi government is operating in a global economy in which retailers and manufacturers can easily shift their purchases to other countries if they consider safety regulations too expensive.

Industrialization has also, however, enabled women in many countries to work outside the household economy for the first time. Despite all the risks of factory work, many women consider a factory job a great improvement over agricultural labor, domestic service, or sex work, the three alternatives that are widely available to poor women in poor countries. Women's ability to earn and control their own incomes changes their lives in many ways, as it undermines the male dominance long inherent in household economies.

The effects of industrialization can be seen by contrasting China and India, which are the world's two largest countries and together contain 36 percent of all people. They have both been agricultural societies for thousands of years, and both fully support the theory that agricultural societies tend to have high levels of inequality. Although there were many differences between the two civilizations, for most of the last couple of millennia their family and gender structures were remarkably similar. Men dominated women and the old dominated the young. A young wife moved into a multigenerational household with her husband's family, where she was expected to serve not just her husband but also everyone else. Well-off women lived in seclusion, perhaps leaving the home only when they married. Lower-status women were less restricted but spent their lives doing hard physical labor. Female infanticide, child marriage, and physical beatings were common.

Recently, however, gender relations in China and India have diverged. In 2013 the United Nations ranked China 37th out of 187 countries in gender equality, while India was 127th (UNDP, 2013a). Other metrics produce somewhat different results, but every indicator suggests that China has become more gender egalitarian than India.

Why the difference? At least three factors are important. First, the Chinese government deliberately chose to empower women and improve their lives.

Declaring that "Women hold up half the sky," Mao Tse-tung revised family law and promoted equal education and work opportunities, and his successors continued these gender-egalitarian policies. Second, the government's population control policies mean that many parents have only one or two daughters, with no sons. Since most elderly people depend on their grown children, parents invest in their daughters' education and employment as an investment in their own future security. Third, the government has promoted rapid industrialization, with factories producing huge quantities of clothing, electronics, and other goods for international markets. Many factories preferentially hire young women, who are seen as more docile and dexterous than men. By 1987 more than 90 percent of urban Chinese women had formal employment, nearly the same percentage as their male peers and much higher than in the United States or any other country (Bauer *et al.*, 1992).

Hundreds of millions of young women have taken factory jobs, despite their long hours and sometimes unsafe conditions. They earned much more in factories than on crowded farms, and their incomes and savings helped fuel China's economic boom. Some women with talent and connections have become wealthy, and in 2008 six of the ten richest self-made women in the world were Chinese (Kristof and WuDunn, 2009: 206). More importantly, China cut its poverty rate from 84 percent in 1980 to 10 percent in 2010, lifting 680 million people (more than twice the population of the United States) above the poverty line (*Economist*, 2013c). Gender inequality certainly still exists. Men own most homes – an important form of wealth – and domestic violence is widespread, with 40 percent of Chinese women who have a husband or boyfriend reporting physical or sexual violence in their relationships. The law generally considers domestic violence a "private" issue, though in 2014 China began to consider its first law intended to reduce domestic violence (Fincher, 2014; *Economist*, 2014o). Although it would be a mistake to paint a completely rosy picture, many Chinese women are earning their own incomes and the increased independence that comes with it.

India has seen no similar transformations. The government has not set itself behind promoting gender equality. Families remain large and male-dominated, with violence against women common both inside and outside the home (Manjoo, 2014). The absence of reliable roads, electricity, and other basic infrastructure has deterred the growth of manufacturing. High-tech centers focus on services that can be powered by local generators and exported over wires, but few Indians have the education necessary for a career in information technology. Even working in a call center requires unusual proficiency in English. The high demand for a limited number of educated workers has increased incomes for those few, but not for the many. Only 30 percent of women work in the formal economy (WEF, 2014: 64), and some men still resist women's employment because they believe women should have no contact with men outside the family (Patel, 2006). The result is a country with very high levels of gender inequality and poverty. Nearly half of the people in India still live on less than $1.50 a day (*Economist*, 2014j).

Some other countries are trying to follow China's example. Bangladesh, for example, is a desperately poor and very crowded country that was formerly part of India and shared its high degree of gender inequality. Wages have been rising in China, and some companies have relocated factories to Bangladesh and other countries in search of cheap labor (Bradsher, 2013). Expanding economic options have made many changes possible in Bangladesh. Girls' enrollment in primary school doubled in just five years, reaching 90 percent in 2005. Life expectancy rose by ten years between 1990 and 2010, while infant mortality fell by half and maternal mortality by three-quarters (*Economist*, 2012c). In 2007 the World Economic Forum rated Bangladesh in the bottom quarter of countries in gender equality, but by 2014 it had risen to the top half (WEF, 2014: 115).

These changes reflect intentional policy choices as well as impersonal economic forces. Bangladesh's economic planners recognize that China and South Korea began to enjoy sustained economic growth about two decades after they opened free education to girls and factory work to young women. The Bangladeshi government provides stipends, known as **conditional cash transfers,** to families that send their daughters to school, and girls are now more likely than boys to attend high school (WEF, 2014: 72). It provides free and voluntary family planning for everyone who wants it. And it has encouraged industrialization and the employment of young women in factories. By making women central to development, it hopes to benefit everyone in the country (*Economist*, 2012c).

Non-governmental organizations, also known as NGOs, have also played important roles. In 1976 a Bangladeshi man named Muhammad Yunus founded the Grameen Bank, which provides **microloans** to poor people, mostly women, who need a tiny bit of capital to start or expand a business. Microfinance programs aimed at women have now expanded to every inhabited continent and have been shown to decrease poverty and domestic violence, increase education for boys and even more for girls, and increase contraceptive use (Khandker, 2005: 23; Hunt and Kasynathan, 2002). Microloans do not solve all problems, and some critics argue that their impact has been over-hyped. Government services (such as schools and clean water) and formal jobs with stable wages and benefits are also essential for lifting people out of poverty, and growing a business to become an employer typically requires larger amounts of credit (Chowdhury, 2009). Poorly administered microcredit programs, like other forms of excessive borrowing, can do real harm (Polgreen and Bajaj, 2010). The evidence suggests, however, that on the whole microcredit programs have benefited the poor, especially women (Khandker and Samad, 2014).

Industrialization in China, Bangladesh, and similar countries is thus benefiting women more than men. Although many of these countries have long-standing cultural practices that discourage women from working outside the home, these prohibitions are changing more quickly in industrializing countries today than they did in the United States when it was industrializing. Many governments and families in poor countries look at Europe and the United States and feel confident that in the long run industrialization will lead to more prosperity. They therefore allow or even encourage young women to take paid employment, and to gain the education that will enable them to contribute even more to their families and countries. The result is not just increasing standards of living, but also women's greater power in their families and communities.

Knowledge-Based Economies

Industrialization opens up opportunities for growing numbers of people to make their living as **professionals**, meaning they sell their expertise rather than their physical labor. In many countries, including the United States, this process has continued to the point that the labor market values and rewards knowledge, creativity, and social skills much more than physical strength. Most American workers now do things for other people, be that cutting their lawns or managing their investments. Some people therefore describe our current economy as a **service economy**. Others call it a **knowledge-based economy** to underline how much it is driven by information and how many of the rewards of work go to people with high levels of education and expertise.

In 1800 men controlled all schools, colleges, apprenticeships, certification programs, professional societies, and formal employment decisions. They were thus able to ensure that all of the people who entered professional work, with its higher prestige and income, were men. In its early stages, therefore, professionalization increased gender inequality.

During the nineteenth century, however, women began to find (or force) their way into higher education and professional careers in the United States and several other countries. Some extraordinary women opened doors by proving their exceptional skills as, for example, scientists or architects. Many women used cultural ideas about women's distinctive talents and responsibilities to argue that certain professions were appropriately part of women's domain. For example, in the 1830s towns began to hire female teachers for their rapidly growing public schools not just because they could pay women much less than men, but also because nurturing children had come to be seen as a feminine activity. (Female teachers remained, however, under the strict supervision of male principals and school boards.) Some women carved out professional niches serving other women – as gynecologists, for example, or professors in women's colleges. Women also created new professions, such as nursing and social work, that expanded upon women's responsibilities for taking care of others. Men still occupied the vast majority of professional positions in 1900, but female employment, financial independence, and political power increased quickly enough that male commentators raised alarms about what they saw as the growing dominance of women (Kessler-Harris, 2003).

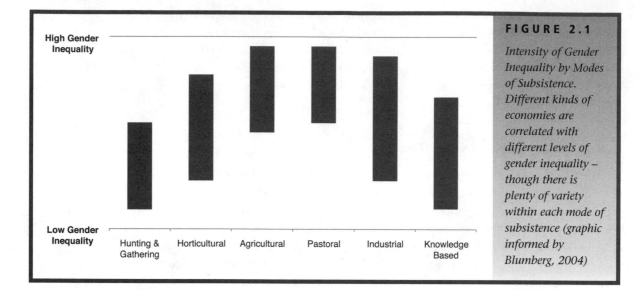

FIGURE 2.1

Intensity of Gender Inequality by Modes of Subsistence. Different kinds of economies are correlated with different levels of gender inequality – though there is plenty of variety within each mode of subsistence (graphic informed by Blumberg, 2004)

Today, millions of women engage in professional work in which they are valued for their knowledge and problem-solving abilities. Companies and countries succeed by competing in an increasingly global economy, and those that do not appropriately employ women and their talents tend to fall behind. The more women gain equal access to higher education and professional employment, the more difficult it is to maintain men's economic, familial, political, and cultural power. The growth of a global knowledge economy has thus significantly decreased gender inequality.

Gender continues, however, to structure work. Even in the most knowledge-based economies, such as the United States and northern Europe, gender still affects how likely people are to work full-time, what work they do, and how much they are rewarded for their work – both in income and in the more intangible qualities of recognition and respect.

The shift to knowledge economies has also increased inequality within each gender by rewarding people with good educations, skills, and professional networks. Income inequality has risen in most countries, while in the United States the income gap between college graduates and non-graduates has expanded dramatically in recent decades (*Economist*, 2012b; BLS, 2012). Parents who attend college themselves are much more likely than non-graduates to have the financial resources and **cultural capital** (i.e., knowledge about how to navigate the more rewarded reaches of their society) to help their own children attend college, so these inequalities tend to be perpetuated from generation to generation.

GENDER AND WORK IN THE CONTEMPORARY UNITED STATES

Gender and Labor Force Participation

In 1950 the United States was a rapidly growing industrial nation. The entire country had become an industrial powerhouse during World War II and employers actively recruited women, both white and black, for almost any job that freed men to engage in combat (Yellin, 2005). After the war many of the new factories were re-tooled for domestic purposes, and the resulting surge of consumer goods created the first mass consumer society in human history.

After the war women were urged to resign from their jobs to make room for returning soldiers, return home, and have children. Many did so, but many returned to the workforce within a few years (U.S. Bureau of the Census, 1975). Previous generations had seen a working wife as un-manning her husband, but rising material aspirations made it increasingly acceptable for wives to help pay for the "extras" of life. A man could now maintain his breadwinner identity if he could pay the basic expenses by himself and his wife earned less than he did, and many people felt it was OK for women to work as long as they also fulfilled their responsibilities as wives and mothers. For the first time, many white women were employed by choice, not necessity. A few had professional careers, but most had more modest jobs, such as working at the local telephone company (Kessler-Harris, 2003).

By the 1960s the shift to a knowledge-based economy was under way. The atom bomb had won the war, and the United States seemed to be in an unending cold war with the Soviet Union. Many people concluded that science and technology were key to U.S. dominance in the emerging world order. The federal government invested heavily in starting and expanding universities, scientific research, and supporting American companies. The industrial economy, meanwhile, began to thin. Engineers and managers constantly invented new ways to be productive – that is, to make more widgets with fewer workers – and automated factories employed fewer people. Other countries sought the benefits of industrialization for their own people, and by the 1970s multinational corporations were beginning to replace older American factories with new ones in countries with lower wages and looser safety standards.

These changes affected different demographic groups differently. Young white men were encouraged to pursue the new jobs in science and engineering, management and government, especially if they did well in school. White male college graduates had many opportunities to advance in jobs that offered good salaries and social status. Until the 1980s there were also plenty of jobs for less-educated white men in such male-coded jobs as manufacturing and construction.

In the 1950s many white middle-class families sent their daughters to college but then expected them to be content using their skills to raise a family. In *The Feminine Mystique* (1963) Betty Friedan famously wrote about "the problem that has no name" – educated women's restless dissatisfaction with a life of milk and cookies. Most women, Friedan argued, need satisfying work – "a job that she can take seriously as part of a life plan, work in which she can grow as part of society" (Friedan, 1963: 282). As many commentators have noted, Friedan's vision was class bound. For working-class people, men as well as women, work may be life constricting rather than life enhancing, and Friedan assumed her readers would hire other women to help take care of their homes and children. Nevertheless, Friedan's basic point was solid: millions of educated American women had talents and skills that were useful beyond their families, and they felt stifled by the prevailing assumption that they should devote themselves to home-making. Growing numbers of college-educated women insisted on access to jobs that would use their educations.

Black men suffered the job losses of de-industrialization most severely. For generations they had been restricted to agricultural work, manual labor, and personal service. Black men slowly got access to industrial jobs as a result of the world wars and the civil rights movement, but careers that required a high school diploma, much less a college education, were generally closed to them (Sugrue, 1996). Most black boys therefore started working as soon as they were big enough to be paid for their efforts. Because a high school diploma did not generally improve their employment prospects they often left school in their teens to work full-time. When the industrial economy was strong it offered plenty of options for healthy men without an education, and in the early 1950s black men were more likely than white men to be employed (BLS, 2013a).

Once factories started to shed workers, however, black men had low seniority as well as dark skin (Sugrue, 1996). In the 20 years after 1967 Philadelphia lost 64 percent of its manufacturing jobs, Chicago 60 percent, and Detroit 51 percent. More than half a million manufacturing jobs disappeared just in New York City (Wilson, 1996: 29–30). The result was a dramatically changed job market for less-educated men. By 1972 black men's labor force participation rate (i.e., those employed or actively looking for work) was only 93 percent of white men's, and by 2012 it was less than 90 percent (BLS, 2013a).

The civil rights movement greatly expanded black women's employment options. Ever since their ancestors had first arrived, involuntarily, in North America, most black women had done agricultural labor and/or worked as servants in white families. Once employment discrimination became illegal in 1964, however, black women pursued the more-desirable jobs that had been closed to them. The degree of occupational segregation between black and white women dropped dramatically between 1940 and 1980, as millions of black women left domestic service to enter female-coded work in schools, hospitals, and corporate and government offices. It continued to drop between 1980 and 2000 as some black women, taking advantage of educational gains, entered managerial and professional positions. Since then, however, the trend toward racial integration has stagnated (Amott and Mattaei, 1999; Alonso-Villar and del Rio, 2013).

As a group, black women have been more successful than black men in moving into "white collar" work. In 2013, 63 percent of employed black women had office, managerial, or professional positions, compared to just 42 percent of employed black men (BLS, 2014a). Black women have long been somewhat better educated than black men, on average, and most of these jobs required a high school diploma or more. In addition, many employers saw black men as potentially uncooperative or threatening, so they were more comfortable pursuing racial diversity by hiring women (Lopez, 2003). And black men themselves were often uncomfortable pursuing jobs they saw as female-coded, such as nursing or secretarial work. If black women wanted to move out of female-coded jobs, however, they faced the double barrier of racism and sexism. Although black men are now less likely than black women to have stable employment, those who manage to work full-time still earn more, on average, than black women who work full-time (BLS, 2012: 64–65).

Immigration to the United States has increased dramatically since 1965. The National Origins Act of 1924 had put tight caps on immigration, particularly from countries outside Europe. The racism inherent in this legislation became less acceptable in the 1960s, and in 1965 the Immigration and Nationality Act allowed much more immigration from Latin America, Asia, and Africa. Some Hispanic families had engaged in gendered migratory work in the southwest since before the United States conquered this area in the Mexican-American war of 1848. For them, men's seasonal migratory work was long traditional (Deutsch, 1987). Other people around the world considered leaving home because of such "push factors" as poverty, war, gang violence, social rigidity, or the unavailability of jobs suitable to their skills. They were attracted to the United States because of such "pull factors" as employment and the hope of education and a better future for their children.

Today, roughly half of all immigrants are women, but the gender ratio varies greatly by country of origin. Men are a majority of immigrants from Mexico and India, while women are a majority from China, the Philippines, and the Dominican Republic. Immigrant men are more likely than native-born men to be in the labor force, while immigrant women from most (not all) countries are less likely than native-born women to have paid employment. This difference is most dramatic among immigrants from Mexico, India, and El Salvador (Immigration Policy Center, 2010: 3, 10).

Typical education levels also vary greatly by country of origin. Immigrants from India are twice as likely as native-born Americans, and ten times as likely as immigrants from Mexico, to have a college degree (Immigration Policy Center, 2010: 7). Hispanic Americans are now more likely than white or black Americans to work in gender-segregated occupations, as immigrants from Latin America are especially likely to work in low-status gender-coded occupations such as landscaping, construction, or housekeeping (Mintz and Krymkowski, 2010–2011). Immigrant women from India and China, in contrast, are more likely than native-born women to have professional careers. Both male and female immigrant workers tend to earn less than native-born workers, but the difference is greater for men. The median immigrant male worker earns 33 percent less than the median native-born male worker, while the difference for women is 17 percent (Immigration Policy Center, 2010: 12; CBO, 2011: 23).

These patterns play out in many local communities across the country. A recent case study in Durham, North Carolina, found that many agricultural jobs were long gone to automation, many manufacturing jobs had been lost to overseas competition, and the loss of effective unions had downgraded the remaining manufacturing jobs. An influx of highly educated male and female professionals created demand for low-paid service and construction workers, especially women to do female-coded childcare and cleaning for dual-career couples. Although black women had traditionally been household servants, they resisted taking such jobs when they had other options. Black men rarely applied to or were hired for jobs as nannies or housecleaners. Instead immigrant Hispanic women filled these positions (Flippen, 2014).

The gender/race coding of different kinds of work thus greatly affects employment patterns. In 2010 the unemployment rate for black men in North Carolina was 22 percent, compared to less than 8 percent for white women. Both race and gender affected unemployment rates, with black and white men more likely than women of their race to be unemployed, and the opposite among Hispanics (Hess *et al.*, 2013: 9). People often say that the economy has created a demand for low-paid workers and immigrants have filled the gap. But with such high unemployment rates among less-educated black people, especially black men, one needs to ask why unemployed black people do not seem to be considered viable candidates for the available jobs.

Together, all of these factors add up to a general pattern of women having more paid employment than in the past and men having less. Men's labor market participation has dropped in every decade since the 1950s. One reason is that de-industrialization decreased the demand for less-educated men in male-coded jobs. Some boys thrive in school, but others do not, and modern society has little need for men who have only their strength to offer. In 1980, 73 percent of white men age 20 to 34 without a high school diploma were employed, but by 2008 only 58 percent of them were. For young black men without a high school diploma the employment rate fell from 56 percent to a shocking 26 percent (Pew Charitable Trusts, 2010: 35).

As the demand for less-educated male workers dropped, growing numbers of them were incarcerated. The number of people in prison quadrupled in 20 years, from about 500,000 in 1980 to 2.1 million in 2000, largely due to the war on drugs and longer sentences. Although people of all colors use and sell drugs at similar rates, enforcement focused on minority communities and white people were generally treated more leniently than black people accused of the same offenses (Alexander, 2010; Stevenson, 2014). By 2000 there were more black men behind bars than in college (Butterfield, 2002). Mass incarceration has driven many black men out of the labor force, as people with prison records have poor employment prospects (Western, 2006; Pew Charitable Trusts, 2010).

There are also happier reasons for men's decreasing work. Unlike in the 1950s, today most men retire rather than working until they die. Social Security and related programs allowed men's average retirement age to fall from 68.5 in the early 1950s to 62.6 in the early 2000s, though in recent years men (and even more women) have become more likely to work after the age of 65 (Gendell, 2008: 42). Meanwhile, life expectancy rose from 46.3 for boys born in 1900 to 65.6 for boys born in 1950, greatly increasing the likelihood that they will enjoy post-retirement years (U.S. Bureau of the Census, 1975: 55). As work becomes less central to men's sense of masculinity, men become more likely to feel like there's more to life than work. Many young men attend college or graduate school, while some take time out of the workforce for other pursuits, such as travel or childrearing.

Women's increasing labor force participation also had multiple causes. Rising standards of living generated demand for teachers, nurses, and social workers, all female-coded fields. Egalitarian ideals and government legislation helped open up other options. The **Equal Pay Act of 1963** required that men and women with the same job be paid the same, while the **Civil Rights Act of 1964** prohibited race and gender discrimination in hiring and promotions. Although discrimination continues, it is far less blatant than in the past, when job ads typically specified whether applicants should be men or women and rejected the other gender. Many women, especially better-educated women, fought for the right to work not just because they wanted to earn money, but also because work can offer many other satisfactions, such as feeling competent and needed.

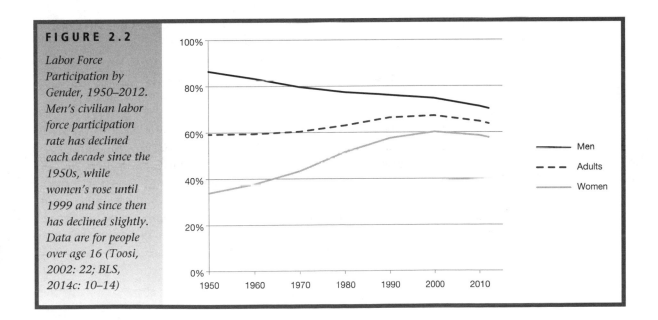

FIGURE 2.2

Labor Force Participation by Gender, 1950–2012. Men's civilian labor force participation rate has declined each decade since the 1950s, while women's rose until 1999 and since then has declined slightly. Data are for people over age 16 (Toosi, 2002: 22; BLS, 2014c: 10–14)

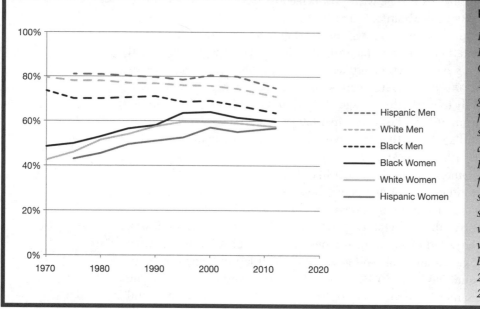

FIGURE 2.3

FIGURE 2.3

Labor Force Participation by Gender and Race, 1970–2012. The gender gap in labor force participation is smallest for blacks and largest for Hispanics. The rates for Asians, not shown, have been similar to those for whites since 1992 when data started to be collected (Aziz, 2009: 18–19; BLS, 2013a, 2013b)

In many cases, though, women work from financial necessity in jobs that they may or may not find otherwise rewarding, and women now hold a majority of working-class jobs (Cobble, 2007). Women today are more likely than in previous generations to be single, divorced, or in a lesbian couple. Most men's incomes have stagnated while the costs of housing, education, and health care have risen, so even women in stable heterosexual marriages are increasingly likely to find that earning money is a necessity (Warren and Tyagi, 2003). In 2012, 14.5 percent of American households – 18 million families – sometimes had difficulty feeding themselves (U.S. Department of Agriculture, 2013: 1).

Family status now affects women's employment rates less than in the past. Women with school-age children are now most likely to have paid work, while women who are widowed, divorced, or separated are least likely to be in the workforce (and most likely to be over age 65). A married woman with a child under age six is only a hair's breadth less likely than other married women to have a job, while never married and formerly married women are more likely to be in the workforce if they have a small child than if they do not. Women are the primary breadwinners in 40 percent of households with children. Nearly two-thirds of these "breadwinner moms" are single mothers, but 37 percent are married women who earn more than their husbands (Wang *et al.*, 2013). (The number of lesbian couples raising children is still too small to make it into such statistics.) Today, 52 percent of women with infants less than a year old also have paid work – 71 percent of whom work full-time (BLS, 2014b).

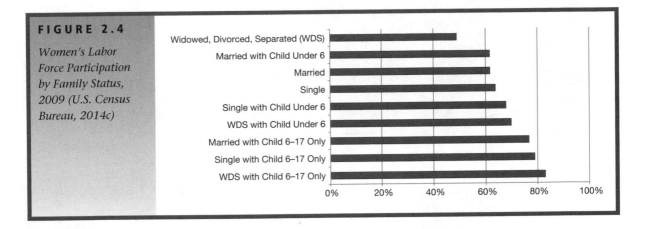

FIGURE 2.4

Women's Labor Force Participation by Family Status, 2009 (U.S. Census Bureau, 2014c)

These patterns too vary among different groups. Black women remain especially likely to continue working after the arrival of a child (Landivar, 2013). Immigrant women are more likely than native-born women to leave the workforce when they marry or have a child, if that child is in the United States. Most immigrant women who have left children behind in their country of origin, however, are employed and send money home for their children's support (Flippen, 2014).

Less-educated mothers are less likely to work outside the home than college-educated mothers, as they more often cannot find work that covers their childcare costs. In 2000, 77 percent of women with a child under age 18 also had a paid job. By 2012 that percentage had shrunk to 70 percent, which some journalists reported as a retreat from women's professional aspirations. Most of this change occurred, however, among less-educated women, while less-educated men were even more likely to leave the workforce during these years. Roughly 5 percent of stay-at-home mothers are in affluent families, but most of the decline in mothers' workforce participation reflects the shrinking options for less-educated workers of all kinds (*Economist*, 2014e).

Gender Segregation of Occupations

Gender continues to affect who does what work. One way to think about the extent of gender segregation is to calculate an "index of dissimilarity" that indicates what percentage of workers of one gender or the other would need to change occupations to create gender parity. This index shows that gender segregation changed little during the first seven decades of the twentieth century, with the exception of the World War II period. Gender segregation declined considerably in the 1970s but much more slowly since 1990, and it is even larger if we include unpaid "keeping house" as an occupation (Cohen, 2004). Today, eliminating gender segregation would require more than 50 percent of either women or men to change their occupations (Blau *et al.*, 2013). For comparison, less than a third of black or white

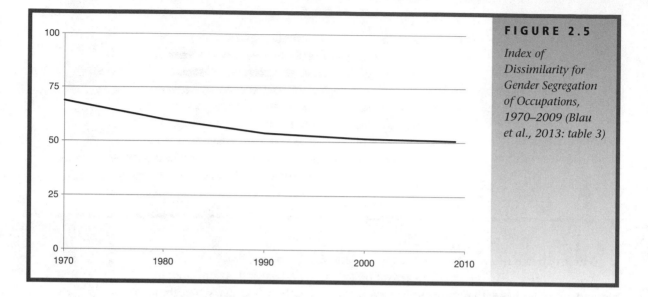

FIGURE 2.5

Index of Dissimilarity for Gender Segregation of Occupations, 1970–2009 (Blau et al., 2013: table 3)

workers would need to change occupations to end racial segregation in employment (Kaufman, 2002; Mintz and Krymkowski, 2010–2011). Gender segregation is thus larger than racial segregation in occupations.

Today, most but not all of the more gender-balanced occupations are "white collar" occupations, such as physicians and managers, that were traditionally male-coded and require a college degree or more. Men are still scarce in the so-called "pink collar" occupations, such as nursing and secretarial work, that were female-coded by 1900. Indeed, social workers and primary school teachers are more predominantly female now than they were in 1980. Women are scarce in engineering, police departments, and "blue collar" jobs, such as welding and construction work, that are seen as demanding some amount of physical strength and stamina but do not require much formal schooling (Coontz, 2012). Men are also more than 85 percent of military personnel, who are not included in the Census Bureau data that is usually used to study the American workforce (DoD, 2013).

White men are disproportionately employed in occupations that give them high authority and high earnings. Their representation exceeds what one would expect if one simply added the effects of being white and being male, suggesting that white men enjoy a synergistic advantage. There was little change in this synergistic advantage between 1983 and 2002 (Mintz and Krymkowski, 2010–2011).

Women are more likely than men to work at all but the highest levels of government. Women are a majority of public-sector workers (57 percent in 2005) but a minority of private sector workers (45 percent) (UNECE Statistical Database, n.d.). Since most police and firefighters are men, the concentration of women outside public safety is even higher. This pattern occurs partly because governments have a large demand for female-coded workers, especially teachers, but also because anti-discrimination laws have been easier to enforce in the public sector. Black women have been particularly successful in finding public-sector jobs: in 2011 they were 8.2 percent of workers in state and local governments but just 5.5 percent of private sector workers. In 2011 one in eight state and local government workers were black, but only one in ten private sector workers, and nearly two-thirds of black public-sector workers were female (Cooper *et al.*, 2012).

Since salaries are the public sector's biggest expense, cutting government budgets means cutting mostly women's jobs. Towns and states laid off more than half a million workers from 2009 to 2012, 70 percent of whom were women (Covert, 2012). Gender patterns can also favor male workers in times of fiscal crisis. When Detroit went bankrupt, for example, retired police and firefighters (nearly all male) were treated more generously than other municipal workers (mostly female) (Davey, 2014).

Gender and the Rewards of Work

Monetary income is an inexact metric for work's rewards, as people are "paid" in respect, power, and prestige as well as money. People care about money, however, not just because of the things it can purchase, but also because it is a symbol of status. In addition, jobs with better working conditions also tend to have larger paychecks. Data about people's financial incomes is therefore, on the whole, a reasonable proxy for how well people are rewarded for their work.

Women continue to earn less than men, even when both are working full-time. In the 1960s female full-time workers earned about 59 percent as much as male full-time workers. Today they earn about 77 percent. This wage gap shrank significantly

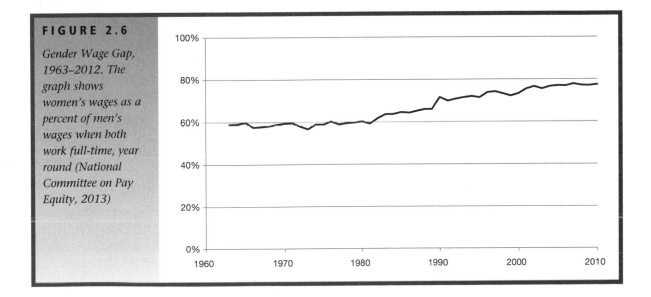

FIGURE 2.6

Gender Wage Gap, 1963–2012. The graph shows women's wages as a percent of men's wages when both work full-time, year round (National Committee on Pay Equity, 2013)

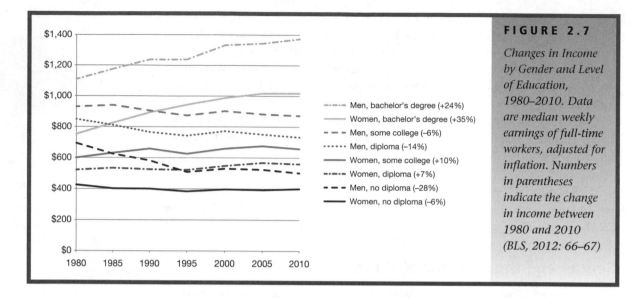

FIGURE 2.7

Changes in Income by Gender and Level of Education, 1980–2010. Data are median weekly earnings of full-time workers, adjusted for inflation. Numbers in parentheses indicate the change in income between 1980 and 2010 (BLS, 2012: 66–67)

in the 1980s but only slowly in the 1990s, and it has been basically stable since 2001 (National Committee on Pay Equity, 2013).

Income inequality within each gender has risen substantially since 1980, especially for men. The average income of male college graduates rose by a quarter in the 30 years from 1980 to 2010, while the average incomes of men without a bachelor's degree fell – by a painful 28 percent for high school dropouts. In 1980 most men earned more than most women, but now women with a college degree generally earn more than men without one. A wage gap still exists at every educa-

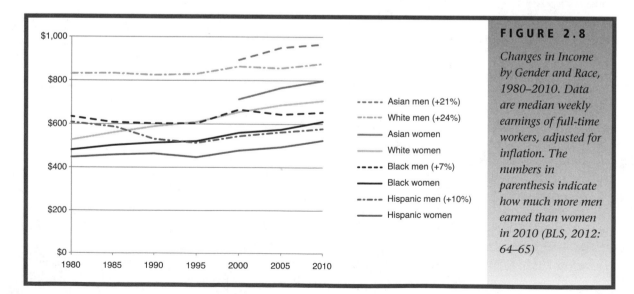

FIGURE 2.8

Changes in Income by Gender and Race, 1980–2010. Data are median weekly earnings of full-time workers, adjusted for inflation. The numbers in parenthesis indicate how much more men earned than women in 2010 (BLS, 2012: 64–65)

tional level, however, as men typically earn 25 to 35 percent more than similarly educated women when both are working full-time.

Although a gender wage gap exists in every race/ethnic group, it is largest for white and Asian people. Racial wage gaps, meanwhile, are largest among men and tend to be self-perpetuating. It is important not to conflate race and class: 40 percent of people living in poverty are white, while 12 percent of black households earn more than $100,000 a year (U.S. Census Bureau, 2012b, 2013b). Generations of disadvantage, however, mean that black and Hispanic families are less likely to have the income and wealth that help send the next generation to college and launch them into professional careers (Lui *et al.*, 2006). White and Asian men therefore tend to benefit more from being male.

Theories about Gender Inequality in Contemporary Work

At least three different factors contribute to the continuing gender segregation of occupations and gender wage gap. One is the gendered expectations and behaviors that individuals bring to the workforce. A second is gender discrimination by employers and colleagues. And a third is the structural assumption that women will do unpaid care work while normatively male workers are free to focus on their paid employment.

Work as Gender Performance

Many men and women make educational and career decisions that reflect their understanding of what it means to be masculine or feminine. Not everyone, of course, chooses a career that is considered gender-appropriate: there are female electricians and male kindergarten teachers. Many people, however, make vocational choices that help them see themselves as appropriately gendered and project a comfortably gendered image to others.

Many men, for example, are drawn to careers that ratify their perception that masculinity means being assertive, in control, strong, tough, competitive, and rational. Many male-coded occupations involve controlling other people (police and soldiers, for example, or executives and politicians) or physical systems (engineering and computer programming). Other male-coded occupations, especially those with lower educational requirements, require physical strength, the ability to tolerate discomfort, and a willingness to take risks, all of which allow workers to display their masculinity through their work.

Women, meanwhile, may be drawn to careers that enable them to display what they see as desirably feminine traits, such as being nurturing, supportive, attractive, empathetic, kind, and self-effacing. Many women choose female-coded occupations that allow them to define themselves as helping other people: they are teachers, nurses and other medical workers, social workers, therapists, and so on.

Men tend to be more reluctant than women to pursue "wrong-gender" occupations. This is partly because male-coded jobs typically offer more pay, prestige, and independence than female-coded jobs, so the financial incentives for women are greater. Many men, however, avoid female-coded fields even when they know the pay and opportunities for advancement would be superior to their other options (Lupton, 2006: 114; Morris, 2012). Twelve of the fifteen occupational categories that are projected to grow most in the next decade have female majorities, including the medical paraprofessional fields that are relatively stable and well-paid (Rosin, 2012: 4–5). In addition, white men (but not black men) in female-coded professions, such as nursing, often receive exceptional mentoring and rise rapidly into the better-paid supervisory positions, an experience sometimes called the **glass escalator** (Williams, 1992; Wingfield, 2009). In the 20 most common female-coded occupations, men earn more than women in all but two (Rivers and Barnett, 2013: 62).

It seems that most men are embarrassed by the thought of doing "women's work" at a level that goes deeper than practical considerations. Kimmel (1994) argues that men constantly scrutinize each other for signs of femininity and homosexuality and that men who enter female-coded occupations fear the disapproval of other men. Men who do undertake female-coded careers use a variety of strategies to overcome the associated discomfort. Male librarians may re-label themselves as information scientists, elementary school teachers may focus on sports, and male nurses may choose an emergency room specialty, which provides the requisite requirement of toughness (Simpson, 2004).

Although men still predominate in the most powerful and best-paid reaches of the workforce, many less-educated men are struggling. In her controversial book titled *The End of Men* (2012), Hanna Rosin argued that men are falling behind because our knowledge-based economy rewards traits that come more naturally to girls and women: social and emotional intelligence, communication skills, and the ability to sit still and focus. Other people believe these gender differences are due to cultural forces. Either way, men who see masculinity as incompatible with education or working beside women are falling behind.

Gender also affects how people do their work. Many men feel that it is important to be competitive, confident, and unswayed by such emotions as fear and insecurity. These characteristics can make men powerful advocates for themselves and their interests, but they can also lead men into unnecessary errors when they dismiss information that is contrary to their existing views. Studies find that men often express more certainty in their opinions than is warranted and over-estimate their own skills and knowledge. Men's gender performances can help them succeed at work – but men can also end up in over their heads. Many women, on the other hand, underestimate their talents and capabilities. Women tend to be less self-confident than men, less willing to advocate for their own interests, and more reluctant to negotiate for more pay or a promotion (Kay and Shipman, 2014a; Babcock and

Laschever, 2007). One study found, for example, that women typically applied for promotions only when they believed they met 100 percent of the qualifications, while men were happy to toss their hat into the ring if they met 60 percent of the qualifications (Kay and Shipman, 2014b: 60).

The felt necessity of performing gender through one's work can thus have drawbacks for both women and men. Many women have chosen careers with low pay, recognition, autonomy, and advancement opportunities. On the other hand, many male-coded jobs that do not require a college degree are disappearing and men's reluctance to enter female-coded occupations can greatly limit their options.

Gender Discrimination and Male Favoritism

Many types of evidence suggest that favoritism toward male workers and job candidates is widespread. One recent study found that both male and female science professors saw female undergraduates as less competent than male undergraduates, even if they had the same skills and accomplishments. They were less likely to offer women mentoring or a job, and when they did hire women they paid them less (Moss-Racusin *et al.*, 2012). The gender wage gap persists even for workers with the most options: young singles, with no children, working full-time in urban areas. At every education level such women earn about 10 percent less than their male contemporaries (Coontz, 2012). Some of this wage gap is because men and women tend to have different majors, with female-coded majors paid less, but it also exists among women and men with identical majors (Corbett and Hill, 2012: 14).

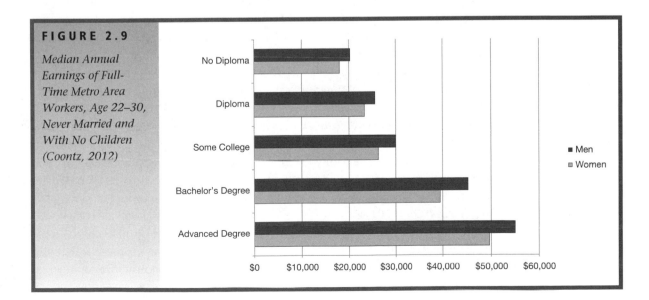

FIGURE 2.9

Median Annual Earnings of Full-Time Metro Area Workers, Age 22–30, Never Married and With No Children (Coontz, 2012)

Favoritism toward men continues throughout people's careers. Men are more likely to receive credit for good ideas, more likely to be sponsored by senior-level mentors, and more likely to be promoted because they are perceived as promising (while women have to actually perform to be promoted). Men are also more likely to be forgiven for mistakes, while women – especially in gender-atypical occupations – are more likely to be branded incompetent if they slip up. Women seen as competent, meanwhile, are often considered unlikeable. Colleagues and managers typically expect women to be caring and nurturing in the workplace, and penalize women who are not, while such behavior in men is generally considered optional. Women are especially likely to face double binds when they are in leadership positions, as both women and men expect women to be deferential and considerate but expect leaders to be forceful and decisive (Rivers and Barnett, 2013: 13–74, 122–124).

While some people argue that women are paid less largely because they more reluctant than men to negotiate for salaries and promotions, other studies indicate that women who negotiate in the same ways men do are often penalized because they are seen as too aggressive. Women generally succeed in accomplishing their goals only when they frame those goals as being for the good of the organization, while men are allowed to be seen as self-promoting (Rosin, 2012: 206–216).

Women's difficulties in receiving promotions commensurate with their abilities and accomplishments has often been called a **glass ceiling**, as many women seem to bump up against a firm though invisible barrier. Recently some women have risen to the top of big corporations, but their numbers are small: women are less than 5 percent of CEOs and 17 percent of board members in Fortune 500 companies (Catalyst, 2014a, 2014b). A woman is more likely to be put in charge when a company is in trouble, apparently on the theory that if things are going poorly it is time to try something different. She is then usually fired and scorned if she cannot turn the company around quickly – a pattern some call a **glass cliff** (Ryan and Haslam, 2005; *Economist*, 2014g).

Gender discrimination today is often unconscious. It is illegal, and many Americans have embraced the idea that women and men should be treated equally in the workplace, but it seems to be pervasive. A study of **trans men** found that some participants reported greater authority, rewards, and respect on the job as males than they had as females, even when they stayed in the same positions, though others faced heightened hostility and marginalization. The masculine advantage was particularly notable for trans men who were tall and white. Even for people who were born female, it seems, being seen as white and male can provide a synergistic advantage (Schilt, 2011).

Racial discrimination is also illegal but also persists (Pager and Shepherd, 2008; O'Sullivan *et al.*, 2014). The dynamics of racial discrimination are complicated, but they seem to have most impact when people are applying for jobs rather than when supervisors are evaluating on-the-job performance. The racial wage gap among young women without a college degree grew in the early 2000s, as less-educated minority women found it increasingly difficult to get a first stable job with benefits and opportunities for advancement (Reid, 2002; Alon and Haberfeld, 2007).

Black men may face a double bind as they present themselves to potential employers. As a gender, men are expected to be assertive, even aggressive, and self-confidence is often a prerequisite for positions of autonomy or leadership. Many white people, however, are inclined to experience assertiveness in black men as threatening, so the same behaviors that benefit white men may be penalized in black men (Lopez, 2003). Black men are just as likely as black and white women to believe they have experienced gender discrimination in the workplace (Pew Research Center, 2013b: 50).

Workplace Organization and Women's Responsibility for Care Work

Women continue to spend more time than men raising children, caring for elders, and doing the other work that is necessary to keep a home functioning (Pew Research Center, 2013b: 22). Many jobs, however, expect long working hours and a worker's perpetual availability. Most professions – medicine, law, finance, and academia – have what Michael Kimmel calls an "invisible masculine organizational logic," as they require many years of intensive training and often expect people to work 60 or more hours a week during the decades when women are best able to have children. Even if employers appear gender neutral in their requirements "the genderless jobholder turns out to be gendered as a man" (Kimmel, 2006: 3). Low-paid service jobs, meanwhile, increasingly use "flexible scheduling," which allows an employer to change employees' working hours week by week. This lack of predictability wreaks havoc on family life and any kind of childcare arrangement (Kantor, 2014).

Women are twice as likely as men to work part-time, with 26 percent of female workers and 13 percent of male workers working less than 35 hours a week (Pew Research Center, 2013b: 21). In some fields, however, increasing competition between both corporations and individuals has created a new norm of very long work hours. In the early 1980s, 9 percent of workers worked 50 or more hours per week, but by 2000 more than 14 percent of workers had such long work weeks. The large majority of the people who engage in this overwork are men. Indeed, some young men choose such careers because they see working long hours at a challenging job as a way to demonstrate masculine toughness. The resulting growth in male incomes accounts for about 10 percent of the current wage gap, largely offsetting the gains women made from increasing their education (Cha and Weeden, 2014: 20).

Mothers are significantly more likely than fathers to report that they have adapted their careers to take care of children or other family members. Indeed,

27 percent of mothers have quit a job to do care work, while an additional 38 percent have reduced their work hours, taken a significant amount of time off, or turned down a promotion. Some fathers also adapt their careers to their family life: 10 percent of fathers say they have quit a job to take care of a family member, while an additional 35 percent have taken one or more of the smaller steps. More than half of fathers, however, report no significant career change due to the needs of their families, while only a third of mothers have never made such changes. Today, 51 percent of working mothers but only 16 percent of working fathers report that being a parent makes it harder to advance in their careers (Pew Research Center, 2013b: 60, 11).

Mothers typically earn significantly less than both fathers and women who are not mothers. One reason is the time they devote to parenting and therefore not to activities rewarded by employers. Mothers earn less, however, even if one controls for their education, skills, and workplace experience. Indeed, mothers experience a **motherhood penalty** of 5–7 percent per child, compared to women who are not mothers but equally qualified. Many employers assume that mothers will be both less competent than other workers and inadequately committed to their job. Because most people still see women as bearing primary responsibility for their children, they expect that mothers, but not fathers, will sometimes be distracted or miss work because of their children's needs. Employers are therefore reluctant to hire mothers and pay them less if they do. If mothers respond to these stereotypes by being hyper-committed to their careers, employers typically see them as lacking in warmth and likeability, as they violate the assumption that a mother should be devoted to her children. Either way, mothers suffer a penalty in hiring and pay (Correll *et al.*, 2007; Benard and Correll, 2010; Correll, 2013). Having a child may well affect a woman's employment prospects and earning potential for the rest of her life (Crittendon, 2010).

Fathers, meanwhile, may receive a **fatherhood bonus**. White and Hispanic men (though not black men) tend to work more hours once a child is born, as they seek to fulfill what they see as a father's responsibility to be a good breadwinner (Coltrane, 2004). Men with no children average 32 hours a week of work, while men with one child average 40 and men with three children average 46 (Pew Research Center, 2013b: 23). This pattern contributes to the fatherhood bonus, but again does not account for all of it. Many employers see fathers as more reliable, responsible, and productive than childless men, as they expect fathers to seek to advance their careers and support their families. They therefore preferentially hire fathers and pay and promote them more than equally qualified non-fathers (Hodges and Budig, 2010).

This daddy bonus is smaller or disappears, however, if a man does not live up to normative images of what a father should be. Men who are white, married, in households with a traditional division of labor, and college graduates in professional or managerial careers receive a larger fatherhood bonus than other men (Glauber,

2008; Hodges and Budig, 2010). A father may be penalized if he displays an interest in doing care work for his family, which both makes him less available to his employer and violates the normative assumption that fathers should be bread-winners, not caretakers. Many employers, for example, discourage fathers from taking more than a few days of family leave when their children are born (Correll, 2013). Black fathers are more likely than white and Hispanic fathers to feed, bathe, diaper, dress, and read to their young children every day, as black parents generally share parenting and money-earning responsibilities more equally than parents in other demographic groups (Jones and Mosher, 2013; Landry, 2000). This may be one reason why black men experience a smaller or nonexistent fatherhood bonus, but it may also be that brown-skinned men simply cannot fulfill most employers' images of "a good father."

CONCLUSION

Access to work, and to the economic rewards and social status that often (but not always) come with it, is a basic human need. In the societies with the most gender inequality, men are defined as owning all land and other assets while women are required to perform large amounts of physical labor within household economies. Industrial and knowledge-based economies generally allow women to earn independent incomes, which shifts the power balance within families and the larger society. Sometimes, though, women are not allowed to work for pay or to control their incomes, and they are often relegated to jobs with worse pay, social status, and working conditions. Gender inequality tends to ease in knowledge-based economies, which reward analytical and interpersonal skills more than physical strength, but it still persists.

Statistics about gender segregation of occupations and wage gaps suggest that gender equality grew substantially in the United States during the last three decades of the twentieth century, but the pace of change slowed around 2000. White men still enjoy a synergistic advantage in high-status occupations and dominate the higher echelons of every field. College-educated men and women are doing reasonably well, on average, though averages can obscure a lot of variations. Many less-educated men of every race, however, are struggling. Their average incomes have decreased in the last generation, and white men can no longer count on earning more than better-educated women. Within each race and educational level men still earn more than women, but the gaps are smaller than they used to be. For people without college degrees, which is most Americans, men's increasing difficulties in finding steady work and their declining incomes have made life harder for everyone.

Develop Your Position

1   Choose either gender segregation of occupations or the gender wage gap. Which of the three basic theories about continuing gender inequality – gender performance, discrimination, and the assumption that women are responsible for care work – do you find most persuasive in explaining this form of gender inequality? Why? Which do you find least persuasive? Why?

2   What is an occupation you might want to pursue? Look it up at www.bls.gov/cps/cpsaat11. pdf. How gender segregated is that occupation? How racially balanced is it? (For comparison, in 2013 the U.S. population was about 63 percent white, 12 percent black, 5 percent Asian, 17 percent Hispanic, and 3 percent other [U.S. Census Bureau, 2014a].) Does this surprise you? Do you think your interest in this occupation is related in any way to how it seems gendered to you? Explain using details from your own background.

3   Are you persuaded by the argument that industrialization today generally decreases gender inequality? Why or why not?

4   What do you know about how your ancestors made their livings? Write down a family tree that includes how people put food on the table, going back as far as you know. Did your ancestors' experiences match any of the patterns and changes described in this chapter? Which ones? How does thinking about your ancestors' experiences add detail to the big-picture patterns we have outlined?

CHAPTER 3

Families as the Crucible of Gender Inequality

INTRODUCTION

Family structures vary widely, not just among societies but also among families within a society, but all families share some basic characteristics. A family is a small group of people that is connected by blood, marriage, adoption, or other long-lasting (but not necessarily permanent) ties. A family shares resources, such as food, tools, and usually a common roof or set of roofs, and it is recognized as a social unit both by its members and by the larger community. A family is responsible for taking care of its members, especially the young but also the old. And a family is a web of ongoing interpersonal relationships in which people often feel affection and loyalty but also experience fear and resentment along with a wealth of other emotions.

We call families the crucible of gender for several reasons. Families are the most intimate context in which people learn, perform, and experience gender. Children are typically raised in families during their earliest years, and the lessons they learn about gender will stay with them, one way or another, for the rest of their lives. Families also typically assign different responsibilities to women and men, with wide-ranging consequences. This chapter will start by sketching four theories about how children acquire gender and three theories about the roles families play in creating and perpetuating gender inequality. We will then look at changing patterns of marriage, childbearing, and childrearing in the United States, ending with a brief comparison with other wealthy countries.

THEORIES OF GENDER ACQUISITION

Although all societies have gender, gender codes vary greatly. Children are clearly not born with the knowledge, for example, that only females wear skirts – especially since in many societies males wear skirts. They aren't born with the knowledge that they are male or female, or even that this distinction matters. Four influential theoretical perspectives have sought to explain how children learn gender and, more broadly, all the things they need to know to become members of their society.

Social Learning

The basic argument of **social learning theories** is that children learn gender (and lots of other things) from other people, in most cases starting with their parents. Adults encourage boys to do "boy" things and girls to do "girl" things, and they use a variety of rewards and punishments to encourage gender-appropriate behaviors. Children also imitate the gendered behavior of same-sex playmates and adults, particularly their mothers and fathers.

Social learning theory is based on a school of psychology called behaviorism, which emphasized the importance of rewards and punishments in learning. By the 1960s many psychologists were skeptical of these theories, since they portray children as basically passive recipients of gender and other messages – something that may not ring completely true if you've spent time with toddlers and young children. They also assume that children are more likely to model their behavior on same-sex parents and playmates than opposite-sex ones, which children in experiments do only inconsistently (Maccoby and Jacklin, 1974). Most psychologists now believe children are not just clay to be molded, but instead have active roles in their own socialization.

Cognitive Development

Cognitive development theories portray children as actively seeking to comprehend the world. These theories are grounded in the work of Jean Piaget, who argued that children go through predictable developmental stages in their ability to think and reason. At age two or three, children begin to see themselves as belonging to a gender and start to apply gender-related labels to themselves and others. Like many other categories that children are also developing during these years, gender helps children sort and interpret information about the world around them. By age six gender has become central to children's sense of personal identity and most children have developed gender constancy, the belief that gender is lasting and that someone who is, for example, female will remain so (Kohlberg, 1966).

The difficulty with cognitive development theories is that they don't explain why sex differences become so important. Why does gender, rather than, say, hair color, become central to a child's sense of self? Surely a child needs some external guidance to make being male or female seem so significant. While social learning theories can go too far in denying the agency of children, cognitive learning theories can go too far in the other direction, neglecting the importance of interactions between children and parents, teachers, friends, and other agents of socialization, such as television.

Gender Schemas

Gender schema theories focus on the mental frameworks that both children and adults use to interpret the world. The term **schema** refers to networks of information that permit some inputs to be processed more easily than others. We absorb information more easily if it fits with what we already believe about the world – with our schemas – than if it challenges us to re-examine things we think we know.

These theories were initially developed by Sandra Bem, a **feminist** psychologist who argued that masculinity and femininity are not opposites, but instead two separate continuums. Most people are neither one nor the other, but instead partake more or less strongly of both clusters. People who are both strongly masculine and strongly feminine Bem called "androgynous," while those with little connection with either spectrum she called "undifferentiated."

Bem argued that children learn their society's gender schema through interactions with parents and others, and thereafter tend to limit themselves to behaviors and modes of thinking that they see as appropriate to their own gender. People who do not adhere to these different "scripts" (ways of thinking, feeling, and behaving) are often stigmatized as deviant and punished in a variety of ways (Bem, 1981). In most societies, part of the script privileges heterosexuality over other kinds of sexuality (Bem, 1995). Bem underlined that these limitations on human experiences and behavior damage not just individuals, men as well as women, but society as a whole. The ideal person, she believed, is able to be flexible rather than bound by gendered schemas and scripts.

Bem believed that it is possible for parents, if they are careful, to deliberately not convey gender schemas and thus prepare their children to pursue happily unconventional lives (Bem, 1995: 334). She and her husband sought to create such an environment for their children. They arranged their teaching schedules to share parenting time equally, monitored their children's books and TV shows, and encouraged them to play with a variety of toys. They also split equally the role of "parent in charge" who was responsible for getting things done, allowing the other parent to do whatever they wanted with the children during their "time off." Their daughter later reported that gender did exist in her psyche, but she also felt she transcended gender regularly (Bem, 1998).

Psychoanalytic Personality Structures

Psychoanalytic theories argue that gender goes deep into the structure of people's psyches. These theories are grounded in the work of Sigmund Freud, who argued that children form their gendered identities between the ages of three and five during a "phallic stage" in which they are deeply interested in the presence or absence of a penis. Both boys and girls see the penis as a desirable symbol of power, as they observe that their fathers (and other men) have higher status than their mothers (and other women).

Feminists have widely criticized Freud for being anti-female and anti-feminist. His theories, they argued, inaccurately turned nineteenth-century cultural conditions (e.g., male dominance and the privileging of heterosexuality) into psychological universals. Some feminists rejected Freudian approaches altogether. Others reformulated them into feminist psychoanalytic theories that, they believe, explain gender patterns without implying that they are inherent in human psychology and therefore unchangeable.

The most influential of these theorists is Nancy Chodorow, who argued that the fact that children spend most of their time with female caretakers (mothers or other women) creates different developmental pathways for girls and boys. Mothers see their daughters as fundamentally similar to themselves – also feminine and likely to become mothers someday. Little girls mirror this perception as they develop a feminine gendered identity by modeling themselves on their mothers. This process gives girls, and later women, a psychological orientation toward connection, relationship, and becoming mothers themselves (Chodorow, 1978).

Young boys, in contrast, find it much more difficult to develop a masculine gendered identity. They spend most of their time with women, so they have to use fragmentary evidence to imagine what it is to be a man. Their resulting gender identity is fragile and strongly defended, as men define themselves by what they are not – they are not women, not their mothers. Male psychological development thus tends to "engender" both an intense fear of and an intense desire for women, and this combination of feelings makes men inclined to see women as objects rather than human beings. Frightened by the possibility of losing their tenuous masculine identity, many men resist cross-gender empathy or thinking about the effects of their actions on women. They therefore participate in gender discrimination and violence (Chodorow, 1978; Lorber, 2011: 159).

These feminist psychoanalytic theories rely heavily on the assumption that children are raised by heterosexual couples and that mothers or other women do most childcare. Recent studies suggest, however, that children raised by lesbian, gay male, and heterosexual couples are indistinguishable in their gender identities and gendered behavior (Farr *et al.*, 2010: 175). Such findings suggest that children's experiences with peers, nonparent adults, and the broader culture are vitally important – and they underline the difficulty of not conveying gender to one's children.

THEORIES ABOUT FAMILIES AND THE ORIGINS OF GENDER INEQUALITY

Inheritance: Patriliny and Matriliny

Some theorists argue that the root of gender inequality is inheritance structures. In **patrilineal** societies family membership as well as land and other property typically pass from fathers to sons. In some patrilineal societies daughters inherit nothing, while in others they may inherit moveable property (household goods, livestock, or money) but not land. In these societies, therefore, men own all or nearly all land and they place a high priority on being able to identify their sons – which means they place a high priority on controlling women's sexual behaviors. In **matrilineal** societies, in contrast, family membership and land typically pass from mothers to daughters. Unlike men, women have little anxiety about being able to identify their daughters. Families in matrilineal societies therefore exert much less control over the sexual behavior of their members. Gender is less significant as an organizing principle in **bilineal** societies, where children inherit from both parents, though fathers may still be concerned about whether the children they are raising are biologically theirs.

The vast majority of people have lived in patrilineal societies. The large literate civilizations of the classical world were all patrilineal: Greek, Roman, Arab, Persian, Indian, and Chinese. So were many smaller-scale societies worldwide. In 1949 an anthropologist estimated that about 60 percent of all human societies have been patrilineal, 30 percent matrilineal, and 10 percent bilineal (Murdock, 1949). More recent studies suggest that 60 percent patrilineal is an underestimate (Ember and Ember, 1971), and certainly larger societies have been much more likely to be patrilineal. Until European colonization, however, the world contained a significant percentage of matrilineal societies, including many but not all Native Americans. Today some communities remain largely matrilineal, including the fourth-largest ethnic group in Indonesia, the Minangkabau. Even they, however, are increasingly affected by the patrilineal norms of their national and global cultures (Sanday, 2003).

Patrilineal societies generally required women to restrict their sexual activities to socially approved relationships, which English-speakers call **marriage**. Unmarried women were expected to be virgins and married women were expected to be monogamous, so that every child could be assigned to his or her biological father. Men, in turn, were expected to provide economic support and physical protection to children born to their wives. Children born outside of marriage were disparaged as "illegitimate," granted many fewer rights than children conceived within marriage, and often heavily stigmatized.

Most patrilineal families were also **patrilocal**, meaning that it was standard for a new couple to live with or near the husband's family (Ember and Ember, 1971). Many traditional societies, including India and China, had multigenerational family structures called **joint families**, in which married sons and their families lived in the same household as their fathers and even grandfathers.

Men's relationships with their male relatives were therefore life-long and multigenerational. Women, in contrast, might lose their relationships with their birth families when they married, or at best could visit occasionally. Families typically arranged marriages, so many spouses met at the wedding or engagement ceremony. A man's loyalties to his father, mother, and brothers thus long preceded, and often superseded, his relationship with his wife. Indications of affection between spouses were generally considered indecent, even in front of other family members.

A young woman was required to obey and defer to everyone in her husband's family at least until she bore sons, and perhaps until her sons were old enough to bring home wives for her to dominate.

Many patrilineal societies developed what anthropologists call **sexual alliance politics**, which means they used sexual relationships as a medium of exchange to create or strengthen social, economic, or political ties. You are probably familiar with the image of a king forging an alliance with another king by marrying his daughter. In many societies, such marriages were part of the warp and weft of ordinary people's lives. Marriages were construed as the transfer of a woman from one family to another, as the bride left her family of origin to join her husband's family, live with them, and provide them labor and children. Families chose marriage partners in order to bind kin groups, create political alliances, and accumulate material resources (Lévi-Strauss, 1969). Only some families had a lot of property to worry about, but even poor men felt they had to control the lives of "their" women if they wanted to retain their status as men. Women thus came to be seen and treated as another form of property (Rubin, 1975).

As objects of exchange women were valuable property, but they could easily lose their value if their chastity were brought into doubt or they refused to be exchanged. Societies that used marriages to structure inter-group relationships therefore placed tight restrictions on women. Elite families preferred to keep women within the household compound, where their behavior could be closely monitored and they were safe from assault by outsiders. Women from prosperous families might never leave the house except when they got married, though typically they could see the sky in an interior courtyard. This seclusion was intended to guarantee that their sexual purity could not be questioned and to maintain their value in the web of sexual/political relationships that underpinned their society. These patterns tended to trickle down into more modest families, as people commonly aspire to higher status by imitating the behavior of their social superiors. Although less wealthy families could not afford to keep women in seclusion, all women were expected to adhere to modesty codes that protected their value to their families (Collins *et al.*, 1993).

Raising a girl was considered a losing proposition, since once she married both her productive work and her reproductive services would benefit a different family. In some societies parents also had to provide a **dowry**, or payment to the groom's family, to get a daughter married. A grown but unmarried daughter diminished the status of the whole family, so families might pay a large percentage of their wealth to find a groom. In other societies the groom's family had to pay a **brideprice**, which provided an economic incentive for raising daughters but underlined that a fertile woman was valuable property. In either type of society, a daughter who did not marry or was sexually dishonored brought permanent shame to the family. For all these reasons and more, families much preferred sons. They often greeted the birth of a daughter with disappointment, and sometimes with infanticide. The more violent the society, the more parents sought to marry off their daughters at a young age, possibly pre-puberty, so that their husbands' families would take on the responsibility of monitoring and protecting their chastity (Hudson and Den Boer, 2004).

Patterns were quite different in matrilineal societies. Most matrilineal societies were also **matrilocal**, meaning women typically lived with or near their female relatives (Ember and Ember, 1971). Men might live with their partners, spend much of their time with their birth families, or live in all-male common houses. Women therefore had life-long relationships with their mothers, aunts, sisters, daughters, nieces, and other female relatives. Women's control of the land and strong relationships with each other gave them significant influence and power. Since a woman could provide for herself and her children with the help of her kin, she was economically independent of her sexual partners.

Matrilineal societies tended to be sexually unrestrictive and egalitarian. Because children belonged to their mothers' families, there was no requirement to identify fathers. Many children were born to well-established couples and had ongoing relationships with their fathers, but a fatherless child was no less accepted by the community. As a Montagnais (Native Canadian) man explained to a Jesuit missionary, "You French people love only your own children, but we love all the children of our tribe" (D'Emilio and Freedman, 1988: 8). Relationships started and ended freely. When Europeans arrived in North America, they were startled that young women in some communities welcomed attractive visitors by inviting them to spend the night with them. These tribes saw sharing sexuality, like sharing food, as a pleasurable way to create positive connections between individuals and groups (Demos, 2000: 12).

The term "marriage" is therefore appropriately applied only to relationships in patrilineal societies, where men are expected to support their biological children and women are expected to be sexually monogamous. People from patrilineal societies often use the terms "marriage," "divorce," "premarital sex," and "illegitimate child" when describing matrilineal societies, but this language is misleading. It is not that matrilineal societies had easy divorces and tolerated illegitimate children. Instead, they imagined the shape and purpose of families differently (Sanday, 2003; D'Emilio and Freedman, 1988: 6–8).

Labor: Reproductive Work

Other theorists argue that the crux of the issue is the assignment of unpaid family based **care work** primarily to women. This approach traces back to Karl Marx, who in the late nineteenth century argued that people in industrial economies are fundamentally divided into two classes. One class is capitalists: people (mainly men) who own the means of production, also called capital. Anything that is used to create other goods, such as a factory or other tools, is part of capital. The other class is workers, who do not own capital and have only their labor to sell. People tend to serve their own economic interests, Marx argued, so capitalists try to pay workers as little as possible for as much work as possible (1867).

Marx's colleague Friedrich Engels extended this analysis to gender (1884). Capitalists, he argued, benefit from women's primary assignment to unpaid care work, which he called reproductive work. Women replenish the workforce both day to day (e.g., cooking and home nursing) and generation to generation (bearing and raising children). They also serve as a reserve army of labor that can be hired when needed and fired at will, and they can be paid much lower wages than men. All of this greatly benefits capitalists.

In the 1970s feminists returned to the question of why it is women who are assigned to unpaid care work. Some argued that the answer lies in a partnership between capitalism and **patriarchy**, which they defined as social relations among men that enable them to dominate women (Hartman, 1979). Patriarchy allowed men to serve their own collective interests by relegating women to the least-compensated and most-exploited positions. Like unpaid slaves, women doing care work were given food, shelter, and clothing, but not wages that they could own and use for their own purposes. Even when women entered the paid workforce they brought with them the expectation that they would be ultimately responsible for meeting the needs of their families. Although some men profit much more than other men from the combination of capitalism and patriarchy, they all benefit from women's unpaid labor. All men therefore have a strong incentive to perpetuate gender inequality and to maintain the alliances between men that enforce it (Rubin, 1975; Lerner, 1986).

Childbearing: Demographic Transition

Other theorists argue that the key issue is what percentage of women's lives they spend pregnant and breastfeeding. In traditional societies most women started bearing children shortly after puberty and continued until they died, as most did not survive past menopause. Pregnancy and breastfeeding are physically demanding, and they become even more so if a woman has already had several children. For most women throughout history, therefore, much of their life-energy went into physical reproduction. Today, however, women in many countries typically have one to three children, or perhaps none, and they live much longer than in the past. If a woman lives for seventy years past puberty, and spends three or four of those years getting a child or two started, she has a lot of time to do other things. From this perspective, gender inequality is likely to ease as family sizes fall.

Nearly all countries have started or completed a demographic transition in which declining death rates are followed by smaller family sizes (Notestein, 1953; Coale, 1973). There are four stages to this process, which usually takes at least a few generations:

> *Stage one: High death rates, high birth rates, stable population size.* Preindustrial societies had high death rates because of infant mortality, infectious diseases, exposure to hunger and cold, and violence. They also had high

birth rates because children were economically valuable and birth control, when desired, was unreliable. The result was a more or less stable population size.

Stage two: Falling death rates, high birth rates, growing population. Changing circumstances reduce death rates. For countries that started this process more than a century ago, and are now wealthy, the trigger was the early stages of industrialization, which improved agricultural production and distribution. More recently, better nutrition, sanitation, and health care (especially vaccinations) have caused death rates to fall in middle-income and even poor countries. Birth rates remain high, however, as parents continue to act on the beliefs that children are the best form of security and that many will not survive to adulthood. Populations therefore grow, sometimes rapidly.

Stage three: Falling death rates, falling birth rates, slowly growing population. Increasing standards of living continue to lower death rates, and over time parents realize that more children are surviving. The greater options available to educated people (and nowadays the spread of compulsory education laws) make parents invest more in raising each child. If birth control is available, many parents choose to have fewer children. The population therefore grows more slowly or begins to stabilize.

Stage four: Low death rates, low birth rates, stable or shrinking population. Parents in many countries now invest so much in raising and educating each child that children are a net economic drain, while birth control is widely available. Many people therefore choose to have just one or two children, or perhaps none. Death rates are low, but birth rates are equal or lower. In the absence of in-migration, therefore, the population is stable or shrinking.

A country with low child mortality has a stable population if its total fertility rate (the average number of children per woman) is at the replacement level of about 2.1. (It is more than 2.0 mostly because some people die before they can reproduce even in the healthiest societies.) All wealthy countries and many middle-income countries are now at or below the replacement level. The only countries outside Africa where the average woman now has four or more children are Afghanistan, Iraq, Yemen, and a few small islands. The country with the highest birthrate is Niger, where the average woman has more than seven children – comparable to American women in the early nineteenth century (World Bank, 2014).

Smaller families increase gender equality in many ways. When women spend less of their life energy on physical reproduction they have more time to earn incomes and pursue personal goals. Relationships become more egalitarian, women have more say in household decisions, and standards of living rise. Parents with only a few children are more likely to educate their daughters and sons equally, thus expanding the options of the next generation (Population Reference Bureau, 2000; Basu, 2002; *Economist*, 2009d).

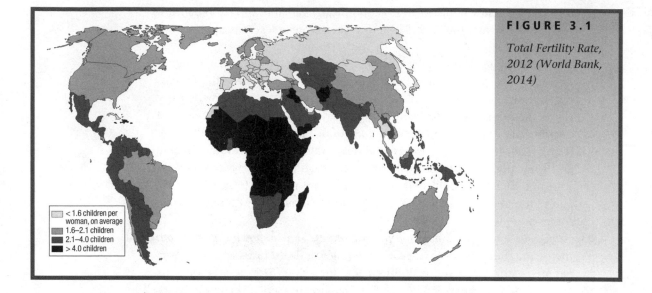

FIGURE 3.1

Total Fertility Rate, 2012 (World Bank, 2014)

Legend:
- < 1.6 children per woman, on average
- 1.6–2.1 children
- 2.1–4.0 children
- > 4.0 children

Households also tend to become smaller, more mobile, and more egalitarian as they are drawn (or pushed) into the international economy. Many young adults move to cities to work and live in apartments or dorms. They may or may not return home, and if they do they are less likely to return to previous levels of filial obedience in multigenerational households. Industrialization thus makes it far more likely that people will choose their own spouses and live in a **nuclear family** (a couple and their children) or even alone. Spouses are on a more equal footing if they have their own household and have to negotiate their own relationship, rather than a wife joining her husband's family and coping with all of his relatives.

The flip side of smaller and less cohesive families, however, is that families are less able to protect their members, and women are often more at risk than men

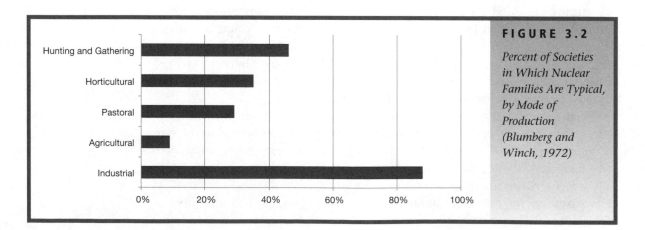

FIGURE 3.2

Percent of Societies in Which Nuclear Families Are Typical, by Mode of Production (Blumberg and Winch, 1972)

when the safety net weakens. Women generally have primary responsibility for taking care of the young, the old, and the sick, and small households mean that each woman has fewer relatives to help buffer the vicissitudes of luck. When young people go off to the city, the elderly mother back home may not get the assistance with domestic tasks that made those responsibilities manageable for previous generations of women. Millions of women have been left raising children by themselves while their husbands travel in search of work. Sometimes men send money home, sometimes not. Sometimes they eventually return home, sometimes not. Millions of girls and women have resorted to sex work because they had no other way to survive, or been sold into sex work because their parents' livelihood disappeared.

Smaller families have made the family's traditional role in taking care of elders less viable. In traditional societies, including the United States until the 1940s, people worked as long as they could and looked to their children for help once they became frail. For most people, especially women, being old meant being poor. A widow in the United States traditionally had dower rights to just one-third of her husband's property. A man kept all his property when his wife died, but widows often found that their dower was insufficient to keep them from hunger. As people had fewer children, even more of them ended up in dire straits in their later years.

Wealthy countries responded to shrinking family sizes by creating collective safety nets that protect their residents from the worst ravages of illness, accidents, unemployment, old age, and untimely death. In the United States, Social Security was created in the 1930s to protect people who could no longer work from destitution. The original program excluded agricultural and domestic workers, so most black people were ineligible, and it assumed women would qualify for benefits as dependents of wage-earning husbands, not on their own account. The system thus preferentially benefited white families with a **breadwinner** husband and homemaker wife. Over time these discrepancies were reduced, but Social Security continues to provide more security for people with more stable employment (Skocpol, 1992).

The purpose of Social Security and related programs was to reduce elder poverty and by that metric they have been largely successful. Before 1940 a majority of Americans over age 65 were poor, but recently the elder poverty rate has been less than 11 percent for women and less than 7 percent for men – substantially lower than the poverty rate for working-age adults and less than half of the child poverty rate (Administration on Aging, 2011: 11; U.S. Census Bureau, 2012c). Without Social Security the elder poverty rate would be about 45 percent (Danziger, 2013). One of the challenges facing middle-income countries with low birth rates, such as China and Brazil, is how to provide a similar safety net even though they are not yet wealthy (*Economist*, 2009b).

Providing financial security for elderly people preferentially benefits women for three reasons. First, women live longer so they spend more of their lives old. Second, in the past older women were much more likely than men to be destitute.

There is still a gender gap in the elder poverty rate, as there is in the poverty rate for working-age adults, but it is small compared to the privations most widows faced in the past. Finally, in many societies women do the majority of informal elder care, as daughters and daughters-in-law are most likely to help elders with groceries, personal care, medical appointments, emotional support, and so on. The more elderly people have unmet needs, the more likely women of the next generation are to reduce their paid employment or quit a job in order to take care of a relative. Since it is often difficult for people over age 50 to rejoin the workforce, many of these caretakers end up in financial difficulty themselves (Searcey, 2014).

Pensions can also benefit female fetuses and newborns. In societies where a son is essential to security in old age, most couples have a strong desire for at least one son. They may not be willing to leave their children's sex – and their own future standard of living – to luck. Many cultures historically condoned female infanticide if a family felt it had enough daughters and wanted to try again promptly for a son, and female infanticide still sometimes occurs (*Economist*, 2010). More commonly, though, families with rising aspirations want one to three children and use sex-selective abortion to ensure that one is a son. In 2008 at least 1.4 million female fetuses were aborted because of their gender (World Bank, 2011a: 15). South Korea was the first country to practice widespread sex-selective abortion, as growing prosperity in the 1970s and 1980s enabled many couples to afford ultrasounds. By 1990 it had a grossly distorted sex ratio at birth, with 1.17 boys for every girl. In 1988, however, South Korea instituted a national pension program and expanded it over the following decade (Yang, 2001: 1). Although it still has a high level of gender economic inequality (ranked 124th out of 142 countries by the World Economic Forum [2014: 9]), sex-selective abortion has become much less common as anxieties about old age have lessened. The sex ratio at birth is now only slightly above normal (*Economist*, 2010; WEF, 2014: 73).

GENDER AND FAMILY IN THE UNITED STATES

Marriage: From Household Economy to Personal Satisfaction

The Europeans who settled in North America had many differences, but on some things they agreed. A family, in their view, was primarily an economic unit governed by the man of the house, of whom there could be only one. (Unlike in China and India, joint families were rare.) Both law and custom gave the husband/father/master authority over every other member of the household, including his wife, children, and servants and slaves if he had them. His primary responsibility was to forge his household into an effective small labor force that would at least survive and hopefully prosper. Affection was nice, but it was not essential. Family relationships were fundamentally hierarchical, with men over women, adults over children, and masters and mistresses over servants and slaves. According to the legal doctrine of **coverture**, a wife was legally subsumed into her husband, who owned his wife's labor, property, and body. In the traditional wedding ceremony a woman promised to obey her husband, and some brides still do.

Men's authority was somewhat mitigated, however, by the requirement that a woman consent to marriage herself, rather than being married off by her parents, and by the tradition of establishing an independent household shortly after the wedding. Parents were deeply involved in selecting spouses, but a woman's consent was considered essential. Young people of both sexes were urged to pay most attention to a prospective spouse's family and prospects, as love was considered a risky basis for this life-shaping decision. Ideally, courting couples felt mutual respect and affection, and love came after marriage (Rothman, 1984).

Most young New Englanders had to work for a few years to acquire the material necessities of a new household, so women typically married around the age of 22 while their grooms were a few years older. Although the husband was clearly in charge, Puritan preachers urged husbands to treat their wives well – to love them as Christ loved the church – and might intervene if they saw a husband as overly harsh or irresponsible (Norton, 1996). Many marriages lasted for decades and produced eight, ten, or more children. Couples knew each other well, and many expressed the mutual love, respect, and gratitude that their community believed characterized the ideal marriage (Ulrich, 1982).

Marriage patterns in the Chesapeake were quite different. The colony constantly received new immigrants, who were mostly male, and many people died young from infectious diseases. Since women were in demand and life was short, many women married for the first time in their teens, often to a man a decade or more older. The average marriage lasted seven years before a spouse died. Women remarried quickly and households often included children from multiple marriages (Carr and Walsh, 1983). Men's power within the household had few limits, as neither religious nor secular authorities thought it appropriate to intervene in what they deemed the "private" arena of family life (Norton, 1996).

Everywhere, children joined the family workforce by the age of four or five and spent most of their time helping their parents and learning the skills considered appropriate to their gender. Both men's and women's tasks were essential to a prosperous household, so parents hoped to have a good balance of girls and boys. The luckiest parents had a girl first, as she would raise the younger children while her mother supervised the household. A string of boys would boost household productivity during their teen years, but they needed to be interspersed with girls or their overwhelmed mother would be unable to fully process the products of their labors.

This economic approach to family life made it possible for slave-owners to describe slaves as part of their "family." It seemed logical to them that economic ties (in this case ownership) should supersede personal emotions. Enslaved people's personal relationships had no legal protections. They did not have access to legal marriage, and masters could sell a child or romantic partner – perhaps for economic reasons, or sometimes as punishment. Enslaved children were profitable, so masters sometimes directed enslaved men to impregnate women or did so themselves. Masters might also reward an enslaved man by giving him a woman and declaring the couple married. Many stories have been told of freed people who, after emancipation, set off to look for a spouse, child, or other loved one. Some freed women, however, used their liberty not to affirm personal relationships, but to put distance between themselves and the claims of a husband assigned to them by a master (Kerber, 1998: 65).

As industrialization separated work life and home life, the ideal of a family as a productive work unit gradually faded and was replaced by the expectation that the husband/father would be a breadwinner outside the home and the belief that a family should be held together by emotional ties of love, loyalty, and mutual caring. Affluent families increasingly defined home and family as an emotional realm that provided a refuge from the competitive demands of money-earning. The ideal nineteenth-century genteel woman was an "angel in the house" who created a haven for her hard-working husband and her innocent children. Many children continued to contribute to the **household economy** – urban children by working in factories or sorting through trash, rural children by doing farm chores. By the twentieth century, however, the ideal was that only adult men would contribute to the economic support of the family.

Love became increasingly central to the meaning of marriage. By the 1830s genteel families were beginning to believe that romantic love – a sense of deep intimacy and yearning – was desirable in courtship as well as marriage. By the end of the century most Americans agreed that people should marry only if they loved each other, not for practical reasons such as needing an income or a mother for one's children. Some marriages of necessity still continued to occur, but they now carried a cultural stigma rather than being the expectation (Lystra, 1989).

In the nineteenth century American culture (like patrilineal cultures everywhere) was largely **homosocial**, meaning that most people over the age of six spent most of their time in single-gender groups. Because of this pervasive gender segregation, people expected their same-gender friends – not their spouses – to best understand their experiences, interests, enthusiasms, and problems. As social life became more gender-integrated (i.e., **heterosocial**) in the twentieth century, however, spouses increasingly turned to each other for the deep understanding and emotional support associated with friendship. Marriage partners became more likely to describe each other as close friends, a pattern that historians call **companionate marriage**.

Since friendship is incompatible with a high degree of hierarchy, the growth of the companionate ideal posed many challenges to men's traditional privileges. Few Americans today share the old beliefs that a woman should consider her husband her lord, a husband has a right to have sex with his wife whenever he wants, or a man should beat his wife if she disobeys him. Instead, marriage is seen as a relationship between more-or-less equals that ideally makes both of its members

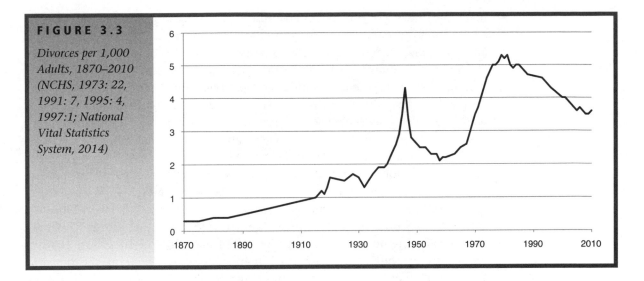

FIGURE 3.3

Divorces per 1,000 Adults, 1870–2010 (NCHS, 1973: 22, 1991: 7, 1995: 4, 1997:1; National Vital Statistics System, 2014)

happy and satisfied. Today most people believe that marriage is, or should be, primarily about love, intimacy, and mutual enjoyment. Such practical things as children and finances remain important, but the essence of a marriage is seen as emotional, not practical (Graff, 1999; Coontz, 2005).

These changing expectations of marriage can be seen in the history of divorce – of what is required to declare a marriage a failure. In the nineteenth century, divorce was an expensive and scandalous process that succeeded only if a spouse could prove serious complaints, typically adultery, cruelty, or desertion. Nevertheless divorce rates started creeping up after 1870. In the 1920s some judges began to grant divorces on the grounds of deep incompatibility. For the first time the courts began to entertain the idea that a marriage that made its members miserable was not fulfilling one of its core purposes (May, 1980). Divorce rates spiked after World War II, as couples who had married in haste before battle came apart, but returned to their previous trend by 1956.

Divorce rates skyrocketed between 1965 and 1980. Many women felt a growing desire for equality and respect in their marriages, which could raise conflict with husbands who felt that being in charge was part of what it meant to be a man. Women were also challenging inequalities in the workplace, which meant more women could afford to leave a marriage if they were sufficiently dissatisfied. Feminists encouraged women in violent marriages to leave rather than accepting their fate, as earlier generations of women had mostly done, and battered women's shelters gave women fleeing abuse a place to go. In the 1970s most states passed "no-fault" divorce laws that allowed people to get divorced without proving the other party had done something wrong. This legal change reflected the growing belief that an unhappy marriage is failing to fulfill the purposes of marriage. And many marriages were unhappy – in part because there was never a time when all marriages were successful, but also because expectations of marriage were changing and spouses did not always change at exactly the same pace. For all these reasons and more, divorce rates doubled in 15 years.

Since 1980, however, the divorce rate has steadily declined. One explanation may be that expectations of gender and marriage are changing less quickly, so couples have less opportunity to get too far out of sync. Another explanation may be that people today experience less pressure to marry, so they are more selective in choosing their spouses. In previous generations most people felt they had to get married, or at least engaged, in order to have intercourse. Today, however, most Americans condone premarital sex (meaning sex when neither partner is married, whether or not the couple is en route to marriage), and more than 90 percent of 30-year-olds have had premarital sex (General Social Survey, 2012; Finer, 2007: 76). Many couples now **cohabitate** (live together without getting married) without stigma and being single is increasingly acceptable. Most people are at least 25 when they marry for the first time, by which point they have had a range of romantic, sexual, and emotional experiences that may help them create good relationships. The declining divorce rate may thus indicate that people are more cautious about getting married and bring more maturity and relationship skills to marriage.

Both men and women are increasingly likely to believe that spouses should always be monogamous. Most patrilineal societies traditionally gave men some freedom to engage in premarital and extramarital sexuality. Monogamy was considered essential for wives, as was virginity for unmarried women, but many societies tacitly accepted that men must be allowed some other outlets – typically with women who were highly stigmatized. In recent decades, however, Americans have increasingly held all spouses to a gender-neutral standard of sexual exclusivity. They have become less tolerant of extramarital sex than people in most other parts of the world, where a certain amount of male straying is still often considered normal (Lamanna and Riedmann, 2009: 133). It is impossible to determine how consistently Americans fulfill these monogamous expectations, as social disapproval makes many people reluctant to admit affairs. Surveys suggest that 8 to 60 percent of Americans have had extramarital sex, suggesting that these surveys are useless (General Social Survey, 2012; Schwartz and Scott, 2013: 173). As a cultural norm, however, Americans' increasing idealization of marital exclusivity, for both sexes, reflects both their increasing gender egalitarianism and their rising expectations of marriage.

The belief that marriage is fundamentally about mutual understanding and emotional fulfillment has underpinned the rapid growth in social approval of same-sex marriages since 2000. If marriage is primarily about two people and their mutual support, then gender is no longer an intrinsic part of the definition of marriage. Many opponents of same-sex marriage argue that it will cause the breakdown of traditional marriage, which is predicated upon the assumption that men and women are fundamentally different. They have, however, the causality backwards. Changes in how people think about marriage and gender led to comfort with same-sex couples, especially among younger people who have embraced the companionate

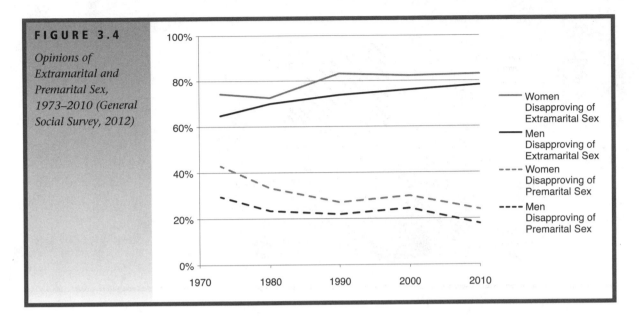

FIGURE 3.4

Opinions of Extramarital and Premarital Sex, 1973–2010 (General Social Survey, 2012)

ideals most fully and grown up in a time when many lesbians and gay men were "out" about their sexual identities.

Many heterosexual people now see their relationships as basically similar to those of their gay and lesbian relatives and friends, which makes depriving same-sex couples of the protections of marriage seem unjust. Many heterosexual people also seek egalitarian relationships for themselves, so they do not want gender to be part of the definition of marriage. A turning point came in 2000, when Vermont became the first state to recognize same-sex relationships as "civil unions." In 2013, 58 percent of Americans, including 81 percent of young adults, believed that same-sex couples should be able to marry (Cohen, 2013). By the end of 2014 a majority of Americans lived in states that recognized same-sex marriages and the federal government gave these marriages equal recognition and rights.

Families today come in many forms. Since 1972 the percentage of Americans who have never married has doubled and the percentage who are divorced quadrupled, while the percentage who are currently married has dropped by a third (General Social Survey, 2012). Nearly a third of American households contain a married couple but no children, a quarter are people living alone, one fifth are married couples with a child under age 18, and the remaining quarter are very diverse (U.S. Census Bureau, 2012d). Even these broad categories include much variety. Married couples may be raising children from a previous relationship. "Unrelated people" may be a cross-sex or same-sex cohabiting couple, or they may be simply housemates. Over the course of a decade many people shift from one category to another, as a child is born or turns 18 and a romantic relationship forms, falls apart, or reforms. A snapshot may look stable, but people's lives often are not.

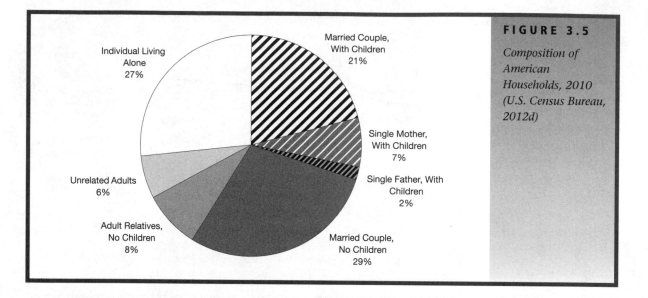

FIGURE 3.5

Composition of American Households, 2010 (U.S. Census Bureau, 2012d)

The Separation of Marriage, Sex, and Reproduction

The percentage of children who are born outside marriage has increased dramatically in recent decades. Before 1970 fewer than ten percent of births were to unmarried mothers. In 2009, 41 percent of women who gave birth were unmarried, as were 53 percent of new mothers under age 30 (DeParle and Tavernise, 2012). Indeed, women's average age of first marriage is now slightly higher than their average age of first birth (Mundy, 2013: 56). Why have these patterns changed so much in just a few decades?

One part of the answer, certainly, is changing attitudes toward sexuality. Since the 1910s, American culture has moved ever more toward celebrating sexuality as a source of pleasure and satisfaction. In the 1950s "good girls" did not have intercourse unless they were married or at least engaged – and the double standard was strong enough that some fiancés would dump women who gave in to their entreaties, arguing that any woman who didn't hold the line until her wedding day was too impure to marry (D'Emilio and Freedman, 1988: 262–263). Today most Americans reject the traditional patrilineal beliefs that women are men's sexual property and that women must be virgins until marriage and monogamous thereafter.

The legal system has changed to acknowledge the reality that sex, marriage, and reproduction are no longer tightly intertwined. In 1965 the U.S. Supreme Court ruled, in *Griswold v. Connecticut*, that married couples have a right to use contraceptives, and in 1973 it ruled, in *Roe v. Wade*, that women have a right to abortion in the first two trimesters of pregnancy. Most patrilineal societies, including the United States in 1970, require a man to support his children only if he is married to the mother at the time of birth. Now, however, child support laws require fathers to provide financial support for all their children. Intercourse and a genetic link, not marriage, establish legal fatherhood. (Genetics alone is not sufficient, as every sperm bank donor knows.)

But acceptance of nonmarital sexuality only explains why the increase in unmarried motherhood *could* happen, not why it *has* happened. Raising a child is a lot of work, and it is even harder without a co-parent to share the load. Why then do so many women end up having children by themselves? And why do so many men help create children to whom they don't commit?

To answer these questions, we need to refine our understanding of who exactly is having children outside marriage. Two observations are particularly important.

First, the large majority of college graduates marry before having children, with just 8 percent of new mothers being unmarried. In contrast, 57 percent of new mothers who have never attended college are unmarried, along with 38 percent of new mothers who have taken college-level courses but did not earn a bachelor's degree. In 2011, 72 percent of black children were born to unmarried mothers, compared to 66 percent of Native American children, 53 percent of Hispanic, 29 percent of white, and 17 percent of Asian (CDC, 2013a: 43). Most Mexican-born American residents have children only after marriage, but their U.S.-born children increasingly resemble other less-educated Americans. The birth rates for married and unmarried Hispanic women recently converged, as they did a few decades ago for married and unmarried black women, while the birthrate for white married women is still higher than that of white unmarried women (CDC, 2012b: 36–37, 46–48). These racial differences disappear, however, among college graduates.

Second, most unmarried mothers are grown women, not teenage girls. Only about 5 percent of unmarried births are to women under age 18. In other words,

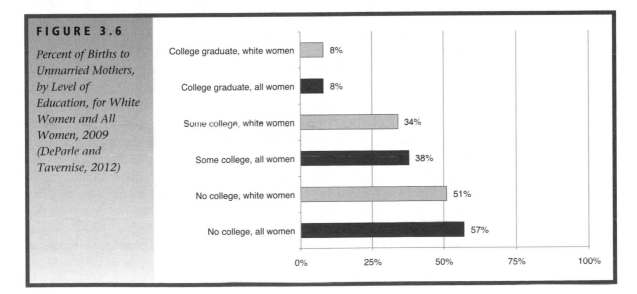

FIGURE 3.6

Percent of Births to Unmarried Mothers, by Level of Education, for White Women and All Women, 2009 (DeParle and Tavernise, 2012)

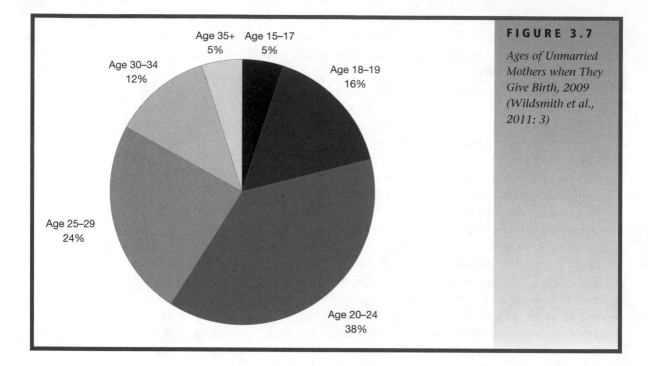

FIGURE 3.7

Ages of Unmarried Mothers when They Give Birth, 2009 (Wildsmith et al., 2011: 3)

the vast majority of unmarried mothers are beyond the typical age of high school graduation. If they dropped out of high school, it is not because they got pregnant and dropped out. Instead, they dropped out and sometime later got pregnant. Pregnancy is more likely to interfere with college plans, but most unmarried mothers are older than the traditional college graduation age of 22. In the past, single motherhood was considered so shameful that a young woman nearly invariably left school or college if she got pregnant, but nowadays many young mothers continue their education despite the challenges of caring for a small child.

These two observations are related to a much broader gap that has opened up between the family experiences of people who have a college degree and people who do not, a gap that we call the **educational divide in family patterns**. In the 1970s education had a noticeable but modest influence on people's chances of such life-shaping experiences as marriage and divorce. Today, the effects are enormous. A woman without a high school diploma is five times more likely than a woman with a bachelor's degree never to marry. If she does marry, she is three times as likely to get divorced. Indeed, divorce rates for college graduates have declined substantially since the 1980s, while they are stable or rising for non-graduates (*Economist*, 2007).

Racial differences exist in these patterns too. A high school diploma has an enormous impact on a black man's chance of getting married, as an extraordinary 59 percent of black male dropouts reach age 40 without marrying, compared to 37

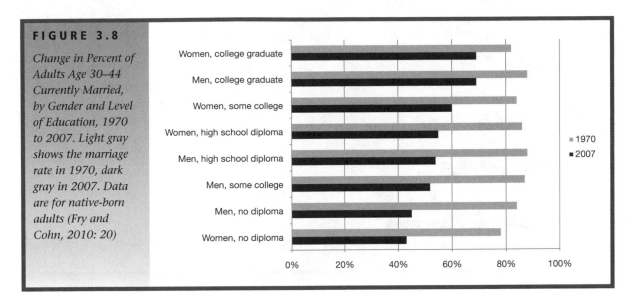

FIGURE 3.8

Change in Percent of Adults Age 30–44 Currently Married, by Gender and Level of Education, 1970 to 2007. Light gray shows the marriage rate in 1970, dark gray in 2007. Data are for native-born adults (Fry and Cohn, 2010: 20)

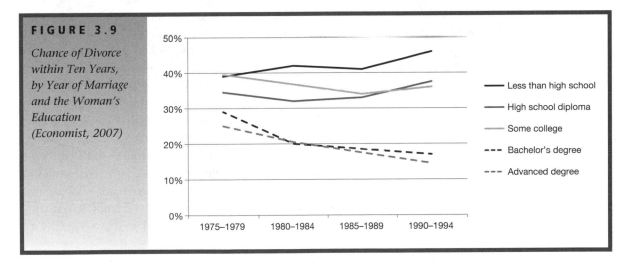

FIGURE 3.9

Chance of Divorce within Ten Years, by Year of Marriage and the Woman's Education (Economist, 2007)

percent of those who just earn a diploma (Stevenson and Isen, 2010). Within each demographic group, more education means both a greater likelihood of marriage and more stable marriages.

So what difference does education make? As we saw previously, men's incomes have been falling unless they have a college degree. Men without a high school diploma now earn only three-quarters of what they did in 1980 – and that is if they can find steady full-time work, which many less-educated men cannot.

Being a good breadwinner is a key component of traditional masculinity. Even today, 67 percent of Americans believe it is "very important" that a man be ready to support a family when he marries, while only 33 percent think the same of a

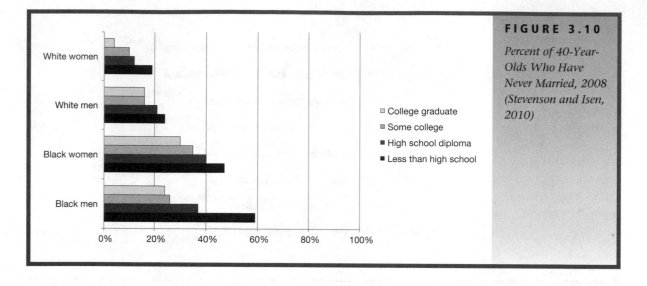

FIGURE 3.10

Percent of 40-Year-Olds Who Have Never Married, 2008 (Stevenson and Isen, 2010)

woman (Mundy, 2013: 60). Since only 30 percent of young men ages 25–29 have graduated from college, most men find that this basic prerequisite for marriageability has become much more difficult to achieve (National Center for Education Statistics, 2013a).

Men's earning power also affects the stability of a marriage. Women initiate most divorces, and both men and women are more likely to file for divorce if the husband is unemployed (Sayer *et al.*, 2011). Less-educated men are increasingly likely to suffer periods of unemployment and underemployment, and being unable to perform the masculine breadwinner role puts their marriages at risk. Indeed, couples are more likely to divorce whenever the wife earns more than the husband (Thaler, 2013). Although most women are employed, they do not carry the same breadwinning expectations and a wife's unemployment does not increase the chances of divorce. If, however, a woman is dissatisfied with the emotional quality of the relationship, having an income makes her more likely to leave (Sayer *et al.*, 2011).

Average ages of first marriage have risen dramatically since 1950, especially for black people. In the first half of the twentieth century black people married younger than white people, but the gender gap was larger than the racial gap. Now the racial gap is larger and the gender gap has basically disappeared for black people, whose median age at first marriage is 30. In any society it is rare for people to abstain from sex until they are 26 or 27 or 30. Indeed, the teen birth rate was three times higher in the 1950s than it is now (CDC, 2001: 10, 2012b: 33). Many of these teens were married, but they were still having sex.

Most people nowadays marry someone who has a similar educational level and earning potential, a pattern sometimes called **educational homogamy**. A man with a bachelor's degree and a professional income is now likely to fall in love with a

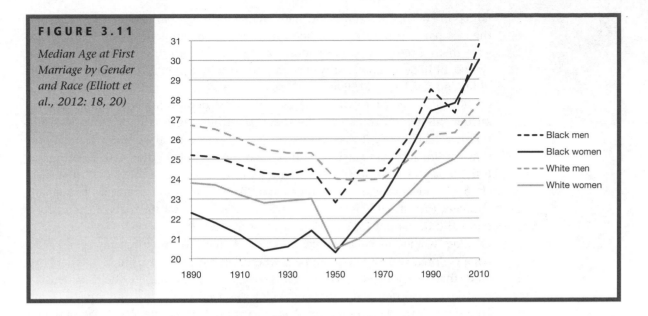

FIGURE 3.11

Median Age at First Marriage by Gender and Race (Elliott et al., 2012: 18, 20)

woman (or sometimes a man) with her own degree and professional income. Less-educated people, similarly, tend to fall in love with people of similar backgrounds. In part, this pattern reflects the simple fact that people tend to meet each other through shared activities, including school or work. It also reflects broader patterns of social segregation, as people with disparate incomes may not feel comfortable socializing, and it reflects the strength of companionate ideals of marriage, which make people want to marry someone who seems similar to them. One result is increased economic inequality between households, as high-earners tend to marry each other and create an even more high-earning partnership. These economic realities shape people's perceptions of the costs and benefits of having children (Carbone and Cahn, 2014).

College graduates tend to plan their childbearing carefully. Most postpone marriage, and perhaps deep romantic relationships, until they have established their careers, as they do not want family entanglements to interfere with their educational and professional goals. They are even more cautious about timing the arrival of children, and a large majority of their children are born into married and financially stable households. College-educated parents generally believe they should send their children to high-end schools and colleges, nurture them intensively, and prepare them for successful professional careers of their own. "Ready for children," in their eyes, is a high standard of financial and emotional maturity that few people reach before their late twenties or thirties (Sawhill, 2014).

People who do not graduate from college are more inclined to have children in their early twenties. Indeed, many less-educated women and men see childrearing as the most satisfying activity available to them. Studies of poor single mothers and fathers in Philadelphia and Camden found that most of them considered parenthood the best part of their lives. Mothers said that having children stabilized them and gave them a sense of purpose and meaning. Fathers said that a new baby was a symbol of hope and possibility, a chance to do things right for the next generation (Edin and Kefalas, 2011; Edin and Nelson, 2013).

Many college-educated people also get a sense of meaning and fulfillment from raising children, of course, but for them parenthood is usually balanced with the rewards of a career. Less-educated people are more likely to have tedious and unrewarding jobs, or to be unemployed. Starting a family in their early twenties has little impact on their long-term earnings, as they are often in jobs that offer little chance of advancement. Since they are unlikely to earn more later if they remain childless, they see little reason to delay the rewards and satisfactions of parenthood (Edin and Kefalas, 2011; DeParle and Tavernise, 2012).

Poor women in Philadelphia, for example, tend to think that the ideal age to have children is between 20 and 25, when one has plenty of time and energy to enjoy them. Some express disapproval of college-educated women who risk infertility by delaying motherhood until later, seeing them as both selfish and unwise. Many young couples are lax around contraceptive use not because they have made a shared decision to have a baby, but because they are attracted to the image of parenthood and see no strong reason to postpone. Mothers often say they had their children a year or two earlier than ideal, but they had no intention of waiting as long as most college graduates do. Nor do they have large families. Most poor women have one to three children and then opt for sterilization – the most reliable form of birth control – once they consider their families complete (Edin and Kefalas, 2011).

More than three-quarters of women without bachelors' degrees have their first child by the age of 25. About half of these women are married when they give birth, while a quarter are cohabiting and only a quarter are "single" in the sense of not living with the father of their child – though fathers often help care for their children even if they don't live with them (Jones and Mosher, 2013: 13–21; Graham, 2014). All of these relationships are less stable than marriages among college graduates. More than a third of the marriages end in divorce, while two-thirds of cohabiting couples have split up by the time their child turns ten (Martinez *et al.*, 2012: 7, 24; Hymowitz *et al.*, 2013; DeParle and Tavernise, 2012). Many relationships founder over tensions around finances and childcare (Edin and Kefalas, 2011).

Today nearly three-quarters of fathers live with all of their children under age 18, while 16 percent live separately and 11 percent have both coresident children and children in another household (Jones and Mosher, 2013: 4, 12). Although three-quarters of one-parent households are headed by mothers, about 2.6 million men are single fathers, 41 percent of whom are cohabiting with a new partner (Livingston, 2013).

Fathers today may be more likely to live apart from their children than fathers were in previous generations, but that does not mean they are less involved in their children's lives. Many men in less affluent eras were often separated from their wives and children by the demands of work. A traveling salesman or Pullman porter, for example, may have resided with his children but rarely been home. Many laborers and domestic servants usually slept where they worked and went home for a visit when they could. Many wealthy fathers provided nice homes for their families in the suburbs, or a summer resort area, while they often slept at the men's club (or at least told their wives they did). Statistics about where men actually were – as opposed to where they were officially resident – are impossible to come by, but families in the past were often more complicated than modern nostalgia suggests (Coontz, 1992). Men who worked 12–14 hour days – or who thought that tending to children was unmasculine – might have a very small role in their children's lives even if they lived with them.

Most fathers today intend to help raise their children, but many less-educated fathers struggle to fulfill breadwinning expectations. The child-support system is predicated on the assumption that men can come up with money if they have to, but that is not always the case. Many less-educated men are unemployed, under-employed, or erratically employed. Nearly a third of the families in the child-support system live below the poverty line, and more than five million noncustodial fathers do not have the financial resources to pay child support. Many of these fathers are directly involved in caring for their children, or want to be, but their inability to provide financial support often causes friction with their children's mothers and/or involvement with the criminal justice system. Men who fail to live up to the masculine breadwinner role can also feel intense feelings of failure and shame (Graham, 2014; Mincy *et al.*, 2015).

All these factors can drive low-income men away from their children. Although most non-coresident fathers help take care of young children, some of them every day, their involvement tends to taper off after children reach school age (Jones and Mosher, 2013: 4, 12–20). If a man has another baby with another woman his hopes for fatherhood tend to focus on the new child, which means his older children may grow up feeling fatherless (Edin and Nelson, 2013).

Children who are born to unmarried mothers tend to do less well than children born to married couples. They are more likely to live in poverty, more likely to have educational and behavioral difficulties, and less likely to graduate from college (Sawhill, 2014). This is not, however, a fair comparison. If most people do not marry until they have achieved a certain degree of financial and personal stability, then people who are married may be more stable not because they are married, but because of things they achieved while they were single. It is not clear, therefore, how much marriage alone would improve children's prospects.

The fundamental issue here is that many lower-income women do not believe that marriage to anyone who is available – nearly always lower-income men – would improve life for them and their children. Many unmarried mothers argue that having a husband would be a disadvantage, not an advantage. They are willing and able, they explain, to support a child, but not to support a husband as well (Carbone and Cahn, 2014; DeParle and Tavernise, 2012).

Indeed, gender patterns within marriage can make it harder for a woman to provide for her children. Although married couples tend to have more income than individuals or cohabiting couples, married women typically earn less than their cohabiting peers and have less ability to affect spending patterns in the household. They also find it harder to leave a man who is violent toward them and/or their children (Lerman, 2002). If money is very tight, the loss of power that can accompany marriage can tip a difficult situation into being impossible.

In short, college-educated and less-educated Americans have similar attitudes toward marriage, but their hopes and expectations play out differently in different economic circumstances. Americans of all social classes now tend to postpone marriage until they believe they can stand on their own feet financially, and until they feel a particular marriage will make them happier than they would be if they were single. They value marriage highly, and they hold marriage to standards of mutual happiness and fidelity that were often unmet in previous generations. Most people feel that men need to be able to support a family before they marry, and most people feel that motherhood is an important source of identity and satisfaction for women. College graduates typically wait to marry until their careers are established, and they delay childbearing until they are ready to prepare their own children for college and careers. Many less-educated people similarly see marriage as a marker of having achieved success in life. Although they often wait a long time for marriage, and some never marry at all, they are less willing to delay or forego the satisfactions of raising children.

Gender and Childrearing: Mothers, Fathers, and Others

Although women have almost always had primary responsibility for childrearing, what precisely that means has varied greatly over the centuries. In the colonial period women and girls cared for infants and small children, all of whom – of both genders – were dressed in long loose gowns. At about the age of seven boys were "breeched": they were presented their first pair of trousers, usually with a small family celebration of their entry into the world of men (Lepore, 2013: 21). From then on fathers had primary responsibility for educating their sons and preparing them for manhood. The ideal mother bore many children, kept them alive, and prepared the girls for productive homes of their own.

Ideals of parenthood changed in the nineteenth century. As fathers took jobs in factories and offices, where small boys were a nuisance, mothers became increasingly responsible for raising their sons as well as daughters. Although large families remained common on farms, where children worked beside their parents, town and city dwellers had fewer children and nurtured them more intensively. In addition to the practical work of keeping everyone fed, warm, and alive, mothers were increasingly expected to do the emotional work that, in the popular phrase, turned a house into a home. The ideal mother now provided moral, intellectual, and emotional guidance to her children and helped them develop the psychological and interpersonal skills they needed to navigate an increasingly complex world.

Fathers, meanwhile, were expected to be breadwinners above all: the ideal father brought home a good income. Fathers were also providers of discipline, which in nearly all families meant corporal punishment. Most non-farming fathers, however, were not involved in the day-to-day lives of their children. Indeed, such involvement was considered unmanly. Women's childrearing skills were attributed to maternal instincts and intuitions, not to acquired knowledge, so if a man displayed such skills he suggested that he was inwardly a woman. For more than a century it was easy to get a laugh by portraying a man in an apron or awkwardly, gingerly holding an infant. Male incompetence in childrearing was a long-standing joke, but it was also a quite serious component of maintaining a masculine identity and its associated privileges.

Although childrearing was done nearly exclusively by females, it was not done exclusively by each child's mother. Except in the wealthiest families, daughters were still expected to help care for younger children. By the age of six or seven a working-class girl often had a younger sibling, or perhaps a niece or nephew, who was her special responsibility. Black mothers often worked outside the home throughout their childbearing years. Sometimes they brought their children to the fields or an employer's kitchen, but often they relied on female relatives to provide food, supervision, and love. Many black children had strong relationships with **other-mothers** – typically a grandmother, aunt, or older sister – who nurtured and guided them (Stack, 1974; Collins, 1990).

As affluent families increasingly expected their homes to be a place of retreat and relaxation, not just an effective shelter and workplace, they developed higher aspirations around cooking, cleaning, and home decoration. Middle-class women therefore spent growing amounts of time creating comfortable and esthetically pleasing environments for their families. It proved impossible, however, to meet the rising standards of comfort and cleanliness with the labor of just one woman. Having a servant or two therefore became an essential mark of middle-class status.

In the colonial period many native-born northern white women had gone "out to service" for a few years as they raised the money necessary to marry and start a new household. For them, being a servant was a stage of life, not a social class (Ulrich, 1982). By the middle of the nineteenth century, however, changing economics and social mores created a greater class distinction between servants and their employers. Servants were now typically immigrant women (in the north) or black women (in the south), as only wealthy families could afford to employ men or native-born white women. Sometimes servants just cooked and cleaned, but often they became involved in childrearing as well.

Middle-class northern families experienced a "servant crisis" in the 1920s. The number of affluent households was growing rapidly. So were industrial opportunities for white women, and most women preferred factory jobs to the close supervision and social isolation common in a servant's life. With more demand and less supply, servants' wages became increasingly unaffordable for middle-class families. Many families resolved these tensions by installing electricity and modern plumbing, which made it possible for a middle-class wife to maintain a house by herself. Numerous mid-century women, however, attested to the loneliness and drudgery of being a full-time homemaker (Strasser, 1982; Friedan, 1963).

In the south it remained common for middle-class families to have black female servants. The south was less industrialized, and black women were excluded from most jobs. Driven by poverty, many black women would work for wages that white middle-class families could afford. Until anti-discrimination laws opened up more options for black women, therefore, childrearing remained a more shared activity in many southern families, both white and black, but it was predicated on black women being paid starvation wages.

By 1970 half of all mothers with school-age children were in the workforce and by 1984 half of all mothers of children under the age of six had joined them (U.S. Census Bureau, 2014c). Fathers, however, were not nearly as quick to take on sharing childrearing responsibilities. Men who had grown up believing it would be unmanly to change a diaper or wash dishes did not necessarily change their gut-level feelings just because their wives got jobs. The culture continued to assume that a man should work full-time in order to fulfill his masculine responsibility to be a breadwinner, and to scorn a man who "lived off his wife," so taking on childrearing tasks usually meant losing leisure time. Although fathers increasingly understood that they were expected to "help out" their wives, most fathers spent less time on childcare than most mothers, even if both were working full-time.

Nor was it just a matter of time spent. Fathers and mothers also tended to interact with children differently. Fathers were more likely to engage in activities that were entertaining or enriching – taking the kids on outings, coaching Little League, watching TV together. Mothers remained responsible for making sure children ate reasonably well-balanced meals, did their homework, brushed their teeth, had dentist and doctor appointments, and so on. In many families children saw dad as the fun parent and mom as the parent who was always making them do things, and not always patiently. The sociologist Arlie Hochschild (1989) dubbed this pattern the **second shift**, arguing that most employed women, especially mothers, effectively work two jobs. Not only do women do more childcare and other domestic work, they are also differently responsible for making sure it all gets done. More recently, Marianne Cooper (2014) pointed out that mothers tend to have final responsibility for making sure that ends meet financially, or for coping if they don't.

The time women devote to housework other than childcare has plummeted. Housekeeping standards declined as the cultural ideal that a good wife has to be a good homemaker faded. By the 1980s women did a lot less vacuuming, dusting, and furniture-polishing than their mothers had. Families at all economic levels used more prepared and processed foods and ate out more. Those who could afford it began to hire part-time housecleaners, thus reversing the long-term trend away from hiring domestic workers.

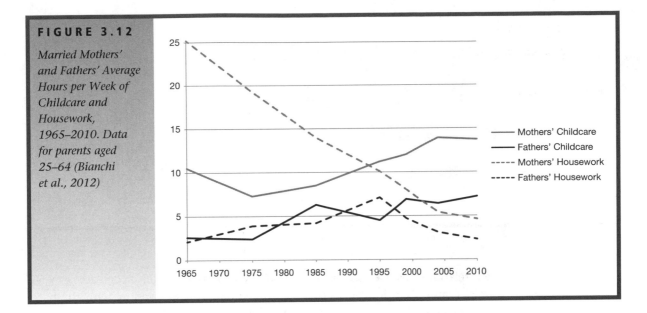

FIGURE 3.12

*Married Mothers'
and Fathers' Average
Hours per Week of
Childcare and
Housework,
1965–2010. Data
for parents aged
25–64 (Bianchi
et al., 2012)*

By the 1980s, however, standards of childrearing were rising. Today, employed mothers spend as much time focused on their children as stay-at-home mothers did in the 1950s (Bianchi *et al.*, 2006). This increase in parenting hours was especially dramatic among college-educated mothers, though it occurred among fathers and non-graduate mothers as well. Many college-educated parents engage in what sociologists call **concerted cultivation** of their children, providing an abundance of stimulating and enriching activities. Less-educated parents, in contrast, tend to expect children to grow up without such intense adult supervision (Lareau, 2003).

These rising parenting standards seem to be related to the increasing inequality and competitiveness of American society. Parents who value professional success are investing more time and money in the socialization of their children than previous generations did. Their hope, it seems, is that children with lots of parent-enhanced activities and accomplishments will be admitted to more selective colleges and have more successful careers (Ramey and Ramey, 2010). Many mothers report feeling social pressure to spend as much time with their children as possible, rely on multitasking to make this possible, and suffer from chronic time stress. In the past many mothers engaged in adult-oriented leisure and community activities, but college-educated mothers now typically integrate their children into their "leisure" time and forego activities that their children don't enjoy (Warner, 2005; Bianchi *et al.*, 2006).

Surveys suggest that today's young women and men are equally focused on their careers, or perhaps the women are more so (Pew Research Center, 2013b: 34). The arrival of a child, however, leads to the **traditionalization** of many (though not

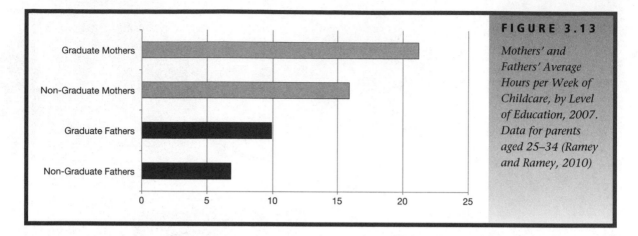

FIGURE 3.13

Mothers' and Fathers' Average Hours per Week of Childcare, by Level of Education, 2007. Data for parents aged 25–34 (Ramey and Ramey, 2010)

all) relationships (Dew and Wilcox, 2011). New mothers usually spend at least a few weeks, and often longer, recovering from the birth and bonding with the baby. Breastfeeding adds to the intimacy of the mother–infant bond and often makes it easier for babies to be soothed by their mothers than their fathers (Rosin, 2009). Fathers who take paternity leave or otherwise get deeply engaged in the hands-on care of their infants tend to be more involved in childrearing for years afterwards, but many employers do not allow paternity leave. Indeed, fewer employers offered paternity leave in 2014 than 2010. Although nearly 90 percent of men take some time off after the birth of a child, perhaps using sick days or personal time, two thirds return to work within a week or less, before they can become accustomed to taking care of their babies (Miller, 2014b). As the years unfold, mothers tend to remain emotionally closer to their children and more responsive to their needs.

Many fathers today are more engaged with their children than their fathers were. The expectation that a father should be a good breadwinner continues, but both scholars and journalists now emphasize that children do better if their fathers are an active part of their lives. Many men of all social classes now feel that it is important to "be there" for their children. In many social circles the stigma on men who take care of children has faded, and there may even be a stigma on fathers who are distant from their children (Edin and Nelson, 2013; Miller, 2014b; Mincy *et al.*, 2015).

Perhaps 125,000 same-sex couples are now raising children together. They are more likely to be racial and ethnic minorities than heterosexual-couple parents, and on average they are not as well off – though of course they vary greatly (Gates, 2013). In 2008, 49 percent of lesbian and bisexual women and 19 percent of gay and bisexual men reported that they have had a biological child. Single-sex couples were less likely to be raising children in 2009 than in 2000, apparently because decreasing social stigma means that lesbians and gay men come out at younger ages and are therefore less likely to conceive a child in a heterosexual relationship that later comes

PHOTO 3.1

Black fathers are more likely than fathers from other groups to feed, diaper, and dress their young children every day (Jones and Mosher, 2013: 13–14) (Source: Shutterstock)

apart (Gates, 2011). The number of adoptions by LGBT parents, however, is rising (Tavernise, 2011).

Same-sex couples are less likely than heterosexual couples to divide household tasks into their traditionally gendered compartments: the person who mows the lawn, for example, is not necessarily the one who takes care of the car. Lesbian and gay couples generally don't split all tasks equally, but instead figure out who prefers to do what eclectically (Mundy, 2013). Studies indicate that children raised by LGBT parents are very similar to children raised by heterosexual parents in their behavior and apparent happiness – though of course there are wide variations within each group (Goldberg, 2010; Farr *et al.*, 2010; Farr and Patterson, 2013).

People other than mothers and fathers continue to do childcare. At least 95 percent of childcare workers are female, and half are themselves mothers. Two-thirds work in a daycare center, while a quarter offer family daycare in their homes (often while caring for their own children), and a tenth are nannies (Braslow *et al.*, 2012). More than 700,000 women now work for a family as a nanny, housecleaner, or other caregiver. Nearly half of these domestic workers are immigrants, many undocumented, and more than half are women of color. They are very vulnerable to exploitation and abuse, with 28 percent of nannies paid less than the minimum wage (Burnham and Theodore, 2012: 10, 41, 18). Unable to afford childcare for their own children, immigrant workers often leave their children with relatives back home (Hondagneu-Sotelo and Avila, 2005).

From the point of view of parents, however, childcare can be quite expensive. Costs vary widely by location and type of care, but in most states full-time infant care in a center costs more than 10 percent of the median income for married couples in that state. It can cost as much as 62 percent of the median income of a single mother (Child Care Aware, 2013: 20–21).

Roughly half of families with a working mother and a child under age five pay for childcare (Glynn *et al.*, 2013: 4). Most families, however, rely at least some of the time on informal arrangements with female relatives or neighbors. The reliability and quality of this care varies widely. Parents may or may not live near their relatives, their relatives may or may not be kind and responsible caretakers, and many grandmothers have jobs of their own. The limited availability of good and affordable childcare makes many mothers work part-time, especially if they have more than one child, but that is not a good option if the family relies on the mother's income for food and shelter (Pew Research Center, 2013b: 23).

A Comparative Perspective: Family Structures and Family Policies in Western Europe and North America

If we look at the 20 bigger countries in Western Europe and North America that belong to the Organization for Economic Cooperation and Development (OECD), we see that the United States is typical in some ways but an outlier in many others. All of these countries share the trend toward unmarried parenthood, and in this regard the United States is near the middle of the pack. Americans are also near the middle on cohabitation rates, though somewhat lower than average (OECD, 2014a). All of these countries have experienced what some people call a **second demographic transition** in which family structures become more diverse, cohabitation and divorce become acceptable, and many children are born outside marriage – all driven by an underlying belief that family life should be emotionally satisfying (Lesthaeghe, 1995).

In other ways, however, the United States is distinctive. American couples are more unstable than couples in other countries, whether or not they are married. The United States has the second-highest divorce rate in the world, second only to Belarus (United Nations Statistical Division, 2011). In many countries cohabitating couples are as stable as married couples, but in the United States they are much more likely to break up. Just 71 percent of American children ages 0–14 live with both parents, compared to an average of 84 percent in Western Europe. The percent of American children who live with neither parent is comparable to that in Mexico (a middle-income country where some parents migrate in search of work) but several times that in most wealthy countries (OECD, 2011, 2014a; DeParle and Tavernise, 2012). American children are also more likely to grow up with a series of men in their lives as their mothers go into and out of relationships, a pattern one sociologist has dubbed the "marriage-go-round" (Cherlin, 2009).

The United States is unfortunately distinguished in other ways too. Infant mortality is higher in the United States than any other wealthy country, and nearly twice the Western European average. The United States has the second-highest child

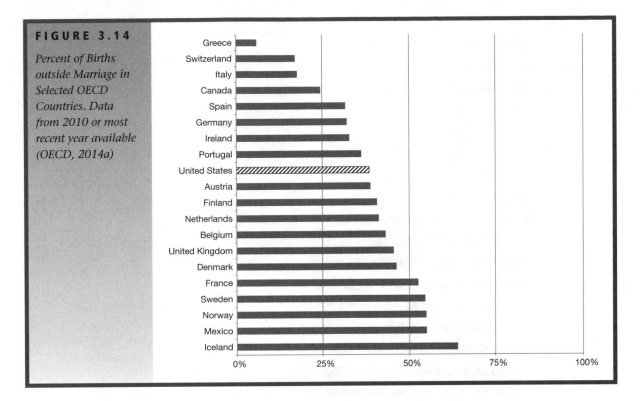

FIGURE 3.14

Percent of Births outside Marriage in Selected OECD Countries. Data from 2010 or most recent year available (OECD, 2014a)

poverty rate among wealthy countries (only Israel is higher). One in five American children lives in poverty, compared to an average of less than one in ten in Western European countries – despite Europe's recent economic troubles (OECD, 2014a).

Some people attribute these difficulties to the challenges of single motherhood, but the United States has a very typical percentage of children born outside marriage. Indeed, that is one of the few family metrics on which the United States is typical. The high level of romantic instability, in both marriages and cohabiting relationships, probably contributes more to American children's troubles. So does the generally high level of inequality. The United States has a higher Gini Index (a standard measure of economic inequality) than any other wealthy country in the world (CIA, 2014a). There are many reasons for this heightened inequality, most of which are unrelated to family structure (Noah, 2012; Piketty, 2014).

The United States is also distinctive in spending less public money on supporting families than any other wealthy country. Most wealthy countries have a variety of policies and programs intended to promote children's wellbeing and help parents balance work and family responsibilities (OECD, 2011). Unlike other countries the United States disperses about 40 percent of its family support in the form of tax breaks, which go primarily to middle-income and higher-income families. Some people argue that public support for families, especially poor single-mother families, creates financial incentives for unmarried women to have children (Murray, 1984,

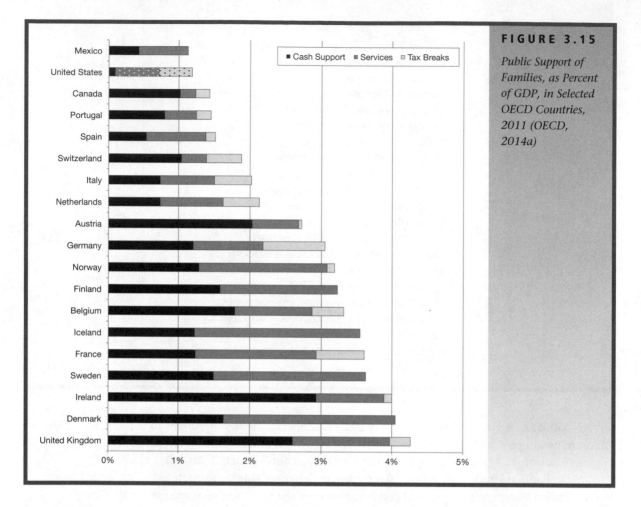

FIGURE 3.15

Public Support of Families, as Percent of GDP, in Selected OECD Countries, 2011 (OECD, 2014a)

2012). The United States provides, however, less support for these families than any other wealthy country, while it has an average rate of unmarried motherhood.

Most wealthy countries have total fertility rates below two children per woman, and many are below 1.5. With low birth rates and long life expectancies, these populations are aging rapidly. People in wealthy countries now expect to stop working while still healthy enough to enjoy retirement, rather than working until they are disabled or dead. Many economists are therefore concerned that the working-age population will soon be too small to support their elders comfortably.

Some countries have tried to encourage motherhood by discouraging women's paid employment. As fertility rates continued to drop, however, it became clear that this approach had backfired. Countries that promote gender-egalitarian policies generally have higher birthrates than those that make it difficult to be a working mother. Sweden, for example, has a total fertility rate of 1.9, compared to 1.4 in Germany, which has historically frowned on mothers working outside the home

(World Bank, 2014). Germany and other countries are therefore trying to improve childcare options and decrease workplace discrimination. Increasing gender equity, they hope, will help stabilize their populations (Bennhold, 2011; OECD, 2011).

One key issue is maternity and paternity leave. With the exception of the United States, all wealthy countries and many less wealthy countries guarantee new mothers at least six weeks of paid maternity leave – with wages covered by the state, not the employer. Maternity leave in Western Europe range from 14 weeks in Switzerland to a year in Great Britain (OECD, 2012: 2). International comparisons indicate that mothers are most likely to leave the workforce if maternity leaves are too short (so many mothers are not ready to return to work when their leave ends), maternity leaves are too long (so mothers' skills atrophy), or childcare is expensive or unavailable (so returning to work may cost more than staying home). Many countries are therefore trying to develop parental leave and other workplace and childcare policies that will help women continue their career growth after having children (OECD, 2011: 129–157). These policies have helped increase women's labor force participation rates in other wealthy nations, even as it has been falling in the United States (Miller and Alderman, 2014).

Like American fathers, many European fathers have been reluctant to take paternity leave, and to be fully involved in caring for their children, for fear of disapproval from employers and peers. In 1995 Sweden reserved a month (now two months) of parental leave just for the use of fathers. Some countries now require fathers to take a certain amount of paternity leave before providing an extended parental leave that can be used by either parent. The goal of such policies is to change cultural norms around motherhood and fatherhood, family dynamics, employers' and colleagues' expectations, and the subtle forces that keep many women from fully using their skills and talents. More than 80 percent of new Swedish fathers now take paternity leave, and studies suggest that a mother's future earnings increase by 7 percent for each month of paternity leave. Germany enacted a similar policy in 2007, and two years later the proportion of fathers taking paternity leave had increased from 3 percent to more than 20 percent (Miller, 2014a; Bennhold, 2010).

American parental leave policies are uniquely stingy and non-universal. Employers with at least 50 employees are required to allow a woman to take up to 12 weeks of unpaid maternity leave if she has worked at the company at least a year and averaged about 24 hours a week. Less than 60 percent of female employees meet these requirements (Kierman et al., 2013: 1). In addition, many eligible new mothers do not take the full leave, either because they cannot afford to have no paycheck or because they are concerned about negative consequences from their employers. Some American employers offer paternity leave and/or paid maternity leave, but that is at the employer's discretion. Much more than parents in other wealthy countries, American parents are on their own (OECD, 2011).

CONCLUSION

Historically, families were economic units as well as the primary place where children were conceived and socialized. Most people lived in patrilineal societies in which men owned land and sought to pass it on to their sons, which meant they put a high premium on female virginity before marriage and monogamy afterwards. Men's control of economic resources, desire for firm paternity, use of women to create inter-family alliances, and assignment of child-rearing responsibilities to women all circumscribed women's lives.

Industrialization and the growth of knowledge economies have transformed family life. Most people now live in nuclear families or even smaller household units, while women no longer spend most of their lives pregnant or nursing. These changes have led to a reconceptualization of the core purpose of families. Especially but not only in wealthy countries, many people today believe that families should be a place for emotional warmth and intimacy and that marriages should be based on love, respect, and mutual self-realization. One result of these rising aspirations is more relationship instability, as people delay marriage until they believe it will be satisfying and have the option of divorcing if it is not. Family forms are more diverse, as people are more likely to cohabit, have children outside marriage, and/or structure their lives around same-sex relationships, which are increasingly recognized as a form of marriage. These interconnected changes increase gender equality, but they can also increase emotional and economic instability.

Develop Your Position

1   The United States was historically patrilineal. About 92 percent of recent brides have taken their husbands' surnames, thus symbolically joining their husbands' families. A 2013 poll found that about 60 percent of Americans said women should take their husbands' surnames, while 34 percent said men should not be allowed to take their wives' surnames (Hallett, 2013). Some people argue, however, that the rising frequency of unmarried motherhood shows that American families are becoming matrilineal – that it increasingly doesn't matter who a child's father is, or even whether the child's father is known, as children are raised by their mothers and their mothers' relatives. Do you think the United States is becoming matrilineal rather than patrilineal or bilineal? If so, do you think this change is overall a good thing, a bad thing, or unimportant? Why? If not, why do you think the United States will remain basically patrilineal?

2   Would you like to see same-sex marriages legalized throughout the United States? If so, why? If not, why not? What do you feel are the strongest arguments of people who disagree with you on this topic?

3   Do you have any theories about why American couples, both married and cohabiting, are more likely to split up than couples in other countries? How might you go about testing those theories?

Develop Your Position – *continued*

4   Sandra Bem's gender schema theory and Nancy Chodorow's feminist psychoanalytic theory imply that more equal sharing of parenting would lead to less gender inequality. Both also imply, however, that conventional gender socialization creates barriers to equal sharing of parenting in the next generation. What, according to each theory, are those barriers? If a heterosexual couple were determined to raise gender-egalitarian children, what does each theory suggest they should do?

CHAPTER 4

Gender and Violence

INTRODUCTION

Gender and violence are clearly connected, but the nature of that connection is both complicated and disputed. In every society, males perpetrate the large majority of acts of violence, including everything from childhood scraps to violent crimes, war, and genocide (Pinker, 2011: 684). Men are also more likely to be targets of violence. Worldwide, men are more than twice as likely as women to die violently: 1,027,000 boys and men and 402,000 girls and women died from violence in 2012 (WHO, 2014a). On the other hand, men's violence against women is a significant factor in maintaining gender inequality. Many societies endorse men's use of violence to control the women in their families. Women are significantly more likely than men to be raped, though men may also use **rape** to inflict humiliation and pain on other men. Around the world, many women limit their behavior for fear of male violence.

Nearly all violence falls into one of five categories, each of which is gendered:

Combat violence. Groups may use violence to expand their territories, capture booty from another group, or protect themselves. Such violence may be called war, raids, or turf battles, depending on the size of the groups involved. In every society, men are a vast majority of combatants (Goldstein, 2001: 1–107).

Group status violence. A group may use violence to dominate another group. Although such violence is perpetrated by some individuals on other individuals, it also helps maintain a broader system, such as slavery, segregation, apartheid, or caste. When an owner whipped a slave, for example, one result of that violence was to intimidate other slaves and prevent challenges to the slave system. In some contexts, men's violence against individual women similarly functions – consciously or not – as group status violence that reinforces men's collective dominance over women. If a woman is killed by her father and brothers because she married a man of her choice, for example, other women will be more likely to submit to arranged marriages.

Social order violence. Most societies condone the use of violence to maintain social norms and discipline individuals who deviate from those norms. Social order violence is usually performed by men, though women may have a role in deciding whether to apply it. **Patrilineal** societies historically expected the male **head of household** to discipline his family members, perhaps with the assistance of younger men. Some modern societies largely delegate social order violence to police and prison guards, most of whom are men. Where governments are weak or corrupt, however, male heads of households may have primary responsibility for maintaining social order even in a complex modern society.

Individual status violence. Individuals may use violence to establish social hierarchies or protect their reputations. Such violence is especially common among groups of young men, who often seek social status by challenging each other to engage in risky behaviors that test their courage, strength, and willingness to endure pain (Courtwright, 1996).

Individual instrumental violence. Individuals may use violence to obtain something practical that they want. Depending on local social norms, such violence may be considered criminal or simply how the world works. Some societies, for example, condone boys and men using violence or the threat of violence to get what they want from female relatives, be that toys, food, or sex.

In this chapter we will start by looking at some of the most prominent theories about why men are much more likely than women to engage in violence. We will then explore the cultural contexts of rape, with a focus on the United States and India, and end with a brief overview of some of the connections between violence against women and international relations.

THEORIES OF GENDER AND VIOLENCE

The Question of Nature

Some people believe that men's greater proclivity toward violence is rooted in genetics and evolutionary history. The basic argument here is that a willingness to use violence enables men to have sex with more women, father more children, and obtain more of the resources that enable those children to survive to adulthood. Whatever genes incline a man toward violence may therefore be handed down to his descendants. Women had more to lose from violence, since if a mother died her children often did too. Although women often engage in verbal aggression that establishes and reinforces social hierarchies, they are genetically inclined to shy away from behaviors that risk serious physical harm (Raine, 2014: 33–35).

People who are inclined toward biological explanations of male violence often point to biological differences between the sexes. On average, men are larger and have more upper-body strength than women, which might reflect the importance of contests of strength in male reproductive strategies. Men also have higher testosterone levels, which many people believe predisposes them to aggression. Some neurobiologists have looked for possible differences in men's and women's brains (the similarities are easy to see), and one study found a difference that might be related to violence (Pinker, 2011: 687). Such scientific studies add detail, but the idea that women are naturally more peaceable than men goes back millennia.

Some **feminist** theorists argue that male dominance over women, backed up by male violence, is the primordial form of inequality among human beings. They cast doubt on the images of egalitarian hunter-gatherer societies put forward by the economics-oriented theorists we discussed earlier. Such societies may have been materially egalitarian, but that does not mean men did not dominate women. Archeological studies indicate that many hunter-gatherers died violently, with 5 to 30 percent of skeletons showing signs of violent deaths, and hunting-horticultural societies were even more violent (Pinker, 2011: 49–50). In her influential *Against Our Will: Men, Women and Rape* (1975), Susan Brownmiller argued that since prehistoric times men have used rape to inspire fear, dominate women, and bond with other men. Ancient bones cannot speak directly to the incidence of rape, but different forms of violence often occur together, and many of the earliest written texts (such as the Bible) refer to rape as a common practice. In this view, the reason some men were able to dominate other men once agriculture was invented was that they had honed their skills by dominating women.

Other theorists, however, cast doubts on biological explanations of men's proclivities toward violence. Scientific research does not, for example, support the popular belief that higher testosterone causes aggression. Artificially raising and lowering testosterone, within normal ranges, does not affect men's level of aggression (Sapolsky, 1998: 153). Men's and women's testosterone levels naturally rise or fall when they engage in competition, but what people experience as competitive is culturally variable (Bateup *et al.*, 2002). One study showed that southern U.S. male undergraduates were infuriated by (and had their testosterone levels raised by) a situation that left northern U.S. male undergraduates and their testosterone levels unaffected (Pinker, 2011: 101). Elevated testosterone levels are thus an *effect* of competitive interactions, not their *cause* (Pinker, 2011: 518–522; Goldstein, 2001: 153–156).

Individuals and cultures vary greatly in their frequency of violence. Many men never engage in any significant violence (toddlers hitting each other does not count). Some women, on the other hand, do. And some cultures are enormously more violent than others. Violent death rates vary from close to 0 percent in some societies to 60 percent in others, but there is no indication that genetic differences account for this diversity (Pinker, 2011: 49–50). Indeed, the warlike Vikings were the ancestors of today's peaceable Scandinavians. Such variations strongly suggest that factors other than biology play a huge role in shaping men's behavior.

FIGURE 4.1

*Male Death Rate
from Violence, 2012
(WHO, 2014a)*

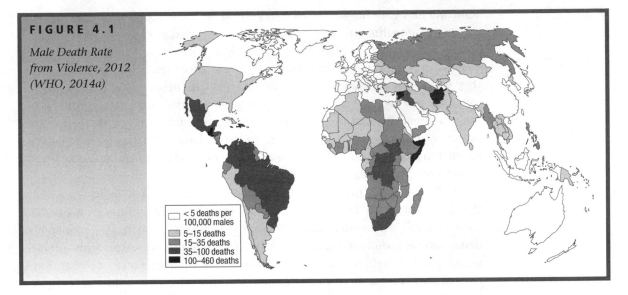

< 5 deaths per
100,000 males
5–15 deaths
15–35 deaths
35–100 deaths
100–460 deaths

Violent deaths here include homicides, inter-group violence, and war, but not suicide. Obviously rates change when a country enters or ends a war. The higher levels of violence in Latin America, sub-Saharan Africa, and the former Soviet Union have, however, persisted for decades or centuries, as has the United States' relatively high level of violence compared to other wealthy countries.

Honor-Based Cultures

Many theorists argue that gendered ideas about **honor** and **shame** drive both men's greater participation in violence and the variation in levels of violence between different cultures. Honor and shame are about how an individual or larger group (such as a family) is seen in other people's eyes. Honor is being respected and esteemed by others, while shame is being seen as degraded and humiliated. Honor accumulates over time, but it is also a fragile thing: just one shameful act can destroy a person's honor.

Honor is highly gendered in patrilineal societies. Women's honor is typically defined in terms of sexual purity, and the most shaming insults for women are words like (to use contemporary examples) "slut" and "whore" that accuse them of sexual impropriety. A man's honor, in contrast, is defined in terms of courage and a willingness to take risks, stand up for himself and others, and fight if necessary. For men, the worst insults typically invoke the closely related concepts of courage, manhood, and heterosexual potency: they are words like "wimp," "coward," "sissy," or "faggot." In the American vernacular, "ballsy" means courageous, while "has no balls" means the opposite (Gilligan, 2001: 56–58).

Men's honor is particularly important in societies that do not have a strong and trusted government that provides **social order**. For most of our readers, if someone robs your house you are likely to call 911 and expect the police to arrest the thief. Throughout most of human history, however, most people have not been able to call on such assistance. Instead, people practiced **self-help justice**: if you were wronged, you figured out who did it, went after them, and retaliated, so that they would not do it again. If you did not retaliate, people would figure out you were easy pickings and come back to victimize you again. Since a man who backed out of a dispute became an easy mark, small slights easily flared up into major fights, especially if there was an audience. Many men therefore engaged in acts of violence in order to protect themselves and their families from future and more serious attacks (Courtwright, 1996: 237; Pinker, 2011: 516).

Male honor can thus more precisely be understood as credibility – the belief that a man or family can and will retaliate for any trespass, minor or major. This kind of honor is essential unless there is a third party, such as a monarch or democratic government, that can be relied on to punish aggressors with sufficient frequency that theft, murder, and other forms of aggression do not pay and men with peaceable reputations can survive. In this context, family solidarity is essential to survival. If the men of the family are seen as unwilling to fight, the family is likely to be impoverished or killed (Pinker, 2011: 34–35).

Honor-based cultures have existed through the millennia and around the world. Many people believe the twentieth century was unusually bloody, but that is true only in raw numbers, not percentages (Pinker, 2011: 48–50). For most of human history, most people lived in violent societies where the need for self-defense was real and present. Men therefore cultivated a reputation for quick and severe retribution that they hoped would prevent others from selecting their families and communities for attack.

Men were assigned responsibility for protecting their families for a variety of reasons. Men's typically greater height and upper-body strength are useful for physical fights and wielding traditional weapons. Most women had young children in their care, and if a mother died her children often did too. Men were therefore more expendable, especially if the society practiced polygyny (the marriage of one man and multiple women), which is more common in societies with high levels of violence. Equally important, women were considered a resource, and they were often captured in battle and distributed as wives or slaves. Men's honor therefore required protecting and defending "their" women. Implicit in this formulation was the idea that women belonged to the men of their group – an idea that persists today (e.g., Faleiro, 2014).

In every society, young single men are most likely to engage in violence. Most of this violence is aimed at each other, as young men jockey for position and establish reputations that will last their lifetimes (Pinker, 2011: 105). Bachelor subcultures tend to have common characteristics whether they are in a mining camp, a prison, a street gang, or an elite boys' school. Single men in groups play hard, take risks, consume alcohol and other mind-altering substances, are touchy about their reputations, test each other for signs of weakness, and frequently erupt in violence. Men who marry become less violent, but low-status males have little chance of marrying if men outnumber women or the economic barriers to marriage are high. Societies that practice female infanticide or sex-selective abortion therefore tend to be more violent, as do societies where many young men cannot afford to marry (Courtwright, 1996; Hudson and den Boer, 2004; Hvistendahl, 2011).

Most violence is moralistic: the perpetrator usually believes that he is enforcing a moral code. The perpetrator is usually a man because enforcing rules and social order is part of most cultures' definitions of masculinity. In many cases, social codes and/or formal laws authorize moralistic violence. Even when an act is deemed criminal, the perpetrator often believes he is punishing the target for some type of misdeed. Men more often, for example, use violence to punish someone for a disrespectful act than to steal their wallet (Pinker, 2011: 83).

Ideas of honor and shame can require men to engage in violence against women. For example, societies that expect women to stay secluded in the home also expect men to beat a woman who steps outside the home without permission. The beating demonstrates to others that their family knows and generally adheres to social codes. If it does not occur, the whole family is further shamed. A woman's indiscretion casts doubt not just on the purity of her female relatives, but also on the ability of her male relatives to maintain order, and thus their masculinity. Men may therefore feel personally attacked if a female relative questions conventional restrictions on women's behavior (Welchman and Hossain, 2005).

If a woman's virginity or marital monogamy is called into question, her male relatives may feel obliged to kill her to restore family honor. "As long as the girl lives within moral codes, she can have as much freedom as she wants," a village elder in India recently explained. "If they are going after love affairs or extra freedom, then they are killed." Because the key issue is the family's reputation, rumors can have dire consequences. "The first time the parents hear that a girl is roaming around," a young woman commented, "they take her home and get her married or else they kill them" (Barry, 2013). As a Jordanian chief justice put it: "Nobody can really want to kill his wife or daughter or sister. But sometimes circumstances force him to do this" (Goldstein, 2001: 366).

In India today, two-thirds of men agree with the statement that a woman sometimes deserves to be beaten, four-fifths agree that a man should have the final word about decisions in his home, and nine-tenths agree that "If someone insults me, I will defend my reputation, with force if I have to" (Barker, *et al.*, 2011: 19). These attitudes are intertwined, and reflect an ancient belief that men must be the enforcers of social order both inside and outside the home. Women are seen as the family's sexual property, and men have both the right and the obligation to enforce social and sexual codes.

American society is not as honor-oriented as many others, but the feeling that a man's honor is besmirched if he cannot control his woman lingers (Herbert, 2002).

Men and women are about equal in committing "minor" violence, such as slapping, but most **partner violence** that results in a trip to an emergency room is committed by men (True, 2012: 10). A third of American female murder victims are killed by a current or former partner, compared to just 3 percent of male murder victims (Meloy and Miller, 2011: 38). A quarter of American women report that they have experienced significant violence by an intimate partner, and such violence is more common in the United States than in most wealthy countries (Black, 2011: 2, OECD, 2014a). Women are most at risk if their partners feel their masculinity has been disrespected or threatened (Campbell, 1993; Meloy and Miller, 2011).

Turning Men into Soldiers

Other theorists argue that the crux of the issue is each society's need to protect itself by turning men into soldiers. In most arenas of life anthropologists have found great diversity in how cultures configure gender: what is feminine in one society may be masculine in another. War, however, seems to be an exception, as men are the vast majority of combatants in all known societies. This is not to say that women never fight. Individual women have long joined war parties, often but not always disguised as men, or commanded armies. Women may fight to defend their children or in irregular wars of resistance or rebellion. Before the twentieth century, however, there is only one known example of a fighting force with a significant percentage of female soldiers – the eighteenth-century Dahomey Kingdom of western Africa, a war-torn society in which women served as the royal bodyguards. Many modern societies allow women to enlist in the military if they want to, but no society has ever drafted large numbers of women and sent them off to battle (Goldstein, 2001: 11–83). Although Israel requires military service from both genders, women are rarely in combat roles (Rudoren, 2013a).

While some people conclude that men have a natural taste for war, others argue that this taste must be acquired. When confronted with the gore of a battlefield, most men feel revulsion and want to run away or freeze (Goldstein, 2001: 253–254). Many soldiers flinch away from killing their opponents, even when they have an easy opportunity to do so (Potts and Hayden, 2008: 70–71). Many combatants return with psychological damage, which has gone by many names over the generations – shell shock, battle fatigue, and now post-traumatic stress disorder (PTSD) (Tick, 2005). At least one in five U.S. veterans from Afghanistan and Iraq report symptoms related to PTSD, and more than 6,500 U.S. veterans kill themselves each year (Kristof, 2012). Men are not, it seems, well adapted by their natures to the experiences of war.

Societies without armies, however, risk being taken over by more warlike societies. To one degree or another, therefore, most societies seek to turn men into soldiers. (There are exceptions: Costa Rica abolished its military in 1948, and a few other countries have followed its example [Barash, 2013].) To help men be effective fighters, boys are socialized to suppress their feelings, especially fear and sympathy.

They are also taught to take pleasure in military culture and to see combat as an opportunity to prove their masculinity by displaying courage and other martial virtues (Van Creveld, 2008). Around the world, soldiers who fail tests of toughness are shamed for being unmanly (Goldstein, 2001: 9, 269; Benedict, 2009: 50).

This process starts young, as cultures "toughen up" boys by subjecting them to a variety of experiences that test their ability to endure pain and shame them for expressions of vulnerability. Most cultures encourage boys to engage in war play and competitive sports that train their bodies while teaching them team spirit and aggression toward outsiders. Some also expect adolescent boys to undergo ordeals that prove their manhood. Associating women with peace, love, and home life further masculinizes violence, aggression, and war. This socialization of all boys to experience masculinity as the ability to suppress emotions, endure pain, and inflict pain on others helps recruit and train soldiers (Enloe, 2007). It also takes a toll on men's personal relationships and makes them more inclined to all kinds of violence (Goldstein, 2001: 251–331).

Slavery, Violence, and Gender in International Perspective

Slavery has existed in numerous societies over the millennia (Patterson, 1982; Walvin, 2005; Black, 2011). The pattern of capturing women to provide sexual and domestic services existed throughout the ancient world that stretched from Morocco through China, and still sometimes occurs (*Economist*, 2009a). The Bible, for example, describes the ancient practice of conquering a city, killing the men, and taking the women, children, cattle, and other goods as booty (Deuteronomy 20:10–14). Although wives, concubines, and slaves had different status and rights, these concepts had certain continuities. In classical Arabic, for example, the term for marriage was *milk al-nikah* while the term for slavery was *milk al-yamin*. The word *milk* refers to sovereignty, ownership, or control, while *nikah* means sex and *yamin* means the right hand (which is the sword hand). A man was allowed to have sex with either his wife or his slave, because in both cases he had legitimate sovereignty (Ali, 2006: xxv).

Other forms of slavery were more based on group membership, often though not always described in terms of ethnicity, race, or caste and inherited through the generations. Slavery could also be a more individual experience, as individuals were entrapped or forced into coerced labor. Although gender was less central to the structure of these forms of slavery, they could also be gendered. Female slaves were typically more vulnerable to sexual exploitation, though attractive male slaves might also be used for sexual purposes. Male slaves were often considered more valuable for hard physical labor. In some contexts, therefore, men were more likely to be enslaved – though their disappearance certainly had consequences for other family members as well (Hochschild, 1998).

Slavery is generally predicated on the threat of violence, but violence is inefficient as a method of labor control, as it may leave recipients incapacitated, dead, or more inclined to sabotage. Effective slave systems therefore also rely on conveying the belief that there is no escape (Oakes, 1982). Enslaved people may, for example, be taken far from their families, subjected to social isolation, and confined behind walls. They may be especially reluctant to flee if they do not speak the local language or are physically recognizable. In the nineteenth century United States, even free-born black people risked being enslaved because of their appearance (Fiske *et al.*, 2013). Women, similarly, have little ability to escape abusive situations in societies where a woman alone will be assaulted, cannot earn a living, or has no options other than sex work.

Although men enact most violence, including most violence related to slavery, violence related to domestic work may be an exception. In the antebellum South, for example, white women were typically assigned responsibility for supervising enslaved women who were doing female-coded work. These relationships ranged from harmonious to highly acrimonious, and some mistresses frequently resorted to whippings out of frustration and rage (Fox-Genovese, 1988: 24, 97, 308–316). Today, many domestic workers tell similar stories of violence at the hands of their mistresses, which in extreme cases is disabling or fatal. Domestic workers are particularly at risk in countries where violence against women is considered normal, but abuse may occur anywhere (McDougall, 2009; DeParle, 2011).

Slavery continues today (M.C. Burke, 2013). Ethnic-based slavery is most prevalent in Mauritania, where it is estimated that around 4 percent of the population remains enslaved (Okewo, 2014). Precise numbers are impossible to come by, as slavery is technically illegal in every internationally recognized country (though not, as of this writing, in areas controlled by the Islamic State [*Economist*, 2014l]). The Walk Free Foundation estimated that about 36 million people worldwide were enslaved in 2014, though critics questioned some of its methods (Walk Free Foundation, 2014: 5; *Economist*, 2014m). The International Labor Organization estimated that the world contains 21 million coerced laborers, 55 percent of them girls and women. More than two-thirds of these people are forced to work for private sector employers doing agriculture, construction, manufacturing, mining, or domestic work. More than a fifth are used for sexual purposes, and the remaining ten percent are military conscripts or in prison labor camps (ILO, 2012: 13–14).

One of the underlying questions here is when to categorize marriage as a form of coerced labor or enslavement. Many societies traditionally did not expect girls and women to consent to marriage. In some of these societies the husband or his family typically paid a **brideprice** to the woman's family, which could be construed as payment for her sexual and domestic services. The Walk Free Foundation includes "forced or servile marriage" in its definition of slavery and slave-like practices (2014: 10), while the International Labor Organization typically excludes forced marriage from its definition of coerced labor (2012: 13). Some organizations include the forced marriage of girls below a certain age in their definitions of slavery, but they are less

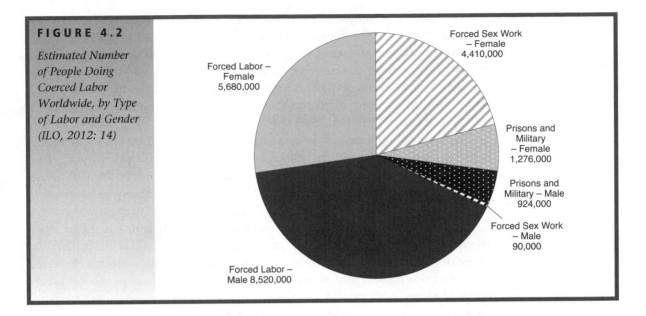

FIGURE 4.2

Estimated Number of People Doing Coerced Labor Worldwide, by Type of Labor and Gender (ILO, 2012: 14)

Forced Labor – Female 5,680,000

Forced Sex Work – Female 4,410,000

Prisons and Military – Female 1,276,000

Prisons and Military – Male 924,000

Forced Sex Work – Male 90,000

Forced Labor – Male 8,520,000

likely to include the forced marriage of a young woman who is 16 or 18 or 20 – though from the woman's point of view the marriage is no more voluntary. Few organizations question whether a married woman who cannot leave a marriage because female-initiated divorce in her country is illegal or otherwise impossible should be counted as enslaved. Many coerced laborers in the private sector originally took the job voluntarily, but they are considered slaves if they are unpaid and not allowed to leave. If women who want to leave abusive marriages but cannot were similarly categorized, the worldwide number of slaves would rise significantly.

Race, Class, Gender, and Violence in the United States

All of the North American colonies expected heads of households (i.e., land-owning men, nearly always white) to control and discipline everyone in their household, including wives, children, servants, and slaves. The Puritans, however, considered disorderly violence incompatible with their goals of a stable, prosperous, and godly society. New England authorities therefore strongly encouraged people to live in towns where neighbors could monitor each other's behavior. Neighbors might intervene if they believed a man was mistreating his wife or another family member, usually using informal social pressures but sometimes bringing a man to court (Norton, 1996: 78, 329). These were not peaceable communities, however, as the magistrates – themselves high-status men – regularly used violence to enforce social order. Men lived within a hierarchy of men and were expected to both submit to authority and (as they got older) exert authority in keeping with the community's expectations.

The southern colonies, in contrast, placed few limits on heads of households (Norton, 1996). Most people lived far from any governmental authority and men were responsible for protecting their families and property. The result was, as it is everywhere government is weak, an **honor-based culture** in which retribution was the law of the land and men considered it their right and responsibility to punish wrongdoers. In the words of a North Carolina proverb: "Every man should be sheriff on his own hearth" (Fischer, 1989: 765).

Violence was generally considered legitimate if wielded by husbands against wives, parents against children, masters against servants or slaves, or gentlemen against common folk. A head of household might or might not be brought to trial if he killed a member of his household, but he was very unlikely to be called to account for violence that was not lethal (Norton, 1996: 51, 80). Violence directed up the social hierarchies, however, was severely punished. In addition, the southern colonies imported more male than female laborers for nearly two centuries, and like bachelors everywhere they created boisterous and sometimes violent subcultures. The result was a society in which violence against lower-status people – women, children, slaves, servants, and poor freemen – was widespread and customary, while violence against the powerful was remarkably rare (Courtwright, 1996: 23; Fischer, 1989: 399–405).

Violence continued after the end of slavery. Gangs of white men beat, whipped, raped, shot, and lynched black men, women, and children and set fire to their schools and homes, while gun ownership for the first time became widespread (Rable, 1984; Williamson, 1986; Patterson, 1999; Bellesiles, 2012). Many states instituted race-specific laws that criminalized certain behaviors when conducted by black people, but not by white people – including unemployment. Black women and, more frequently, men might be arrested for loosely defined crimes like "vagrancy" (which might mean changing employers without permission) and consigned to forced labor camps for months or years, thus re-establishing slavery by another name (Blackmon, 2008). City officials tacitly tolerated prostitution, gambling, and other illegal activities in black neighborhoods, while racial discrimination in housing made it impossible for black people to leave high-crime areas (Muhammad, 2010: 226–268).

By the 1890s a racial gap in crime statistics had appeared and sociologists and journalists were discussing whether black people were inherently more criminal than white people (Muhammad, 2010: 1–14). Stories about black men's atrocities, especially the rape of white women, fueled and justified the exclusion of black people from neighborhoods, schools, jobs, and political power. Often, though, these stories seemed location-less and apocryphal – always occurring in the next town over (Gilmore, 1996: 91). White men's violence against black people, meanwhile, was typically categorized as maintaining social order, not as crime (Williamson, 1986).

In the 1920s to 1960s millions of black people left the South both to escape the violence and to seek work in the North's growing industrial cities (Wilkerson, 2010). They brought with them not just the general southern culture of honor but also a race-specific expectation that government would not protect them. For generations they had been whipped, raped, and killed with impunity, and no less so in the age of Jim Crow than in the centuries of slavery. While police often treated black men and women as criminals until proven otherwise, they often showed little interest in finding or prosecuting people who hurt black people. Black communities were thus both overpoliced and underprotected (McGuire, 2010; Crenshaw, 2012). They therefore developed honor-based systems of self-help justice in which men retaliated for wrongs done to them and theirs. As always, communities that lacked trustworthy governments had relatively high levels of violence (Pinker, 2011: 84–85, 94–100, 115; Rios, 2011; Patterson, 2015).

Taken as a whole, the United States today is more violent than other wealthy societies, for reasons that go deep into the country's history and understandings of masculinity (Courtwright, 1996; Herbert, 2002; Strain, 2010). Geographic variations are, however, larger than racial differences and comparable to gender differences. Scholars consider murder rates one of the most reliable ways to compare the intensity of violence in different locations or times: other kinds of violence may not be reported, but it is hard to ignore a dead body. If we use murder rates as our guide, many northern states are similar to Western Europe. Louisiana is at the other end of the spectrum, comparable to Russia or Mexico. Cities are generally more violent than suburbs and rural areas, with the most troubled cities comparable to the parts of Latin America that are plagued by drug-funded gangs (Pinker, 2011: 87–94).

Violence is more common in communities that are poor and/or economically declining. Partner violence, for example, can occur even in the most affluent of

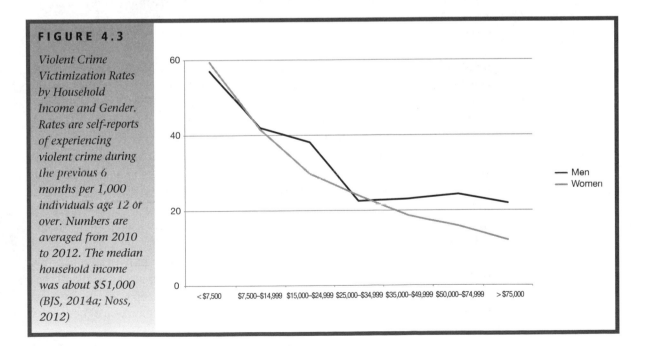

FIGURE 4.3

Violent Crime Victimization Rates by Household Income and Gender. Rates are self-reports of experiencing violent crime during the previous 6 months per 1,000 individuals age 12 or over. Numbers are averaged from 2010 to 2012. The median household income was about $51,000 (BJS, 2014a; Noss, 2012)

— Men
— Women

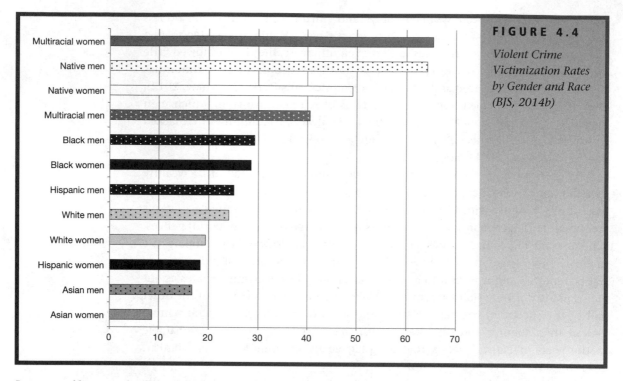

FIGURE 4.4

*Violent Crime
Victimization Rates
by Gender and Race
(BJS, 2014b)*

*Rates are self-reports of experiencing violent crime during the previous 6 months per 1,000 individuals age 12 or over.
Numbers are averaged from 2010 to 2012, since the sample is too small to produce consistent numbers for the smaller
demographic groups. Numbers for the Native, Asian, and multiracial groups should therefore be treated with caution,
though the pattern is reliable.*

families, but it is more likely when families are economically stressed or socially isolated (Sokoloff and Pratt, 2005; Renzetti and Larkin, 2011; True, 2012; Catalano *et al.*, 2009). Women have more ability to leave a relationship if they have an income of their own, access to housing, and social supports. Men who attack their partners, meanwhile, are often unemployed or underemployed, and they often lack – or are losing – money, friends, education, and other resources that convey social status. When a man feels he has little value in the wider society, he may be sensitive to feeling devalued by a personal interaction and more likely to react violently if he feels disrespected (Campbell, 1993: 108; Pyke, 1996; Gilligan, 2001: 56–65). Across the board, people are less likely to be victims of violence if they have more income, with the biggest gender gap in wealthier households.

Both race and gender affect people's likelihood of being victims of violent crime, with Asian and white people facing the smallest risks. Men are more likely than women to be victims in all single-race groups, but the gender gap is smaller for black people than other groups. Multiracial women, on the other hand, face the highest risks of all.

Surveys of crime victims indicate that about 29 percent of violent perpetrators are black, though black people are only 13 percent of the population (Ghandnoosh, 2014: 13; U.S. Census Bureau, 2014e). About 39 percent of individuals arrested for violent crimes are black, suggesting that black people who engage in violence are more likely than other people to be arrested – or perhaps that a significant percentage of those arrested have not engaged in violence (FBI, 2013; Stevenson, 2014). Because black people are more likely than white people to be poor, it is difficult to disentangle the effects of race and social class. Some studies, for example, find that black women's greater risk of experiencing partner violence disappears if one controls for social class, while others find the opposite result (Benson *et al.*, 2004; Pearlman *et al.*, 2003; Hampton *et al.*, 2005: 132).

Violence within a community tends to be self-perpetuating, as children who are subjected to violence are much more likely to engage in violence themselves. Children absorb social norms and often (though certainly not always) behave as they see others behave. In addition, there is evidence that exposure to violence physically changes people. Neurological studies of men who have engaged in violent crime suggest that their brains show characteristic differences from the brains of nonviolent men. These differences have some genetic heritability, but they are also highly correlated with childhood physical and sexual abuse as well as parental neglect, poverty and malnutrition, exposure to lead and cadmium, and certain kinds of brain injuries (Raine, 2014: 134–272).

Violence is also perpetuated by images of masculinity. Victor Rios (2011) studied black and Hispanic teenage boys in Oakland, California, and found that they – especially the black boys – were subjected to intense scrutiny by police and other authority figures who assumed they were incipient criminals. The police officers, Rios argued, were performing a harsh form of masculinity in which they sought to display their own manhood by being tough, combative, and physically violent toward teenagers and young men of color. Teachers and other mentors urged boys to embrace a working-class form of masculinity in which they proved their manhood by working hard, earning money, respecting authority, and accepting their subordinate status with grace. The dearth of jobs, however, made it extremely difficult for youths to demonstrate their masculinity by **breadwinning**. Instead, respecting authority seemed to mean accepting the criminalization of their behaviors and appearance (even when they had committed no crime) and giving up their claim to manly dignity by acting submissively. Many youths rebelled by embracing a hypermasculine identity that equated manhood with physical strength, psychological toughness, and aggression toward others, both men and women. What Rios calls a "youth control complex" thus created the aggressive, violent, and sometimes criminal behavior that it was ostensibly intended to prevent.

Many psychologists believe that boys and men who engage in violence are often defending themselves against feelings of shame and inadequacy. Masculine men are supposed to be breadwinners for their families and they are supposed to control the world around them. Many men find socially approved ways to achieve these goals:

by building a house, programming a computer, or making trades on Wall Street. Men who grew up in disadvantaged neighborhoods and school systems, however, often find it very difficult to meet these basic expectations of masculinity. Most of these men share the mainstream expectations, and they often feel deeply shamed by their inability to meet their own and other people's standards (Edin and Nelson, 2013; Patterson, 2015). Some men compensate for chronic feelings of failure and powerlessness by engaging in masculine-coded displays of toughness, which sometimes turn violent (Pyke, 1996; Gilligan, 2001: 56–65).

Girls and women in harsh environments may also protect themselves by projecting a tough persona, which some sociologists consider a female performance of masculinity. Girls and women, however, also face a gendered pressure to be "good" (Jones, 2009, 2010). Many families and schools allow boys to engage in a certain amount of physical aggression as long as they do not go too far, and male peer cultures have codes of proportionality that usually keep violence in check: honorable men fight in certain ways, but not in others. Girls, however, are generally not supposed to fight at all. Most girls internalize the message that aggression is unfeminine and they must squelch their anger. Most women therefore do not engage in physical violence until they reach a level of frustration, fear, or fury that bursts through these inhibitions. Because girls do not learn the male rules of engagement, when girls and women finally lash out they often fight differently than their male peers would in the same circumstances. Many men therefore experience women's violence, when it does occur, as unpredictable, excessive, and irrational (Campbell, 1993). These gender differences may decrease in future generations, however, as the anti-bullying movement challenges the traditional "boys will be boys" attitudes toward childhood violence.

RAPE AND CULTURE

Rape in Historical Context

In the 1970s many feminists accepted Brownmiller's argument (1975) that rape is a cultural universal and that all men benefit from women's fear of rape. The anthropologist Peggy Sanday, however, considered this analysis both overly pessimistic and overly complacent. If rape is due to men's inherent nature it will always exist, but Sanday (1981b) surveyed studies of 95 traditional tribal societies and found that rape was nearly unknown or even incomprehensible to respondents in several of them. It is possible, she concluded, for men not to rape.

Rape free and **rape prone societies** differed in other ways too. Societies in which rape was extremely rare had low levels of other kinds of interpersonal violence, saw men and women as complementary, valued women's contributions to their communities, and treated women with respect. In societies that practiced rape, interpersonal violence of many kinds was common, men and women were seen as separate social groups, women were construed as men's sexual property, and rape was considered a legitimate way for men to punish women who disobeyed them, rejected sexual overtures, or were on the losing side of a battle (Sanday, 1981b). Rape was thus not an isolated phenomenon, but part of a larger cultural pattern.

Before the twentieth century, most societies defined rape in terms of men's sexual rights, not a woman's consent or non-consent. The word "rape" derives from a Latin word meaning "violent theft," and rape was illicit sex that violated the property rights of a woman's family (Freedman, 2013: 3). Being raped shamed the woman and her family, so if a woman accused a man of rape it was generally her reputation that suffered most – unless, perhaps, he made it right by marrying her. In the Bible, for example, a man who rapes a virgin is instructed to pay 50 shekels to her father and marry her. Only if the woman is betrothed or married is rape a capital crime, and the woman is put to death too if the act occurred within city walls, where presumably she could have cried louder for help (Deuteronomy 22:22–28).

Honor cultures classically distinguish between women who possess honor (who deserve protection, even if they do not always receive it) and women who have lost their honor (who are available for sexual use by any man, since no more harm can be done to a woman who has lost her purity). In many cultures a woman who was raped was expected to commit suicide, and if she did not do so her male relatives were expected to kill her to restore the family's honor. In many cases the only alternative was leaving her family (so they could claim she had died) and working as a prostitute.

These patterns continue today, though they are increasingly contested. Several countries allow men accused of rape to avoid prosecution by marrying the victim (UNICEF, 2011: 3; U.S. Department of State, 2012: 43). In much of Asia and Africa a woman who has been raped (by someone other than her husband) is considered deeply and permanently shamed. Many police still believe that rape charges are generally best settled by persuading the rapist and the victim to marry. Some still believe there is no harm in raping a woman whose purity has already been taken, so women who report a rape face a significant risk of being raped again in police custody (Harris, 2013a). Police may even encourage families to kill a girl who has been abducted (*Economist*, 2012a).

Traditional courts sometimes ordered a woman to be raped to punish her family, whether or not she did anything wrong. In 2005, for example, a local Pakistani court ordered a woman to be gang-raped to punish her family for the allegation that her younger brother had had sex with a higher-status woman. Instead of killing herself in shame, as was expected, the woman spoke out against the injustice of her experience. Her story stirred outrage in Pakistan and strengthened an already-building campaign to change laws and practices related to rape. Many Pakistanis now agree that women should not be raped, but others resist changes to older ways of thinking about sex, consent, and family membership (Masood, 2006).

Mass rape often occurs during wars and other inter-group conflicts. In the ancient world, women captured during war were often raped on the spot and then distributed to the soldiers. Since rape shamed the whole family, it was an effective tactic of both war and inter-family conflicts (Hudson and den Boer, 2004: 7). Mass rape can be used tactically to drive communities off land, extract information, or coerce cooperation, and it can be used as propaganda to humiliate men who have failed in their role as protectors. It can also be a form of male bonding, generating the intense emotions that make men more willing to fight and die for each other. Commanders may therefore encourage mass rapes to increase solidarity among the troops (Study of the Secretary-General, 2006: 53; Kristof and WuDunn, 2009: 83–86).

Mass rape occurred during most modern wars. More than 20,000 women were raped when Japan conquered Nanking in the 1930s, and perhaps as many as 500,000 women during the 1994 genocide in Rwanda. During World War II German officers allowed their men to rape and plunder on the eastern front, where they considered the natives genetically inferior, and the Soviets reciprocated by raping at least 100,000 women when they took Berlin. In some parts of the Congo three-quarters of the women have been raped, and in some parts of Liberia more than 90 percent of the women and girls over age three. Bangladesh, Bosnia, Sudan, Sri Lanka, Syria, Iraq – the list continues to grow (Goldstein, 2001: 362–368; Potts and Hayden, 2008: 136; True, 2012: 115; Study of the Secretary-General, 2006: 54; Kristof and WuDunn, 2009: 85).

Rape is not, however, a universal accompaniment of war. The early European settlers in North America were surprised to learn that white women who were captured by Native Americans were never sexually assaulted. Rape and sexual coercion were culturally unacceptable in the Native communities of the eastern seaboard, including in times of war. Native women were, however, vulnerable to rape by white men, as some settlers considered rape a right of conquest (Sanday, 1981b; Ulrich, 1982: 97; D'Emilio and Freedman, 1988: 8–9).

In the United States, women who brought charges of rape used to be subjected to intense scrutiny for any hint of complicity or previous indiscretions, however minor. In 1906 the Michigan Supreme Court ruled that if at any point the woman ceased resisting, even for a moment, the act was not a rape (Meloy and Miller, 2011: 47). It was widely believed that women frequently accused men of rape after regretting consensual sex, and courts typically reasoned that a woman who consented to sex with one man had permanently lost the right to refuse sex to other men. Even little girls were often accused of "bad character" if they charged their fathers or other men with rape (Freedman, 2013: 23–24). Most women concluded that reporting a rape would make their lives worse, not better. They therefore tried to keep the rape a secret, even from their closest relatives. One result was that perpetrators were rarely identified or punished.

Rape began to be explicitly politicized in the 1830s, when abolitionists used images of the sexual vulnerability of enslaved black women to help build a moral argument against slavery. In response, several states modified their rape statutes to insert the word "white" before "woman," thus legally defining nonconsensual sex with non-white women as not rape (Freedman, 2013: 28). After emancipation, white supremacists used images of brutal black men ravishing innocent white women to build support for racial segregation and the political and civil disenfranchisement of black men. Black men, they argued, were incapable of the self-control necessary to exercise the rights of citizenship (Freedman, 2013: 8).

Both white and black women tried to challenge the traditional impunity of "libertines": higher-status white men who assumed that lower-status girls and women were their playthings. Because courts considered such men honest and sexually desirable, they usually accepted their claims that the females had consented. One of the arguments of the women's suffrage movement was that if women could vote they could revise the laws to protect themselves from harassment and assault (Freedman, 2013: 2, 57).

Some people even began to question the equation of marriage and sexual consent. "Free love" advocates argued that love and consent, not marriage, defined sexual morality, but most people considered their views scandalous (Sears, 1977). More common, but still rebellious, was the view that only love could sanctify sex, so a woman should not be obliged to have sex with a husband she did not love (Horowitz, 2002: 266). Some people argued for what they called "voluntary motherhood" – that a wife should be able to refuse sex unless she wanted to become pregnant. Distributing contraceptive information was criminalized in the 1870s, so many women had children unwillingly (Brodie, 1994: 253–288).

The most mainstream of these currents was the **temperance** movement, which was also a campaign against male violence. Nineteenth-century men drank abundantly, and many women had frequent experience of men's drunken rages. Challenging a man's right to discipline his wife and children was going too far for the culture of the time: only the most extreme feminists suggested that a man should not be allowed to beat his wife. Blaming "demon rum," however, externalized the problem. It was the liquor, not the man. Everyone understood that men were less likely to beat their wives and children if they stayed sober. And if men did not spend money on alcohol, there would be more money for food and heat, so maybe less reason for marital conflict. A subtext, only sometimes explicit, was that women should not be subjected to men's drunken advances either on the streets or in their homes (Epstein, 1981: 127–128).

Through most of the twentieth century popular opinion and expert commentary agreed that rape was rare and unimportant. In the 1920s medical schools taught that women's rape accusations were often lies or fantasies. In the 1960s a popular criminologist claimed that alleged rapes were typically "victim-precipitated" as women signaled availability and then later claimed rape (Freedman, 2013: 230–274). In 1972 a majority of survey respondents judged that forcibly raping a stranger in the park was more acceptable than selling LSD (Pinker, 2011: 408). In the 1980s nearly half of college-age men acknowledged that they had engaged in sexual coercion, defined as "ignoring a woman's protest, using physical aggression, [or] forcing intercourse" (Parrot and Cummings, 2006: 43). Such behavior was not generally called rape, but "forced intercourse" was quite common.

In the 1970s women identified rape as a widespread problem and sought to redefine what counted as rape. Only consensual sex, feminists insisted, should be considered moral and legal. They argued that forced sex within marriage is rape and gradually got legislatures and courts to agree that "marital rape" is a legitimate category rather than a contradiction of terms. They also created new terms, such as "date rape" and "acquaintance rape," that validated women's experiences that too often social interactions became coercive or violent. By the 1990s growing numbers of women and men were talking about the sexual exploitation they had experienced as children, usually at the hands of a parent, teacher, coach, clergy member, or other authority figure. Sexual abuse of children, feminists argued, is not a rare and private matter, but reflects large cultural patterns that eroticize children and give men excessive power and privilege (Freedman, 2013: 276–288).

Feminists identified an interlocking network of beliefs, attitudes, and behaviors that condone and encourage rape, which they called **rape culture**. Women, they argued, have a right to physical and sexual autonomy and should not be seen as men's property. They criticized language and imagery that suggest sex is something men do to women, rather than something that people do together. Sex, they insisted, is freely chosen. If it is not freely chosen it is violence, not sex. They denounced the assumptions that women often lie about rape and that when a woman says "no" she often means "yes." And they insisted that it is the rapist, not the victim, who should feel shame.

On a practical level, feminists organized to change laws and to provide medical and legal assistance to rape victims. They created rape crisis centers and insisted that rape victims should be treated with kindness and empathy, not blame. They developed new training materials for police, emergency room workers, and other people who are likely to come into contact with victims. They organized "Take Back the Night" walks and argued that women should be able to go about their lives without fear of violent attack.

The frequency of rape has dropped by nearly 80 percent since 1980. The solid black line in the graph in Figure 4.5 is based on a national survey that asks Americans about their experiences of crime during the previous six months (BJS, 2013). Women are now much less likely to report a rape than they were before 1990, though there has been little change since 2000. The dashed black line is based on rapes reported to the police. Even today most rapes are not reported, but evidence suggests (not surprisingly) that victims are more likely to report rapes if they are treated well rather than stigmatized (Clay-Warner and Burt, 2005: 150). The number of police reports nearly doubled between 1973 and 1992, as women became more willing to make reports, but since then has declined roughly in tandem with the decline in

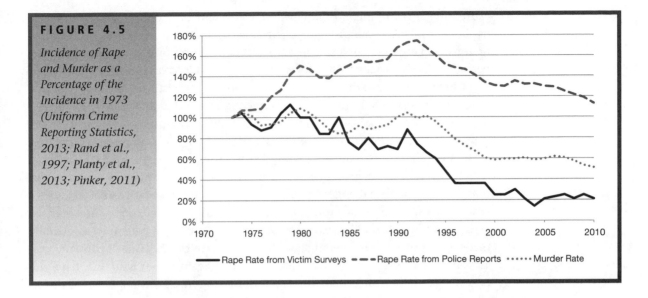

FIGURE 4.5

Incidence of Rape and Murder as a Percentage of the Incidence in 1973 (Uniform Crime Reporting Statistics, 2013; Rand et al., 1997; Planty et al., 2013; Pinker, 2011)

survey-reported rapes. Most other forms of violence have also decreased in recent decades, but not as much as rapes. The dotted gray line is the murder rate, which has fallen by nearly 50 percent since the 1970s – an impressive change, but not as large as the change in rapes.

Other forms of gender-related violence have also declined more quickly than the murder rate. The frequency of serious partner violence, for example, fell by two-thirds between 1993 and 2005, paralleling the decline in rape. In 1987 half of all Americans agreed that it is sometimes appropriate for a man to discipline his wife by hitting her with a belt or stick. Just ten years later only one in six still held that opinion (Pinker, 2011: 408–410). It seems likely that some of the decrease in gender-related violence was caused by the same factors that drove the more general decrease in violence, while the rest was caused by changes in attitudes toward gender.

Rape in the Contemporary United States

Definitions of rape continue to be debated. Until 2012 the FBI defined rape as "the carnal knowledge of a female forcibly and against her will," which was generally understood to refer only to penile/vaginal intercourse. Since the 1970s, however, most states and police departments – as well as victims' advocacy groups and feminist organizations – have expanded their understanding of rape to include forcible penetration of any kind (including anal and oral), penetration when the victim is incapacitated by alcohol or other drugs, and the possibility that men as well as women can be raped. The key issue, many people now agree, is whether both parties consented to the act. Using different definitions in different jurisdictions caused much confusion, so the federal government now encourages everyone to use a more inclusive definition: "penetration, no matter how slight, of the vagina or anus with any body part or object, or oral penetration by a sex organ of another person, without the consent of the victim" (FBI, 2012; Savage, 2012).

People continue to disagree, however, about what constitutes consent. Cultural mores are in flux, and both women and men may feel that a woman who engages in some level of sexual activity gives up her right to say no to intercourse. Many women have experienced lasting physical and psychological harm from experiences they did not name as rape. Men who identify as heterosexual may be even more reluctant to acknowledge a rape, to themselves as well as others, as they may feel that being raped challenges their sexual and gender identity (Rabin, 2012). Researchers who try to determine the frequency of rape therefore do not start by asking blunt questions like "have you been raped?" or "have you raped someone?" Instead, they ask less threatening questions that focus on the issue of consent, such as "have you ever been forced to have intercourse against your will?" or "have you ever had sex with someone who was too drunk to refuse?" In many cases, people who answer "yes" to such questions do not view the incident as rape (e.g., Krebs *et al.*, 2007: 5-21).

The issue of alcohol use can be especially vexed. There have been millions of instances of men having sex with women, or sometimes men, who were unconscious or incapacitated by alcohol, cold medicines, surgical anesthesia, or other drugs, legal or illegal. Being unable to protect oneself does not constitute consent. Drinking alcohol, though, creates a continuum of changes, not an abrupt transition from completely sober to unconscious. Part of the definition of inebriation is impaired judgment, and people who have nonconsensual sex after drinking are particularly unlikely to define it as rape. One study found that just 2 percent of female undergraduates who were sexually assaulted while they were incapacitated reported their experiences to the police, compared to (a still small) 13 percent of women who were sexually assaulted by physical force (Krebs *et al.*, 2007: xvii).

Nonconsensual sexual acts that do not involve penetration can have also real consequences. Many recent studies describe all nonconsensual sexual acts as **sexual assault**, which includes both rape and other nonconsensual touching (such as forced kissing or groping a breast or other body part), which is technically called **sexual battery**. The term **sexual harassment** is sometimes reserved for verbal expressions only – catcalls, unwanted sexual commentary, and so on – but other people use it to include various forms of unwanted touch. Here too definitions vary.

Studies of men who engage in sexual harassment suggest that many do it for the ego boost. Asserting dominance over a woman, it seems, makes them briefly feel better about themselves. Others do it for tactical reasons: to drive women out of a male-coded job or a social environment that they think should be for men only. A small minority are engaging in "rape testing": if the woman responds by freezing in fear they will continue, while if she responds assertively they will try to find a more pliable victim (Langelan, 1993: 45–48). Being groped is not the same as being raped, but it often makes the recipient feel uncomfortable or violated. Indeed, the goal of many harassers is to make their target cringe, and a woman may not know until the episode is over how serious the attack will be. Sexual harassment can thus be part of a continuum of sexual violence (Baker, 2008; Roy, 2010).

Nearly one in five American women has been raped. Sexual battery is even more common, with 45 percent of women reporting they have been sexually assaulted. About 1.1 percent of American women – 1.3 million women – experienced rape or attempted rape in 2010. Alcohol or other drugs facilitated about 60 percent of these assaults, while the rest involved violence or threats of physical harm. Women are most at risk between the ages of 16 and 20. Their risk more than doubles if they identify as bisexual rather than heterosexual or lesbian, and their risk is somewhat higher if they are multiracial or Native, though the racial/ethnic difference is smaller than for other kinds of violent crimes. The vast majority of perpetrators are men, and the woman usually knows him personally (Black *et al.*, 2011: 18–24; Walters *et al.*, 2013: 10; Rennison, 2014).

Although men are much less likely than women to be raped, one in 71 men reports that he has been raped sometime in his life. More than a quarter of male victims were first raped when they were aged ten or less, and roughly 440,000 men (compared to 2.7 million women) report that they were raped as children. Sexual battery is again more common, with more than one out of five men reporting such assaults. Gay and bisexual men are roughly twice as likely as heterosexual men to be sexually assaulted. Nearly all rape victims report male perpetrators, but women perpetrate about a quarter of the incidents of sexual battery on men (Black *et al.*, 2011: 3, 19–25; Walters *et al.*, 2013: 1, 13).

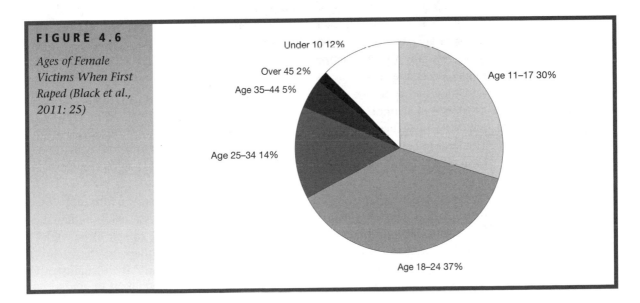

FIGURE 4.6

Ages of Female Victims When First Raped (Black et al., 2011: 25)

Under 10 12%

Over 45 2%

Age 35–44 5%

Age 11–17 30%

Age 25–34 14%

Age 18–24 37%

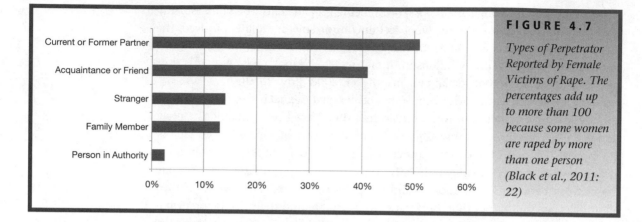

FIGURE 4.7

Types of Perpetrator Reported by Female Victims of Rape. The percentages add up to more than 100 because some women are raped by more than one person (Black et al., 2011: 22)

Like other forms of violence, rape and sexual assault are more frequent when people are disadvantaged in other ways. Women without a high school diploma are more than four times as likely to be raped as women with a bachelor's degree, while women with a household income of less than $7,500 a year are six times more likely to be raped than women with a household income of more than $75,000 a year. It has sometimes been suggested that college students are more likely than other women their age to be raped (Krebs *et al.*, 2007: 1-1), but more precise studies indicate that women aged 18 to 22 are about 30 percent more likely to be raped if they are not enrolled in college (Hart, 2003: 2; Rennison, 2014).

An often-cited study of campus rape (based on an online survey at just two universities) found that 19 percent of female undergraduates reported that they had experienced at least one attempted or completed sexual assault since entering college, a proportion that rose to 26 percent among seniors. Nearly 12 percent of the women had been raped – 8.5 percent reported a rape while they were incapacitated by alcohol or occasionally other drugs, while 3.4 reported a rape that was physically forced. Although men reported fewer sexual assaults than their female peers, the gender gap was smaller than in other studies: 6.1 percent of men said they had been sexually assaulted since arriving at college, usually with the assistance of alcohol. Only 2.5 percent of college men acknowledged committing any kind of sexual assault, while 1.8 percent acknowledged committing a rape. The large majority of confessed perpetrators said that both they and the victim had been drinking before the incident (Krebs *et al.*, 2007: 5-2, 5-3, 5-5, 5-27, 5-28; *Economist*, 2014p).

Female victims typically knew the perpetrator, and in almost a fifth of the cases he was someone she was dating. Women who had been threatened, humiliated, or hurt by a dating partner were much more likely to be raped. Women who experienced sexual assault before college (16 percent of respondents) were also much more likely to be assaulted during college, which is compatible with many other studies indicating that women who have previously been raped face a greater risk of being raped again, especially but not only if they were assaulted as children (Krebs *et al.*, 2007: 5-8, 5-10, 5-15; Classen *et al.*, 2005).

Social circles can either encourage or discourage rape. The campus study found that more than half of the alcohol-assisted rapes occurred at parties, as did more than a quarter of the rapes by physical violence, and belonging to a sorority, attending fraternity parties, and going to bars all significantly increased women's chances of being raped (Krebs *et al.*, 2007: 5-16). It seems that other partygoers must have at least condoned aggressive behavior, and perhaps egged it on. It is easy to imagine, however, a party at which rape is not within the range of possible activities. Studies indicate that members of some fraternities and athletic teams are more likely than other young men to assault women, while membership in other fraternities and teams has no such effect (Humphrey and Kahn, 2000). The problem is not belonging to a fraternity or playing sports per se, but the rape-conducive attitudes encouraged by some social groups, many of which also encourage excessive alcohol use (Locke and Mahalik, 2005). Indeed, some fraternities actively try to create a culture in which denigration and assault are unacceptable (Khadaroo, 2014).

High rates of sexual assault in the military have also raised concerns. Although women have served in one way or another in all U.S. wars, the military did not begin to integrate women into regular units until the 1970s. The feminist movement was challenging women's exclusion from many sectors of society, including military service, at the same time as the humiliations of the Vietnam War led to a new focus on military effectiveness. Successful military leaders have always known that wars are won not by brute strength alone, but by superior technology, strategy, logistics, and intelligence. From a rational perspective, including women in the military made sense (Goldstein, 2001: 93, 166–168). More than 200,000 American women served in Iraq or Afghanistan, and by 2012 women were 14.6 percent of active duty service members (Bellesiles, 2012: 312; Patten and Parker, 2011; DoD, 2013: iii).

It is common for men in all-male occupations to resist the arrival of female colleagues by engaging in sexual harassment and social exclusion, and the military was no exception (Baker, 2008). The presence of female soldiers, even in small numbers, challenged the equation of soldiering with masculinity, and some men responded with an aggressive form of hypermasculinity. About a third of the female soldiers in Iraq told researchers that other U.S. soldiers had raped them, while 90 percent reported sexually demeaning remarks that could be relentless (Benedict, 2009: 5–6). Some women resorted to carrying knives to protect themselves not from the enemy, but from their colleagues (Potts and Hayden, 2008: 131). Many women feared that reporting assaults would be ineffective at best and might lead to worse attacks or their own dismissal (Draper, 2014).

The Pentagon has tried to reduce sexual assaults. By 2012 the large majority of both women and men said that their leadership had made it clear that sexual assault is unacceptable, and the number of official reports was rising – which some officials considered a welcome sign that norms were changing (DoD, 2013: 5; Steinhauer, 2013). Researchers estimated that in 2014 about 19,000 service members experienced some kind of unwanted sexual contact, including 4.3 percent of women and 0.9 percent of men. About a quarter of them reported the incident (a higher rate than in many civilian studies), but more than 60 percent of the women who made reports said they experienced some kind of retaliation afterwards (DoD, 2014a: 6, 2014b: 117). At this point it is unclear whether the military as a whole has a larger sexual assault problem than the civilian population, but individual service members may be more vulnerable to repeated victimization and retribution because they cannot leave their assignments without the permission of their superiors.

Sexual assault is also salient in many prisons and juvenile detention facilities. Indeed, the threat of sexual violation seems to be part of the punitive regime. In 1999, Amnesty International was sufficiently concerned about the sexual abuse of women in U.S. prisons that it published a report titled "Not Part of My Sentence." Among other things, they found that many guards (41 percent of whom were male) subjected prisoners to unnecessary vaginal searches in the name of security (Amnesty International, 1999: 7–9). Guards may even use strip-searches to intimidate visiting lawyers (Stevenson, 2014: 195). Many police and probation officers raise the specter of prison rape, with its symbolic emasculation as well as physical pain, in their interactions with young men on the streets (Rios, 2011: 140).

Studies of people in prison may be less reliable than most sociological studies, as respondents may fear retribution from guards if they answer honestly. That said, the research suggests three likely conclusions. First, some institutions have much higher sexual assault rates than others, probably because of differences in institutional cultures and procedures. In some juvenile facilities nearly a third of the youth are sexually assaulted, while in others sexual assault is practically nonexistent. Second, assault rates vary for different demographic groups. Youths are more likely to be assaulted than adults, women than men, boys than girls, and LGBT people most of all. Third, total sexual assault rates are perhaps two to five times higher than for the general population, but some individuals are victims of many assaults. If a youth was previously assaulted in a different institution he or she faces more than a 50 percent risk of being sexually assaulted (Beck *et al.*, 2013a, 2013b).

The literature on male-on-male rape emphasizes that the vast majority of perpetrators identify as heterosexual and use sexual assault to assert dominance over other men (Matthews, 2013; Gilligan, 2001: 63–64). As one prosecutor commented, "The acts seemed less sexually motivated than humiliation or torture-motivated" (Dao, 2013). Although they have sex with men, perpetrators do not see their heterosexuality as called into question, apparently because they identify heterosexuality with being aggressive and in control. Perpetrators usually target men they see as insufficiently masculine, so men in an environment where the threat of rape is ambient have a strong incentive to appear tough, aggressive, and heterosexual.

Being raped can have a huge range of physical, practical, and psychological consequences, including physical injuries, missing school or work, medical and legal fees, STDs, pregnancy, leaving a home, job, course, or university that feels unsafe, fear, depression, PTSD, alcohol and drug addiction, and suicide (Krebs *et al.*, 2007: viii, 2-6). Effects may last for years, as both women and men are more likely to report frequent headaches, difficulty with sleeping, and poor physical and mental health if they have been raped (Black *et al.*, 2011: 3).

Rape also affects every woman who limits her activities for fear of being raped. Women typically fear crime more than men do, even though men are significantly more likely to be victims of violent crime. Men's fear of crime tends to vary depending on the perceived risks of a situation, while for many women the fear of rape looms large and makes the world seem a threatening place (Lane *et al.*, 2009: 172; Truman *et al.*, 2013: 7). To prevent rape, women may avoid going out alone after dark, being alone with a man they do not know well, or taking a job that would require them to go to unfamiliar places. Such measures are of limited effectiveness, since women are most likely to be raped by a partner or friend. Nevertheless, the fear of rape leads many women to constrict their lives. Women's ambient fear of rape thus increases men's relative power and privilege, even though most women are never raped and most men never rape.

Some people believe that the United States is still a "rape culture" that tacitly condones or even encourages sexual assault. American media, they argue, make sexual violence against women seem like a normal expression of masculinity. Many people trivialize the consequences of sexual assault, suggesting that "boys will be boys" or that only rape by a weapon-bearing stranger is "real rape." Women who say they have been assaulted are often scrutinized for any hint of complicity, as if they are to blame and only their perfect behavior can make them not deserve to be raped. A variety of gender-related beliefs, sometimes called "rape myths," legitimate sexual assault by promoting variations on the themes of "she asked for it," "he didn't mean it," "it wasn't really rape," and "she lied" (Locke and Mahalik, 2005; McMahon and Farmer, 2011; Department of Health and Human Services, 2011).

Other people argue that rape is not characteristic of American culture, but of a small and atypical group of men, many of whom rape repeatedly. Researchers found that 6.4 percent of men attending a community college and 13 percent of men enlisting in the U.S. Navy self-reported that they had engaged in acts that meet the legal definition of rape. They typically knew their victims and used alcohol or drugs to incapacitate them. About two-thirds of the rapists had perpetrated more than one rape – averaging six rapes each – and most had also engaged in other violent acts (Lisak and Miller, 2002: 78–79; McWhorter *et al.*, 2009: 204).

Psychological studies indicate that men who rape women differ from other men in a variety of ways. They are more likely to have experienced family violence and abusive fathers as children, display high levels of hostility toward women, lack empathy, and use language that links sex and dominance. Nearly all endorse a variety of beliefs that hold women responsible for rape. They anticipate pleasure from sexually dominating women, but many do not ejaculate or have difficulty maintaining an erection during the rape, supporting the theory that their primary goal – like that of men who rape men – is to dominate and inflict pain, not to experience sexual pleasure (Lisak and Roth, 1990; Bownes and O'Gorman, 1991; Lisak and Miller, 2002; Chiroro *et al.*, 2004).

There are elements of truth in both of these analyses. The fact that the frequency of rape dropped by nearly 80 percent in just one generation suggests that cultural effects are powerful. Many men as well as women were re-examining their beliefs about gender, and many men came to believe that women should be able to make their own sexual decisions. Many men also came to feel more empathy with women, as they listened to women's stories, questioned long-established beliefs about the differences between men and women, and got to know women as friends and colleagues as well as lovers. Young men grew up with different experiences and expectations than previous generations. When men see women as equals, they do not want to rape them.

Gendered ideas about sexuality can, however, still lead to sexual assault. Some men still feel that they have a masculine responsibility to initiate sexual interactions and that women who are properly feminine do not make sexual initiatives, but instead accept or reject male overtures. Some men also feel that they have to prove their masculinity by having heterosexual sex, also known as "scoring." These images set up men to keep making overtures until they receive a very firm rejection – at which point they have pushed over the boundary of non-consent.

Some women, meanwhile, feel that it is very important to be attractive to men, so they pursue a sense of self-worth by dressing and behaving in ways that they hope will make men attracted to them. If they engage in sexualized interactions in order to reinforce their feminine identity and sense of self-esteem, rather than because of sexual interest, they are set up for confusion about what they want and don't want sexually. Desiring approval and acceptance, they may not perceive clearly when they are uncomfortable with a situation or be able to articulate that discomfort. If they are with a man who feels it is his masculine responsibility, or right, to keep going despite female resistance, sexual assault is likely.

When men or women speak about such experiences with people who share these gendered assumptions, they often receive the message that such patterns are to be expected. Many college administrators, military officers, and police have encouraged women who report nonconsensual sex with someone they know to think about it in terms of poor communication. Such responses can lead women to internalize blame for the assault. Their ensuing self-doubt, not infrequently eased by alcohol, may be one of the reasons that women who have been raped are likely to be raped again (Krebs *et al.*, 2007: 2-6).

In 2011 the Department of Education warned colleges and universities that if they did not do more to address sexual assault they could be found in violation of **Title IX**, which guarantees gender equity in federally funded educational programs. Faculty and administrators, often with little training, have been asked to adjudicate crime accusations as if they were student discipline issues. The results can be deeply unfair to both rape survivors and alleged perpetrators, some of whom are innocent. They can also mean that perpetrators go on to rape again (Rubenfeld, 2014;

Economist, 2014o; Krakauer, 2015). Growing public dissatisfaction has recently led some police departments to embrace new approaches to investigating rape accusations, which can rapidly lead to more reports if women learn that they will be listened to rather than forced to either prosecute or not prosecute (Van Syckle, 2014).

One of the most consistent research findings is that rapes tend to cluster. Rape is more common in some social groups than others, and both perpetrators and victims tend to repeat their experiences. Most men never rape, but some men rape repeatedly. Perhaps, then, it makes sense to speak of "rape subcultures": social circles that propagate beliefs that encourage rape, and in which rape is relatively common. Only some men live in these subcultures and most men never rape. But men who are hostile to women, many of whom grew up in violent families themselves, can usually find peers and Internet sites that reinforce their views. Rape reduction efforts often encourage bystanders to intervene if they see abusive behavior (White House Task Force, 2014: 9–10). It is even more effective to create social norms that make nonconsensual sex unappealing, as it is for most American men today.

Nearly all women, however, live with the awareness that they could be raped and are affected, both emotionally and practically, by fears of rape (Lane *et al.*, 2009). Women may therefore live in a "rape culture" whether or not rape is common in their social circles.

Rape in India

Definitions of rape and the acceptability of rape are also being contested in many other countries around the world. The issue of rape in India became a matter of national and international discussion in 2012, when a young woman in Delhi (in northern India) got on a bus and was brutally and fatally raped with a metal rod. Jyoti Singh was a college student studying physiotherapy. Her father had supported her education in every way he could, including selling land to pay her tuition fees. She had gone to see a movie with a male friend, Awindra Pandey, who was severely beaten but survived (Barry and Sharma, 2013; J. Burke, 2013). She belonged to one of the lower castes, now politely known as Dalits (Fontanella-Khan, 2014). This case encapsulated many of the issues roiling India today.

Northern India has had high levels of inter-group violence, social inequality, and gender inequality for millennia. Geography helped make the area subject to both invasions and internal wars, while the Hindu caste system – a highly stratified system of ranking families and individuals – placed a high priority on female sexual purity. Since children inherited the caste of their fathers, a woman who was not chaste polluted the whole caste structure. Many men in the higher landowning castes, however, considered it their prerogative to rape lower-caste women, especially those considered "untouchable" (Fontanella-Khan, 2014). Marauding groups of men sometimes captured women – perhaps because they wanted wives, sex, or money, or perhaps as a way to strike at the honor of the women's families. Families that could therefore kept their women behind walls (Hudson and Den Boer, 2004).

Caste discrimination was officially banned decades ago, yet it persists in ways both obvious and subtle. People rarely marry across caste lines and caste affects both politics and patterns of violence (Sankaran, 2013a; Burke and Chaurasia, 2014). A 2007 study in Uttar Pradesh found that 90 percent of the women who reported a rape were Dalits (Fontanella-Khan, 2014).

Physical, psychological, and sexual violence against female family members has been long common and condoned by community norms (Manjoo, 2014). In a recent survey 57 percent of teen boys said that beating one's wife is acceptable and 53 percent of teen girls agreed (Chandrashekar and Vij, 2013). One in four men report having participated in sexual violence, including 14 percent who said they had sexually assaulted their partner within the previous year (Barker *et al.*, 2011: 46).

Reports of many kinds of gendered violence have increased in recent years and decades, though that might be in part because the women are increasingly likely to report them (*Economist*, 2012a). **Dowry deaths** – in which wives are killed as punishment for an inadequate dowry – have apparently become more common, perhaps because rising material aspirations have placed families under more financial pressure (Rastogi and Therly, 2006; Manjoo, 2014: 4). Acid attacks – in which a man throws concentrated acid on a woman who has rejected his marital overtures or sought a divorce – became a problem as acid used in textile production became widely available. The man usually targets the woman's face, so if the attack does not kill her it leaves her grotesquely disfigured and possibly blind – and therefore unmarriageable (Thakur, 2008).

Traditional women from respectable families did not leave their homes unless they were accompanied by a male relative – partly for fear of assault, but also because the presence of a chaperone prevented rumors that might damage a woman's reputation even if nothing else happened. Today, however, growing numbers of women want to be able to go to school, work, stores, and so forth, on their own. The result is a cultural contest over whether a woman can maintain respectability, and a claim to personal integrity, in public spaces. Many women, especially in the northern areas, report that they are frequently subjected to intense sexual harassment, including attempts to strip them of their clothes, when they walk on public streets. Indian men and media often call this behavior "eve-teasing," which implies it is playful and harmless. The frequency and intensity of sexual assault, however, can make women reluctant to step outside their homes (Roy, 2010; Chandrashekar and Vij, 2013). Most married women still do not visit a nearby neighborhood or village unless they are accompanied (Harris, 2014a).

Jyoti Singh has become a symbol of Indian women's aspirations. With the financial and moral support of her family, she pursued education and a career instead of getting married in her teens. Instead of staying in her home, she attended classes and went to malls. Instead of avoiding all contact with men who were not relatives, she invited her friend Pandey (from a much higher caste) to go to a movie (J. Burke, 2013).

The assault on the bus began with a challenge to Pandey: "What are you doing out roaming with a girl on her own?" (J. Burke, 2013). From the point of view of the attackers, Singh and Pandey were engaging in immoral behavior, so punishing them was part of the traditional masculine role of enforcing moral codes. According to honor-based logic, forcing sex on Singh was acceptable since she had already displayed her lack of purity by spending the evening with an unrelated man. The brutality of the attack, however, underlines the depth of anger triggered by Singh's presence.

All of this took place in the context of large and growing economic inequality. Nearly half of the people in India live on $1.50 or less a day, and half of the children are underweight from malnutrition (*Economist*, 2014j; UNICEF, 2014). The middle and upper classes, however, increasingly participate in a global consumer culture, with all its pleasures. Historically, lower-status men could reassure themselves that at least they were better than women, but self-assured women walking the streets and going to movies belie that belief.

Many observers suggest that public violence against women reflects the growing disruption and isolation of poor men's lives. Like Singh's attackers, most men who are accused of assaulting women in public are poorly educated and describe women in public spaces as immoral and therefore deserving attack (Jacobson, 2013: 193). India, one Indian journalist explained, is full of men who are "untethered from their distant villages, divorced from family and social structure, fighting poverty, exhausted, denied access to regular female companionship, adrift on powerful tides of alcohol and violent pornography, [and] newly exposed to the smart young women of the cities, with their glistening jobs and clothes and casual independence" (Sankaran, 2013b).

The men who killed Singh grew up in impoverished villages with inadequate schools, moved to Delhi, took a variety of menial jobs, and had poor marriage prospects (J. Burke, 2013). India has many more men than women, due to sex-selective abortion and neglect of female infants, so many poor men will never marry. This is a terrible deprivation in a society where families are the primary source of both emotional intimacy and economic security. Gender segregation remains strong in many communities, so even friendships with women are forbidden. Men have few images of sexuality that are related to tenderness or intimacy. Married couples traditionally do not express affection in front of their families. Kissing is rare in Bollywood films, as it is considered indecent, while rape scenes are common (Timmons and Gottipati, 2012). Many poor men have sex only with prostitutes, who are seen as shamed women who protect the virtue of honorable women. All of these intertwined patterns leave many men impoverished emotionally as well as financially.

It is important to be cautious here. Many Indian men do not fit these images. Many men, like Singh's father, are embedded in families and communities and try to do well by the women in their lives. International surveys indicate that women in many other middle-income countries, such as Colombia and Egypt, are more likely than Indian women to report sexual violence and beatings by their husbands (Harris, 2014b). Other rapidly changing countries with high levels of social inequality, such as South Africa, have also had surges of sexual violence, as young men who feel powerless and disenfranchised use gang rape to reassert their sense of masculinity (Altman, 2001: 8). India is far from alone in these problems, and many Indians disapprove of them just as much as international observers.

Since "the rape on the bus," as it has come to be known, thousands of Indian women and men have spoken out against rape and the culture of sexual harassment and violence that supports it. They have called on men to stop assaulting women. They have called on police and government officials to enforce laws against violence against women and to stop victimizing women themselves. And they have challenged the widespread assumption that rape indelibly shames a woman.

Rape and the fear of rape have shaped India's culture (and many other cultures) for at least two thousand years. Reliable statistics do not exist, but it is likely that rape has increased in recent years as growing numbers of women abandon traditional prohibitions intended to protect them and their families from shame. Many of these women have the support of their families, including their fathers and brothers, but that does not necessarily protect them from assault by other men who resent these changes. In the past, people rarely spoke about rape. Today, rape is a widely discussed political issue because women's desires to go to school, go to work, and move in public spaces is part of a much broader challenge to traditional hierarchies of gender, age, and caste.

VIOLENCE AGAINST WOMEN AND INTERNATIONAL RELATIONS

Violence against women is now a significant theme in international relations. Many people who are concerned about poverty and economic development now see violence against women as keeping families and nations in poverty. Gendered violence interferes with girls' and women's ability to get an education, earn an income, limit their family size, and participate in family and community decision-making. It makes it less likely that children will be fed adequately, given clean water, or sent to school (True, 2012: 14). Many international organizations have concluded that ending violence against women is not just an important human rights issue, but also a key to economic prosperity (Pickup, 2001; Penn and Nardos, 2003).

Many women around the world have welcomed this growing awareness that violence against women is a problem, not just a cultural tradition. They have drawn on an international language of human rights to assert that they too should live free from violence. Some women have used international institutions, the Internet, or feminist groups located in wealthy countries to support their local organizing efforts. In many countries, governments have at least in theory accepted the principle that violence against women should be discouraged.

On the other hand, many people in formerly colonized countries distrust the motives of wealthy countries. Colonizers often claimed that their own gender practices were more "civilized" and their rule would rescue local women from oppression by local men. People in England, France, and the United States told stories about the burdens and horrors faced by women in other societies – stories that entertained and shocked their listeners, but also ratified the idea that European and American cultures were superior to other cultures and therefore deserved to spread throughout the world (Spivak, 1988). The fact that Middle Eastern and Asian societies were not identical to European societies was used to justify conquering them (Said, 1978).

It is a long-standing pattern, going back at least to ancient Greece, for groups to discredit their opponents by decrying their deviant gender practices. In recent decades, criticizing sexism in other countries has often been used to provide ideological justification for political, cultural, and even military interventions (Bhattacharyya, 2008). In the weeks after 9/11, for example, the American media were suddenly saturated with images of Afghan women in burkas, which allowed the subsequent invasion of Afghanistan to be framed as war of liberation for women. Taliban rule was indeed horrific for women, but few Americans seemed to care about gender inequality in Afghanistan until after 9/11 – which suggests that the new interest had more to do with American war aims than an abiding commitment to

PHOTO 4.1

Artist Ann Telnaes warned in 2001, as the United States was planning to invade Afghanistan, that women in Afghanistan – though indeed oppressed – had much to lose from war (Source: Ann Telnaes with permission)

gender equality (Faludi, 2007: 49–53). Many Muslim women, in Afghanistan and elsewhere, felt that the stereotype of oppressed Muslim women was used to rain down death and suffering on innocent women, men, and children (Abu-Lughod, 2010; Ahmed, 2011: 223).

Some women in poor countries accuse Westerners of focusing too much on violence against women. Their real problems, they argue, are a lack of economic opportunities, clean water, and sufficient food, exploitation by corrupt governments and corporate elites, and the horrors of war. Some women (and men) complain that Westerners seem to care a lot about freedom of dress and sexuality, but have little interest in more basic necessities, such as a right to food, shelter, and not being bombed (Volpp, 2005: 44; Esposito and Mogahed, 2007: 127). Indeed, gendered violence looms larger in the lives of Western women. Partner violence and rape cause perhaps a fifth of all health problems for women aged 15 to 44 in wealthy countries, but closer to 5 percent in developing countries, where women are much more likely to suffer and die from hunger, infectious diseases, pollution, childbirth, and war (Study of the Secretary-General, 2006: 64).

Indeed, criticizing gender inequality in other countries can backfire. Some people defend what they see as traditional gender practices as part of their broader resistance to foreign political, cultural, economic, and military domination. Allowing women to take paid employment, choose their own husbands, or wear Western-style clothing, for example, may be seen as a capitulation to Western dominance. Extremist groups like the Taliban seek to impose draconian restrictions on women as part of a quest to recreate an imaginary cultural authenticity. Most people do not go that far, but it is common for people to resist changes in women's behavior more than changes in men's behavior in the name of cultural autonomy. Ironically, the "traditional" patterns now defended are often themselves a product of previous intersections between local and colonialist practices. But the more people feel under attack, the more they defend themselves (Jacobson, 2013).

War always increases violence against women. Men are much more likely to die as combatants, but the more a war affects civilians the more women and children die as well, whether from bombs, disease, or hunger. Rape is often used tactically in war zones, and the chaos of war often leads to other kinds of violence as well. The number of honor killings in Iraq, for example, rose dramatically after it was invaded in 2003 (Seager, 2009: 31). Violence against women typically increases in civilian areas during wartime, apparently because of the cultural celebration of aggressive forms of masculinity, and increases again with the return of veterans, especially if soldiers have been traumatized by violence or a lack of jobs makes it difficult for them to re-establish a civilian identity (Pickup, 2001: 142–147; Sontag and Alvarez, 2008; Duroch et al., 2011).

Conversely, societies that are more gender-egalitarian tend to have less war. Women are not always pacifists. Indeed, women can be just as emphatic as men in equating masculinity with courage and a willingness to kill (Enloe, 2000). Women are more likely to prefer less violent options, however, and the more public opinion is divided on an issue the larger the gender gap (Goldstein, 2001: 329). Societies that include women in political decision-making may thus be less likely to choose war when the need is not compelling. Cultural factors are at least as important. Egalitarian societies place less emphasis on establishing masculinity through demonstrations of manly honor. They discourage violence against women and other interpersonal violence, so men do not regularly experience themselves as agents of violence. They do not engage in sex-selective abortion or infanticide, and their balanced gender ratios and female employment allow young men to marry more easily and spend less time in all-male peer groups. All of these characteristics lessen the likelihood of war as well as other kinds of violence (Hudson and den Boer, 2004; Potts and Hayden, 2008: 122; Pinker, 2011: 686; Hvistendahl, 2011).

CONCLUSION

In almost all contexts, violence is associated with masculinity. Women do sometimes engage in violence, but it is rare for a woman to feel – or for her observers to feel – that violence is part of being feminine. Men, on the other hand, often demonstrate their masculinity by engaging in a wide range of violent activities – from fistfights to flying fighter planes, hunting to football, policing to rape. Especially when they are young, men often use tests of strength, courage, and toughness to establish and maintain social hierarchies with other men. Historically, most cultures expected men to use violence and the threat of violence to dominate and control women. Some cultures and subcultures still do.

The frequency of violence, however, varies greatly from one culture to another, as does which forms of violence are considered appropriate and legitimate and which are deemed undesirable or criminal. In some cultures and subcultures, men rarely engage in violence once they reach an age where they are capable of self-control. Furthermore, as we have seen with the example of rape within the United States, levels of violence can change significantly within just one generation. Although no culture has completely eradicated violence, cultural norms and images greatly affect how likely men are to use violence to achieve their goals.

Develop Your Position

1   How would you explain the fact that men commit the large majority of violence? What evidence presented above helps you understand this disparity? What more would you like to know?

2   How would you define a "rape culture"? Using that definition, do you think the United States currently is or has a rape culture? Why or why not?

Develop Your Position – *continued*

3   Imagine that you lived in an honor-based society, such as America's west in the nineteenth century or Afghanistan or Pakistan now, and you wanted to reduce rates of violence over the next 20 to 30 years. What would you do? What if you were an outsider – someone who cares about that society but is not fully part of it? What course of action do you think might be most effective for an outsider?

CHAPTER 5

The Control of Sexuality

INTRODUCTION

Sexuality is related to reproduction, the ability of some female bodies to create other human beings, but human sexuality is far more than just a means of reproduction. Sexuality is also entwined with such inward experiences as attraction and love, perception and fantasy. It is framed by powerful social, cultural, economic, and political forces. And it is one of the primary ways in which people mediate relationships.

Our focus in this chapter is on **sexual cultures**: on how different societies think about sexuality, the values and norms they promote, and the behaviors they encourage or discourage, require or prohibit. Sexual cultures affect individuals on a very deep level – not just what they do or do not do with their bodies, but also how they experience themselves as sexual human beings and how they understand their relationships with other people. Many theorists believe that sexuality is key to understanding both gender and gender inequality precisely because sexuality weaves together the realms of mind (thought and imagination), body (sensations and actions, always interpreted by the mind), and culture (patterns of behavior and expectations we learn from our society). We will start by sketching five theoretical approaches to thinking about the relationships between sexuality, gender, and power. We will then offer some historical and cross-cultural perspectives on two topics that have been controversial both in the United States and around the world: same-sex behaviors and sex work.

THEORETICAL PERSPECTIVES ON SEXUALITY, GENDER, AND POWER

Sexual Control and Sexual Purity in Patrilineal Societies

Patrilineal societies make a bargain between the sexes: men will be economically responsible for their children, while women will not present men with children who are not theirs. They therefore have to guarantee that most babies will be assigned to the correct biological father. There can be some dereliction of duty without breaking down the system, but not too much. Patrilineal societies therefore require respectable women to be virgins before marriage and sexually monogamous after marriage. Women's sexuality, and the reproductive capacity it implies, is seen as a family resource. Before marriage a girl's family must guard her virginity and preserve her value on the marriage market. After marriage a husband has the right to have sex with his wife and to restrict her relations with other men.

These requirements are arbitrated by concepts of female purity, **honor**, and **shame**. Any illegitimate contact with a man can leave a woman impure – shamed in the eyes of her society, her family, and herself. In many societies (including the United States until recently, and arguably even now) a woman is considered dirtied if she has been misused by a man, whether or not she consented. The result is that patrilineal societies contain two classes of women. One class – wives and future wives – are expected to be sexually pure and receive some protection from men's sexual overtures as long as they stay within prescribed bounds. The other class of women is considered sexually available but not marriageable. This division between "good women" and "bad women," sometimes called the **virgin/whore dichotomy**, can be observed in patrilineal societies around the world.

Some patrilineal societies expect men to be monogamous too, but most tacitly or explicitly accept men's nonmarital relations. Well-off men in many societies have concubines or mistresses: women who are supported by one man and expected to be monogamous, but do not have the full rights and status of a wife. Many societies also allowed well-off men to have sex with their slaves or servants or other lower-status women. **Prostitution** and other forms of **sex work** have existed for millennia, with customers of all social classes.

For women, an *appearance* of monogamy is necessary to prevent doubts. Women are therefore expected to project an aura of inaccessibility that is commonly called modesty. The most extreme modesty codes require that a woman never be seen by a man who is not her husband, blood relative, or an eunuch, but only prosperous families can maintain that level of seclusion. Most women worldwide need to work, and peasant and servant women require mobility. In many societies, therefore, a woman's degree of seclusion and covering reflects her family's status.

Marital sexuality, on the other hand, may be quite public. The idea that sex is a private realm of personal self-expression works best if a married couple has their

> **Codes of modesty that have existed in the United States and elsewhere:**
>
> - Cover legs, arms, and chest
> - Bind and cover hair
> - Cover face
> - Sit with legs together
> - Do not reveal that you have legs
> - Never bend over
> - Do not appear in public if you look pregnant
> - Do not make eye contact with a man
> - Speak quietly and gently
> - Do not speak to a man unless you have been formally introduced
> - Do not speak in front of men who are not your relatives
> - Stand and sit separately from men in public spaces
> - Sit separately from men within the home
> - Do not leave your home without a chaperone
> - Do not leave your home except in an enclosed vehicle

own bedroom, but many people have lived in houses with one or two rooms for the entire family. Sex is therefore frequently observed, or at least heard. Some societies also have defloration rituals in which a bride is supposed to bleed and the bloodied sheets are displayed to others as proof of her virginity.

Patrilineal societies differ in their beliefs about whether women enjoy sex. The Puritans, for example, believed that women are more lustful than men, while the Qur'an describes sexuality as a comfort to both husbands and wives (2:187). Many patrilineal societies, however, expect women to find sex distasteful. Some societies in central and northern Africa practice **female genital cutting**, which can make intercourse quite painful, while women in parts of sub-Saharan Africa, Saudi Arabia, and a few other countries may use traditional medicines to dry out the vagina before sex (UNICEF, 2013; Kun, 1998). In these and other societies, female sexual pleasure is considered a possible precursor to adultery and therefore dangerous.

Patrilineal societies also vary in how intensely they enforce the taboo on nonmarital sexuality. Some societies put a single woman to death if she becomes pregnant, while others leave her no option other than prostitution. The Cheyenne (one of the Native American tribes of the Great Plains) strictly segregated women and men, including siblings, after puberty and if a man suspected his wife of adultery he could "put her on the prairie" to be gang-raped by his comrades (Hoebel,

1960: 27–31; Sanday, 1981b). Other societies tacitly allow premarital sexuality as long as it leads to marriage, or make it possible for an unmarried mother to regain respectable status if she finds a man who will marry her and "make her an honest woman." French courtly society was famous for celebrating the true love found in extramarital affairs (as opposed to the practicality of arranged marriages) while also preserving a husband's right to be irate.

It is thus reasonable to speak of societies as more or less intensely patrilineal. The more a society requires all children be conceived within marriage, the more it values female sexual purity and restricts girls' and women's activities in the name of modesty and honor.

Compulsory Heterosexuality

Some theorists argue that the crux of the issue is what Adrienne Rich (1980) termed **compulsory heterosexuality** – the fact that women in most societies do not have any real choice about whether to be sexually involved with men. Compulsory heterosexuality, these theorists argue, binds women into intimate, unequal, and often dangerous relationships with men. It makes women define themselves in relationship to men and devalue their relationships with other women. It also makes women see themselves as objects of men's desire and therefore too willing to accept men's treatment of them as objects (Dworkin, 1987). The problem is not heterosexual desire and pleasure per se, but the whole context in which those desires and pleasures take place – all of which are designed to make women sexually, emotionally, and reproductively available to men (Bunch, 1975; Rubin, 1975; McKinnon, 1982).

This lack of choice is obvious in cultures where women are commonly married without their consent, either by the agreement of their fathers or by capture. Some patrilineal societies simply require parental permission before marriage – especially from the bride's father, who is often described as "giving away" his daughter. Many societies, however, arrange marriages. Young adults may or may not be consulted or have veto power, and grooms are more likely than brides to have some role in choosing their spouses. Most cultures assume that a man has a right to have sex with his wife and to force her if she tries to refuse. When a girl or woman is married without her consent, and then required to have sex with her husband, heterosexuality is compulsory indeed.

Even in societies where women have some choice of husbands, not getting married is rarely a viable option. Since most societies give men control of land and other property, most single women have no way to survive. Women are expected to earn their keep by getting married, having sex, bearing children, and doing other work assigned to wives. Parents feed and house daughters for a while, but most parents expect a daughter to marry once she reaches a certain age. Daughters who resist marriage come under verbal pressure: nagging, incessant questions, and scorn for "old maids." Highly stubborn daughters may also be beaten, starved, or expelled from the family home, but that level of coercion is rarely necessary. Most girls internalize the cultural message that it is important to get married before it is too late, so they share the quest for a husband.

Under these conditions, women do not really have a choice about whether to have sex or not. They may acquiesce or resist, with more or less happiness, but the social pressures to engage in sex are so intense that it is problematic to describe women's choices in terms of "consent." If one cannot say no, one cannot really say yes either.

American women experience a variety of economic and social pressures to marry, all of which were much stronger in the 1970s than they are now. At the time it was rare for a single woman to earn enough to support herself comfortably, so many women looked to marriage for economic security. Most Americans – indeed most people worldwide – considered homosexuality deviant and immoral, and in most states same-sex relations were illegal. Women in lesbian relationships often faced heavy social stigmas, including rejection by their families, socially approved discrimination by employers, and sometimes violence. Single women beyond a certain age were also targets of mockery, as they were deemed society's "leftovers" that no man had found desirable enough to marry.

Women were encouraged to look to men and heterosexual relationships for validation of their self-worth. Being attractive made a woman valuable. Many young women focused on their physical appearance and romantic lives, rather than pursuing educational and career paths that would enable them to be financially self-sufficient. With their hearts set on marriage, even before a potential husband was in view, many middle-class women did not plan for the possibility of an independent life (Holland and Eisenhart, 1990). Although most women had female friends, those friendships were supposed to take a back seat to romances. Indeed, women's competition for men's attention and approval often pitted them against each other. The institution of heterosexuality thus narrowed women's options even for women who had no difficulty feeling sexual attraction for individual men.

Men have also experienced their own forms of compulsory heterosexuality, though usually with more room for choice and negotiation. Families in patrilineal societies expect men to marry women, perform sexually, father children, and continue the family line. Men often have some influence over the timing of marriage and the selection of their spouse, but marriage per se is generally a requirement. Frequent pregnancies are often considered a sign of masculine vigor, and a man who fails to impregnate his wife soon after the wedding, and a sufficient number of times thereafter, may be shamed as unmanly. Indeed, many societies expect men to display their masculinity by expressing sexual interest in women not their wives. Men are supposed to be always interested in and ready for sex: in a recent survey 91 percent of Indian men said a man should be embarrassed if he could not get an erection (Barker *et al.*, 2011: 19).

Almost all societies expect men to make sexual initiatives. Being hetero-sexually assertive, even aggressive, can be a way to gain status in the eyes of male peers. Being rejected by a woman, however, can feel even more humiliating if it is a symbol of failure as a man. For men too, the institution of heterosexuality can be burdensome.

Economics and Sexuality

Other theorists argue that societies' sexual norms typically fit and serve their changing economic needs. These sexual norms often focus on women's bodies, both because women produce babies (always of economic significance) and because men control most laws, businesses, media, religious institutions, and other mechanisms of institutional change. The United States, for example, has had three sexual eras, each of which reflected changing economic interests.

Bastardy in the Colonial Era

Colonial-era laws criminalized just about every sexual act that was not part of marital reproduction – fornication, adultery, rape, sodomy, bestiality, "self-pollution" (i.e., masturbation), and so on. In reality, though, prosecutions for most of these crimes were rare. If one looks at the cases that were actually presented, it becomes clear that the authorities' highest priority was preventing births to unmarried white women. British common law required towns and counties to provide enough food and warmth to destitute residents so that they would not die. Since single mothers faced a high risk of destitution, the authorities tried to prevent single motherhood. Once again the Chesapeake and New England colonies pursued this shared goal in different ways.

In the Chesapeake, sexual restrictions generally applied only to white women who became pregnant outside of marriage. White men had nearly unlimited power over other members of their households, and that extended to the sexual realm too. About one in five female indentured servants was punished for bearing an illegitimate child, typically by being whipped and having her indenture extended to compensate her master for the inconvenience. Authorities rarely tried to identify the father, perhaps because when they did he was usually married – and often the master. Premarital pregnancy among free white women was acceptable as long as the couple married, and 20 to 30 percent of brides were pregnant. (In England at the time the rate was about 20 percent.) A free white woman who could not produce a groom, however, was fined, whipped, and scorned (Thompson, 1986: 54; Carr and Walsh, 1983: 100–103; Norton, 1996: 346; Katz, 1983: 29–66; D'Emilio and Freedman, 1988: 30–31).

Unlike white women, enslaved black women were not expected, or allowed, to protect their chastity and not punished if they became pregnant. This was a mixed blessing, as it reflected their total exclusion from the white-defined community: no one worried if a black child died of hunger as black children were of no public concern. Black men's sexual behavior was considered even less consequential, as their children had no rights and cultural images of threatening black male sexuality did not emerge until slavery became controversial (Freedman, 2013: 20).

New England's sexual culture was both more restrictive and more egalitarian. Married men were expected to be monogamous, and although Puritans accepted a certain amount of intimacy during courtship they drew a harsh line at anything that might produce a pregnancy. Men and women were held equally accountable for an unmarried pregnancy. If the man were single, as he nearly always was, he came under intense pressure to marry the mother and usually did so before the child was born, while fines and whippings were administered equally to both members of the couple. These restrictions were successful, as less than two percent of brides were pregnant in seventeenth-century Massachusetts (Ulrich, 1990: 148; Norton, 1996: 346; Thompson, 1986: 70).

Sexual Self-Control in the Early Industrial Era

Sexuality became a topic of greater cultural discussion in the late eighteenth and nineteenth centuries, especially in the northern parts of the country where industrialization and urbanization arrived first. A third of the brides were pregnant in some parts of New England in the late eighteenth century, and parents were even more dismayed by the growing ability of a young man to disappear into a nearby city if he did not want to get married (D'Emilio and Freedman, 1988: 43–44; Ulrich, 1990: 148–160).

Similar patterns emerge whenever a region is industrializing. As teens and young adults spend more of their time outside family settings, they are less subject to hour-by-hour supervision by their elders and therefore get to make more of their own sexual decisions. If parents want to control young people's sexual behavior, they need to do it by instilling sexual codes and beliefs rather than in-person supervision.

In the United States, the result was a flourishing of literature preaching the importance of sexual self-control. Young men of the aspiring classes were urged to direct their energies toward productive work in the new industrial marketplace. Any kind of seminal emission, they were warned, drained a man's life-energy and his ability to be a productive worker. Even marital sex should not occur too frequently, lest it deplete a man's vital powers and produce too many children (Rosenberg, 1973; Barker-Benfield, 1972). Masturbation was yet more dangerous, as it symbolically represented a turning inward, into a realm of imagination and desire, away from society's claims (Laqueur, 2003). In a highly competitive and rapidly changing world, men were urged to work hard, be thrifty, and sire no more children than they could raise and educate appropriately.

People acknowledged that many men would find it difficult to practice this degree of self-restraint, but they expected women to make it possible. Although earlier generations had expected women to enjoy sex every bit as much as men, sexual reticence now became part of genteel women's gender identity. Ladies were required to dress, speak, and move with decorum. Nineteenth-century literature often claimed that women are or should be sexually pure, innocent, and passive – responsive to a loving husband, but otherwise immune to sexual passions (Cott, 1978).

The industrializing economy offered rewards to men and women who could practice self-discipline and deferred gratification – who could save up a bit of money, deploy it wisely, and start themselves on the path to wealth. There was a lot more to the story than that, of course, but nineteenth-century "self-made men" prided themselves on beginning with nearly nothing and turning it into something. The economic ideology of the time preached the importance of frugality, restraint, and self-control, all of which translated into the sexual realm.

This genteel sexual culture was highly class-specific. It was the culture of ladies and gentlemen – of families that were prospering from the opportunities opened up by industrialization and wanted to make sure their children would do the same. Working-class sexual culture was more earthy and practical, as crowded urban neighborhoods provided little leisure time and no privacy, while elite men enjoyed diverse sexual pleasures (Stansell, 1982; Duberman, 1989). For the growing middle class, however, sexual self-control became part of proving one's moral worth.

Sexuality and Consumer Culture

By the turn of the twentieth century, however, the United States was developing a consumer-oriented economy. Industrialization created mass markets – first for practical products like flour and clothing, and then for an ever-expanding array of household goods, entertainments, and personal technologies. Over time, a growing percentage of the population could afford comforts and luxuries, not just necessities. Indeed, the health of the economy increasingly depended on such people spending freely, as consumer spending would shrink dramatically if people purchased only what they needed to stay alive. Cultural norms therefore shifted to encourage people to spend money on a wide variety of products, often redefining as necessities things that did not exist in earlier eras. One result is longer and more pleasant lives, due to everything from toothbrushes to smartphones. Another result is a culture that urges people to pursue pleasure, self-gratification, and happiness.

Sexuality is often used to sell goods and services. Since the 1920s ads have used sexual imagery to sell products, implicitly promising viewers that they would be more attractive if they wore the right clothes, used the correct personal care products, or drove the right car (Marchand, 1985). Many entertainers use sexuality to sell their music, movies, and other experiences. When sexuality is the primary focus of a product we call it pornography or erotica, but the line between erotica and, say, a music video can be blurry. Numerous medical treatments are offered to stimulate sexual interest and function, as low sexual interest is now defined as a problem rather than a virtue (Colgate, 2004; Calasanti and King, 2005; Jutel, 2010).

Many theorists have discussed how women are damaged by media-driven understandings of beauty (e.g. Wolf, 1992). Most girls feel a need to make themselves

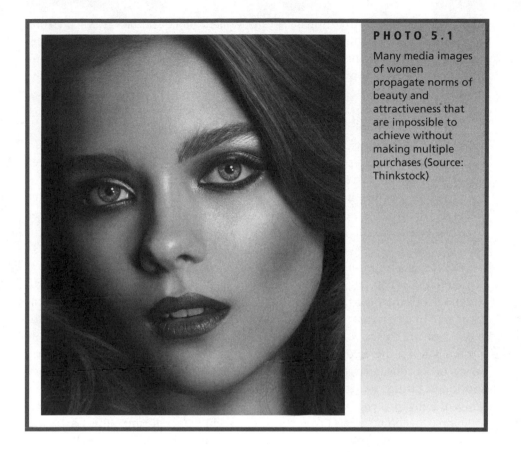

PHOTO 5.1

Many media images of women propagate norms of beauty and attractiveness that are impossible to achieve without making multiple purchases (Source: Thinkstock)

beautiful, often starting by the age of six or eight – long before they are ready for adult sexuality. Surrounded by media images that are unattainable without artificial assistance, girls and women tend to become dissatisfied with their own bodies. Indeed, much advertising works by raising feelings of dissatisfaction and anxiety while suggesting that these uncomfortable feelings would be soothed by purchasing particular products. Many girls and women spend a significant percentage of their income on clothes, cosmetics, shoes, jewelry, haircuts, manicures, diet books, diet aids, exercise videos, gym memberships, perhaps even cosmetic surgery. Some of these activities can be dangerous, especially when pursued to excess. The pursuit of beauty also distracts girls and women from other activities and goals that could be more rewarding.

Modern American sexual culture describes itself as liberated and liberating. Individuals, not families, are considered the primary sexual decision-makers, and women as well as men are encouraged to take pleasure in their sexuality. Some theorists argue, however, that modern pressures to be sexual are themselves coercive (Foucault, 1978; White, 1993). Sexual desire is, of course, natural to human beings, as it is to all animals, but not all cultures place such a high importance on sexuality or consider it so central to personal identity. Modern Americans face strong pressures to be sexually active, consider sexuality essential to their sense of self, and look to sexuality as an important source of happiness and satisfaction. Advertisements and other media often portray sexuality as a source of vitality and a solution to feelings of boredom, loneliness, or meaninglessness. Actual sexual experiences cannot always live up to the heavy expectations placed upon them. The combination of high promise and frequent disappointment can, for some people, prove addictive, as they compulsively seek enticing but elusive rewards.

These lessons are gendered. Men are supposed to be sexually assertive, even aggressive, and they can be pressured into sexual interactions by their peers and by an internalized belief that real men always want as much sex as they can get. Women, meanwhile, are often evaluated by their attractiveness, and women deemed attractive often struggle to make no mean no in a culture that considers yes the default answer.

What men and women have in common is equally important. The ubiquity of commercial sexual imagery encourages people to experience sexuality as a commodity, something that can be bought and sold. Sexuality often occurs in the context of interpersonal relationships, of course, but people are also urged to define and experience their own sexuality separate from others, or to enjoy the sexuality of people they do not know. The search for sexual self-expression and pleasure makes people better consumers, but it can also alienate people from themselves, each other, and longer-lasting sources of satisfaction. While the re-definition of sexuality in terms of individual choice and the pursuit of pleasure has, on the whole, increased individual freedom, especially for women, seeing oneself and others as sexual objects can also contribute to sexual exploitation and violence, as well as deep loneliness.

Sexuality, Danger, and Gender

Many people, including some feminist theorists, believe that sexuality is more dangerous for women than for men. Some roots of this feeling are quite practical. Men have proven more likely than women to walk away from unwanted children, so one sexual encounter can leave a woman with a child to raise alone. An encounter that starts as consensual can turn violent, as some men – and some cultures – feel that a woman who engages in any sexual activity has forfeited her right to say no to intercourse. In addition, a small but important minority of men enjoys sexual sadism and even murder. The stakes for women can be high indeed.

Other feminist theorists, however, argue that the pervasive **sex negativity** of Western cultures is fundamentally a system of control. The idea that sexuality is a dangerous, degrading, and destructive force justifies dehumanizing and punishing any person who engages in sexual behaviors outside the "charmed circle" of what is deemed natural, normal, and good (Rubin, 1984). One of the easiest ways to declare oneself virtuous and righteous is to denounce others for their sexual misbehavior. Although sexual moralists often wrap themselves in the cloak of religion, the Bible and Qur'an talk much more about the immorality of poverty and excessive economic inequality than about sexual issues. Many politicians and preachers, however, put much more energy into regulating sexual behavior than promoting economic justice (Wallis, 2005). This sex-negative discourse distorts all public discussions of sexuality and its implications. It has justified ostracizing and in some cases killing people for homosexual relationships or other forms of sexuality deemed deviant, and it has led to recurrent attempts to restrict access to contraception and abortion, especially for anyone who is not deemed perfectly virtuous. In this view, the association between sexuality and female danger is rooted in the millennia-old belief that sexuality, especially outside of marriage, is shameful for women.

Debates about the significance and effects of pornography reflect these different perspectives. In the 1980s some feminists sought to make pornography socially unacceptable or even illegal. Pornography, they argued, is inherently degrading to women and trains men to see and treat women as sexual objects. Its imagery is often violent and encourages rape and other forms of violence against women. Many feminists quoted Robin Morgan: "Pornography is the theory and rape is the practice" (Lederer, 1980; Griffin, 1981; MacKinnon, 1987).

Other feminists, however, argued that the assumption that explicit sexual imagery is inherently degrading to women reflects the age-old idea that women must be sexually pure – an idea that underlies a multitude of efforts to control women's bodies and behavior. Pornography became much more available during the decades when the frequency of rape declined, casting doubt on that proposed causal connection (Kutchinsky, 1991). Lesbians and other sexual minorities have been especially likely to argue that sexually explicit imagery, whether called pornography or erotica, can be an important part of women's exploring and enjoying their own sexuality. Instead of trying to suppress sexual imagery and behavior, they argued, feminists should try to encourage a sex-positive sexual ethic grounded in how people treat each other, mutual consent, and mutual pleasure (Rubin, 1984; Heyward, 1989). Although pornography is now widely available on the Internet, 66 percent of Americans tell pollsters it is morally wrong (*Economist*, 2009c; Newport and Himelfarb, 2013).

Similar differences of perspective shape debates about the significance of casual heterosexual encounters that are not expected to lead to ongoing relationships. College students often call such encounters "hooking up," while poor Philadelphians more often call them "relating" (Edin and Kefalas, 2011). Some observers see hookups as a triumph of sex on men's terms – the casual pleasure without human connection that men are stereotyped as preferring. Critics also warn that hookup culture encourages sexual exploitation and assaults. If people believe that casual sex is common, it is easier for a man to overcome a woman's reluctance by such arguments as "everyone is doing it." Men are more likely to engage in physical coercion, or to use alcohol to confuse or incapacitate women, if they do not care about the women they are having sex with (Kalish and Kimmel, 2011; Freitas, 2013; Zimmerman, 2014).

Other observers, however, argue that many women are willing and active participants in hookups and should not be construed as passive parties or victims. Young women with professional aspirations may prefer to avoid the demands of romantic relationships during the years when they are getting educated and starting their careers. Such relationships can be greedy for time and attention, while hookups enable young women to enjoy occasional sexual pleasure without putting their professional goals at risk (Taylor, 2013).

Three-quarters of college students report that they have hooked up sometime during their college years, most of them one to four times. A third of these encounters included intercourse, and a third did not include any genital contact. It is not clear whether casual encounters are more common now than they were forty years ago, when they might have been called "one night stands" or "making out at a party." Nor are serious relationships going out of fashion: three-quarters of undergraduates report an exclusive relationship that lasts at least six months sometime during their college years (Armstrong *et al.*, 2010; Fortunato *et al.*, 2010: 263).

Media alarms about "hookup culture" may thus say as much about adult anxieties about young women's sexuality as anything else. Sex-negative ideology makes many people feel that sexuality, especially female sexuality, is distasteful unless it occurs in the context of a loving relationship. If people are viscerally uncomfortable with pleasure-oriented female sexuality, they may prefer to see women – and especially teenage girls – as objects of male lust rather than as sexual agents.

The persistence of double standards can, however, put girls and women in a double bind. Most girls feel a pressure by their mid-teens to prove that they are sexually attractive by being sexually active, but a girl who is too sexually active risks getting a "bad reputation" or being labeled as a "slut." Girls targeted by such labels often feel shame and guilt, and they may be victimized by peers who perpetuate the old belief that it is OK to misuse females who are already impure. Girls and women still tend to suffer more from sexual missteps, while boys and men are more likely to be forgiven for their mistakes (Tannenbaum, 1999). Females are supposed to be available but not too available, sexy but not too sexy, and the location of the line varies in different communities. Indeed, it may vary for different individuals. A recent study found that undergraduate women were much more likely to brand other women as "sluts" or "trashy" if they came from working-class backgrounds, while women from affluent families could engage in the same behaviors without stigma (Armstrong and Hamilton, 2013).

Some people argue that permissive sexual mores have liberated men more than women. Since the 1950s, American men have increasingly rejected the traditional patrilineal understanding that men get sexual access to "respectable" women only if they promise to financially support and raise their children (Ehrenreich, 1983). The availability of contraception and abortion allows a man to think of the birth

FIGURE 5.1

Percent of Adolescents Who Have Had Intercourse by Each Age. Boys are slightly younger than girls when they first have intercourse, on average, but ages vary widely and a quarter of young people have not had intercourse by their 21st birthdays (Guttmacher Institute, 2013a)

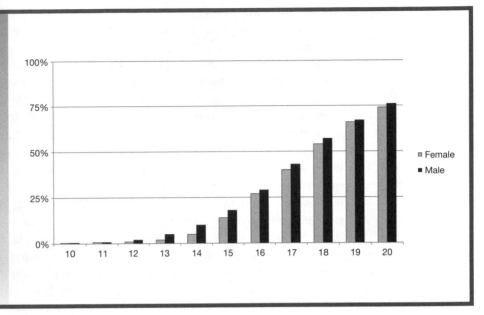

FIGURE 5.2

How Much First Intercourse Was Wanted. Women are much less likely than men to report that their first experience of sexual intercourse was fully wanted, and one in nine women reports that it was unwanted. More than a third of men, however, also report mixed or negative feelings (Martinez et al., 2011: 31)

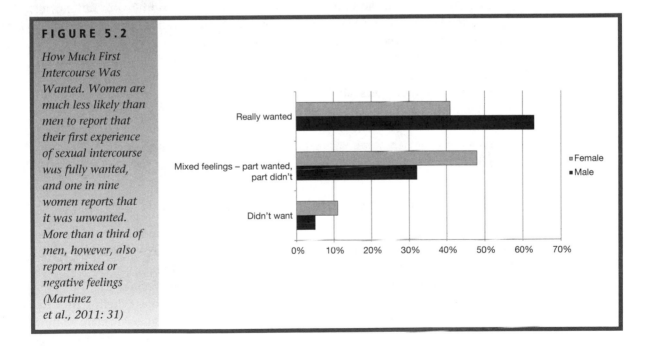

of a child as a woman's choice, rather than as the consequence of his own actions. If a child is the woman's choice, the father may also see it as her financial and practical responsibility (Edin and Nelson, 2013). Women may therefore see changes in sexual norms and practices, especially the legalization of abortion, as a threat to their ability to hold men sexually and financially accountable (Dworkin, 1978).

Many people, in many societies, believe that restrictive sexual morality is in women's interests, as it requires men to take responsibility for their sexual behavior. As we have seen, the recent rise of gender egalitarianism has been correlated with a growing belief that married men as well as women should always be monogamous (General Social Survey, 2012). Politicians may now be driven from office because of extramarital affairs, which previous generations silently tolerated. Public opinion increasingly condemns sexual exploitation and violence. Recent scandals over clerical sexual abuse of children, for example, reflect a profound change in ethical standards: behavior that in previous generations was tacitly accepted as within normal range, meriting only a slap on the wrist and a change of assignment, is now considered unacceptable. All of these cultural and political shifts aim to make the world safer for women and children by limiting male sexual privileges.

Some theorists suggest, however, that too much focus on women's sexual vulnerability should be considered a red flag. Gender equality would require a full acknowledgement that women are capable of sexual desire and initiative, and also that boys and men can find sexual activities awkward, disturbing, or unwelcome. The tendency to discuss sexuality in terms of female vulnerability and danger is not simply an objective reflection of reality, but also a legacy of the patrilineal tendency to see men as sexual agents and women as sexual objects – the idea that sex is something men do to women. Boys and men are also vulnerable to peer pressure, cultural forces, and troubling emotions. Women – even young women – often make sexual choices, and are not just fragile beings who need to be protected. Even when those choices do not work out as hoped, or are constrained by circumstances, they are still choices, and sometimes they do bring pleasure, satisfaction, and even joy.

Globalization, Individualism, and Sexuality

Some theorists suggest that **globalization** has triggered a worldwide argument over the principle of individual self-control, especially as applied to women (Jacobson, 2013). Around the world, globalization has increased cultural gaps between social classes. College-educated elites participate in a cosmopolitan culture facilitated by airplanes, computers, multinational brands, and global media. Whether they live in Los Angeles or Paris, Beijing or São Paolo, urban professionals share many cultural styles and often have more in common with their peers in other countries than with the poor of their own countries (T. Friedman, 2005). Lower-income people, meanwhile, have little chance of travel or participating in the global consumer culture. In 2010, 1.2 billion people lived on less than $1.25 a day, and several billion people are poor by American standards (*Economist*, 2013c). Even poor people, however, often have a growing awareness of what is happening elsewhere, as they contrast their own existence with what they see on TV and among the educated classes.

In many cases, globalization has empowered women and disrupted long-standing gender inequalities. Industrialization, urbanization, and education give women more options and decrease the power of families and traditional local political and religious authorities, who were nearly always men. The Internet and other global media expand women's horizons, help them connect with other women, and encourage them to question traditional ways. Ideas about liberty and equality help women challenge age-old assumptions of male dominance in family, work, and public life. Globalization has also spread the ideas that individuals rather than families should make sexual decisions, that sex and pregnancy can be separated, that women as well as men should pursue sexual pleasure, and that sexually stimulating images are acceptable in public – indeed, part of the warp and weft of a modern economy.

Cosmopolitan culture values individual self-control and self-determination. It sees the individual as the center of the world, and it encourages men and women to define and develop themselves through education and career choices, fashion and consumerism, travel and other experiences. It encourages sexual self-expression and the casual mixing of the genders. It sees individuals as sovereign over their own bodies, minds, and spirits.

All of this is especially radical for women. Although both men and women were traditionally expected to suppress individual desires and perform their duties, the constraints on women were usually much tighter. In many traditional cultures, women were effectively owned by their fathers and husbands. Modern cosmopolitan culture expects women to own themselves, and it expects men to honor the decisions women make about their bodies, work, and self-identities.

Some men welcome such changes, but others feel them as an affront to deeply held values. The issue here is not just practical – men's loss of power and privilege as women gain access to education, independent incomes, contraception, and other tools of self-determination. Traditional patrilineal cultures value honor and duty, family and community, chastity and gender segregation. They see gender as a fundamental division decreed by God and nature, and they believe that family-enforced sexual controls are essential to family and social stability. For men who are emotionally rooted in honor-based cultures, women's self-ownership can feel like a violation, an appalling tear in how the universe is supposed to be (Jacobson, 2013).

These emotions drive the violence against women by extremist groups around the world. Afghan culture, for example, has always been restrictive of women, but the Taliban's preferred regime is far more misogynistic. It is the creation of young men who grew up in refugee camps and fantasize about a golden age when everything (including females) was under control (Ansary, 2002: 269–171). As we argued earlier in our discussion of rape in India, men are much more likely to engage in vicious assaults on women if they feel displaced in a world out of control (Jacobson, 2013).

It is not just militants, furthermore, who sometimes interpret controlling women as resisting globalization. Many people in formerly colonized countries associate cosmopolitan cultural styles with Western economic, political, and cultural domination. They may also associate these styles with the unaccountable power of their own countries' elites, who were often educated in Western universities. Many people have sought to return to traditional gender patterns to signal their opposition to oppressive foreign and local rulers. Sometimes, though, these traditions are so long gone that they have to be reinvented (Ahmed, 2011).

Around the world, however, many people have embraced ideas of individualism and human rights, with their implicit gender egalitarianism and affirmation of sexual self-determination. The desire for freedom that drove the pro-democracy movements in Egypt and Iran, for example, includes personal and sexual dimensions. Young couples hugging or holding hands in Cairo are also embracing a world in which personal happiness is important, men and women can be openly fond of each other, and individuals make their own sexual choices. Families are the primary source of security in countries where governments do not provide the rule of law and a functional economic framework. They therefore still have a lot of coercive power over their members, especially women, but the boundaries can increasingly be negotiated (Wright, 2011; El Feki, 2013).

SAME-SEX BEHAVIORS AND SEXUAL IDENTITIES

Heterosexual relations are important in every society, since children are both essential and a lot of work. Same-sex relations have also, however, occurred in most or all societies. Data here are far more abundant for men than for women. Historians and anthropologists have found evidence of male–male relationships wherever they have gone looking for them, but we often have little or no evidence about women's personal lives. Women in many societies were considered unimportant, and most women were illiterate and left no trace in historical records. We do have examples of female–female relationships from many times and places, but they are less often documented than male–male relationships – which does not necessarily mean they were less common.

It is important to distinguish here between same-sex *behaviors*, which are widespread, and homosexual *identities*, which exist in only some times and places. A behavior is what people do, while an identity is part of how people think of themselves and others. In the modern United States, a young person who is beginning to experience sexual desires can ask the question, "Am I homosexual or heterosexual?" These identities exist in the culture, independent of any individual, and they suggest that who one is attracted to is a significant element in defining who one is. Other cultures, however, have thought about same-sex behaviors in many different ways.

Same-Sex Behaviors in Traditional Societies

Four basic ways of framing same-sex desires and actions appeared in traditional cultures. We call these patterns gender-crossing, tribal repressive, urban permissive, and anxious repressive. Each of these patterns emerged independently in multiple societies around the world that shared certain other characteristics.

Gender-Crossing

Many traditional societies recognized "third sexes" in which men took on women's gender roles, often including sexual relations with men. Some societies also allowed women to take on men's gender roles, including sexual relations with women, but that was apparently less common – or perhaps that is an issue of documentation. We mentioned previously the *hijras*, who were considered neither male nor female, in what is now India and Pakistan (Nanda, 1990). Many Native American societies included individuals who took on the clothing, work, and family roles of the other gender. These "two spirits," as they are now often called in English, were usually free to engage in sexual relationships with either men or women (Williams, 1986; Roscoe, 2000). Some indigenous communities survive in the southern Mexican state of Oaxaca, where men who live as women are known as *muxes* and are often seen as possessing special intellectual and creative gifts (Lacey, 2008). Wherever these patterns occurred, same-sex relationships were seen as a possible consequence of gender fluidity, not a defining attribute of individuals.

Tribal Repressive

Many honor-based tribal societies were and are highly intolerant of same-sex behaviors, which they associate with other forms of sexual deviance. Although two men or two women do not risk producing an illegitimate child, the idea that sexuality might be a matter of individual choice rather than family duty raises the possibility that individuals might pursue other sexual interests as well. Indirectly, then, same-sex behaviors may be seen as threatening the sexual culture that guarantees the legitimacy of children, the solidarity of kinship networks, and social and individual security. Same-sex relations sometimes occurred in these societies, but if they were discovered their participants were often punished or killed.

Urban Permissive

Many urban societies create space for men, and perhaps women, to engage in same-sex relations. Cities have economic and political structures that transcend families, so urban dwellers are not completely dependent on their kin for work, safety, and other elements of survival. Family controls therefore become less restrictive, both because they are less needed and because they are harder to enforce. In addition, cities create prosperous classes that can enjoy such luxuries as art, literature, fashion, and social life. Urban societies encourage their residents to consider what might bring them pleasure, which often includes sexuality – and not necessarily marital sexuality. For some people, same-sex relations are part of the broader pleasure-orientation and relative freedom of urban life.

Until the twentieth century, however, people who enjoyed same-sex relations were also expected to fulfill their family responsibility to marry and produce children. The historian John Boswell (1980) did an extensive search for evidence of same-sex relations in ancient and medieval Europe. With the exception of a few clergy, the vast majority of the men he identified were married fathers. Most lived in societies that did not expect monogamy of married men. Some husbands had nonmarital relations with women, others with men, others with both, and the distinction was not necessarily significant. Some societies even celebrated male–male eroticism as more virtuous than the reproductive sexuality associated with marriage. Many classical Greeks, for example, assumed that men who are attracted to other men are also attracted to such manly virtues as courage and strength, and are therefore better warriors than men who are effeminized by their connections with women. Sufi poetry similarly used male–male erotic imagery to express the ideal spiritual relationship between man and God.

Boswell found much less evidence of relationships between women. Some societies considered female–female relations compatible with monogamy because they did not risk pregnancy and were therefore deemed insignificant. Sometimes these relationships enjoyed some level of social acknowledgement, but nearly always their participants remained within their heterosexually structured families. It seems likely that many other relationships left no trace in historical records, but there is no way to estimate how many.

Anxious Repressive

Not all urban societies, however, are tolerant of same-sex behaviors. Societies that are concerned about economic or cultural decline often identify same-sex relations as one source of the problems. Urban cultures often retain threads of ancient honor-based ideas about sexuality. Such concerns may be muted as long as things are going well, but they can rise to the surface when a society is under stress.

Hostility to homoeroticism rose dramatically, for example, during the decline of the Roman Empire. It also surged during the centuries of the Crusades and Inquisition and witchcraft trials, as numerous communities expelled, killed, or suppressed anyone perceived as deviant (Boswell, 1980: 269–334). More recently, countries disrupted by economic and political changes have often become more homophobic. **Homophobia** literally means fear of the same, and it may manifest simply as discomfort, but it can also take more actively hostile forms. It tends to be particularly virulent when people feel insecure and hope that reasserting honor-based sexual values will help restore personal and familial stability.

The scriptures of all three Abrahamic religions – Judaism, Christianity, and Islam – emerged in honor-based societies and contain passages that suggest same-sex behaviors are part of a general breakdown of social order. Actual Jewish, Christian, and Muslim communities, however, have varied widely in their attitudes toward same-sex behaviors, from welcoming to tolerant to hostile. Those that are hostile often claim that their attitudes come from scripture, but that is not a full explanation. Some religious people argue that abundant scriptural teachings about the importance of love and honoring the divine in everyone take precedence over a few passages with words that do not mean now what they did then. People who beat or kill people for same-sex relations rarely do the same to rich men, who are far more clearly and frequently condemned in the Bible and Qur'an. Although religious leaders may preach homophobia, it is more closely correlated with certain social patterns (honor-based societies and urban cultures under stress) than with any religious tradition.

Homosexual Identity and Gender Policing in the United States

For most of the nineteenth century, Americans did not see people who engaged in same-sex sexual relations as different in kind from other people. Some (though not all) Americans expressed moral condemnation of any kind of sexual behavior that was not directly related to marital reproduction, but that included a lot of possibilities. They did not think of people who engaged in same-sex relations as a separate group any more than, for example, people who engaged in oral sex – which many people considered unnatural and degrading and morally reprehensible, but not the basis of a personal identity.

Three different patterns of what modern Americans might consider homosexual relations seem to have existed in the nineteenth century. American society was largely **homosocial**, meaning people were expected to spend most of their time with and form their closest relationships with other people of their own gender. Many men and women had an intimate friend of their own gender with whom they expressed love openly, shared kisses and caresses and a bed when convenient, and wrote letters that to our eyes seem quite passionate. Whether we should consider these relationships "sexual" is often a matter of interpretation, as we rarely know what exactly these friends did in bed or how they interpreted their physical intimacy. What was important, in the eyes of their own society, was that they fulfilled the family obligation to marry and have children. But many women and men clearly valued the emotional and physical intimacy of these romantic friendships (Rotundo, 1993: 76–91; Smith-Rosenberg, 1985: 53–76).

Another pattern was more recreational. Pleasure-seeking activities were common among young men living in all-male institutions, such as schools, colleges, ships, mining camps, and the military (Freedman, 2013: 170). Some of these relationships were fleeting, but others might last for years. They had a different tone than romantic friendships, however, as the letters they left behind are more raunchy than sentimental and often refer to adventures with multiple people, perhaps of both sexes (Duberman, 1989). By the end of the century New York offered men a variety of options for commercial sex, casual encounters, and short-term or long-term relationships (Chauncey, 1994).

A third pattern was domestic. As we have seen, in the colonial period marriage was generally a prerequisite for establishing a working household of one's own, as it brought together two sets of complementary gender-coded skills. Industrialization, however, made it possible for people to earn wages and live outside a household economy. Some people (most of the ones we know about are women) took advantage of this new autonomy to form a domestic partnership with someone of their own gender (D'Emilio, 1992: 3–16). As early as 1807 two women set up a home and a tailoring business in a small town in Vermont and eventually won recognition from their neighbors as a well-regarded couple. Today they still share a tombstone (Cleves, 2014). Such lives were more available, however, after 1880, when more women were educated and could make a decent living. Some professional women formed socially recognized partnerships with other women. Such a partnership was known as a **Boston marriage** (Faderman, 1981: 190–230).

The idea that these various experiences reflected a fundamental sameness emerged slowly. It started in 1880s Germany, where Berlin offered sexual diversity similar to New York's and a few professional men – now called sexologists, or scientists of sex – tried to bring intellectual order to this diversity. They were inspired by taxonomists, who had brought order to the study of biology by assigning each species of plant and animal a distinctive name, illuminating the relationships between them, and allowing scientists in different places to know whether they were speaking about the same thing. Categorizing humans proved more slippery than categorizing animals, however, and sexual nomenclature remained abundant and inconsistent (Katz, 1983: 147–148; Sedgwick, 1990; Chauncey, 1994).

It was not until the 1920s that the concept of **homosexuality** and its necessary cousin, **heterosexuality**, became widespread in the United States. Women got the vote in 1920, sparking a wave of cultural anxiety about whether women's liberation had gone too far. The first two generations of college-educated women had nurtured a women's world of colleges, settlement houses, and other predominantly female environments in which women pursued professional careers and social change. Most early female graduates felt they had to choose between career and marriage, and those who chose careers typically found their closest relationships with other women. Although most nineteenth-century people were troubled by women who chose not to marry, they often saw women's romantic friendships and domestic partnerships as admirable reflections of women's loving feminine natures (Smith-Rosenberg, 1985: 53–76).

In the 1920s, however, mainstream culture began to think about women's relationships in explicitly sexual terms. The growth of a consumer-oriented economy made sexuality much more visible and celebrated than in previous generations. Newspapers wrote about the importance of "sex appeal," as Freud's many followers declared that sexual repression was unhealthy for women as well as men. Many people asked new questions about what women were doing with each other in bed, and they did not like the answers. Writers suggested that lesbianism was the logical but appalling conclusion of women's quest for autonomy and gender equality, and warned parents not to let their daughters become too educated or independent-minded lest they develop unnatural lusts. Many women's organizations – social, educational, professional, cultural, and political – folded as women's loyalties toward other women came to be seen as suspect. The new attention to lesbianism was thus part of a cultural and political backlash against women's growing power (Smith-Rosenberg, 1985: 245–296).

Men too came under increasing pressure to prove their heterosexuality by pursuing women (White, 1993). Friendship patterns became increasingly **heterosocial** as men and women socialized together and same-sex friends became more cautious with each other. Men, especially, were required not to show signs of tenderness toward other men, while women, long considered more emotional, were allowed a little more leeway. Homosexuality was increasingly seen as a distinctive and unacceptable identity rather than related to many kinds of immoral (but widely practiced) sexual pleasures.

By the 1950s people who were suspected of homosexuality were often rejected by their families, labeled as mentally ill, fired from their jobs, or beaten on the streets. Homosexuality was now strongly associated with gender deviancy, and people who did not conform to the conventions assigned to their gender were suspected of homosexuality. Even little children were subjected to scrutiny – underlining that the issue was no longer sexual behaviors but an underlying nature or identity that was deemed pathological. Boys came under special pressure not to try on their mothers' clothing or otherwise imitate their mothers, as any sort of feminine-coded behavior became an indicator of homoeroticism. Taunts like "sissy" and "pansy" taught boys that they had to be constantly masculine. Girls might have more leeway to be "tomboys" and enjoy masculine-coded active play, but by adolescence they too came under intense pressure to prove that their sexual desires were "normal" by looking and behaving in feminine ways.

Homophobia thus affected women and men, girls and boys, whatever their own personal erotic inclinations. Everyone had to perform heterosexual social and family roles and keep their distance from others of their own gender. Women suffered more economically, as their employment options narrowed and fear of lesbianism kept them from organizing with other women. Men suffered more emotionally, as mid-century masculinity prohibited any sign of tenderness toward other men. People who really were attracted to those of their own gender suffered most, as they were often rejected by their families and potential employers unless they married and successfully appeared heterosexual. Homophobia thus functioned as a form of gender policing, as families, employers, and neighbors imposed harsh penalties on individuals who did not live up to gendered expectations of appearance and behavior – whatever they did in bed (Pharr, 1988).

Identity Politics and Queering Categories

In the 1950s some brave men and women began to organize around what they generally called "homophile" identities, to emphasize love (*philos*) rather than sexuality. By the 1960s the preferred terms were generally lesbian (for women) or gay (sometimes meaning men distinctively and sometimes either gender). Activists emphasized the importance of "coming out," or identifying oneself to others, instead of seeking the fragile safety of secrecy. Most people who considered themselves gay or lesbian, however, lived "in the closet," hiding their identities and relationships from employers, neighbors, and even family members (D'Emilio, 1983).

Coming out gained a new urgency for many gay men in the 1980s, as the AIDS epidemic grew. At first the cause was completely unknown, but epidemiologists and journalists soon associated AIDS with "the four H's": Haitians, homosexuals, hemophiliacs, and heroin users. The stigma attached to three of these groups complicated early efforts to limit the epidemic. Many people felt AIDS was unimportant if it affected only these marginal groups (which was never true, but that was the popular image), and some felt it was appropriate punishment for sin (Shilts, 2007).

In the United States, as in most other middle-income and wealthy countries, HIV infected and killed more men than women and the most common mode of transmission was (and still is) male–male sex – a fact that made many people acknowledge and discuss for the first time the frequency of such relationships (CDC, 2013b: 17–18). AIDS devastated many gay communities, as hundreds of thousands of men died before effective treatments were developed. But AIDS also galvanized community development, as numerous groups formed to care for the sick and demand political and cultural changes. Gay men and their allies organized to press for medical treatment, research funding, educational campaigns, and a reduction in the stigma that made life even more miserable for people with HIV and impeded diagnosis, treatment, research, and prevention. The activist group Act Up embraced the slogan "Silence = Death." If gay men did not speak up, they warned, even more people would die.

Identity-based politics brought many successes. Many cities developed gay and lesbian communities with their own businesses, organizations, and social structures. Activists focused on many specific goals, including ending employment discrimination, funding for AIDS research and treatment, lowering the suicide rate among gay teens, and recognizing same-sex relationships and parenting rights. As lesbians

PHOTO 5.2

Today AIDS disproportionately affects people – women as well as men – who are poor, people of color, and/or victims of violence (CDC, 2013b: 7; Meyer *et al.*, 2011) (Source: Thinkstock)

and gay men came out in large numbers, many heterosexuals discovered that some of their friends and relatives were homosexual. They were usually quite decent people, which made it difficult to maintain repulsive stereotypes.

Broader cultural changes aided the growing acceptance of homosexuality. Many people were embracing a sexual ethic based on the principles of pleasure and consent, which made them increasingly reluctant to condemn consensual relationships. Growing egalitarianism also made it harder to claim that men and women are so fundamentally different that gender has to be the building block of every family. Sympathetic media depictions of lesbians and gay men both reflected and reinforced these trends.

The gay rights movement stimulated politically freighted arguments about the causes of sexual orientation. There is no doubt that culture affects people's sexual behaviors, attitudes, and self-perceptions, but people differ in their beliefs about how profoundly culture affects sexuality. Some people – often called **essentialists** – believe that the shape and texture of our sexual impulses are basically inborn, though culture may limit or suppress sexual behavior. Other people – often called **constructivists** – believe that cultural shaping of sexuality goes deeper than that: that culture can actually create sexual impulses and potentials that would not have emerged in a different context. For example, once the words and concepts "homosexual" and "heterosexual" became widespread, people had to define themselves in relationship to them, which changed at least their self-images and quite possibly their behavior. In short, constructivists believe that how we think, speak, and behave changes who we are, so there is no inner core underneath all the layers of culture. Essentialists believe that each person has a resilient inner core of sexual truth, which remains the same no matter what.

Many people who support equal social, economic, and legal rights for gay men and lesbians have used essentialist arguments. Sexual orientation is, they argued, biologically determined, not a personal choice, and people should not be penalized for something they cannot control. Many of their opponents, in contrast, argued that homosexual identity can be changed by therapy, religious faith, or strength of will, and that people should be urged – or compelled – to become heterosexual. In some circles, therefore, the belief that homosexuality is (or is not) genetic in origin became unquestionable because of its political implications.

Most historians, however, believe that homosexual identity is culturally constructed – it did not even exist 150 years ago. In this view, sexuality is similar to language. Humans have innate desires to communicate using language and to connect with each other physically, but how we do so reflects our environment in many ways. After a certain age certain patterns feel reflexive, but that does not mean they were genetically determined. Sexual diversity, from this perspective, is more like religious diversity than like skin color: it reflects deep and value-laden parts of human experience, and it can evolve, but it cannot be chosen at will. Although people can decide whether or not to *act* on attractions, they cannot decide whether or not to *feel* attractions, any more than they can decide to change what they do or do not believe about the nature of the universe. Constructivists argue that lesbians and gay men should be treated well not because their identities were genetically foreordained, but because all people should be treated well.

By the 1980s some people were arguing that identity-based politics, though it can achieve important goals, also has self-defeating limitations. Organizing around an identity reinforces its intellectual and cultural salience as a meaningful category. In reality, however, many – indeed most – people do not fit into the existing categories. Evidence suggests that most people experience some level of attraction to both women and men at some time in their lives. In a highly homophobic culture many people suppress awareness of their same-sex attractions, but the less taboo such attractions are the more willingly people acknowledge them. Similarly, many people who identify as lesbian or gay at some point experience cross-sex attractions. Some people use the word "bisexual" to identify themselves or others who acknowledge that they can be attracted to both sexes. Other people, however, ask why people should be labeled by the sex of the people they are attracted to, as if that were their most important (or only important) feature. It is rare for anyone to be attracted to all members of a sex, implying that most of us have other criteria for attraction.

Some people have embraced the word "queer" as a way to indicate that they do not fit the conventional categories of sex, gender, and/or sexual orientation. Like lesbian feminists, many queer people believe that most women have been socialized into heterosexuality and that compulsory heterosexuality underpins an oppressive sex/gender system that affects every aspect of life. They also believe that most men have been socialized into and damaged by compulsory heterosexuality. Creating alternative lesbian and gay subcultures, they suggest, is only a small improvement, as it leaves intact the assumptions that heterosexuality is normal, homosexuality is alternative, and all people can fit into some small number of boxes. Adding a few more boxes is not a solution to the problem (Wilchins, 2004).

From this perspective, the achievements of identity politics are inherently limited. Women's movements, gay and lesbian movements, even transgender movements, presume that these categories say something meaningful about human experience. They may be necessary to protect individuals from violence and other forms of oppression, or to create safe spaces for self-expression. In the long run, however, they reinforce the categories on which oppression is built. True liberation, queer people argue, would mean acknowledging human diversity and not using categories to limit the potentials of individuals' lives.

Globalization and Sexual Identities

Attitudes toward homosexuality now vary greatly around the world. As the chart in Figure 5.3 shows, there is a significant correlation between a country's wealth and its acceptance of homosexuality, but also significant regional variations. Europeans and Latin Americans are more likely than their wealth would predict to approve of homosexuality. Many of these countries prohibit employment discrimination on the basis of sexual orientation and recognize same-sex marriages. Positive attitudes are not universal, and some gay and lesbian people report exclusion from their families, rejection by employers or schools, violence by family or strangers, or harassment by police – especially if they are gender-nonconforming. The broad trend of these societies, however, is toward not just tolerance but active acceptance of same-sex relationships.

Attitudes tend to be much more negative in Africa, Muslim countries, and Russia. Gay sex is illegal in 78 countries, and is grounds for execution in five (*Economist*, 2014k). Indeed, in many places gay and lesbian people are experiencing increasing hostility, violence, and legal persecution. In 2013, Russia made it illegal to "propagandize" "nontraditional" sexual relationships among minors or to say that traditional and nontraditional relationships are equivalent. Although the legislation did not specify what it meant by "nontraditional" or "propagandize," the law was generally understood to criminalize any representation of homosexual relationships in the media or public spaces (Kramer, 2013). In the same year, Uganda and Nigeria passed bills imposing long prison terms on people convicted of homosexual acts (Cowell, 2014). People in countries where homosexuality is criminalized are often subjected to violence by neighbors and police if they are suspected of homosexuality. Such suspicions may be raised by gender-nonconforming clothing or behavior, not just actual relationships.

Global media have offered people around the world not just images of gay men and lesbians, but also the basic concept that homosexuality is a sexual identity. People who become aware of same-sex desires often use these globalized media

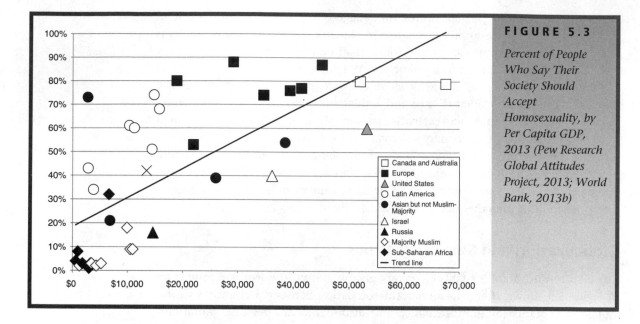

FIGURE 5.3

Percent of People Who Say Their Society Should Accept Homosexuality, by Per Capita GDP, 2013 (Pew Research Global Attitudes Project, 2013; World Bank, 2013b)

images to construct identities for themselves. Many English-speaking gay men in Southeast Asia, for example, describe themselves as being part of a global gay culture: they read gay American authors, celebrate the gay bars of Paris, and hope to attend the Gay and Lesbian Mardi Gras in Sydney, Australia. Indeed, some people have moved to the United States because they see it as a place where gay men and lesbians are safe and accepted (Corrales and Pecheny, 2010: 19; Altman, 2001: 45, 93).

These "modern" cosmopolitan identities often displace older and indigenous ways of thinking about homoerotic desires (Altman, 2001: 86–88). In pre-Columbian Mexico, for example, Xochiquetzal was the goddess of love and nonreproductive sexuality, including male–male relations. Spanish colonists brought with them Catholicism, which condemned same-sex behaviors, and the Inquisition, which considered sodomy a serious crime and publicly strangled and burned people who were judged guilty of the practice (Murray, 2010: 61–62). In recent centuries the blended Mexican culture allowed men to pursue sexual pleasures as long as they maintained their public status as men. Husbands were not expected to be monogamous. Indeed, a prominent politician sparked a bit of a scandal in 1997 when he suggested that men should be faithful to their wives (Dillon, 1997). If a man was an *activo*, meaning he had an active/insertive role in sex, he could have sex with either women or men without calling his masculinity into question – as long as he did not talk about what he was doing. A *pasivo* who allowed a man to penetrate him, in contrast, was highly stigmatized. He was considered like a woman, and therefore fair game to be controlled, beaten, raped, and otherwise used by "real" men. A good wife, in the popular view, accepted her husband's extramarital activities, took care of her family, and was sexually passive, monogamous, and *abnegadas*, meaning long-suffering and self-sacrificing. The denigration of *pasivo* men thus reflected a pervasive gender hierarchy (Carrillo, 2002: 24, 139–153; Murray, 2010: 63).

In the 1970s some Mexican men from the middle and upper classes, who first had access to global media, rejected the traditional division between *activo* and *pasivo* and referred to themselves *internacional*. By the 1990s many Mexicans used imported words such as *homosexual*, *lesbiana*, or *gay* to describe what they now considered a sexual identity rather than a gender identity. Mexico City, Guadalajara, and other cities contained gay bars and other meeting places, some of which were so fashionable that heterosexual people mingled there too. Popular *telenovelas* and movies began to portray gay characters sympathetically and to explore what it might mean for a family to accept its homosexual members (Carrillo, 2002, 2013; Corrales and Pecheny, 2010: 65).

In 2008 the Organization of American States adopted a resolution condemning all violence and other human rights violations based on sexual orientation or gender identity. The Gay Pride parade in São Paolo, Brazil, that year attracted more than 3 million people (Corrales and Pecheny, 2010: 435). TV talk shows now consider tolerance of gay and lesbian people a sign of cosmopolitan modernity – of belonging to the globalized world, with its promises of individual prosperity and freedom (Carrillo, 2013). Distrust, exclusion, and violence still exist, but many urbanites now consider such attitudes backward (Malkin, 2010).

PHOTO 5.3

The Gay Pride parade in São Paolo, Brazil, filled the streets (Source: Thinkstock)

Similar patterns have occurred in many other countries. Travelers and activists observe what is happening in other parts of the world and bring home attitudes and strategies that they adapt to their local circumstances and needs (De la Dehesa, 2010: 176). The Internet accelerated this process and has been especially helpful for lesbian women in more traditional countries, many of whom were isolated before they found each other online (Friedman, 2010: 313).

Stable democracies, gender egalitarianism, and sexual individualism tend to grow together. One of Latin America's most popular feminist slogans – "Democracy in the country and in the home" – was coined by Chilean feminists in 1983, as resistance was growing to the dictatorship of Augusto Pinochet, and explicitly linked the demand for democratic politics with a challenge to male dominance within families (Baldez, 2010: x). Both pro-democracy movements and young democratic governments have promulgated ideas about individual freedom and human rights, which echoed on the personal as well as governmental levels.

Gender inequality has certainly not disappeared in Latin American democracies, but it is no longer so taken for granted in families, workplaces, and the law. "[I]t's easier nowadays for women," a Brazilian woman explained, "to insist on proper behavior from men. We don't have to accept machismo and sexism" (*Economist*, 2013b). Latin American sexual cultures have become more liberal, as indicated by increasing approval and practice of contraception and cohabitation, and more restrictive of old-fashioned male sexual privileges, such as sexual harassment and unilateral nonmonogamy. As in the United States, the growth of a sexual ethic based on mutual pleasure and consent, rather than sexual shame and gender hierarchy, has encouraged acceptance of gay and lesbian relationships as well as nonmarital heterosexual relationships (Carrillo, 2002, 2013).

Countries with high levels of hostility toward lesbians and gay men, in contrast, tend to have shaky democracies or autocratic regimes, high levels of gender inequality, and a general suspicion of outsiders. Many see themselves as the victims of centuries of colonization or (in the case of Russia) military conflict and invasion. Proponents of anti-homosexual laws and practices often claim they are defending their local culture against foreign contamination and Western cultural imperialism (Altman, 2001: 43; Kramer, 2013; El Feki, 2013: 224). In Uganda, for example, awareness of Western support of civil rights for gay people fueled local support for anti-homosexual legislation, in some cases including the death penalty (Kron, 2012).

Ironically, Westerners brought to many of these countries beliefs and laws that were more restrictive than the indigenous cultures. Recent anti-homosexual campaigns in Africa and Southeast Asia have often been led by Christians, including American missionaries, but Christianity itself was originally an import from the West that has shaped what are now often considered "traditional" attitudes toward gender and sexuality (Mugisha, 2011; Gettleman, 2010; *Economist*, 2013d). In the sixteenth century the Mughal emperor of India, Babur, wrote the first known

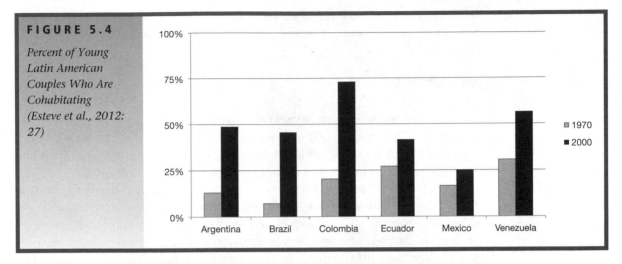

FIGURE 5.4

Percent of Young Latin American Couples Who Are Cohabitating (Esteve et al., 2012: 27)

The rapid growth in cohabitation represents a remarkably quick decay of the idea that a woman is permanently disgraced by sex outside the family-approved and Church-sanctioned bonds of marriage. Percentages are based on heterosexual couples in which the man is age 25–29.

Muslim autobiography, in which he eloquently described falling in love with a young man, which he evidently considered comparable to falling in love with his wife (Thackston, 2002). British colonizers criminalized homosexual acts in 1861, a law that India's Supreme Court upheld in 2013 over the protests of Indian gay rights advocates (Harris, 2013b). It is such laws, not same-sex eroticism, that were imported by outsiders.

Cosmopolitan lesbian and gay identities have been invaluable to people who want to build their lives around same-sex relationships, but they have also entailed a sense of loss for people who appreciated indigenous ways of interpreting and constructing same-sex relations (Altman, 2001: 88–95). Some Latin American men, for example, regret the passing of the old days, when an *activo* could enjoy whatever sexual pleasures he desired as long as he married and appeared *macho* (Corrales and Pecheny, 2010). Some men in Egypt and other Muslim countries find that they are now scrutinized for signs of homoeroticism in ways they were not in the past. Effusive physical affection between members of the same gender has long been considered normal in Middle Eastern cultures, but city-dwellers now sometimes ask questions that previously would not have occurred to them (El Feki, 2013: 216–277).

Many activists in non-Western countries consciously draw on local traditions around homoeroticism as well as cosmopolitan gay and lesbian identities. Using local history and language helps counter opponents who construe homosexuality as a foreign import, and some people find local cultural traditions familiar and comfortable (Altman, 2001: 95; Corrales, 2002: 293–306). Although globalization has created worldwide ways of talking about sexuality – and worldwide debates over what forms of sexual expression are acceptable – the international language coexists with many other ways of experiencing and interpreting sexuality.

SEX WORK

The term **sex work** refers to any sexual activity that is performed in exchange for money, food, clothing, drugs, or other material rewards. It covers a wide range of activities with dramatically different amounts of pay, control over customers and the working environment, and risks of violence, STDs, and pregnancy.

People who regularly sell intercourse (the usual meaning of the word **prostitution**, which we will use to distinguish these sex workers from others, though some people consider the term pejorative) may work on the street, in brothels, for escort services, in contacts arranged by their families, or independently via the Internet. Sex workers may also perform in pornography, provide in-person noncontact entertainment such as stripping or pole-dancing, or engage in sexual activities that do not include intercourse, such as lap-dancing or dominatrix sessions. Sex work may be their primary form of income, or it may be a sideline that supplements other income. Some sex workers are unpaid and enslaved, and they may be trafficked for other people's profit either within their own country or across national borders (M. C. Burke, 2013). People in dire circumstances, such as war zones, may trade sex for a meal or a place to sleep, an exchange sometimes called **survival sex**. Drug-addicted women may trade sex for their next hit. Impoverished parents may sell a daughter for marriage or prostitution if they see no better way for their families to survive. At the other extreme, attractive women or men may find high-end prostitution an efficient way to earn a living while pursuing other goals, such as an educational degree or a creative career. The seemingly simple term "sex work" thus encompasses a vast range of experiences.

The boundaries of sex work can also be unclear. How sexually explicit does a movie have to be for its actors to be considered sex workers? Does a woman who marries because she sees no other way to eat and keep a roof over her head count as a sex worker? Some people think of themselves as sex workers and some have organized to demand respect, control over their working conditions, and freedom from violence (Chateauvert, 2013). Many people, however, who exchange sex for money or food see this process as simply one of the ways they survive, not part of their identity (Altman, 2001: 102–103).

Sex work is more common in some contexts than others. It tends to flourish in cities and is often a significant part of the economy of rapidly growing cities, with their extremes of wealth and poverty (Altman, 2001: 11). Sex workers also tend to find customers wherever large numbers of single young men are clustered. In the nineteenth-century American West, for example, women in towns and cities provided for the sexual as well as other desires of cowboys, miners, and soldiers, while port towns catered to sailors. During the Vietnam War Bangkok became a popular destination for soldiers' "rest and recreation," and since then it has been a center of international sex tourism. Cultures that require strict segregation of the sexes and late marriage of men create a demand for alternative outlets for unmarried men. Traditional Islamic law, for example, recognized a variety of forms of "temporary marriage" under contracts that might last as little as an hour and legitimated intercourse in exchange for financial compensation. These practices continue today (El Feki, 2013: 180–197).

In the United States, the growth of cities in the nineteenth century created new opportunities for recreational sexuality, especially but not only in New York. Some women lived in female-controlled brothels, which usually offered music, dancing, and alcohol as well as sex. These women often had long-term relationships with men they knew well and could hold to certain behavioral standards (Cohen, 1998: 69–86). Other working-class women bartered sexual favors, usually not including intercourse, for food, money, or other gifts in exchanges that might or might not be articulated explicitly. Most of these women also had other forms of employment, but women's wages were so low that it was difficult to survive on them alone. Girls in working-class neighborhoods grew up in a sexualized street culture in which it was impossible to be unaware of the possibility of earning a bit of money by pleasing men (Stansell, 1982: 171–192). By the end of the century New York also offered men a variety of commercial venues catering to same-sex interests (Chauncey, 1994).

The moral purity movements of the late nineteenth and early twentieth centuries attempted to eradicate commercial sexuality, but mostly succeeded in driving it into the arms of organized crime. Women increasingly relied on male pimps to protect them from the violence of vice squads, customers, and other men. They often had less control over when and how they worked, and sometimes were subjected to violence by their pimps. Although prostitutes were highly stigmatized, prostitution remained widespread. In 1948, 69 percent of men surveyed said that they had paid for sex (*Economist*, 2014a).

Today most American men never patronize prostitutes. A 2006 survey found that only 15 percent of men reported that they had ever paid for sex. Declining demand has led to declining prices. A century ago an average street prostitute earned about $25,000 a year in today's dollars, which was nearly four times as much as a retail shop worker. Now a street prostitute might earn about $18,000, which is only $2,920 more than a full-time minimum wage worker. There is, however, a huge range in prices, from $15 to $1,000 or more per trick. A high-end escort today might earn $200,000 a year, or about half as much as her predecessor a century ago (*Economist*, 2014a). The decline in prostitution is often attributed to the more permissive sexual culture, which means most men can have sex without paying for it – and often in more satisfying ways.

The decrease in prostitution in the United States and other wealthy countries has been more than compensated for by its increase in low and middle-income countries. Rapid economic and social changes have driven many people into the sex trade, which is often a means of survival for people who have been displaced by industrialization, deindustrialization, urbanization, migration, or war. Rising economic inequality creates supplies of both customers and vendors, while cheap international travel brings together people near the extremes of wealth and poverty. Brazilians even have a term for the combination of tourism and commercial sex: "prosturismo" (Altman, 2001: 107–112; Seabrook, 2001).

The demographics of sex work are impossible to identify precisely, but the majority of sex workers are women. A significant minority, however, are men – perhaps 10 percent (Altman, 2001: 110). Another significant minority are transgender people, usually male-to-female. Around the world, many transgender people are excluded from their families and formal employment and have no financial options other than sex work.

The large majority of customers are men. Not only do men tend to have more time and money for leisure activities, but most societies consider it much more appropriate for men to pursue sex purely for the sake of pleasure. Most commercial sexual services cater to men pursuing heterosexual pleasures, but some are designed for gay men or for men who do not identify as gay but appreciate a sense of transgression.

Some customers, however, are women. Male prostitutes serving women are most often found in international tourist destinations, where they, like local women, often hope for an ongoing relationship that will gain them entry to a wealthy country with better opportunities (Altman, 2001: 110). More commonly women purchase pornography, which they may prefer to call erotica, or attend adult entertainment venues. Some pornography is designed for lesbian women. Whatever their sexual identities, some women consider pornography or other sexually explicit experiences part of exploring their own sexuality and liberating themselves from conventional patrilineal expectations of female sexual purity and reticence.

Sex workers are often highly stigmatized. In most cultures, the word "whore" or an equivalent is one of the worst insults one can throw at a woman. People who actually are whores are often treated as outcasts, undeserving of basic protections or civility. The conventional patrilineal equation of female honor with sexual purity means that many people see sex workers as without honor or rights worthy of protection. Many are ostracized by their family and peers, and they often face intense discrimination in housing and employment. Their outcast status can make it impossible for them to leave sex work if they want to (Chateauvert, 2013).

Violence against sex workers is common. Many people seem to believe that it is acceptable to beat, rape, or rob sex workers, as they are not "good" women, and police often provide no protection. Indeed, police often consider sex workers fair game for rape, physical abuse, and extortion. In Bangladesh more than 50 percent of street-based sex workers are raped by police or other men in uniform each year. Papua New Guinea even has a word – *lainap* – to describe the gang rape of a sex worker by police. One study found that 10 percent of police said they had participated in a *lainap* within the previous week. The lack of police protection means that customers, pimps, and neighbors know that they can exploit sex workers with impunity. The frequent violence contributes to the high rate of HIV infection among sex workers. Even those who successfully insist on condoms during consensual sex – which not all can – cannot require condoms during rapes (WHO, 2005).

Some sex workers are coerced. The International Labor Organization estimates that 4.5 million people worldwide are engaged in forced sex work, of whom 98 percent are female (ILO, 2012). Deception, sexual shaming, psychological manipulation, and violence can all be used to obtain compliance. Girls and women may be offered a nonsexual job in another city or country and discover once they get there that they are expected to engage in sex work. They may be beaten, raped, or starved until they submit. In many cases they do not have the finances to return home, and they may also feel that once they are no longer virgins it would be too shameful – or dangerous – to return to their families. Sometimes destitute parents sell their children, knowing or not knowing that they are headed for sex work. Or boyfriends may turn out to be pimps (Kristof and WuDunn, 2009: 3–69; U.S. Department of State, 2013).

Cultures with restrictive sexual ethics tend to have more coerced sex work. Such cultures do not allow premarital sexual intimacy with "respectable" women. Many have growing populations and stagnant economies that do not provide enough jobs, especially for men who are not well educated, but require men to be able to support a family before they marry. Prostitution functions as a "safety valve" that reduces social unrest while protecting higher-status women. Since sex work is highly shaming for both women and their families, procurers often use fraud and coercion to draw in new workers and meet customer demand (Kristof and WuDunn, 2009: 3–16). One international study found that 27 percent of men in India (a highly restrictive country) reported that they had paid for sex, of whom 34 percent suspected that the sex worker had been forced or sold into prostitution and 48 percent suspected she was under age 18. Customers in Mexico and Brazil (less restrictive countries) were much less likely to suspect coercion (7 or 8 percent) or underage workers (14 or 17 percent). This difference was not due to the frequency of prostitution, as Mexican men were less likely than Indian men to report paying for sex (18 percent had done so) while Brazilian men were more likely (56 percent) (Barker *et al.*, 2011: 50).

Some people argue that sex work should be illegal and that such laws should be strictly enforced. Tolerating prostitution, they argue, is tantamount to accepting the enslavement, exploitation, and infection with HIV of millions of girls and women (Kristof and WuDunn, 2009: 23–34). The United States requires all international organizations that receive funds to combat HIV/AIDS through the President's Emergency Plan for AIDS Relief (PEPFAR) to sign a pledge that they are "opposed to prostitution and related activities," which it deems "inherently harmful and dehumanizing" (Global Commission on HIV and the Law, 2012: 40). In 2013 the Supreme Court struck down this provision for U.S. organizations on free speech grounds, but it still applies to organizations outside the United States (Wetzstein, 2013).

Some people, however, believe that sex work should be legal and regulated like other occupations: no child labor, no forced labor, and health and safety protections for all workers. Criminalization, they argue, encourages stigmatization of sex workers and creates an environment in which violence is tolerated. Prostitution is already illegal, they point out, in India, Thailand, and other countries where it is ubiquitous. Sex workers do not have the protection of the police and courts, but instead work in a climate of harassment and fear. Indeed, police often threaten sex workers with arrest if they do not provide sex or money on demand. Many sex workers are beaten and raped by police or incarcerated in institutions where they are sexually and physically abused. Women of color and trans women are particularly likely to be branded as prostitutes and subjected to arrest, incarceration, forced "rescues" (even if they do not want to be rescued), and other human rights violations. Criminalization also makes it more difficult to leave sex work, as people who are considered criminals are barred from many forms of employment, housing, and educational programs (Chateauvert, 2013; Grant, 2014).

Criminalization also makes it much harder for sex workers to organize and advocate for their own interests, including safer sex practices, or to receive health care and other needed services. Some sex workers do not use condoms because they know that possessing condoms would be used against them if they were detained, while PEPFAR's anti-prostitution pledge forces organizations to choose between U.S. funding and supporting sex workers in advocating for themselves (Provost, 2012). In 2005 Brazil rejected $40 million in HIV funding from the United States because it considered the prostitution pledge counter-productive (Chateauvert, 2013: 19). The World Health Organization and several other international organizations have called for decriminalizing sex work, which they argue would help curb HIV, improve working conditions, make health services fully available, and reduce the stigma, discrimination, and violence attached to sex work (WHO, 2012; Forbes and Patterson, 2014; Global Commission on HIV and the Law, 2012).

In 1999, Sweden criminalized buying sex but decriminalized selling sex, a model that has been followed by Norway and Iceland and considered by several other wealthy countries. Iceland also outlawed strip joints in 2010. These countries have generally permissive sexual cultures: two-thirds of children in Iceland are born outside marriage, and condoms are sold next to supermarket checkouts. Many of their residents, however, draw a sharp line between commercial and noncommercial sexuality and argue that sex workers should be considered victims deserving of compassion and assistance (*Economist*, 2013a).

These critics argue that sex work should be seen as an inherently exploitative manifestation of larger systems of gender and class inequality, and often racial inequality as well. Many sex workers, they point out, were sexually abused as children. They often come from poor families, are poorly educated, and turn to sex work because of a lack of other options. In many countries they are disproportionately members of racial or ethnic minorities – African American women in the United States, for example, or Native Canadian women in Canada. Sex workers suffer from high levels of depression and post-traumatic stress, and they often feel that they cannot leave the trade. Some observers believe that the "Swedish model" of criminalizing customers has reduced both prostitution and sex trafficking, while others believe that it has driven sex work further underground or to nearby countries (Waltman, 2012; Global Commission on HIV and the Law, 2012: 38).

Many sex worker organizations and their supporters reject the idea that all sex workers are victims who need to be rescued. Most sex workers are not coerced, and the large majority of coerced laborers are not in the sex industry. Activists and governments, however, often focus on the plight of coerced sex workers, who can be construed as helpless females, and ignore the much larger number of men and women who are forced to work in factories, agriculture, armies, or domestic work (ILO, 2012; U.S. Department of State, 2013). Arguments for criminalization often conflate sex work and sex trafficking, which ignores the important difference between consent and coercion (McNeill, 2014). When the United Nations' Special Rapporteur on Violence against Women was asked to report on violence against women in India, she (among many other things) critiqued the equation of sex work and trafficking and advised decriminalization (Manjoo, 2014: 6, 19).

Some people suggest that the belief that sex work is inherently more degrading and exploitative than other forms of work is rooted in conventional patrilineal ideas about female sexual purity. The ethicist Martha Nussbaum points out that nearly everyone, unless they are independently wealthy, exchanges the labor of their bodies for money in one way or another. The idea that sex work is inherently demeaning to women, she suggests, reflects gender and class prejudices – and distracts from addressing the real needs of sex workers (Nussbaum, 2012).

Attitudes toward sex work thus reflect different fundamental beliefs about sexuality. People who believe that women should be sexually pure tend to be morally offended by sex work and believe it should be illegal. People who believe that sexuality is often dangerous for women, or that commercial sexuality is distasteful, are likely to agree that sex work should be illegal. People who believe that sex work is part of a much larger system of making women sexually available to men, on men's terms, are likely to prefer the Swedish model of criminalizing purchasing sex, but not selling it, as part of a broader statement of gender equality. People who believe that sexual liberty is an unambiguous good are likely to prefer decriminalization on libertarian grounds. People who believe that norms of female purity are primarily a way to control women's sexuality are likely to see decriminalization as affirming women's right to control their own bodies.

CONCLUSION

Sexuality is one of the primary arenas in which people around the world are debating the implications of individualism. Traditional patrilineal societies expected families to tightly control women's sexuality and guarantee the paternity of each child. Many modern societies, however, argue that individuals should be able to control their own sexuality. Some people resist this transition because they experience it as a threatening breakdown of social order. Other people worry that sexual individualism leaves women yet more vulnerable to sexual violence, single parenthood, and sexual exploitation. Around the world, though, political and economic individualism tend to be associated with sexual individualism. The result is a growing acceptance of sexual diversity and self-determination, including same-sex relationships.

Develop Your Position

1 Are there sexual activities that would be accepted in your social circles if done by a boy or man but considered a source of shame if done by a girl or woman? Can a girl or woman's reputation be ruined by a single event? Can a boy or man's? Would you say there is still a double standard in the United States?

2 Do you think married men in the United States are now expected to be monogamous, or can they get away with straying? Does marriage per se make a difference, or are the expectations the same if a couple is living together or otherwise in a serious relationship? Are the standards the same for men and women, or is there still a gender difference here?

3 How would you make the argument that compulsory heterosexuality still exists in the United States today? How would you argue that it no longer exists in the United States? Which of these arguments is more compelling to you?

4 Do you think prostitution and other forms of sex work should be legal or illegal? Why?

5 Are you more essentialist or constructivist in your understanding of sexual identity? Why? Are you more essentialist or constructivist in your understanding of gender? If your answers to these two questions are different, why?

6 We have made the argument for four different arenas being the crux of the issue in causing gender inequality: work and control of economic resources, family structures, violence, and control of sexuality. Which of these arguments do you find most persuasive? Why?

PART II

Consequences

CHAPTER 6

Life and Death Matters
Consequences of Inequality

INTRODUCTION

Most of this book is about how gender affects people's lives, but this chapter will focus on how gender affects who gets born and when and how people die. Gender inequality, along with other forms of inequality, is a significant cause of premature death worldwide. Premature death is obviously important in and of itself, but it also is important because it is a signal about the quality of people's lives. If girls are more likely than boys to die of malnourishment, for example, they are also more likely to suffer from malnourishment but not die from it. Generally speaking, the harder people's lives are, the more likely they are to die prematurely.

Data about mortality are relatively available and reliable. People everywhere notice when someone dies, and the World Health Organization and other international organizations have worked for decades to collect data about why people die and how premature deaths could be prevented. Data about quality of life issues are far more complex and difficult to compare across different places and times. This chapter will therefore focus on patterns in dying, though it will interweave some quality of life issues – especially related to whether women can control their own reproductive capabilities. We will start by outlining five basic theories about how gender can kill, and then examine how inequality affects life expectancies both globally and in the United States.

FIVE WAYS GENDER KILLS

Devaluing Female Lives

Many societies consider women less valuable than men, sometimes with lethal consequences. Each year more than 1.4 million couples use the growing availability of ultrasound machines to selectively abort female fetuses (World Bank, 2011a: 15). Where food is limited males are often fed more and better meals, and 54 percent of the 558,000 people who died from malnutrition in 2012 were female (WHO, 2014a). Nearly 300,000 women die from pregnancy and childbirth each year, and most of these deaths are preventable (WHO *et al.*, 2012: 25). Roughly one-third of women worldwide have been assaulted by an intimate partner, with a wide range of consequences for their physical, psychological, and economic health. More than 40,000 women are killed by their husbands, boyfriends, or other family members each year, and more than two-thirds of the people killed by intimate partners are women (Catalano *et al.*, 2009: 2; Garcia-Moreno *et al.*, 2005; UN News Centre, 2014). Both by actions and by neglect, the low value placed on female lives leads to about 4 million "missing women" each year, as well as many other miseries (World Bank, 2011a: 15).

Masculinity and Risky Behavior

Men's performances of masculinity increase their risks of dying in many ways. About 500,000 people are killed by other individuals each year, roughly 80 percent of whom are men both globally and in the United States. Men are six times more likely than women to die in combat, which killed 119,000 people in 2012, and twice as likely to die from suicide, which killed 804,000 people (WHO, 2014a).

Men are more likely to engage in a variety of risky behaviors, as young men in many societies tend to challenge each other to prove their masculinity by feats of strength and daring (Courtwright, 1996). Several feminist studies of men have observed that working-class men, who have little access to the markers of achievement enjoyed by higher-status men, are especially likely to display a "taste for risk" that increases their status among peers but can be both physically and socially dangerous (Lorber, 2011: 228). This equation of masculinity with risk-taking means that men are nearly twice as likely as women to die of unintentional injuries (which kill 3.7 million people a year worldwide), and nearly three times as likely to die in road accidents (which kill 1.25 million). Men's "excess deaths" from injuries, both intentional and unintentional, add up to about 3.4 million men a year (WHO, 2014a).

Men are also more likely than women to use a variety of dangerous substances. Many societies, including the United States historically, consider smoking tobacco a masculine behavior and disapprove of women who indulge. In the 1960s some tobacco companies began to market cigarettes to women as a sign of female empowerment, using slogans like "You've Come a Long Way, Baby." Smoking rates are now nearly equal in the United States and many other wealthy countries, but worldwide men are still five times more likely than women to smoke. In China, for example, 61 percent of men and 4 percent of women smoke. Smoking is estimated to kill about 5 million people a year worldwide, the large majority of them men (Hitchman and Fong, 2011).

Drinking alcohol, especially in large quantities, is also widely associated with masculinity. Men are more likely to drink at all, to drink frequently, and to drink in large quantities, and men with inequitable gender norms are more likely to abuse alcohol (Barker *et al.*, 2011: 36). Here too gender differences are decreasing in countries that are becoming more egalitarian, but even in wealthy countries men are more likely to have problems with alcohol (WHO, 2014b). Worldwide, about 2.3 million men and 1.0 million women had alcohol-related deaths in 2012, and men are also more than twice as likely as women to die from other forms of drug addiction and abuse (WHO, 2014c: 8–9, 54; WHO, 2014a).

Men who believe it is important to be tough and independent may be unwilling to request or accept needed medical care. Studies of middle-aged men in the United States suggest that the more they idealize masculinity the less likely they are to seek preventative care (Springer and Mouzon, 2011). Studies in sub-Saharan Africa suggest that many men resist getting tested and treated for HIV because they believe men should be fearless and autonomous. Men's after-infection life expectancy is shorter than women's because they are less likely to get timely treatment – which also makes them more likely to infect their partners (UNAIDS, 2012: 70–71).

Powerlessness, Isolation, and Chronic Stress

Gender inequality can more indirectly lead to premature death by causing chronic stress. Stress affects nearly every organ and system in the body, including the cardiovascular system and immune system, so chronic stress pervasively increases the likelihood of illness and death from many causes (Sapolsky, 1994). Conversely, being well connected with other people can lower stress, illness, and death rates. People who have several close relationships generally live longer, and are more likely to survive heart attacks, breast cancer, and other serious ailments than people with no or fewer friends (Parker-Pope, 2009). Men who define themselves largely in terms of their employment, at the cost of their personal relationships, tend to have less resilience in times of medical or economic turmoil (Wade, 2013).

One of the most common sources of chronic stress is feeling powerless or isolated, which sociologists describe as lacking **social status** and **social capital**. Social status refers to our rank vis-à-vis other people. Societies have all sorts of ways to rank people – who earns more, who has what color skin, who is what gender, as well as more individual characteristics. All of us are part of multiple hierarchies in different parts of our lives, and our sense of our status shifts depending on our context. Social capital refers to the resources created by personal connections and group memberships that help people solve problems and achieve their goals. In other words, the more people you know who are inclined to help you, the more you can get advice and assistance in dealing with challenges, small or large, and the more likely you are to succeed in your undertakings (Putnam, 2000: 19–24).

Most societies assign women a lower social status than men, though the magnitude of that difference varies. Women also typically have less social capital. Men are more likely to have the wealth, employment status, and political power that enables them to shape their own lives and do favors for others. Patrilocal societies give men life-long relationships with their male relatives, while women are often seen as burdens by their families of origin and outsiders by their families of marriage. Women's isolation is most intense in societies that practice female seclusion, in which higher-status women may never leave their homes except when they get married. Around the world, women are much more apt than men to be diagnosed with depression, as many women struggle with difficult economic circumstances, constant demands to care for family members, rapes and other assaults, and feelings of powerlessness and isolation (WHO, 2014b; 2004).

Societies with higher levels of inequality tend to have more illness, suicide, murder, and many other forms of unhappiness. To a significant degree, people's contentment with their lives comes from the comparisons they make with other people, not just their own circumstances. For example, poverty itself can affect people's health: if you do not have the money to get the antibiotic you need, you are much more likely to die from an infection. But relative poverty also affects people's health, even if they have adequate food, medical care, and other basic necessities. Being low status in a highly unequal society creates chronic stress, with all its many consequences. Societies that have been fractured by violence and political strife have especially low expectations of mutual assistance outside families. Social capital requires trust and reciprocity, while high levels of inequality and instability make people isolate themselves and protect their own personal interests (Sapolsky, 1994: 353–583; Wilkinson and Pickett, 2009).

In the United States today, being married adds seven years to a man's life expectancy and two years to a woman's. Marriage makes men less likely to engage in risky activities and more likely to have social support and connections. Most of the marriage benefit for women, however, disappears if one controls for family income. If a man's wife dies his own chance of death rises abruptly, while women may or may not experience a similar widowhood effect (Christakis and Fowler, 2009: 86–89). Such observations suggest that marriage is an important source of social capital for many American men, but may or may not be so for women.

Gendered Medical Systems

Until the 1990s, most medical research was done on male animals and humans. Most researchers were men, and they argued that their analyses would be more complicated if they tried to account for variations in reproductive hormones in female subjects. They therefore did most basic research, investigations of specific diseases, and drug studies in exclusively male pools of animals and human volunteers – or sometimes not volunteers, as black men and women were sometimes used for medical research with or without their consent and awareness (Dally, 1991; Smith, 1995; Washington, 2007; Skloot, 2010). Most research that included women focused on reproductive biology or on supporting gender roles by identifying differences (not similarities) between men and women (Bleier, 1984; Tuana, 1989). Most physicians were also men, and until the 1970s they tended to expect patients to submit to treatments without questioning medical authority.

In the 1970s feminists identified sexism in medical care as a major cause of women's ill health and sometimes death. A self-help movement encouraged women to learn about their own bodies and participate actively in their own health care. *Our Bodies, Ourselves* became a best seller in 1976, has been translated into more than two dozen languages, and is still in print after selling more than four million copies (OBOS, 2014; Pincus, 2005). Some women started women-run clinics to provide contraceptives, abortions, and obstetrics and midwifery services. Other women agitated for mainstream medical organizations to pay more attention to women's needs and interests, especially during childbirth and the treatment of female-specific cancers. Feminists also insisted that health research should include women, and in 1987 the National Institutes of Health (NIH) began to encourage scientists to include women in clinical studies (NIH, 2014).

Women are now more than half of the participants in NIH-funded research, but they are often under-represented in trials by drug companies and medical device manufacturers, and basic research still relies heavily on male lab animals and cell cultures. When a drug comes to market, therefore, researchers and physicians typically know much more about its effects and side effects in men. Women often respond differently to medications, with different benefits, dangers, and ideal dosages, but these differences generally become apparent only after the drug has been approved and clinicians observe more severe problems among their female patients. In 2014 the NIH told scientists that their studies must include female lab animals and cell cultures, and they must ask whether their results suggest sex differences. For the next decade or more, however, women will remain more likely than men to suffer adverse drug reactions (Rabin, 2014).

Medical research and clinical care have thus been predicated on the assumption that men's bodies are the norm. In wealthy countries, menstruation, childbirth, and menopause have been simultaneously under-researched and highly medicalized, with drug companies and surgeons eager to provide treatments. Although women receive significantly more health care than men, they are less likely to receive high-quality care for heart attacks and other important health needs (Owens, 2008).

Mental health care, on the other hand, can be gendered in ways that disadvantage boys and men. Young boys are encouraged to show their masculinity by being physical and active, but if their behavior becomes disruptive they may be diagnosed as hyperactive and treated with Ritalin or other psychotropic drugs. Older boys, especially if they have brown skin, may be arrested and imprisoned for behaviors that in previous generations were considered ordinary adolescent thoughtlessness (Khadaroo, 2013). Both boys and men may feel that crying and other forms of showing sadness are unmasculine, so they may externalize depression into aggression or violence. Girls and women are more likely to display the behaviors considered characteristic of depression, and therefore to receive a diagnosis and treatment for depression, while boys and men who are battling similar feelings of worthlessness and despair may be deemed antisocial or criminal (Real, 1997; Lester *et al.*, 2014). Although girls and women are more likely to experience suicidal thoughts, boys and men are more likely to successfully follow through on them. In the United States there were 34,000 male suicides and 9,000 female suicides in 2012 (CDC, 2012c; WHO, 2014a).

Gendered Body Images

Many people suffer health consequences, and some die, in the pursuit of gendered standards of attractiveness. History is full of examples of unhealthy practices that were embraced in the name of feminine beauty, from corsets to foot-binding to cosmetics that contained arsenic or lead.

Today more than 125 million girls and women, mostly in central and northern Africa, have undergone **female genital cutting**, also known as FGC or female genital mutilation. In the most extensive procedure, called **infibulation**, the clitoris and labia are removed and the genitals sewn shut, leaving only a small hole for urine and menstrual fluids. These girls will later need to be cut again in order to have intercourse or give birth. Some girls die from infection after the procedure, which is typically done at home and often without anesthesia, and some die later from scarring-related complications of childbirth. Cutting short of infibulation is both more common and less dangerous, but removing genital tissue without anesthesia can be traumatic even if the girl is not then sewn shut (UNICEF, 2013).

In communities that practice FGC, a young woman who has not been cut may be socially scorned and considered unmarriageable. An international campaign to change public opinion means that fewer teenage girls than middle-aged women have been cut, some communities are shifting away from infibulation to less comprehensive forms of cutting, and growing numbers of both women and men oppose the practice, especially if they are younger, better educated, wealthier, or live in urban areas. Many families, however, still consider FGC an unavoidable social requirement (OHCHR *et al.*, 2008; UNICEF, 2013).

In the United States the surgical pursuit of beauty focuses on women's faces, breasts, hips, and abdomens. In 2012 more than 10 million American women had cosmetic surgery or related procedures, including 458,000 women who had their breasts enlarged or lifted. More than 90 percent of the people who undergo cosmetic surgery are women (American Society for Aesthetic Plastic Surgery, 2012: 9). The death rate from cosmetic surgery is small, but surgery is never risk-free and often uncomfortable.

Many Americans use diet and exercise to shape their bodies. In moderation, of course, limiting calories and getting exercise are healthy practices. When taken to extremes, however, they can lead to metabolic imbalances that can damage the heart, kidneys, and other organs and even cause death. An estimated 10 million American women suffer from eating and exercise disorders. These disorders used to be seen primarily among young women, who come under the strongest pressure to be attractive, but their incidence has recently grown among males and women of middle age or older (Hudson *et al.*, 2007; Parker-Pope, 2011; Osgood, 2013). For men, the goal is often an appearance of muscularity. Some boys and men over-exercise and/or take steroids to build up muscle mass, while some practice excessive dieting in order to increase muscular definition by eliminating subcutaneous fat. Women are more likely than men to worry about their weight, but that gender gap is smaller than it was a generation ago (Brown, 2012).

One of the prevailing theories is that eating and exercise disorders are an attempt to assert control over what one can – one's body – in a life that feels out of control (Orbach, 1986; Brumberg, 1988). A national study of high school students found that 25 percent of girls and 11 percent of boys reported eating or exercise behaviors that could damage their health. Boys were much more likely to report worrisome behaviors if they were not white. There were fewer racial differences among girls, but Native American girls were particularly at risk (Austin, 2008). These patterns support the idea that eating and exercise disorders are a reflection of low social status and its accompanying insecurities.

GENDER DIFFERENCES IN LIFE EXPECTANCY: A GLOBAL PERSPECTIVE

Overview

Looking at life expectancy – how long the average man or woman can expect to live – gives us a broad-brush perspective on the level of gender inequality in different countries. As Figure 6.1 shows, women live longer than men in almost all countries, but how much longer varies widely. Males naturally have a somewhat higher death rate than females at every age, which nature compensates for by creating more males to begin with. More males are conceived, more miscarry as fetuses, more are born, more die in infancy, more die of heart attacks in middle age, and so on (Bruckner and Catalano, 2007; Blue, 2008; Kirkwood, 2010). With the best possible life circumstances and health care, the natural gender gap in life expectancy is probably in the range of 4 to 7 years, though it is impossible to give a precise number since there is no place where culture does not affect people's lives. Most countries, however, have gender gaps that are larger or smaller than the natural one.

The largest male disadvantages are found in countries that were once controlled by the Soviet Union. The biggest gap is in Russia, where women live 11.4 years longer than men, on average. Men also have relatively short life expectancies in some Latin American countries, due in part to violence related to the illegal drug trade – though femicide (men killing women because they are women) has also increased in recent years (UNDP, 2013b: 2).

Women are disproportionately likely to die young in a broad swath of countries from Africa through Asia, which together contain about half of the world's population. Some people look at this map and conclude that the problem is poverty.

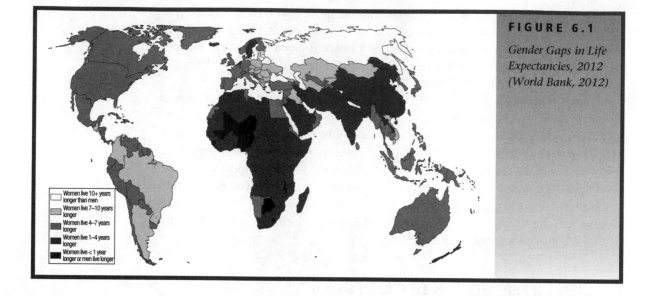

FIGURE 6.1

Gender Gaps in Life Expectancies, 2012 (World Bank, 2012)

Legend:
- Women live 10+ years longer than men
- Women live 7–10 years longer
- Women live 4–7 years longer
- Women live 1–4 years longer
- Women live < 1 year longer or men live longer

Indeed, about two-thirds of the 75 countries in which women live less than four years longer than men have a per capita income of less than $2,000 a year. Both men and women tend to have hard lives in such places, but women's relatively low life expectancy accurately suggests that the burdens of poverty and illness fall harder on women. Ten of these countries, however, are relatively affluent, with per capita incomes of $20,000 to $91,000. (For comparison, the U.S. per capita income is about $50,000.) So poverty is far from a full explanation (World Bank, 2013a).

Other people look at this map and conclude that the problem is Islam. Nearly 40 percent of countries in which women are disadvantaged have Muslim majorities, compared to 24 percent of all countries (Pew Forum, 2012a: 45–50). The importance of cultural patterns is perhaps most visible in Saudi Arabia and its oil-rich neighbors. These countries have plenty of money to provide for their residents' nutritional and medical needs, and both women and men regularly live into their 70s. In Saudi Arabia, however, the gender gap in life expectancy is 3.7 years, while in Bahrain, Kuwait, Qatar, and the United Arab Emirates it is 2.02 or less (World Bank, 2012). These are countries in which women's lives are highly restricted by both law and social customs, and the small gender gap suggests their lives are shortened by the multitude of health problems caused by constricted lives and chronic stress (Sapolsky, 1994).

Most countries in which women are disadvantaged, however, do not have Muslim majorities. The two largest such countries are predominantly Hindu India and predominantly Confucian/Communist China, which together account for more than a third of the world's population and contain more people than all the Muslim-majority countries put together. Women have shorter lives than men in just three countries: one is Muslim-majority while people in the other two practice

Christianity and/or indigenous African religions. There are Muslim-majority countries in which men are disadvantaged or the gender gap falls within the range considered natural. Clearly Islam is not our answer. To explain what is happening here, let us start with the country in which men are most disadvantaged: Russia.

Why Men Die Young in Russia

Russia has had an exceptionally large gender gap for decades. Men's and women's life expectancies rose steadily in the middle decades of the twentieth century, as they did in most countries, but men's began to decline in the 1960s while women's continued to grow slowly. At the end of the Soviet era (1991) the gender gap was 11 years (74 for women to 63 for men). After the collapse of the Soviet regime women's life expectancy fell by more than two years while men's fell more than four, creating a huge gender gap of 13 years (Shkolnikov and Meslé, 2010).

On a biological level, men's increased mortality was primarily due to cardiovascular diseases and various forms of violent death (accidents, suicides, etc.), most of which were associated with high levels of alcohol consumption (Shkolnikov and Meslé, 2010). From a bigger perspective, however, it is clear that social and economic changes drove the changes in men's longevity. Men's lifespans rose in the 1980s, when the most liberalizing of the Soviet leaders, Mikhail Gorbachev, was in office (Haaga, 2000). Their sharp decline in the early 1990s coincided with the vast disruptions associated with the dissolution of the Soviet Union and the embrace of (relatively) free-market capitalism. Some normalization during the middle 1990s allowed men's life expectancy to rise a bit, but it fell again after Russia's economic crisis in 1998 (McKee and Shkolnikov, 2001). While the cause of death on the death certificate might have been a heart attack or an alcohol-induced traffic accident, the fluctuations associated with Russia's changing political and economic conditions are too big and too consistent to be coincidental.

Not all men were equally affected by these changes. It was primarily less-educated men who died at early ages, while better-educated men had mortality rates that were similar to their counterparts in Western nations. The increased male mortality also affected primarily men of working ages. Infant mortality, for example, did not increase more among boys than girls. And unmarried men, whatever their level of education, were affected more than married men (McKee and Shkolnikov, 2011).

These variations point to the roles of social capital and status. By the 1960s the Soviet Union had become a highly unequal "hour-glass society" in which the men at the top – the ruling Communist Party functionaries – enjoyed good connections and high status, while the rigidity and arbitrariness of the regime left many men feeling powerless. Inequality increased even more after the collapse of the Soviet Union, as some better-connected men became extremely wealthy but vast numbers of men suffered from unemployment and underemployment and felt like they had little control over their lives. Their sense of powerlessness and despair led to binge drinking, violent and risky behavior, and the classic stress-related chronic diseases (McKee and Shkolnikov, 2001; Kennedy *et al.*, 1998).

Women's life expectancy also declined after 1991, but not as dramatically. The Soviet regime preached (though did not always practice) gender equality and many Soviet women worked outside the home, which gave them some degree of economic independence. Soviet women also spent much more time than men taking care of their families, and women's double burden of work and family responsibilities was often exhausting. When the country and economy went through rapid and disorienting changes, however, women's interpersonal relationships gave them more resilience in difficult times. Most women were embedded in networks of women that gave them social capital – both the objective ability to call in favors if they needed to, and the more subjective feeling of having meaningful connections (Goodwin and Emelyanova, 1995).

The gender gap in Russia is still large but it has narrowed in the last decade. Both men's and women's life expectancies have increased, but men's more than women. Women in post-Soviet countries are now more likely than women elsewhere to report more exhaustion, worry, and dissatisfaction with their health than the men of their country (Mendes and McGeeney, 2012). Although men are still more likely to die from many causes related to alcohol and tobacco, women are now more likely than men to die from cardiovascular diseases (WHO, 2014a). These findings suggest that Putin's regime is re-establishing male dominance and that the gender gap in life expectancies may continue to narrow.

Gender Inequality and HIV in Sub-Saharan Africa

HIV is a global epidemic, but it is especially virulent in sub-Saharan Africa, where it has killed more than 23 million people. This region has an eighth of the world's people but two-thirds of those living with HIV. Nearly one in twenty adults are infected with HIV, 58 percent of them women (UNAIDS, 2012: 8). Men's life expectancy in South Africa dropped four years between 1990 and 2000 (from age 59 to 55) while women's plummeted eight years (age 67 to 59) (WHO, 2013). Many of these deaths were caused by HIV or violence – or both at the same time, as many women contract HIV through rape.

Gender inequality is one of the fundamental reasons why HIV has been so devastating in this region. Sub-Saharan Africa has a long history of colonization and in many places slave trading, both of which used violence to subordinate local populations and make them profitable. The result is a legacy of deep inequality, low social trust, and violence (Hochschild, 1998; Fukuyama, 2014). Obtaining national independence does not by itself heal these breaches in the social fabric. Nor does it necessarily create effective political and economic institutions or open up new opportunities for work and the sense of self-worth it brings.

As in Russia, many men react to feelings of powerlessness and despair by engaging in risky and violent behavior that damages themselves and others (Centre

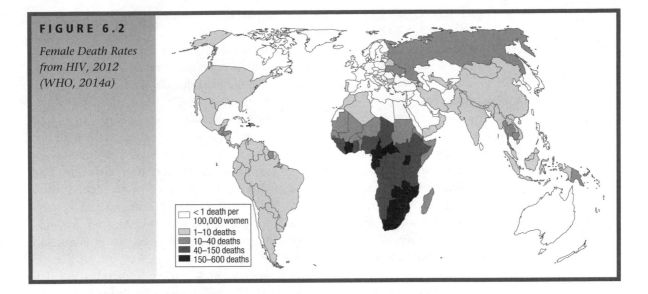

FIGURE 6.2

Female Death Rates from HIV, 2012 (WHO, 2014a)

< 1 death per 100,000 women
1–10 deaths
10–40 deaths
40–150 deaths
150–600 deaths

for the Study of Violence and Reconciliation, 2009: 2–3). Prevailing images of masculinity encourage HIV transmission by portraying "real men" as sexually voracious, fearless, and autonomous. Many men pursue sexual activities but are unwilling to admit their lack of knowledge about HIV or get tested or treated (UNAIDS, 2012: 70–71). They also resist condom use, and not just because it interferes with male pleasure. In communities that see the ability to father children as a sign of masculine virility, men may be reluctant to do anything that prevents conception even if they know they are HIV-positive (Altman, 2001: 78).

Women, meanwhile, are expected to defer to men and have little ability to make choices about sex, health care, and other aspects of their lives. Cultural norms see women as men's sexual property. Women but not men are expected to be monogamous, and a wife is required to have sex with her husband whenever he wishes (Pickup, 2001: 15). Some communities require a new widow to have sex with or marry her husband's brother or another near relative, and either partner in these mandated couplings may become infected (LaFraniere, 2005; Ayikukwei, *et al.*, 2008; Agot *et al.*, 2010). The most effective ways to prevent HIV transmission are avoiding sex with someone who is infected, condoms, and male circumcision, which reduce the chances of transmission by 50 to 60 percent (Joint United Nations Programme on HIV/AIDS, 2010: 7). In countries where women generally do not have the ability to say no to sex, men control all three of these approaches.

Women are inherently more vulnerable than men to contracting HIV through heterosexual intercourse, but cultural factors can increase that vulnerability. Foreplay may be minimal or nonexistent if women's sexual pleasure is considered unimportant or undesirable, and sex without sufficient lubrication is more likely to create vaginal abrasions through which the virus can enter. HIV infection is also more likely if other vaginal infections or STDs are untreated, as they often are in poor countries with inadequate health care systems.

Rape is an especially effective way of transmitting HIV through injuries to the woman's vagina. About a quarter million women were raped during the 1994 genocide in Rwanda, often by multiple men, and about 70 percent of the women who survived were infected with HIV (Wang, 2010: 326). That conflict spilled over into the Democratic Republic of the Congo, where about two million women have been raped (Gettleman, 2011). Many men who rape do so repeatedly, and they rarely use condoms, so they have a high risk of contracting HIV. A quarter of the men in South Africa acknowledge that they have raped, half of them more than once, and a fifth of South African women report that they were raped by the age of fifteen (Lindow, 2009; Kristof and WuDunn, 2009: 6). The belief that sex with a virgin will cure AIDS is widespread through much of Africa and southern Asia, and creates a special incentive for men who know or suspect they are infected to rape young girls (Study of the Secretary-General, 2006: 49).

The premium placed on female monogamy makes many husbands reject their wives if they have been raped. Women who have been expelled from their homes may end up doing sex work to survive, which again increases their risks of HIV (Wang, 2010).

Gender inequality also interferes with medical treatment. Antiviral therapies are now quite effective at saving lives and preventing transmission to a sexual partner or fetus, but many women who want testing or treatment do not receive it because they fear their husbands will beat or abandon them if they suspect they are HIV-positive. Many communities consider HIV-positive women immoral, even though it is common for monogamous wives to contract HIV from their husbands. Women who are known to be infected are often subjected to verbal and physical abuse by their families and communities, and many report intense feelings of shame and suicidal thoughts. Many women therefore die earlier than they might, while many babies are infected unnecessarily (UNAIDS, 2012: 70–71, 75).

Giving girls and women information and other resources makes them significantly less likely to contract HIV. In many countries it is common for teenage girls to take up with "sugar daddies," older men who offer them financial resources in the context of a sexual relationship. As a health worker in Uganda put it, "Here we say sex is a poor girl's food" (Wax, 2005). Many of these men are HIV-positive, so girls aged 15 to 19 are five times more likely to be infected with HIV than boys their age. One program in Kenya simply informed schoolgirls that older men are more likely to be infected with HIV. The result was a two-thirds reduction in the number of girls who got pregnant by a sugar daddy, and presumably a similar decrease in HIV infection (Banerjee and Duflo, 2011: 114). Another program in Malawi found that giving young women and their families a small amount of money per month (between $5 and $15) reduced their chances of being infected with HIV in the next 18 months by more than half. Even a small income, it seems, liberated young women from the need to find a sugar daddy (*Economist*, 2012d).

Most programs funded by the U.S. government, however, have emphasized the importance of abstinence and monogamy, which are often financially or physically unattainable for young women. Such programs generally fail to reduce the incidence of risky sex, pregnancy, and HIV infection (Banerjee and Duflo, 2011: 113; Kristof and WuDunn, 2009: 137). Worse yet, their approach reinforces gendered ideas that have helped drive the HIV epidemic, such as the belief that women are impure if they have sex outside marriage. The emphasis on abstinence means that many young women in countries with high rates of HIV infection do not even know that condoms can offer protection (UNAIDS, 2012: 18, 73). Ideas about sexual purity can thus interfere with empowering girls and women to save their own lives.

The good news is that the AIDS epidemic is beginning to ebb, both globally and in sub-Saharan Africa. In 2011, 1.2 million people died of AIDS in sub-Saharan Africa, which is one-third less than in 2005. The number of new infections was 25 percent lower in 2011 than in 2001, due to both behavioral changes and antiviral therapies (UNAIDS, 2012: 10–11). More than a million deaths a year, though, is still a very significant toll and quite disruptive to these societies.

The Missing Girls of India and China

Perhaps 160 million women are missing in Asia due to sex-selective abortion – perhaps more, perhaps fewer, but certainly enough that their absence affects their countries (Hvistendahl, 2011). Under natural conditions, something like 1.05 boys are born for every girl. As Figure 6.3 shows, the ratio of boys to girls is much higher in China, India, and a variety of smaller countries in southern Asia and southern Europe. Fewer boys than expected are born in sub-Saharan Africa, several Caribbean islands, and Kazakhstan. This is probably because male fetuses are more likely to miscarry when pregnant women are malnourished or under stress, as women often are in societies with high levels of gender inequality and social inequality (Song, 2012; Bruckner *et al.*, 2010). It is certainly not because of sex-selective abortion.

The ancestor of sex-selective abortion is female infanticide, which was condoned by many traditional societies and still sometimes occurs today (*Economist*, 2010). Many families considered raising daughters a waste of scarce resources, since adult sons supported their parents while daughters were married off to other families, often with a dowry payment as well. In India, upper-caste families were particularly likely to practice female infanticide, as these families were required to marry daughters up in the caste structure, suitable husbands were scarce, and an unmarried daughter brought shame to her family. Female infanticide was also particularly common in areas that frequently suffered from war or raids, with their accompanying capture and rape of girls and women. Many families concluded that it was better to lose a daughter at birth than to feed and raise her and lose her humiliatingly later. Some villages raised no girls at all, which meant that wife-capture was often the only way for young men to marry, thus fueling the cycle of violence. Female infanticide was rare or unknown in many Muslim communities, as the Qur'an emphatically

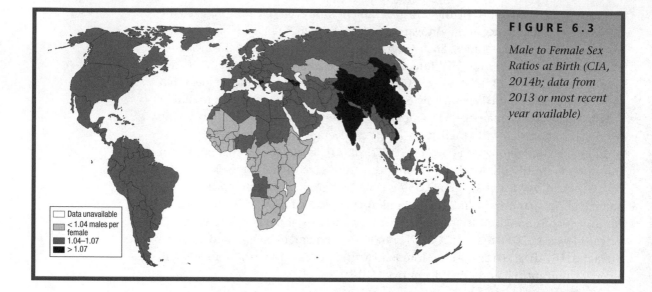

FIGURE 6.3

Male to Female Sex Ratios at Birth (CIA, 2014b; data from 2013 or most recent year available)

prohibited it. In some places, however, it was so deeply entrenched that it persisted even after people converted to Islam (Hudson and den Boer, 2004).

Today, the growing availability of ultrasound technology has made it possible for couples to determine the sex of a fetus and abort it if it is the undesired sex – nearly always female. Family sizes are shrinking around the world. When couples expect to rely on a grown son to support them once they get old, and they also expect to have only one or two children, they have a strong incentive to use sex-selective abortion. In India, for example, 76 percent of men and 81 percent of women consider it "very important" to have at least one son, primarily to carry on the family name and to provide support in old age (Nanda *et al.*, 2014: 60).

The high frequency of sex-selective abortion in China has often been blamed on its "one child" policies, but women in China average nearly 1.7 children, comparable to women in Canada or Denmark (World Bank, 2014). Sex-selective abortion has been illegal in China and India for years, but the laws have had little impact. The key issues seem to be whether couples have a strong son preference and whether they can get access to ultrasound machines and abortions, legal or illegal (Bongaarts, 2013). It seems likely that sex-selective abortion will continue either until these countries have universal pension systems that their residents feel they can rely on, or until sons and daughters are seen as equally able and willing to support their parents. China is closer to this goal than India, but it is not close (Hudson and den Boer, 2004; Hvistendahl, 2011; *Economist*, 2014c).

Neglect also takes its toll. In most of the world boys are more likely than girls to die before the age of five, as they are biologically more vulnerable to congenital abnormalities, premature birth, and infectious diseases. In India, however, girls are more likely to die young, while in China girls and boys die at nearly equal rates

(WHO, 2014a; *Economist*, 2013f). Nearly half of the children in India are physically stunted due to inadequate nutrition, and under these conditions even relatively subtle forms of neglect can affect a child's chances of survival (Rawe *et al.*, 2012: iv). Women typically breastfeed boy babies longer than girl babies, so boys are better nourished and have more protection from water-borne diseases (Banerjee and Duflo, 2011: 122). Parents may also be less willing to invest in medical care for a daughter; two-thirds of the newborns in India's neonatal intensive care units are male (Harris, 2014b). Two-thirds of the people who die from malnutrition in India are female, as are 59 percent of those who die from diarrhea, one of the biggest killers of children in poor countries (WHO, 2014a).

Childbirth

Childbirth is an intrinsically risky proposition, and no country has managed to eradicate maternal deaths altogether. As Figure 6.4 shows, however, women's chances of dying in childbirth vary greatly – from two deaths per 100,000 births in Estonia to 1,100 in Chad. In 20 countries (Afghanistan plus 19 in Africa) women face a more than one in 40 lifetime chance of dying from pregnancy or childbirth. Part of the issue here is poverty, which affects health in many ways, but that is not the whole story. Tajikistan has about the same per capita income as Chad, but there only 65 women die per 100,000 births (WHO *et al.*, 2012: 32–34; World Bank, 2013a).

Regions with high levels of maternal mortality also tend to have large numbers of childbirth injuries. More than two million women in Africa and Asia live with untreated fistulas, openings between the vagina and bladder or bowel that drip urine or feces uncontrollably. These wounds are caused by obstructed labor that in a wealthy country would be remedied with a cesarean section, but in many places

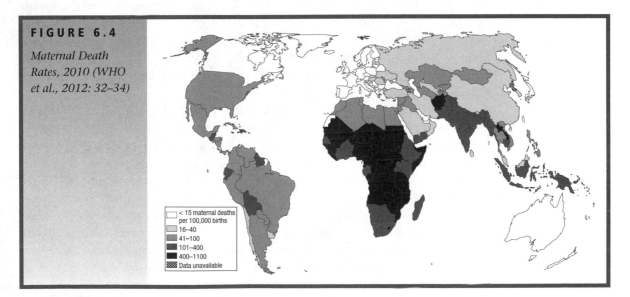

FIGURE 6.4

Maternal Death Rates, 2010 (WHO et al., 2012: 32–34)

< 15 maternal deaths per 100,000 births
16–40
41–100
101–400
400–1100
Data unavailable

a woman either pushes the baby out or dies. About 50,000 women each year develop fistulas, and in most cases their babies are stillborn or die within a week. Unable to control their wastes, women with fistulas are often socially ostracized and sometimes die from infection or starvation. Although fistulas can be repaired surgically these procedures are unavailable to many women in poor countries (UNFPA, 2012: 31–37).

Many different factors increase the chances of death, fistula, and other serious complications. Childbirth is more dangerous if women give birth before their bodies have fully matured. Although the frequency of child marriage is decreasing worldwide, in 2010 a quarter of young women (ages 20 to 24) had been married before the age of 18, and a third of teen brides were not yet 15 (UNICEF, 2014). Malnutrition, genital cutting, and a variety of diseases also increase the dangers of pregnancy and childbirth. Literacy makes it easier to learn and integrate information about everything, including how to keep oneself healthy, but women are more likely than men to be illiterate or very poorly educated. In addition, many women in areas with high maternal mortality do not receive prenatal care or have a trained attendant present when they give birth. If women are seen as vessels for making babies, and it is assumed that women's suffering is inevitable, childbirth may be seen as a natural process that does not need special attention. Although most births do succeed without medical interventions, many women in poor countries die from complications that could be treated if they had medical care.

All of these factors are related to poverty as well as gender inequality, and the example of Sri Lanka helps us separate their effects. An island country just south of India, Sri Lanka is a low-income country with a per capita GDP of about $2,400 a year (World Bank, 2013a). Since the 1930s it has made a priority of creating a nation-wide health system, with clinics in rural areas, centralized hospitals, ambulances, well-trained midwives, and careful statistics about maternal deaths. It has also made a priority of educating its people, including its girls. In Sri Lanka 90 percent of women and 93 percent of men are literate, compared with 51 percent of women and 75 percent of men in nearby India (WEF, 2014: 70). Sri Lanka's gender gap in life expectancy is 6.2 years, suggesting that gender inequality has little effect on death rates (World Bank, 2012).

In Sri Lanka about 39 women die for every 100,000 who give birth, while most countries with similar incomes have maternal death rates two or three times higher. This is not because Sri Lanka spends more on health care than comparable countries, but because it uses its resources more effectively. India's maternal death rate, for example, is six times higher than Sri Lanka's, though it spends significantly more on health care (Kristof and WuDunn, 2009: 117). India has not managed to create reliable sanitation and health care institutions: a recent study found that 78 percent of hospitals had no soap available at their hand-washing sinks (Harris, 2014b). Maternal death rates in Sri Lanka are still two to ten times higher than those seen in wealthy countries, which is probably due to its relatively low income. But if all countries brought their maternal death rates down to the levels of Sri Lanka, that would save the lives of approximately 200,000 women each year (WHO *et al.*, 2012: 32–36).

This is not an unreasonable hope. The number of women dying in childbirth declined by 47 percent between 1990 and 2010 as a result of an international campaign to provide all women adequate medical care, sanitation, and contraception. It takes time to change public opinion, educate both practitioners and families, and build an effective public health infrastructure, but it can be done if there is sufficient will and funding. Progress has, however, been slower than many people had hoped. In 2000 the United Nations set a goal of decreasing maternal mortality by 75 percent between 1990 and 2015 and providing universal access to reproductive health care by 2015, neither of which proved possible (WHO *et al.*, 2012: 1). Sri Lanka's success, however, underlines the importance of valuing women's lives, as it shows that even a poor country can make dramatic changes if it has the political will to do so.

Reproductive Control

A woman's life is greatly affected not just by how many children she has, but also when and under what circumstances she has them. Without contraception, many sexually active women get pregnant soon after they stop breastfeeding. A constant cycle of pregnancy and breastfeeding is exhausting, as is raising a large number of children. Frequent childbearing is even more depleting if a woman is malnourished, engages in hard physical labor, and frequently suffers from infectious diseases, which is the plight of poor women in many countries.

As we saw earlier, different types of societies have different ideal and average family sizes. In traditional societies many couples did not try to limit their family size. Sometimes, though, couples tried to space out births or stop having children once they felt their families were large enough. Some women used herbs and extended breastfeeding to try to prevent conception, and some used various techniques to try to abort an unwanted pregnancy. Some men practiced *coitus interruptus*, withdrawing from the woman right before ejaculation. All of these techniques reduced family sizes but were not fully reliable. The most effective method was to abstain from sex for extended periods (Brodie, 1994; Mohr, 1978: 3–7).

In industrialized countries, many people see children as expensive to raise and educate and expect to rely on pensions and savings in their old age. They therefore tend to have one or two children, or perhaps none. Worldwide, women nowadays have an average of 2.5 children – half of the five children that they averaged in the 1960s (UNPD, 2013). Within each country, wealthier couples tend to have fewer children. In Nigeria, for example, families in the wealthiest quintile (top 20 percent) have an average of 4.0 children, while families in the poorest quintile average 7.1 children (World Bank, 2011b: 2).

Although many couples make decisions about family size together, it can also be a source of significant tension. In poor and middle-income countries men generally express a preference for more children than women do – if women are interviewed separately. If couples are interviewed together the wives generally agree with their husbands. Many women in these countries prefer contraceptives they can conceal from their husbands, such as injectable hormones and implants, and they are more likely to request or accept contraception if they are seen alone by medical personnel (Banerjee and Duflo, 2011: 116–117).

Images of masculinity may make men resist contraceptive use. Many traditional cultures consider fathering children an important sign of virility. A man may therefore fear being mocked, to his face or behind his back, for impotence if his wife stops getting pregnant. In addition, some communities associate contraceptive use with extramarital relationships, so a man may fear that if it becomes known that his wife is using contraceptives the neighbors will assume that she is having affairs and he is a cuckold. In many villages it is difficult to keep anything private.

A vasectomy (male sterilization) is often the safest, cheapest, and easiest way for a couple to stop having children once they consider their families complete. Some men, however, feel that they would be unmanned if they were incapable of impregnating a woman. Tubal ligations (female sterilization) are more painful and hazardous than vasectomies. Nevertheless, 19 percent of couples worldwide use tubal ligations and only 2 percent use vasectomies (United Nations, 2013). (In the U.S. the figures are 27 and 10 percent, respectively [Guttmacher Institute, 2014a].)

About one in eight married women worldwide wants contraception but does not have access to it. Most of these 110 million women live in Asia or Africa. Sometimes husbands forbid their wives from using contraception, while in other places contraceptives are not available because of some combination of poverty, a general lack of medical services, and social norms forbidding their use. The situation of women who have sex outside of marriage for any reason (rape, money, or desire) is even more vexed, as they may be ostracized if they get pregnant but often face steep legal and cultural barriers to obtaining contraception. The world contains about 400 million unmarried women, mostly teenagers, many of whom have little or no access to reproductive information and services. With so many barriers to contraception, more than 40 percent of all pregnancies are unplanned (United Nations, 2013; WHO, 2011b: 10–11).

One indicator of how often women have unwanted pregnancies is abortion rates. Unwanted pregnancy affects women more than men not just because of the obvious biological reasons, but also because all societies require women to take primary responsibility for childrearing, whether or not they wanted the child or even consented to sex. Giving an infant up for adoption is sometimes an option, but in many places it is highly stigmatized or logistically impossible. Many women continue unwanted pregnancies, and 39 percent of women live in countries where abortion is legally available on request. In 53 countries, however, abortion is legal only to save the woman's life, and in four countries it is illegal even then (WHO, 2011b: 4).

In 2008 about 22 million women resorted to illegal abortions, 47,000 of whom died. In the United States abortion is about as safe as a penicillin injection and far safer than giving birth. In Egypt, by contrast, abortion is illegal except to save the life of the woman, but it is estimated that about 15 percent of pregnancies are aborted and 10 percent of pregnancy-related deaths are due to abortion. In other words, abortion is still safer than childbirth, but not by much (El Feki, 2013: 162, 165). In Africa nearly one out of every 200 women who has an abortion dies, compared to less than one in 100,000 in the United States (WHO, 2011b: 19, 28, 30).

As Figure 6.5 shows, abortion rates are generally higher in countries where abortion laws are moderately or strongly restrictive. The big exception is Eastern Europe, where contraception was often unavailable under Soviet rule and many women relied on abstinence and abortion to control their family size, a pattern that apparently continues (WHO, 2011b: 26). Making abortion illegal does not necessarily make it more common, of course. Instead, it seems likely that restrictive abortion laws reflect larger social attitudes and practices that make it more likely that a woman will get pregnant when she strongly does not want a child. If women and their reproductive capacity are considered men's property, women have little control over whether they have sex and they are more likely to consider abortion a necessity – even if it is illegal and unsafe and poses a serious risk to their own health.

Here too things are changing. Most importantly, contraceptives are becoming more widely available, though progress is slow and sometimes does not keep up

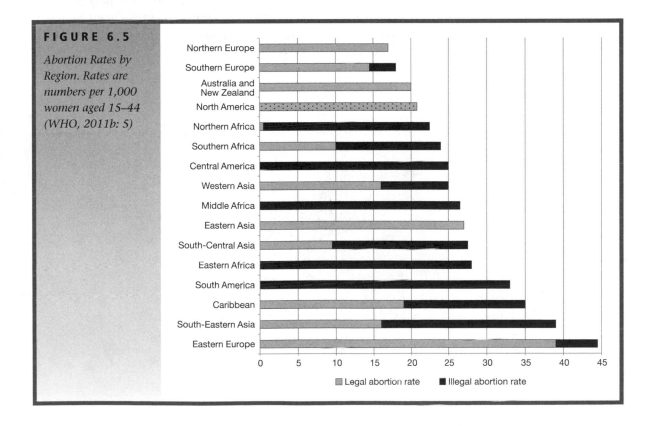

FIGURE 6.5

Abortion Rates by Region. Rates are numbers per 1,000 women aged 15–44 (WHO, 2011b: 5)

with the growing number of women reaching reproductive age (Ahmed and Sarker, 2013: 42). Although no contraceptive is perfectly reliable, death rates from abortion drop when women have access to modern contraception (WHO, 2011b: 10).

In addition, medical abortions using drugs are increasingly available, both in clinics and informally. These drugs have multiple purposes and are available without a prescription in many drugstores around the world, even in countries where abortion is illegal, and growing numbers of women know about their alternative uses. Though self-administration has its own risks, it is safer, more private, and cheaper than illegal surgical abortions, which are often performed by inadequately trained practitioners in insufficiently sterile environments. Both medical and surgical abortions are safest when they occur under medical supervision, but political realities make that impossible in many countries (IPPF, 2008: 16–20; Kristof, 2010; Eckholm, 2013).

Suicide

Here is one final way to think about how gender affects people's well-being: how likely people are to end their own lives. More people die from suicide than all other forms of violence put together, and men are nearly twice as likely as women to kill themselves (WHO, 2014a). This does not mean that men are more unhappy than women. Indeed, in most countries women are more likely than men to report chronic sadness, and they are much more likely to do so in a fifth of countries (Mendes and McGeeney, 2012). As we have noted previously, however, men are more likely than women to engage in violence of almost every kind, including violence toward themselves.

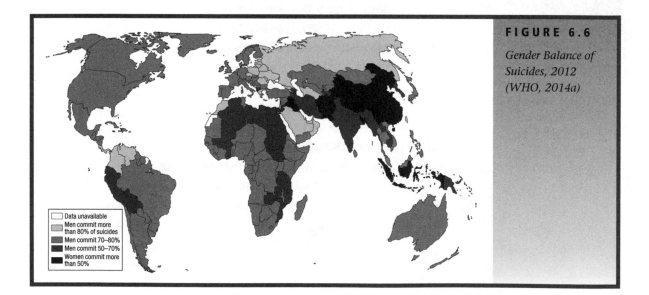

FIGURE 6.6

Gender Balance of Suicides, 2012 (WHO, 2014a)

Comparisons of the gender ratios of suicides can be suggestive about where women and men find their lives most difficult. In the 1990s China had one of the highest suicide rates in the world, but now it has one of the lowest. The most dramatic change was among young rural women, whose suicide rate dropped by around 90 percent and is now similar to that of rural men. The option of urban employment has, it seems, liberated many young women from feeling trapped in abusive and violent families. From a global perspective, however, near-equality in suicide rates suggests that rural women in China still have hard lives (Phillips *et al.*, 2002; Fish, 2013; *Economist*, 2014h).

Figure 6.6 should be treated with a bit of caution, as there are all sorts of reasons that suicides may not be reported accurately. Where suicide is considered shameful families may choose to obscure what happened, and sometimes it is impossible to determine with certainty whether a death was intentional, accidental, or somewhere in between. In many cases, however, the patterns suggested by this map align with other metrics of gender inequality. Once again the former Soviet states look bad for men. The six countries in which women are more likely than men to kill themselves are Afghanistan, Bangladesh, China, Indonesia, Iraq, and Pakistan. In Iraq women are twice as likely as men to commit suicide (WHO, 2014a).

GENDER AND HEALTH IN THE UNITED STATES

Gender, Race, Class, and Life Expectancy

From a global perspective, life expectancies in the United States are good but not exceptionally good. In 2012 the average man could expect to live to 76.4 and the average woman to 82.2, which is longer than most of the world but shorter than in 43 countries, including China and some other middle-income countries (World Bank, 2012). The gender gap is 4.8 years, which is somewhat small but may be within the natural range. Here too, life expectancies reflect not just how long people live but also, in a broad-brush way, how healthy they are along the way.

In the United States, race has always affected life expectancy. As Figure 6.7 shows, until the 1940s the gender gap was relatively small and was dwarfed by the racial gap. In 1900 the average white male lived nearly 50 percent longer than the average black male. The gender gap expanded after World War II but has since narrowed somewhat. For white people, it peaked in the 1970s at 7.8 years and by 2010 had declined to 4.8 years. For black people, the gender gap peaked in 1991 at 9.1 years, which suggests a state of society that was highly unhealthy for black men. The black gender gap has since moderated to a more reasonable 6.2 years, which is still much larger than the white gender gap. In 2010 the racial gap was 4.7 years for men and 3.3 years for women. This gap may have some genetic basis but it is mostly due to social and cultural issues, including poverty and discrimination, quality of nutrition and housing, chronic stress, and differences in preventative

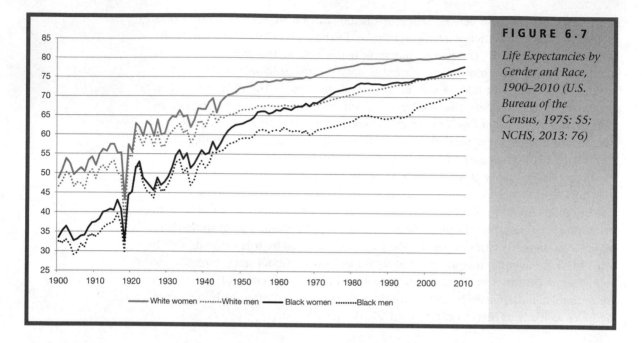

FIGURE 6.7

Life Expectancies by Gender and Race, 1900–2010 (U.S. Bureau of the Census, 1975: 55; NCHS, 2013: 76)

——— White women ········· White men ——— Black women ········· Black men

health care and treatment of acute illnesses (McNeil, 2011; Velasquez-Manoff, 2013).

There are also large differences within each racial grouping, as people with more education and income tend to live longer lives with fewer debilitating illnesses (Scott, 2005). Indeed, the "education gap" now dwarfs the gender and racial gaps. White men with a college degree live 12.9 years longer than those with no diploma (80.4 versus 67.5 years), while white women have an education gap of 10.4 years (83.9 versus 73.5) (Tavernise, 2012). If we look just at people without a high school diploma, life expectancy for white women has dropped by five years since 1990, and for white men by three years. Life expectancies for black women have been basically stable, while they have risen for black men and Hispanic people of both genders. Indeed, the white–black racial gap has basically disappeared among people without a diploma (Tavernise, 2012).

It is very rare for life expectancies to fall in countries that are not undergoing a war, epidemic, or economic crisis. For the one in eight white Americans who have not finished high school, however, it seems that the changes of the last two decades have been life-threatening, especially for women (Ryan and Siebens, 2012: 7). As we discussed earlier, there is a lot of concern about the ability of less-educated men to thrive as the United States transitions ever more to a knowledge-based economy. Women's education levels and incomes are rising, while incomes are falling for men without a college degree (BLS, 2012: 66–67). If we look at changes in life expectancies, however, women without a diploma seem to be doing worse than men without a diploma.

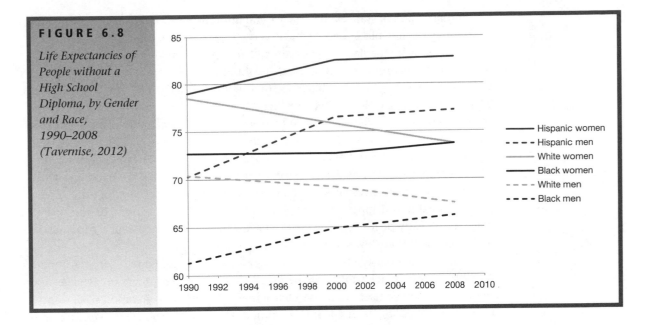

FIGURE 6.8

Life Expectancies of People without a High School Diploma, by Gender and Race, 1990–2008 (Tavernise, 2012)

Legend:
— Hispanic women
---- Hispanic men
— White women
— Black women
---- White men
---- Black men

When researchers tried to identify the mechanisms behind the decline in life expectancy among less-educated white women, two factors stood out: unemployment and smoking. Unemployed women are more likely than employed women to die even if they have the same income and health insurance coverage from other sources. The researchers suggested that employment is protective because of its more intangible benefits, "including a sense of purpose and control in life, as well as providing networks that help to reduce social isolation" – which we have been calling social capital (Tavernise, 2013). A separate study found that Americans are more socially isolated than they were a generation ago, and this change is especially marked among white women without a diploma (McPherson *et al.*, 2006). Many of these women, it seems, are now too busy, sick, or depressed to maintain the social relationships that sustain health (Potts, 2013).

Smoking rates have dropped in almost every demographic group, but have actually increased among less-educated women (Scott, 2005; Tavernise, 2013). The fact that smoking reduces life expectancy is well known, even to smokers. People who feel powerless, however, are more likely to engage in risky behaviors, and smoking offers immediate comfort with only a future hazard of disease. A similar factor is fatal overdoses from prescription drugs, which have increased dramatically among white people since 1990, especially among women (Tavernise, 2013). Since 2002 white people have been more likely than black people to die from drug overdoses, and legal prescription drugs have killed more people than illegal drugs (McNeil, 2011). Drug abuse, addiction, and overdoses are also symptoms of social isolation and despair (Hart, 2013).

Similar issues of status and social capital underlie black men's relatively low life expectancy. Some black people have very high status, including most notably President Barack Obama, but they are still relatively unlikely to have prestigious degrees, high incomes, and other markers of high status. Young black men aged 22 to 30 are more than twice as likely as their white and Hispanic contemporaries to be jobless (Western, 2006: 90). The stereotype that black men are dangerous or criminal affects how they are treated by teachers, employers, police officers, judges, and people walking down the street. Incarceration rates for black men have risen dramatically since 1980, largely due to new laws that prescribe harsh sentences for what were previously considered minor offenses (Alexander, 2010; Khadaroo, 2013). All of these experiences make people feel powerless, which profoundly affects people's health and longevity (Velasquez-Manoff, 2013). The immediate cause of black men's early deaths may be heart attacks or emphysema, HIV or a gun. But the deeper cause is their low social status.

Some people believe that black women are now doing better than black men. As we have seen, black women are better educated than black men, on average, and their earnings have risen more than black men's in the last generation (U.S. Census Bureau, 2014b; BLS, 2012: 64–65). Looking at life expectancies, however, calls this conclusion into question. Life expectancies are rising more quickly for black men than black women, and they are stagnant for black women without a high school diploma (NCHS, 2013: 76; Tavernise, 2012). These observations suggest that less-educated black women are struggling at least as much as their male peers, and that the recent focus of racial justice efforts on improving the prospects of black men should be extended to black women as well.

The high life expectancy among Hispanics, despite their relatively low incomes, is sometimes called the "Hispanic paradox." Cultural factors seem to be very important here. For example, Mexican-Americans are healthiest if they live in neighborhoods with many other Mexican-Americans, while their health deteriorates if they live in mixed communities and assimilate into American culture. Although Mexican-American neighborhoods are often poor, they also tend to have strong kinship networks and community institutions, with high levels of employment and family stability and low use of alcohol, tobacco, and other recreational drugs (Eschbach et al., 2004; Franzini et al., 2001). The fact that Hispanic women live, on average, five years longer than Hispanic men suggests that they benefit from their communities' strong social capital as much as the men do.

Communities that are predominantly black or Native American, in contrast, have relatively low life expectancies. Black men in racially mixed suburbs live nearly three years longer than black men in predominantly black urban neighborhoods, though for black women this gap is only a year. The gender gap among urban black people is about eight years, well into the range that is unhealthy for men. Native Americans who live on or near reservations have life expectancies comparable to those of suburban black people, while Asians have the longest life expectancies and a relatively large gender gap of six years (Murray et al., 2006).

TABLE 6.1 *Rates of Sudden Death from Destructive or Risky Behavior, 2007 (CDC, 2011, 2012a)*		SUICIDE	HOMI-CIDE	DRUG OVER-DOSES	VEHIC-ULAR ACCI-DENTS	FIRE-ARM RELATED INJURIES	TOTAL
	Black men	8.7	41.4	15.8	23.2	38.5	127.6
	Native American men	23.2	11.7	12.6	40.0	11.1	98.6
	White men	22.9	3.7	18.7	21.5	16.3	83.1
	Hispanic men	8.9	12.5	9.5	19.5	13.4	63.8
	Native American women	6.2	4.0	11.5	18.8	1.7	42.2
	White women	6.1	1.8	11.4	8.8	2.9	31.0
	Asian men	8.9	3.4	2.3	9.5	5.1	29.2
	Black women	1.7	6.4	7.5	7.3	3.8	26.7
	Hispanic women	1.8	2.5	3.4	7.0	1.5	16.2
	Asian women	1.8	1.4	1.7	5.3	0.7	10.9

Note: All rates are deaths per 100,000 people.

Another approach to these issues is to look at how likely people of various demographic groups are to die from risky or destructive behavior. Accidents, substance abuse, suicide, and murder are usually considered different causes of death, but if one looks at these categories closely the edges start to blur. When someone dies from a drug overdose or gun accident, for example, the death may not be considered a suicide unless a note accompanies it. How often, though, does a drug overdose reflect a desire to die, or at least a lack of desire to continue living? Sometimes car accidents are simply accidents, but sometimes they are a result of risky behavior and a similar disinterest in preserving one's life. Homicides can also be a reflection of despair, pain turned outward instead of inward. Taken together, these behaviors are nearly twelve times as likely to kill black men than Asian women, but both Native and white women are more at risk than black women. Native men have the highest risk of suicide, while white men have the highest risk of drug overdoses. The topography of despair is complex (Lester *et al.*, 2014).

In short, race and class now affect Americans' life expectancies – and presumably general health – more than gender. With the exception of urban African Americans, every contemporary gender gap we have mentioned is within the 4 to 7 year range that is considered possibly natural. The gaps by race and social class, however, are definitely not natural and can change significantly within just a few decades.

Childbirth

American women's chances of surviving childbirth are good but not exceptional. In 2010, 21 women died for every 100,000 births, giving the United States a higher maternal mortality rate than 49 other countries. American women were four times more likely than Polish women to die from pregnancy and childbirth, though Poland's per capita income was only about a quarter of the United States' (WHO *et al.*, 2012: 32–34; World Bank, 2013a).

Maternal death rates declined during most of the twentieth century, due to improved nutrition, medical care, and sanitation, but they have roughly doubled since 2000. Some of the most detailed data comes from California, where an eighth of American births occur. As Figure 6.9 shows, black women are far more likely to die in childbirth than other women and have experienced the sharpest increase in death rates. Even among non-black women, however, the increase in death rates is statistically significant.

Social class is a significant factor: 11 percent of the women who gave birth in 2002–2003 and 31 percent of the women who died did not have a high school diploma. Black women, however, had a higher chance of dying whatever their education level. Also of concern is the change among U.S.-born Hispanic women. In 1999 their death rate was lower than that of both white women and foreign-born Hispanic women, but since 2005 it has been higher. This trend may reflect increased assimilation into U.S. culture. The death rate is lowest for Asian women, and they and foreign-born Hispanic women have experienced the smallest increase since 1999 (CDPH, 2011: 2–5, 26, 35).

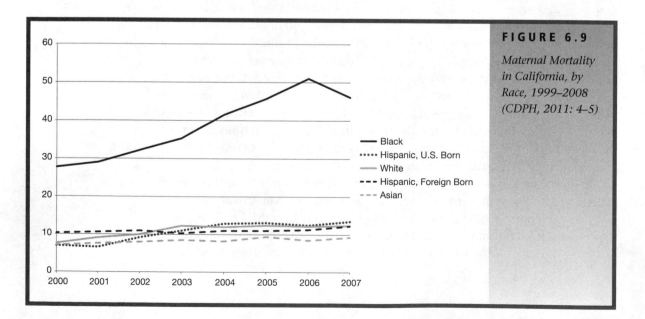

FIGURE 6.9

Maternal Mortality in California, by Race, 1999–2008 (CDPH, 2011: 4–5)

Legend:
— Black
····· Hispanic, U.S. Born
— White
- - - Hispanic, Foreign Born
-- - Asian

California's researchers concluded that four factors had increased the state's maternal death rates. First, improved reporting procedures meant that more pregnancy-related deaths were recorded as such. Second, women were giving birth at older ages and with higher rates of obesity, hypertension, and diabetes, which affected their risks. Third, more women were being affected by detrimental social factors, such as social isolation, chronic exposure to environmental hazards, and the stresses associated with racism and low social status. Finally, the quality of health care was inconsistent, with both overuse and underuse of medical interventions (CDPH, 2011: 8).

Since the 1970s, some women have critiqued the over-medicalization of childbirth, arguing that childbirth is a natural process that is usually successful without medical interventions. Hospital procedures, they argued, often serve the interests of doctors and hospitals, not women and babies, and reflect a deep distrust of women's bodies and disregard for women's well-being. The frequency of medical interventions continued to climb, however, and in recent years a third of all births have been by cesarean section. Some cesarean sections, of course, are necessary, but they pose dangers to both mothers and infants. The cesarean section rate ranges from 7 to 70 percent in different U.S. hospitals, while women with low-risk pregnancies have a 2 to 36 percent chance of having a cesarean section, depending on which hospital they go to. Such wide variations suggest that many women receive suboptimal maternity care (Tavernise, 2013).

The U.S. maternal mortality rate is twice or more – sometimes much more – of the rate in most of Western Europe and much of Eastern Europe, and infant mortality is also significantly higher in the United States (WHO *et al.*, 2012: 32–36; OECD, 2014b). Outcomes are particularly good in the Nordic countries, where trained nurse-midwives provide all women comprehensive prenatal care, birth attendance, and home visits after birth. These nurse-midwives work cooperatively with specialist physicians who take over if there are major complications, but most births occur without significant interventions (Högberg, 2004; Moorhead, 2006). Reformers often suggest that Europe's lower death rates are due to tax-funded national health systems that guarantee health care for all residents. With the exception of Bulgaria, however, every country in Europe also has substantially less economic inequality than the United States (CIA, 2014a). It is therefore difficult to disentangle the effects of medical practices per se from the broader health effects of living in a society with less inequality and higher levels of social cohesion. The conclusion that more American women than necessary die in childbirth is, however, inescapable.

Reproductive Control

Most Americans today use contraception and believe it should be widely available. With an average of 1.9 children per woman, many Americans practice contraception for decades and 89 percent believe it is morally acceptable (Newport, 2012a).

Although Catholic doctrine disapproves of artificial contraceptives, 99 percent of sexually experienced American Catholic women report that they have used contraceptives and two-thirds of Catholics believe that employer-provided health insurance plans should be required to include contraception coverage (Jones and Dreweke, 2011; Markoe, 2012).

Roughly half of U.S. pregnancies, however, are unintended, three-fifths of which are "mistimed" – that is, a couple wanted to have a child but not yet (Guttmacher Institute, 2013b). Each year about 5 percent of American women of reproductive age have an unintended pregnancy, and more than half will have an unexpected pregnancy sometime in their lives. Indeed, North America is the only region of the world in which unintended pregnancies have not declined in recent years (Singh *et al.*, 2012). Women are more likely to have an unintended pregnancy if they are under age 25, poor or low income, have less education, are black or Hispanic, or are cohabiting with a man, especially if they are cohabiting before the age of 20 (Finer and Zolna, 2011). Women living in poverty are five times more likely to have an unintended pregnancy than women whose incomes are at least twice the poverty line (Guttmacher Institute, 2013b).

Only 5 percent of unintended pregnancies occur when modern contraception was used correctly and consistently. Nearly half of the women with unintended pregnancies, however, report that they used contraception in the month when they got pregnant, and many couples use contraception inconsistently even though they are quite aware of how pregnancies occur (Guttmacher Institute, 2013b). The simple-seeming distinction between "intended" and "unintended" thus obscures the reality that human intentions may be more blurry than clear.

The most common contraceptive in the United States is the pill. Although it is very effective when taken consistently, in actual life about 9 percent of women using the pill become pregnant each year. The failure rate is especially high among teenagers, one out of eight of those who become pregnant each year they are on the pill (Guttmacher Institute, 2014a; Winner *et al.*, 2012). One of the issues is that the pill requires a woman every day to make a choice not to become pregnant. If one day she is too busy dealing with work or one of life's little crises to remember to take the pill, or if one day she feels a strong emotional yearning for a baby, she may end up pregnant (Griego, 2014). Pills also require doctors' prescriptions, insurance coverage, and often copayments. Renewals often require medical appointments and pharmacy visits, which may be challenging to fit into busy or chaotic lives. All of this is even harder if a young woman wants to hide her contraceptive use from parents or other family members. Pills may also have unpleasant side effects that create an emotional resistance to taking them. For all of these reasons and more, women sometimes skip a pill or fail to renew a prescription promptly. They may not even know that just one missed or too-delayed pill can make them vulnerable to pregnancy (Edin and Kefalas, 2011). The result is nearly one million unintended pill-related pregnancies each year (Guttmacher Institute, 2014a).

Many American women do not know about or have access to the most effective contraceptive techniques (Sawhill, 2014). If given appropriate information and insurance coverage, many young women will choose a long-acting reversible contraceptive (LARC) – an IUD or hormonal implant, which typically last 3 to 5 years (Secura *et al.*, 2010). LARCs are highly effective and require attention only every few years, so they allow a woman to make a choice once and then carry on with other aspects of her life. Only 4 percent of American women of reproductive age use LARC, however, and LARCs are less available in the United States than in other wealthy countries (Guttmacher Institute, 2014a; Winner *et al.*, 2012). One barrier is that many practitioners do not know about LARC and do not offer it to their patients (Harper *et al.*, 2008). Up-front costs can also be a barrier, though in the longer run LARC is often more cost-effective than condoms, pills, and other kinds of reversible birth control – and certainly far cheaper than raising a child (Trussell *et al.*, 2013). Women using the pill or patch are twenty times as likely as women using LARC to have an unintended pregnancy (Winner *et al.*, 2012).

Colorado has recently made a concerted effort to make LARC available to low-income residents, and this program is credited with causing a 30 percent drop in teen birth rates (Griego, 2014). Such programs can provoke resistance, however, among people who believe that women should be virgins until they are married. Although only 11 percent of Americans say they disapprove of contraception, political opposition to providing reproductive health care to unmarried women can be intense.

In the United States, about 40 percent of unwanted pregnancies (i.e., 20 percent of all pregnancies) end in abortion and nearly one in three women has an abortion at some time in her life (Guttmacher Institute, 2014b). The abortion rate declined 8 percent between 2000 and 2008, which is part of a long-term trend. The abortion rate among poor women, however, rose 18 percent during these years. One reason, it seems, was that many poor women faced increased difficulties in accessing contraception. Another reason was that poor women were increasingly likely to be homeless, juggling multiple jobs, or otherwise in life situations that made managing an infant seem impossible (Jones and Kavanaugh, 2011; Jones *et al.*, 2013).

Attitudes toward abortion have changed dramatically over the years. Before modern medicine a pregnancy could not be confirmed until "quickening," when the woman first felt the fetus move and Catholics and Protestants believed the soul entered its body. Most people felt that until quickening it was a woman's right to try to "bring down her menses" if she wanted to, though the available techniques were unreliable and could be dangerous. Abortion was criminalized after the Civil War as part of a much larger "moral purity" movement that sought to eradicate contraception, prostitution, pornography, adultery, and reproductive information (Mohr, 1978; Brodie, 1994).

By the 1950s and 1960s growing numbers of women were dying from illegal abortions. Sexual mores were changing, as were ideal family sizes and the costs of raising and educating children. Contraception, however, was less reliable than it is now and often unavailable, especially but not only for unmarried women. The Supreme Court ruled in 1965 that married couples have a right to use contraception but did not extend that right to unmarried women until 1972. Even where contraception was legal it might not be locally sold or physicians might not be willing to prescribe it. Although many men no longer believed that abstinence until marriage was appropriate or acceptable, unmarried women who became pregnant were highly stigmatized, especially in white communities (Solinger, 1992). Many married women also had abortions when they felt they could not physically or financially manage another child and needed to take care of the ones they already had (Reagan, 1997).

Feminists argued that the ability to control reproduction was necessary if women were to be able to set the course of their own lives. Even non-feminists, however, were increasingly concerned about the number of deaths caused by illegal abortion, as many people had heard such stories from their extended social circles. In 1973 the Supreme Court's *Roe v. Wade* decision legalized abortion before the third trimester, before the fetus is viable outside the womb. This decision made abortion both safer and more widely available, but it also became a flashpoint in the ensuing "culture wars" between those who embraced the principles of women's rights and autonomy and those who felt that family relationships based on gender are natural, God-given, and under threat (Reagan, 1997).

Today, opinions about abortion vary widely but there is only a small gender gap, with 55 percent of women and 53 percent of men saying abortion should be legal in most or all situations (Pew Forum, 2013a). Education has a much larger impact, as people who attended college, especially graduates, are much more likely than less-educated people to believe that early abortions should always be legal, which fits with their belief that it is important to time the arrival of children carefully (Gallup, 2010). College graduates are, however, much less likely than less-educated women to actually have abortions, with an abortion rate just a little more than half that of women without a college degree (Jones and Kavanaugh, 2011).

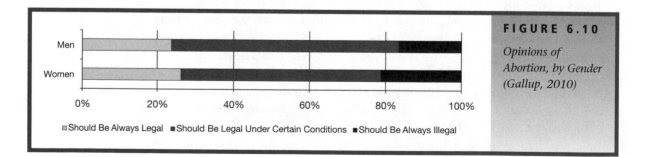

FIGURE 6.10

Opinions of Abortion, by Gender (Gallup, 2010)

CONCLUSION

Gender inequality affects life expectancies in many and complicated ways. Around the world, men are more likely to die violently or from risky behavior, and they are particularly affected in the former Soviet Union with its high levels of male alcohol consumption and parts of Latin America with high levels of violence. The "missing boys" who are not born in sub-Saharan Africa may also reflect gender inequality as well as poverty. In most of Asia and Africa, however, females are more likely to die prematurely from sex-selective abortion, infanticide, malnutrition, neglect, HIV, preventable deaths related to pregnancy, and a wide range of stress-exacerbated illnesses.

Other forms of inequality also affect life expectancies. Race, class, and where one lives all affect people's chances of dying prematurely, sometimes more than gender does. The variations in gender gaps among different demographic groups, and the fact that they can change in just a few decades, underlines the difficulty of determining the natural gender gap in life expectancies.

Develop Your Position

1 We suggested five ways in which gender inequality might shorten people's lives: actions and inactions that reflect a low value placed on women's lives, codes of masculinity that encourage risky behavior, the chronic stress that comes from low social status and low social capital (and their associated experiences of powerlessness and isolation), gendered assumptions built into medical systems, and the excessive pursuit of gendered images of attractiveness. Which of these factors, if any, have you seen in action? Can you think of other ways in which gender inequality might shorten women's or men's lives?

2 Does the argument that social status and social capital affect longevity ring true to you? Why or why not?

3 The gender gap in life expectancy in the United States is 4.8 years, which is on the short side. Do you find it plausible that in the United States women might have their lives shortened by gender inequality more than men? Why or why not?

4 Take another look at Table 6.1. What do you think you can learn about gender, race, and despair in the United States from examining this table? Where, for you, does it raise questions that it cannot answer?

PART III

Continuity and Change

CHAPTER 7

Learning and Performing Gender in School

INTRODUCTION

Broadly speaking, education is all the ways that young people acquire the skills, knowledge, and attitudes they will need as adults. Many traditional societies did not have formalized schools. Instead children learned from their families and neighbors, as men taught boys and women taught girls gender-specific skills. Families still provide informal education in complex modern societies, and some parents choose to home-school their children or cannot afford to send their children to school. Most children today, however, attend formal educational institutions, which have important roles in socializing the next generation, creating economic opportunities, and conveying cultural values. For the purposes of this chapter, therefore, we will use "education" as shorthand for "schools, colleges, universities, and other components of formal educational systems."

There are three basic theories about the relationship between education and gender inequality, each of which is also applicable to other forms of social inequality. One theory – education as gender socialization – argues that schools and colleges reproduce gender inequality over the generations. Steeped in the gendered expectations of their culture, educational institutions both overtly and subtly teach gendered messages and offer better opportunities to male students, thus preparing them for higher-status and higher-income careers. A second theory – education as skill development – argues that education decreases gender inequality by giving girls and women the skills they need to earn independent incomes. As we have seen, the ability to earn money gives women more independence and power within their families. A third theory – education as citizenship development – acknowledges the importance of skills but considers mindset even more important. Educated women believe they have some ability to control their lives, so they are more likely to assert themselves within their families and communities.

This chapter will explore a variety of issues related to how education both perpetuates and undermines gender inequality. We will start by looking at how education historically empowered women in the United States, as well as the concerns raised by the 1880s that boys were falling behind educationally. We will discuss recent concerns about a **hidden curriculum** that disadvantages girls and women, and how gendered choices of college majors affect men's and women's future earning power. We will offer three case histories that explore the intersections between gender, class, and race in contemporary American high schools and help explain why girls from less-privileged backgrounds are now more likely than their male peers to graduate from high school and go on to higher education. We will conclude with a survey of gendered patterns of education worldwide.

A BRIEF HISTORY OF GENDER AND EDUCATION IN THE UNITED STATES

Mass Education and Women's Empowerment

For most of American history, education was unequal by design. From the 1630s to the 1970s girls were excluded from the highest forms of education, whatever that was in a given era. Coeducation has been standard at the lower levels since the nineteenth century, but teachers and textbooks made it clear that they had different goals for different groups. Schools for white students expected boys to become productive workers, while girls were to become good wives and mothers. Schools for racial minorities, meanwhile, prepared both boys and girls to work in the lower ends of job markets that were segregated by gender. Until the 1970s most public and private schools offered gender-segregated classes, with girls learning how to do domestic work while boys learned industrial arts or science.

Increases in education, however, tended to reduce gender inequality. Being literate (able to read and write a simple sentence) and numerate (able to do basic arithmetic) greatly expands anyone's options in life. The more universal literacy became, the more it included women. Until the 1820s men monopolized all occupations that required education other than teaching very young children to read. As women gained more education they were able to push their way into a wide variety of other occupations, starting with teaching slightly older children but eventually including all secular professions. Educated women also developed the organizational, financial, and leadership skills that enabled them to form their own organizations and pursue their own goals. The reform movements of the nineteenth century owed much to schools that taught girls how to read books, speak in public, and argue for their positions. Girls' education also affected boys, as boys who attended school with girls – and competed with them for academic honors – became less vulnerable to the age-old belief that females are intellectually inferior and therefore must defer to men.

American education has experienced four major waves of expansion. The first wave occurred in seventeenth-century New England. Puritans believed that every individual should be able to read the Bible, so they aimed for universal reading and came close to it. Gender differences opened up, however, once children could read. Most boys and some girls attended town-funded primary schools that taught writing and arithmetic, but many parents felt this higher level of education was unnecessary for their daughters, whose labor was needed at home. Wills typically specified that girls should be taught to read and sew while boys should be taught to read, write, and figure (Ulrich, 1982: 44). In 1795, 90 percent of New England men could write their own name, but only 45 percent of women could do so (Tyack and Hansot, 1992: 25). Grammar schools, which prepared boys for college, did not admit girls. Nevertheless, the fact that reading was nearly universal made New England unusually well educated and egalitarian by world standards.

The southern colonies, like most of the rest of the world, did not have any public schools. Wealthy families hired tutors and governesses to teach their sons and daughters the very different responsibilities of a land-owing man and a young lady. Most people, however, were servants, slaves, or tenant farmers, and the elites believed literacy would make them unsuited to their station in life. "I thank God," wrote Virginia's governor William Berkeley, "there are no free schools nor printing, and I hope we shall not have these [for a] hundred years; for learning has brought disobedience and heresy . . . into the world, and printing has divulged them, and libels against the best government. God keep us from both!" (quoted in Taylor, 2001: 147).

The second wave of educational expansion began in the 1820s, also in the northern states. These areas were industrializing, and school reformers argued that the entire country would benefit if all boys learned the practical skills and moral principles (diligence, discipline, efficiency, etc.) that would make them productive workers in the new economy. Girls, meanwhile, needed to be prepared for their growing responsibilities as mothers. Although colonial-era fathers had supervised the education of their children, especially their sons, nineteenth-century mothers bore primary responsibility for childrearing. A mother, many people now believed, shaped her children's character and therefore the future of the young country. Girls needed to be educated, both intellectually and morally, if they were to raise their sons to be democratic citizens and successful workers and their daughters to be successful mothers.

Such arguments were obviously highly gendered, but they did mean that most northern towns established public schools. Most of these schools were coeducational because that was cheaper than single-sex schools, and most parents educated their daughters almost as much as their sons. By 1850 nearly all white children in the Northeast and Midwest learned to read and write, long before female literacy rates began to increase in most parts of Europe (Tyack and Hansot, 1992: 46–47, 50). Compared to every other aspect of society education was remarkably gender egalitarian, as children's educational opportunities were determined more by their location and their family's economic resources than by their gender.

Most children, however, had little or no access to schooling if they had darker skins or lived in the South. Nationwide, about 14 percent of free black boys and

11 percent of free black girls attended school (Tyack and Hansot, 1992: 50). Most southern schools were private, white, and single-sex (McCandless, 1999: 9). In 1850 the white female literacy rate in what would become the Confederacy ranged from a low of 64 percent in North Carolina (the white male rate was 78 percent) to a high of 86 percent in Mississippi (92 percent for men) (Tyack and Hansot, 1992: 52).

Enslaved African Americans treasured literacy, as it enabled them to read a newspaper or the Bible, correspond with loved ones separated by sale, and perhaps write a travel pass or otherwise challenge the slave system. As white people became more concerned about slave revolts, southern states passed laws that prescribed stiff punishments both for any slave who could read and for anyone who taught a slave to read. Nevertheless, some slaves learned surreptitiously and their literacy rate on the eve of the Civil War was probably 5 to 10 percent (Anderson, 1988: 16; Fairclough, 2001: 4). This was an impressive accomplishment under the circumstances, but the large majority of black people, both free and slave, remained illiterate.

The third big wave of educational expansion began after the Civil War. African Americans saw education as key to their advancement both as individuals and as a people, and they set about educating themselves as soon as they could. All that was necessary was someone who could read, a stick, and an empty patch of ground, and hundreds of thousands of children and adults flocked to quickly gathered classes. More could be achieved with a schoolhouse, some books, and a teacher who had a couple years of schooling, and the freed people spent a remarkable percentage of their meager new earnings on schools. Literacy was now vital for reading employment contracts and soon, for men, ballots. Even more, literacy was a symbol of freedom (Anderson, 1988: 17–18).

Some white people felt deeply threatened by black people's aspirations for education and the economic, social, and personal improvement that accompanied it. Gangs of white men torched many black schools and threatened, whipped, and shot their teachers, both white and black. As the brief period of Reconstruction came to an end, white politicians sought to starve black schools of resources or shut them down (McAfee, 1998: 14, 153). The North had required formerly Confederate states to create public school systems as a prerequisite for returning to Congress, and some southern elites began to support the idea of public education for poor white people, lest they be surpassed by black people. In every region, however, most white people vehemently rejected racial integration in schools. The result was a highly segregated system in which black schools were inferior by any objective measure. In Mississippi, for example, black people were 60 percent of the school-age population at the turn of the century but received only 19 percent of public school funds (McCandless, 1999: 39).

Other white people – primarily northern philanthropists and Protestant missionaries – helped start and support schools for freed black people. Many white northern Protestants inherited the Puritan faith in education as key to both individual advancement and social cohesion. In their view, one of the country's biggest challenges was assimilating millions of culturally diverse people, including not just former slaves but also Native Americans, Spanish-speaking people who lived in territories annexed after the Mexican-American War, and millions of immigrants from Europe and Asia. Most immigrants did not speak English and many were Catholic or Jewish, which to native-born Protestants was foreign indeed. In each case, white Protestants concluded that education would help incorporate these groups into American society, make them economically productive, and curb their disruptive potentials. As the country became larger and more diverse, they believed education would keep it from spiraling apart.

One of their goals was to inculcate what they considered correct gender roles. Their schools explicitly taught gender, including the correct work to be done by men and women, men's leadership in families and communities, husbands' sole responsibility for money-earning, the importance of proper mothering, and the demand on women to be simultaneously deferential to men and moral exemplars within their families and communities. The communities in which these schools operated had many different ways of doing gender, including the division of work and parenting responsibilities. In the eyes of white Protestants these other gender patterns were deviant and inappropriate. Indeed, they considered these gender practices one of the fundamental reasons why racial, ethnic, and religious minorities were less prosperous than the white Protestant majority. If men and women did not fulfill their gendered responsibilities, they believed, families would naturally fall into economic and moral poverty. White Protestants therefore considered teaching gender an essential part of a much larger process they called "Americanization," which included transforming how minority groups spoke, ate, dressed, earned their livelihoods, and raised their children.

Most schools for minority students emphasized what people at the time called "industrial arts" – that is, practical skills that could be used to make a living. Schools for Native Americans taught boys farming and carpentry while girls learned how to be housewives and domestic servants (Crawford, 1999: 31). Schools in New Mexico (which had recently been annexed, along with the people living there) taught boys how to tend poultry and gardens, which were traditionally women's work in Mexican communities. They taught girls Anglo-style domestic skills and urged girls to accept economic dependence and a life of homemaking and motherhood (Deutsch, 1987: 64–77). Schools for African Americans and for immigrants similarly taught boys how to do manual labor in farms and factories, while girls were taught how to do housework on the assumption that they would become domestic servants and then wives (McAfee, 1998).

Most schools for minorities assumed that the prospects of their students were limited. They sought to train children to be good workers and mothers, but few offered students the academic opportunities necessary to graduate from high school, much less be admitted to college. Their mission was to create a skilled, disciplined, and productive working class, and to help their students flourish as much as they

PHOTO 7.1

These Apache children in Anglo-style clothes and hairstyles studied at the Carlisle Indian Industrial School (Source: National Archives, 1886)

Native American children received cultural instruction in everything from English to table manners. Note how the girls are gracefully bent toward each other. Two of the three look away from the camera and one girl's arm rests on another's lap in a typical nineteenth century-sentimental posture. The boys (with one exception) sit upright, look straight at the camera, and separate their knees and arms to take up space. These children have been taught how ladies and gentlemen sit.

could within that class. They assumed, however, that the nation's cultural, intellectual, and political leaders would remain white Protestants. Schools for white Protestants were much more likely to offer courses in mathematics, classical and foreign languages, oratory, and other fields intended to help students learn how to think precisely and express themselves effectively.

Schools of every kind sought to instill in children values that were useful in the emerging industrial economy. Most families everywhere still practiced agriculture, often in ways that had been traditional for centuries. They taught their children values suitable to their way of life, including family and group solidarity, acceptance of natural rhythms, respect for tradition, and not wasting energy by working harder than one needed to. The modern economy, however, wanted workers who would take new kinds of jobs, travel far from their families if necessary, and meet the demands of time clocks and overseers. Schools emphasized the importance of hard work, punctuality, self-discipline, and deferring gratification. They also taught students that they should attempt to advance themselves in life, even if that meant leaving behind their families and communities. In schools for minorities, many teachers saw their mission as inculcating a backwards people with values that were more suitable to the modern world (McAfee, 1998: 13).

On a practical level, many of these schools offered their students useful skills that could help them and their families. Skilled workers earned more than unskilled workers, so the trades taught to boys had real economic value. The lessons in housework helped girls get and keep positions as domestic servants, and highly skilled servants earned more than other female workers. By the end of the century the emerging field of home economics was discovering and teaching important information about nutrition and sanitation. Girls who learned germ theory (which was then a new idea taught by schools, not parents) and the basics of nutrition were more likely to see their own children survive to adulthood.

The price, however, was high. Schools founded by white Protestants sought to create cultural uniformity by insisting that all children speak only English, embrace white Protestant cultural patterns, and learn white Protestant religious practices. Parents who spoke other languages, had other cultural traditions, or practiced other religions often felt that schools were trying to take their children away from them. For example, public schools typically began each day with Bible readings and Protestant hymns, which Catholics, Jews, and freethinkers (today called agnostics or secularists) considered distinctively Protestant liturgical practices. Many Catholic parishes started Catholic schools, for which they sought public funding. Protestants blocked this funding on the grounds that public schools should be nonsectarian, but many non-Protestant parents felt the public schools were already sectarian (McAfee, 1998: 27–78). In the 1870s reformers and the federal government concluded that Native American children should attend boarding schools that would separate them from the tribal ways of their elders and assimilate them into American society. By the 1920s more than 80 percent of Native American children attended schools whose stated goal was the extinction of Native American cultures (Adams, 1995: 27).

Some parents welcomed the opportunities offered by schools, limited though they were. Others resisted cultural indoctrination by trying to keep their children out of school, with more or less success. Others, especially African Americans, sought to create schools that would teach their own values. Black communities had animated conversations about whether it was best to prepare their children for the world as it is or encourage them to challenge the rules of that world. Some black people argued that they would accomplish most if they accommodated themselves to the realities of a racist country and used industrial education to lift as many of the next generation as possible out of dire poverty. Others argued that some black schools should provide a highly rigorous academic education that would prove black people are capable of high levels of achievement, disprove myths of black inferiority (often believed by black as well as white people), and create a black leadership class that could press for full civil and political rights. These positions are often associated

**PHOTOS
7.2 & 7.3**

Strong black female educators included Mary McLeod Bethune (left) and Anna Julia Cooper (right). (Sources: State Archives of Florida, Florida Memory, and Smithsonian Institute)

In 1906 Mary McLeod Bethune founded the Daytona Literary and Industrial School for Training Negro Girls. Later she was the first president of Bethune-Cookman College, which grew out of her training school but stressed academic excellence and was (like most black schools and colleges) coeducational. She was also an advisor to three U.S. presidents. In 1906 Anna Julia Cooper, who was born a slave, was fired from her position as principal of the Washington Colored School for her belief that black children deserve as rigorous an education as white children.

with Booker T. Washington and W.E.B. DuBois, respectively, but thousands or perhaps millions of black people participated in these conversations.

The fourth wave of educational expansion occurred after World War II, and this time it included mass attendance at college. The country's leaders were concerned that an influx of veterans into the workforce would plunge the country back into economic depression. Congress therefore passed the G.I. Bill of Rights, which offered veterans housing assistance, loans to start businesses, unemployment payments, and both tuition assistance and cost-of-living stipends for those who wanted to attend school or college. Most women who had served in the war were informed that they were not considered veterans and not eligible for veterans' benefits, so 97 percent of the students sent to college by the G.I. Bill were men. Black male veterans faced racial quotas and outright exclusion from most educational institutions, so they often could not use the scholarships to which they were theoretically entitled. By 1956 nearly 8 million veterans – nearly all white men – had taken advantage of the educational benefits, which cost the country $14.5 billion but created an unprecedentedly large middle class (Patterson, 1996: 68; Bellesiles, 2012: 256; Irving, 2014: 32–37).

Women's college attendance also expanded during the post-war years. College was seen as a good place to meet a husband with good prospects, and many college-educated men preferred a moderately educated wife. Women were, however, expected to leave a course or a job if a man wanted the position, especially but not only if he was a veteran or married. They were also encouraged to major in home economics or a liberal art, rather than prepare themselves for a career and make a prospective husband fear competition. Many colleges offered women courses in interior decoration and other ornamental topics. Women were much more likely than men to drop out without earning a degree, especially if they married during their college years, as many did. Brides typically left college to work and support their husbands' education, and people joked that women went to college to receive their M.R.S. degree and later a Ph.T. ("Putting Hubbie Through"). Most graduate and professional schools had quotas limiting women to a small percentage of their student bodies, and some did not admit women at all (Patterson, 1996: 367).

Each of these waves of expanding education was followed by an expansion of women's economic and political activity. Nineteenth-century opponents of girls' education often warned that a woman who had learned math and literature might not be satisfied with spending the rest of her life thinking about babies and cooking, and they were correct. Some women parlayed their education into professional careers. Others became skilled volunteers and social activists, as women filled the ranks of the reform movements and not-for-profit organizations that would shape the twentieth century. By the 1960s, however, growing numbers of college-educated women were dissatisfied with their lives. The more women were educated, the more glaring was the inconsistency between what they could do and what society said they should do. And thus the modern feminist movement was born.

The "Boy Problem"

In the 1880s commentators began to observe that girls had surpassed boys educationally. White teen girls were more likely than their brothers to be literate. Although women born in slavery never achieved the same literacy rates as men born in slavery, by 1900 three-quarters of black adolescent girls could read and write, compared to two-thirds of black adolescent boys. Girls were also much more likely to graduate from high school, which at the time was a significant academic accomplishment. By the 1890s girls were receiving two-thirds of high school diplomas and a disproportionate share of academic awards (Tyack and Hansot, 1992: 46, 53, 114, 138).

The gender gap was largest in black families. Educated black men might be teachers or ministers, but other professions were closed to them by the country's racial regime. Most black men worked in the fields or did other manual labor, while some started businesses of their own. As the Jim Crow regime settled in, however, black men who were too successful faced a growing danger of lynching – that is, being tortured to death. Graduating from high school suggested a young man had aspirations, which could attract hostile attention from white people. Since a diploma rarely expanded a black man's employment options, and might get him killed, most black boys left school as soon as they were big enough to be helpful in the fields.

Getting a diploma could, in contrast, transform the life of a black woman, as it enabled her to be a teacher. Uneducated black girls and women either worked in the fields, which everyone agreed was physically grueling, or worked as domestics for white families, where sexual harassment and assault were common. Black schools preferentially hired female teachers, as they learned from experience that white people tended to find black men threatening and white school boards were more likely to release funds if appealed to by well-spoken and carefully dressed women. Although women were occasionally lynched, their risk was smaller than that of black men. Many black families therefore channeled their limited resources into educating their daughters (Tyack and Hansot, 1992: 88–89).

Similar economic patterns held in white families. Girls increasingly needed a diploma in order to teach, which was the best profession open to them. Companies were also beginning to hire white women to do clerical work, and they preferred high school graduates. A white woman without a diploma had a choice between domestic service and factory work, both of which offered long hours, low wages, low respect, and exhausting labor. If a girl thought she might have to work for her living, even for just a few years, a diploma greatly improved her options. White men, on the other hand, could get jobs with decent wages even without a diploma.

When asked why they had left school, teenage males talked about wanting to be men. Being a man, they felt, meant earning money and being self-sufficient or contributing to the family income, rather than depending on one's parents. It meant being boisterous rather than submitting to schools' expectations of decorum. And it meant pleasing peers rather than obeying female teachers. "Pressure from other boys," an early sociologist observed, "was sometimes so strong as to warp an actual desire and liking for school into the general pattern of rebellious hatred. Girls, by contrast, could safely like school" (quoted in Tyack and Hansot, 1992: 177). Working-class boys were especially likely to leave school in their early or mid-teens. Many felt that high school was irrelevant to their goals, and they were eager to advance to the money-earning respect of manhood (Tyack and Hansot, 1992: 171).

Women's interest in education elicited concern among educators, journalists, and other observers. White men were supposed to be the natural leaders of the country, but women were rapidly proving themselves men's intellectual equals. College enrollments expanded rapidly after the Civil War, as higher education was recognized as necessary for the country's scientific and technological development, increasingly complex economy, and aspirations toward world leadership. A college degree was far from essential, but it was increasingly important for intellectual, political, and cultural leadership. Women's interest in college expanded much more quickly than men's. In 1870 only a fifth of college students were women, but a decade later women were a third of the nation's student body. Many people feared the result would be female supremacy. "If we are not to have a comparatively ignorant male proletariat opposed to a female aristocracy," two educators warned in 1900, "it is time to pause and devise ways and means for getting more of our boys to attend high school" (quoted in Tyack and Hansot, 1992: 174).

Educators tried many approaches to solving the "**boy problem**" by making high school more attractive to boys. They preferentially hired male teachers, to counter the prevalent complaint that female teachers had "feminized" the schools. They added physical education to the curriculum and organized team sports based in the schools, in the hopes that boys would stay longer if they felt loyalty to school-based athletic teams. They chose reading assignments that featured male protagonists, and rewrote math textbooks to feature activities that were stereotypically masculine, such as fishing. Some experimented with all-male classes and all-male schools, which were promoted as a way to improve boys' academic performance and professional opportunities (Tyack and Hansot, 1992: 179–200).

Many coeducational colleges made similar shifts in response to women "taking over." To attract and support male students they changed admissions policies, curricula, hiring practices, athletic programs, dorms, and criteria for student awards. Women might be tolerated in small numbers, but the more they achieved the more they were excluded both formally and informally (Kerber, 1997: 231; Kenschaft, 2005: 187–189). These efforts were successful. Although nearly half of all college students were female in 1920, their presence declined thereafter and did not reach equality until 1980.

The content of education became more gender-specific in the 1920s. High school girls were increasingly required to take home economics courses, while college women were urged to make home economics their major. This new field was full of ironies. It was part of the white Protestant campaign to homogenize American

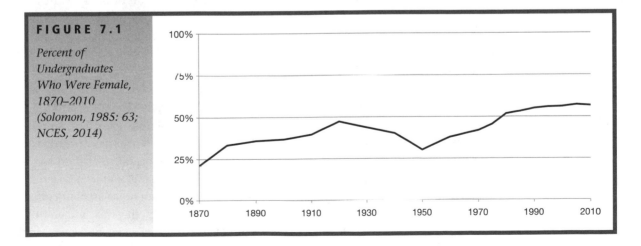

FIGURE 7.1

Percent of Undergraduates Who Were Female, 1870–2010 (Solomon, 1985: 63; NCES, 2014)

families, but it also saved millions of lives by teaching girls about new discoveries in nutrition and sanitation. It reinforced traditional gender roles by teaching that women's lives should be primarily domestic, but it also underlined the importance of women's work to all of society. It created tens of thousands of new jobs for female teachers, but it also narrowed women's employment as women with other qualifications found that they were shunted into teaching home economics. Home economics became a safe way for a young woman to attend college – which increasingly was where young men with high future earnings could be found – while signaling that her real goal was marriage, motherhood, and home-making, not a career (Stage and Vincenti, 1997).

GENDER AND EDUCATION IN THE CONTEMPORARY UNITED STATES

Gender in the Hidden Curriculum and College Majors

Since the 1970s, feminists have tried to eliminate instruction in gender from schools. In 1972 Congress enacted **Title IX**, which prohibited gender discrimination in any educational program that receives federal assistance, which is nearly all of them. No longer were schools allowed to require only girls to take home economics, or to admit only boys to courses on carpentry, physics, or basketball. Feminists also critically examined textbooks and other educational materials, which typically focused on the achievements of boys and men and ignored girls and women, with perhaps the exception of an occasional profile of a famous man's wife.

Both Title IX and shifting public opinion created dramatic changes in curricula. Many math textbooks, for example, now use an equal number of male and female names in examples and problem sets. Most history textbooks provide both information about individual notable women and a sense of how ordinary women's lives have changed over time. Similar changes have occurred in many other fields. While textbooks still sometimes contain gendered assumptions and stereotypes, they are now relatively subtle – unlike in 1970, when they were explicit and common (Clark *et al.*, 2004, 2005a, 2005b).

Gendered assumptions remained pervasive, however, in what some people call the "hidden curriculum" – the unintended, and perhaps unconscious, lessons conveyed in classrooms (Basow, 2004; Margolis, 2001). For example, classroom studies suggest that most teachers tend to give girls and boys different types of feedback on their work. Girls are more likely to be praised for the appearance of their work – for neat handwriting, for example. Boys are more likely to be praised for the content of their work or for being smart. Both teachers and students tend to attribute girls' good grades to their diligence and hard work, not to native intelligence and ability. If a boy is having difficulties with an assignment his teacher is likely to ask him leading questions or urge him to try harder, while if a girl is having difficulties her teacher is more likely to do part or all of the assignment for her (Sadker *et al.*, 2009: 172, 197).

Most teachers also discipline boys more frequently and more firmly. Boys are more likely to be scolded, sent to the principal's office, or otherwise punished, and girls agree that boys are more likely to be "picked on" by their teachers (Sadker *et al.*, 2009: 20). Most teachers describe boys as more energetic and rambunctious than girls, and it is true that many (but not all) boys are more physically active than their female classmates. Some people believe this difference has biological origins, while others argue that these beliefs can be self-fulfilling prophecies. If parents and teachers expect boys to be more active and girls to be more obedient and kind, children incorporate such beliefs into their own gendered identities. A boy's misbehavior may be seen as both annoying and somehow appropriate, a sign that he is a real boy, while adults may see identical behavior by a girl as more deeply disturbing. Children pick up on such signals, making it impossible to determine how they would have acted in the absence of adult input.

These different classroom experiences affect girls' and boys' self-images and self-confidence. Girls learn that they will be praised for diligence and being "good," but they also receive subtle and repeated messages that they are not intelligent enough to rise to real challenges. Boys are more likely to see themselves as innately smart and talented, but also more likely to position themselves in opposition to school authorities and adult expectations. By the time they reach high school boys are less likely to do homework and more likely to cut classes, talk back to teachers, play class clown, get into fights, and be suspended or expelled.

This self-image as smart but non-deferential contributes to boys' higher dropout rate and can be self-destructive (Sax, 2007). When not excessive, however, it can give men a level of self-assertion that can be helpful in the workplace. As adults, men tend to overestimate their abilities and knowledge, while women tend to have less confidence than reality warrants. Overconfidence can lead men to reject helpful advice or ignore important information that does not match their pre-existing opinions, but it can also give men the emotional resilience required to take on challenges, handle criticism, and try again after failures. Lacking such self-confidence, women are more likely to unnecessarily doubt themselves and seek the approval of others (Kay and Shipman, 2014b).

These differences have important consequences during the college years. Nearly two-thirds of male freshmen rate themselves as above average in intelligence, compared to less than half of female freshmen. Women tend to work harder in college, while men spend more time on leisure activities. Women tend to have better grades in college than their SAT scores would predict, while men do worse. Although women have higher average GPAs and are more likely to graduate, many women conclude during their college years that they are not as smart as they thought they were and scale back their career aspirations. Men are less likely to revise their self-evaluations, perhaps because they are more likely to attribute their failures to lack of effort rather than lack of ability (Sadker *et al.*, 2009: 183, 245–248).

Gender significantly affects people's choice of college majors. Women are two-thirds or more of the majors in the "helping professions" of health, education, psychology, and social work, while men are two-thirds or more of the majors in the highly analytical fields of computers, mathematics, and engineering.

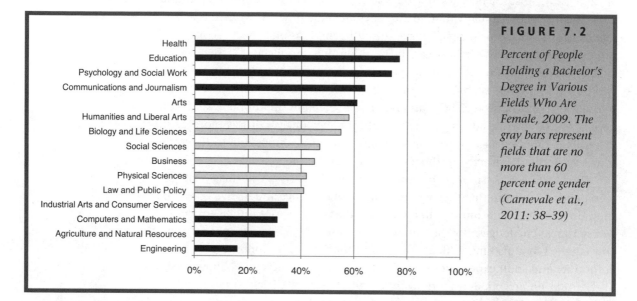

FIGURE 7.2

Percent of People Holding a Bachelor's Degree in Various Fields Who Are Female, 2009. The gray bars represent fields that are no more than 60 percent one gender (Carnevale et al., 2011: 38–39)

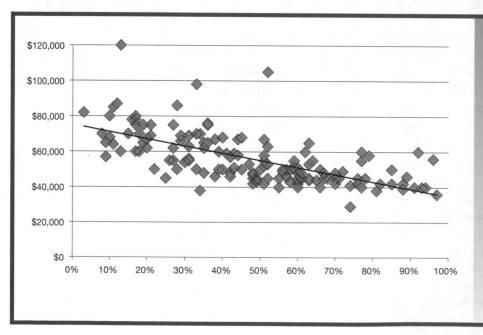

FIGURE 7.3

Median Incomes of Majors, by Percent Female, 2009. Salaries represent the median annual income of full-time workers with a bachelor's degree and no advanced degrees. The female-dominated majors with incomes around $60,000 a year are in health related fields (Carnevale et al., 2011: 46–179)

These choices affect men's and women's lifetime earnings. Figure 7.3 compares the average incomes of full-time workers who have a bachelor's degree in various majors with the gender balance of those majors. As you can see, the more women choose a major the less it tends to pay.

Some people argue that the gender gap in incomes is largely caused by undergraduates' performance of gender as they choose college majors. Many women feel more comfortable if they are able to present themselves as caring about other people and/or artistic. Many men are less daunted by the intellectual and emotional challenges of fields where failure is clear and common: computers do not care what sort of person you are, just what code you wrote. These gendered preferences may reflect years of receiving different kinds of praise, support, and criticism from teachers, but by the college years they are deeply ingrained in people's personalities.

Gendered choices of majors do not, however, fully explain income inequality. As Figure 7.4 shows, there are also significant wage gaps within each field, always to men's advantage (Carnevale *et al.*, 2011: 46–179).

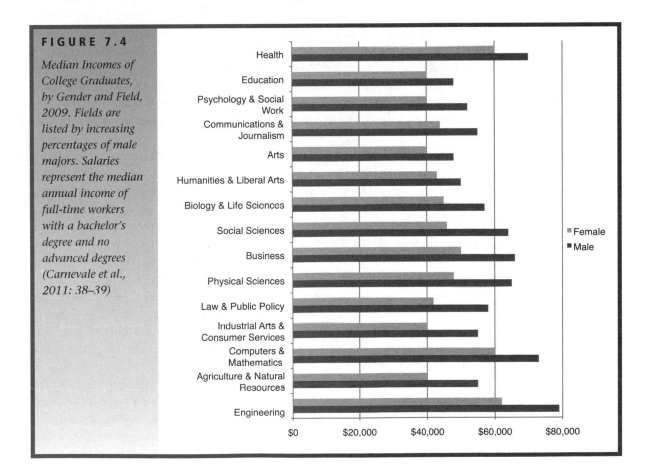

FIGURE 7.4

Median Incomes of College Graduates, by Gender and Field, 2009. Fields are listed by increasing percentages of male majors. Salaries represent the median annual income of full-time workers with a bachelor's degree and no advanced degrees (Carnevale et al., 2011: 38–39)

The "Boy Problem" Continues: Three Case Studies

If one looks only at the number of degrees awarded, women are now doing better than men (Goldin *et al.*, 2006). Women are still more likely than men to have completed high school or an equivalent – 91.5 percent of women aged 25 to 29 have a diploma, compared to 88.3 percent of young men that age. Women also predominate at the higher levels of education. In 2012 women received 62 percent of associates' degrees, 57 percent of bachelors' degrees, 60 percent of masters' degrees, and 51 percent of doctoral and professional (M.D., law, etc.) degrees. Today 37 percent of women but only 30 percent of men aged 25 to 29 have a bachelor's degree (NCES, 2013a, 2013b).

This educational gender gap is small or nonexistent, however, among higher-status families. Affluent parents send most of their children to college, and elite colleges enroll roughly equal numbers of men and women (Morris, 2012: 4). Men are still more likely than women to earn the professional degrees that are most lucrative (U.S. Census Bureau, 2013c). At the highest reaches of the educational system, men and women are in balance or men may still have an advantage.

The differences are seen elsewhere. As Figure 7.5 shows, racial gaps in educational attainment are at least as significant as the gender gap. Data on parents' educational and income levels are not collected as consistently as data on students' racial identities, so it is impossible to authoritatively disentangle the effects of class and race. Scattered evidence suggests, however, that class effects are significant and perhaps growing. One study found that women were 52 percent of lower-income white undergraduates in 1996, but 56 percent in 2004, just eight years later (Sadker *et al.*, 2009: 202).

In part, the educational gender gap reflects the different economic incentives facing different demographic groups. Since women earn less than men pretty much no matter what they do, they may decide to stay in school longer in order to obtain an income level they consider acceptable (Coontz, 2012). For women, earning a bachelor's degree typically boosts their earnings both immediately and in the long run. Male undergraduates who drop out and work full-time, however, can often earn about as much as a man with a brand-new bachelor's degree. Their earnings will likely plateau at a lower level than if they finished the degree, and in the long run male graduates typically earn much more than non-graduates. In the short run, however, men's better immediate opportunities may make them more reluctant to take on college debt to fund an increasingly costly college education. Women may be more willing to invest in their education because the penalties for not doing so are more evident (Dwyer *et al.*, 2013).

The economic returns on a bachelor's degree vary greatly depending on which college one attends, and some colleges actually have a negative return on investment (*Economist*, 2014d; PayScale, 2014). The worst scenario, financially speaking, is starting college, taking on debt, and dropping out without a degree. Students with marginal qualifications (who for reasons we discuss below are more likely to be male)

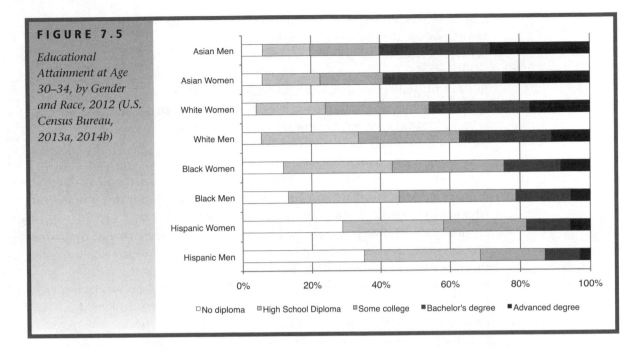

FIGURE 7.5

Educational Attainment at Age 30–34, by Gender and Race, 2012 (U.S. Census Bureau, 2013a, 2014b)

may therefore do better economically if they forego college. Young adults from affluent families, meanwhile, usually attend high-quality schools that prepare them for high-quality colleges with a large return on investment. They also tend to be less anxious about both immediate bills and their long-term livelihood. Gender therefore has less impact on their educational choices.

Not all behavior, however, is driven by economic incentives. Gender can also affect young people's educational decisions by shaping their values, preferences, priorities, and beliefs. These patterns cannot be measured in numbers, so understanding them requires us to look more closely at what is happening in lower-status communities. We will therefore offer here three brief summaries of recent ethnographic studies of lower-income high schools. Together, they help us see how gendered expectations can play out in different contexts.

Male Privilege and Gendered Achievement in a Rural White Town

One high school was located in a predominantly white and economically depressed former coal town in Appalachia. Boys and girls typically responded in different ways to the limited opportunities available in their area. Ever since the mines had closed, nearly all boys had aspired to work in the construction trades. Being a man, they felt, meant being able to do hard physical labor and provide for their families, so they wanted work that would be physically challenging. Most boys realized, however, that there was not enough construction work to go around and they felt realistic anxieties about their futures. Girls, meanwhile, tended to be less resistant to change, perhaps because the old regime had rewarded them less. Most girls were willing to leave the town to pursue education and jobs elsewhere, while boys were reluctant to leave the only place they knew. Men and women, girls said, should earn equal incomes and be equal within the family, while boys felt that a man should be the primary breadwinner and head of the family – even though they saw that many men could not fulfill the provider role (Morris, 2012).

Most girls saw school as a route to a good occupation and economic independence from men. Since they saw academic achievement as leading to a better life, they generally worked hard and followed school rules. Two-thirds of the students who hoped to attend a four-year college were girls (Morris, 2012: 78–82).

Many boys, however, were more focused on proving their masculinity. Anxious that they would never be able to earn a good wage, they instead sought to prove their manhood by demonstrating their toughness, physical vitality, and willingness to take risks and tolerate physical pain. Outside school they got into fights, raced four-wheelers, and otherwise pursued risky physical activities. Inside school they focused on athletics. They took a carefree attitude toward schoolwork, regularly forgetting books, assignments, and tests and expressing disdain for school rules.

Indeed, most boys saw book learning and following rules as feminine traits, and often claimed that boys are naturally not good at schoolwork. "I think girls have a God-given talent to study!" one boy explained. "I can't study though. At all" (Morris, 2012: 84). For this boy, and many of his classmates, doing poorly in school helped prove that he was a real man. Although easy academic success from natural intelligence was acceptable, studiousness called a boy's masculinity into question. Boys who were attentive and hardworking students were taunted as "gay" (Morris, 2012: 71).

The school encouraged boys' disconnection from academic work by celebrating their nonacademic activities more than girls' academic accomplishments. School displays featured boys' athletics, thus reinforcing boys' perception that sports are of vital importance. Although some girls played sports too, their events received much less attention (Morris, 2012: 88–90). Academic success was the only way for a girl to get recognition, but even that validation was undercut. Teachers consistently characterized boys as more intelligent, while they attributed girls' successes to their diligence, not their abilities. Girls often described themselves as "dumb" and boys as naturally smart (Morris, 2012: 60, 140–145). Boys saw girls' orientation toward academic achievement, with the white-collar jobs it might open up, as sign of feminine laziness and inferiority. "Girls don't think about fightin' or think about hard work," one boy explained. "They're thinkin' office type jobs, you know. Accounting, business, stuff like that – the easier . . . type stuff" (Morris, 2012: 42). Boys thus did less well in school – and had fewer options later in life – because their community valued them and their interests more highly than girls.

Making an Impression and Submitting to Authority in a Black Urban Neighborhood

Similar patterns appeared in a predominantly black inner city high school in the Midwest, but with two important differences. First, the school was large and it was easy to feel anonymous, so the peer culture emphasized the importance of being known for something. Boys could achieve this recognition in a variety of ways, including intelligence, athletics, fighting, being a class clown, a gangsta persona, or verbal dexterity in "riffin'." Like the rural white boys, however, their masculinity was called into question if they were seen to study or do homework, so good grades had to come from a natural gift, not hard work (Morris, 2012: 124). Girls, meanwhile, had fewer acceptable pathways to recognition. Like the rural white girls, they saw schoolwork as leading to a decent career and financial independence, and they considered diligence and self-discipline feminine traits. Many girls therefore tried to distinguish themselves by doing well in school (Morris, 2012: 128).

The second big difference between the schools was the urban school's emphasis on crime control. Although the rural area had a lot of illegal drug use and other crimes, school authorities generally ignored these issues. The black school, in contrast, was full of surveillance cameras and security officers. People arriving at the white school were greeted with a big sign celebrating the boys' sports teams, while the equivalent sign outside the black school declared, "This is a Drug Free and Weapons Free Area." The white school nearly always dealt with student discipline in-house, while in the black school it was common for students who defied school rules to be led out in handcuffs by police officers (Morris, 2012: 23, 108, 124).

This crime-control emphasis affected boys and girls differently. Both white and black boys felt that masculinity required them to have a casual or defiant attitude toward authority, to test and break rules, and to respond assertively if they were belittled (Morris, 2012: 40, 69). In both schools – and in many others – boys who were seen as insufficiently tough and assertive became walking targets for their peers (Sadker *et al.*, 2009: 20). Girls lost less status by deferring to authority figures, since obedience was considered a feminine trait. The crime-control regime in the black school required students to act subordinate many times a day – e.g., wait in lines, submit IDs, and obey demands. Boys rebelled more often than girls, and they were punished more consistently and severely for their misbehavior. Boys in the black school were frequently arrested for offenses that the white school tolerated, or for resisting aspects of the disciplinary system that did not exist in the white school. Many black boys therefore gained criminal records, which increased their disconnection from school. One young boy was expelled because he had a plastic bullet on a keychain that he had gotten at Disney World: in Orlando it was a toy but in his school it was a weapon (Morris, 2012: 110). In this school, therefore, boys became more disaffected than girls not because their other activities were more highly valued, but because they were constantly scrutinized for signs of insubordination and criminality.

Female Responsibility and Male Autonomy/Isolation in Caribbean New York

Patterns were again similar and different in a New York City high school that enrolled primarily low-income second-generation immigrants from the Caribbean. The appearance of most of these students suggested African ancestry, but their culture was shaped by their families' immigrant experiences. Here too, male privilege translated into boys doing less well than girls academically, while racial stereotypes affected boys and girls differently (Lopez, 2003).

Girls were expected to take responsibility for childcare and housework, as their mothers worked long hours in low-paying jobs. Girls also frequently served as translators and intermediaries for their elders. Though these duties could be burdensome, by the time they reached high school most young women saw themselves as competent and were proud of their responsibilities and accomplishments (Lopez, 2003: 115–116).

Girls' warm relationships with their mothers helped them form good relationships with their teachers, most of whom were also women. Sometimes these relationships led to jobs or internships. More often girls were funneled into "pink collar" vocational programs, such as practical nursing or secretarial work. These curricula did not prepare them for college, but they did enable girls to gain work experience in hospitals and white-collar firms and to meet women who had achieved social mobility through education (Lopez, 2003: 55, 172).

Boys were exempted from domestic tasks, so they had more leisure time than girls but also fewer experiences that made them feel capable and proud. Apartments were overcrowded, and bedrooms were generally given to females while males slept in the living room and were expected to be out of the home during the day. Boys therefore tended to be more disconnected from their families. Their time was their own and they spent much of it engaged in leisure activities with other boys and young men in public spaces. They frequently experienced aggressive and even violent interactions, including racial taunting, businesses that chased them off the premises, and police brutality. Many people shunned them, thus regularly reminding them that dark-skinned males are seen as menacing (Lopez, 2003: 25–29, 131–134).

With or without a high school diploma, young men generally could get only the lowest levels of service jobs (such as working in grocery stores) or informal jobs (such as being a messenger). Many did work that was unstable, poorly paid, or even dangerous. Education did not seem like a way out of low-level work, since male graduates had no better jobs. White employers, boys concluded, are often reluctant to hire dark-skinned men, seeing them as unreliable or even dangerous (Lopez, 2003: 145, 161, 152, 172).

In school, boys were disciplined far more frequently than girls. The school was low on books, desks, computers, and sanitation, but it had metal detectors, tall fences, and dozens of security personnel who used bullhorns to tell the students to

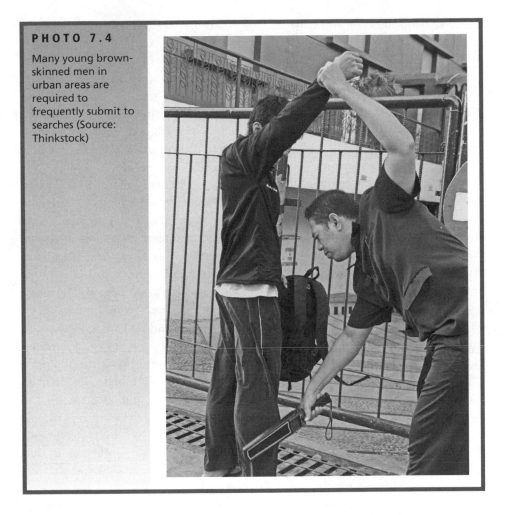

PHOTO 7.4

Many young brown-skinned men in urban areas are required to frequently submit to searches (Source: Thinkstock)

move quickly to their next class. Students referred to their school as "Riker's Island," an infamous New York prison. In reality many school rules applied to boys but not to girls. Male security guards were not allowed to touch female students, but they regularly apprehended and physically constrained male students. In addition, boys were more likely to get into conflicts with their peers. Since boys saw school authorities and police as hostile and arbitrary, they did not trust those authorities to protect them. Instead, they lived in an **honor-based culture** in which they felt they had to respond strongly to signs of disrespect or risk being marked as weak and easy to exploit. While girls could seem to ignore racial epithets and other insults, boys felt they had to defend their honor or risk escalation. Even small scuffles could lead to prison time (Lopez, 2003: 50, 53, 72–77; Pinker, 2011: 82–85).

Most students felt that the curriculum was dumbed down and boring. Some girls responded by doing more than was required and demanding an education. Boys, however, could not appear studious without threatening their masculinity, and they had little confidence that school would help them get a better job afterwards. Many therefore focused their need for a sense of accomplishment elsewhere – such as work, athletics, or pursuing girls (Lopez, 2003: 42, 105). Indeed, young Hispanic men aged 16 to 24 are much more likely than any other demographic group to work full-time at that age (Saenz and Ponjuan, 2009: 74). Like European immigrants in the nineteenth century, many feel that they have little to gain by remaining in school and delaying the money-making status of manhood. Girls, meanwhile, realize that dropping out of school would condemn them to a lifetime of low-paid female-coded jobs, so they see education as a path to a better life.

In all three of these communities masculinity represented a network of privilege and constraint that served to make boys devalue academic achievement. Masculine privileges enabled them to focus their time, energy, and day-to-day goals on sports and other leisure activities. Masculine constraints made it seem unacceptable to work hard on schoolwork. Teachers in all schools tend to see boys as their primary disciplinary challenge, and in the urban schools discipline translated into a behavioral control regime that bore down especially heavily on boys and regularly required all students to act subservient to authority figures – which was in direct tension with the masculine requirement to be independent and subservient to no one. Some people call the result a "school to prison pipeline" that channels young people of color, especially young men, into the criminal justice system and often a lifetime of irregular employment and incarceration (Rios, 2011; Knefel, 2013). Even boys who avoid serious disciplinary problems are less likely than girls to have the academic preparation required to attend or succeed in college.

Meanwhile, all of these communities associated femininity with being responsible and hardworking, but not with being talented. Most girls were seen as dull compared to boys, who were celebrated for their athletic skills, risk-taking behavior, native smarts, sense of humor, and other personal characteristics. As long as girls were "good" their teachers assumed they were doing fine and did not need personal attention – unlike the boys, who were seen as having more potential both for brilliance and for making trouble. By the end of high school, most girls had developed a modest but achievable career plan that would enable them to modestly support not just themselves, but also future children. As we have seen, many lower-status women decide by their early twenties that they have achieved enough financial stability to be ready for a child or two, but resist taking on responsibility for supporting a man as well (DeParle and Tavernise, 2012). Under other circumstances many of these young women could have done well in a more demanding college and professional career, but they learned by their teens that such ambitions were not for them (Cookson, 2013).

Equally important, the mediocrity of many American school systems – especially those in disadvantaged neighborhoods – makes it difficult for students from less-privileged backgrounds to use school as a stepping stone to economic and social mobility. Wealthy parents can pay for tutors and enrichment programs for their children, but low-income students generally need public schools to educate them. If their schools focus more on athletics than academics, options are foreclosed not just for students who direct their aspirations into sports, but for all students (Ripley, 2013).

GENDER AND EDUCATION IN A GLOBAL PERSPECTIVE

Gender, Literacy, and Primary Education

In many countries, the gender gap in education is still about literacy. Nearly 800 million adults are illiterate, two-thirds of whom are women (UNESCO, 2011: 6), and roughly half of the world's people live in countries where men are more likely to be literate. In India, 75 percent of adult men can read and write a simple sentence, but just 51 percent of adult women, while gender gaps of 10 to 30 percentage points are common throughout most of Africa (WEF, 2014: 69). Such discrepancies have huge implications, as people who are illiterate have limited economic options and must rely on other individuals for information about the larger world – be that a name on a ballot, the words on a drug label, or the wages listed on a receipt.

Educating girls has been found to be one of the most effective ways to reduce poverty, hunger, and premature death. Most obviously, education increases women's economic productivity. Literacy and numeracy are prerequisites for most formal jobs,

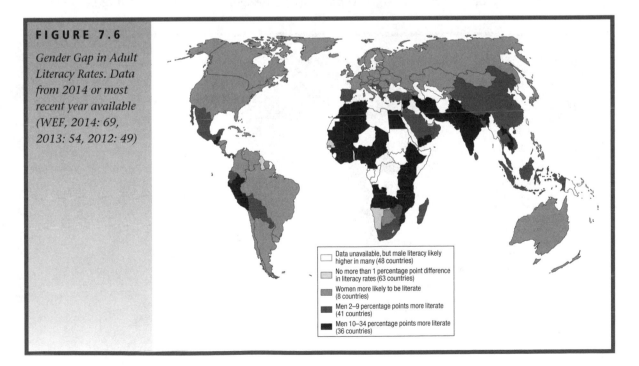

FIGURE 7.6

Gender Gap in Adult Literacy Rates. Data from 2014 or most recent year available (WEF, 2014: 69, 2013: 54, 2012: 49)

Data unavailable, but male literacy likely higher in many (48 countries)

No more than 1 percentage point difference in literacy rates (63 countries)

Women more likely to be literate (8 countries)

Men 2–9 percentage points more literate (41 countries)

Men 10–34 percentage points more literate (36 countries)

and additional skills open up a wider range of occupations, but even women who do subsistence farming are more productive if they have a primary-level education (Patrinos, 2008: 59). Nearly half of the reduction in hunger between 1970 and 1995 is attributed to improvements in girls' education (De Schutter, 2013: 2). Educating girls also does more than educating boys to increase contraceptive use, reduce family sizes, and improve the health of the next generation (Population Reference Bureau, 2000). Each year of girls' schooling reduces infant mortality, for example, by 5 to 10 percent (Patrinos, 2008: 58).

In recent decades many governments and non-governmental organizations (NGOs) have embraced the goal of making primary education universal for girls as well as boys. Much progress has been made. Gender gaps in primary school enrollment are now small or nonexistent not just in wealthy countries, but also in nearly all of Asia, Latin America, the Caribbean, and the Middle East. Even in India boys are only slightly more likely than girls to attend primary school (87 percent vs. 84 percent). Primary school enrollments in China are now much more affected by official residence (urban vs. rural *hukou*, or residency permits) than gender, as 87 percent of both boys and girls attend primary school (WEF, 2014: 70; *Economist*, 2014f).

The goal of universal primary education remains, however, elusive. In 2011, 67 million children of primary school age did not attend school – 53 percent of them girls and 43 percent of them in sub-Saharan Africa (UNESCO, 2011: 6). Although several African countries have eliminated this gender gap, others still have big disparities. The largest gender gap is in Angola, where 97 percent of boys but just

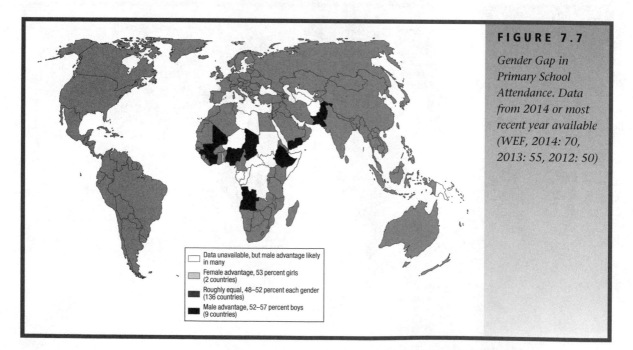

FIGURE 7.7

Gender Gap in Primary School Attendance. Data from 2014 or most recent year available (WEF, 2014: 70, 2013: 55, 2012: 50)

Data unavailable, but male advantage likely in many

Female advantage, 53 percent girls (2 countries)

Roughly equal, 48–52 percent each gender (136 countries)

Male advantage, 52–57 percent boys (9 countries)

74 percent of girls attend primary school. Gender gaps are also significant in Pakistan, Yemen, and very likely Afghanistan, though good data are not available there (WEF, 2014: 70).

Roughly half of primary school age children who are not in school live in areas that have recently suffered war or civil strife (United Nations, 2014a: 17). Parents are understandably reluctant to let their children leave home if they face a significant chance of kidnapping or death, and schools in conflict zones sometimes close. In addition, countries that are militarily or politically unstable often have high levels of sexual violence. Parents who fear sexual assault may send their sons but not their daughters to school, as even young girls may not be immune to rape.

Both poverty and belonging to a disadvantaged ethnic group also make it less likely that children will attend school, and more so for girls than boys (World Bank, 2011a: 12–14; United Nations, 2014a: 17). Most countries have eliminated school fees at the primary level, but parents often have to pay for books, paper, pencils, clothes, and shoes, and they have to forego children's assistance in the household economy. More than a third of the world's people live on less than two dollars a day, and they may find such sacrifices challenging or insurmountable. Girls' labor is especially essential in households without clean piped water in the home, as carrying water is usually considered a task for girls and women.

In the poorest countries the economic returns from primary education are almost twice as high for boys as girls. Many families are reluctant to let women work for pay, and income-producing activities for women with only a primary-level education can be hard to come by. Once a country starts to industrialize the returns on primary education are higher for girls than boys, as factories hire young women who have a few years of education, but in the poorest countries primary school may not increase a girl's earning power at all (Patrinos, 2008: 61–62). Wage-based analyses ignore the health benefits of girls' schooling, but if a poor family can afford to send only some children to primary school it may make economic sense to choose boys. In addition, boys are usually freer to move around the community and engage in income-generating activities that help offset their school costs (Kirk, 2008: 157).

Another issue that affects girls more than boys is the painfully low quality of education in many countries. Teachers often have little incentive to cover the assigned material or to make sure students are learning. Books and other instructional materials may be inadequate or nonexistent, and many teachers are minimally educated themselves (Baker and Safi, 2008). A study of several low- and middle-income countries found that a fifth of the teachers were absent on any given day (Rogers and Vegas, 2009: 3). Under such circumstances children can attend school for years but learn little. Almost half of the children in Peru finish ninth grade, but only 15 percent become literate by the standards used in industrialized countries. In Ghana, 37 percent complete ninth grade but only 5 percent become literate (Hanushek, 2008: 34; Tembon, 2008: 7). Similarly disappointing school results have been documented in India, Pakistan, Kenya, and many other countries (Banerjee and Duflo, 2011: 75–76).

Such low-quality schooling brings few benefits to students and leads to high dropout rates, especially for girls (Hanushek, 2008: 27; Lockheed, 2008: 121). Girls are nearly always needed at home, as the work assigned to women is usually inexhaustible, so school has a higher opportunity cost for girls. If parents see that their daughter is not learning, they may conclude that keeping her home would be of greater benefit to the family, especially if her work frees her mother's time for more crop tending, market trading, or paid employment. Providing books and teacher training improves both quality and attendance, and even a small amount of teacher training can make a big difference. For example, the Afghan Institute of Learning offers a 24-day teacher-training program that reduces the typical time it takes children to learn to read from three years to three months, thus greatly increasing both the rewards of school and the likelihood that girls will remain enrolled (Yacoobi, 2008: 193, 197).

Gender and Secondary Education

The gender dynamics of secondary education vary greatly, but three large patterns are visible. First, two dozen wealthy and middle-income countries, most but not all in Europe, send 90 percent or more of their teenagers to high school with little or no gender gap. Second, boys are more likely to attend high school in much of central Africa and southern Asia, where poverty and gender inequality are high and most countries send less than half of their teens to secondary school. Third, and between these two extremes, are the majority of countries, which send between 50 and 90 percent of their teens to high school, and, by and large, have a female advantage that ranges from tiny (as in the United States) to 55 percent female students (WEF, 2014: 71; World Bank Data, 2014).

At least two factors can contribute to girls being more likely to attend high school. First, in some countries the financial return on a diploma is higher for girls. Especially if it is still sufficient to qualify as a teacher, a diploma can liberate a woman from the extremely low wages common in low-skill female-coded job markets. One study found that the economic returns of secondary education were 50 percent higher for girls in developing countries (Patrinos, 2008: 61–62). Teenage boys may conclude that their time is better spent working than in school – especially if the quality of instruction is poor and they are learning little (Banerjee and Duflo, 2011: 71–101).

Second, many countries with female majorities have **conditional cash transfer** (CCT) programs, in which a small stipend is given to the mother of a family (or the father if there is no mother) if the household meets certain conditions – typically sending school-age children to school and taking all children for basic medical care. The largest and earliest CCT programs are Mexico's *Oportunidades* (founded under the name *Progresa* in 1997) and Brazil's *Bolsa Família* (founded in 2003), both of which include millions of families. These programs have been so successful in reducing poverty and increasing schooling that they have been imitated in nearly all Latin

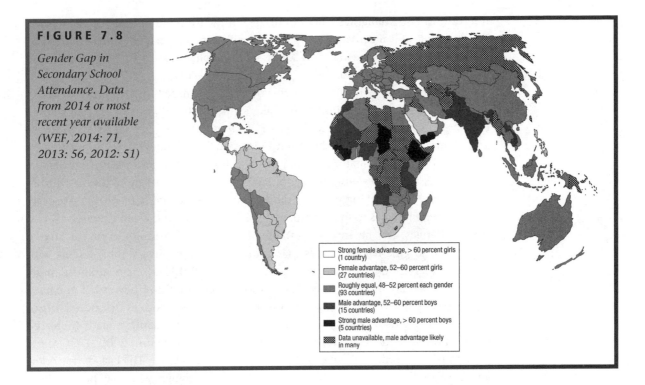

FIGURE 7.8

Gender Gap in Secondary School Attendance. Data from 2014 or most recent year available (WEF, 2014: 71, 2013: 56, 2012: 51)

Legend:
- Strong female advantage, > 60 percent girls (1 country)
- Female advantage, 52–60 percent girls (27 countries)
- Roughly equal, 48–52 percent each gender (93 countries)
- Male advantage, 52–60 percent boys (15 countries)
- Strong male advantage, > 60 percent boys (5 countries)
- Data unavailable, male advantage likely in many

American countries as well as several other countries around the world. Mexico, Turkey, and Pakistan provide larger stipends for girls as an incentive for their parents to free them from household labors. Bangladesh and Cambodia originally covered girls only, as a way to reduce gender inequality, but once they were successful in raising girls' secondary school attendance they expanded to include poor boys as well. Even where CCT programs are not gender-specific they often increase girls' enrollments more than boys (Fiszbein and Schady, 2009: 1, 4–18, 81–82, 131). Pilot studies in Malawi and Morocco found that even small and unconditional cash transfers to poor families increased girls' school attendance. Parents in these countries, it seems, do not need to be forced to send their daughters to school, but many need financial assistance to do so (Banerjee and Duflo, 2011: 80).

Boys are more likely to attend secondary school in countries that are at war and/or have high levels of other forms of violence. Rape is common in high-conflict zones, and sometimes girls are kidnapped to be the "wives" of soldiers or sold as wives to others. Many parents are afraid to let their teenaged daughters out of their sight. Parents in high-rape zones often prefer to get a daughter married at a young age, before her virginity is forcibly taken, and few girls attend school once they are married, even if they have not yet reached puberty (Kirk, 2008: 156). Families in rural areas often live far from schools, especially secondary schools. Parents may be willing to send a son on a long walk every day, but feel that is unsafe for a daughter. They may also be willing to send a son to board with relatives near the school, but not want to lose a daughter's labor from the family. Even school can be a risky place. Roughly half of Tanzanian and Ugandan women report that they were abused by male teachers, while one in fifteen South African women report that they were raped by a teacher (Mannathoko, 2008: 131; Kristof and WuDunn, 2009: 62, 182).

A lack of sanitary facilities can also be a serious impediment for menstruating girls and women in poor countries, where schools often do not have restrooms. A billion people worldwide, more than half of them in India, have no access to toilets and commonly relieve themselves outdoors, which encourages infectious diseases, malnutrition, and premature death, as well as making girls and women vulnerable to sexual assault (*Economist*, 2014i). In Pakistan, for example, more than a third of schools have no drinking water or sanitary facilities (Ashraf *et al.*, 2011). Modesty codes require females to find an isolated place to relieve and clean themselves, and the challenges can be insurmountable. Many sexual assaults occur in shared restrooms, so girls need facilities that combine enough privacy for modesty with enough supervision to deter rapes (Mannathoko, 2008: 136–137). In addition, many girls and women in poor countries cannot afford anything beyond homemade sanitary supplies, which are awkward to handle in public spaces. In some parts of Africa, giving girls' underwear and reusable or disposable sanitary pads increased their school attendance (Kirk, 2008: 176; Kristof and WuDunn, 2009: 172). Many girls drop out of school at puberty, even if they did well earlier. The lack of restrooms also contributes to the high absenteeism of female teachers, who may be unable to work during their periods (Kirk, 2008: 170).

In some areas, the biggest barrier to girls' high school attendance remains traditional ideas about gender. From Morocco through China, women past the age of puberty were traditionally expected to stay in or near home, where their virginity could be monitored and protected. Girls were generally considered marriageable shortly after puberty, or even before. Where these ideas and practices persist, most often in villages and rural districts, few girls attend secondary school.

Girls may also face opposition from people – women as well as men – who fear the society-changing effects of educating girls. Sending girls to school changes the gendered balance of power within families and communities, and ultimately nations. Literacy makes a woman less dependent on the men in her family, but most men find that the benefits of girls' primary education – such as higher family incomes and child survival rates – outweigh the drawbacks. Secondary school can be quite a different issue. The more girls are educated, the more they think and act for themselves, and the more likely they are to demand a say in how their household is run, how many children they have, how their children are raised, and in larger decisions that affect their community.

Some schools try to teach girls to be obedient and deferential, and they may be somewhat successful in instilling such gendered norms. Even if they try to be "good" women, however, women who have more knowledge and more options tend to act differently than those who live more cloistered lives.

Other schools, furthermore, see girls' education as part of a larger project of women's empowerment and community improvement. Sakena Yacoobi, for example, is one of the most influential educators in Afghanistan. She began to teach while Afghanistan was under the control of the Taliban, when educating girls was illegal but hundreds or thousands of Afghan women created home schools that surreptitiously taught girls how to read, write, sew, and other practical money-making skills (Yacoobi, 2008: 185; Lemmon, 2011). Yacoobi now leads the Afghan Institute of Learning, which provides education, health services, and training programs to more than 300,000 Afghan people a year – primarily but not exclusively women and girls. Her vision of education is expansive:

> When empowered through education, women are able to overcome their circumstances and their self-doubt and exercise more autonomy over their lives . . . In a practical sense, women and girls must learn to read and write and must learn skills that will help them find work. However, it is far more important for women and girls to receive education that will open their minds to analyze, think critically, and consider people and events in new ways. This type of education will allow women to make real choices about their actions and their lives. (Yacoobi, 2008: 195, 197)

Not everyone, of course, wants women to be able to make real choices about their actions and their lives. Parents and community leaders may be wary of the changes that come from educating girls. Some men cherish the dreams of their daughters and sisters and do everything they can to help them come true, while other men resist any reduction of the male privilege they consider their birthright. Many fathers are somewhere in the middle – willing to support their daughters so far, but not too far. Mothers too may be fearful about changes and suspect their daughters will be happiest and safest if they do not stray too far from the well-worn paths. In some countries, it still takes courage to send a daughter to high school.

Indeed, a few countries – as of this writing, Afghanistan, Pakistan, Nigeria, Syria, and Iraq – have active militant movements that seek to end girls' education, especially above the primary level. The names of the Taliban (literally "Students") and Boko Haram ("Western Learning is Sinful") indicate that they take very seriously the socializing effects of education. In their view, what children learn today is what society becomes tomorrow. Tolerating schools that are influenced by international values and norms will therefore destroy their cultures. Boys, they believe, should attend schools that teach religious and traditional values, while girls should not attend school at all.

The Taliban has bombed or burned more than a thousand schools in Pakistan and Afghanistan and has raped, poisoned, and beheaded female students (Walsh, 2014; Alvi-Aziz, 2008; Bearak, 2007; Hamid, 2012). In 2012 the Taliban shot in the head Malala Yousafzai, then a 15-year-old Pakistani schoolgirl who, with her parents' strong support, had spoken out in favor of educating girls. She survived and went

PHOTO 7.5

Sakena Yacoobi with a schoolgirl in Afghanistan (Photo by William Vazquez, supported by a grant from the Abbott Fund. Used with permission)

on to win the Nobel Peace Prize for her international advocacy of girls' education (Yousafzai and Lamb, 2014). In 2014 Boko Haram kidnapped nearly 300 secondary school girls, declared them slaves, and threatened to sell them as wives. "Western education should end," a spokesman declared. "Girls, you should go and get married" (Nossiter, 2014). The goal of such violence is not just to shut down specific schools, but also to intimidate all girls in these areas from attending school.

China, in contrast, shows what can happen to a poor country when a government seeks to end gender inequality in education and employment. Nine out of ten Chinese women were illiterate in 1949, when Mao Tse-tung assumed power. His government built huge numbers of new schools and universities and encouraged women to work outside the home (Zhou, 2003). Unlike in the United States and many other countries, girls and boys received equal encouragement in math, science, and related fields and performed equally well on standardized tests (Tsui, 2007). A 1998–1999 survey of urban eighth graders from single-child families found that there were no gender differences in parental expectations, the children's

PHOTO 7.6

China's schools encourage all students to succeed in science, math, and technology (Source: Thinkstock)

own educational aspirations, or educational outcomes (Tsui and Rich, 2002). These attitudes are even spreading to rural areas, which changed less quickly than the cities (Hannum *et al.*, 2009).

Gender, Higher Education, and Employment

Most college students worldwide are female. Men and women are equally likely to attend college or university in just a handful of countries – including Iran, which is not otherwise known for gender equality. Men are a majority, sometimes a large majority, of college students in poor countries that have high levels of gender inequality and low rates of college attendance, such as India, Pakistan, and most countries in Africa. Men are also a majority in two wealthy countries, South Korea and Japan. In the large majority of wealthy and middle-income countries, however, women are significantly more likely than men to go to college (WEF, 2014: 72).

Several of the countries with the largest percentages of female college students are wealthy petroleum producers in which women's lives are quite constricted. The extreme case is Qatar, where 87 percent of college students are women. Like its near neighbor, Saudi Arabia, Qatar is an absolute monarchy that practices a highly restrictive form of Islam. Although Qatari women are better educated than Qatari men, their families often forbid their working outside the home and they hold only about 10 percent of the country's professional and technical positions (WEF, 2014: 64, 68, 72). In these countries, young women's greater interest in education probably reflects their appreciation of opportunities to get out of the house and think about

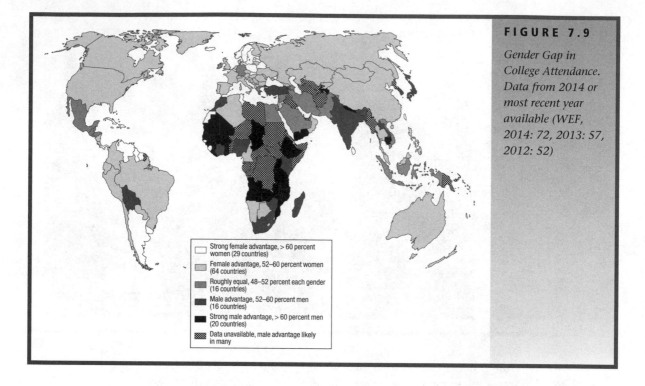

FIGURE 7.9

Gender Gap in College Attendance. Data from 2014 or most recent year available (WEF, 2014: 72, 2013: 57, 2012: 52)

something other than family life. Since young men can have an active social life outside school, they have less incentive to stay in school.

In many poor countries, in contrast, intense workplace discrimination discourages women from attending college. The economic return from university education averages 25 percent higher for men than women in developing countries, since women usually face high levels of opposition if they try to take what are seen as men's jobs in the professions or government (Patrinos, 2008: 61–62). Resources in these countries are quite limited, and both families and legislatures tend to conclude that sending men to college is more worthwhile.

Education and work patterns in most wealthy and middle-income countries resemble those in the United States. The growth of a global knowledge-based economy has greatly increased demand for workers with a college education or more, while gender discrimination in the workforce, though definitely present, is less than it used to be. Women therefore have economic incentives to get an education that enables them to escape the low wages of low-skill female-coded work.

Women may or may not receive greater financial returns from college – the data on that are too complex to be conclusive. It seems, though, that girls in these countries tend to find it easier and more attractive to prepare for college, as they often possess more of the **non-cognitive skills**, such as diligence and an ability to work for future rewards, that are rewarded in school and facilitate college readiness. Girls and women tend to work harder and to have more patience for routines and rules, while boys and men are more likely to have disciplinary problems and to be diagnosed with learning disabilities. The result in many countries is that the pool of male undergraduates seems to be leveling out while the pool of female undergraduates continues to grow (Becker *et al.*, 2010; Pekkarinen, 2011).

Some people suggest that men's relative lack of non-cognitive skills, and consequent lower level of college attendance, is due to biological differences between the sexes (Rosin, 2012). The fact that more than 85 percent of men go on to higher education in Finland and South Korea – both countries known for their effective teaching and high educational standards – suggests, however, that most men are biologically capable of high levels of academic work (WEF, 2014: 72). Instead, women's greater willingness to work hard, submit to authority, and defer gratification is probably due to the gendered socialization that girls and boys continue to receive in families and schools.

In Japan and South Korea, however, gender discrimination in the workforce is sufficiently intense that it discourages women from pursuing higher education. Nearly all young women in these countries graduate from secondary school, but they later come under strong social pressure to spend their days intensely mothering one or two children. Men, meanwhile, are expected to work long hours for their employers. Statistics suggest that Japan and South Korea have more gender inequality than any other non-Arab wealthy countries. Both countries also rank lower in global gender inequality indices than they did a decade ago, as much of the world has reduced gender gaps more quickly than they have. Their exceptionally low birth rates, combined with two decades of economic stagnation in Japan, have called into doubt the viability of this model. Indeed, Japanese women today are almost as likely as men to be employed. Childcare, however, is extremely difficult to find, and most women work part-time in poorly paid jobs. With so many impediments to women's professional success, Japan and South Korea are the only wealthy countries in which women are less likely than men to deem college a good investment (WEF, 2014: 16, 72, 221, 229; Tabuchi, 2013; *Economist*, 2014b).

CONCLUSION

Gender inequality in education seems to be nearly universal. Indeed, it may be impossible to eradicate as long as gender inequality continues in workplaces, families, and teachers' psyches. Education has often helped reproduce gender inequality, as well as inequalities of race and social class, through differences in attendance, formal curricula, and many different aspects of the hidden curriculum.

In the grand scheme of things, however, expanding education typically leads to a significant increase in women's economic, cultural, and political power. Schools are often more gender egalitarian than other social institutions, including work and family structures. The skills and attitudes that girls develop in school expand not just their employment opportunities, but also their ability to help shape decisions in their families and communities. As women become more educated, it becomes much harder to confine them within narrow expectations defined by gender.

Indeed, some people worry that education will lead to a reversal of gender hierarchies, with better-educated women running the world and men left behind (Rosin, 2012). There are reasons to be concerned about lower-status men in the United States and other countries, and ideas about masculinity – held by teachers and police officers as well as students and parents – do seem to be interfering with the ability of some boys to shape productive and satisfying futures for themselves. It is important to remember, however, that men still have higher wages than women within every racial group, and that white men from affluent families are doing very well indeed. If the problem is defined as women's desire to educate themselves and have interesting careers and satisfying lives, the solution may be to limit women's options. If, however, the primary problem is images of masculinity that limit and damage the lives of lower-status men, the solution is to change these images of masculinity. And if the primary problem is the ways that intersecting hierarchies of race and class constrain both men and women, the solution will require reducing inequality within each gender.

Develop Your Position

1   Think about gender patterns in your own high school. In what ways were they similar to the gender patterns discussed in this chapter? In what ways were they different? Do you think gender affected your academic performance in high school? Do you think it affected your male and female peers? How?

2   Based on what you have read in this chapter and your own experiences, do you think American schools favor girls or boys or neither? Why? What do you think are the strongest arguments that someone who disagrees with you could make?

3   What are three college majors you have considered? Look up their gender balance and expected incomes for men and women in "What's It Worth? The Economic Value of College Majors" (http://cew.georgetown.edu/whatsitworth). Does this information affect how you feel about these majors? Why or why not? How important are gender issues to you in your choice of major and career?

4   Re-read the three theories about the relationship between education and gender inequality in the second paragraph of this chapter. Which of these theories now rings most true to you? Why? Would your answer be different if you were asking about the relationship between education and inequalities of social class or race?

5   We claim in our conclusion that "[s]chools are often more gender egalitarian than other social institutions." Does this seem correct to you? If not, what other institution(s) would you say is (are) more egalitarian? If so, can you explain why educational institutions are relatively egalitarian?

CHAPTER 8

Gender, Power, and Politics

INTRODUCTION

Broadly speaking, politics is how people use power to make something happen. Politics can exist within any group of people, including small groups like families, workplaces, and religious congregations. For the purposes of this chapter, however, we will use "politics" to refer to the use of power within geographical communities, from villages to nations to the earth as a whole. Today, politics is male-dominated in every country. Men hold the majority – in some places the large majority – of political offices, and they have a disproportionate impact on laws, policies, judicial opinions, and everyday political decisions.

One of the most basic forms of politics is the military or strongman model. A military leader and his men conquer an area, and then he and his heirs rule it and defend it against other potential conquerors. The ruler expects his subjects to support him and his soldiers through taxes, looting, or other levies, but the subjects have little or no voice in governance. If a ruler controls a large region we call him a king or emperor, while if his territory is small we call him a warlord. In either case, the basic principle of this type of politics is "might makes right": the ruler rules because he controls the soldiers. Although women have sometimes ruled as queens or warlords, the vast majority of strongmen have been men. Successful strongmen, furthermore, typically embody a "tough" form of masculinity: they are authoritative, ruthless, and willing to use violence to enforce their will.

Another basic form of politics is deliberative assemblies, in which communities come together to discuss an issue and formulate a plan of action. Around the world, numerous societies have independently developed traditions of councils, town meetings, *shuras*, and so on. In most societies, though, only men were expected to

PHOTO 8.1

This second-century Roman victory column represents men engaged in a Germanic assembly known as a thing. Only men participated, and the horses and spears were a visual reminder of the importance of being able to back up decisions with military force (Source: Müller-Baden, 1904)

participate in these conversations. Men owned most or all land and wealth, they were considered the heads of their families, and they were soldiers, former soldiers, or potential soldiers. They were therefore considered the important stakeholders in community decisions. Some societies allowed women and children to observe the men's deliberations, and perhaps to speak if given special permission, but other societies excluded women altogether. Some traditional societies, including the Igbo of West Africa and the Iroquois of North America, had separate women's councils that governed what was considered women's domain. These dual-sex political systems, however, were atypical and rarely survived colonization (Okonjo, 1976; Demos, 2000). Until the twentieth century it was exceedingly rare for men and women to engage in political deliberation together on anything resembling equal terms.

Modern democracies use elections to create assemblies whose members are expected to represent the interests of their constituents. When democracy began it was assumed that voters would be land-owning heads of households. In North America, as in England, the common law doctrine of **coverture** held that a married woman had no legal existence apart from her husband. Each household had only one head: the husband/father/master, who had authority over his wife, children, and workers (Norton, 1996). Women very occasionally voted if they were unmarried (usually widows) and owned property, and were therefore deemed the head of their household. By the 1830s, however, the movement for "universal manhood suffrage" for white men, whether or not they owned property, had firmed up the boundaries that excluded women and non-white men. Women and black men, it was said, were perpetually child-like in their need for protection and supervision, while white men naturally embodied autonomy, rationality, and courage (Kerber, 1998). White male legislatures, meanwhile, enacted laws that granted white men more options and freedom than others.

Women's suffrage movements in the United States and other early democracies eventually secured the right to vote, while women have been able to vote from the beginning in countries that have recently transitioned to democracy. Democracy is, however, more than voting. Its basic principles include rule by the majority with protection of the rights of individuals, freedom of expression and belief, and the rule of law. Whether women are equally covered by these principles is still a live question in much of the world. A recent study found that nearly half of the 100 countries surveyed still gave women fewer economic rights than men, and some countries, such as Saudi Arabia, still consider women legal minors for many purposes (Hallward-Driemeier *et al.*, 2013a: 2; Coleman, 2010: 205, 283). Even where women have equal formal rights, they are less likely than men to run for or win political office.

This chapter will focus on how women have sought to increase their political power and how political power continues to be gendered. It will start by examining the many women's movements that occurred in the United States in the nineteenth and twentieth centuries. It will look at how political practices and opinions are gendered in the United States today. It will then turn to a global perspective and explain why many multinational organizations have focused on women's empowerment as a necessary prerequisite for other goals, survey some of the multitude of gender-related grassroots organizations, and examine the impact of women in political office.

GENDER, POWER, AND POLITICS IN THE UNITED STATES

Women's Entrance to Politics, 1820–1930

Although some women participated in the political debates of the revolutionary era, they were nearly always the wives or daughters of politically active men and worked in relationship with their male relatives. It was not until the 1820s that significant numbers of American women began to organize as women to pursue self-defined goals. Foreign visitors in the 1830s were amazed by the way Americans seemed to create groups for every purpose. Nowhere else were people as likely to form voluntary associations: to see something that could be improved and start a group to improve it. Since social life was generally gender segregated, most of these groups were single sex.

Education was a great help, as it enabled people to take notes, learn from written documents, and better organize their thoughts. Groups were also much more common in towns and cities, where neighbors could gather without traveling long distances. Most voluntary associations were therefore in the north, where industrialization encouraged urbanization and near-universal literacy arrived generations earlier than it did elsewhere. Because nearly all white northern women could read and write by 1850, they had the basic skills required to start a politically effective group.

Women learned other skills from experience. Joining a mothers' club or sewing circle was reasonably non-controversial. It took women away from home for a few hours, but it could feel like an extension of women's devotion to domestic life. In these clubs, women talked about their lives, developed relationships with other women, and learned how to organize a meeting and lead a discussion. Sometimes they addressed shared problems or started a new group for a special purpose. As time went by, women started and joined an enormous number of societies devoted to charitable purposes (e.g., providing food, coal, nursing aid, or burial expenses), educational purposes (starting schools, Sunday schools, and adult programs), and social reforms (anti-slavery, temperance, women's rights, etc.).

All types of women's organizations, even the most innocuous, thus helped women develop **social capital**. Women's expanding relationships with other women gave them more independence from their families and more ability to imagine and execute projects in their communities – in other words, more political power.

Many nineteenth-century women used arguments based on gender to claim larger roles in their communities. Some elaborated the idea of God-given gender differences into a **"cult of domesticity"** that they used to expand their influence and power within a women's world. Were women children's primary educators? Then they needed to be well educated themselves. Were women naturally responsible for children? Then they should have a say in schools, religious education, and whether their sons would be sent off to war. Other women took an even more expansive view of women's responsibilities. Were women the moral guardians of society? Then they should be able to curb drunkenness, wife beating, prostitution, gambling, and other vices. Were women supposed to serve others, especially the weak? Then they could not ignore enslaved Africans or Native Americans who were being dispossessed of their land. When told to be quiet and obedient, these women countered that they had a responsibility to make their voices heard (Cott, 1977; Epstein, 1981).

The anti-slavery movement proved especially effective at creating women's rights leaders. A few courageous black people who had escaped slavery toured the North speaking about the horrors they had experienced and witnessed. In the 1830s "decent" women could speak only in front of other women, not to what was termed a "promiscuous" group. Black women therefore met with women's groups, where they emphasized the sexual vulnerability of enslaved women – a topic that could not be mentioned in front of men. Many white female abolitionists were motivated not just by a general sense of injustice, but also by a gendered empathy with black women who had suffered public nakedness, rape, and forced separations from their children (Jeffrey, 1998).

As they fought for the rights of other women, white female abolitionists became more aware of the constraints of their own lives. White male abolitionists were deeply divided about whether women should be active in the abolitionist movement. Some abolitionists (women as well as men) believed women should be invisible, not just because of their own gendered senses of propriety but also because they feared that transgressing gender norms would discredit the movement and set back the cause of ending slavery. Other abolitionists believed that the strongest argument against slavery was the principle of universal human rights, which included women (Kraditor, 1969).

Given courage by what they considered the importance of their cause, some abolitionist women broke new ground. In 1838 Angelina Grimké became the first American woman to speak before a legislative body (Lerner, 1971). In 1841 Lydia Maria Child became the first female editor of a major newspaper, the *National Anti-Slavery Standard* (Karcher, 1994). In 1855 Lucy Stone and Henry Blackwell released at the time of their wedding a statement repudiating unjust marriage laws that gave husbands legal custody of their wives' bodies, children, and property. The custom of women's taking their husbands' surnames, they argued, is a symbol of female subordination, so Stone kept her own name (McMillan, 2015). Some of these early feminists were inspired by the different gender patterns they observed among their Native American neighbors (Wagner, 2001; Karcher, 1994).

Often, though, women were stymied by male opposition – and some were radicalized by it. When Lucretia Mott and Elizabeth Cady Stanton traveled to London for the first World Anti-Slavery Convention the organizers refused to allow them to participate. Instead they sat in the balcony, watching the convention they had crossed an ocean to attend. Eight years later, in 1848, they helped organize the first major women's rights convention in Seneca Falls, New York, which adopted a Declaration of Sentiments modeled on the Declaration of Independence. "[A]ll men and women are created equal," it asserted as it decried unjust laws and practices around voting, marriage, divorce, employment, property ownership, education, religious leadership, sexuality, and proper behavior (Declaration of Sentiments, 1848; Tetrault, 2014).

Men too formed and joined numerous voluntary associations, sometimes with the same goals as women's groups. Over the course of the century, however, many men backed away from broad civic activities as they focused their time and identities on their work (Bender, 1993: 6). By the 1870s men were most likely to participate in three types of groups. All-male unions and professional societies promoted the interests of men in specific occupations. All-male political parties were membership organizations that used parades, picnics, and other public events to build group solidarity. And perhaps one in five men belonged to all-male fraternal lodges, such as the Odd Fellows or Freemasons, whose elaborate rituals allowed men to express nurturing, paternal, and spiritual impulses that were otherwise suppressed by prevailing codes of masculinity (Carnes, 1989: 1, 149). As men stepped back from civic life women stepped forward into a vast range of volunteer roles. Women generally needed male official leadership and men's financial resources in order to, for example, start a hospital or a school, but unpaid female volunteers did much of the legwork.

Most organizations were segregated by race as well as gender. Black men won the legal right to vote after the Civil War, and during the brief period known as

Reconstruction many voted and some served in public office. Once Reconstruction ended, however, it became physically dangerous for black men to show any interest in politics. Black women were seen as less threatening, so they had somewhat more leeway to organize themselves through churches and women's clubs. By the end of the century they were also on average better educated than black men. Women with high school educations played especially important roles in black communities, as they used schools, church groups, women's clubs, and benevolent societies – and later civil rights groups and tenant organizations – to try to improve the lives of their people. Male ministers were usually the most visible leaders, but most of the people who had developed the skills required to run community and activist organizations were women. Numerous black women preached messages of self-help, community uplift, and social justice (White, 1998; Higgenbotham, 1993; Gilkes, 2000; Landry, 2000).

The cause that attracted the most women was **temperance**, which many women defined as prohibiting the sale or consumption of alcohol. Nineteenth-century men drank a lot of alcohol, and drinking was strongly associated with masculinity. It was believed that alcohol makes its imbibers active, aggressive, and competitive, all qualities highly valued in men but problematic in women (Barr, 1999: 14). Some communities deemed it unfeminine for women to drink at all, while others allowed women to drink moderately in their homes. With the exception of prostitutes, however, women were barred from the public taverns and men's clubs where men drank socially and abundantly. Many wives resented the amount of money that their husbands spent on alcohol, even when food and heat were scarce. Married women's employment options were extremely limited, and many poor women saw their husbands' frequent tavern attendance as threatening their children's survival. In addition, the combination of alcohol, peer pressure, and the misogynistic rhetoric common in drinking halls frequently fueled violence against wives and children. Most women were not yet prepared to argue that male authority per se should be limited, but many channeled their anger at men's power and privilege into the temperance movement (Pleck, 2004: 49–66; Stansell, 1982).

Numerous women also became involved in activities that historians call "municipal housekeeping." By the 1880s many cities had become filthy and dangerous. Drinking water was often contaminated with sewage and industrial chemicals, as sewers were rare and factories discharged their untreated wastes into rivers. Roads were often covered by rotting garbage and dead animals. Milk often carried tuberculosis or was diluted with water, chalk, and other substances. Many children died from diarrhea, malaria, measles, and other childhood diseases, while people of all ages died from tuberculosis and the epidemic diseases that swept through each summer. Women were considered responsible for the health of their families, but many women rightly concluded that the biggest threats to health came from outside the home. Women therefore organized to press for clean water, sewage treatment, garbage collection, industrial waste regulations, food regulations and inspections, vaccination campaigns, and numerous other public health measures.

As mothers and homemakers, they argued, they had a right to try to make the larger community clean and safe for their children (Addams, 1910).

White men were more likely to see politics as a tool for economic advancement. Every road, bridge, port, and railroad required significant funds, and their precise locations were often the product of much political maneuvering (Larson, 2001). By the 1870s party rhetoric was full of masculine imagery, urban machines regularly paid voters for their votes, and both parties celebrated loyalty to one's "friends" as a manly virtue. Other men, especially in rural areas, considered party politics corrupt and preached the value of frugality, which to them meant government should do as little as possible and leave decisions to families and communities – that is, them. They too defined political virtue in terms of manliness, which in their eyes meant being prudent, responsible, and autonomous (Baker, 1991: 24–55).

White women and men thus developed divergent political cultures. Many women found the boisterous masculinity of the political parties distasteful. Politically active women believed that government should provide reliable public services and curb men's drunkenness and violence. Government, they argued, would work better if it were non-partisan and guided by research and expertise, rather than party loyalties. Some men shared these goals, and historians call 1890 to 1920 the "Progressive Era" because of their many political reforms. Many men, however, were more inclined to treat politics like a team sport or to see government as infringing on their freedom, autonomy, and masculinity. They did not want government to regulate where they could throw garbage or how they milked their cows. They did not want to pay higher taxes to support water treatment plants or other public projects. And they did not want laws that would limit their ability to behave as they pleased toward women and children (Baker, 1991; Pleck, 2004).

By the 1890s growing numbers of women were becoming frustrated by their political disenfranchisement. The age-old argument that women were insufficiently rational to engage in democratic governance rang increasingly false as women became better educated than men. Growing numbers of women were going to college, and the first generations of graduates, though small in numbers, were showing that women could succeed in a variety of professional careers. Women had accomplished an enormous amount through organizing themselves, petitioning legislators, and changing public opinion, but they kept running into limits. They increasingly wanted to be able to vote for – or against – the politicians who created laws.

Anti-suffragists made many arguments for reserving the vote for men. Some claimed that giving women the vote would undermine family unity. Some argued that women are too absorbed by their responsibilities as wives and mothers to spare time for public activities. Some insisted that voting should be reserved for those who might put their lives on the line to protect the country as soldiers. (Suffragists pointed out that no country would survive unless women put their lives on the line in childbirth.) Some referred to scripture or other religious precedents. Fundamentally, though, they feared that women's suffrage would place new limits on men's behavior and subject men to rule by women.

Women's suffrage came gradually. First some towns allowed women to vote for school boards, thus acknowledging that women had a gender-specific interest in the education of children. Wyoming gave women the vote in 1869, and most western states and territories followed suit over the next 45 years. Many Westerners saw women's contributions as essential for developing these newer parts of the country. For them, women's suffrage was part of a broader rejection of conventional restrictions. Even in the east and south growing numbers of men supported (white) women's suffrage, especially if they agreed that government should provide good public services and that the political parties were distastefully corrupt. Giving women the vote, such men hoped, would "clean up" male patterns of politics and improve government and society. With western members of Congress already representing women, and others afraid of what might happen if they proved too intransigent, Congress passed the nineteenth amendment, giving women the vote, in 1919 and it was ratified a year later.

PHOTO 8.3

By the 1910s vast numbers of women – and also male supporters – turned out for woman suffrage marches (Source: Library of Congress, 1915)

Many people expected that a women's voting bloc would change the shape of politics. Congress made sure to pass the eighteenth amendment prohibiting the production, transport, and sale of alcohol before giving women the vote. Another women-oriented piece of legislation was the **Sheppard–Towner Act**, which in 1921 established maternal and child health centers throughout the country. Women's groups, churches, and labor unions had worked for years to establish a nationwide program providing health care to mothers and babies. Maternal and infant mortality were higher in the United States than in most other industrialized countries, and advocates argued that many of these deaths could be prevented if all mothers received prenatal care and instruction in infant care. Jeannette Rankin of Montana, the country's first Congresswoman, introduced the bill in 1918 and it passed Congress by a large margin soon after women got the vote (Skocpol, 1992: 494–512). Women's values, it seemed, were transforming the country.

The women's voting bloc, however, failed to appear. As anti-suffragists had predicted, women voted similarly to their male relatives and were less likely to vote at all. The National American Woman Suffrage Association turned itself into the League of Women Voters, which promoted voter education, open government, and rational analyses of policy outcomes. Carefully non-partisan, the League did not support individual candidates and did little to elevate women into political office. Although it had many local successes, it failed to change the masculine tone of politics (Young, 1989). The 1920s turned out to be a time of backlash against women. Colleges overtly favored male students while employers and professional associations squeezed many women out of professional work. Women's organizations of many kinds were accused of being old-fashioned or of promoting inappropriate intimacies – that is, lesbianism. Women were urged to be sexy when young and good mothers once married, but definitely not **feminists**, a word coined around 1910 (Cott, 1987: 13–16).

Politicians soon stopped worrying about attracting women's votes. The American Medical Association lobbied strenuously against the Sheppard–Towner Act and its mother-baby clinics. Before the Act was passed physicians had argued that prenatal care and well-baby care were unnecessary. Once the clinics proved that prenatal care and well-baby care saved lives, physicians argued that the clinics were unfair competition for their private practices, where they could charge mothers for these services. Congress de-funded the clinics in 1929 (Skocpol, 1992: 512–522). Most people agreed that prohibition fueled organized crime and corruption, and overwhelmed courts and prisons, without much affecting alcohol consumption. Prohibition was repealed in 1933 and with it the critique of male abusiveness that had fueled the temperance movement for nearly a century. Women continued to organize politically around a wide range of issues, especially the exploitation of women in the workplace (Cobble, 2007; Cobble *et al.*, 2014). But most political observers agreed – some with relief, others with deep disappointment – that women's political power had ebbed.

Second-Wave Feminism

The second wave of women's quest for political power began in the 1960s. Once again, it was triggered by a combination of women's increasing education and a movement for racial justice. By the 1950s middle-class families commonly sent their daughters to college, but young women graduated into a world in which job advertisements were segregated by gender and employers considered it appropriate to reject, or even fire, a woman if a man wanted the job. This contrast between their relatively egalitarian education and their adult opportunities made many women feel that something had to change (Coontz, 2011). The civil rights movement also made many women, of all races, ask about their own lives the same questions that black men and women were asking about racial inequality. Why should the body a person was born into be grounds for disrespect, violence, and limited opportunities?

One of the key phrases of second-wave feminism was "the personal is political." As women talked with each other, they learned that many other women shared what they had thought of as their own personal problems. In many cases, they realized, their individual experiences reflected larger patterns of power and privilege. Through these "consciousness raising" conversations, they developed what C. Wright Mills (1959) called a **sociological imagination** – the capacity to link their personal experiences to larger social issues. When women could not find jobs with responsibilities and wages that matched their abilities, it reflected gender discrimination in the workforce. When mothers were overwhelmed by sole responsibility for their children, it was caused by a gendered division of labor. When women were treated without compassion by physicians, it reflected sexism in the medical system. When many women reported that they had been molested or raped by their fathers, it revealed men's excessive sexual privilege and power within families. By seeing their own problems in a larger perspective, many women became less self-condemning and more determined to change the systems that had created so many problems for them and other women.

Feminist women and men engaged in an enormous range of activities intended to challenge gender inequality and improve women's lives, and hundreds of books have been written about their varying philosophies, tactics, and accomplishments (e.g. Schneir, 1994; Rosen, 2006; Collins, 2011). Five currents, however, stand out as especially large and influential: liberal feminism, radical feminism, black feminism, multicultural and class-critical feminism, and different voice feminism.

Liberal Feminism

Liberal feminists argued that women should be treated as individuals, not as members of a group called "women." They acknowledged that some biological differences between the sexes are real and affect people's lives, but they argued that the effects of these differences are now relatively minor. With small families and long lifespans, most modern women spend only a small percentage of their lives pregnant or breastfeeding. Many liberal feminists suspected that theorizing about other possible biological differences, such as math skills or propensities toward violence, is mostly driven by a desire to justify pre-existing **stereotypes**. The most important thing, they argued, is to see people as individuals. Governments, schools, employers, families, and other institutions should not discriminate on the basis of gender, but instead should allow all individuals to pursue whatever goals they chose, as long as they did not hurt others. In short, liberal feminists sought to create a level playing field that would give individual women the same rights, freedoms, and opportunities as individual men.

These ideas and values were rooted in the political philosophy called **political liberalism**, which has four basic principles: every individual has inalienable human rights, all people should be equal in the eyes of the law, individuals should generally have as much freedom as is compatible with the freedom of others, and citizens should be able to participate in collective self-government. These ideas emerged during the eighteenth-century Enlightenment and shaped the Declaration of Independence and Constitution. Liberal feminists understood that when the Constitution was enacted it was assumed that the "individuals" to whom these principles applied were white men, but they considered that a failure of the nation's founders. The principles of liberalism, they insisted, should apply to all.

Liberal feminist activism led to vast legal changes. Gender discrimination in hiring, firing, pay, and promotion became illegal. Women gained the right to use contraception or have an abortion. Publicly funded schools were required to offer equal opportunities to girls and boys. Banks were required to consider female applicants for a mortgage, credit card, or commercial loan. It became a criminal act for a man to beat his wife or have sex with her against her will. Police, hospitals, and courts were required to treat women who had been raped like crime victims rather than women shamed. Such laws could not end gender inequality, or even completely eradicate the practices they banned. They did, however, change the framework within which women and men lived their lives.

Liberal feminists also sought to reduce gender discrimination and stereotypes in ways that were unrelated to government. They asked the men in their families to share the life-maintaining work of cooking, cleaning, and childcare. They raised awareness of the everyday "put-downs, micro-inequities, and micro-aggressions" that erode women's confidence, enthusiasm, and potential. They wrote innumerable articles and books documenting the injustices of women's lives and proposing alternatives. They pursued careers as doctors and teachers, social workers and clergy, lawyers and legislators, and used their skills to help other women navigate discriminatory institutions or create new ones.

Liberal feminists expressed great optimism about human potential. They believed men could learn to treat women as equals, and that women could step up to take good advantage of the opportunities available to them. Many liberal feminists were white college graduates who experienced gender discrimination as the greatest limitation of their aspirations. A future society without discrimination, they imagined, would enable every individual to pursue her or his dreams.

Radical Feminism

Radical feminists argued that male dominance is universal and fundamental in human societies. They used the term **patriarchy** to refer to the web of relationships between men that men use to advantage themselves and oppress women. While they recognized that some men benefit from patriarchy more than others, they argued that all men benefit from the exploitation of women and participate in maintaining male privilege. They also argued that men's domination of women is the original form of human inequality and the model for all others. They pointed to evidence that men in hunting-gathering societies use systemic violence against women, including rape. Patriarchy, they concluded, preceded all other human hierarchies, and men's experience in dominating women enabled them to establish the other hierarchies of class, caste, race, and tribe (Rubin, 1975; Brownmiller, 1975). Many radical feminists suggested that a tendency toward dominance and violence is intrinsic to male psychology, while others implied that it might be a product of universal masculine socialization. In either case, they doubted that anti-discrimination laws and rules would make much of a difference.

Some but not all radical feminists were **lesbian feminists**, who argued that the crux of the issue was **compulsory heterosexuality** – the multitude of social forces that pressure women into heterosexual relationships (Rich, 1980). The solution, they believed, was to create communities of women who would love and support each other. Some women became "political lesbians," who pursued romantic relationships with other women not because of an innate sexual orientation but because they wanted to give their best energies to other women. A few women became separatists and tried not to engage with men at all. Most lesbian feminists, however, remained connected with the larger society while nurturing women's organizations. Not all women who were lesbians and feminists were lesbian feminists, but many felt a resonance between their love of specific women and their commitment to the wellbeing of women as a group.

Many radical feminists worked hard to build institutions that would empower women and build an anti-oppressive society from the ground up. They started and led women's health clinics, rape crisis centers, domestic violence shelters, women's bookstores and publishers, women's newspapers and journals, women's studies programs, women's music festivals, women's bars, women's sports teams, women's community centers, and numerous other organizations. Their goal was not just to help individual women, but to challenge the underlying systems that create inequality of all kinds.

Liberal feminists also helped build these community organizations, and the various flavors of feminists sometimes worked well together and sometimes came into conflict. While liberal feminists saw their goal as eliminating gender discrimination, radical feminists were more likely to describe themselves as trying to eradicate all forms of oppression and hierarchy. Radical feminists generally wanted to keep the institutions they nurtured separate from government, which they saw as not just male-dominated but inherently oriented toward hierarchical ways of being in the world, while liberal feminists were more likely to see government funding as a way to expand and stabilize services. Radical feminists often felt that liberal feminists took for granted their privileges granted by race, class, heterosexual identity, age, physical ability, and other differences among women. Liberal feminists often felt that radical feminists were overly idealistic and in their own way overly narrow-minded. Such tensions around philosophy and tactics could prove either creative or destructive.

Black Feminism

Rosa Parks is often described as a sweet old lady with tired feet who one day in 1955 did not want to give up her seat on the bus and thereby sparked the Montgomery bus boycott. In reality, Parks was an experienced organizer for the NAACP (National Association for the Advancement of Colored People) who had been working for years to end sexual violence against black women by white men. At the time most black women suffered from being at the bottom of three intertwined hierarchies: gender, race, and class. Most black women labored long hours for scanty wages and were not covered by labor laws that regulated hours, wages, and safety conditions in predominantly white jobs. In addition, white men harassed and raped black women with impunity. Few courts would take a black woman's word against that of a white man, and if a black man tried to protect his wife, sister, or mother he might well be killed. These experiences helped fuel the uprising that became known as the civil rights movement (White, 1998; McGuire, 2010).

Although black women had long been deeply involved in organizing their communities, and remained so throughout the 1960s, the best-known civil rights and Black Nationalist leaders were men. Men's prominence in a movement that was probably majority female had multiple roots. Many black men and women shared the general American belief that leadership and authority were properly masculine characteristics, so they expected women to defer to men. Many activists also believed that performing gender "properly" was important for appealing to white Americans. Women therefore wore skirts and heels to demonstrations, while men wore suits and ties, and only men were put forward as spokesmen. On a deeper level, many black people felt that black men had been unmanned by white America's depriving them of masculine prerogatives available to white men. Black men had little ability to provide for their families economically, control the activities of their female relatives, protect "their" women from violence, or assert their will in public spaces. Even when they had gray hair, black men were commonly addressed as "boy." For many black men the assertion, "I am a man!" was a powerful rejection of the country's racist regime – but it also implied dominance over black women (Estes, 2005; White, 1998; McGuire, 2010).

Black feminists challenged the presumption that black liberation could come through male dominance. In her controversial *Black Macho and the Myth of the Superwoman* (1978), Michelle Wallace argued that the civil rights and Black Nationalist movements did not fulfill their aspirations precisely because black men suppressed women's full involvement. Instead, they created a myth of black female strength and invulnerability. Black mothers were revered for the backbreaking work and loving determination with which they raised their children, but at the same time inhumanly strong black women were blamed for the weakness of black men. Black women, Wallace argued, are survivors but not superwomen, and black macho is self-defeating. Five years later Alice Walker's *The Color Purple* (1983a) again sparked controversy by vividly portraying sexual violence by a black man against a black girl. Critics argued that her popular novel, followed by an equally popular movie, reinforced racist images of black men as violent and criminal. Black feminists countered that black women would continue to suffer as long as the exploitation, degradation, and violence to which they were so often subjected remained invisible and unmentionable – and as long as the myth of the strong black woman made their suffering seem inconsequential.

Black feminists were equally critical of the racism and class-based assumptions of the white women who dominated the feminist movement. Both the liberal feminist emphasis on individual autonomy and the radical feminist quest to create an alternative feminist lifestyle could alienate women who valued their existing lives, relationships, and communities (hooks, 1984: 17–31). College-educated white feminists were very interested in opening up professional careers to women, breaking through glass ceilings, and celebrating the "first" women in numerous careers – the first woman astronaut, surgeon general, president of an Ivy League university, and so on. White feminists often spoke as if employment were the key to women's liberation. Sometimes they justified this opinion by arguing that women with independent incomes could leave abusive marriages, or that work was important for human self-fulfillment. Black women had been working hard for generations, however, and they knew that work was often neither liberating nor self-fulfilling. Very few people would choose plucking chickens, for example, as a path to self-actualization, and yet it must be done. Most women were not white college graduates and did not have access to professional careers for reasons well beyond their gender. "When the middle-class white woman said 'I want to work,' in her head was a desk in the executive suite," explained Michelle Wallace, "while the black woman saw a bin of dirty clothes, someone else's dirty clothes" (1978: 126).

Many black feminists spoke compassionately about the challenges faced by black men in a racist society and the need for racial solidarity. They understood, but did not excuse, that people who have been hurt often hurt others (e.g., hooks, 2004). They discussed hair texture and images of beauty, professional accomplishments and the complexities of class, the pain and the integrity of African American families, loving women and loving men, raising children, poetry, spirituality, and numerous other topics (e.g., hooks, 1981, 1989; Smith, 1983; Lorde, 1984; Collins, 1990). Some fought against involuntary sterilizations and other abuses that black women experienced in the medical system, while others worked in labor unions to secure better wages and working conditions (White, 1990; Smith, 1995; Cobble, 2007). Alice Walker suggested that black women might embrace the term "womanist," which she partially defined as: "A woman who loves other women, sexually and/or nonsexually . . . Sometimes loves individual men, sexually and/or nonsexually. Committed to survival and wholeness of entire people, male *and* female . . . Womanist is to feminist as purple is to lavender" (1983b: xi–xii).

Multicultural and Class-Critical Feminism

In the 1980s many feminists of all racial and ethnic identities began to try to follow bell hooks's admonition to look "from margin to center" (1984). They recognized that women do not all share a common experience, and argued that a true feminist movement would have to recognize and address the "multiple jeopardies" faced by women who were not just female, but also black, brown, poor, poorly educated, disabled, and/or lesbian (King, 1988). This approach is often called **multicultural feminism**, as it involves articulating and affirming the experiences of women of many different heritages, especially those that have been marginalized (Moraga and Anzaldua, 1984; Kirk and Okazawa-Rey, 2012).

Many feminists, however, were (and are) more concerned about economic and class issues than the term "multicultural" – with its implicit focus on "culture" – suggests. Hierarchies of gender, race, and class, they argued, are all fundamental to

American society, and one cannot understand either the past or the present without examining the intersections between these interrelated systems of oppression (Crenshaw, 1991). Some feminists argued that the root cause of inequality is capitalist patriarchy and called themselves **socialist feminists** (Eisenstein, 1979; Hansen and Philipson, 1990). The term "socialism" has, however, never become popular in the United States, and most feminists who pursued class-critical analyses did not describe themselves as socialists. There is no one widely accepted word to describe feminists who believe that feminism has to include challenging many intersecting hierarchies, including class. Many such feminists simply call themselves feminists.

Many multicultural feminists are concerned about what Diana Pearce (1978) called "the feminization of poverty." Both in the United States and around the world, women are more likely than men to be poor (Goldberg, 2009). Female-coded occupations usually have low wages, and many women have family responsibilities that make it impossible for them to work full-time – or more than full-time, which is often what would be required to pay for rent, groceries, and other necessities at prevailing wages. Women of color face the double burdens of racism and sexism in the job market, while schools in low-income communities of all colors often do not prepare their students for college and professional careers. Roughly a quarter of women of color live below the poverty line, as do more than a third of children of color (Entmacher *et al.*, 2012: 13).

Because so many women – especially but not only women of color, especially but not only mothers – cannot earn enough to survive, they and their children often rely on public services, including subsidized housing and food stamps, to make ends meet. The welfare rights movement of the 1960s and 1970s argued that poor women have a right to be treated with respect and to have the resources they need to raise their children, even if they had been disadvantaged by racist and sexist educational systems and job markets (Orlech, 2005; Nasaden, 2011). By the 1980s, however, the politics of welfare reform focused on reducing single motherhood and pushing women into paid employment (Murray, 1984; Morgen *et al.*, 2009; Collins and Mayer, 2010). Many Americans were expressing concern about the impact of women's employment on their children, and as we have seen standards of parenting were rising among college graduates, especially for mothers (Lareau, 2003; Ramey and Ramey, 2010). The 1996 **Personal Responsibility and Work Opportunity Reconciliation Act**, however, required low-wage mothers to devote more time to paid work (Collins and Mayer, 2010). Today many mothers effectively have three jobs: caring for children (sometimes without a spouse or live-in partner), paid employment (often with erratic hours that are incompatible with childcare facilities, which are often unaffordable anyway), and navigating the awkward and sometimes hostile bureaucracies that determine whether their children are eligible for publicly funded food, housing, childcare, and other services and necessities (Nasaden, 2011).

Stereotypes related to gender, race, and class often underpin the institutional structures and political decisions that perpetuate inequality (Lin and Harris, 2010;

Harris-Perry, 2011; Bonilla-Silva, 2013; Caliendo, 2014). For example, the stereotype that black women tend to be sexually irresponsible and have a lot of children helps justify public welfare policies that are much stingier than in other wealthy countries, which historically had racially homogenous populations and less stigmatization of lower-income people. The total fertility rate of black women (1.90 in 2012) and white women (1.89) are, however, nearly identical. A small gap existed in 1995, when images of fast-breeding "welfare queens" were used to justify pushing poor mothers into low-wage jobs, but even then black women's total fertility rate was 2.13 – or just slightly over replacement level (Martin *et al.*, 2013: table 4). The image of poor women and black women as bad mothers has fueled the growing incarceration of mothers, which often sends their children into the foster care system (Roberts, 2012). Although women are still much less likely than men to be incarcerated, women's incarceration rate has grown more quickly in recent decades (Sentencing Project, 2012). Multicultural feminists argue that feminist politics must expose these kinds of connections and challenge all of the intersecting hierarchies that damage people's lives.

Different Voice Feminism

In 1982 Carol Gilligan published her extremely influential *In a Different Voice: Psychological Theory and Women's Development,* in which she argued that women and men have different moral sensibilities and draw on different ethical principles when making decisions. Women, she suggested, tend to think in terms of an "ethic of care," which is focused on relationship and meeting people's needs, while men tend to think in terms of an "ethic of rights," which focuses more on rules and individual autonomy.

Gilligan and many other women came to be known as **different voice feminists**. While liberal feminists preferred to minimize the significance of differences between women and men, different voice feminists saw gender differences as deep and important. Some drew on theories of evolutionary psychology to suggest that women evolved characteristics that helped their children survive, such as emotional connection, generosity, and protectiveness. Others drew on Chodorow's theories about male and female development, arguing that women are more attuned to relationship in any society in which women do most of the parenting – which thus far is all of them. Others focused on women's own experiences of mothering, suggesting that motherhood tends to be core to women's identities and affects how they interact with other people generally, not just their own children. Whatever their theory of origins, they believed that women and men have fundamentally different ways of being in the world and that women's ways are inherently valuable (Belenky *et al.*, 1986).

Different voice feminists argued that the world has been damaged by an overemphasis on men's values and perspectives. Many pointed out that wars have always been led and started by men and are often driven by gendered images and motivations. Women, they believed, are more inclined toward collaborative and nonviolent approaches to resolving intergroup and international conflicts (Ruddick, 1989; Anderlini, 2007; Enloe, 2007). Many also argued that the root cause of our planet's ecological problems is masculinity's emphasis on distance, control, and domination. We will not be able to address the underlying causes of environmental destruction, they suggested, until we heal the alienation from nature created by men's illusions of autonomy (Griffin, 1978; Merchant, 1980).

Different voice feminists thus sought to empower women not just as a matter of individual justice, but also because they believed women's voices are needed in the public realm. Unlike liberal feminists, who often imagined that the ideal society would provide a level playing field for more-or-less androgynous individuals, different voice feminists affirmed and promoted many of the values traditionally associated with femininity. The world would be a much better place, they argued, if public policies reflected women's values of relationship, nurturing, and meeting people's true needs. Indeed, many believed that the future of the planet depended on giving women more cultural and political power.

Feminism Today

Americans today dispute the meaning and significance, successes and failures, of feminism. Whether women should have equal legal rights is no longer a live question: 97 percent of Americans say they should (Pew Research Center, 2010). If presented with a standard dictionary definition of feminism – "do you believe in the social, economic, and political equality of the sexes?" – two-thirds of American women and nearly half of the men say yes (YouGov, 2013). A more subtle definition of feminism would include believing that gender inequality still exists and that changes should be made to lessen it. Here too most Americans qualify. Two-thirds of Americans believe that gender inequality exists today and that more changes would be needed to give women equal rights and equal pay for the same work – goals that most Americans endorse. Black women and men are especially likely to perceive gender inequality, with 83 percent of black men and 86 percent of black women saying more change would be needed to create gender equality in the workplace (Pew Research Center, 2010, 2013b: 28–29). Only 38 percent of women and 18 percent of men, however, use the word "feminist" to describe themselves (YouGov, 2013).

One issue is generational. By the 1990s some young adults – including some daughters of feminists – were beginning to feel that the feminist concerns of the 1970s were dated (Walker, 1995; Henry, 2004). Today anyone under the age of 40 was born after the major feminist legal victories and raised in an era when many schools and families endorsed gender-egalitarian values, however imperfectly they acted on them. Many young adults celebrate diversity, believe in tolerance and egalitarianism, and volunteer their time for a wide variety of causes. Many are, however, more likely to focus their political and organizational energies on issues they consider important to their generation, such as economic inequality, climate change, or police brutality, than to join traditional feminist organizations. If they see feminism as defined by the issues that were important in the 1970s they may not consider themselves feminists.

Some people believe that gender equality has been sufficiently accomplished. Anyone who still calls herself a feminist, some argue, is going well beyond the original feminist goal of equality to vilify men, seek special privileges for women, and demean women by portraying them as victims rather than free agents (Young, 2014). Indeed, 28 percent of men and 19 percent of women say they consider the word "feminist" an insult (YouGov, 2013).

Other people believe we are living in a time of backlash or a "soft war" against women (Faludi, 2006; Rivers and Barnett, 2013). Gender discrimination in the workforce remains pervasive and persistent. The culture wars over abortion have recently spread to contraception and affect women's ability to access all kinds of reproductive health care. Violence against women, including rape, is still widespread, and often treated as a misunderstanding rather than an act of violence. Media still portray women as focused on home, family, and fashion, while running many stories about the end of feminism and high-powered women "opting out." Some critics suggest that all changes related to gender (especially the ones they dislike) are due to the feminist movement, though economic forces and other cultural trends have also affected women's and men's lives. Feminists have never been as omnipotent as their harshest critics imply.

It seems fair to conclude that feminism is still a significant part of American society, though the tone and content of feminist conversations are often different now than in the 1970s. Ideals of gender egalitarianism are now deeply entrenched, but so is gender inequality. Not everyone agrees that more gender equality would be desirable, and not everyone who would approve of more gender equality feels motivated to help bring it about. But more than a quarter of Americans – a third of them men – describe themselves as feminists, and many more endorse egalitarian values and try to live by them at least some of the time.

GENDER, PUBLIC OPINION, AND POLITICAL PARTICIPATION IN THE TWENTY-FIRST CENTURY

Although women and men voted similarly for the first sixty years after women's suffrage, a gender gap emerged in 1980. Women are now significantly more likely than men to vote for Democratic candidates. Indeed, in the last four presidential elections a majority of women voted for the Democrat while a majority of men voted for the Republican.

Public opinion polls help us understand the factors behind this gender gap. Poll results need to be used cautiously, as people's answers rarely capture the full

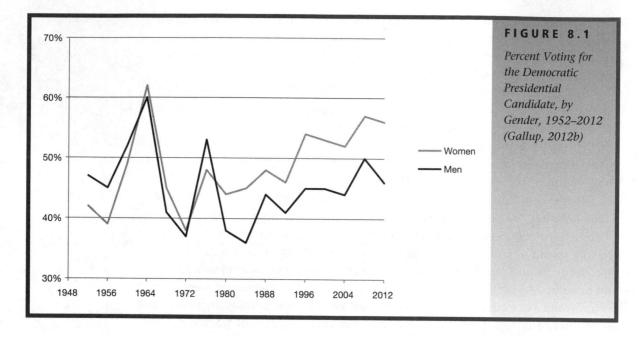

FIGURE 8.1

Percent Voting for the Democratic Presidential Candidate, by Gender, 1952–2012 (Gallup, 2012b)

complexity of their beliefs and behaviors and may change in response to what may seem like small differences in wording. Gender patterns that appear in dozens of polls, however, probably reflect something real.

Men and women today express similar though not identical opinions on most so-called "moral issues." With regard to abortion, for example, women are somewhat more likely to hold absolute positions – abortion should be always legal or always illegal – while men are more likely to embrace the middle ground that abortion should be legal under some but not all conditions (Gallup, 2010). Women are also somewhat more accepting of homosexuality (Pew Research Center, 2013a). The differences between genders, however, are small compared to the differences within each gender. These issues are therefore unlikely to drive the substantial differences in men's and women's voting patterns.

One of the most robust gender gaps in public opinion is that men are more likely to support going to war, and have been for generations (Goldstein, 2001: 322–330). In 1991, for example, 60 percent of men but 45 percent of women supported the first U.S. invasion of Iraq (Moore, 2002). Closer study suggests that women are more conditional in their support for war. Women are more likely to support a military action if it has international approval or they consider it a humanitarian intervention, while these factors have less effect on men's opinions (Brooks and Valentino, 2011). Before the second U.S. invasion of Iraq, for example, nearly half of the women polled said the United States should invade only with United Nations authorization, while men were more willing to go it alone (Moore, 2002). If voters see the Republican Party as more likely to support a strong and active

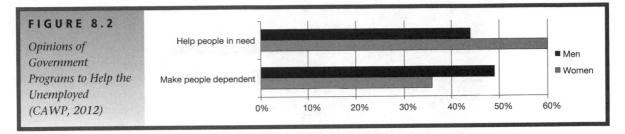

Do you think government programs to help the unemployed do more to help people in need get back on their feet or do more to make people dependent on such assistance?

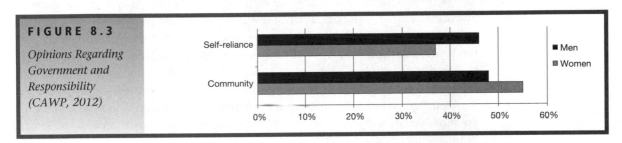

Do you think the United States is more successful when the government emphasizes self-reliance and individual responsibility, or when the government emphasizes community and shared responsibility?

military, these differences may make men more inclined to vote Republican. The fact that the gender gap in opinions about war existed long before the gender gap in voting patterns suggests, however, that it is not the only factor.

A similarly pervasive gender gap appears in opinions about the role of government. Women are more likely to believe that government should provide public services for everyone and a safety net for those in trouble, while men are more likely to be skeptical about the helpfulness and effectiveness of government programs. These differences appear both in questions about specific programs and in broader philosophical questions (CAWP, 2012).

Women are also more inclined to approve of government limitations on individual behavior. This gap is particularly evident in opinions about gun control. A majority of men say there should be few or no restrictions on gun ownership, while a majority of women say there should be major restrictions on guns or they should be limited to people who need to carry them for their employment. Men are three times as likely as women to own guns, with 37 percent of men and 12 percent of women reporting that they personally own firearms (Pew Research Center, 2013c: 16).

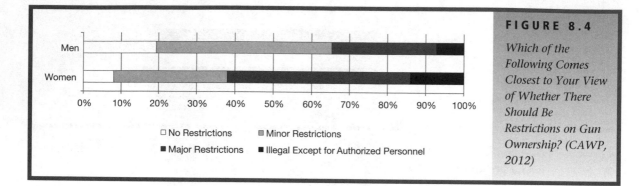

FIGURE 8.4

Which of the Following Comes Closest to Your View of Whether There Should Be Restrictions on Gun Ownership? (CAWP, 2012)

Men are generally less connected with the political process, at least as measured by voting and party affiliation. Until the 1970s men were more likely than women to vote, but since 1980 the reverse has been true. Although voting has dropped across the board, the decline is especially marked among men. Men are also more likely to describe themselves as political independents than as either Republicans or Democrats. Among men who identify with a political party, the majority alternates between Democrats and Republicans every few years. Women's political affiliations are more stable, with more women identifying as Democrats than as Republicans or independents (CAWP, 2012).

Political scientists have long observed that public opinion tends to move opposite to government policies. When government programs are generous the public calls for more frugality, while when government programs are frugal the public calls for more generous support. Most of this shift occurs among men. Gender gaps are therefore largest when public spending increases, as men are more eager to call for retrenchment. They decrease when public budgets are cut, as both men and women call for the restoration of programs they care about but men's greater responsiveness moves them closer to women's position (Kellstedt *et al.*, 2010). These correlations support the theory that different beliefs and feelings about the role of government help drive the gender gaps in political behavior.

Gendered differences of opinion about the role of government go back to the nineteenth century and are probably related to long-standing gender patterns. Many men have inherited images of manhood that define masculinity in terms of autonomy and independence: a man is the head of his household and the ruler of his hearth. They are therefore inclined to frame government as potentially infringing on their freedom and want to limit its scope. If Chorodow's and Gilligan's psychological theories are correct, men are deeply concerned about establishing interpersonal distance and prefer an ethic of rights that focuses on what individuals do and do not deserve. Women's family experiences, meanwhile, make them see people as inherently interconnected, not as fundamentally independent individuals who can choose whether to be in a relationship with others. (No infant can choose to be independent.) They therefore tend to prefer an ethic of care and responsibility

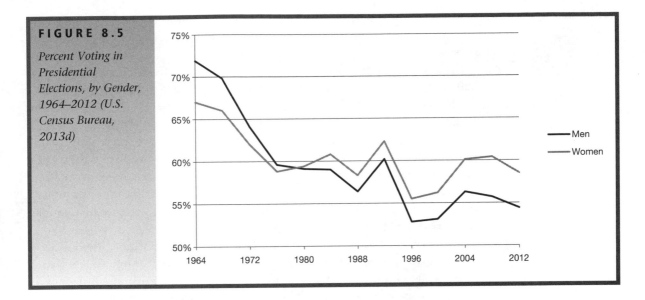

FIGURE 8.5

Percent Voting in Presidential Elections, by Gender, 1964–2012 (U.S. Census Bureau, 2013d)

that focuses on supporting good relationships and meeting everyone's needs. Political opinions then mirror interpersonal psychology. Men tend to be more concerned about carving out individual rights and delineating where government may not intrude, while women tend to want to use government to support families and communities and take care of people (Chodorow, 1978; Gilligan, 1982; Kathlene, 2001).

The gender gap in voting patterns did not emerge, however, until around 1980, so gender psychology cannot be the full story here. At least two major changes help explain the shift. First, feminists affirmed that women have a right to think and act for themselves rather than obeying their husbands and fathers. As women became more assertive in many arenas of life, they became more confident in their abilities to draw their own political conclusions. Second, women's responsibilities expanded. Since 1970 women have entered the workforce in large numbers, rates of divorce and unmarried motherhood have risen, and women have continued to have primary responsibility for the care of children, the elderly, and family members who are sick or disabled. Many women now juggle hefty work and family responsibilities, and they want public institutions to help make this possible.

Cuts in social services disproportionately affect women. Since women are generally assigned final responsibility for the wellbeing of their families, it tends to be women who try to fill in the gaps when life gets hard or complicated. Good public schools, childcare, health care, and so on, help everyone flourish and thus make it easier for women to fulfill their family responsibilities. Dysfunctional schools and other public institutions, on the other hand, add to women's burdens. Long or unpredictable commutes, for example, make it harder to juggle day-to-day logistics. Women are also disproportionately likely to be poor, and every hurdle is harder if one is poor. In addition women are more likely to have public sector jobs, and therefore to lose their incomes when government budgets are cut (UNECE Statistical Database, n.d.).

The key issue, some observers suggest, is the ratio between responsibilities and resources. Unmarried women – who are increasingly likely to be raising children – are especially likely to believe that governments should help their citizens and to favor Democratic candidates. In the 2012 presidential election they preferred Obama to Romney by a remarkable 36 percentage points. Men have, on average, more income, wealth, and leisure time than women and fewer care-taking responsibilities. While "leave me alone" may appeal to men, women are more concerned about being abandoned with responsibilities that are beyond their abilities. In a time when many women are working harder than ever, they want government to help their families survive and flourish (*Economist*, 2013e).

Women are, however, much less likely than men to run for or hold elective office. In 2013 women were less than a fifth of members of Congress, less than a quarter of state legislators, less than a tenth of state governors, and less than an eighth of big-city mayors. Women have the highest representation on school boards – a local office, often unpaid, with a primary responsibility for children – but even there they are a minority (Lawless and Fox, 2013: 1; Sparks, 2014).

Women's political representation is not increasing. The number of women in elective office began to grow slowly in the 1980s and grew more quickly in the early 1990s. Since then, however, it has basically plateaued (Lawless and Fox, 2013: 23). School boards are often stepping-stones to other political offices, so their composition is considered a predictor of future trajectories. There are, however, about the same proportion of women on school boards now as in the 1980s (Sparks, 2014; Henderson, 1985). Political incumbents have great advantages in recruiting donors, volunteers, and voters, and they typically win re-election if they seek it. The large majority of incumbents are men, and the low turnover rate makes it difficult for women to increase their political representation. Incumbency advantages do not, however, explain why the number of women in office increased in the 1980s and 1990s but not in recent years.

One factor is that men are more likely to receive support, both moral and financial, in running for office. About a fifth of Americans still believe that women are not well suited to politics, and male college students are significantly more likely than their female classmates to be encouraged by parents, professors, and others to consider running for office later in life (General Social Survey, 2012; Lawless and Fox, 2013: 12–13). One study identified women and men who were mid-career professionals in the fields that are most likely to run for office: law, business, education, and activism. Although all were well qualified to become political candidates, men received more encouragement to do so from every direction – colleagues, family members, party officials, and so on (Lawless and Fox, 2012: 12). Once they decide to run, male candidates typically are able to raise more money than female candidates (Center for Responsive Politics, 2013b).

Another factor is that men express more self-confidence around politics, as they do across the board (Kay and Shipman, 2014a). Almost a quarter of undergraduate men claim they will know enough to run for public office after a few years in the workforce, but less than a tenth of undergraduate women express similar confidence (Lawless and Fox, 2013: 14). Among mid-career professionals who were carefully matched for credentials and experience, 73 percent of men and 57 percent of women believed they were qualified for public office. Men were also substantially more likely to consider running even if they described themselves as unqualified, while most women considered good qualifications a prerequisite for throwing their hats into the ring (Lawless and Fox, 2012: 9). From childhood on up, women are more likely to be encouraged to be modest and warned against tooting their own horns, while men are expected to become proficient at self-promotion – a necessary skill in politics (Kay and Shipman, 2014a).

If women receive opportunities and support only if they are truly exceptional, while men can advance their careers if they are merely good, the average woman in the field will be superior to the average man. Even though they typically raise less money than their male opponents, female candidates seem to be just as likely to be elected to office, at least below the presidential level. This finding suggests that the general caliber of female candidates is indeed higher (Lawless and Fox, 2012: ii, 24).

Women may also be discouraged by a variety of other issues related to gender. Women's greater family responsibilities may make them more reluctant to attend lots of evening meetings or commute to a state or national capital, while women who have forged strong relationships in their communities are more likely than men to resist giving them up to pursue state-level office (Forster, 2009). Women express more distaste for several aspects of campaigning, while men are more likely to describe themselves as possessing personal traits that are useful in politics, such as competitiveness and a thick skin (Lawless and Fox, 2012: 10–11). Female politicians can find it difficult to balance the normatively masculine quality of being physically and emotionally "tough" – which is essential both on the campaign trail and in political office – with voters' feelings (and perhaps their own) that a woman must not be unfeminine. The militarized language of many political campaigns resonates with the long association between masculinity and war. In addition, many women believe that female politicians receive biased media coverage and are less likely to win than equally qualified men (Lawless and Fox, 2012: 7–8). If their hurdles are higher, their chances of success lower, and the process distasteful, why start?

Finally, men are more likely than women to believe that formal politics is a good use of their time, energy, and money. One study asked undergraduates what career they would choose if their goal was to make their community or country a better place. Young women were almost three times more likely to say they would work for a charity than run for political office, while young men ranked these options about equally (Lawless and Fox, 2013: 16). Women are more likely than men to

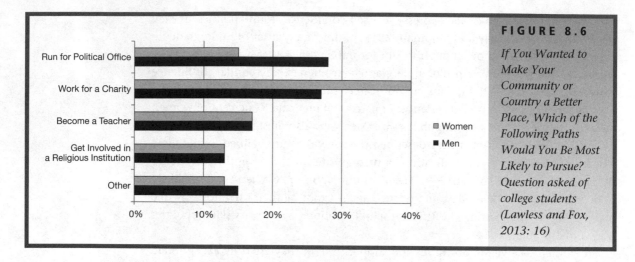

FIGURE 8.6

If You Wanted to Make Your Community or Country a Better Place, Which of the Following Paths Would You Be Most Likely to Pursue? Question asked of college students (Lawless and Fox, 2013: 16)

donate to charities and to volunteer their time, and 78 percent of female charitable donors believe that contributing to charities has a greater impact than contributing to political candidates (Hawthorne, 2012; Women's Campaign Forum, 2007: 4). Men, meanwhile, are twice as likely as women to make political donations and their average donation is larger (as is their average wealth). Men provide 70 percent of campaign funds and are two-thirds of the big donors who give more than $2,500 and get more attention from candidates (Center for Responsive Politics, 2013a). Both genders give most of their money to male candidates, but women are almost twice as likely as men to contribute to female candidates (Women's Campaign Forum, 2007: 3).

The gendered patterns of politics are thus somewhat ironic. Women are more likely to believe that government can and should be a proactive force for good, and they are more likely to engage in the political process at the basic level of voting and party affiliation. They are, however, less likely to engage at the deeper levels of running for office or even contributing to candidates. One reason is that many women believe that NGOs are a more effective way to improve the world. It is also, however, because men receive more encouragement to put themselves forward and more cash and other support if they do so.

GENDER, POWER, AND POLITICS IN A GLOBAL PERSPECTIVE

Grassroots and International Organizations

Women all over the world have started and joined innumerable local groups that seek to improve women's lives. Some women have started schools to educate girls and women, while others have used labor unions, workers' cooperatives, micro-finance groups, and professional associations to improve women's incomes and working conditions. Some have set up clinics and trained practitioners to provide contraceptives, childbirth attendants, and other forms of health care. Some have organized to end sexual harassment, rape, domestic violence, and female genital cutting. Some have started childcare centers or provided clean water and safe sanitary facilities. Some have lobbied to change laws that constrain women's lives, especially customary laws around family life and economic rights. Some have created peace in communities torn by war and intergroup violence. In these and many other ways, millions of women around the world work on the issues they consider most important for women in their communities (Armstrong, 2013; Moghadam *et al.*, 2011; World Bank, 2011a).

As in the United States, these groups have created social capital and sociological imaginations. Women who communicate with other women can identify shared problems, put their own experiences in a larger context, and work together to make changes. Even working on a relatively small project, such as installing a water well, expands women's skills, confidence, and political power, which makes them better prepared to take on the larger problems of their society.

Political scientists consider the existence of **civil society** – a layer of social organization that is larger than families but not tightly linked with the state – essential to the formation and preservation of a non-totalitarian government. Authoritarian regimes typically seek to control or eliminate the ability of their subjects to congregate in groups that are not state-sponsored, and the resulting social and intellectual isolation helps sustain the power of the regime. Successful democracies, on the other hand, have social and civic associations that distribute power and knowledge more widely (Arendt, 1951).

Similar patterns strengthen or moderate the power of families and tribes. In traditional societies, people often had little opportunity to build relationships of mutual trust or assistance outside their own families, tribes, or local communities. Because of male dominance within the family, family decision-making often meant men's decision-making. Families become less central and powerful, however, when people organize with other people across family lines. If women are not allowed to congregate with other women outside their families, but instead are confined to their home compounds, they live in what is for them an authoritarian regime. This exclusion of women from the public sphere also has larger implications, as societies with high levels of gender inequality tend to have difficulties establishing a stable, peaceful, and democratic state (Hudson *et al.*, 2012; Ní Aoláin *et al.*, 2011).

All major international institutions now consider empowering women essential for global prosperity and security. They recognize that is extremely difficult for a family or community to work its way out of poverty if its women suffer from poor health, inadequate education and employment opportunities, and high levels of gendered violence. Countries that develop the talents of girls and women and bring them into the workforce can, in contrast, make remarkable advances in two generations. In 2000 the UN's General Assembly overwhelmingly approved eight Millennium Development Goals, one of which was: "To promote gender equality and the empowerment of women as effective ways to combat poverty, hunger and disease and to stimulate development that is truly sustainable" (United Nations, 2000). All of the world's leading development institutions have since endorsed these goals (United Nations, 2014b).

Arguments for gender equality are both principled and practical. The World Bank (2011a), for example, argues that gender equality should be a core development objective both because women's lives matter in themselves and because increasing gender equality improves economic productivity, life expectancies for men as well as women, and children's health, education, and future potential. Higher incomes, its analysts point out, do not necessarily reduce inequality. Instead, empowering women requires intentional changes in institutions and attitudes. The United Nations' Food and Agriculture Organization has estimated that agricultural productivity in sub-Saharan Africa would rise by 20 percent if women had equal access to land, seed, and fertilizer. Since 2002 it has "mainstreamed" gender equity into all of its activities not just because the majority of poor people are female, but also because programs that include or target women have proven most effective in reducing hunger (FAO, 2009). As former U.S. Secretary of State Hillary Clinton put it, "Gender equality is both the right thing to do and the smart thing to do" (USAID, 2012: iv).

Governments and NGOs of all kinds are acting on the evidence that giving women more control over money, land, and other assets significantly improves children's lives and therefore a country's future. Studies suggest that when women in poor countries gain more access to money they tend to spend it on the nutrition, health, and education of their children, while men are more likely to spend additional income on recreation, including alcohol, tobacco, and commercial sex. In the poorest families a child's probability of survival increases by 20 percent if his or her mother controls the household budget (De Schutter, 2013: 2). Most countries therefore give **conditional cash transfers** to the mother of the family, if she is alive, while most microfinance organizations preferentially or exclusively lend to women (De Brauw *et al.*, 2012; Coleman, 2010: 3–31).

Many countries have reduced legal restrictions on women's abilities to own or inherit property, open a bank account or start a business without a husband's consent, or otherwise function as independent economic agents. Some such restrictions remain, however, in roughly half of the world's countries, especially in the Middle East, southern Asia, and sub-Saharan Africa. Progress on improving women's legal rights tends to be particularly fast in the five years after each country ratifies the Convention on the Elimination of All Forms of Discrimination Against Women (CEDAW), which was passed by the UN General Assembly in 1979 (Hallward-Driemeier, 2013b: 2–3, 12). Almost all countries have ratified CEDAW, with the United States and Iran being notable exceptions.

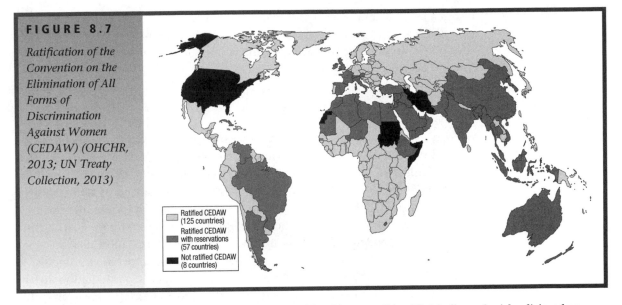

FIGURE 8.7

Ratification of the Convention on the Elimination of All Forms of Discrimination Against Women (CEDAW) (OHCHR, 2013; UN Treaty Collection, 2013)

Ratified CEDAW
(125 countries)

Ratified CEDAW
with reservations
(57 countries)

Not ratified CEDAW
(8 countries)

The most common reservations are provisions that are considered incompatible with Muslim or Jewish religious law, affect succession to a throne, provide for international dispute resolution, or are believed to favor women.

Women's grassroots organizations benefit from large international organizations in many ways (Naples and Desai, 2002). Sometimes local women receive grants or assistance in learning effective organizational techniques, such as how to keep good financial records. More often they get information, ideas, and inspiration from women's groups in other parts of the world. Especially as the Internet and mobile phones have become increasingly widespread, women have shared huge amounts of information about what is happening in their own communities, stories about changes and setbacks, and strategies that have worked. International organizations facilitate such communication by sending staff, setting up Internet connections and training local women in computer use, and publishing information in many different languages. They promote the basic concepts of political liberalism, human rights, and gender equity, as the phrase "Women's rights are human rights" has echoed around the world. They also spread the idea that voluntary associations can exist and make real changes.

This international context can raise local resistance. Men especially, but sometimes women, may see efforts to improve women's lives as reflecting foreign values and influences. Increasingly, though, international organizations recognize that they need to let local people take the lead and develop language and programs that feel suitable to their own context. The evidence strongly suggests that many women around the world want better lives for themselves and their children. Wherever they have freedom of mobility and speech, women work with each other on local projects – and increasingly they work with local men too. As they tap into a larger context and learn more about what people are doing elsewhere, their aspirations tend to grow. Women's groups face obstacles of many kinds, but they have played an essential role in increasing women's political, economic, and social power (Coleman, 2010; World Bank, 2011a).

Women in Political Office

Women's participation in formal politics varies greatly around the world, as do political systems more generally. Women have the highest political representation in the Nordic countries, with the rest of Western Europe, Latin America, and the Caribbean all comparable to each other, on average, and ahead of the rest of the world (Torregrosa, 2012). The only country with no women in its national assembly (Qatar) is a monarchy in which the assembly has very limited powers. The three countries with gender-balanced assemblies (Rwanda, Andorra, and Cuba) are small or tiny, and Rwanda and Cuba are ruled by their (male) autocratic presidents. In democracies with more than 100,000 residents, women's participation in the national legislature ranges from 10 percent in Brazil to 45 percent in Sweden (Inter-Parliamentary Union, 2014).

More than a third of the world's countries have had a female president, prime minister, or similar head of state in modern times. Their actual power has ranged from minimal (Nyam-Osoryn Tuyaa was acting prime minister of Mongolia for just eight days) to equal to that of any male politician (Germany's Chancellor Angela Merkel has affected all of Europe). Most Asian female heads of state have been the wife, widow, or daughter of a previous male head of state. Indira Gandhi, for example, was both India's fourth prime minister and the daughter of its first.

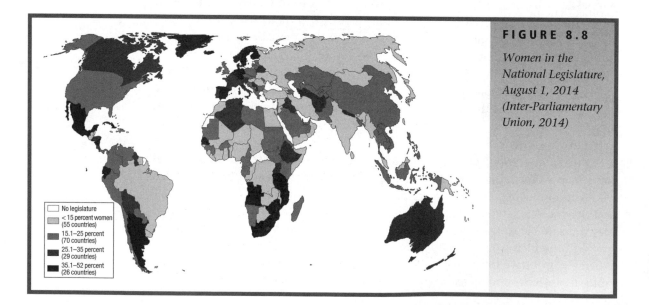

FIGURE 8.8

Women in the National Legislature, August 1, 2014 (Inter-Parliamentary Union, 2014)

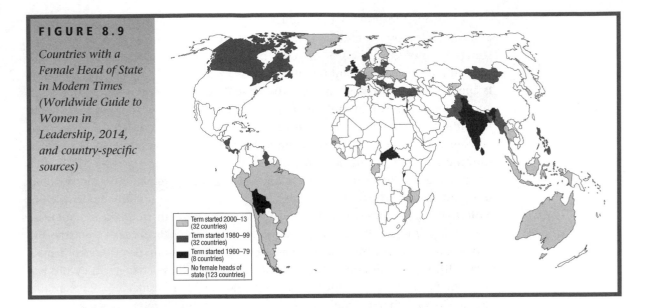

FIGURE 8.9

Countries with a Female Head of State in Modern Times (Worldwide Guide to Women in Leadership, 2014, and country-specific sources)

Term started 2000–13 (32 countries)
Term started 1980–99 (32 countries)
Term started 1960–79 (8 countries)
No female heads of state (123 countries)

Such patterns reflect the importance of families in politics and can also help men. Indeed, Indira was succeeded by her son. Outside Asia, however, most female heads of state did not follow a male relative.

Some of the countries in which women have relatively high – though not equal – political participation are long-time democracies in which women gradually gained political power. Starting in the nineteenth century, feminist movements changed attitudes toward gender, won women's suffrage, and helped elect women to office. The percentage of female Members of Parliament (MPs) slowly increased, reflecting women's growing power not just in formal politics but also in families, workplaces, and civil society (Dahlerup, 2006). The countries in which women have the highest political participation also have unusually low levels of economic inequality, reflecting a generally egalitarian political and economic culture (CIA, 2014a).

Some of these gradual-process countries eventually instituted gender-quota systems that seek to guarantee women a certain share of legislative seats, but the results of these systems vary depending on the depth of public support. In France, for example, the law requires that 50 percent of the seats in most elections go to women. The law has such weak public support and enforcement mechanisms, however, that only 25 percent of French MPs are female (McCann, 2013; Inter-Parliamentary Union, 2014). Sweden, with 45 percent female MPs, has a voluntary quota system that political parties follow because of some combination of believing in gender equity and knowing they will be punished at the polls if they do not. Finland, with 43 percent women, has no official system promoting gender equity (QuotaProject, 2014).

The United States took the gradual path toward female political participation, and women's representation remains lower than in every European country except Hungary. As of 2015 the United States has never had a female president, though women have held important Cabinet positions such as Secretary of State. Congress is about 18 percent female, making the United States noticeably below the world average of 21 percent. Even if we look just at countries that have no official system for promoting women, almost half have a larger percentage of female MPs (Inter-Parliamentary Union, 2014). Their cultures, it seems, are more conducive to women running for and winning political office.

Most countries with a relatively high percentage of female MPs did not take the gradual path. Instead, they are young democracies or semi-democracies in which the male-dominated political leadership chose to dramatically increase women's political visibility sometime since 1990. These "fast-track" countries use gender quotas or seats reserved for women to enforce a certain percentage of female MPs. Although local feminist movements applauded these changes, they did not have the power to achieve them (Dahlerup, 2006). China's leadership, for example, decided in 2007 that its National People's Congress would be no less than 22 percent female, though it is widely understood that the Congress mostly rubber-stamps decisions made behind the scenes (QuotaProject, 2014; Bristow, 2009).

Politicians rarely give up power for no reason, of course. Many of these countries have experienced war or serious civil strife, and their leaders sought to quell inter-group tensions and prevent future political violence by promulgating democratic ideas of individualism and equal rights under the law. These values were extended to women because the leaders believed their countries' stability depended on promoting the principle of universal human rights. Women's presence in government came to be seen as an important symbolic statement of equality and inclusiveness (Dahlerup, 2006). South Africa's post-apartheid constitution, for example, is radically egalitarian and specifies that political and judicial bodies should "broadly reflect the gender composition of South Africa" (Constitution of the Republic of South Africa, 1996). Though the political parties' gender quotas are purely voluntary, about 40 percent of South Africa's MPs are women (Inter-Parliamentary Union, 2014).

Another factor is that many international donors, investors, and lenders make their assistance conditional, either implicitly or explicitly, on the promotion of good government practices and the empowerment of women. Gender quotas presumably cover both bases at once. Several Latin American countries have instituted gender quotas with little discussion and no pressure from women's organizations, apparently in response to such international norms (Paxton and Hughes, 2007: 184; Welborne, 2010).

Not everyone believes that quotas are an effective way to increase women's political power, as opposed to simple presence. Critics are concerned that political parties may nominate poorly qualified women who are overly dependent on their parties and reluctant to speak out. Quotas may also serve as a ceiling, rather than

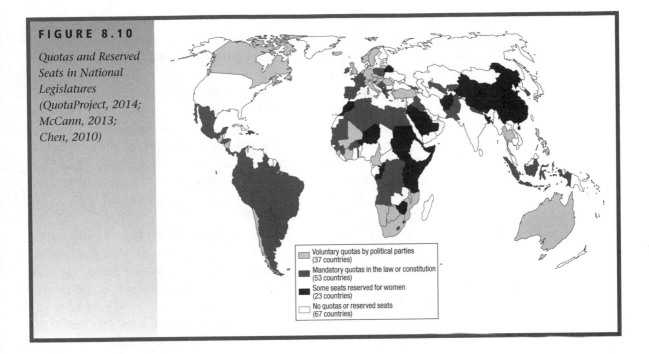

FIGURE 8.10

Quotas and Reserved Seats in National Legislatures (QuotaProject, 2014; McCann, 2013; Chen, 2010)

Voluntary quotas by political parties
(37 countries)

Mandatory quotas in the law or constitution
(53 countries)

Some seats reserved for women
(23 countries)

No quotas or reserved seats
(67 countries)

floor, on women's political participation. Supporters argue, however, that quotas are the most effective way to increase the number of women past a "token" level, that societies will benefit immediately from women's participation in decision-making, and that over time voters will recognize that women are performing well and elect more of them (McCann, 2013).

Studies suggest that the presence of female MPs usually has a limited impact on policy outcomes. In Rwanda, for example, female MPs have been able to introduce additional topics for discussion but rarely to enact legislation, though perhaps the symbolism of their presence will have long-term ripple effects (Devlin and Elgie, 2008; Burnet, 2008, 2012). Female MPs in Tanzania have raised a variety of issues of concern to women in their country, including discriminatory property laws and mild punishments for sexual offenders, but succeeded only when an issue served men's interests too. Beholden to political parties for their seats, they had weak connections with grassroots organizations and little real power (Meena, 2003). An international study concluded that female MPs had some success in developing more "gender sensitive" policies around domestic violence but otherwise had little policy impact, especially where grassroots women's organizations were weak (Waylen, 2007). Globally, most countries with more than 25 percent female MPs have also lifted all gender-specific legal restrictions on women, but six of the ten African countries that are over that threshold still limit women's property rights or other legal rights (Hallward-Driemeier, 2013a: 42).

In the United States, institutional contexts seem to affect office-holders' goals and accomplishments more than their gender. Both male and female mayors, for example, display such stereotypically feminine characteristics as being highly oriented toward relationships and caring about the quality of schools and other public services (Beck, 2001). Female and male legislators tend to express similar views regarding bills that are seen as benefiting women, but women may put more effort into enacting them – or may hold back for fear of being gender-stereotyped (Carroll, 2001; Thomas and Welch, 2001). Researchers can occasionally identify bills that succeeded because of women's gender-related political leadership, but these measures have wide support among men too (for example, guaranteeing that a new mother can stay in the hospital for 48 hours after childbirth) (Tolbert and Steuernagel, 2001).

One reason for women's limited policy impact may be a lack of critical mass, as various studies suggest that to affect legislation women need to hold at least 25, 30, or even 60 percent of legislative seats (Childs and Krook, 2008; Hallward-Driemeier, 2013a: 3; Sparks, 2014). Another issue is that differences within each gender outweigh differences between the genders. Although women generally support good public services, for example, women have been at the forefront of the Tea Party movement to cut public spending. Men are more likely to tell pollsters they support Tea Party goals, but women are more likely to organize and lead chapters (Skocpol and Williamson, 2012: 42–43). Conversely, many American men, including legislators, have embraced gender-egalitarian ideals, even if they do not always live up to them. Laws promoting gender equality are most likely to be enacted when strong organizations outside government can persuade (or scare) a majority of legislators, male as well as female, to vote for them.

The strongest evidence that having women in government can affect policy outcomes comes from India, which created a convenient experiment by randomly mandating that some villages, but not others, must elect women to head their village councils. The councils were previously all-male and even within families women were unaccustomed to making decisions on their own. Indeed, campaign literature typically featured the candidates' husbands, and many of the early women selected were illiterate or otherwise expected by the men of the village to be pliable. Nevertheless, these women did make a difference. The village budgets were fixed, and did not change, but women provided more public services for the same amount of money. They especially increased the services that women cared more about, such as clean water, but they also increased the services that men cared more about, such as improving roads. They were also less inclined to take bribes. Later, after these experiences, these villages were slightly more likely to elect women of their own free will (Chattopadhyay and Duflo, 2004; Banerjee and Duflo, 2011: 250–260).

One way to interpret these seemingly contradictory results is that women in rural India typically have so little voice in community decisions that putting a few women into political office makes a measurable difference. In Rwanda and the United States and other countries where gender inequality is less intense, however, women already have a political voice, so the effects of a little more voice may be statistically unidentifiable. Equally important, the political process in the United States is much more complicated than in a rural Indian village, so individual politicians have limited impact. Even the president is constrained in many ways, and a state legislator even more so.

The biggest impact of women in political office may thus be cultural. Female politicians may not act differently than male politicians. If they do act in subtly different ways, on average, those differences may not produce any legislative differences. But seeing women in government, or in high-level corporate offices, gradually erodes the age-old association between men, authority, and power.

CONCLUSION

Human relationships are the foundation of political power in all its many forms. In most traditional societies men's social and political relationships with other men supported their power within families and the economic realm. These networks enabled men to set and enforce rules for their families and communities. They also enabled some men to rule others, and often to create large inequalities between men of different classes, castes, races, and/or ethnicities. Some traditional societies gave women their own domains of power, which were usually grounded in women's shared cultivation of fields and/or the shared running of a market. The more women's work and social life was confined to their families, however, the less they were able to affect what happened in their communities.

For nearly 200 years some women have been working – intentionally or not – to increase women's social capital and political power. All around the world, women's groups have sought to improve their communities in a vast number of ways – from clean water to good schools, increasing incomes to ending violence. Numerous women have discovered that accomplishing their goals requires resisting restrictions placed on them as women: whether they can speak in public, own land, vote, enter professional careers, be listened to respectfully, win political office, and so on. Many women have balanced the desirability of working with men (and their sometimes much greater resources) on shared goals against the desirability of having spaces where women can listen to each other and define their own priorities without male interference. Today many men worldwide support women's empowerment because they have been convinced of the justice of egalitarian ideals, because they realize women's empowerment can benefit men and especially children too, or some combination thereof.

Develop Your Position

1 Are you persuaded that grassroots organizations are important for social capital and political power? What grassroots organizations have you observed directly? What have they accomplished? What are their limitations?

2 Which of the types of feminism we described above – liberal feminist, radical feminist, lesbian feminist, black feminist, multicultural feminist, class-conscious feminist and different voice feminist – is closest to your worldview? Why? Do you consider yourself a feminist? Why or why not?

3 Do you think countries should try to increase the number of women in elective office? Why or why not? What methods do you think would be effective in the United States?

4 Do you imagine that you might at some point run for political office yourself? Why or why not? If your biggest goal were to make your community or country a better place, what would you do? Do you think gender affects your answer?

CHAPTER 9

Religion and Gender Inequality

INTRODUCTION

Religion presents a paradox to people who are concerned about gender inequality. On the one hand, all of the world's largest religions preach and practice gender inequality. Their scriptures contain passages that indicate women are less valuable than men and should be subordinate to men in their families and communities. They have typically excluded women from certain religious rituals and forms of religious leadership, and they have often encouraged misogynistic beliefs and practices. The roots of these religions are thousands of years old, and they perpetuate long-traditional values and beliefs, including male dominance, into the modern age (Carter, 2014; Armstrong, 2014).

On the other hand, women are the majority of devout and committed religious practitioners in most societies. Women are more likely than men to say that religion is important to them and to participate in religious practices regularly, while men are more likely to have no religious affiliation or to celebrate only major holidays. In the United States this gender difference has existed since colonial days and can now be seen in every age cohort and most native-born demographic groups. It also exists in a large majority of countries around the world (Putnam and Campbell, 2010; Newport, 2012b).

This gender paradox is part of an even larger paradox. Throughout history, religions have reinforced many kinds of human hierarchies. Numerous kings and emperors have claimed to rule by right of divine favor. God has (people claimed) instructed people to kill others who do not share their religion, nationality, tribal affiliation, or political allegiance. God has mandated that slaves obey masters, the young obey the old, the poor obey the rich, and women obey men. God has required human sacrifices and infanticide. God has ordered the whipping of women who allow a stray bit of hair to show and the stoning of women who become pregnant outside marriage, even if by rape.

On the other hand, many movements for justice have been inspired and nurtured by religious messages about the inherent worth and equality of every

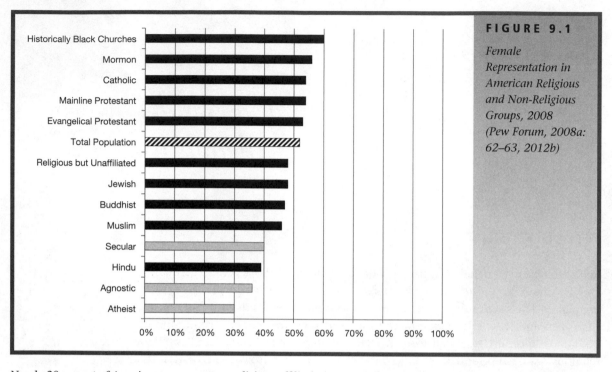

FIGURE 9.1

Female Representation in American Religious and Non-Religious Groups, 2008 (Pew Forum, 2008a: 62–63, 2012b)

Nearly 20 percent of American men report no religious affiliation, compared to 13 percent of women, and their numbers are growing rapidly. Men are a majority of American Buddhists, Hindus, Jews, and Muslims, but together these add up to less than 5 percent of the population. The big difference is in Christianity, as 82 percent of women but 74 percent of men describe themselves as Christian.

human being. God's promise of justice sustained Martin Luther King, Jr. when his home was bombed. God's unconditional love sustained Mohandas Gandhi when he nonviolently stood up to the British and fasted to quell inter-religious violence in his homeland – and when he sought to include women and the "untouchable" castes in the mainstream of Indian life. Religious faith has also inspired millions, probably billions, of people to serve others. Mother Teresa exemplified a life devoted to serving the poor, while on a smaller scale ordinary women and men around the world have lived their faith by practicing compassion. Religious faith has also given many people the strength to get through their days. Karl Marx famously called religion "the opiate of the masses," and many critics of religion have argued that it encourages people to accept their oppression rather than rising up against it. Others counter that physical and emotional survival are prerequisites for everything else, and that personal faith and religious communities have often aided both (Armstrong, 2009; Campbell, 2014).

Religious symbolism is often multilayered. Many generations of African American women, for example, wore elaborate church hats to worship services.

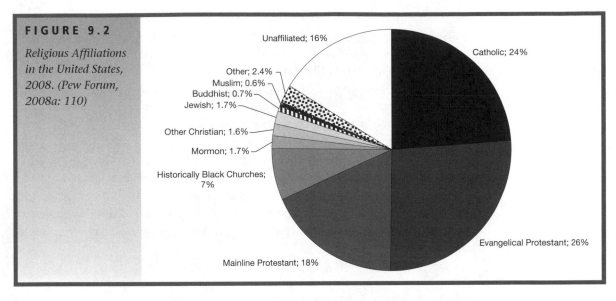

FIGURE 9.2

Religious Affiliations in the United States, 2008. (Pew Forum, 2008a: 110)

Unaffiliated; 16%

Other; 2.4%
Muslim; 0.6%
Buddhist; 0.7%
Jewish; 1.7%

Other Christian; 1.6%

Mormon; 1.7%

Historically Black Churches; 7%

Catholic; 24%

Evangelical Protestant; 26%

Mainline Protestant; 18%

More than three-quarters of Americans identify as Christian (solid colors in the chart above) and a sixth have no religious affiliation (white)

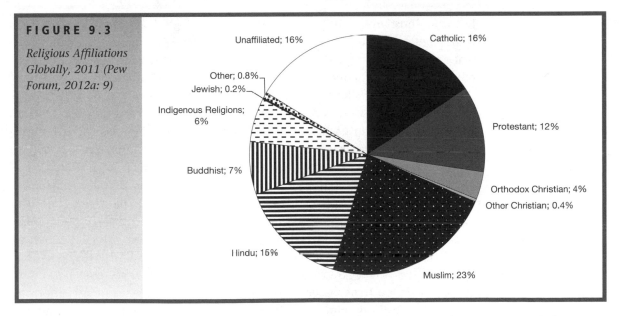

FIGURE 9.3

Religious Affiliations Globally, 2011 (Pew Forum, 2012a: 9)

Unaffiliated; 16%

Other; 0.8%
Jewish; 0.2%

Indigenous Religions; 6%

Buddhist; 7%

Hindu; 15%

Catholic; 16%

Protestant; 12%

Orthodox Christian; 4%
Other Christian; 0.4%

Muslim; 23%

Almost a third of people worldwide are Christian. Almost a quarter are Muslim, and another near quarter Hindu or Buddhist. A sixth have no religious affiliation. About 6 percent practice a religion indigenous to their area, a religion that is often but not always polytheistic.

One root of this tradition was a biblical passage that requires women to cover their heads. Another root was the pervasive degradation of African Americans, which made dressing up for church a statement of personal self-respect and collective dignity. Church hats, also called "crowns," were thus a symbol of both subordination and self-worth (Freedman, 2014; Collier-Thomas, 2010). In this and many other examples, the *meanings* people attach to a behavior are complex, even contradictory, but they are more important than the behavior itself.

This chapter will explore a variety of issues related to gender inequality and religion. It will start by examining two key theological issues that have been widely discussed by feminist critics of religion and feminist people of faith: gendered images of the divine and gender in the Bible. It will then explore how voice and leadership have been gendered in several influential American religious traditions, starting with the Puritans. It will then turn to gender and gender inequality in Islam, the second-largest religion worldwide.

GENDER AND THEOLOGY

The Gender of God

Judaism, Christianity, and Islam all trace their theological and historical roots back to the figure of Abraham in the Hebrew Bible, and a little more than half of the world's people identify with one of these Abrahamic religions. Although these religions have many differences, they share some core similarities. One of their most distinctive characteristics is monotheism: they teach that there is one God and only one God (although Christians teach that the one God has three aspects). Most of the rest of the world's religions are either polytheistic (they recognize multiple deities) or nontheistic (they do not focus on deities). Within Abrahamic religions, however, the nature of that one God is critically important.

Most but not all God-imagery in Abrahamic religions is coded masculine. Christians, Muslims, and Jews typically refer to God using masculine pronouns such as "He" and "Him." Two of the three elements of the Christian Trinity are distinctively masculine – the Father and the Son – while common titles like "Adonai" and "Lord" connote a masculine authority figure. Christian visual images of God are nearly always male. (Judaism and Islam strongly discourage such images, as they consider God too transcendent to be portrayed visually.) There are exceptions to this pattern. The Holy Spirit, for example, has been described as masculine, feminine, and neither, and Judaism and Islam likewise have feminine or neutral ways of referring to divine energy and presence. The large majority of God-language, however, implies that God is male.

Feminist theologians argue that gender-neutral God-language is more theologically sound on at least three grounds. First, the consistent use of masculine language implies that men are more God-like, valuable, and holy than women. Such language encourages men to over-estimate their own value and think of themselves as superior to women – and women to do the opposite. Gender-neutral language suggests instead that women and men are equally made in the image of God (Plaskow, 1979). Second, imagery that implies God is male blurs the difference between divine and human and contributes to the human tendency to invoke God to serve our own purposes. The issue here is the *pattern* of imagery. If people use a wide range of descriptions of God, human and transcendent, masculine and feminine, that diversity reminds hearers and speakers that all human attempts to understand the divine are partial and imperfect. If, however, people use just a few images, familiarity makes those images feel correct and others unacceptable. People can end up overconfident that they know God's nature and will – a behavior that in other contexts is called blasphemy (Ruether, 1983; Morton, 1985). Third, because human societies associate masculinity with authority and violence, masculine imagery for God makes it easy for humans, especially men, to invoke God to support their own use of authority and violence. Some feminist theologians argue that masculine God-language – especially hierarchical terms like "Lord" – therefore promotes not just gender inequality, but the whole pattern of using religion to reinforce human hierarchies (Starhawk, 1982).

It seems likely that many of the earliest human images of a divine Creator were female. Women's role in creating human beings is obvious to all, while men's role takes longer to figure out and is not self-evidentially essential. Numerous polytheistic religions have spoken of a divine Mother who gave birth to humanity and/or the physical world, with or without a male consort. Some feminists argue that the Abrahamic religions' exaltation of a deity separate from the world is the root cause not just of human hierarchies, but also of a human alienation from nature that allows environmental exploitation and degradation. They have sought to re-awaken polytheistic sensibilities as a way to re-infuse all of existence – female and male, human and not – with a sense of sacredness (Starhawk, 1982; Allen, 1986; McFague, 1987).

Some archeologists and theologians believe that until about 6,000 years ago Europeans worshiped a Great Goddess and lived in peaceful communities that were either gender-egalitarian or matriarchal. People of this era created stone figures with large breasts, buttocks, and pubic triangles, which may have been goddesses and/or fertility charms. Seeing the divine in female form, some argue, helped people live in harmony with the earth and each other (Stone, 1976; Gimbutas, 1982; Eisler, 1987). Other archeologists, however, believe that these conclusions about how people lived and thought go beyond the evidence. Appreciating sexualized female bodies, they argue, does not necessarily mean that ancient people worshiped a supreme Goddess or held women in high esteem. The presence of weapons and fortifications, and the high percentage of violent deaths in prehistoric archeological sites, belies the image of prehistoric societies as a peaceful Eden (Steinfels, 1990; Pinker, 2011: 49–50). A more cautious analysis suggests that most cultures started out recognizing a diversity of divine beings and unseen forces, female and male and neither (Armstrong, 1993: 3–78). Even in the Bible we can read about women baking cakes for the queen of heaven (Jeremiah 7:18).

The example of India shows that it is possible to both worship a goddess and denigrate women. Hinduism recognizes several goddesses as well as gods, and many Hindus engage in devotional practices centered on feminine images of the divine. As we have seen, however, India has a high level of male dominance. Indeed, some people attribute this gender inequality to Hindu teachings. The Hindu Code of Manu required all females to be under the control of men. Only sons were allowed to perform certain essential funeral rites for their parents and prayers for their ancestors, which is one of the reasons parents have long preferred sons (Hudson and den Boer, 2004: 72–75). The Hindu concept of *pativratya* taught that a woman's only route to divine favor was through utter devotion to her husband. Some communities took the idea that a woman has no life beyond her husband to its logical conclusion and

PHOTO 9.1

The goddess Durga is often portrayed as a warrior riding a tiger or lion. Images of divine female power did not, however, translate into high levels of power for Indian women (Source: Thinkstock)

expected a widow to join her husband's funeral pyre (Dhruvarajan, 1989). Other people argue that gender inequality in Hinduism has been overemphasized by Western observers and that Hinduism has always offered women a multitude of opportunities for satisfying religious lives (Leslie, 1991). Even if some women found strength and inspiration in feminine divinities, however, most social and familial power remained in the hands of men.

It is thus too simplistic to assume that the existence of feminine images of the divine equates to respect for actual women. It does seem likely, however, that overwhelmingly masculine imagery within monotheistic traditions reinforces male religious, social, and political power. The Abrahamic religions point to God as that which is ultimately valuable, true, and good. If God is also understood to be more like men than women, it makes sense that people would experience men as more valuable than women.

Gender in the Bible

The Abrahamic religions regard scripture as central to their faiths. This understanding of scripture is not shared by all other religions, but it gives scripture enormous cultural as well as religious influence. Much early feminist theological work focused on identifying and critiquing gender inequality in the Bible, which critics argued is one of the deep sources of American culture and therefore of American sexism. Other readers, however, asked whether the Bible might also contain resources that would help women and men of faith create a more egalitarian society – and whether such a society might actually be closer to God's intentions. In the last few decades similar work has been done with the Qur'an, but we will focus on the Bible here and return to the Qur'an later in this chapter.

The Bible clearly reflects a patrilineal society in which men were the heads of households and occupied nearly all leadership positions. The Ten Commandments, for example, construe women as men's property: "you shall not covet your neighbor's wife, or his manservant, or his maidservant, or his ox, or his ass, or anything else that is your neighbor's" (Exodus 20:17). Men chose their daughters' husbands and required virginity of women before marriage and monogamy afterwards, while men were free to have children with multiple women.

The Hebrew Scriptures frequently represent women as a source of impurity and danger. Menstruation and childbirth make a woman and everything she touches ritually unclean, and more so if she bears a daughter than a son (Leviticus 15:19–24; Leviticus 12). A bride who is not a virgin is to be stoned to death because she has brought shame to Israel (Deuteronomy 22:13–21). These texts also contain many stories of the rape, murder, and brutalization of women (Dinah, Tamar, Lot's daughters, Jephthah's daughter, the Levite's concubine, etc.). If we understand scripture as providing exemplary models of how to live, then violence against women seems to be part of God's intended order (Trible, 1984).

The Christian Bible endorses male authority in families and the church. Two passages, known as the "household codes," prescribe hierarchy in the household: husbands over wives, parents over children, and masters over slaves. Wives, children, and slaves are required to demonstrate their faithfulness to God through obedience to their superiors, while men are to think of themselves as like Christ and treat their subordinates kindly (Ephesians 5:22–6:9; Colossians 3:18–4:1). I Timothy states that no woman may teach or have authority over men (2:11–12). I Corinthians adds that women may not speak in a church (14:34–35) and makes explicit a cosmic hierarchy that places men above women:

> I want you to understand that the head of every man is Christ, the head of a woman is her husband, and the head of Christ is God . . . For if a woman will not veil herself then she should cut off her hair . . . For a man ought not to cover his head, since he is the image and glory of God; but woman is the glory of man. (For man was not made from woman, but woman from man. Neither was man created for woman, but woman for man.) (I Corinthians 11:3, 6–8)

Those who look for gender inequality in the Bible can thus easily find it. If they want to use the Bible to support male dominance today, they can quote applicable texts. If they want to dismiss the Bible as irredeemably sexist, that argument can be made. Other approaches are, however, possible.

For example, Jewish tradition encourages complex readings of biblical texts. Jews have endlessly interpreted and commented on biblical texts, and on biblical commentaries, and thus built up layers of meanings that are seen as complementary, not contradictory. Adding new interpretations is thoroughly in keeping with traditional Jewish approaches to scripture.

Take, for example, the familiar story of Adam and Eve. Over the centuries this story has often been interpreted to justify men's dominance over women. God created Adam first and then formed Eve from Adam's rib to be his helpmate. Men are therefore primary, while women are secondary and created for the good of men. Eve's tasting of the forbidden fruit shows her moral weakness, and thus that of all women. Men must therefore rule over women.

Other interpretations have, however, been suggested. If Eve was created from Adam's side, perhaps that indicates she was intended to be his equal. If Eve ate first from the tree of the knowledge of good and evil, perhaps that is a mythological retelling of women's key role in the domestication of plants and the creation of agriculture – which did make many people's lives harder, but also allowed much larger populations than were possible in the hunter-gatherer world of Eden. Eve's attraction to the tree of knowledge echoes many a goddess of wisdom. The book of Proverbs characterizes Wisdom as female, as do many other texts from the ancient world. A multitude of readings of this story are possible – some egalitarian, some justifying male dominance, some celebrating Eve's pursuit of knowledge, and many more (Kvam *et al.*, 2009).

Equally important, Jewish traditions do not assume that we are always supposed to see biblical figures as exemplary. Indeed, a recurrent theme is covenant made and covenant broken: the people fail to live up to God's expectations, are punished, and are then offered another chance. Perhaps the Bible's "texts of terror" – such as Lot offering his daughters to be gang-raped (Genesis 19:8) – are meant to teach that misogyny and violence are some of the many ways in which men have fallen from God's path (Trible, 1984).

The New Testament also includes multiple messages. Although it states that women must keep silent in the church, it also names a dozen women who hosted the original house churches, evangelized, discussed theology, or were described as a deaconess, an apostle, or "fellow workers" of Paul (Colossians 4:15; Acts 12:12, 16:40, 18:26; Romans 16:1–15; Philemon 1:2; Philippians 4:2–3). Clearly women were active in the leadership of the early church and respected for their gifts.

One key passage asserted that all people are equal: "There is neither Jew nor Greek, there is neither slave nor free, there is neither male nor female; for you are all one in Jesus Christ" (Galatians 3:28). Many people have interpreted this dictum as applying only on a spiritual level or in the afterlife, but others have embraced it as an egalitarian ideal toward which all Christians should strive. Some scholars believe the household codes and other hierarchical prescriptions were not part of the original writings but were added later, in a different generation, by men who were reacting against women's prominence in the early church and seeking to consolidate their own religious and familial authority (Fiorenza, 1979: 32–33).

The Gospels indicate that Jesus included women in his close circle of followers, sometimes over the objections of the men around him. His conversations with the sisters Mary and Martha show that he approved of women pursuing spiritual life (Luke 10:38–42). He was also deeply compassionate toward women. At one point his opponents brought before him a woman who had committed adultery and reminded him that the law of Moses required that she be stoned. Jesus replied, "Let him who is without sin among you be the first to throw a stone at her." The crowd edged uncomfortably away and Jesus told the woman that he did not condemn her (John 8:3–11). In *Jesus Was a Feminist* (2007), Leonard Swidler argued that Jesus consistently treated women as the equals of men, even when that meant violating the social customs of his time.

Women were more physically and spiritually present than men during Jesus's crucifixion and resurrection. A woman anointed Jesus with expensive oil during his last supper. When the (male) apostles protested the expense Jesus told them that she had prepared his body for burial and that wherever the gospel was preached this story would be told in her memory (Mark 14:3–9). In other words, it was a woman – not the apostles – who recognized the significance of Jesus's last meal. The Gospels agree that several women stayed near the cross during the crucifixion (Matthew 27:55, Mark 15:40–41, Luke 23:49, 55–56, John 19:25). They also agree that women first went to the tomb, saw that the stone had been rolled away, and encountered an angel and/or saw and spoke with the risen Christ. The apostles would not believe the women's accounts and took longer to comprehend the significance of what was happening (Matthew 28:1–10; Mark 16:1–11; Luke 24:1–12; John 20:1–18). Peter even denied that he even knew Jesus (Mark 14:68). Although the canonical Gospels are attributed to men, they suggest that Jesus's closest and most perceptive followers were women (Fiorenza, 1988).

A skeptical eye can raise many questions. For example, the Gospels say that Jesus selected only men to be apostles, which has often been used to argue that only men are allowed to be priests. But what about Junia, whom Paul described as an apostle (Romans 16:7)? What was the role of Mary Magdalene, who figures in so many stories and apparently was one of Jesus's most trusted followers? What more would we know of the woman whom Jesus said we would all remember for anointing (and truly recognizing) him if those who recorded the story had not all been men? What other stories about women did the compilers of the Gospels omit as uncomfortable or unimportant?

Many Jewish and Christian women have concluded that their desire for gender equality does not require them to forswear their faith and everything they value in it. God's revelations, they argue, have been experienced and interpreted within the context of human cultures, and those cultures have been male dominated. Men have often distorted religious traditions in order to support their own human desire for power. It would be more true to God's intentions to return to the scriptures, ask new questions of them, and re-interpret religious traditions with the faith that God intended good for all humanity, not just men (Fiorenza, 1984; Plaskow, 1991; Hunt and Neu, 2014).

GENDER, VOICE, AND LEADERSHIP IN U.S. RELIGIOUS COMMUNITIES

Whether women and men should have equal voice and visibility in religious communities is still a highly contested question. Every Abrahamic religion has had bans on women serving as clergy, an umbrella term that includes priests, pastors, ministers, imams, and rabbis. Many branches still do, and approximately half of religiously affiliated Americans today belong to communities that do not allow female clergy (Pew Forum, 2008a: 152). (Religious institutions are exempt from laws prohibiting gender discrimination when they hire staff to engage in religious activities, though not when hiring people for secular tasks, such as bookkeeping [Pew Research Center, 2011a].) Only 11 percent of American congregations were led by women in 2012, a proportion that has remained more or less stable since the 1990s (Masci, 2014).

Serving as clergy is not, however, the only way to exert religious leadership or to have a religious voice. Indeed, the role of clergy varies enormously in different traditions and times. Catholics have an ordained priesthood that claims a direct

TABLE 9.1		
Can Women Serve as Clergy in the United States? (2014)	Catholics	No
	Orthodox Christians	No
	Jews	
	Conservative and Reform	Yes
	Orthodox	No
	Muslims	No
	Protestants	
	Episcopalians	Yes
	United Church of Christ	Yes
	Baptist	
	Southern Baptist Convention	No
	American Baptist Church	Yes
	Lutherans	
	Evangelical Lutheran Church in America	Yes
	Missouri Synod Lutheran Church	No
	Methodists	
	United Methodist Church	Yes
	Primitive Methodists	No
	Presbyterians	
	Presbyterian Church (U.S.A.)	Yes
	Presbyterian Church of America	No
	Historically Black Churches	
	African Methodist Episcopal	Yes
	National Baptist Convention	Mostly no
	Founded in the nineteenth century United States	
	Latter Day Saints (Mormons)	No
	Seventh Day Adventists	No (under discussion)
	Christian Scientists	Yes

Sources: Masci, 2014; Braude, 1993: 61; Levy, 2003; Banks, 2013; Primitive Methodist Church, 2014.

lineage back to the apostle Peter and a unique ability to perform sacraments. Mormons recognize every adult male member as a priest. Muslims have no equivalent of ordination and require only that an imam be able to lead prayers, though the most respected imams are religious scholars. Most Protestants vest significant power and authority in lay leadership. Catholics, Orthodox, and Episcopalians have monastic orders of women as well as men.

ROLE	%
May be head clergy	58
May preach at main worship service	67
May hold all volunteer positions that a man might hold	76
May teach by herself a class with adult men in it	85
May be a full-fledged member of the main governing body	86

TABLE 9.2

Leadership Roles Allowed to Women in American Congregations (2012)

Note: Numbers represent the percentage of congregations answering "yes" (National Congregations Study, 2012).

Understanding the extent to which women have a voice in religious communities therefore requires examining both clergy and the broader texture of religious life. Some traditions assign specific religious responsibilities to women as a group, while others allow individual women to step forward into a variety of positions, formal and informal. The Abrahamic religions have been and still are male dominated, but that sweeping generalization deserves many qualifications.

Puritans

The Puritans believed that gender hierarchy is divinely ordained. People should, they argued, live exactly according to the Bible, stripping away everything else as unwarranted accretions. Preachers referred frequently to passages that instructed women to obey their husbands, be silent and submissive, and cover their heads as a mark of humility. The ideal woman, they taught, was meek, chaste, and very hard working. Although women were a majority of church members, they sat separately from the men, often in a gallery, and were not allowed to have any leadership roles either in the church or the larger community (Ulrich, 1982: 54). One of the few women who dared to express her own religious thinking, Anne Hutchinson, was excommunicated and banished from Massachusetts (LaPlante, 2005).

In the bigger picture, however, Puritanism decreased gender inequality in two important ways. First, Puritans believed that every individual should be able to read the Bible, so they taught girls to read at a time when the vast majority of women worldwide were illiterate. They even taught some girls to write their names and do arithmetic. They recognized that such skills would help a woman be more productive, and they considered economic prosperity a sign of God's favor. They thus set New England, and by extension the United States, on a path toward educating daughters as well as sons.

Second, Puritans placed real limits on men's power within families. Although they gave all formal authority to men, they also believed men were obligated to use that authority well and took seriously the New Testament injunctions that a husband should love and cherish his wife as Christ loved and cherished the church (e.g., Ephesians 5:25). Individual freedom was not a Puritan value. Because they believed God would punish an entire community if it tolerated sin in individuals, Puritans enforced ethical behavior as well as religious observance. Neighbors chastised men who were seen as lazy, imprudent, or not in control of their tempers. Preachers required men to confess and atone for behavior they considered physically or verbally abusive, and if the behavior persisted the magistrates ordered public punishment (Norton, 1996). Some men left Puritan settlements because they wanted more personal freedom, which was rarely an option for women without male assistance. Men who stayed, however, faced pervasive religious/social norms and strong sanctions if they broke those norms.

No such limitations existed in the southern colonies, which were officially Anglican but in reality mostly secular. Plantations were large, roads were scarce, and most people were not free to travel. Virginia in 1650 had one priest for every 3,239 people, and a century later there were only two churches in the entire colony of Georgia (Taylor, 2001: 179; Davis, 1977: 212). Most people lived and died without stepping foot into a church. Those few who did attend Sunday services – mostly white and relatively affluent – regularly heard that God had ordained the social hierarchies that placed male over female, white over black, and rich over poor (Heyrman, 1997: 11). Neither churches nor secular authorities sought to limit men's authority within the household, and southern men could do pretty much whatever they chose to their wives, children, servants, and slaves (Norton, 1996). In short, gender inequality was high in the Puritan colonies, but it was even higher in less-religious colonies.

Quakers

The Society of Friends, also known as Quakers, described God as an inner light or divine spark within every human being. In their meetings for worship they sat silently until and unless someone felt moved by the spirit to speak. Anyone could speak if so moved, and both men and women participated in meetings for business and might be recognized as elders. There were no ordained clergy, as Quakers taught that every individual is directly responsible for his or her own relationship with the divine.

Males and females sat separately during worship, so that they would not distract each other, but they typically occupied different sides of the meetinghouse rather than placing women behind or above the men. The largest meetings, such as the one in Philadelphia, eventually had separate meetinghouses for each gender, with women and men having separate meetings for business in which they conducted their own affairs as well as shared meetings for shared business. Quakers thus practically and symbolically placed the genders as equals – different, but neither superior to the other – and expected both genders to participate in the spiritual and practical leadership of their community. Although only men held political office, Quaker women expected to have a voice in community decisions.

Quakers were the dominant religious group in the early years of Pennsylvania, where they welcomed other people to their communities and guaranteed them freedom of thought and worship. By the time of the Revolution, therefore, Quakers had lost their political predominance. Though they were thereafter relatively small in numbers, their commitment to egalitarian ideals and personal witness gave them disproportionate cultural impact, especially in social reform movements. Quakers freed their own slaves by the 1780s and in 1783 petitioned Congress to end the "complicated evils" of slavery, 80 years before the Emancipation Proclamation. Many early advocates for women's rights were Quakers, including four of the five organizers of the 1848 Seneca Falls Convention. Quakers described all people as spiritual equals, asked individuals to listen carefully to the voice of conscience even when it contradicted prevailing customs or secular authorities, and expected talented women to provide leadership.

Early Evangelicals

By the middle of the eighteenth century, all of the colonies – soon to be states – had evangelical religious movements that emphasized the importance of personal conversion and an individual relationship with God. The Baptists, Methodists, Presbyterians, Separates, and New Lights had many differences, but they all taught the importance of a second birth that (ideally) transforms both individuals' relationships with God and how they live their lives. The most important part of religion, they argued, is not correct belief, but the individual's personal relationship with God.

Evangelical religions were relatively egalitarian by the standards of their time. All converts were expected to tell their spiritual stories and reflect publicly on the state of their souls. Although social norms generally barred women from speaking publicly before a mixed-sex audience, evangelical men and women listened with rapt attention when a new sister testified to the power of God working in her heart. Although white people generally assumed that black people had nothing worth saying, evangelicals celebrated God's divine grace even when it manifested itself within brown skin. Although young people were generally expected to defer to the experience and wisdom of their elders, evangelicals delighted in the spiritual prowess of "young gifts" in their teens and twenties. In no other corner of American society did the young, black, or female receive such a respectful hearing. Not surprisingly, disproportionate numbers of women, black people, and young people were drawn into the new churches (Heyrman, 1997: 41).

Anyone who showed a gift for eliciting conversions was encouraged to practice that skill. Black men could be preachers, deacons, and exhorters, and could even vote on church business, though they were not allowed to exert disciplinary authority over white members. Methodists intermittently tried to bar church members from holding or selling slaves, arguing that only God can have sovereignty over a human soul. Women were generally not permitted to preach or vote, but they could publicly pray, prophesy, and exhort – which could be quite difficult to distinguish from preaching. John Wesley, the founder of Methodism, endorsed women preaching locally, but not becoming itinerant ministers. Even literacy was not required, and some of the early preachers were quite eloquent even though they could not read the Bible (Heyrman, 1997: 15, 68, 116–154).

From the point of view of outsiders – especially white men who owned property – evangelicals could seem like radical levelers. Slave-owners, especially, did not appreciate the message that all people are equal in the eyes of God. A related issue was a deep conflict over ideals of masculinity. As we have seen, the southern colonies had developed a culture of honor in which each man was in charge of his household and fiercely independent. The evangelical churches, in contrast, taught that the ideal man was moral, pious, and self-controlled, and they expected all members to submit to church discipline. Church committees investigated reports of physical abuse and sexual impropriety, thus requiring men to account for how they treated other members of their families. Many property-owners ran itinerant preachers off their lands as quickly as they could (Heyrman, 1997: 206–252).

Over time, preachers began to make accommodations for local mores. In 1804 Methodists started to print two editions of their core book, the *Discipline*. The northern edition continued to denounce slavery and forbade members from buying or selling slaves, while the southern edition omitted those passages (Heyrman, 1997: 155). The Methodists, Baptists, and Presbyterians all split in the 1830s and 1840s, creating northern denominations that criticized slavery and southern denominations that embraced it. Southern evangelicals quoted the Bible: "Slaves, obey in everything those who are your earthly masters" (Colossians 3:22). Northern evangelicals could not find such explicit biblical passages criticizing slavery, but instead appealed to underlying principles of love and equality. Neither found the other's position acceptable. As the Civil War approached, both Southerners and Northerners fervently believed God was on their side (Chesebrough, 1991).

Everywhere, evangelical churches became more focused on increasing their institutional stability, enhancing the authority of the clergy, and recruiting men. The majority of the early converts were women, many of them young and/or black. Such members could provide neither social prestige nor stable financial support. As the churches sought to become respected American institutions, preachers saw attracting men, with their greater financial resources and social authority, as essential for their success. They expressed increasing concern that evangelical teachings might encourage too much self-confidence in women. Baptist women lost the right to exhort their congregations, Separates no longer appointed eldresses, and Methodist women were more firmly discouraged from preaching. Many churches also stopped investigating rumors of sinful acts committed on private property, instead affirming the right of patriarchs to rule their households as they saw fit. The same quest for status led white-dominated congregations to exclude black people, who formed their own congregations and denominations (Collier-Thomas, 2010). Although women remained a majority of church members and their obituaries chronicled their many contributions, the churches concentrated authority among men (Heyrman, 1997: 156–169, 206–252).

Nevertheless, evangelical churches continued to contribute to the erosion of gender inequality. Some evangelicals still believed that the principle that all people are equal in the eyes of God has social implications. The Seneca Falls women's rights convention, for example, took place in a Wesleyan Methodist chapel. More generally, people's experiences in freely gathered congregations led to the explosive growth of many other freely gathered associations – charitable societies, social reform groups, and so on. As we saw previously, these religious and secular voluntary associations empowered women, taught them important leadership skills, and drew them into informal and formal politics.

Roman Catholics

Roman Catholicism has undergone many changes during its nearly two millennia of history (Macy, 2007; Parker, 2008). By the time it arrived in North America religious leadership was centralized in three categories of celibate religious professionals. Only ordained priests could perform sacraments, including offering the Eucharist (understood to be the body and blood of Christ) during a Mass. Local priests were the first step in a Church hierarchy that culminated in the Pope, and until the 1960s it was unquestioned that all of them would be male. Both women and men, however, could participate in monastic orders. Male monks usually lived in communal settings, though the New World offered some adventurous monks and priests the opportunity to explore unfamiliar territory and seek to convert Native Americans. Female nuns lived cloistered lives focused on prayer, while sisters combined prayer with service to the needy, such as running a school or hospital. Both always lived with other women religious, but sisters necessarily interacted with lay people while nuns were secluded from most contact with the outside world. Lay people were encouraged to attend Mass, pray, and engage in other devotional practices, but they rarely had any voice in religious leadership.

The first sisters in the New World arrived in what is now Quebec City in 1639 and started a convent that educated Native and French children. These and later sisters' lives were full of contradictions. They promised and practiced obedience, yet as a group they had more autonomy than any other European or Euro-American women of their time. They worked within a hierarchy that preached male supremacy, while they created and ran important institutions. They enacted rituals of gender subordination, deferring to male priests, but they also created a women's world in which women made decisions that mattered, became highly learned by the standards of their time, and educated the next generation. They taught girls to be dutiful wives and mothers, while they themselves were unmarried and built lives focused on other women. Although only men could be priests, for children educated in Catholic schools religious authority often had a female face.

The Second Vatican Council (1962–1965) changed Catholicism in numerous ways. One of its goals was to narrow what many had come to see as an excessive distance between religious professionals and lay people. Priests were instructed to conduct the Mass in local languages rather than Latin and to face the congregation rather than the crucifix. Many priests experimented with worship elements intended to move the congregation emotionally, such as new styles of music and homilies. Monks and sisters were encouraged to update their habits or to wear secular clothes, as a symbol of being contemporary rather than medieval. Discipline within the orders was eased, as was discipline in Catholic schools.

Since then, far more men and women have left the priesthood and religious orders than entered them. In 2014 there were about 49,900 sisters in the United States (down 72 percent since 1965), 38,300 priests (down 35 percent), and 4,300 brothers (down 65 percent) (CARA, 2014). This dramatic decline in religious personnel, while the number of American Catholics continued to grow, placed serious strains on Catholic parishes, schools, and other institutions. By 2009 the average age of American priests was 63 (Gautier *et al.*, 2012). The number of priests being ordained each year began to increase around 2000, but it is still not large enough to replace priests who are dying or leaving the priesthood. The decline in women religious is even sharper, as there were 30,000 fewer sisters in 2014 than 2000 and their median age is over 75 (CARA, 2014; CICLSAL, 2014).

The reasons for these declines are many and disputed, but the Church's teachings about gender and sexuality are certainly among them. A majority – sometimes a large majority – of American Catholics disagree with the hierarchy's restrictive teachings about contraception, abortion, divorce, gay marriage, whether priests should be allowed to marry, and whether women should be ordained as priests (Univision, 2014). Catholic women born since 1962 are more likely than their male peers to disagree with the hierarchy's positions. Indeed, "millennial" Catholic women (born between 1981 and 1995) are more likely than Catholic men their age to never attend Mass – a striking exception to the general pattern that women tend to be more devout than men. Before the 1970s, when the feminist movement opened up many secular professional careers to women, becoming a sister could be a relatively attractive option for a Catholic woman with a talent for leadership. Today, however, women's options are more restricted within the Church than in the secular world (Wittberg, 2012).

A related question is how much sisters should be able to follow their own understanding of God's call. In 2008 the Vatican undertook an "Apostolic Visitation" to communities of women religious in the United States. A preliminary report in 2012 charged the Leadership Council of Women Religious, which represents a majority of American sisters, with discussing forbidden topics, such as women's ordination and ministry to homosexual people. The sisters, the Vatican argued, focused too much on social justice and not enough on the Church's teachings about sexuality, and they made statements that "disagree with or challenge positions taken

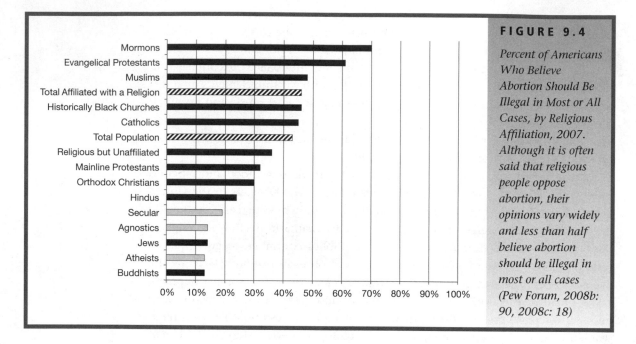

FIGURE 9.4

Percent of Americans Who Believe Abortion Should Be Illegal in Most or All Cases, by Religious Affiliation, 2007. Although it is often said that religious people oppose abortion, their opinions vary widely and less than half believe abortion should be illegal in most or all cases (Pew Forum, 2008b: 90, 2008c: 18)

by the Bishops, who are the Church's authentic teachers of faith and morals" (Congregation for the Doctrine of the Faith, 2012). Many observers felt that one of the fundamental issues here was whether the all-male and all-celibate bishops should have the sole authority to define "faith and morals." Some sisters dedicate themselves to what they consider moral causes, including ending the risk of nuclear war, advocating for acceptance of lesbians and gay men in the Church, and social programs that show compassion for people who are poor or struggling (Piazza, 2014; Campbell, 2014). Most American Catholic laypeople are more aligned with the sisters than the bishops: they approve of contraception and gay marriage and believe government should do more to help the poor (Newport, 2012a; Univision, 2014; Pew Forum, 2008b: 92, 102). The final report from the Vatican was broadly positive about the activities of American sisters, while acknowledging the need for more "respectful and fruitful dialogue" between women religious and male clergy (CICLSAL, 2014).

The Church has responded to the growing egalitarianism of American Catholics and the paucity of priests by opening up to females many roles that used to be reserved for males. Girls may now be altar servers (formerly known as altar boys), while women may read scripture during Mass or assist in the distribution of communion. Both intentionally and by force of circumstance the Church has greatly expanded the voice and influence of lay people. Many of those lay people are women, some of whom hold positions of real power and responsibility. The Church has recently created a new category of lay professional (i.e., paid) ministers, who may not perform sacraments but regularly do pastoral counselling, teach, prepare sacraments, and engage in many other aspects of ministry. Approximately 80 percent of lay professional ministers are women. Their numbers grew rapidly until about 2005, but much more slowly since then, and several training programs have recently closed (CARA, 2014; Wittberg, 2012).

The Church continues to insist that gender is a theologically significant category. Most religious authorities are now careful to avoid traditional arguments about women's inferiority and impurity, but instead argue that God intended men and women to be different but equally important. Pope Francis, for example, has praised women's distinctive moral strength, sensitivity, and intuition. He expressed appreciation for women's increasing public responsibilities while also emphasizing their "irreplaceable role in the family" (Pope Francis, 2014).

Although 45 percent of Catholics worldwide approve of women's ordination, the hierarchy considers discussions of female ordination unacceptable (Univision, 2014). In 1994 Pope John Paul II declared that the Church has no authority to ordain women since Jesus chose only men as apostles, a position that is now axiomatic to Church teaching on the issue (Novak, 1993; Butler, 2007). Indeed, Pope Francis excommunicated a priest for advocating women's ordination just a few months after he ascended to the papacy (Roewe, 2013). Some theologians argue that it should be possible to ordain women as deacons, though that practice was eliminated more than 800 years ago (Macy *et al.*, 2012; Zagano, 2012). Some women who consider themselves loyal Catholics have sought training and ordination through the Womenpriest movement (Roman Catholic Womenpriests, 2014). It seems likely, however, that the hierarchy will refuse to consider any form of female ordination for the foreseeable future.

Jews

Judaism has not had a priestly class since the fall of the Second Temple in CE 70. Instead, traditional Judaism expected all adults to engage in numerous gender-specific religious rituals. Women ideally kept a kosher kitchen daily, lit the Sabbath candles weekly, observed a variety of prohibitions during menstruation and purified themselves in a ritual bath (the *mikvah*) monthly, and conducted a yearly cycle of holidays that included special foods and other home-based rituals. These religious practices infused family life with spiritual meaning. Men, meanwhile, ideally devoted themselves to religious study, scholarship, and prayer, both alone and with other men. Because only men had the obligation to read the Torah and pray, only men counted toward a *minyan* (the ten men required to recite certain prayers). Women could voluntarily attend public prayers (though some believed entering a synagogue was forbidden during menstruation), but they sat in a separate section and their presence did not lessen men's gender-specific obligations. A rabbi was honored as a teacher and scholar, but any man could lead prayers. In short, both women and men were expected to be religious leaders within their separate domains.

In the United States, many Jews ended up living in religiously mixed communities, which undermined the old patterns. When Jews were segregated, by choice or discrimination, the entire neighborhood participated in the ritual rhythms that wove religion into everyday life. In mixed neighborhoods, however, most Jews let go of many of the home-based and women-led rituals – kosher meals and *mikvah* baths, Sabbath rests and a full calendar of holidays. As these rituals faded, both religious practice and the religious instruction of children became more centered in synagogues.

The traditional definition of synagogues as a male space became more problematic when they were no longer balanced by an abundance of women-led religious rituals, and many Jews came to see the exclusion of women from public religious practices as anachronistic. Reform synagogues began to replace the separate women's gallery with "family pews" in the 1850s, and women soon became a majority of those attending services. In 1922 Rabbi Mordecai Kaplan, the founder of Reconstructionist Judaism, conducted the first public American *bat mitzvah* – the female equivalent of a *bar mitzvah*, the coming-of-age ceremony that indicates a Jewish male is old enough and educated enough to understand the Torah. The first American female rabbi was ordained 50 years later (Goldman, 2014).

Today, Reform and Reconstructionist congregations have embraced the principle of gender equality, though like other Americans they are not always perfectly egalitarian in practice. Conservative congregations are also largely gender egalitarian, though they are more likely to make some exceptions. These communities have reinterpreted Jewish religious law to allow women to engage in practices that were traditionally reserved for men, such as publicly reading the Torah and leading prayers, wearing ritual garments such as *tallit* and *tefillin*, and serving as a rabbi or cantor. *Bat mitzvah* celebrations are now common, and some families conduct naming ceremonies for newborn daughters that are similar to the male *brit* but do not include circumcision. Home-based rituals are harder to study than synagogue-based rituals, but it seems likely that they too are more gender-egalitarian than in the past, though women probably still do most of the cooking. Some women have even resuscitated the old *mikvah* baths, reinterpreting them not as a symbol of monthly defilement but as an opportunity for spiritually connecting with other women and the rhythms of one's own body. Despite traditional teachings that marrying and raising children are religious obligations, 92 percent of Reform Jews and 80 percent of Conservative Jews now say homosexuality should be socially accepted (Pew Research Center, 2013d: 101).

Orthodox Jews reject all of these reinterpretations. They believe religious law is unchanging, that women's voices should not be heard during public worship, and that both women and men should continue their gender-specific religious practices. Most try to live in communities that support these practices: where men can walk to synagogue on the Sabbath, women have a *mikvah* bathhouse, and community norms support gender segregation and large families. About 30 percent

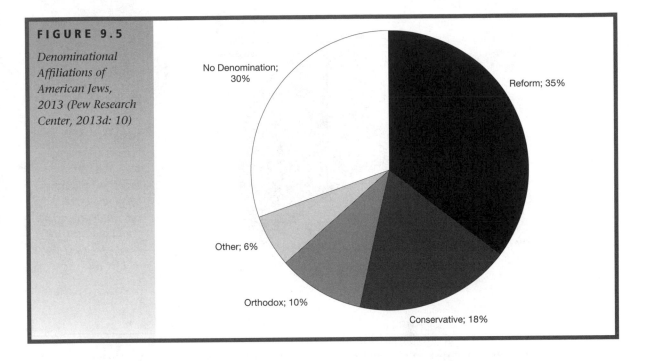

FIGURE 9.5

Denominational Affiliations of American Jews, 2013 (Pew Research Center, 2013d: 10)

No Denomination; 30%

Reform; 35%

Other; 6%

Orthodox; 10%

Conservative; 18%

of Jews in New York City are ultra-Orthodox. Their "modesty committees" enforce traditional female dress codes and require women sit in separate sections at the back of buses (Lipka, 2014; Berger, 2013a, 2013b). Such disputes are much more heated in Israel, where the ultra-Orthodox were 11 percent of the population in 2011 but their rabbis control marriage and family law. Police there may arrest women who engage in traditionally male rituals, such as wearing a prayer shawl or praying at the Western Wall of the Temple. Israeli Orthodox men may also insist on separate seating not just on buses, but also airplanes (Rudoren, 2013b; Sommer, 2014). The differences between different types of Judaism are thus enormous.

Muslims

Religious practices in traditional Islam were not as gender-patterned as those of traditional Judaism, as both genders were expected to engage in the five core religious rituals: prayer, fasting, charitable giving, the pilgrimage to Mecca, and the statement of faith. Only men, however, were urged to attend public prayers at a mosque and listen to sermons explicating religious texts. Women were expected to perform their prayers at home, interwoven with their domestic duties. They went to mosques not during the times of community prayer, but for private prayers and devotions (and not while menstruating). What some scholars call "women's Islam"

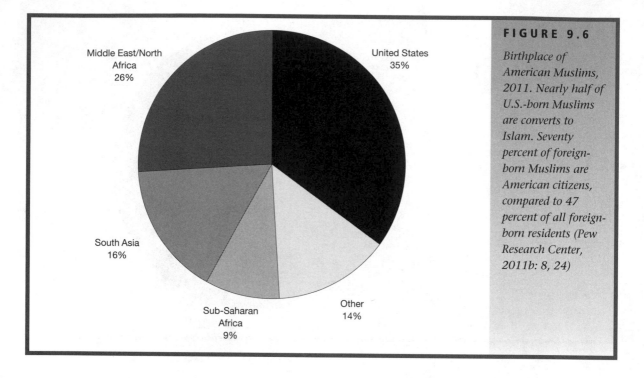

FIGURE 9.6

Birthplace of American Muslims, 2011. Nearly half of U.S.-born Muslims are converts to Islam. Seventy percent of foreign-born Muslims are American citizens, compared to 47 percent of all foreign-born residents (Pew Research Center, 2011b: 8, 24)

was thus grounded in oral traditions and daily practices. Women tended to consider Islam a way of living and being, a moral code and devotional practice. "Men's Islam" or "formal Islam," meanwhile, was more textually oriented and more controlled by scholars and clergy, though for many men too Islam was primarily a way of life (Ahmed, 1999: 120–133).

Like American Jews, American Muslims are discovering that living in religiously mixed neighborhoods makes mosques increasingly important as centers of religious and community life. Women have therefore begun to attend public prayers, though they do so less consistently than men. Men and women sometimes pray together in homes, but more than 90 percent of American Muslims agree that women should pray separately from men in mosques, with half believing they should be separated by a wall or curtain (Pew Research Center, 2011b: 26, 30). Muslim prayer is quite physical: it includes bending and prostrating, and worshippers are shoulder to shoulder in a tight line. Nearly all Muslims feel it would be indecent for women and men to come into contact during prayer or for a woman to lead public prayers and prostrate herself in front of men. Women do, however, hold a wide variety of other leadership positions in American mosques, and the continent's largest Muslim organization, the Islamic Society of North America, elected its first female president in 2006.

Many Muslim women and men are seeking to distinguish gender practices that are central to their religion from those that are cultural and can be changed. Although this is a worldwide conversation, it is particularly prominent in the United States. American mosques may include immigrants from all over the world, which makes it clear that there is not just one type of traditional Islam. Interacting with people from other backgrounds, both Muslim and not, generates new perspectives on what is core and what is peripheral to Islam (Rauf, 2005; Karim, 2009). Indeed, most American Muslims agree that there is more than one way to interpret Islam and that other religions can also lead to eternal life (Pew Research Center, 2011b: 28, 29). Like other Americans, American Muslims are increasingly embracing egalitarian ideals. They reject the stereotypes that Muslim women are always downtrodden and Muslim men are always domineering, and they object to the assumption that Muslim people are more sexist than others. But they also increasingly question gender inequality in their own communities and see male dominance as a cultural, not divine, practice (Abou El Fadl, 2005; Wadud, 2006; Ali-Karamali, 2008; Hammer, 2012; Mattu and Maznavi, 2014).

Modern Protestants

Reflections of the pre-Civil War split in American Protestantism are still visible today. Denominations rooted in formerly Confederate states are more likely than others to argue that the Bible should be read literally, to endorse gender hierarchies, and to be opposed to women's ordination. Southern Baptists, for example, teach that a wife should "submit herself graciously" to her husband and determined in 2000 that women should not serve as pastors, a provision that individual congregations are not obliged to follow but most do (Southern Baptist Convention, 2000; *New York Times*, 2000). Churches that forbid women's ordination typically point to biblical passages that prohibit women from teaching or speaking in church, arguing that God intends such instructions to apply to the modern world. They also cite passages requiring wives to obey husbands, though they rarely cite parallel passages requiring slaves to obey masters.

A few denominations, including Congregationalists and Universalists, ordained women in the nineteenth century, but female ordination was rare until the 1970s (Noble, 2001; Zikmund, 2003; Masci, 2014). Churches that ordain women argue that the Bible should be read in its historical and cultural context and that individual passages should be interpreted in the light of fundamental principles, such as love and justice. The United Methodist Church, for example, teaches that the heart of faith lies in scripture, tradition, personal experience, and reason, and no one source pre-empts the others. Although United Methodists acknowledge that some biblical verses prohibit women's ordination, they also recognize that several biblical practices (e.g., slavery, polygyny, and anti-Semitism) now seem morally and ethically objectionable. The Christian principle that all persons are equal in the eyes of God, they argue, calls believers to fully include women in every aspect of church life, including ministry (Gulley, 2014; McAnally, 2014).

About 20 percent of mainline Protestant churches are now led by female clergy (Banks, 2014). Female clergy tend to serve smaller congregations. Many are chaplains or assistant ministers, and they generally earn substantially less than male clergy. They also face a variety of less quantifiable challenges. Congregations often expect female clergy to be universally nurturing and have difficulties with their exerting legitimate authority, while women often face assumptions that they cannot be a "real minister." Many male ministers still have wives who devote themselves to volunteer work in the congregation. Although this "two for the price of one" arrangement has become less universal in recent years, congregations with a female minister may not be sure how to relate to a minister's husband with his own career. Some hiring committees also worry that female clergy will discourage men's attendance, a particular concern in denominations that are shrinking (Fiedler, 2010; Bolding, 2012; Smith, 2013; Park and Willhauck, 2013).

Many commentators have observed that there seems to be a "stained glass ceiling" excluding women from high-status pulpits. In 2006 the Episcopal Church elected Bishop Katharine Jeffers Schiori to its highest position, and in 2014 women were called to be the senior pastors of three of the country's most prominent churches. Some observers hope that this is a sign that mainline Protestants are finally becoming fully comfortable with women exerting religious authority, while others suggest that women are gaining such positions only because mainline Protestantism is shrinking in numbers and influence (Banerjee, 2006; Banks, 2014).

Although clergy play important roles in most Protestant churches, many congregations also have strong traditions of lay ministry and lay governance. Like female clergy, lay women can be disempowered by expectations that women must always be nice and must always take care of others. In many congregations today, however, women are not just a majority of members but also a majority of volunteers, and they make many of the decisions that shape the life of the congregation. They also do most religious education, and thus decide what children will be taught about their religious tradition. It is unusual nowadays to find a director of religious education who is male – or who is paid as much as clergy.

GENDER AND ISLAM

Gender in the Qur'an

Like the Bible, the Qur'an originated in a patrilineal society in which women were considered men's property. One verse describes women as men's fields and says a man may have sex with his wife whenever he wants, unless she is menstruating (2:222–223). Men may divorce their wives at will but a woman who wishes a divorce must go through a more complicated process (4:128, 4:35). One of the

Qur'an's most quoted verses requires women to obey men, but its precise meaning has been long disputed. Even native Arabic-speakers disagree over the meaning of several key words. One translation is:

> Men have authority over women because God has made the one superior to the other, and because they spend their wealth to maintain them. Good women are obedient. They guard their unseen parts because God has guarded them. As for those from whom you fear disobedience, admonish them and forsake them in beds apart, and beat them. Then if they obey you, take no further action against them. (Dawood, 1990: 4:34)

Some of the contested words here are "authority," "superior," and "beat." Indeed, some scholars argue that this passage was intended to limit men's behavior in a society where they had few such limitations (Abou El Fadl, 2005). Most readers, however, believe this passage allows husbands to use corporal punishment, at least in moderation (Fish, 2011: 106).

A good case can be made, however, that the Qur'an's theology is gender egalitarian. Several passages state that women and men are spiritual equals and emphasize that they have exactly the same religious duties (e.g. 33:35). The Qur'an's typical word for both "an individual" and "humanity" is *insan*, which is gender non-specific though it is often translated into English as "man." In its creation stories, women and men were created at the same time. Indeed, God created humanity as spouses "that you might live in peace with them, and planted love and kindness in your hearts" (30:21). Although the name Allah is grammatically masculine, the two ubiquitous descriptions of Allah, *ar-Rahman* and *ar-Rahim* (often translated as Compassionate and Merciful) both derive from the word for "womb" and have decidedly feminine connotations (Sells, 1999: 21, 37, 202).

Many teachings that are attributed to the Qur'an look different if one reads the actual passages. For example, the Qur'an prescribes identical punishment for men and women who commit adultery: a hundred lashes and afterwards they can marry only other adulterers (24:2–3). It was only after Muhammad's death that the Muslim community started stoning women for adultery – a punishment prescribed in the Bible, not the Qur'an (Deuteronomy, 22:20–24; Ansary, 2009: 50). Many communities punish women more severely or men not at all, though the Qur'an requires equal punishment. The Qur'an was also concerned about protecting women from false accusations. It required four witnesses to support adultery charges, while a person who made an unsupported accusation was to receive 80 lashes and barred from ever again giving testimony (24:4). Pakistan's Hudood Ordinance turned the intention of this verse on its head by requiring a woman who claimed she was raped to produce four male witnesses who agreed it was a rape, or be prosecuted for extramarital sex (Masood, 2006).

The Qur'an requires both men and women to be modest (24:30–31), but it does not say that women should cover their faces. Arab people of both genders traditionally used cloths to cover their heads, which is wise where the sun is intense, but the Qur'an makes only one reference to this practice and does not (unlike the Bible) connect it with female subordination.

The Qur'an also does not say that women should be segregated from men. In the seventh century elite families throughout the Mediterranean world commonly secluded their women. As Muhammad became prominent some of his male followers thought it inappropriate that his wives mingled and socialized with everyone. Muhammad defended their freedom, and he frequently talked with them and other women about religious and other matters. On at least two occasions he declined a dinner invitation unless his wife Aisha was invited too. Sometimes, though, hostile people sexually harassed his wives as a way to impugn his authority. One night, at a time of high stress in the community, Muhammad had a revelation that separated his wives from all others: "If you ask his [the Prophet's] wives for anything, speak to them from behind *hijab* [a curtain or screen]. This is more chaste for your hearts and their hearts. You must not speak ill of God's apostle, nor shall you ever wed his wives after him" (33:53–54). The Qur'an encouraged other widows to remarry once they knew whether they were pregnant, so this prohibition was intended only for Muhammad's wives (2:234). "Wives of the Prophet," it underlined, "you are not like other women" (33:32). In the centuries after Muhammad died, however, many Muslims began to apply these strictures to all women (Armstrong, 2006: 115–116, 148, 166–171; Ramadan, 2007: 118–121).

Many Muslims who have gender-egalitarian inclinations argue that the teachings of the Qur'an have been distorted by the sexist assumptions of its readers and interpreters, and that actually following the Qur'an would be much better for women. This is a safe argument to make within Islam. Muslim tradition considers the Qur'an authoritative, and there is a long history of critiquing current social practices by arguing that they are illicit deviations from the Qur'an. In addition, Muslim tradition has always taught that passages in the Qur'an should be understood in the context in which they were revealed. For more than a thousand years scholars have used *hadith*, stories about Muhammad's words and deeds, to interpret the intended meaning of various passages. When feminist women and men draw on *hadith* to contextualize verses, and call on contemporary Muslims to live up to the teachings of the Qur'an, they place themselves squarely within Muslim interpretive traditions (Wadud, 1999; Mattson, 2008; Hidayatullah, 2014).

Some Muslims go further. Kecia Ali, for example, argues that the Qur'an and *hadith* should be treated not as "repositories of regulations to be applied literally in all times and places" but as "sources of guidance for Muslims in transforming their societies in the direction of fairness and justice" (Ali, 2006: 156). Khaled Abou El Fadl argues that the Qur'an consistently endorsed, out of all the social arrangements that were imaginable in Arab culture of the time, the options that were most equitable and advantageous for women. It did not seek to revolutionize gender relations, but it dramatically improved women's lives. It banned female infanticide, gave women property rights and ownership of their dowries, guaranteed protections to wives, widows, and divorced women, allowed women to initiate divorce, required that women inherit half as much as their male kin (which was enormously better than the common practice of treating widows as part of their husband's estates), and repeatedly exhorted men to treat women with kindness. Being faithful to the Qur'an, Abou El Fadl concludes, means following its example by choosing the most equitable social arrangements that we can imagine in our own time and place (Abou El Fadl, 2005: 250–274).

Gender Inequality in Muslim-Majority Countries

Many Americans believe that there is a connection between Islam and gender inequality, and this belief has some grounding in reality. Muslim-majority countries tend to have more gender inequality than other countries by many possible metrics, and the difference persists even if one controls for socioeconomic variables, such as GDP per capita (Fish, 2011: 174–201). According to the United Nations, 43 percent of the 30 countries in which gender inequality is highest have Muslim majorities, while none of the 30 countries in which gender inequality is lowest have Muslim majorities. For comparison, 24 percent of all countries are majority Muslim (UNDP, 2014; Pew Forum, 2012a: 45–50). In most Muslim-majority countries between 75 and 95 percent of respondents tell pollsters that a woman must always obey her husband (Pew Forum, 2013b: 93).

Historical evidence indicates, however, that gender inequality was high in Muslim-majority areas long before Islam came into existence. Islam began in the Arabian Peninsula, which was at the center of an ancient band of civilization that stretched from Morocco through China. Surrounded by inhospitable oceans, deserts, mountains, and steppes, this ancient world was bound together by land-based trade routes along which ideas as well as material goods traveled (Ansary, 2009: 1–16). Islam, like Judaism and Christianity, started within a culture in which male supremacy was already well established (Ahmed, 1992: 9–38). As Figure 9.7 suggests, it spread out from its Arabic birthplace along pre-existing land and sea trade routes. Different areas were more or less amenable to conversion. Islam made little headway, for example, in the more populous areas of what is now China. Until China's Communist revolution, however, all of the countries rooted in these ancient civilizations retained high levels of gender inequality. The largest of the highly unequal countries – India – is predominantly Hindu, while 50 percent of the 30 countries in which gender inequality is highest have Christian majorities. The connection between religion and gender inequality is thus anything but simple.

Religions can be very effective at perpetuating traditions. When people believe that a practice is required by their religion, it is invested with an aura of sacredness or even inevitability – it is part of how the world is ordered. In addition, most forms of Islam, like many forms of Christianity, teach that there will be a day of judgment

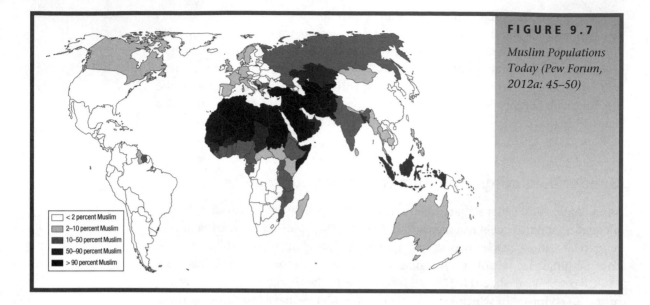

FIGURE 9.7

*Muslim Populations
Today (Pew Forum,
2012a: 45–50)*

Legend:
< 2 percent Muslim
2–10 percent Muslim
10–50 percent Muslim
50–90 percent Muslim
> 90 percent Muslim

after which good people will be rewarded for eternity and bad people will be punished for eternity. If one believes in such a religion, challenging religious authorities means risking an infinity of torment.

Some people conclude that decreasing gender inequality and improving the quality of women's lives requires secularization, greatly weakening or eliminating the role of religion in society. Since the nineteenth century, some Muslim reformers have pointed to European and American models of family and social life, as well as technology and law, as preferable to local traditions. Women, they argued, should be free to socialize with men, attend school and have professional careers, and wear Western-style clothes (Ansary, 2009: 247–268).

Several twentieth-century rulers aggressively pursued agendas of women's emancipation, universal education, technological advancement, and reducing the power of religious leaders, all of which they believed would help free their people from widespread poverty, illiteracy, and other ills. Most of these rulers, including Iran's Reza Shah Pahlavi and Egypt's Hosni Mubarak, were highly authoritarian and stayed in power only with the assistance of their militaries, secret police, prisons, and torture squads. They came from an elite class that was highly Westernized, often attending Western universities and sending their children to Western-style schools, and they embraced female emancipation in part because it helped them gain the support of the United States and European governments (Ansary, 2009: 269–316; Coleman, 2010: xii, 49–50, 248–250).

Secularization also helped them consolidate power. In the traditional Muslim empires, clergy and religious scholars served as a counterbalancing force to state authorities. Modern rulers resisted such restrictions on their power, so they sought to control the clergy and scholars. They confiscated the endowments that supported Cairo's ancient university, Al-Azhar, and several other centers of religious learning, thus ending a millennium of financial and intellectual independence (Feldman, 2008; Abou El Fadl, 2005: 35–37). The undermining of traditional religious scholarship and authority has, among other things, made room for the rise of more extremist forms of Islam (Armstrong, 2014).

Today some Muslim women and men, especially those who have lived in Western countries, believe that secularization is key to decreasing gender inequality. They face, however, an uphill battle. Based on their experiences with secular regimes, many less-elite Muslims consider secularization, authoritarianism, Westernization, feminism, gross economic inequality, abusive prisons, and feelings of cultural inferiority to be all part of a single package. Arguments that Islam should become less important because it is unfair to women therefore tend to be received poorly (Ahmed, 2011; Coleman, 2010: xxxi–xxxiii, 250–252).

Efforts to shift people's understanding of Islam have been more successful. Although schooling is becoming more widespread, many adults in poor countries still cannot read, or cannot read well. In addition, many have never been exposed to a translation of the Qur'an into their own language. If they only hear Arabic recitations, but do not know Arabic, they must must rely on other people to inform them about what the Qur'an says. Reformers can be very effective at changing opinions if they cite the Qur'an and come across as reasonably impartial (Coleman, 2010: 161–174).

For example, promoters of girls' schooling quote passages from the Qur'an that proclaim the importance of education for both sexes and *hadith* that describe Muhammad teaching women. Many local mullahs have become enthusiastic supporters of girls' education, sometimes allowing girls' classes to meet in the mosque if no school is available. Roughly 90 percent of men and women in Egypt, Yemen, Afghanistan, and several other countries now say that girls and boys should have equal access to education (Yacoobi, 2008; Yousafzai, 2014; Gallup, 2012a: 8; Coleman, 2010: xxiv).

Muslim women's groups have promoted access to family planning by citing the Quran's teachings about health and cleanliness (Coleman, 2010: 173). They have also countered long-traditional beliefs that Islam requires female genital cutting (though most Muslims do not practice FGC and the tradition pre-dates Islam) by pointing out that it has no basis in the Qur'an. Religious authorities in Egypt, Senegal, Sudan, and other countries have taken strong stands against FGC, declaring it un-Islamic and seeking to change the attitudes that support it. The prevalence of FGC is declining, though patchily (UNICEF, 2013: 67–73, 84–112; Ali, 2006: 97–111).

People working to end partner violence, rape, honor killings, and other forms of gendered violence emphasize the Qur'an's statements about women's rights and the importance of kindness (Koofi, 2012; Shadid, 2014). They also hold up the example of Muhammad, who is considered an exemplary figure whose behavior all Muslims should emulate. The *hadith* indicate that Muhammad universally treated women with kindness and respect, enjoyed conversation with his wives and other women, and was disgusted by men who beat women, though he apparently despaired of ending that practice (Ramadan, 2007: 211–213; Armstrong, 2006: 158).

The differences among Muslims today are wide and deep. Reza Aslan (2005) argues that Islam is now undergoing its own Reformation, as the spread of literacy and the Internet are proving as disruptive to the Muslim world as Gutenberg's invention of the printing press in 1450 was to Christendom. Protestant-Catholic violence continued through the twentieth century, though the worst of it was over by around 1700.

Differences of opinion about gender relations and the proper roles of women and men are now entwined with much larger disputes over theology, international relations, and the desirability of individualism. Many extremists know little about Muslim history or traditional theology, as most are poorly educated in both religious and secular terms. Most of the men who started the Taliban, for example, were war orphans (from the Soviet invasion of Afghanistan) who grew up in refugee camps in Pakistan. Like other traumatized children, many grew up to be violent adults. Their behavior says more about the legacy of war than the legacy of Islam (Armstrong, 2014). The traditional religious scholars, though steeped in a culture of male supremacy, have less misogynistic views and are more open to arguments based on the Qur'an. They struggle, however, to make their voices heard in the new competition for attention (Jacobson, 2013; Abou El Fadl, 2005).

Muslim women are almost as likely as Muslim men to want Islamic law, called *sharia*, to be either the only source of legislation in their countries or a primary (but not only) source of legislation (Gallup, 2012a: 12). By the late nineteenth century, Western colonizers had imposed their own legal systems throughout much of the Muslim world, so many Muslims see returning to *sharia* as a way to regain local autonomy and cultural self-respect. Many also believe that *sharia*, properly interpreted, is a better guarantor of personal and social justice than Western-style laws. Because of their history, they associate Western law with authoritarianism, economic inequality, and social injustice. Yet many Muslims have also embraced ideas about individualism, liberty, and equality that are more central to Western legal traditions than to *sharia* (Mufti, 2013). In many countries Muslims who believe that *sharia* should be the law of the land are more likely to embrace a variety of restrictions on women – but not in all countries (Pew Forum, 2013b: 99).

Muslims vary greatly in what they think *sharia* means and how they believe it should be applied. For example, the Qur'an specifies that men's share of any inheritance is to be twice the size of women's, on the grounds that only men are responsible for supporting their families. In about half of Muslim-majority countries, however, most Muslims believe that women and men should have equal inheritance

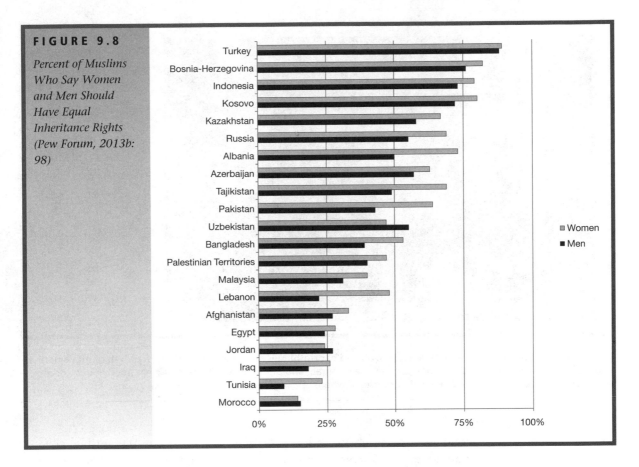

FIGURE 9.8

Percent of Muslims Who Say Women and Men Should Have Equal Inheritance Rights (Pew Forum, 2013b: 98)

rights, often on the grounds that women now share responsibility for family support. In most countries women are more likely than men to approve of equal inheritance, but even that is not a universal (Pew Forum, 2013b: 98; Alami, 2013). Muslims thus differ in how authoritative they consider one of the Quran's most unequivocal specifications of gender inequality. In a 2010 poll 71 percent of people in Muslim-majority countries said that women and men should have equal legal rights. This is significantly less than the 96 percent who agreed in countries with only small Muslim minorities, but still a significant majority (Pew Research Center, 2010).

Like African American women's church hats, Muslim women's head coverings have many simultaneous meanings. They probably started with the simple need to protect heads from the hot sun, but came to be associated with modesty codes intended to protect women's purity. By the 1960s many elite families saw them as a symbol of backwardness, as most elite women wore Western-style clothing that reflected their families' economic, political, and cultural affiliation with the West. Women in rural areas, like the poor and servant classes in cities, continued to wear

PHOTO 9.2

These two women in Aleppo, Syria, suggest some of the range of clothing styles worn by observant Muslim women today (Source: Thinkstock)

The woman on the left wears a modern-style hijab and her clothing is quite compatible with freedom of movement and visibility. The woman on the right wears an abaya, niqab, and black gloves, which make her anonymous and interfere with ordinary activities like eating or seeing where one is going.

traditional clothes – abayas in many Arab regions, burkas in Afghanistan, chadors in Iran, loose headscarves and salwar kameez further east. In the 1970s some prosperous women, usually college students, began to wear the hijab – a tightly wrapped headscarf – as a symbol of religious and cultural pride and cross-class solidarity (Ahmed, 2011).

Today, many women consider the hijab a religious obligation, even if their mothers or grandmothers went uncovered, and many also consider it a rejection of Western cultural and political domination. Some also view it as a rejection of what they consider the West's excessive sexualization of women, which they see frequently in Western media. Some women wear the hijab tactically as a symbol of piety that enables them to expand their freedoms in other ways, as a *hijabi* is much better positioned to invoke religious arguments in favor of her own, or other women's, schooling, employment, freedom of movement, freedom from violence, contraceptive use, and so on. In some places the hijab is no longer optional, as an uncovered woman faces intense social pressure and/or sexual harassment and assault. Women in the most violent places, however, generally wear an abaya or burka, which covers them more fully. The meaning of hijab thus varies greatly, but for some women it remains a symbol of collective pride and personal self-determination (Ahmed, 2011).

CONCLUSION

The world's largest religions are all rooted in ancient cultures that were strongly patrilineal and restrictive of women. Traditional religions provide many resources for those who seek to assert male supremacy in the modern world, and they have often been used to justify gender hierarchies, male control of women, and even violence. Traditional religions also, however, provide many resources for those who believe that the divine will is on the side of mutual compassion, justice, respect, and kindness – especially if practitioners focus on the often-repeated central themes of their religious heritage rather than turning individual verses from ancient texts into law. Many women and men draw on religion to create opportunities for joyful celebration with their families and communities, provide solace in times of grief, offer times of quiet and centering in the midst of daily cares, make their lives feel more meaningful, and remind them of what is truly important. Some also draw on religion to challenge gender inequality and other forms of inequality. They juxtapose religious teachings about what should be with society as it is, and call for change.

Develop Your Position

1 Many people who are trying to move their own religious traditions in a more egalitarian direction distinguish between religion and culture, arguing that male-dominated cultures have distorted religion. Do you think it is useful to distinguish between religion and culture? How would you make the distinction between religion and culture clear? Use one of the examples above to explain how distinguishing between religion and culture helps us understand people's experiences – or how it does not.

2 Do you think it is possible for a religion to be patriarchal and oppressive *and* for women to find that religion a source of comfort, community, and inspiration? Why or why not?

3 Some women try hard to stay inside their religious tradition and make it work for them, even when they recognize that their tradition is patriarchal. Other women instead choose to create new religious communities and traditions or leave organized religion altogether. How might you explain why different women make different choices about how to respond to sexism in their religious traditions?

CHAPTER 10

Displaying and Constructing Gender in the Media

INTRODUCTION

Media are forms of mass communication, including TV, movies, social media, books, advertisements, and even product packaging. For people in modern societies, media are an important source of information about the world. They shape our imaginations in ways both obvious and subtle, and they inform our sense of what is likely and possible in our own lives. Media can therefore be very effective at both reinforcing and challenging gendered norms.

Media are particularly important in the socialization of children. Young children develop their fundamental sense of gender identity from the ages of 3 to 5, and for most children this age the most formative influences are their families, other caretakers, peers, and media. A recent study found that children ages 2 to 4 spent an average of 1½ hours a day watching TV or DVDs, half an hour using computers or mobile devices, half an hour being read to, and 18 minutes listening to music (Common Sense Media, 2013: 15). Families vary greatly, of course, and any such statistics are only approximations, but it seems safe to say that media are a significant presence in the lives of most young Americans.

Media are also important for adolescents, who use media to learn about the world beyond their own families and communities. For many, media provide emotionally salient reference points as they figure out what is considered normal and how their own appearance, interests, and behavior measure up. And media affect adults as well, as American adults average more than 11 hours of media exposure a day (eMarketer, 2014).

This chapter will start by looking at how different media structures affect men's and women's access to those media. We will then go on to examine how **stereotypes** work both in people's psyches and in American media, and some of the ways in which media have changed in response to feminist critiques. These first three sections will focus on the United States, while in the final section we will look at some of the complicated ways in which media globalization has changed people's experiences of gender in other parts of the world.

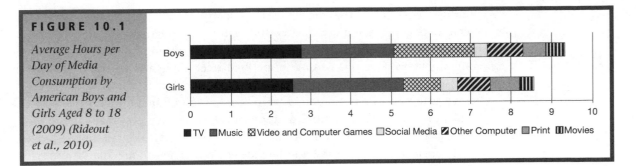

FIGURE 10.1

Average Hours per Day of Media Consumption by American Boys and Girls Aged 8 to 18 (2009) (Rideout et al., 2010)

Girls spent an average of 7.6 hours a day with media and boys an average of 7.9 hours. The totals above add up to more than that because of media multitasking.

GENDER, MEDIA ORGANIZATIONS, AND MEDIA ACCESS

As a general rule, men tend to predominate more in media that require more resources. For example, blogging requires only access to a computer, an Internet connection, and some skills that are easily and cheaply learned. American women and girls author more blogs than men and boys by a small but significant margin (Sysomos, 2010; Nielsen, 2012). Working on a TV show, on the other hand, requires not just expensive equipment but also professional contacts. In 2013 women were just 28 percent of the "behind the scenes" workforce at broadcast TV networks (WMC, 2014: 45).

At least three different types of resources are relevant here: money, skills, and social capital. Men have always been more likely to have the money required to fund a project, the social networks required to get funding from others, and the clout that comes from being a funder or potential funder. In the past, women were typically shut out of the educational and networking opportunities that would enable them to develop their skills. Nowadays they do not face such blunt exclusion, but they often encounter a pervasive pro-male favoritism. Men's ideas are often taken more seriously than those voiced by women, and men are generally offered more responsibility, visibility, and second chances after mistakes (Rivers and Barnett, 2013). Such factors may be particularly important in creative fields, where judgments about quality and significance can be quite subjective (Dargis, 2014). The larger the bureaucratic organization involved in media production, the more such everyday devaluing of women's contributions can accumulate over the course of a career.

Print Media

Until the twentieth century mass media meant printed media: books, newspapers, pamphlets, magazines, and so on. In the colonial period men owned nearly all printing presses, just as they did almost all property. Most publications were religious literature or government documents, and men had a monopoly on both genres. A few women, however, found their way into print by writing things that their male contemporaries were not writing. Anne Bradstreet published a book of poetry in 1650, and women also created a new literary genre known as "captivity narratives." Native groups sometimes captured white women or children either for ransom or to adopt into their communities, and some of these women eventually found their way back to the colonies and wrote about their experiences. Their narratives proved highly popular at the time and now provide us invaluable – though hardly unbiased – insights into both colonial and Native cultures (Derounian-Stodola, 1998). Later, as the revolution approached, a few women participated in the torrent of writing about politics, but most of the "founding fathers" were indeed fathers (Zagarri, 2015).

Printing presses became more affordable in the nineteenth century, which opened up new opportunities for female writers in both the commercial and "reform" press. With the invention of magazines and cheap books, and nearly universal female literacy in the north, commercial publishers were increasingly willing to take a risk on female authors. Many educated women found writing more attractive than the manual labor and personal subordination involved in most jobs open to women. Writing could be done at home, perhaps anonymously, so most people saw it as less indecent than occupations that required a woman to expose herself to the public eye. Women wrote about a fifth of best-selling novels in the nineteenth century – a remarkable percentage in an era when women had made only token inroads into other professions (Mott, 1947: 303–315). Harriet Beecher Stowe's *Uncle Tom's Cabin* (1852) was the best-selling book of the century, after the Bible, and galvanized the anti-slavery movement (Tompkins, 1985).

Equally important, small groups of reformers could now afford to purchase their own presses and publish materials that were too controversial for commercial publishers. Many, but not all, reformist men were willing to include talented and hard-working women in their ranks, and the first female journalists started by working for abolitionist and Transcendentalist newspapers (Marshall, 2005, 2013). Frederick Douglass's abolitionist journal even included a statement of gender equality in its masthead: "Right is of no sex – Truth is of no Color" (Emery and Emery, 1988: 153). After the Civil War, women started journals of their own to advocate for access to jobs, divorce, suffrage, and other women's rights. These journals helped activists share information, refine ideas and arguments, and build coalitions in a time when travel was difficult and expensive.

Men still reserved for themselves, however, the roles of critics and cultural arbiters. Many felt that women's writings could not be considered real literature and agreed with Nathaniel Hawthorne when he complained that America had been taken over by a "damned mob of scribbling women." In *How to Suppress Women's Writing* (1983), Joanna Russ surveyed the wide range of techniques that have been used to make it difficult for women to write, to deny that women wrote, to disparage the quality of their writing, and to make female authors seem anomalous or deviant.

Today, the gender balance of authors varies greatly by genre. Women write the large majority of romance novels, which are the best-selling genre of adult literature and read primarily by women (Romance Writers of America, 2013). Women also write most children's books and have received about 70 percent of all Newbery Awards, which have been awarded for outstanding children's literature since 1922. Illustrators of children's picture books, however, are more likely to be men, and men have received 59 percent of the Caldecott Medals or honors for outstanding illustrations (Association for Library Service to Children, 2014).

Male authors predominate in adult non-fiction and literary fiction. One study of 13 publishing houses found that only one came near gender parity and women were a quarter or fewer of the authors at eight (Franklin, 2011). Book reviews and book reviewers are if anything even more skewed. For example, men were 84 percent of both book reviewers and authors of books reviewed by the *New York Review of Books* in 2010 (VIDA, 2011). Women write about 40 percent of best-selling novels, which is substantially higher than their representation in book reviews (Hawes Publications, 2014). This discrepancy suggests that novels with little best-seller potential are more likely to be published and reviewed if they are authored by men. More than 80 percent of non-fiction best sellers are written by men, which is more in keeping with their representation in book reviews.

Two-thirds of the people in newspaper newsrooms are men, a proportion that has not changed since 1999. Although women are now 59 percent of journalism majors, they are only 38 percent of reporters. Female journalists most often report on lifestyle, culture, and health topics, while men predominate in reporting on

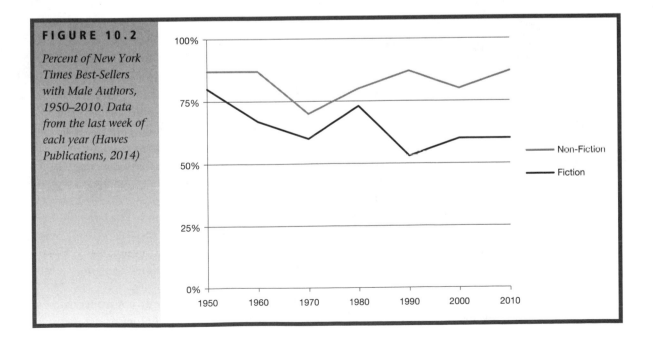

FIGURE 10.2

Percent of New York Times Best-Sellers with Male Authors, 1950–2010. Data from the last week of each year (Hawes Publications, 2014)

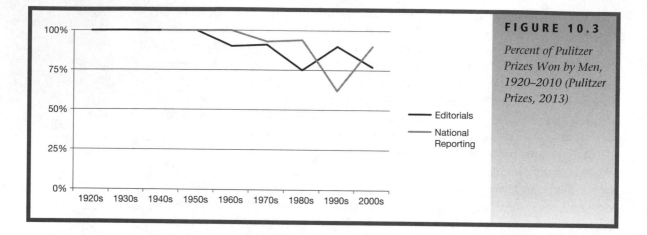

FIGURE 10.3

Percent of Pulitzer Prizes Won by Men, 1920–2010 (Pulitzer Prizes, 2013)

politics, sports, foreign policy, crime, and technology. Men are especially over-represented among sports reporters, three-quarters of whom are white men (who are just a third of the adult population). Only 27 percent of the widely read opinion columnists are women. Men are also much more likely to be quoted in news articles, with only 19 percent of *New York Times* articles including any quotes from women (WMC, 2014: 6, 19, 22, 24, 33; Carnevale *et al.*, 2011: 85). Women began to receive the highest accolades in journalism only after the second-wave feminist movement helped legitimate their presence in the workforce. Men won only 60 percent of the Pulitzer Prizes in national reporting in the 1990s, though that number returned to 90 percent in the 2000s.

Twentieth-Century Media

Early twentieth-century inventions opened up to ordinary Americans a breadth of sensory delights that had previously been unimaginable. Radios, movies, record players, and TVs provided visual and auditory pleasures. They also exposed people to a much bigger world than had previously been accessible. For the first time, ordinary people could see and hear New York, Chicago, or the Emerald City.

Women appeared as artists from the very beginning, but the vast majority of people employed in these new media were men. Most films included a female romantic lead or dancing beauties, and perhaps a mother or a maid, but men appeared in a much larger number and wider variety of roles. The film industry therefore employed many more actors than actresses (Lincoln and Allen, 2004). Some female vocalists found appreciative audiences, but female instrumentalists were rare and male singers generally more popular. Until the 1990s women sang only a fifth of Top-30 songs (Billboard, 2011).

Behind the scenes, all of these media were staffed and controlled almost exclusively by men during their golden ages. The new technology was expensive, and only men had the wealth to own a movie studio or record company. The vast majority of executives and managers were men, as were the vast majority of scriptwriters and songwriters, directors and producers, technicians and stagehands. For each actress who glowed with feminine beauty and sexuality, there were dozens of men who provided her clothing, applied her makeup, wrote her words, told her how to move, controlled the camera, and hired her in the first place.

Men continue to be over-represented in today's films. Men had 70 percent of the speaking parts in the 100 top-grossing films of 2013 – a proportion that has remained basically unchanged since the 1970s. Only 15 percent of films had stand-alone female protagonists, while 71 percent had stand-alone male protagonists and 14 percent had both male and female protagonists (WMC, 2014: 48–49).

Women are even more under-represented behind the scenes. Women were just 6 percent of directors in 2013's top 250 films. Of the 85 winners of the Best Director Oscar between 1929 and 2013, only one was a woman (Kathryn Bigelow for *The Hurt Locker* in 2010). Men are about 90 percent of film writers, 83 percent of film editors, and 97 percent of cinematographers. Men are also a majority of film critics – 78 percent on the popular website Rotten Tomatoes (WMC, 2014: 42, 44).

The situation is somewhat better on TV, but still far from equal. Women had 43 percent of primetime TV speaking roles in the 2012–2013 season, an historic high. Although 29 percent of TV news directors are now women, and all of the major networks have at least a third female anchors and correspondents, female reporters are typically assigned the "softer" news (such as human interest and health) while men usually report political and economic stories (WMC, 2014: 47, 26, 72; Desmond and Danilewicz, 2010). Three-quarters of the guests invited to speak about political issues are men. Behind the scenes, women are 23 percent of TV creators, including 30 percent of writers, 11 percent of directors, and 38 percent of producers. Shows with at least one female creator have more female characters in their casts, as they average 47 percent female characters, compared with 41 percent in shows where only men work behind the scenes (WMC, 2014: 30, 47).

Women in large media organizations face the same sorts of challenges as women working in other types of bureaucracies (Ferguson, 1984; Cantor and Cantor, 1992: 68–81). Advancing to a decision-making role in movie production, for example, typically requires many years of learning the ropes, cultivating relationships and the respect of important others, and negotiating workplace politics. Even if women are only slightly disadvantaged in each interaction, the cumulative effect of hundreds of small incidents each year make it less likely that women will be hired, promoted, and recognized for their work (Rivers and Barnett, 2013). In addition, many employers expect a level of time commitment that is not feasible for women who have family responsibilities: the "normal" career is actually a male career, with either the flexibility of a single man or a woman at home to take care of family needs (Acker, 1990). These characteristics are not unique to the media world, but they mean that most big-market media imagery continues to be generated and controlled predominantly by men.

Twenty-First Century Media

Computer-based media offer both unprecedented reach and unprecedented diversity. On the one hand, a globally popular creation, such as Psy's music video "Gangnam Style," may be seen by more than a billion people. On the other hand, the Internet has created what economists call a "long tail" market, in which it is possible to make a living by catering to the tastes of a small number of people who may be geographically scattered (C. Anderson, 2005). Even more people participate in amateur media production as they post films, short essays, or photographs to social media sites.

The creators of the new media structures are predominantly male. More than 80 percent of computer programmers and software designers are men (BLS, 2013c). The video game industry is particularly male dominated, as men are 84 percent of artists and animators, 89 percent of game designers, and 96 percent of audio developers (Matulef, 2013). Only about 14 percent of video game characters are female, and highly sexualized images of women are often used as "background decoration" or to titillate presumptively heterosexual male players (Downs and Smith, 2010; Sarkeesian, 2014).

Both women and men, however, use the new media in large numbers. Men are more likely than women to play computer games, for example, but 45 percent of gamers are female – though evidence suggests that some games appeal primarily to males or females (Entertainment Software Association, 2013: 3). Surveys consistently show that a majority of social media users are female, but 74 percent of women and 70 percent of men reported using social media in 2013 (Duggan, 2013). Most sites are more popular within one gender or the other, but the most popular appeal to large numbers of both genders: Facebook (58 percent female), YouTube (54 percent male), and Twitter (62 percent female) (McCandless, 2012).

These media enable both women and men to experiment with gender in a variety of ways. Game players, for example, usually construct masculine or feminine avatars, which may or may not match the gender they occupy in ordinary life. One

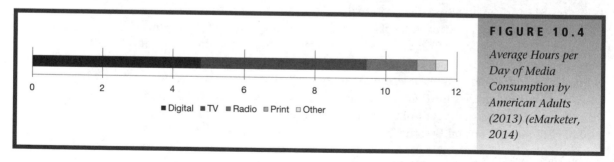

FIGURE 10.4

Average Hours per Day of Media Consumption by American Adults (2013) (eMarketer, 2014)

2013 was the first year that American adults spent more time with digital media than TV – not by much, but the trend is clear.

recent study found that 23 percent of male players and 7 percent of female players had played cross-gender avatars. Most men made their feminine avatars stereo-typically beautiful and more emotionally expressive than their masculine avatars – perhaps because they enjoyed looking at a female-shaped body as they played, but it is possible that men who play at being women may have their stereotypes con-founded as well as reinforced (Martey *et al.*, 2014). While girls and women are less likely to adopt a masculine identity online, they may use online personas to try out different ways of being feminine. Some adolescent girls, for example, use chat rooms and social media sites to experiment with being aggressive or sexually assertive in ways that might be more challenging or dangerous in an offline environment (Ringrose and Barajas, 2011).

In many cases, though, people who appear female online find that they become targets for aggressive behavior. When researchers set up fake accounts in chat rooms they found that female usernames were 25 times more likely to receive sexually explicit or threatening messages than male usernames (Hess, 2014). A study of teenagers found that 36 percent of girls and 23 percent of boys had personally experienced some form of cyber bullying, with the biggest difference that peers were more likely to spread unpleasant rumors about girls (Lenhart, 2007: 3).

Women who write about gender issues online risk receiving a torrent of harassing messages, including rape and death threats – sometimes with their home addresses highlighted. Men may also receive threats online, and 27 percent of the individuals who have reported threats to a volunteer organization called Working to Halt Online Abuse are male. When women are targeted, however, the language is often sexually explicit and virulently misogynistic (Hess, 2014). Women are more likely to receive mob attacks, with hundreds or thousands of people harassing them, or to be subjected to "revenge porn," the circulation of naked or suggestive photos as a threat or punishment (Citron, 2014). When Anita Sarkeesian, a gamer and journalist, released a Kickstarter-funded series of YouTube videos on the portrayal of women in video games, she received numerous graphic threats and eventually left her home in fear for her safety. Some female game designers have also received threats that were sufficiently violent and detailed that they felt it wise to go into hiding (Lewis, 2012; North, 2014; Suellentrop, 2014).

Some people suggest that the virulence of these attacks on female gamers reflects the decline of a gamer culture focused on young men. Game companies realize that girls and women are an expanding market and are diversifying their products, while some educators are using games to get girls into coding (North, 2014; Tiku, 2014). Some men, it seems, react fiercely against what they experience as a female incursion into a properly masculine world (Kimmel, 2013).

Many analysts point out that the diversity of the Internet makes it possible for people to surround themselves with news and opinion pieces that they agree with, which may be contributing to the political polarization of the United States (e.g., Miller, 2014c). Similar patterns occur around gender issues, with different subcultures of the Internet engaging in very different conversations. The Internet has enabled women to connect with and learn from each other, but it has also enabled men who are resentful of women to fuel each other's anger. This reaction can also transfer offline. One mass murderer justified his rampage by using misogynistic ideas he repeatedly read online – including that men are oppressed by women's unfair distribution of sexual favors and that men should get sex by isolating and intimidating women (Marcotte, 2014). Only a small minority of American men approve of misogynistic violence, either online or offline, but the Internet makes it easy for them to find each other and to reinforce each other's opinions.

The easy access and "long tail" of the new media thus have many gendered implications. On the one hand, both women and men, girls and boys, have more opportunities to express themselves than ever before. At their best the new media enable people to connect, learn, and try on different ways of being in the world. On the other hand, technology also makes it easy to harass and intimidate other people, and online behavior can have offline consequences. Both the inclusive and the exclusionary forces are powerful.

GENDERED STEREOTYPES IN THE MEDIA

The Power of Stereotypes

Stereotypes are "pictures in our heads" that we use to categorize and imagine other people. Although the content of our stereotypes comes from our culture, the tendency to categorize sensory input is hard-wired into our brains and necessary for navigating a complicated world. Indeed, stereotypes are often benign or helpful. When shopping, for example, you trustingly hand over your credit card to someone who triggers your stereotype of "salesclerk." Unfortunately, people also acquire stereotypes that are harmful, and most of us retain them even if we want to be non-sexist and non-racist.

One influential line of recent research has focused on **implicit stereotypes** – associations that affect our cognitive processes even though we are not consciously aware of them. Most Americans nowadays disavow blatant racist and sexist beliefs. If, however, a computer presents them with faces and words and asks them to create a specified pairing, nearly 75 percent of Americans are faster at pairing white faces with positive words and black faces with negative words than vice versa. This cognitive delay for the counter-stereotypical pairing occurs not just among many people who want to be non-racist, but also among many people who are black. Similarly, 75 percent of men and 80 percent of women find it easier to pair words related to men and work, and words related to women and family, than vice versa (Banaji and Greenwald, 2013: 47, 115). This deep association of *men = work* and *women = family* may encourage both men and women to unconsciously favor men in the workplace. It may also make women feel subtly uncomfortable with pursuing a career, or men feel subtly uncomfortable if they prioritize family life.

Other research has explored a phenomenon called **stereotype threat.** People handle challenges more poorly if they feel anxious about confirming an unfavorable stereotype about their group. For example, women who fill out a questionnaire related to gender before taking a difficult math test perform worse than women who fill out a neutral questionnaire. Watching commercials that contain stereotypical images of women has a similar effect. Racial stereotypes are similarly powerful. Stereotype threat was first identified among black students, but white men who are told, before taking a test, that Asian people tend to do better than white people show a marked decline in their scores. Being afraid of fulfilling a stereotype, it seems, makes people think about the stereotype rather than the challenge in front of them. It raises self-doubt, triggers rumination about whether those doubts are justified, and makes people excessively monitor their own performance as they try to suppress their anxiety. All of this can be seen in brain scans (Steele, 2010: 92–93, 124–125, 144).

These researchers argue that unconscious stereotypes may now be the most powerful driver of gender and racial inequality in the United States (Banaji and Greenwald, 2013: 157–167; Steele, 2010: 191–202). Although intentional discrimination was common in the not very distant past, Americans today rarely consciously and intentionally discriminate against others on the basis of race or gender. They tend to be uncomfortable, however, when interacting with people who are acting in gender-atypical ways or are of a different racial background. Understandably, people prefer to interact with people who do not make them uncomfortable. People also continue to be more likely to do favors for people who look like them, and over a lifetime those favors add up to substantially different outcomes.

Unconscious bias may even have lethal effects. In an experimental video game, participants were told to "shoot" armed targets and "not shoot" unarmed targets, all of whom were male. Participants more quickly and accurately decided to shoot an armed target if the target was black, and more quickly and accurately decided not to shoot if the unarmed target was white (Correll *et al.*, 2002).

It is possible to reduce unconscious stereotypes. Warm interactions with people from different groups, for example, can shift perceptions of both those other groups and one's own. Repeated exposure to counter-stereotypical individuals (female scientists, for example, or dads caring for their toddlers) can gradually create new associations that displace the older images, weaken implicit stereotypes, and make people less vulnerable to feeling judged by their group membership. Education about unconscious stereotypes also helps, as it enables people to reflect on their own responses and over time modify them. Some medical professionals, judges, and juries, for example, have been encouraged to self-monitor to offset their unconscious biases, with some success (Staats, 2014: 20–21; Banaji and Greenwald, 2013: 164).

By the time they are adults, however, people's cognitive processes are resilient, much like a rubber band that can stretch but easily returns to its original shape. Repressing biased thoughts can, ironically, make them more powerful, while exposure to stereotypical images reinforces unconscious associations. For most people, not acting in response to long-internalized stereotypes requires conscious intentionality, seeking out non-stereotypical experiences and imagery, and sometimes self-forgiveness (Staats, 2014: 20).

Gendered Images in the Media

Most media are full of stereotypical images that reinforce unconscious stereotypes. What matters is the *pattern* of images, not any one image in isolation. For example, when most of the media images of people in authority are male, those images reinforce an assumption that people in authority are naturally and appropriately male. If media images of authority figures were gender-balanced, the half that would still be male would no longer be stereotypical. Media are not, of course, our only source of stereotypes. Most authority figures are still male in the non-media world too, and many people can feel uncomfortable with a woman who uses authority in the same ways as a man in her position would. The media images, however, help stabilize the stereotype and maintain the status quo.

Media stereotypes often have a foot in real-world patterns. To feel realistic media need to have some connection with people's experiences, but then their use of stereotypes can distort viewers' sense of what is typical. As it has long been said, art imitates life – but life also imitates art.

For example, some gay men commonly use feminine-coded behaviors and styles that are called effeminate. Other gay men never use such patterns, while some use them in some contexts and not in others (at a party, for example, but not at work). If gay men in the media are usually effeminate, that is a stereotype. It is an easy way for media creators to signal that a character is gay, but it grossly over-simplifies life. In the absence of other input, a boy who is attracted to other boys may conclude that being gay necessarily means being effeminate. If, however, media regularly portray gay men with a wide variety of activities and styles, then the occasional portrayal of a gay man being playfully effeminate is simply part of exploring the diversity of human experience.

Similarly, many (but not all) women do sometimes enjoy making themselves attractive to men, but many media portray an abundance of young women who are scantily clad and have little purpose in the story other than to be attractive to men. Such media reinforce the stereotype that women are naturally sexual objects, and they encourage female viewers who want to be like celebrities to dress in sexually provocative ways. Just exploring themes of sexuality and attraction, however, is not necessarily stereotypical – depending on how it is done and how often media portray other aspects of women's lives.

Most people understand that many media images are fictional, and that profit motives often determine what appears in media products. Nevertheless, it is very difficult not to let what we see and hear shape our imaginations. Good media creations engross our attention and feel emotionally real, no matter how our brains may analyze them afterwards. Even mediocre media creations linger in our unconscious memories and help shape our assumptions about what is commonplace.

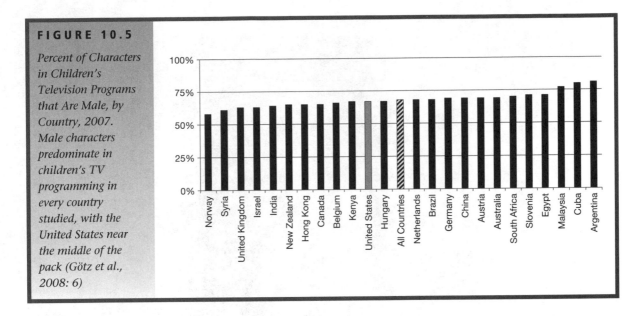

FIGURE 10.5

Percent of Characters in Children's Television Programs that Are Male, by Country, 2007. Male characters predominate in children's TV programming in every country studied, with the United States near the middle of the pack (Götz et al., 2008: 6)

Media scholars use a variety of techniques to study the content of media messages, collectively known as content analyses. One of their most consistent findings is that female characters are relatively scarce in most media (Collins, 2011). Female characters have hovered at about 30 percent of film roles and 40 percent of TV roles for decades. Most children's TV is even more unbalanced, with two male characters or more for every female (Smith *et al.*, 2013: 15). Critics argue that these consistent imbalances suggest to viewers that girls and women are less important, active, and interesting than boys and men.

Twentieth-century mass media tended to represent females in a relatively narrow range of roles. An extreme but telling example is the Smurf cartoons, in which dozens of male Smurfs exemplified various occupations and traits but for many years there was only one Smurfette. Most films and TV shows defined women by their relationships with men. Nearly all women were sweethearts, wives, mothers, ingénues, princesses, seductresses, or servants. They were usually young and beautiful, though some were old, ugly, and either evil or inconsequential. Even talented actresses found that their options were limited once they no longer glowed with youthfulness (Lincoln and Allen, 2004).

Men occupied a much wider range of roles – some based on their family and romantic lives, but many related to work, war, politics, or other activities deemed masculine. Romantic leads were typically tall, dark (hair, not skin), and handsome, which meant an angular jawline and muscular body. Movies and TV thus helped promulgate standards of masculine as well as feminine attractiveness. The media also contained, however, many other types of male characters, who displayed much of the diversity of human personalities, activities, and levels of attractiveness.

PHOTO 10.1

Like this young woman wearing an animal-print bikini to listen to music, black women are especially likely to be portrayed in highly sexualized ways that suggest they are animalistic (Gill, 2007: 79) (Source: Thinkstock)

"Generic" characters were nearly always male, while female characters were typically defined by their femaleness.

Race is embedded in these stereotypes. "Women" are stereotypically beautiful, delicate, gentle, faithful, in charge of their own homes, vaguely ineffective, and deserving of male protection. "Black women" are none of these things (Harris-Perry, 2011). Throughout the twentieth century women who were neither white nor black were rare in media, and most black female characters embodied one of three stereotypes. Many were shapely young females bursting with indiscriminate and animal-like sexuality (Bounds Littlefield, 2008). Others were ever-nurturing "mammies" – overweight, asexual women with large breasts who devoted themselves to serving white families. And others were brash, domineering, ugly, and inexplicably (for white viewers) angry. These recurrent images portrayed black women as foreign and unreadable "others" whose deeper motivations could not be understood (Collins, 1990: 67–90).

A recent study by *Essence* (a magazine aimed at black women) found that the image readers now encounter most frequently in the media is the "baby mama" – young and irresponsible – but most black women they know personally do not resemble this stereotype (WMC, 2014: 42–44; Walton, 2013). Indeed, many black women take on huge responsibilities for caring for other people, often in challenging environments with inadequate housing and schools and in the face of continual suspicion that they are "bad mothers" – another stereotype frequently applied to black women (Crenshaw, 2012).

Men of color have long had their own triptych of roles. Nineteenth-century blackface minstrel shows and twentieth-century radio and TV shows like "Amos and Andy" portrayed black men as buffoons: gullible and ineffective, but always cheery and ready for a laugh at themselves. Villains were often swarthy – African American, Mexican, Asian, Arab, or indeterminately dark. "Good" dark men, meanwhile, were typically butlers or sidekicks, whose quiet competence and asexuality lent dignity to their masters. The most famous Native American character remains Tonto, the nearly silent and always trustworthy companion to the white Lone Ranger. Here too gender stereotypes were normatively white: "men" were supposed to be muscular, dominant, and take-charge sorts who shaped the world around them, but dark-skinned men who displayed these characteristics were nearly always malevolent and dangerous anti-heroes.

The stereotype of dark men as criminal continues today, and both TV shows and news media provide distorted images of the connections between gender, race, and violence (Monk-Turner *et al.*, 2010). Although only 10 percent of violent crimes involve a black perpetrator and white victim, 42 percent of violent crimes reported on television have this profile. The large majority of homicides are intraracial and both the offender and the victim are usually male, but media coverage dwells on the relatively rare instances of black male perpetrators and white female victims. This is not just because media like unusual stories, as murders that are even more atypical – of white men by white women, for example – receive less coverage. Instead, media reinforce the trope of dangerous black men and vulnerable white women (Ghandnoosh, 2014: 22–23).

These stereotypes have significantly affected both public policy and individual behavior. The more white people associate crime with black people the more likely they are to support harsh punishments for criminals (Hetey and Eberhardt, 2014). The number of people in American prisons and jails has increased by more than 500 percent since 1980, and black people tend to experience harsher judgments at every stage of the criminal justice system. In 2012 black men were six times as likely as white men to be imprisoned, while black women were more than twice as likely as white women to be behind bars. Even preschools tend to punish black 4-year-olds more severely than white 4-year-olds (Alexander, 2010; Crenshaw, 2012; Sentencing Project, 2014; Powell, 2014).

It would perhaps be easy to conclude that mass media have always propagated sexist and racist stereotypes, but reality is more complicated. Even when they were nearly entirely run by white men, commercial media sometimes pushed at the boundaries of what was culturally acceptable. Katharine Hepburn, with her daring slacks and sharp banter, became a star in the 1940s because she was seen as more than just beautiful. Her film roles portrayed her as intelligent, articulate, and a woman to reckon with, and magazines let fans know that she was so in real life too. Aretha Franklin's compelling song, "Respect," provided a self-affirming image of black female power and topped the charts in 1967, while Sydney Poitier took the black male image of quiet competence into then-novel positions of authority, such as a physician treating white patients. More recently, news coverage of the killings of Trayvon Martin, Michael Brown, and Eric Garner raised awareness of black men as victims, not victimizers. Although production companies tend to be wary of too much controversy, they have learned that touching carefully on social issues can boost sales. Mass media with money behind them – and investors who want to turn a profit – are never radical, but they have exposed many Americans to images and possibilities they would not have encountered in their own communities.

On the whole, however, media have been a powerful force for propagating and reinforcing stereotypes. Today some media represent men and women in counter-stereotypical roles, but the familiar patterns are easy to fall into. In recent movies, for example, female characters are generally younger than male characters and are much less likely to be shown in leadership positions. Male characters are nearly twice as likely as female characters to be represented as having an occupation, even though women and men are now nearly equally likely to be in the workforce (WMC, 2014: 48–49; Smith and Choueiti, 2011; Smith *et al.*, 2013: 2).

One of the most ubiquitous stereotypes today is that women are willing sex objects. Female singers in music videos, for example, typically engage in sexual displays that include suggestive dancing, sultry looks, and sexual "self-touching." Music videos featuring black female artists are even more intensely sexual than those with white female artists (Turner, 2011). Male singers, in contrast, rarely display themselves as sexually available (Wallis, 2011). In the top 100 films of 2012, 29 percent of the actresses and 7 percent of the actors wore sexually revealing clothing, while actresses were three times as likely as actors to appear naked or partially naked. Hispanic actresses are particularly likely to be dressed provocatively. The percentage of teenage girls who are dressed seductively or appear at least partially naked on-screen has surged in recent years, and teens (aged 13 to 20) are now more likely than young women (aged 21 to 39) to be presented provocatively in films (WMC, 2014: 36, 40, 44).

Although white men continue to be portrayed in a wider variety of ways than other groups, they too can be affected by damaging stereotypes. One cluster of stereotypes represents young white men as lazy slackers who are emotionally clueless. Another cluster represents white men as super-competent and in charge – thus suggesting that any white man in real life who is not super-competent and in charge is a failure. Another cluster represents men of all colors as isolated individuals in a dangerous world whose best defense lies in their willingness to use violence.

Some critics suggest that media increasingly glamorize violent masculine stereotypes because traditional white male heterosexual authority is being challenged – and therefore share responsibility for mass shootings, gay bashings, and other forms of real-world violence (Katz, 1999; Kimmel, 2013).

Gendered Stories in the Media

Media also provide recurrent story lines that people use to understand the world and their own lives. Truly new stories are rare. Indeed, people often find truly new stories uncomfortable and do not like them. Most media creators understand the unspoken rules of their genre, and they seek to attract a large (and profitable) audience by offering intriguing details that attract interest while re-working familiar story lines. Audiences, in turn, use these deeply familiar stories to help frame and interpret their own experiences and options.

Many of these stories convey unspoken messages about gender. For example, media often tell the story of a woman who throws herself into a career or a cause until the right man comes along, at which point she gives up her work for love. We much less frequently are told stories about a man who gives up his work for love. Such stories convey messages about the appropriate life-paths for men and women that are no less powerful because they are often unconscious.

Perhaps the most common story is of a man and woman falling in love. Most people encounter this story thousands of times, which reinforces the image that it is natural and appropriate for men and women to fall in love with each other – rather than, say, fall in love with someone of their own gender, or devote their lives to God and good works (a popular story in earlier eras, but not in ours). This recurrent story informs readers and viewers about what is common, typical, and appropriate in heterosexual romances.

Media aimed at children often tell this story in terms of a princess being rescued by a prince, with whom she lives happily ever after. When frequently repeated, such stories subliminally teach girls that they are incapable of taking care of themselves and that they need a prince or other masculine savior to save them. They teach boys that females are weak and passive and that their own role in life is to protect women – and to tell them what to do. The first three Disney princesses, Snow White (1937), Cinderella (1950), and Aurora of *Sleeping Beauty* (1959), all depended on princes for their salvation. There were only three titular female characters in Caldecott Medal books of the 1950s and 1960s: *Madeline's Rescue* (Bemelmans, 1954), *Cinderella, or the Little Glass Slipper* (Brown, 1954), and *Sam, Bangs and Moonshine* (Ness, 1966). All three were rescued, though only Cinderella by a prince. This "damsel in distress" trope continues to be very common in video games, which often ask players to fight monsters and solve puzzles in pursuit of a passive female (Sarkeesian, 2013).

Romance novels are very popular among adult female readers. In 2012 Americans purchased twice as many romances as mysteries, and three times as many romances as classic literary fiction (Romance Writers of America, 2013). Janice

Radway did a content analysis of romance novels that many readers deemed satisfying (1984). Their narratives, she found, typically portray a heterosexual relationship in which the man initially seems distant, indifferent, or even cruel, but the woman (and the reader) later learns that these characteristics are really signs of his deeper caring and love. Their relationship undermines the heroine's previous social identity and reconstructs it in terms of a loving relationship with the hero, usually (except in Christian romance lines) after a passionate sexual affair.

Most romance readers, Radway pointed out, are women who, while increasingly in the workforce, still devote much of their lives to nurturing others while receiving little nurturing in return. Readers find escape in the novels – a treasured chance to take some quiet time for themselves and an affirmation that relationships are important. They also find a welcome reinterpretation of the indifference, anger, and perhaps cruelty that they experience in their own relationships with men, as the novels encourage them to see such behavior as signs as of an underlying attachment. Romance reading, Radway concluded, can be seen as a form of resistance to or compensation for the dissatisfactions that are common in women's lives. Romance heroes imaginatively supply the tenderness and attention that many wives no longer receive. The story lines assuage readers' fears of male dominance by presenting dominant males who, underneath it all, harbor tender feelings. Romances thus help readers reconcile themselves to their own less than satisfying relationships by learning to read male distance as a sign of male caring.

The Profitability of Gendered Images

Advertising aimed at children tends to be strongly gendered, with most toys and clothes clearly coded as being "for boys" or "for girls." Theorists suggest that children's products and their associated advertisements stimulate sales by raising children's anxieties about whether they are behaving in sufficiently gendered ways and promising to soothe these anxieties by the acquisition of appropriate toys and clothes. Young children are in a developmental phase in which they seek information about gender (and other things) and affirmation that they are performing gender (and other social roles) correctly. The intensity of their interest in gender reflects how salient gender is in the world around them. Toy stores offer girls makeup, fashion playthings, and princess costumes, while boys are offered vehicles, power toys, and superhero costumes. Girls' products are packaged in pink and sparkles, while boys' products are packaged in blue, other primary colors, or military camouflage. Ads aimed at girls depict them in a home or another indoor setting, while ads portraying boys are more likely to be set outside. In these and many other ways, advertisements and products teach children not just gender codes but also the underlying premise that gender is important (Cross, 1997: 231; Kahlenberg and Hein, 2010: 844).

Advertising aimed at adults, meanwhile, tends to emphasize the importance of gender-coded attractiveness. This pattern began in the early years of the twentieth century, when for the first time many Americans had some discretionary income. Before the 1910s, advertisements usually just stated the availability, price, and/or quality of a product. Since then, advertisers have sought to create and expand markets by evoking emotional associations and manipulating customers into sending discretionary dollars in their direction (Marchand, 1985).

One of the earliest common advertising hooks was to raise viewers' anxieties about their attractiveness in order to sell cosmetics, clothes, shoes, and an abundance of new personal care products, such as toothpaste and deodorant. You are not sufficiently beautiful, adverts suggested to young women; let us sell you something

PHOTO 10.2

Many ads, for everything from feminine hygiene products to cars, informed women that the best body type was slender, youthful, and tall (Source: Attic Paper, 1929)

that will help. Although many Americans had previously felt that too much concern with personal appearance was a sign of vanity, the new beauty culture urged young women to see themselves as artworks and to adorn themselves accordingly.

Ads and other media have long suggested that women should be slender and men should be muscular, but these standards have become more stringent over time. In the 1950s Marilyn Monroe was considered an ideal of feminine beauty, but her curves were quite curvy compared to modern models like Anne Hathaway or Kate Moss. In the 1950s the average *Playboy* centerfold or Miss America had a body mass index (BMI) of 20, which was not that much smaller than the average BMI for adult women of 22. By the 1990s, however, the "ideal" BMI had shrunk to 18 while actual women had grown substantially larger, with an average BMI of 26 (Spitzer *et al.*, 1999). *Playgirl* centerfolds, meanwhile, increased in size and muscularity, presumably reflecting a shift in ideal male body types. Men's actual body sizes also grew – though the actual bodies did so by gaining fat and the ideal ones by gaining muscle (Katz, 1999). John Wayne cut a dominating on-screen male figure in the 1950s, but his muscularity would be dwarfed by several of today's celebrities, such as Vin Diesel or Dwayne "The Rock" Johnson.

Today's advertisements often emphasize the importance of – and raise anxieties around – being sexually active. Many ads portray young women as willing sex objects and pose them in sexually suggestive ways. Such ads can be used to sell products both to men (who are implicitly promised sexual access to beautiful women) and to women (who are implicitly promised not just beauty but sexual freedom) (Mager and Helgeson, 2011: 248). Advertisements aimed at older adults, meanwhile, are full of suggestions that if they are losing their hair, skin tone, or sex drive they should try various cosmetics, medical treatments, or other remedies. Like advertising aimed at younger adults, these messages seek to sell products by raising viewers' uncertainties about their sexual desirability and whether they are doing gender and sexuality in the "right" ways. Since 1979 the film-maker Jean Kilbourne has released a series of films that document the ways ads encourage the objectification of women's bodies, erode women's self-esteem, and even legitimize physical abuse (Kilbourne, 2010).

Many other media, of course, also use gendered images and sexuality to make a profit. Numerous films, TV shows, and music videos rely on scantily clad female bodies to attract viewers, just as painters and sculptors have for centuries. Fashion magazines play upon girls' and women's desires to be attractive to men. Many comic books, movies, and video games celebrate hyper-masculine heroes who display feats of muscularity unattainable by ordinary men. When highly gendered images sell well, publishers are inclined to create more of them.

The Effects of Media Imagery

Many people find it intuitively plausible that media affect how people feel about gender. If, for example, one sees thousands of images of skinny white women who are presented as attractive, and few images of other sorts of beauty, it makes sense that one would come to feel that feminine beauty requires being skinny and white. Viewers who become dissatisfied with their own bodies may simply not enjoy life as much as they might, but they may also engage in practices that can be dangerous. As we have seen, young women and young men who are not white are especially likely to engage in excessive dieting or exercise (Austin *et al.*, 2008). Some women conclude that their natural bodies are unacceptable and seek surgical interventions. Not every individual, however, responds to media images in these ways. One recent study, for example, suggested that adolescent Hispanic girls were less vulnerable to feeling negative about their own appearance after seeing sexualized images of thin white women if they had a strong sense of ethnic identity (Schooler and Daniels, 2014). Proving precisely how media affect ideas and behaviors is thus quite complicated.

For example, studies have found that teenage girls are more likely to have negative body images if they frequently read fashion magazines or watch music videos (Tiggeman and McGill, 2004; Tiggeman and Slater, 2004). One easy interpretation is that unrealistic images of women make girls feel dissatisfied with their own bodies. Statisticians often point out, however, that "correlation doesn't prove causation." It is possible, for example, that girls with negative body images are more likely to read fashion magazines, as they are attracted by the magazines' messages of self-improvement. In other words, a negative self-image might be either the *effect* or the *cause* of media consumption – or possibly both, in a positive feedback loop. It is also possible that some third circumstance causes both results. For example, living with a mother who is obsessed with feminine standards of beauty might lead to both reading fashion magazines and a negative body image. The magazines would then be correlated with negative body images, but would not cause them. These "correlation studies," as sociologists call them, can thus be difficult to interpret.

Some researchers attempt to deal with these methodological problems by creating experiments, but these studies often have problems of their own. Lee *et al.* (2011), for instance, exposed male participants to scenes from TV crime dramas and found that men who viewed scenes of sexual violence expressed less support for traditional gender stereotypes than those who viewed other types of scenes. The TV viewing preceded the questions and it was unlikely that the two groups (randomly created) had something else that distinguished them. It would be nice to think that portraying sexual violence in a disapproving context might have a salutary effect on men's attitudes. As the researchers acknowledged, however, it is possible that participants guessed the purposes of the experiment and therefore gave what they considered socially acceptable answers (2011: 4). Other studies have found that watching TV violence desensitizes viewers and increases the potential for aggression (American Psychological Association, 2013). Since what we really care about is how people are affected by the millions of media images they see in their lives, studies that focus on exposure to a single image do not tell us much.

The most persuasive evidence that media can affect attitudes and behavior comes from studies of real-world experiences. MTV's *16 and Pregnant*, for example, is a popular reality show about the bumpy lives of teenage girls who get pregnant. The show premiered in 2009 and by the end of 2010 the areas of the country with highest viewership showed not just an increase in Google searches and tweets about birth control, but also a sizable reduction in teen births (Kearney and Levine, 2014). This study had a built-in time element: the show came first, the reduction in teen pregnancy came later. It also offered a mechanism: the increased interest in birth control. It thus provided highly plausible confirmation that media messages can affect viewers' behavior. Perhaps not coincidentally, *16 and Pregnant* was directed and produced by women (*16 and Pregnant*, 2014).

RESPONSES TO CRITIQUES

Since the 1960s feminists have criticized the ways women are excluded from media careers, the under-representation of female characters, and the stereotypical ways in which both females and males are portrayed. Some feminists also highlighted media distortions related to race, especially but not only the stereotypical representations of black women. Eventually feminists also critiqued the near invisibility of and disparaging stereotypes applied to lesbian women and gay men, though such issues were not yet on the table for most feminists in 1970. In 1985 the lesbian feminist cartoonist Alison Bechdel proposed what came to be known as the "Bechdel test." One of her characters would attend movies only if they met three criteria: (1) they have at least two women, (2) who talk with each other, (3) about something other than a man. Few movies passed the test (NPR, 2014; Hickey, 2014).

Feminists agitated for women to be hired as news anchors, talk show hosts, and other roles that had traditionally been reserved for men. They also created new audiences and markets for female musicians, film producers, and other creative artists. The price of media technology was beginning to fall, which made it possible for some women to go independent rather than relying on the big male-dominated houses for access. Feminist musicians, for example, created their own record labels, distributors, booking companies, venues, journals, and women's music festivals. *Ms. Magazine* created an essential forum for feminist writers. Even in the mainstream media female artists got more opportunities, support, and attention. Women have been much more likely to sing Top-30 songs since 1989 (Billboard, 2011).

Some feminists focused on children's media, which they considered key to creating the next generation's images of gender. Many pointed out that female characters in Disney movies displayed body shapes that were humanly impossible and set up girls to feel that their own bodies were inadequate. Others suggested that the hypermuscularity of superheroes prepares boys for similar feelings of inadequacy – which may lead them to over-exercise or use drugs to build up their own bodies, or to be overly aggressive in their interactions with others. Others focused on the

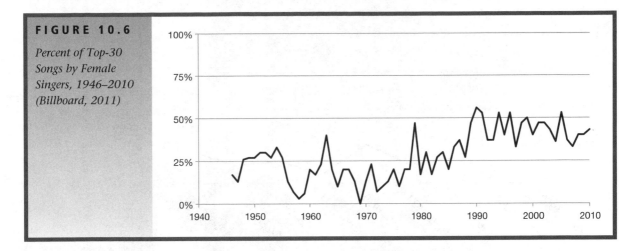

FIGURE 10.6

Percent of Top-30 Songs by Female Singers, 1946–2010 (Billboard, 2011)

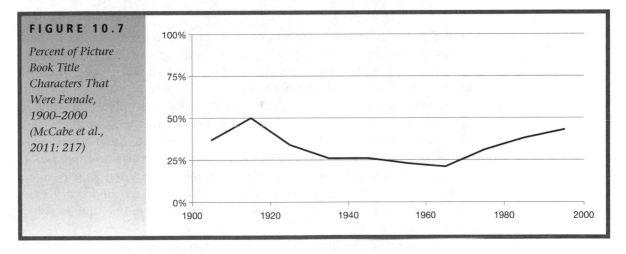

FIGURE 10.7

Percent of Picture Book Title Characters That Were Female, 1900–2000 (McCabe et al., 2011: 217)

ubiquitous plots in which girls/women/princesses are at risk until they are rescued by boys/men/princes. Others focused on school textbooks, which often suggested that men had done nearly everything of interest in the past or consistently used stereotypical gender images when presenting word problems in math. Others focused on children's books, which had many more male than female characters, or children's TV, which was even more imbalanced.

Some of the most significant changes occurred in children's literature. As the chart in Figure 10.7 shows, children's picture books were equally likely to feature female and male title characters in the 1910s. Female visibility plummeted, however, in the 1920s, which were a time of backlash against women's political and cultural power. In the 1950s and 1960s less than a quarter of title characters were female, and the female characters that did exist were usually depicted in stereotyped positions of dependence and/or domestic settings (Weitzman *et al.*, 1972).

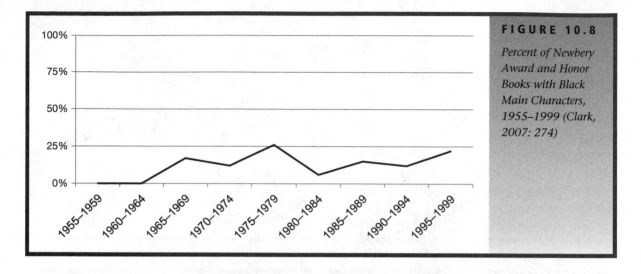

FIGURE 10.8

Percent of Newbery Award and Honor Books with Black Main Characters, 1955–1999 (Clark, 2007: 274)

The percentage of female characters began to rise as the second-wave feminist movement took off, and was beginning to approach equality by 1995 (McCabe *et al.*, 2011: 217). Subsequent studies indicated, however, that this progress plateaued during the first decade of the twenty-first century (Clark *et al.*, 2013).

The nimbleness of the children's book medium is underscored by its responsiveness to critiques growing out of the civil rights movement. In 1965 Nancy Larrick justifiably called children's books an "all-white world." Within just a few years, however, the percentage of black protagonists in award-winning books was fluctuating around the percentage of black people in the American population. The award-giving body, the American Library Association (ALA), undoubtedly gets some of the credit for this shift, but some is also due to the authors and publishers of children's books.

The content of children's books has also changed, as they increasingly tell stories that girls and boys, women and men, may use to frame their lives in non-traditional ways. Female protagonists have been far more active, creative, and independent in Caldecott honor books of recent decades than they were in the 1950s and 1960s. We find death-defying tightrope walkers in *Mirette on the High Wire* (McCully, 1992), and social activists like Rosa Parks in *Rosa* (Giovanni and Collier, 2005) and Harriet Tubman in *Moses: When Harriet Tubman Led Her People to Freedom* (Weatherford and Nelson, 2006). By the 1990s, female and male characters in award-winning books displayed similar levels of activity, independence, competitiveness, persistence, and creativity (Clark *et al.*, 1993, 2003).

In 1982 the ALA introduced the Coretta Scott King Award for picture books by black illustrators and children's books by black authors, and in 1996 it created the Pura Belpré Medal for Latino and Latina illustrators. These awards help guide minority children and their parents to stories about black and Latino/a characters. Like white women, black and Latino authors and illustrators are more likely than white men to depict female characters – often as a majority of their main characters – and their female characters generally do gender even less stereotypically than female characters in contemporary Caldecott books (Clark *et al.*, 1993, 2003, 2013).

When writing for older children, black women have been especially likely to address the topic of oppression. For example, Sharon Draper's 2006 *Copper Sun*, a King Award winner, follows a young enslaved adolescent character from the massacre of her family by slavers, to her rape by sailors on a slave ship, to work upon a southern plantation that includes submitting to the sexual predations of the plantation owner's teenage son. Nothing similar exists among recent Newbery Medal winners by white women. Black female authors are also much more likely than their white counterparts to show that oppression – and resistance – persists into the present day (Clark *et al.*, 2008).

Several factors help account for the relative flexibility of children's literature. The medium is relatively inexpensive, and a talented author or illustrator may submit a book to publishers without going through the years of training that are required in more bureaucratized media. Barriers to entry are thus relatively low. In addition, women are the majority of editors, publishers, librarians, judges, and reviewers of children's books (Sanderson and Wilson, 2014). The majority of non-institutional purchasers are almost certainly also women, as mothers and grandmothers typically choose books for the children in their care. Shifts in women's priorities are therefore reflected quickly in market forces, as well as in the sensibilities of writers and editors. When many mothers wanted non-stereotypical stories for their children, writers and publishers soon provided them.

Questions have been raised, however, about whether boys are being deterred from reading because children's literature is now so much shaped by women. Today's children's books, critics argue, are unlikely to contain elements that appeal to boys. Some teachers have observed that boys may become restless when reading a book with a female protagonist, while girls are generally fine with reading about boys. Some people attribute these patterns to boys' inherent natures, while others point out that most adults are more willing to support girls in stepping out of traditional female limitations than to support boys in taking on traditionally feminine (and lower-status) roles. Adults are more likely, for example, to give a little girl a truck than a little boy a Barbie. Girls thus learn that it is OK to do "boy things," at least in moderation, while parents and other adults convey discomfort with a boy's desire to do "girl things." Whatever the roots of these gender differences, the relative egalitarianism of children's literature has produced calls for schools to preferentially select books that boys (according to the stereotypes of boys) will enjoy (e.g., Sanderson and Wilson, 2014).

Other children's media have also changed in response to feminist critiques. The recent Disney princess films, for instance, portrayed multicultural princesses (Mulan, Pocahontas, and Tiana) pursuing war, diplomacy and business, even as they also engaged in more traditional romances. Although women's bodies still have impossible proportions, characters like Anna and Elsa in Disney's "Frozen" are anything but passive and inactive. The highest-grossing film of 2013, and the highest-grossing animated film of all time, "Frozen" turns the classic heterosexual romance on its head, as the sisters discover that their love for each other is the "true" love needed to release the spell. The prince, it turns out, is not to be trusted. Perhaps not coincidentally, the screenplay for "Frozen" was written by a woman (IMDB, 2014).

The Nickelodeon network, which is devoted to children's programming, has embraced both multiculturalism and "gender-neutral" programming as part of its brand. In 1991 Nickelodeon marketed "Clarissa Explains It All," a sitcom featuring a teen girl, as a break-out show that would attract boys as well as girls while affirming "girl power." As one of its executives explained, Nickelodeon seems to have a lot of female protagonists because it has a roughly equal number of female and male protagonists – and it has proven that boys will watch shows about girls. The network frames its non-stereotypical approach as a non-political way to attract all children as viewers. "We care less about gender in our programs and more about kids" (Banet-Weisner, 2007: 123–125; Sandler, 2004). Although Nickelodeon's programs are comparatively gender-neutral, they are surrounded by the standard gender-stereotypical toy advertisements (Kahlenberg and Hein, 2010).

Media aimed at adults have also changed, though more patchily. Less than half of the movies produced in the last 20 years have passed the Bechdel test – and the percentage doing so has not increased since 1995. Movies that pass the Bechdel test typically have smaller production budgets than those that do not, but offer a somewhat larger average return on investment. In other words, the industry seems to resist funding films that feature women, but such films tend to do well at the box office (Hickey, 2014).

TV also offers several examples of successful shows that challenged stereotypes. *The Oprah Winfrey Show* (1986 to 2011) became the highest rated talk show in history (King World, 2004). Intelligent, perceptive, and witty, Oprah undermined, on a daily basis, negative stereotypes about black women. More recently, TV shows have sympathetically portrayed lesbian women (*E.R.* in 1995), gay men (*Will and Grace* in 1998), bisexuals (*Sex and the City* in 1998), and transgendered characters (*Orange is the New Black* in 2013). TV shows did not include appealing LGBT characters until LGBT people had gained a certain amount of social acceptance, but these characters in turn increased social acceptance. Many of these progressive portrayals are thanks to the relatively few women who have made it into positions of power in TV studios. Jenji Kohan, for example, created *Orange is the New Black*, while Gail Mancuso won the 2013 Best Director Emmy for *Modern Family*, a comedy that portrays gay partners and their adopted daughter and an interracial marriage.

Individuals working in large organizations often find that it is difficult to change practices in the face of financial and cultural pressures. For example, most editors of magazines aimed at teenage girls are women. When asked about girls' critiques of the magazines' unrealistic images, especially with respect to body size, several editors expressed sympathy with their readers' concerns. They cited, however, pressure from other constituencies, including photographers, copywriters, and their corporate sponsors. They also argued that readers could and should read past the stereotypical images and reap benefits from the magazines' larger messages (Milkie, 2002). It is relatively easy to add the occasional article urging female empowerment. Much harder is keeping a magazine aimed at female readers afloat if one rejects advertising (often supported by associated articles) that sells products by raising readers' anxiety about their appearance.

MEDIA GLOBALIZATION AS AN AGENT OF CHANGE

Media globalization occurs in at least two different ways. First, long-established media are still expanding into some parts of the world. Some rural villages, for example, acquired electricity and TV just in the last 20 years, and some still do not have them. New local markets rarely have the finances to create their own programming, so they typically import shows from elsewhere. The arrival of TV and

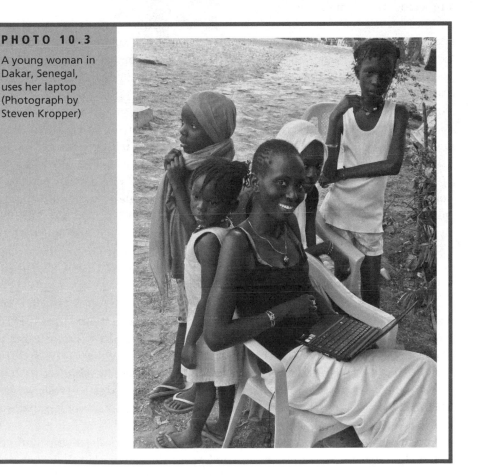

PHOTO 10.3

A young woman in Dakar, Senegal, uses her laptop (Photograph by Steven Kropper)

movies thus brings areas that have been relatively isolated more into the sphere of influence of larger cosmopolitan centers. Second, some newer technologies have rapidly spread around the world. Cellphones did not take off in the U.S. market until the 1990s, but by 2013 roughly 6 billion out of the world's 7 billion people had access to cellphones (far more than had access to toilets) (Rainie, 2013; UN News Centre, 2013). These more interactive technologies enable information to flow in multiple directions.

Homogenization

Some people argue that the fundamental effect of media globalization has been to create an increasingly homogenized global popular culture. Indeed, successful movies and TV shows may now be seen worldwide. "Frozen," for example, was released in China, Morocco, and Bangladesh less than three months after its U.S. premiere (IMDB, 2014). The gendered messages – and other messages – in global media now affect people around the world and give the media-making centers unprecedented cultural power.

Researchers have confirmed that the arrival of global media can change local ideas and practices related to gender. For example, Fiji, one of the world's least populous island nations, had no TV until the 1990s. Like people in other traditional societies accustomed to hard physical labor, Fijians considered plumpness attractive, especially on women. In wealthy countries calories are plentiful and many people do desk jobs, so thinness tends to be a sign of higher status, as it indicates access to the leisure required for careful food selection and exercise. In Fiji thinness was traditionally associated with hunger and privation, and telling someone she had "skinny legs" was an insult (Becker, 1995, 2004). Fijians saw ample curves as a sign of prosperity and social status, a welcome indicator that one did not need to be constantly engaged in the pursuit of food. Norms of female attractiveness changed quickly, however, after American TV programs arrived on Fiji's main island in 1995. By 1998, 74 percent of Fijian teen girls said they were "too big or fat" and, by 2007, 45 percent of them reported purging in the previous month to control their weight (*BBC News*, 1999; Ireland, 2009). They wanted, they explained, to look like the thin actresses in primetime dramas (Goode, 1999).

Like *16 and Pregnant* in the United States, the introduction of TV to Fiji allows a clear time-separation between the cause (watching American shows) and the effects (girls feeling they have to be thin to be attractive and developing eating disorders). Correlational studies from Egypt (Ford *et al.*, 1990), Japan (Kirjike *et al.*, 1998), Tonga (Craig *et al.*, 1999), Lebanon (Afifi-Soweid *et al.*, 2002), and India (Shroff *et al.*, 2004) similarly suggest that the spread of Western media has propagated Western ideals of attractiveness, and that these ideals are associated with eating disorders that were previously rare in non-Western societies.

Media globalization can also tap into long-standing local patterns and give them additional force. For example, a preference for lighter skin tones has been documented in numerous societies around the world. The origins of this wide-spread (but not universal) "colorism" – the preferential value and treatment given to people with lighter skin – are complicated but include at least two roots. First, sunlight darkens skin, so people who work outdoors tend to have darker skin than those who spend most of their time indoors. As we have noted, agricultural societies tend to have high levels of social inequality in many dimensions, with high-status people largely exempt from agricultural labor. Lighter skin can thus be a sign of higher status, especially among women in societies that prefer female seclusion and/or consider female agricultural work degrading. Many societies have long considered lighter-than-average skin a desirable trait in a marriage partner and have particularly associated lightness with female beauty and desirability (Aoki, 2002; Li *et al.*, 2008). Second, these preferences were reinforced in societies that were invaded and/or colonized by lighter-skinned people. European and American colonization was accompanied by, and often legitimized by, Euro-American ideas about race (Thompson and Keith, 2001; Parameswaran and Cardoza, 2009). Many scholars believe that the caste system in India originated with the arrival of lighter-skinned Aryans who dominated the native Dravidians and other indigenous peoples, though the historical roots of the caste system, and its connections with skin color, are complicated (Bhattacharya, 2012: 124–127). Although colorism is related to racism, it has its own distinctive dynamics and should not be conflated with racism (Glenn, 2009; Bhattacharya, 2012; Norwood, 2013; Russell-Cole *et al.*, 2013).

Although skin-lightening methods have been used in some societies for centuries, only in the modern era could they be turned into a mass market. International corporations have aggressively advertised skin-lightening creams to women in Asia and Africa, suggesting that lighter-skinned women are more beautiful, more attractive to men, and even more successful professionally. It has been estimated that more than 60 percent of Indian women between the ages of 16 and 35 have used a skin-lightening product, and for many years these products enjoyed double-digit sales growth in India. Although girls and women are the primary audience, Unilever introduced a similar product aimed at men in 2005 (Li *et al.*, 2008; Glenn, 2008; Parameswaran and Cardoza, 2009; Thappa and Malathi, 2004).

Such creams are a luxury in countries where many families still live in or near poverty, but young women may feel that using cosmetics is essential for social acceptance, finding a good husband, or getting a decent job. Skin lighteners can also have a variety of health effects, some of which are occasionally fatal (Olumide *et al.*, 2008). Indian feminists have criticized the practice of skin lightening and they seem to be having some success in shifting cultural norms. In 2012 the fairness cream market shrank in India. The general skin-care market continued to grow, however, as many women continued to purchase products whose advertisements offered them not just beauty but social status and self-esteem. As in the United States, the advertising industry knows that raising girls' and women's anxiety about their attractiveness and social acceptability can be quite profitable (Leistikow, 2008; Li *et al.*, 2008; Singh, 2013).

Diversification

Other people argue that the fundamental effect of media globalization has been to open up options for individuals. Media expose people to information, ideas, and images from other parts of the world, including other parts of their own country, and make it harder to believe or claim that local practices are inevitable or universal. They thus disrupt the power of local traditions and local traditional authorities, including fathers, clergy, and village leaders. "It has always been done this way" is a less compelling argument in the face of overwhelming evidence that other people do things differently.

For example, soap operas – drama series that portray the daily lives of an ongoing group of characters – often portray everyday problems for women and men in their society. One of the most widely watched TV shows in India is "Because a Mother-in-Law Was Once a Daughter-in-Law," which tackles head-on the gender and generational tensions within Indian families. South Africa's "Soul City" has dealt extensively with the HIV-AIDS epidemic, while Kenya's "Makutano Junction" has had episodes focusing on touchy topics like what happens when a husband drinks up the family income. Such shows are especially popular among women and attract viewers precisely because they address difficult topics that are relevant to people's lives. Their focus on the trials and tribulations of ordinary life enables them to articulate women's concerns, portray family dynamics, and explore controversial social themes. By exploring problems and possible solutions on-screen they help ordinary women and men name, discuss, and act on problems in their own families (Rivadeneyra, 2011: 210). Soap operas can even be designed to have an impact: a government-sponsored soap opera in Tanzania succeeded in increasing discussion about and use of contraceptives (World Bank, 2011b: 314).

The impact of *telenovelas*, as they are called in Latin America, has been especially well documented in rural areas of Brazil. Between 1991 and 2003, researchers tracked when TV arrived in each village, when children began to be named after characters in popular *telenovelas*, when women gave birth, and when couples divorced. The *telenovelas* emphasized themes of freedom, female emancipation in the workplace, and the importance of being an individual. They portrayed smaller families than were common in rural areas and characters who were unhappy in their marriages left them. The researchers discovered that the arrival of these *telenovelas* was followed within a few years by a decrease in fertility and an increase in divorce. Rural women, it seemed, found the greater freedoms of urban life attractive, and the *telenovelas* inspired them to consider making more proactive choices in their own lives (Chong and La Ferrara, 2009; La Ferrara *et al.*, 2012).

The arrival of cable TV in rural Indian villages may have had a wider range of effects. Researchers observed rapid increases in girls' school enrollments and decreases in fertility within just a few years after the arrival of TV. Village women reported less tolerance for violence against women, more female autonomy (for example, being able to leave the house without permission), and less preference for sons (Jensen and

Oster, 2007). One might quibble about some of these findings. It is possible, for example, that women reported changes in attitudes because they guessed what researchers wanted to hear. Behavioral changes like higher girls' school enrollments and fertility declines were part of long-term trends and might have happened anyway. They accelerated, however, soon after families started watching TV shows that portrayed the better lives enjoyed by smaller and better-educated families.

The Internet, with its multidimensional flow of information and opinions, can be even more disruptive. We have already mentioned the role of the Internet in women's and GLBT political organizing, as people on every continent have learned from each other's experiences. Both women and men are also using the Internet to improve their own communities in a multitude of ways, some of which are related to gender. The online HarassMap project, for example, was started in response to sexual harassment in Egypt and provides women a way to report, map, and build community opposition to sexual harassment. As of 2014 the HarassMap model had inspired efforts in 28 other countries (HarassMap, 2014; Fahim, 2012).

The Internet and traditional news media often combine to raise awareness of a particular story that symbolizes a larger problem. We mentioned earlier, for example, the "rape on the bus" in Delhi in 2012. Millions of other women were raped that year, but this particular story captured many people's imaginations. Both in India and around the world, millions of people used social media to share news, rumors, and opinions. Social media interest attracted reporters and editors from the formal media, and their reporting fueled more social media attention. This spiral allowed the story to spread worldwide in a way it could not have before the Internet. This one incident, only somewhat unusual in its brutality, thus sparked much broader conversations about sexual violence, gender attitudes, and inequality – conversations that focused on India but also echoed in many other countries around the world.

Each year provides several similar examples of incidents that become scandals – a focus of collective and sustained attention that heavily stigmatizes a perceived moral transgression (Adut, 2008). Gender-related scandals rarely reflect new behavior. Indeed, the underlying patterns of behavior are often, within their own circles, experienced as normal and common – perhaps not morally exemplary, but within customary practice. Rape in fraternities, rape in the military, rape by athletes, domestic violence, father-daughter incest, the sexual impunity of clergy, coaches, and celebrities; veterans' vulnerability to psychological distress, substance abuse, and violence; football players' vulnerability to concussions, brain damage, and erratic behavior; the killing of young black men – all of these things have been visible to many observers and participants for many years.

A scandal erupts when a particular incident triggers mass interest. The collective attention and moral indignation crystalize around one rape, with all its particularity and detail, not around the broad concept of rape. Media have a financial interest in provoking scandal, as emotion-raising stories of wrong-doing attract readers and viewers. From the point of view of the target of scandal the resulting publicity can seem quite unjustified: why me when so many other people did much the same thing?

The intense public conversation both raises awareness of the broader behavior pattern and increases the moral judgment attached to it. Over time, behavior that was once normal comes to be deemed unacceptable. In a sense, then, media scandals are another form of homogenization. The village council in Pakistan that sentenced a woman to be gang-raped as punishment for allegations against her brother did not think they were doing anything remarkable or newsworthy. Many other village councils had done the same thing. What was traditional in rural Pakistan, however, was shocking for many Americans. And for many Pakistanis it was a tradition they were no longer comfortable with – just as many Americans are no longer willing to look away when a man pummels his girlfriend or a celebrity is accused of raping multiple women (Nyhan, 2014).

Gender-related traditions are being contested all around the world, and global media enable local debates to receive widespread publicity. For those traditionally in power, the result can be new constraints and expectations of accountability. For women and other traditionally disadvantaged groups, however, global media can both increase their awareness of possibilities and open up pathways that were not previously available.

CONCLUSION

Media often give viewers skewed impressions of the world. Advertising is especially likely to propagate stereotypical images, as many advertisements raise gendered anxieties in order to sell products that promise to ease those anxieties. Media that are created in large organizations are also particularly likely to be dominated by men and to be conservative in their creative choices, as their profitability depends on reaching a broad audience. When people see lots of stereotypical images, their implicit stereotypes are strengthened and they become more vulnerable to experiencing stereotype threat. Media thus reinforce stereotypes and all of their detrimental effects, help socialize children into gendered expectations, and perpetuate gender inequality.

Media can also, however, bring about significant changes in people's thoughts, feelings, assumptions, and behaviors. Because they are emotionally powerful, media images and stories shape people's perceptions of the world and of the choices available to them, sometimes surprisingly quickly. Exposure to non-stereotypical characters weakens implicit stereotypes and makes people less vulnerable to feeling judged by their group membership. The mass media are still dominated by white men, but not as much as they used to be. The new electronic media are much cheaper and easier to access, and they enable people to communicate with each other both within groups and across many types of difference. As a wider variety of people become involved in media creation, they tell a broader range of stories.

Develop Your Position

1   Make a list of the last ten movies you have seen. How many pass the Bechdel test?

2   Can you remember times when your own feelings of inferiority or superiority affected how well you did something? Does the concept of stereotype threat ring true to you? Why or why not?

3   Do you believe you have implicit stereotypes related to gender, race, age, religion, sexual orientation, and/or disability? Find out by taking some of the implicit stereotype tests available at https://implicit.harvard.edu/implicit/takeatest.html. What did you learn from this experience?

4   What is your favorite TV show, music group, or magazine? How does it affect or reflect your own ideas of what makes a woman or man attractive? Do you find it plausible that media images of attractiveness might sometimes motivate individuals to engage in unhealthy behaviors?

5   How concerned are you about stereotypical media portrayals? Why? Are you more concerned about stereotypes of women, stereotypes of men, or both equally? What do you think could or should be done to reduce the harmful effects of media stereotypes? Do you think there should be special attention given to media aimed at young children?

6   Does the finding that MTV's *16 and Pregnant* produced a decline in teen birth rates surprise you? Why or why not?

CHAPTER 11

Acting Out Gender Through Sports

INTRODUCTION

Sports, also known as athletics, are physical activities that are guided by rules and typically competitive. On a surface level the goals of sports are usually quite mundane: get a ball from here to there, for example. Like religions, though, sports invest behaviors that are unimportant in themselves with many layers of meaning. Both participants and spectators may be emotionally caught up in the flow of the game, reacting collectively to moments of skill or disappointment and caring deeply about who wins or loses.

Team sports can create and reinforce powerful feelings of group solidarity. Just wearing red flags or blue flags can be enough to create teams that people identify with and root for, but in many cases teams represent pre-existing social groups – different schools or colleges, tribes or nations. Sports then can be a form of competition for social status, with both participants and spectators feeling like the rank of their whole group is affected by the outcome of the game. Such feelings can be particularly intense in international competitions, especially the Olympics, where different countries and systems symbolically compete for pre-eminence. When international tensions are high, sports may serve as a proxy for war – an alternative and much less destructive way to use physical prowess to assert national dominance (D'Agati, 2013). The partying and sometimes looting that occur after high-profile games between teams representing different universities indicate, furthermore, that emotions can run strong even when nothing substantive is at stake. Athletes thus often serve as standard-bearers for a larger group, as athletic success is often experienced as mark of superiority not just for the individual but also for the groups with which he or she is affiliated.

The most celebrated athletes are almost always men. This is not just because the largest human beings are male: as any sports fan knows, skill and training trump raw size and strength. Athletes are cultural symbols as well as human beings, and they are seen as embodying strength, skill, courage, persistence, dominance, and other virtues that many cultures associate with masculinity. To one degree or another, most societies use sports to create a **gender boundary** – a marker of the purported divide between "real men" and "real women" (Potuchek, 1997: 17).

In some societies, sports are an all-male world in which women are excluded even from spectatorship. In ancient Greece, for example, all free men were expected to compete in sports and develop the physical fitness that would enable them to defend their city-state if necessary. The gymnasium was the focal point of free men's social lives, as men regularly gathered to exercise and compete in the nude. For many men it was also a center of their erotic lives, as older and younger men commonly had sexual relationships that, in their culture, symbolized allegiance to manly virtues, male solidarity, and independence from women. Women had no place in this athletic culture and could not even watch the Olympics or other public competitions, while enslaved men provided necessary services but were not allowed to compete with free men. Sports thus symbolized, among other things, the freedom to participate in public life – unlike male slaves and women, who were constrained both by constant work and by their exclusion from public spaces. Athletics, military preparedness, and citizenship were intertwined (Spivey, 2004: 47–53; Crowther, 2007: 45–57).

Today, most sports teams are segregated by sex. This segregation is sometimes justified on the grounds that women are not as big and strong as men, and therefore should not be forced to compete with men. Individuals vary widely, however, and teams have often excluded women even if they were better athletes than some men on the team. Children's teams, furthermore, have often been sex-segregated, even though 9-year-old girls and boys have the same range of sizes. Segregation may also be justified on the grounds that physical intimacy between men and women is inappropriate even if it is non-sexual, or that there is no way to avoid sexualized behavior or assault if men and women share a sports field. Such arguments underline the cultural anxiety that drives gender boundaries – the desire to clearly distinguish and separate men and women.

Many girls and women have fought to get access to athletics programs. One reason is simply that many girls and women, like many boys and men, enjoy challenging themselves physically. The endorphin rush that accompanies physical exertion is gender neutral. Another often-proffered reason is that sports can be positive socializing agents. Since the nineteenth century, boys in the United States (and many other countries) have been encouraged to play amateur sports as a way to build their character, prove their masculinity, and develop relationships with peers that will serve them well in later life. Sports have been thought to engender values of persistence, initiative, self-control and responsibility (Zarrett et al., 2009), as well as a tolerance for failure (Bartko and Eccles, 2003) – all useful traits for academic and professional success in Western societies. Liberal feminists have argued that girls and women should be allowed similar opportunities to develop highly rewarded values, behaviors, and social capital.

Even more fundamentally, women's exclusion from sports, and more recently their marginalization within low-status teams and leagues, has long been a symbol of female inferiority and subordination. The idea that men are naturally stronger than women – as proven by sports and military performance – has often translated to the idea that men should naturally be in charge. When women excel athletically, or even just when girls play Little League, they symbolically challenge the presumptions that male dominance is natural and women are second-class citizens.

Athletes may, however, be denigrated as well as celebrated. In some societies physical strength and skill really are essential for success in life: hunters who develop their coordination and stamina through competitive games also increase their ability to bring home meat. In such societies the celebration of successful athletes tends to be whole-hearted. In other societies, including the United States today, people who engage in physical labor tend to be near the lower end of social hierarchies. The more a society values self-control, intellect, and distance from the physical world, the more it may look down on athletes as overly physical and therefore inferior.

A quintessential example is the Roman Empire, where gladiator tournaments entertained the elites and masses. Most gladiators were slaves, usually men but sometimes women. Owned by others, they were forced to engage in a dangerous blood sport that often ended in maiming or death. Within this framework they could gain a certain amount of social status, as many gladiators were trained athletes who were admired for their skills. The gap between them and free male citizens was, however, enormous. Many free male spectators saw the bloody spectacle of gladiator competition as, among other things, confirmation of their own civility and superiority – and therefore fitness to be in charge. Against such men (and occasionally women) the Roman free man could affirm his own superior form of masculinity (Kyle, 2007).

Some commentators suggest that a similar pattern exists in the United States today, as black Americans are strikingly over-represented in the "tougher" and more dangerous team sports. In 2013, for example, 67 percent of NFL (National Football League) players were black, as were 77 percent of NBA (National Basketball Association) players. Black people were, in contrast, 13 percent of the American population – and just 8 percent of MLB (Major League Baseball) players. Although the precise numbers vary year by year, these patterns are persistent (Lapchick *et al.*, 2014a, 2014b, 2014c). Some critics suggest that the popularity of black players in the most vigorous sports reflects a cultural association between dark skin and animal-like physicality that aids the athletic careers of some individuals but overall does a lot of harm (Messner, 2007b).

Some critics argue that American athletics have become a profit-making juggernaut that reinforces many different hierarchies. Although some individual black athletes have gained fame and fortune, the large majority of coaches, team owners, sports journalists, marketers, university administrators, and others who control and profit from athletics remain white men (Powell, 2007). Many concerns have been raised about the exploitation of black college athletes to entertain predominantly white alumni and raise money for their institutions (Hawkins, 2010). More broadly, some critics argue that the institution of sport has shaped understandings of black masculinity that have helped perpetuate racial inequalities (Smith, 2005; Powell, 2007). As we have seen, many young lower-income men, both black and white, see athletics as one of the few pathways to cultural respect and financial security that are open to them, but far more teenagers dream of an athletic career than can actually have one (Morris, 2012). When public schools in lower-income communities channel their financial resources into athletics programs, and encourage students to focus their desires for achievement on sports, they weaken their academic programs and deprive their students – athletes and non-athletes – of the chance to develop skills that are more likely to help them flourish in an international economy (Ripley, 2013).

The "sports/media complex" has also marginalized female athletes and reinforced gender hierarchies both on and off the field. Sports media provide much more coverage of men's sports than women's sports, and typically treat male athletes as "real" athletes while emphasizing female athletes' sexuality rather than athleticism. Women are typically portrayed as supporters of men's athletic activity – as cheerleaders, spectators, or sexual rewards for victors (Jhally, 1984). Sports culture celebrates physicality and the use of force, and many college and professional athletes live in a nearly all-male world in which misogynistic rhetoric is more common and acceptable than in many other parts of American society. The result, some argue, is an athletic subculture that tolerates violence against women and encourages the dehumanizing attitudes that can lead to rape, assault of intimate partners, and other forms of violence (Benedict, 2004; Fuller, 2009; Smith and Cooper, 2010).

In short, sports are often contested ground in ways that go far beyond the games themselves. This chapter offers a gendered history of sport in North America, a gendered approach to understanding sports in the United States today, and brief discussions of the role of gender and sports in the British Empire and the modern Olympics. We will focus on the ways sports both reproduce and challenge hierarchies of gender, race, class, nationality, and sexuality.

A BRIEF HISTORY OF GENDER AND SPORTS IN NORTH AMERICA

Sports and Gender Boundaries in Native America, the British Colonies, and the Early Republic

Native Americans

Gender boundaries were relatively porous in Native American sports. As we saw earlier, Native American communities – like most small-scale societies – used gender to organize work and family life, with distinct but complementary tasks assigned to each gender. Gender boundaries were blurrier when it came to sports, which were arguably more important for Native Americans than for most people today. There were sports for men and sports for women, but these boundaries were regularly crossed, and both men and women frequently participated in individual or small-team sports such as running, swimming, horseback riding, and canoeing (Oxendine, 1988).

Lacrosse was primarily but not exclusively a men's game, and it was played in virtually every corner of the North American world. Major contests would involve hundreds of men, all of whom trained for weeks or months for this very rough sport. Teams often represented different villages and matches might be seen as preparation for battle, or they might be used as an alternative to actual fighting for resolving disputes between villages or tribes. Like the United States and the Soviet Union during the Cold War, Native Americans could thus use sports as a proxy for war. Matches could also take on the character of rites of passage for young men. Women sometimes played lacrosse, which is remarkable for an activity that was otherwise such an important marker of masculinity (Oxendine, 1988; Vennum, 1994).

Two sports that were primarily played by women were double ball and shinny, which some people believe is a forerunner of the field hockey played today. These games might occur on fields as large as a lacrosse field – sometimes as long as a mile – and like lacrosse they might have as many as a hundred players on a side and were watched and wagered on by both men and women. They demanded quick feet and reflexes and enjoyed high status, as did the women who played them well. Men

PHOTO 11.1

Seth Eastman's 1850 "Ball Play of the Dahcota Indians" (Minnesota Historical Society)

were more likely to play double ball or shinny than women were to play lacrosse. Like lacrosse, shinny was sometimes played by men and women simultaneously (Oxendine, 1988: 22–26).

The English Colonies and the Early Republic

The European colonists brought with them two distinctive class-based sports cultures. On the one hand, elite men engaged in hunts and contests that allowed them to display their military skills and privileged status. Only aristocrats, for example, were allowed to hunt big game, and commoners that defied game laws might be hanged. Elite women were spectators at most – sometimes the ladies fair to whom gentlemen displayed their chivalry, other times excluded altogether. On the other hand, both men and women participated in a folk culture of games and festivals. Folk football, a forerunner of soccer, was played on Shrove Tuesday (the last day before Lent) as far back as the twelfth century in England and France, and included much pushing and shoving on the part of men and women alike (British Embassy, 2006). During spring festivals men alone might wrestle, fight with poles or staves, or lift barrels, but girls were perhaps equally likely to engage in foot races. Women were the primary participants in stoolball, which is thought to be a forerunner of both cricket and baseball. Peasant women and men worked hard, and when they had the opportunity they played hard too (Guttmann, 1991; Nichols, 2001).

The Puritans of New England disapproved of all of this. They belonged to the newly emerging middle class – not aristocrats, not peasants, but merchants and small landowners – and they frowned on what they saw as the decadence of the elite and the profligacy of the poor. They purged the calendar of all holidays and festivals, arguing that the Bible declared Sundays a time of rest and worship but all the other traditional holidays had no biblical justification. They even prohibited celebrating Christmas. Six days a week were for work, they taught, and the seventh was for God. Hunting and fishing – which some elite Europeans had considered leisure activities – they condoned as productive work, since the meat and furs were needed. But good men were diligent and somber, and good women even more so (Delaney and Madigan, 2009: 46–47).

The Chesapeake colonies, in contrast, continued both folk sports and elite sports, though at first in attenuated forms due to the exigencies of settler life. Within a few decades, however, these colonies had a high degree of social stratification and landowners held great power over workers (indentured servants earlier, slaves later). With this stratification came a hierarchy of sports that was enforced by both law and social custom. Horse racing was reserved for large landowners. While slaves and servants could observe, they were not allowed even to bet on the results. As in Europe, hunting had its own strict hierarchy. Only large landowners could hunt stags. Lesser landowners could hunt foxes, and so on. Large landowners thus asserted their dominance over lower-status white men by, among many other things, legally barring them from high-status leisure activities (Fischer, 1989: 360–364).

White and black common men drew on the folk sports of Europe and Africa, sometimes with some influence from Native Americans as well. Slaves and servants could not participate in the elite sports, but they could run, wrestle, box, and play many different types of games involving balls, all of which their social superiors considered ungentlemanly. Most games were organized by the participants. Sometimes, though, masters would arrange a boxing or wrestling match that pitted slaves from different plantations against each other, with the owner of the winner commonly claiming the loser as his prize (Griffith, 2010).

Women almost never participated in any of these activities. Elite women certainly could not participate in gentlemen's sports. Enslaved women enjoyed dancing, cooking, and weddings, but there is no evidence that they engaged in races, ball games, or other sporting activities (Griffith, 2010). White female servants were more socially isolated than black slaves, many of whom lived in slave quarters separate from the "big house" and could develop their own community ties in their scant off hours. White female servants usually lived intimately with their mistresses and were at their beck and call for every hour of the day. And women of every class were to be humble and obedient, not competitive and self-assertive.

Regional differences began to fade as Puritanism lost its hold. In the eighteenth century some northern men gained a modicum of respected leisure through the use of servants, laborers, and even slaves. Like their genteel southern and British counterparts, some of this new elite played cricket, fenced, bred horses for racing, and otherwise expressed their masculinity through public competitions. Wealthy women, like their southern counterparts, might ride horses for exercise but not competitively. Men and women of the laboring classes now might sled, boat, or "throw balled stockings," though women's time-consuming domestic responsibilities meant they had less opportunity than men for any kind of leisure (Hoffert, 2003: 439).

In the nineteenth century, industrialization created new opportunities for commercial entertainments. Many people labored long hours in factories or offices and had little time for sleep or leisure. Others, however, benefited from the economy's increasing productivity, and the growing cities created concentrations of people with sufficient surplus income and time to purchase amusements. Entrepreneurs organized horse and harness racing in New York City in the 1820s, while the wealthy founded cricket, tennis, and yachting clubs. College students, all male, began to organize intramural sports teams. These teams were created by students, not administrators or faculty, and reflected a successful effort to develop an anti-academic subculture. Sports were an extension of a network of other student-created organizations, such as fraternities and literary societies, that encouraged privileged young men to feel that "only men were important" (Horowitz, 1987: 41). Sports activities were rough-and-tumble, with few rules and no protective gear. Many young men prided themselves on their resulting bruises and even broken bones, which were considered a sign of hearty masculinity.

Masculinity and the Formalization of Athletics

The post-Civil War period posed many challenges to traditional sources of white men's masculine pride. Most men found themselves working for other men throughout their lives, so the definition of manhood as "self-making" through independent work became much more problematic. Black men were constitutionally granted the civic rights that only white males had previously enjoyed. Although by the 1880s most black men had been cowed into not trying to exercise those civic rights, the intensity of white men's response to black enfranchisement suggests how deeply many of them felt threatened (Williamson, 1986). The growing women's movement was also perceived as threatening men's privileges. Women were entering occupations traditionally reserved for men and girls and women were proving to be superior students. Women were also clamoring for political rights, the prohibition of male drunkenness, and limitations on male violence.

White men increasingly turned to sports as an arena in which to define a positive masculinity that was independent of the worlds of work, black people, and women. By the 1880s many people worried that middle-class men were being physically weakened by office jobs and spiritually weakened by a lifetime of subordination to workplace authorities (Douglas, 1977). Sports allowed men to cultivate their physical strength, assert their will without threatening their employers, and maintain an image of men as inherently stronger and more vigorous than women. The urban middle class, especially, embraced sports both for their own young men, whose vigor and masculinity needed to be bolstered, and for the immigrant populations, who needed to be socialized to American ways. Channeling male aggression into sports would, they hoped, temper the dangerous potential of a growing urban working class (Hoffert, 2003: 441).

American-style football was always a male activity. The game originated in no-holds-barred mass scrimmages between freshman and sophomore college students. It had its intercollegiate kickoff in 1869 in a game between Rutgers and Princeton, and it quickly dominated intercollegiate sports. These competitions gave spectators a sense of fierce college loyalty, and players a sense of manly heroism, that earlier intramural events could not equal. Players typically attacked each other en masse, with minimal protective equipment, and proudly displayed their resulting injuries as badges of masculine honor (Hoffert, 2003: 442). "Prizefighting doesn't compare in roughness or danger with football," asserted John Sullivan, the heavyweight boxing champion of the 1880s (Stewart, 1995). Many commentators at the time worried that too much education would soften elite men (Douglas, 1977). Football enabled college students to counter such anxieties by displaying masculine toughness as they gave and received physical punishment (Horowitz, 1987).

Baseball, on the other hand, evolved from children's games, using a ball and a stick, that were brought from England and traditionally played by both boys and girls. As one sports historian observed, "Although modern baseball is primarily American, urban, and male, its roots are medieval, English, rural and female"

(William Baker, quoted in Guttman, 1991: 48). Several baseball leagues flourished after the Civil War. Business owners sponsored men's teams to represent their companies and instill values of hard work and sobriety in their workforces (Hoffert, 2003: 440–441). Women's teams became standard fare at women's colleges after the Vassar Resolutes were founded in 1866, five years after Vassar's own founding. Several women's and mixed-gender teams formed in the 1880s, including some black women's teams, and the semi-pro Chicago Bloomer Girls barnstormed against men and women's teams of all races. Softball was invented in 1887 by a group of young Chicago men who wanted to practice baseball skills indoors. With its smaller field, requiring less running and shorter throwing, it was soon seen as a feminized version of baseball. Many men and boys, however, played softball, while some women and girls continued to play baseball. In 1911 A.G. Spaulding created the myth that Abner Doubleday invented baseball in 1839 and that it had always been a men's game. It took, however, some masculine imagination to rewrite baseball as a male sport (Ring, 2009).

Black and white players sometimes played together during the Reconstruction era immediately after the Civil War, which was a time when racial boundaries were in flux in many ways. By the 1880s, however, most sports teams reflected the "Jim Crow" rules that white people were imposing throughout the country. White men's hegemony in baseball was well entrenched by the time the major leagues started the first World Series in 1903, and no black or female player could join the major teams. Black men therefore formed black baseball leagues, whose teams played throughout the country until Jackie Robinson broke the color bar in 1947. Within a few years the black leagues were dismantled in the pursuit of integration (Hoffert, 2003: 444–445).

Basketball was a more intentional creation, as Dr. James Naismith invented it in 1891 to give young men a vigorous workout. Basketball was initially thought to be a non-contact sport, in contrast with football. It grew in popularity on the collegiate scene during the first three decades of the twentieth century, coming to supplant baseball and track as the second most popular collegiate sport by the 1930s.

Unlike football, basketball was soon adopted by women. Unlike baseball, it quickly diverged into two gender-specific versions of the game. In 1892 Senda Berenson, a physical education teacher at Smith College, created a version that emphasized team play over individual heroism and was less physical than the men's game (Molina, 2005). Women's basketball quickly became popular, as its focus on cooperativeness rather than individual athletic prowess resonated with players', coaches', and spectators' perceptions of women's capabilities (Cahn, 1995: 85–87).

Black and white men also played in segregated teams and developed different brands of the game. The black version favored jumping skills, while the white version emphasized dribbling, faking, lay-ups, and set shots. White players and audiences frowned upon the jump shot and dunk, which they considered illegitimate. In 1967, when college basketball was beginning to integrate, the National Collegiate Athletic Association (NCAA) introduced what came to be called the "Alcindor rule," which outlawed dunking. According to the NCAA, dunking gave black players like Lew Alcindor (later Kareem Abdul-Jabbar) an unfair advantage: black players might be tall, but white players were more civilized. Strictures on the "unnaturalness" of the black man's game proved to be only temporary, as nine years later dunking became legal again. Such disagreements over rules were not just about the game per se, but also about who has the authority to determine what behavior is deemed legitimate and valued (Delaney and Madigan, 2009: 201).

By the 1880s high school administrators were realizing that sports might help them solve their **boy problem**. As we saw earlier, girls were doing better, on average, than boys scholastically and staying in school longer, partly because boys without a diploma had many more attractive employment options. Sports teams fostered school pride, thus increasing boys' connections with the school community. They also provided an alternative source of masculine meaning that competed with the rewards of going to work. School administrators therefore encouraged school athletics – and took control of them – by providing their own gymnasiums, playing fields, coaches, and equipment (Horowitz, 1987: 199ff.; Tyack and Hansot, 1992: 166, 192).

Segregation, both legal and de facto, meant that black and white players rarely competed against each other. The roles of racism and the media in the construction of manliness became particularly evident in 1910, when the black prize fighting champion, Jack Johnson, faced the former white champion, Jim Jeffries, who was billed as the "Great White Hope." This fight was widely portrayed as a competition "to determine which race could produce the most virile specimen of manhood" (Hoffert, 2003: 444). White journalists read Johnson's victory as a humiliation of white manhood, while black people hoped that his success would lead to more respect for other black men. After Johnson finally lost his title in 1915, the boxing establishment made sure there would not be another black champion for 20 years.

Early black athletes who competed with white athletes were never just runners or ball players: they were also symbols of their community's desire to be recognized as human beings. The hopes of many African Americans were lifted in the 1930s, when two black men became national heroes by defeating German athletes. Jesse Owens won four gold medals at the 1936 Olympics, and in 1938 Joe Louis defeated Max Schmeling for the heavyweight championship of the world. Many white Americans rooted for Owens and Louis. Although most white people at that time saw African Americans as "others," in international competitions African Americans could be part of "us." Besides, some white Americans were becoming sufficiently concerned about Nazi claims of Aryan superiority that they toned down their own assertions of white superiority. Nevertheless, American society and sports remained largely segregated.

Women's Sports, 1920–1970

The 1920s are sometimes described as a Golden Age in sports, and women's sports experienced a lower-case version of this golden age. Women were challenging gender hierarchies in many ways, and one of the many results was a "first wave of athletic feminism" that allowed some women to gain access to the training they needed to turn their native talents into actual accomplishments (Messner, 2007a: 44). Swimming proved to be a sport in which women could break records that had been set by men. In 1924 Sybil Bauer broke the men's world record in the backstroke, and in 1926 Gertrude Ederle swam the English Channel much faster than any of the five men who had swum it previously. These women were both admired for their athleticism and criticized for their "mannishness," a derisive term that disparaged their femininity and their heterosexuality (Cahn, 1995: 33).

Two major factions drove women's sports participation. Foremost were female physical educators in high schools and colleges. Many women of this era made their careers by serving other women, and sports was no exception, as it was generally considered indecent for young women to be coached by men. Most female P.E. instructors advocated moderate amounts of exercise for all young women, rather than challenging the few that showed high levels of athletic talent to excel. They seem to have acted out of genuine concern for their charges. They argued that a sedentary life was bad for women's physical and mental wellbeing, but like many of their contemporaries they worried that too much exercise would harm women's health, especially during menstruation. They also, it seems, sought to avert criticism about the masculinizing effects of athletics by keeping girls' and women's sports low key and minimally competitive. Many argued that women's sports should be exclusively intramural, which would maintain women's dignity and modesty by not subjecting them to competition and spectatorship.

Some commercial promoters, meanwhile, hoped to draw ticket-buying audiences by creating and promoting women's leagues. These promoters were nearly always male and had very different interests than the female P.E. instructors: they wanted to make money by celebrating winners. The most successful promoters drew audiences numbering in the thousands (Cahn, 1995: 92–93). In the 1940s Philip Wrigley and Arthur Meyerhoff organized the All-American Girls Professional Baseball League. To the delight of the spectating public, they employed a strategy that had been used by other promoters to avoid the charge of "mannishness": emphasize players' feminine attractiveness. Players were required to take a charm school course, keep their hair long, and wear short (some might have said immodest) skirts when they played. The combination of athletic skill and respectable but sexy femininity worked for about a decade. In the 1950s, however, national efforts to restore a more purely domestic femininity made it seem out of place and the league died out (Cahn, 1995: 140–163).

Indeed, women's access to athletics generally proved fragile. As we saw previously, a backlash against women's political and economic achievements grew during the 1920s and many kinds of women-oriented organizations, including women's sports teams, came to be seen as politically and sexually suspect. The Depression deprived women's sports of financial support, while media criticism of female athletes' mannishness took its toll on both players and public opinion. By the late

PHOTO 11.2

The 1940s All-American Girls Professional Baseball League fended off accusations of "mannishness" by emphasizing the players' feminine attractiveness as well as athleticism. Here, Sophie Kurye, who stole 201 bases for the Racine Belles in 1946, swipes third base (Photo provided courtesy of The Center for History)

1930s many predominantly white high schools and colleges had discontinued interscholastic competitions for women. Some female athletic programs became exclusively intramural, while others disappeared entirely. Girls who received little athletic encouragement became less likely to seek out either amateur or professional opportunities as adults. By the early 1950s many of the women's leagues and tournaments had vanished.

Predominantly black institutions, however, were not so discouraging for female athletes. Unlike white communities, which always had the lingering sense that good women were delicate and needing of protection, black communities generally valued strength in women. Finances were always tight at historically black colleges, but they still managed to support sports programs for women as well as men. The Tuskegee Institute, for example, started a women's track team in 1929 and invited both women and men from other colleges to its Tuskegee Relays and Meets (Cahn, 1995: 118–119).

In the 1950s black women were two-thirds of the country's female representatives in international track and field competitions, including the Olympics, though they were only 10 percent of all women (Cahn, 1995: 120). Althea Gibson, a black woman from South Carolina, integrated tennis in 1950 and won the women's singles championship at Wimbledon in 1957. The media paid little attention to black women's early international achievements, but this approach became impracticable when Wilma Rudolph and other female athletes from Tennessee State University, a black college, dominated the 1960 Olympics. Sometimes dubbed "the fastest woman in the world," Rudolph won three gold medals in track and field events in front of national TV audiences. Like it or not, black women were representing the country, and often winning.

Another constituency that stayed with women's sports was lesbians, white as well as black. Local sports teams became important refuges for many lesbians during the virulently homophobic decades of the 1940s, 1950s and 1960s. Amateur sports provided opportunities for women to interact primarily with other women, without babies in tow. Some heterosexual women enjoyed sports too, of course, but women who did not have heterosexual interests could find sports an especially refreshing change from the otherwise unrelenting celebration of heterosexuality, family life, and heterosocial relations. Playing softball or bowling, they could at least meet other women. Many young women also learned to name their attractions, identify the signals that indicated others were so inclined, and develop personal and romantic relationships. Amateur athletics thus gave lesbian women a social space, rare elsewhere, in which they could create a shared culture and positive identity (Cahn, 1995: 185–206). Lesbians who wanted to play on school or professional teams, however, had to remain strictly closeted, as any woman who did not appear married faced harsh scrutiny and unpleasant accusations (Griffin, 1998).

GENDER AND SPORTS IN THE CONTEMPORARY UNITED STATES

Bringing Girls and Women into Sport

The second wave of the feminist movement sparked a second wave of athletic feminism and began to equalize opportunities for female athletes – though sometimes in ways that marked women's bodies as different from and inferior to men's (Schultz, 2014). Women's professional tennis took off in 1968, with the beginning of the open era that permitted professional athletes to play in long-standing tournaments, including Wimbledon and the U.S. Open. (Previously only amateurs could play in such tournaments.) In 1970 Billie Jean King led a boycott to address pay inequities in professional tennis, as women then received about one-tenth the prize money that was available in men's pro tennis tournaments (Delaney and Madigan, 2009: 183). Inspired by other campaigns for women's access and equal treatment, women founded their own Women's Tennis Association and equalized prize money in most major tournaments. In 1973 King defeated Bobby Riggs, a retired male pro, in a match known as the "Battle of the Sexes," which drew 48 million TV viewers and demonstrated the high quality of the women's game. It became increasingly difficult to claim that men were always better athletes than women – and therefore implicitly superior in other ways as well.

The 1972 passage of **Title IX** turned out to be transformative for women's sports. The **Civil Rights Act of 1964** had declared that discrimination on the basis of sex (as well as race, color, religion, and national origin) was illegal, but it required repeated clarifications. Two female members of the House of Representatives and

PHOTO 11.3

Kathrine Switzer was almost thrown out of the 1967 Boston Marathon by a race organizer, who told her to "Get the hell out of my race." One of her male running companions blocked him and enabled her to finish the race, becoming the first woman to do so (Source: Associated Press; Peralta, 2012)

advocates of women's rights, Edith Green and Patsy Mink, were instrumental in the drafting and passage of Title IX, which simply stated: "No person in the United States shall, on the basis of sex, be excluded from participation in, be denied the benefits of, or be subjected to discrimination under any educational programs or activities receiving federal financial assistance." The statute does not mention sports, and its sponsors were more concerned about women's employment than women's athletics, but the biggest immediate effect of Title IX was girls' and women's increased participation in sports.

In 1971 about 310,000 girls and women played high school and college sports and the United States was represented in the Olympics by 318 men and 85 women. In 2012, forty years after Title IX, 3.4 million girls and women participated in high school and college sports (Dangerfield, 2012). Female U.S. Olympians outnumbered males, with 268 women and 261 men, for the first time in 2012. Women won 56 of the United States' 104 medals that year, including 29 of its 41 gold medals (Nhan, 2012). Talented American women were now able to make a living in such sports as basketball, track and field, and tennis. Serena Williams, the African American gold medalist in tennis, had already earned over $36 million in prize money and more than $130 million overall (including endorsements) during her 10-year career (Said, 2012).

Just as the first wave of athletic feminism engendered backlash, however, so has the second. Most obvious was a campaign by the NCAA to have athletic departments excused from complying with Title IX on the grounds that men's programs would suffer irreparably. The federal government took three years, until 1975, to decide against the NCAA, and then it gave athletic departments three more years to comply with the law. Many high school officials also dragged their feet. In 1984 the Supreme Court ruled that Title IX did not apply to programs (such as athletic programs) that did not directly receive federal funding even if the larger institution did receive it. Congress responded by passing the Civil Rights Restoration Act of 1988, which once again demanded that schools and colleges receiving federal dollars aim at eliminating gender discrimination in all programs, including sports (Cahn, 1995: 246–281).

Women's sports still lag behind men's sports. In 2006, boys were 58 percent of participants in high school athletic programs and 57 percent of participants in college programs (Stevenson, 2007). Women's teams, furthermore, generally receive less money and other resources than men's teams. One study found that male athletes at 27 Division I colleges typically received $598 more in scholarship aid than female athletes, while coaches of male teams earned an average of $190,310 more than coaches of female teams (Hattery, 2010). The breakdown of societal patterns of gender segregation also created disproportionate opportunities for male coaches as the number of women's teams expanded. In 1972, when Title IX was passed, 90 percent of women's teams were coached by women. By 2011, that figure had dropped to 40 percent (Lapchick, 2010).

Some of these differences reflect disparities in the prestige associated with various sports. Masculinized sports, such as football and basketball, still receive far more institutional support than sports that are more gender equitable, such as soccer and tennis. Differences also exist, however, within each sport. The same study found that the operating budgets for men's basketball teams were on average $275,050 higher than those for women's basketball teams (Hattery, 2010).

Most women's professional teams struggle with the interlocking problems of low budgets, inconvenient venues, little or no TV coverage, and a thin fan base. They also face the problem that many sports fans believe female athletes lack the strength, speed, and skill of male athletes – a perception that can be reinforced when female athletes are promoted as good role models for girls rather than as great athletes who play interesting games. Promoters of women's sports, however, point out that many men's teams and leagues also played in relative obscurity for decades before developing a reliably enthusiastic (and profitable) fan base. They acknowledge that it may be harder now to gain attention, in this era of innumerable entertainment options, but argue that it can be done with sufficient support and persistence. The WNBA (Women's National Basketball Association), for example, has received both financial and moral support from the NBA since its founding in 1996. Today six of the 12 WNBA teams are profitable and in 2013 WNBA games attracted more TV viewers than men's Major Soccer League matches (Springer, 2014).

Most women's teams today, though, have little or no TV coverage. They may live-stream games, or even upload videos to YouTube, but the formal media continue to give grossly disproportionate coverage to men's sports. NFL games, especially, raise enormous amounts of money for TV networks, sponsors, team owners, players, and the league. These financial incentives translate into intensive coverage of men's football and other sports, which keeps women's sports from catching the public's attention and, in turn, its financial support. While there are spikes in the amount of coverage given to women's sports, the attention soon fades and therefore fails to translate into financial success (Springer, 2014).

Media coverage of women's sports also differs in quality as well as quantity, as it continues to focus on athletes' sexuality and feminine attractiveness, or lack thereof (Schultz, 2005). More than 95 percent of sports commentators are male, and their language often encourages viewers and listeners to engage in what is effectively sexual voyeurism (Messner *et al.*, 2003; Fuller, 2009). Magazines like *Sports Illustrated* and *Playboy* hire female athletes to pose nude or in sexually provocative poses as often as they can. The 2014 *Sports Illustrated* swimsuit edition included a section entitled "50 Years: Of Beautiful Athletes" that featured a soccer player, basketball player, and surfer in swimsuits that were almost there. One study showed images of female athletes in action to some adolescents and young adults and sexualized images of athletes to others. The athletic images led viewers to empowering talk about what they could do, while the sexualized images led to negative assessments of their own bodies (Daniels, 2009).

Female sports culture can thus turn into yet another iteration of the cultural fixation on female appearance. The "aesthetic fitness" movement that emerged in the 1990s urges women to exercise so they will look good, while the skin-tight sports bras, yoga pants, and other exercise wear that have become fashionable reveal the details of women's bodies and allow viewers to compare and evaluate every curve and bump. These sports-related norms and clothing styles have yet again fueled unrealistic expectations of feminine beauty (Schultz, 2014).

Some sociologists believe that participating in organized sports is correlated with academic or even professional achievement. Girls and boys who play sports in high school are more likely to graduate from high school and college (Hartmann, 2008; Mueller, 2007). One study interviewed young adults 10 to 20 years after graduating from high school and found that those who had considered sports important during their high school years were significantly more likely to hold a bachelor's degree and had higher incomes than those for whom sports had been unimportant. The gap in college graduation rates was larger for men (46 percent to 31 percent), but quite noticeable for women (59 to 48 percent) (Lutz *et al.*, 2009). Sports can provide social capital: relationships that keep students in school and help them succeed afterwards. Life skills learned through sports (e.g., persistence, initiative, leadership, teamwork, and the capacity to deal with setbacks) may also translate to workplace success (USADA, 2012: 35). One study found that both women and men who played varsity or junior varsity sports in college were significantly more likely than non-athletes of their gender to consider running for political office later in life (Lawless and Fox, 2013).

Other sociologists, however, have raised many questions about these findings. Some studies suggest that students with higher socioeconomic status and grade point averages are more likely to join high school sports programs (Crosnoe, 2002; Sabo *et al.*, 1989). Athletes may therefore tend to have higher academic, financial, and professional success because of who chooses to join sports programs, or the quality of the schools in which sports programs are well-funded and widely available, not because of the effects of playing sports. Other studies find that the effects of sports participation vary greatly among different demographic groups and sports programs. For some groups under some circumstances, playing sports is correlated with academic difficulties, substance abuse, and violent behavior (Hartmann, 2008; Miller *et al.*, 2006). One study that tried to identify the effects (rather than the correlations) of sports participation found that sports had a positive effect on the educational attainment and earnings of white female and black male students, a negative effect on white males, and no effect on black females or Hispanic males or females (Eide and Ronan, 2001).

Some sociologists argue that it is important to examine how intensively students are engaged with sports. Being a "jock" – that is, putting a lot of time into sports and building a significant part of one's identity around athletic performance – may have significantly different effects than just being an "athlete," that is, participating in athletic programs in a less intense way. One study found that jock identity, but not athletic participation, was correlated with binge drinking and violent behavior, especially for boys (Miller *et al.*, 2006). Another study found that female athletes reported higher grades than female non-athletes, while this effect was reversed among male athletes. Female and black male students who identified as jocks reported lower grades, while jock identity had no effect on the grades of white males (Miller *et al.*, 2005). Results in this area are sufficiently diverse and inconsistent that there is no consensus about their implications. Certainly, though, one should not conclude that athletic participation always leads to other desirable effects.

Defining Masculinity(ies) Through Sport

In the last 70 years, at least two factors have increased the salience of sports in Americans' images of masculinity. First, the spread of television led to the broadcasting of many sports and a dramatic expansion of sports spectatorship. The last couple of generations of men have spent considerably more of their lives engaged with sports than previous generations. Though much of that engagement has taken the form of watching games on TV, it means that sports have a substantially higher cultural profile than they could before the rise of broadcast media. Second, for many American men work is no longer a satisfying arena on which to base their sense of masculinity. Women are now about half of the workforce, men can no longer count on earning more than women, and growing numbers of men are not in the workforce at all. Many men have experienced a crisis of masculinity, as breadwinning has become a flimsy basis on which to build a masculine identity or assert masculine power, so they are looking for alternatives (Kimmel, 2013). Sports – especially but not only in their televised forms – have become a culturally approved way to declare the distinctiveness and importance of men (Messner, 2007a).

Critics argue that TV sports programs and their associated commercials offer a narrow view of masculinity. A content analysis of sports programs and commercials concluded that most embody and perpetuate five intertwined beliefs that together constitute a "Televised Sports Manhood Formula" (Messner *et al.*, 2007). First, men are important: sports announcers and their subjects are almost exclusively male. Second, white people are important: most commercials are about white people. Third, women are sexy props or prizes for men: witness cheerleaders on the sidelines and women's roles in commercials. Fourth, aggression wins and violence is not only acceptable but desirable. Fifth, it is manly to sacrifice one's own body and to punish the bodies of others.

Anything that one sees over and over starts to feel familiar and therefore normal. People who watch a lot of sports are therefore likely to incorporate these gender-related beliefs into their working models of the world. Messner (2007c: 87–88) argues that boys are particularly vulnerable to internalizing these messages because they, according to Nancy Chodorow's (1978) theory of gender socialization, have

PHOTO 11.4

Many young men, especially but not only black men, have been encouraged to focus their identities and their aspirations for achievement on sports and muscularity (Source: Thinkstock)

a greater need than girls to find ways to differentiate themselves from their nurturing mothers and are therefore alert for messages about what it means to be masculine. Boys who spend little time with their fathers, or whose time with their fathers is dominated by watching sports, may be especially likely to internalize the standards of masculinity promulgated by sports media.

Many boys are urged to participate in sports during their school years. As we have seen earlier, many school cultures – especially those in lower-status communities – encourage boys to focus on developing their physical prowess rather than their intellectual skills. Glorifying boys' athletics reinforces the idea that boys are and should be active, tough, and the center of attention. Many boys dream of athletic careers, which are glamorous but highly selective, and thereby lose out on developing other capabilities that would lead to more plausible livelihoods (Morris, 2012). All students, athletes and not, are disadvantaged if administrators focus their attention, creativity, and financial resources on sports programs rather than academic programs (Ripley, 2013).

Similar concerns have been raised about college "student-athletes," especially in profitable sports like football and men's basketball, where demanding practice and playing schedules may leave participants little time for classwork. Critics argue that black men, especially, are recruited to provide entertainment for alumni (and thus encourage alumni donations), given an inadequate education, subjected to the risk of concussions and other life-changing injuries, and then discharged (with or without a college degree) into an adult world for which they are ill prepared. The NCAA has instituted a variety of measures that aim to increase college graduation rates for all athletes and to reduce the racial gap in graduation rates, but disparities persist. In 2013 the University of Texas awarded a bachelor's degree to 90 percent of its white football players but just 44 percent of its black football players (Jackson, 2014). Just passing courses, furthermore, is not the same thing as becoming educated, if the faculty experience strong pressures to give passing grades to profitable athletes.

Some cultural critics suggest that many white male spectators feel a special satisfaction in watching black men engage in the more physically aggressive "contact sports." On the one hand, they identify with professional athletes as fellow men and see them as symbols of their own physical superiority to women. On the other hand, they also see black athletes as racially different (and often different in class as well) and feel superior to them as symbols of a relatively uncivilized form of manhood. Although the violence that occurs on the sports field is codified by rules, it nonetheless conforms with and reinforces the cultural stereotype of black men as brutal and violent. The "tough" persona of many black athletes off the field is commercially successfully because it taps into these stereotypes (Messner, 2007b).

Other explanations of black men's over-representation in contact sports focus on the different opportunities and motivations available to boys and men of different races and social classes. Messner (2007b) interviewed former high school and college athletes and found that the decision about whether or not to pursue sports intensively reflected rational choices about the kinds of masculinity available to different young men. The chances of attaining a professional sports career are extremely remote. In the late 1980s – when his interviewees were making their decisions – approximately three in 100,000 high school athletes moved on to a professional athletic career. Putting one's eggs in this basket was therefore a losing strategy if one had viable alternatives. Most of the upper-class (and predominantly white) men reported that they realized the pursuit of an athletic career was, in the words of one respondent, like "pissing in the wind," while pursuing an education would more reliably lead to the status of a successful American man (Messner, 2007b: 57). Later in life, these men used their interest in sport to do "dominance bonding" with other high-status males and to maintain their belief that men, generally, were superior to women – at least in their potential for violent sport. They themselves, after all, once had such potential that they freely gave up for other opportunities.

Many men from less privileged backgrounds, on the other hand, reported pursuing athletic careers, which were usually unfruitful, because they perceived sports as providing their best opportunity for attaining a respected masculine role, both in the present and in the future. Rhonda Levine (2010) argues that high school coaches in lower-income communities are often important sources of social capital and **cultural capital** – knowledge about how to navigate the more rewarded aspects of one's society, such as how to apply to college. It makes sense, she concludes, for young black people to attach themselves to sports teams, if they have the necessary athletic ability, since these programs often offer them resources that are not available to non-athletes. In poor urban neighborhoods, many young black men see no other way to pursue educational and economic advancement.

The emphasis on toughness and risk-taking in many men's sports can leave athletes with significant physical problems. Perhaps as many as one in five high school football players experience concussion each year and even those who do not may suffer neurological impairment (Talavage *et al.*, 2013). About half of all NFL players retire because of injury, while two-thirds suffer an injury whose pain never fully goes away. Six in ten suffer from concussion – often multiple concussions – and many of those will later in life suffer from memory loss or dementia (Steele, 2002). Athletes and former athletes are also more likely than other men to drink heavily and engage in other risky behaviors, which can have implications for both short-term and long-term health (Lutz *et al.*, 2009; Crosnoe, 2002).

The emphasis on toughness can also take a toll on others, as communities often seem to condone violent behavior by high-status athletes. In 2007, after more than fifty NFL players had been arrested in the previous season, the NFL instituted a new personal conduct policy in which players could be disciplined for transgressions even if they had not been found guilty in court. In practice, players were punished more severely for accusations of drug possession or drunk driving than for accusations of partner violence, which often were not punished at all (Pennington and Eder, 2014). NFL players (like other high-income people) are much less likely than most men their age to be arrested, but the difference is smaller for domestic violence and sexual assault than most other crimes (Morris, 2014). When athletes are charged with domestic violence, football and basketball players are less likely than other athletes to end up incarcerated. Perhaps surprisingly, black football and basketball players are even less likely than white football and basketball players to be incarcerated (Smith and Cooper, 2010). Black men are generally treated harshly by the criminal justice system and are more likely to be imprisoned, and imprisoned for longer, than white men who commit the same crimes (Alexander, 2010). Being a high-status athlete, it seems, can disrupt this usual pattern – perhaps because part of the entertainment value of black athletes is a racialized aura of barely controlled brutality.

Related patterns operate on the high school and college level, where successful athletes are often local celebrities. Smith and Cooper (2010) argue that elite male athletes live in a **Sportsworld**, a highly gender-segregated institution in which men have little contact with women other than cheerleaders. They therefore have few opportunities for the companionable interactions with women that encourage cross-gender understanding and sympathy. In *Our Guys* (1997), Bernard Lefkowitz did an ethnographic study related to the gang rape of a mentally disabled 17-year-old girl by 12 popular white athletes in an affluent suburb. He concluded that at least three attributes of male team sports make such brutality more likely. First, male athletes tend to engage in misogynistic joking and "dominance bonding" that celebrates imposing one's will on others. Second, this banter leads to a suppression of empathy in encounters with actual girls and women. Third, parents, teachers, and peers cut successful male athletes considerable slack. Their high social status makes people unwilling to criticize them, punish them for misbehavior, or otherwise disrupt their chances of winning games. Many successful male athletes thus end up with both a sense of impunity and a lack of empathy for others, especially women.

Not all athletes, however, participate in these patterns. Different sports and different teams have different cultures. Some encourage hostility to women, rape-supportive attitudes, and sexual assaults, but others do not (Murnen and Kohlman, 2007; Humphrey and Kahn, 2000). When athletes with high status and visibility behave poorly toward women, all athletes may get tarred with the same brush.

Most sports teams encourage aggressive heterosexuality (Aitchison, 2006). Male athletes, including young boys, have often been subjected to homophobic taunts like "pansy," "fag," and "gay" if they make a mistake or are less than fully dedicated to the game. The prevalence and virulence of homophobia can be enhanced by the physical intimacy of the games and locker rooms, where men come into close contact with each other's bodies but have to be careful to define themselves as interested only in sports (E. Anderson, 2005; Branch, 2011). Many men – not just athletes –

feel that potentially being the object of another man's desire, even if nothing is said, symbolically equates them with women, and some men feel deeply threatened by such lessening of their status. Indeed, some criminal defendants have used "gay panic" arguments to defend themselves against assault and even murder charges: the realization that another man was homosexual, they argued, was so emotionally overwhelming that they should not be expected to refrain from violence (Lee, 2008).

Many gay and lesbian athletes have done their best to remain closeted, often at great personal cost (Griffin, 1998; E. Anderson, 2005). Others created alternative forums, including the Gay Games, an Olympics-style international competition that was started in 1982, welcomes participants whatever their sexual identity, and has become one of the most important international institutions for LGBT people (Symons, 2010). In 1994 the Gay Games attracted 11,000 participants from 40 countries and half a million spectators (McKinley, 1994). The feminist movement, with its critiques of homophobia, helped open up space for lesbian athletes and fans in professional sports. In 2014 the WNBA announced plans to specifically court LGBT fans, thus becoming the first professional league to openly target this demographic (Springer, 2014). Men's leagues remain more uncomfortable with homosexuality, with very few openly gay players. A pro basketball player came out in 2013, as did a prospective pro football player in 2014, and their announcements were widely viewed as courageous and newsworthy (Branch, 2014). As in so many ways, the Internet has both made it easier for LGBT athletes and fans to find each other and harder to keep secrets, as websites like Outsports.com advocate for LBGT athletes and rapidly spread rumors.

The assumption that sports can and should be segregated by sex has been increasingly called into question by transgender and genderqueer players who challenge the premise that people's genders can be assigned by looking at their bodies. The NCAA now officially encourages colleges to ensure that transgender individuals have equal access to all academic and extracurricular activities, including sports, but also seeks to preserve women-only competitions. Drawing on what it frames as the objective and disinterested findings of science, the NCAA allows individuals who are transitioning from male to female to participate on women's teams only if they have been taking testosterone-suppressing drugs, which reduce muscle mass, for at least a year. Those who are transitioning from female to male may take physician-prescribed testosterone, which otherwise is a banned substance, but are then ineligible for women's teams. A team with both male and female participants is a "mixed team," which may compete in men's championships but not women's championships. The NCAA encourages coaches, players, administrators, and media to use the pronouns preferred by individuals, enact gender-neutral dress codes, preserve individuals' privacy and confidentiality, and reject all discriminatory or harassing behavior (NCAA, 2011). These norms have yet to become universal, but their existence is a challenge to the celebration of masculinity that has been embedded in sports culture.

GENDER AND SPORTS IN GLOBAL PERSPECTIVE

Sports and Masculinity in the British Empire

Sports played at least two important roles in the British Empire, which in the nineteenth century stretched around the world. First, the British elite saw team sports, such as cricket, rugby, and soccer, as the best way to prepare boys and young men for the empire's literal and metaphorical battlegrounds. These sports cultivated strength, speed, and the ability to keep calm and make decisions under pressure, all of which were useful qualities in warriors. They also taught boys how to work in groups and function in hierarchies where they were expected to both obey and exert authority, which were useful preparation for their future roles in civil as well as military governance. Sports were widely seen as a test of masculine character, "a measure of a man's valor, capabilities and virility" (McDevitt, 2004: 13). The ability to tolerate pain, cold, hunger, and other discomforts demonstrated that a boy had the toughness required to serve the empire no matter what. By the middle of the nineteenth century, therefore, a "games revolution" had taken root in the British private schools that trained England's leadership class (Simri, 1983: 16).

Second, sports were also a way to assert national superiority. British colonial administrators saw themselves as exporting "civilization" to an unruly world. Among many other things, they brought their games to colonies as diverse as Ireland, South Africa, India, Australia, and the West Indies. By playing the sports of empire they asserted their moral and physical superiority over their subjects. Like the Greeks and Native Americans, the British used sports as a surrogate for war. If the locals could be kept sufficiently cowed by demonstrations of British prowess, actual violence would not be needed to keep them in check. Sport was only one of the ways in which the British sought to display their superiority and deter uprisings, but it was a very visible one.

British sports also, however, provided colonized men a venue in which they could assert their own masculinity and declare themselves the equals – or even superiors – of their colonizers. The Irish nationalist "Gaelic Revival" movement led to, among many other things, the creation in 1884 of the Gaelic Athletic Association. The indigenous games of hurling and Gaelic football became symbols of resistance against British cultural imperialism and helped forge a vigorous image of Irish masculinity. Whereas the British had been inclined to dismiss Irish men as effeminate, now the Irish disparaged their occupiers in the same terms. South Africa and New Zealand decided to challenge British sports dominance on the Brits' home turf – rugby – and by 1906 they had produced teams that toured Britain and soundly defeated British squads. Their feats elicited public worries in the British press about the manliness of British men – worries not unlike those expressed about white American men when Jack Johnson beat Jim Jeffries in 1910 (McDevitt, 2004).

In each case, the politicization of sport underlined the importance of excluding women from competitions. If sport was war by other means, then women certainly had no place in it. A group that allowed women to compete in sports implicitly feminized its soldiers, which was serious business indeed when the new nationalist ideology was teaching that each nation (a group of people who share a history and often a language) should have its own state (a geographic region that it controls). Around the world, both colonizing and colonized men asserted their rights to rule by asserting their masculinity and excluding women not just from the symbolically laden team sports, but also from the public sphere more broadly defined. Women, men asserted, were too fragile for strenuous exercise, even though the majority of women survived through hard physical labor. Women were therefore also unfit to exert political authority, which ultimately rested on the ability of soldiers to conquer and control territory. As men struggled with each other for political, cultural, and military power, they expressed a shared aversion to effeminacy, and often to actual women.

Some women shared the growing interest in sport, but women's sports had very different symbolic meanings. By the closing decades of the nineteenth century individual sports that required little exertion, such as archery or croquet, were generally considered acceptable ways for a wealthy and fashionable woman to show off her figure, clothing, and gentility. Tennis and golf eventually became acceptable pastimes as well, though few could afford them. Bicycle riding was increasingly popular among

PHOTO 11.5

In the 1890s the Gibson Girl on her bicycle was an image of female liberty (Source: Library of Congress, 1895)

women as well as men during the latter part of the nineteenth century. The first women's bicycle race was held in France in 1869, but most female riders were amateurs who delighted in their new freedom of leisurely movement (Simri, 1983: 22).

As in the United States, however, objections to women's sports participation were both numerous and durable. Some people claimed that athletic women were too masculine or worried that their participation in sport threatened a masculine sphere of activity. Many expressed concerns about immodest and provocative dress. Bloomers, divided skirts that were especially popular among bicycle riders, were scorned as both ugly and indecent. Bathing suits were a new invention: previously men had swum naked and women had not swum at all. The early suits covered women's bodies from their necks to their wrists and toes, with skirts down to their knees, but they were still highly controversial. Women's bathing suits that revealed an ankle were legally actionable in 1890s Britain. But perhaps the greatest fears concerned women's presumed delicate constitutions. Sports, critics warned, might damage the reproductive organs and sap energies that were better used in the improvement of one's home and family (Simri, 1983: 17–19; Hargreaves, 2002: 53–65).

Gender and the Modern Olympics

The history of the modern Olympics movement encapsulates the international struggle for gender equality in sports. The first modern Olympics took place in Athens in 1896. They were initially a male-only affair, though unlike in ancient Greece women were permitted to be spectators – and male participants were clothed. Female athletes, their founder always believed, would be invading a male sphere (Simri, 1983: 32–35).

Women just barely gained entrance to the Paris Olympics in 1900, thanks to the insistence of the French hosts. Twelve women from four countries (France, Great Britain, Bohemia, and the United States) competed in two events, golf and tennis, and were just 2 percent of the athletes. Women's participation grew haltingly. There were significant steps up in 1928 and 1976, reflecting the international influence of first-wave and second-wave feminism. It was not until 2004, however, that women were more than 40 percent of Olympians. In 2012 women were allowed to compete in 140 out of 302 Olympic events – up from just 39 in 1968.

Women's increasing participation required both activism by women's organizations and growing acceptance, particularly by the media, of women athletes. Until 1924 the inclusion of any women's events was based on the host country's wishes, as the International Olympic Committee (IOC) preferred to reserve the Olympics for men. In 1921 a French woman named Alice Milliat organized the Fédération Sportive Féminine Internationale (FSFI), which agitated for women's permanent representation in the games. The FSFI ran its own Olympics for women in Paris in 1922 and a second in Gothenberg, Sweden, in 1926. Both of these events proved to be popular draws. The IOC consequently relented and agreed to make women's events, particularly in track and field, permanent fixtures. The 1928

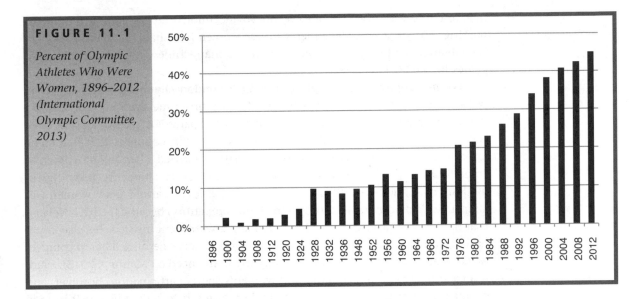

FIGURE 11.1

Percent of Olympic Athletes Who Were Women, 1896–2012 (International Olympic Committee, 2013)

Amsterdam games included five women's track and field events (Teetzel, 2011; Simri, 1983: 47–54). Unfortunately, one of these events, the 800 meter run, was lost for the next 32 years when three competitors fell after completing the race and male organizers took this as proof that women could not run such long distances. Women had much more access to training and other support by 1984, when the American Joan Benoit won the first Olympic marathon (26.2 miles) for women.

In many cases, women were sent to the Olympics and other international competitions most enthusiastically by (male) political leaders who saw them as useful for political goals. Totalitarian regimes, including Nazi Germany, China, and the Soviet Union, developed sports programs for elite female athletes in order to demonstrate the virtues of their systems and counter international criticisms around human rights. Images of successful and happy women allowed these regimes to suggest that they were better than democratic countries at promoting gender equity (which China and the Soviet Union arguably were) and therefore better guarantors of human liberty (a more debatable claim).

Many countries felt that fielding winning teams was a signal of national strength and military as well as physical prowess. Contests between the United States and the U.S.S.R. were especially freighted throughout the Cold War, and in 1980 the United States and 61 other countries boycotted the games held in Moscow (Zinser, 2008; D'Agati, 2013). In 1957, during China's formative "Great Leap Forward," the country's Sports Ministry declared a "Great Sports Leap Forward." Its goal was to catch up with the world's best sporting powers in just ten years (Hong, 2003). This initial target proved unachievable, and mainland China boycotted several Olympics due to geopolitical struggles over the status of Taiwan. In 1984, however, China was able to send 216 athletes to the Olympics (which were held in Los Angeles and boycotted by the Soviet Union) and placed fourth in medal rankings (Zinser, 2008). Since then Chinese women have held up "half the sky" in the Olympics and they won more gold medals than Chinese men in Beijing's own games in 2008 (Clarey, 2012).

Women approached equality in the 2012 London Olympics, where about 45 percent of the athletes were female and for the first time every one of the 204 participating countries sent at least one female participant (IOC, 2013). The last three holdouts were Saudi Arabia, Qatar, and Brunei, Muslim countries that had come under significant international pressure and finally allowed a handful of women to compete as long as they wore "modest" dress. Disputes about the meanings of modesty continued even after the games began, as a 16-year-old Saudi woman was almost blocked from participating in the judo competition because the IOC declared that the *hijab*, or headscarf, that her father and government insisted she wear could be dangerous on the mat. After some negotiation, officials permitted her to compete while wearing a form of *hijab* that held tightly to her head (O'Mahony, 2012). Saudi Arabia strongly discourages girls' and women's sports participation, however, and Wojdan Shaherkani, who was trained by her father, held only a blue belt in judo and was defeated by her opponent in 82 seconds. Some people asked whether such inexperienced athletes should be allowed to participate in the Olympics, especially after an undertrained woman from Qatar was injured while running a race. Others, however, felt that these women's participation was an enormous victory, no matter how poorly they performed (Robertson, 2012; Associated Press, 2012).

As we suggested earlier, women's participation in business, academia, the media, and other fields has been limited by systemic preferences for men. Similar patterns appear in sports, including the Olympics. In 2012 women won more medals than men in all three of the top-ranked countries – the United States, China, and Russia – but in the fourth-ranked country, Great Britain, women won just 22 of 65 medals. Great Britain's policy was to provide government support to more elite male than female athletes, on the grounds that more competitions were open to men and men had more opportunities to develop the skills that make them potential winners (Hartmann-Tews and Pfister, 2003: 274). This policy perpetuated the male-dominated status quo: men were given more funding because they had more opportunities. New Zealand took a different approach, making all athletes, male and female, eligible for comprehensive government support if they were one of the top ten competitors worldwide in their sport and gender (Thompson, 2003). Women won six of New Zealand's 13 medals in 2012, suggesting that a more merit-based system produces more balanced results.

CONCLUSION

Sports have many implications that extend well beyond the playing field. Some societies have used sports as relatively egalitarian opportunities for physical activity, group interaction, and shared fun. In many societies, however, sports have been used to celebrate masculinity and toughness, symbolically assert a group's or nation's dominance, and police the boundaries between men and women. Achievement in sports can be an attractive way for boys and men to pursue social status and material rewards. While these opportunities are especially important for those who have few other options for achieving social respect and economic success, they can also help foreclose other pathways to social mobility. Sports can also be a way for relatively privileged spectators to congratulate themselves on their distance from and superiority to competitors whom they view as more bestial – whether they be gladiators in the Roman era or football players today.

Girls' and women's growing access to sports, demanded by many women and facilitated by Title IX legislation, is part of a much larger effort to break down the gendered prescriptions that have constrained so many people's lives. School sports and community athletic programs give girls and women opportunities to develop their more physical and competitive inclinations, which can help them break free from some of the more limiting aspects of expected femininity. Lesbian women, in particular, have often found sports a welcome reprieve from the broader culture's emphasis on heterosexual romance, family life, and expectations of feminine attractiveness. Women's professional sports, however, have struggled to gain the media and fan attention that makes them financially sustainable. The equation of sports with masculinity and strength, more than skill, has discouraged women's participation at every level. It has also helped justify male dominance on the grounds of male physical superiority.

Develop Your Position

1   Do you think sports are currently a key area in which males develop a masculine identity? Why or why not? Do you think sports are more central to the development of a masculine identity for low-income males and males of color than for wealthier or white males? Why or why not?

2   Do you think sports are now an arena where females can gain a sense of feminine identity? Why or why not?

3   What do you think are the most important factors that have made it difficult for women's professional sports leagues to succeed? Do you expect these leagues will have more success in the next 20 years? Why or why not?

4   We have suggested that sports are often a medium for intergroup competition that extends well beyond the playing field. Have you seen that pattern in action? Where? Do you think the sports contest increased people's experiences of intergroup competition, or did it more provide a structured venue for pre-existing competitive impulses to play out?

PART IV

Looking Toward the Future

CHAPTER 12

Possible Futures of
Gender Inequality

INTRODUCTION

Where is gender inequality headed in the future? No one really knows. Sometimes the world changes in unexpected ways. Looking back later, people can usually see some hints of what was to come, even if they did not recognize the signs at the time. Sometimes, though, truly unpredictable events come out of nowhere. We do not presume to know what history-changing events might occur in the future.

We can, however, look at the trends of the recent past and ask where they seem to be headed. If something has been changing at a fast or slow pace for a while, it is plausible to guess that it might continue changing at something like that pace. If, however, something changed quickly in the past and more recently slowed down, it might be heading toward a plateau. If one looks at a situation and thinks, "I don't see how that can last," chances are it will not.

In this final chapter, therefore, we will trace some of the recent trends related to gender inequality and their possible implications, with a focus on the underlying determinants of those trends. Many of these underlying factors suggest that gender equality is likely to continue to grow. Others, however, suggest that change may be difficult in certain arenas, or even that gender inequality might increase. Overall we suspect that the arc of history will bend toward gender egalitarianism and equality, but that trajectory is not inevitable.

TRENDS TOWARD GREATER EQUALITY

As we have seen, gender equality has increased dramatically in the United States in the last half-century. In 1960 gender discrimination was pervasive, overt, and taken for granted. It was perfectly legal for employers to reject female candidates just because they were women, or to pay women less than men, and most did. Female professionals were rare in every field and men held nearly all positions of authority and leadership. Women had no legal right to say no to sex with their husbands and some states prohibited contraception even for married couples. A woman who had sex outside of marriage risked social ostracism, especially if she got pregnant, while a woman who accused a man of rape risked having her entire life raked over the coals in court. Most Americans agreed it could be appropriate for a man to use corporal punishment to discipline his wife.

Today, two-thirds of American women and nearly half of American men say they believe in the social, economic, and political equality of the sexes (YouGov, 2013). Most Americans agree that men and women should be paid the same for the same work (though the question of what that means in practice can be vexed). Female professionals are no longer an oddity in most fields, and most families assume that girls as well as boys need to be prepared to make a living. Women now receive a majority of bachelors' and graduate degrees, suggesting that their professional visibility and achievement will continue to grow. Many Ivy League universities – which in 1960 did not admit female undergraduates – now have or have had female presidents. Many large companies have or have had female CEOs, and in 2008 Hillary Clinton was taken very seriously as a candidate for president of the United States.

Laws now recognize women's rights to refuse sex, use contraception, and obtain an abortion, though sometimes it is difficult to turn those legal rights into actual access. Americans have increasingly embraced a sexual ethic based on the principle of consent, and most now consider premarital sex morally unproblematic. The stigmatization of unmarried mothers has decreased dramatically, though not disappeared, and nearly half of all children are now born to unmarried women. Most Americans now believe that people should be able to marry whomever they love, and by the end of 2014 same-sex marriage was an option for the majority of Americans. Growing numbers of Americans believe that sexual coercion and family violence are always unacceptable, and the frequencies of both rape and serious partner violence have decreased dramatically, though neither has disappeared. Growing numbers of American men believe it is important for fathers to be actively involved in raising their children. In short, gender discrimination still exists, but it is far more patchy, subtle, and challenged.

Economic forces suggest that gender equality will continue to increase. It seems very likely that the U.S. economy will generally continue to reward people with cognitive and interpersonal skills more than people who are physically strong. Many companies are realizing that the less they discriminate in hiring and promotion the more likely they are to get the best available person into each position – whatever their gender, race, or sexual orientation – and therefore the more likely they are to succeed against their competitors. Being non-discriminatory also helps avoid lawsuits and bad publicity. And evidence is growing that a diverse team of decision-makers often makes better decisions. These economic incentives all lean toward more gender equality over time.

As we have seen, women continue to earn less than men at every educational level, due to some combination of (usually unconscious) discrimination, the continued assumption that children are primarily women's responsibility, and men's and women's performance of gender through their educational and career choices. Increasing gender equality would therefore presumably increase women's incomes. One of the reasons for the narrowing gender gap, however, has been the loss of jobs previously performed by less-educated men due to technological innovation and the growth of an international economy. When boys feel that trying to do well in school is incompatible with masculinity, or when schools focus on athletics more than academics, young men end up ill prepared for the current job market. In a society where gender was less important they would presumably feel less pressure to perform their masculinity by focusing their energies on sports, high-risk activities, or other ways of demonstrating toughness. For the young men who have had the most tenuous connections with the workforce, therefore, increasing gender equality might improve their economic prospects. Increasing racial equality would be similarly helpful for people with brown skins: it is not just their own performances of masculinity and femininity that can get in their way, but also how others stereotype them.

Most Americans – especially young Americans – now espouse egalitarian ideals and feel it is generally wrong to discriminate on the basis of gender, race, or other group memberships. Both individual behavior and institutional arrangements do not always live up to those egalitarian ideals, and as we have seen unconscious stereotypes can have powerful effects even on people who want to be egalitarian. It seems likely, however, that the longer such ideals are culturally normative, the more broadly and deeply they will affect individual and collective behavior. Not everyone shares these ideals, and for many people they are mixed with other deeply held assumptions about how the world works. Increasingly, though, people who hold to older ways are discovering that standards of behavior are changing. For example, the media have recently been full of stories about sexual assault on college campuses and domestic abuse by athletes not because these behaviors are new, but because they are newly considered as newsworthy.

Cultural ideals can ebb as well as flow, of course, but it seems likely that gender egalitarianism will persist. As we have seen, capitalistic economic systems tend to nurture individualism – the belief that individuals, not families or larger social units, should make their own decisions. Most successful capitalistic societies also end up embracing the principles of democracy and political liberalism, which extend individualism to the political level. The example of China suggests (at least thus far) that it is possible for a country to embrace industrialization and capitalism, and the liberation of women from family domination that typically ensues, without accepting political individualism. In the United States, however, ideas about self-determination, inalienable human rights, and equality under the law are deeply woven into the culture. The extent to which these principles have applied to women and many different types of minorities have varied greatly over time. When, however, Americans claim that all people should have equal rights, freedoms, and opportunities, they invoke values that are core to the country's economy and political system. One way to read American history is as a gradual expansion of the rights and principles guaranteed by the Constitution to all Americans – a process that has often been contested, but is unlikely to utterly reverse itself.

On a psychological level, egalitarianism is rooted in broad feelings of empathy. When people feel that members of another group (gender, race, nationality, species, etc.) are fundamentally unlike them, they can be quite indifferent to the suffering of others. In its narrow forms, empathy motivates people to do favors for other members of their own groups – their family, class, gender, and so on. As the circle of empathy expands, however, people's desire to see others do well broadens. One result is that people increasingly embrace abstract principles of rights and justice, which apply to everyone. Many experiences can nurture empathy, including personal relationships (friends and colleagues from various groups) and media (journalism, novels, movies, etc.) (Pinker, 2011: 571–692).

Americans today live in a heterosocial world in which men and women commonly study, work, socialize, and live together both romantically and not. They therefore have many opportunities to experience each other as real human beings and discover commonalities. Most Americans also have enormous exposure to media products that ask them to look at the world from multiple points of view. It seems very unlikely that American culture will revert to the pervasive patterns of gender segregation that inhibit cross-gender empathy. Indeed, the recent rapid increase in social acceptance of homosexuality and same-sex marriage reflects a growing feeling that gender is not essential even within family life. If men and women are truly equal, why should the law care about the genders of two people who love each other? Although gay marriage is most important for gay couples and their children, it also reveals a fundamental shift in understandings of gender, which affect everyone.

Gender equality has also increased dramatically on a global level. From Latin America to Asia, many countries are experiencing a mutually reinforcing cycle of women's increasing economic opportunities, increasing educational levels, decreasing fertility rates, increasing life expectancies (reflecting better health more generally), and increasing legal rights. Each of these trends tends to promote the others. Women are more likely to have paid employment, for example, if they are decently educated, have just a few children, are in good health, and are not circumscribed by legal restrictions (such as needing a husband's permission to have a job). Women's incomes, in turn, increase the education of daughters, men's and women's desires for small families, women's health, and women's participation in family and community decision making. The fact that these changes are interlocking, each reinforcing the others, suggests that they are likely to continue. Indeed, gender patterns are changing more quickly in many developing countries than they did in the United States at similar stages of development. In the United States, for example, it took more than a century for the average family size to drop from six to three children. The same transition took 35 years in India and less than 20 years in Bangladesh, as incentives, aspirations, and behavior changed dramatically in just one generation (World Bank, 2011a: 7–12).

As we noted earlier, all large international institutions (such as the United Nations and World Bank), most large NGOs (such as the Gates Foundation), and most national governments now espouse the idea that increasing gender equality and women's empowerment are essential for reducing poverty and promoting national prosperity and well-being. Study after study has shown that giving women access to land, fertilizer, credit, education, jobs, contraception, and other resources increases families' incomes, countries' economic productivity, and children's health and education, thus preparing countries for even more economic growth in the next generation (e.g., World Bank, 2011a: 3–6). It is now nearly a cliché in international circles to say that economic development has to start with girls and women. This widespread institutional commitment to gender equality, which is seen as not just as an end in itself but also as key to other much-desired goals, means that significant quantities of money, creativity, and rich-world professional careers are now devoted to women's empowerment. It seems likely that this institutional momentum will continue to promote girls' education, contraception and maternal health care, women's access to land and paid employment, violence prevention programs, and numerous other efforts to redistribute power for the benefit of girls and women.

TRENDS TOWARD STAGNATION

There are, however, also signs that the path toward gender equality may have reached a plateau in the United States. As we have seen, many different metrics of gender inequality changed quite significantly between 1970 and 2000 but little or not at all since them. Women's political representation, for example, has changed little since the 1990s. The incidence of rape, as reported in victim surveys, fell dramatically between 1980 and 2000 but since then has basically leveled off. Women's workforce participation, women's wages as a percentage of men's, and gender segregation of occupations have all stagnated. Men and women continue to perform gender in their choices of majors and career paths, their balancing of work and family responsibilities, and their willingness to take risks or to apply for positions for which they are not fully qualified – and women who fail to negotiate successfully the competing demands to be leaders and to be feminine are often shot down. Married mothers still do twice as much childcare as married fathers, with little change since around 2000. Mothers are even more disproportionately responsible for most children who are born outside marriage, which now is nearly half of all children. Although mothers are now the sole or primary breadwinners in 40 percent of American families with children, 51 percent of poll respondents say that children are better off if their mothers do not work and stay home – compared to just 8 percent who say children are better off if their fathers do not work and stay home (Wang et al., 2013).

We have repeatedly pointed to the Nordic countries as proof that it is possible for a society to be substantially more gender-egalitarian than the United States.

Strong feminist movements in these countries have promoted gender equality for more than a century, and today their governments are committed to the principles of gender equity and support for all families. Even in the Nordic countries, however, there are substantial differences in the amounts of paid work and care work done by men and women. Swedish women, for example, spend twice as much time on childcare, on average, as Swedish men. They give about 40 percent more time to housework and 30 percent less time to paid employment (World Bank, 2011a: 19). Some people argue that long maternity leave policies, common in Europe but not in the United States, encourage the association of women with childcare and make employers wary of hiring reproductive-age women (Miller, 2014a). Sweden, however, offers both mothers and fathers ten weeks of paid leave after the arrival of a child, though many fathers do not take all of their leave (OECD, 2012: 2). Around the world, women bear a disproportionate responsibility for housework and caring for people who are young, old, or sick. This expectation that women will do most care work affects women's educational and career choices even before they have children, and it helps perpetuate gender segregation of occupations and the gender wage gap. The fact that it persists even in the most egalitarian of countries suggests it would be difficult to eradicate.

This gendered division of care work and economic resources may also put limits on how much or how quickly gender equality can increase in developing countries. If one includes both paid and unpaid work, women in most countries work more hours than men (World Bank, 2011a: 17). Women who take on more work outside the home may experience no lessening of their cooking, cleaning, and family care responsibilities, and their resulting exhaustion may make them reluctant to press harder for economic opportunities. Worldwide, 34 percent of men and 18 percent of women work full-time for an employer, the form of work that generally provides most income and stability (Ray, 2014). Gendered norms about appropriate behavior are often reinforced by institutional factors, such as discrimination in labor markets (including the gender-segregated social networks that help people get jobs), a lack of childcare facilities, and a lack of labor-saving (and health-saving) services like electricity and clean drinking water from a tap inside or near the house. Government provision of job training and placement services, decent and affordable childcare, and reliable utilities and transport can significantly increase women's access to paid employment and thus help set in motion the cycle of incentives and changes that lead to greater gender equality. Such services require, however, not just money but also competent governance. The interlocking factors maintaining gender inequality can thus prove quite persistent indeed.

Indeed, gender inequality tends to be most intense in communities that are disadvantaged in other ways. For example, female disadvantage in education has disappeared among higher-income families in nearly all countries, while it can be quite significant in poor families. In India, the top two income quintiles have no gender gap in median educational achievement. In the poorest income quintile, however, boys receive an average of 6 years of education while girls receive an average of just 1 year. Globally, almost two-thirds of out-of-school girls belong to ethnic minorities in their own countries. In these severely disadvantaged communities, economic opportunities of any kind are slim, public services miserable, and gender inequality intense. Poverty and gender inequality are thus mutually reinforcing, and the cycle between them can be very difficult to disrupt in communities that are marginalized or stigmatized (World Bank, 2011a: 12–14).

TRENDS THAT MIGHT INCREASE GENDER INEQUALITY

It is possible that gender inequality will grow in the future, at least in some locations. Men are less likely to support opportunities for women when they feel like their own opportunities are inadequate or shrinking. We mentioned earlier that the incidence of rape in India seems to be rising as poor men take offence at the increasing freedom, opportunity, and affluence of more-educated women. A 2010 (before the Arab Spring pro-democracy uprisings) study of Arab men in six countries found that most agreed that women and men should have equal legal rights and that women should be able to hold any job outside the home for which they are qualified. Men's support for women's freedoms was highly correlated with their own levels of employment, education, and life satisfaction, but not with their religious views. The more men were struggling themselves, the less willing they were to share what they experienced as limited resources with women (Gallup, 2012a: 13–16). Around the world, many other examples suggest that men who experience their own conditions as declining may take out their anger and disappointment on women – sometimes through violence, sometimes just by trying to ensure that what opportunities remain go to men.

Generally speaking, women benefit more than men (but probably not as much as children) from **social order**: the ability of a society to provide housing, schools, clean water, medical care, safe streets, the rule of law, and a basic level of predictability for all its people. In these environments, women are able to fulfill their family responsibilities and have some time, energy, and attention left over to pursue their own goals. Conversely, women tend to suffer more from conditions of political and economic instability, chronic conflict, and war. The lack of a trustworthy government encourages the growth of an **honor-based culture** that validates male dominance. Men are more likely to be violent toward women when their own lives are insecure, and in many war zones they use rape as a weapon. When women lack physical safety and material resources, they become both more dependent on their male relatives and less able to provide for their children, who in every society are ultimately a female responsibility.

If the world becomes more violent and/or more impoverished, gender inequality will probably increase, at least in the areas so plagued. In 2011, Steven Pinker showed that human societies have experienced less war, murder, and other forms of violence over time, whether time was measured in decades, centuries, or millennia (2011:

1–377). Since then, however, there has been an upsurge of violence in some parts of the world, as a series of events have destabilized a swath of countries from Mali to Pakistan. These countries have long suffered from high levels of social inequality, poverty, and government corruption, and their high birthrates mean they contain large numbers of unemployed, underemployed, and unmarriageable young men. Early experiments with establishing democratic governance proved fragile and unable to quell discontent. History shows that elections alone cannot create the economic and governmental institutions, and related shifts in attitudes and practices, that allow a nation to prosper and resources to be shared more equitably. Such changes take both time and intentionality, but the impoverished are not always patient and the privileged are not always willing to risk real change.

It is possible that the recent increase in violence will prove to be a temporary blip and that the forces Pinker identifies as responsible for the decline in violence will resume their long-term trends. It is also possible, however, that violence and disorder will continue to grow. The civil war in Syria was triggered in part by a long-term drought that displaced a million people into already crowded and strained cities (Friedman, 2014). The Pentagon has recently predicted that climate change and its associated droughts, fierce storms, and crop failures will lead to more desperate poverty, hunger, mass migration, social and political instability, and demands on the American military (Davenport, 2014). Environmental stresses, especially when combined with rapid population growth or ineffective and corrupt governance (which typically occur in the same countries), may mean that the world will experience more violence and disorder in upcoming decades than it did in the recent past.

The United States may not be exempt from these patterns. In general, countries that are able to give most of their residents a gradually increasing standard of living develop a political culture that nurtures social mobility, tolerance of diversity, democratic governance, and egalitarianism. When people experience serious economic difficulties, however, they tend to become more rigid, self-protective, and intolerant, and they often seek scapegoats to blame for their unhappiness (B. Friedman, 2005). Income inequality is growing in the United States and shows no sign of abating. For example, the bottom 80 percent of the income curve saw their incomes fall from 2010 to 2013, which statistically was a time of economic growth – but all of the growth, and more, went to the wealthiest 20 percent of Americans, especially the top 10 percent (Irwin, 2014). For many men, these declining circumstances represent an end to the old bargain that if a man worked hard he could earn not just a living for his family, but also respect as a man. Men who still believe in the old image of men as breadwinners – and therefore as respected heads of their families – may feel humiliated and emasculated if changed economic circumstances mean they are unable to live up to their own expectations of masculinity. Many men feel cheated, and some erupt with rage against the people they see as winners in the modern economy: women (Kimmel, 2013). If the United States continues to provide a declining standard of living to many of its residents, it is possible that intergroup resentments of many kinds may rise.

CONCLUSION

Gender equality increased dramatically in the United States and most other countries in the twentieth century, and our guess is that it will continue to increase in the twenty-first century. It would be difficult for the increase in the United States in the next 50 years to be as dramatic as that of the last 50 years, simply because so much has already changed. It is possible that gender equality in the United States will never reach the level of the Nordic countries, which are more egalitarian in many dimensions and more inclined to use public resources to help individuals and families flourish. It is even possible that economic difficulties and growing economic inequality may lead to a successful backlash against women's aspirations. It seems most likely, however, that the combination of a knowledge-based economy and increasingly entrenched egalitarian ideals will mean that gender equality continues to grow over the coming decades.

Around the world, many other countries are experiencing similar patterns. The growth of a global economy, with its associated industrial and knowledge-based development, is creating new economic opportunities for women. Increasing health and education, declining fertility, and greater political participation are all both consequences and causes of women's employment. Global media, international institutions, and international travel are also encouraging the spread of individualism and egalitarianism. As people's aspirations rise they tend to have just one or two children, and within a couple of generations they tend to invest equally in their daughters and sons. Women's disproportionate responsibility for family care work seems to be persistent, but even that moderates as families get smaller and women gain more economic and political power.

Not everyone, however, considers this increasingly individualistic and egalitarian world desirable. Redistribution of power and resources can be threatening to those who are accustomed to being advantaged. Individualism weakens families and communities, which may seem like a reasonable price to pay in prospering societies but less so where life is hard. When a society is in turmoil it is quite possible for women to lose freedoms and rights previously achieved. Societies are more likely to become tumultuous when they have high degrees of social and economic inequality, corrupt and unresponsive governments, environmental stresses, and/or rapidly growing populations. These tensions tend to reinforce each other, and they can prove explosive.

The future of gender inequality is thus intertwined with the future of many other kinds of inequality. Countries that can provide social order and economic opportunities to most of their residents will probably see gender equality continue to grow. Societies with large disparities between different classes, ethnicities, or religious groups may, however, prove more unstable, and one result may be the increasing suppression of women.

Develop Your Position

1   What is your educated guess about where gender equality is headed in the United States in the next 50 years? Do you think it is likely to increase from here? Decrease? Stay about the same? Why?

2   What dimensions of gender inequality now seem most important to you? For example, we wrote earlier about the gender gap in how much men and women earn, even if they have the same education. Does gender inequality in income seem key to you, or are there other aspects of gender inequality that seem more important?

3   Do you agree with our conclusion that peace, social order, and a lack of large inequalities between different social groups is conducive to gender equality? Why or why not?

4   Below is a map of the world. Choose three colors and fill in the map. Where do you think gender equality is likely to grow in the next 50 years? Where do you think it will stay about the same? Where do you think it will decrease? Where do you have no idea where it is headed? Why?

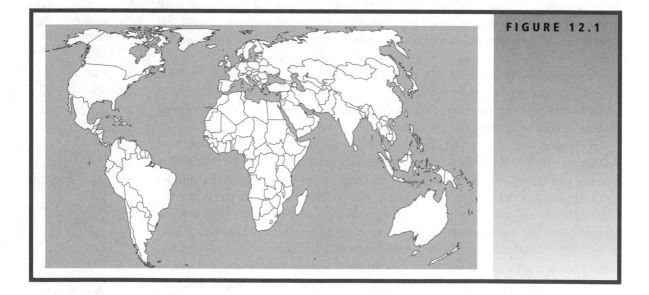

FIGURE 12.1

GLOSSARY

agriculture growing crops with the aid of plows and large domesticated animals, or more recently machinery.

bilineal referring to societies that trace family membership and inheritance through both parents.

black feminists people who critique both racism and sexism, see them as intersecting systems of injustice, and seek to promote the well-being of black women.

Boston marriage long-term and socially recognized partnerships that some professional women formed with other women in the late nineteenth century.

boy problem American boys' relative educational underachievement, first problematized in the late nineteenth century and re-problematized in the twenty-first century.

breadwinner the masculine-coded expectation in industrial and knowledge-based societies that a good husband and father will be able to provide primary or exclusive financial support for his family.

brideprice payment from a groom or his family to the bride's family at engagement or marriage.

care work work (usually unpaid, typically in families) that nurtures other people, including raising children, cooking food, caring for elders, etc.

cisgendered adjective referring to people whose gender identities are in line with their physical sex.

Civil Rights Act of 1964 a federal law that prohibited discrimination by race, color, gender, religion, or national origin in schools, workplaces, elections, and public accommodations.

civil society a layer of social organization that is larger than families but not tightly linked with the state.

code femininity or **rewarded femininity** the ideal form of femininity that is most rewarded in a society.

code masculinity or **hegemonic masculinity** the ideal form of masculinity that is most rewarded in a society.

cognitive learning theories theories that argue that children actively seek to comprehend the world, including ideas about gender.

cohabitate to live with a sexual partner without marriage.

colonialism the control of one society and its people and economy by another.

companionate marriage marriage based on the belief that marriage is similar to close friendship and is, or should be, primarily about love, intimacy, and mutual enjoyment.

compulsory heterosexuality the web of social pressures that push women into sexual relationships with men, and men with women.

concerted cultivation the effort that many college-educated parents in the United States today make to provide their children with an abundance of stimulating and enriching activities.

conditional cash transfers government stipends that are conditional upon the receivers' actions, typically sending children to school and medical appointments.

conflict perspectives theoretical perspectives that examine how groups of people manipulate institutions to benefit themselves and disadvantage others.

constructivism theoretical perspectives based on the belief that cultures create shared meanings and understandings of the world. Constructivists believe that gender, race, sexual identity, etc., are cultural constructions, not immutable realities created by God or nature. See also **essentialism**.

coverture the English Common Law doctrine, inherited by the British colonies and the United States, under which a woman's legal existence is subsumed in her husband when she marries.

cult of domesticity the nineteenth-century middle-class ideology that women should devote themselves to – and have sovereignty over – a feminine domain of home, family, children, and morality.

cultural capital knowledge about how to navigate the more rewarded aspects of one's society.

cultural lag the inconsistencies and discomforts that occur when some aspects of a culture change more quickly than others.

culture a society's characteristic ways of thinking, feeling, and behaving.

demographic transition a period of change during which declining death rates are followed by smaller family sizes.

different voice feminists people who believe that women and men have different moral sensibilities and draw on different ethical principles when making decisions, and that women's ways of being in the world should be affirmed and promoted.

dowry payment from a bride's family to the groom or his family at engagement or marriage.

dowry deaths the killing of women due to inadequate dowries.

educational divide in family patterns the gap that has emerged in the United States between college-educated and less-educated people in age of marriage, age of childbearing, unmarried parenthood, and related behaviors and expectations.

educational homogamy the tendency to marry someone who has a similar educational level and earning potential.

Equal Pay Act of 1963 a federal law that prohibited gender discrimination in pay.

essentialism theoretical perspectives based on the belief that each person has intrinsic qualities created by nature and/or God. In the case of gender, essentialists believe that women and men are different not just in their reproductive capacities, but also in their basic natures. See also **constructivism**.

family economy an economic system based on the expectation that all members of a family will function as an economic unit, typically under the direction of a male **head of household** who owns all property and directs the work and lives of other family members. A similar term is "household economy," but not all members of a household economy are necessarily members of the family that defines that household.

family wage a wage sufficient to support a whole family and enable a man to fulfill his breadwinner role; a major goal of men's union movements in the nineteenth and early twentieth centuries.

fatherhood premium the additional earnings and other workplace privileges that may be given to fathers on the assumption that they want and need to be good **breadwinners**.

female genital cutting the removal of some or all of the external female genitalia. Also known as FGC or female genital mutilation.

feminine displaying qualities culturally associated with women.

feminists people who believe in the social, economic, and political equality of women and men, believe that inequalities advantaging men exist, and want change.

functionalism a theoretical perspective based on the belief that every element of a society serves useful functions and contributes to the stability of the society.

gender the many meanings cultures assign to sex. Sociologists use "**sex**" to distinguish between females and males, while "gender" distinguishes between feminine and masculine.

gender boundary anything that marks the purported divide between men and women.

gender inequality hierarchies based on gender.

gender roles social expectations associated with each gender category.

gender schema theories theories that argue people develop gender **schemas**, or networks of information about gender, that make them selectively process new inputs related to gender.

gender segregation of occupations the tendency of many occupations to have workers who are predominantly one gender or the other.

genderqueer referring to people who mix and match masculine and feminine signals and performances.

glass ceiling the experience of many women that they reach a certain level in the workplace and cannot rise higher, while men of equal or lesser capabilities and performance continue to rise.

glass cliff the experience of some women that they are given challenging or impossible assignments in the workplace and then blamed and fired if they fail to achieve them.

glass escalator the rapid rise to supervisory positions that men in female-coded occupations often enjoy.

globalization the growth in international travel of money, objects, people, and ideas.

Griswold v. Connecticut the 1965 Supreme Court case that found that married couples have a right to use contraceptives.

head of household the person, nearly always a man, to whom ownership of most material goods is assigned in family or household economies.

hegemonic masculinity or **code masculinity**   the ideal form of masculinity that is most rewarded in a society.

heteronormativity   the cultural ideology that urges people to think of themselves as women or men, feminine or masculine, and heterosexual but not homosexual.

heterosexuality   a sexual identity defined by sexual and/or romantic attraction to people of the other gender.

heterosocial   cross-gender friendships, or the expectation that people will spend most of their time in a mixed-gender social environment.

hidden curriculum   the unintended and often unconscious lessons conveyed in classrooms.

homophobia   fear of or discomfort with homo-eroticism, hostility towards people who are believed to experience homoeroticism.

homosexuality   a sexual identity defined by sexual and/or romantic attraction to people of the same gender.

homosocial   same-gender friendships, or the expectation that people will spend most of their time with and form their closest relationships with people of their own gender.

honor   high respect or esteem in the eyes of others.

honor-based cultures   cultures in which honor is important and individuals or families are expected to retaliate against threats and insults.

horticulture   growing crops with the aid of hoes and other light tools, but not plows or large domestic animals.

household economy   an economic system based on the expectation that all members of a household will function as an economic unit, typically under the direction of a male **head of household** who owns all property and directs the work and lives of other household members. A similar term is "family economy," but not all members of a household economy are necessarily members of the family that defines that household.

hunting-gathering   an economic system in which people rely on collecting and hunting wild foods.

implicit stereotypes   associations that affect the speed of our unconscious cognitive processes even though we are not consciously aware of them.

industrial societies   economic systems focused on the making of goods other than food.

infibulation   the removal of the clitoris, the labia minora, and most of the labia majora.

intersectionality   theoretical perspectives that focus on the ways multiple intersecting identities and hierarchies shape people's experiences.

joint family   a multigenerational family with parents, adult children, and the children's spouses and children all in one household; can occur in either patrilineal/patrilocal or matrilineal/matrilocal forms. Contrasts with **nuclear family**.

knowledge-based economy   an economy that is driven by information and typically rewards people who are adept at processing information. Many knowledge-based economies are also **service economies**.

lesbian feminists   people who believe that the root of women's oppression is compulsory heterosexuality and the ways it binds women into intimate, unequal, and often dangerous relationships with men.

liberal feminists   people who believe that equality will be achieved if women are treated as individuals, not as members of a group called "women."

male privilege   the advantages that come to men simply by virtue of being men.

marriage   a socially and legally recognized sexual and economic partnership; the term is typically associated with patrilineal societies that expect women to be monogamous within marriage and men to support their biological children.

masculine   displaying qualities culturally associated with men.

matrilineal   referring to societies in which family membership and land typically pass from mothers to daughters.

matrilocal   referring to societies in which women typically live with or near their female relatives.

microloans   small loans to poor borrowers who are considered bad credit risks by traditional banks. Microloans are often intended to start or expand small business ventures.

motherhood penalty   the reduced earnings and employment opportunities experienced by mothers, compared to other women with equal education and workplace experience.

multicultural feminists   people who articulate and affirm the experiences of women of many different heritages, especially those who have been marginalized.

non-cognitive skills   skills useful for pursuing education that are independent of the ability to think, such as diligence, patience, and a willingness to submit to authority.

nuclear family   a small family consisting of just a couple and their children. Contrasts with **joint family**.

othermothers   women other than biological mothers – typically grandmothers, aunts, or older sisters –

who nurture children; often important in African American communities.

partner violence   violence by a current or former romantic, sexual, or marital partner.

pastoral   societies in which food comes primarily from raising larger animals such as cows or camels, sheep or goats.

patriarchy   social relations among men that enable them to dominate women; a system of power that benefits men.

patrilineal   referring to societies in which family membership and land typically pass from fathers to sons.

patrilocal   referring to societies in which married couples typically live with or near the husband's family.

Personal Responsibility and Work Opportunity Reconciliation Act   a 1996 federal law that, among other things, placed a 5-year cap on receiving welfare benefits and required low-wage mothers to devote more time to paid work

political liberalism   the beliefs that every individual has inalienable human rights, all people should be equal in the eyes of the law, individuals should generally have as much freedom as is compatible with the freedom of others, and citizens should be able to participate in collective self-government.

productive work   work that creates goods and/or generates income. See also **reproductive work**.

professionals   people who sell their expertise rather than their physical labor.

prostitution   the practice of regularly selling intercourse in exchange for money, food, or other material rewards. See also **sex work**.

psychoanalytic theories   theories that argue that gender goes deep into the structure of people's psyches.

race   a cultural construction that assigns cultural meanings to inherited aspects of physical appearance, such as skin color and bone structure.

radical feminists   people who believe that patriarchy is universal and fundamental to human societies, that the system of power created by **patriarchy** led to all other hierarchies of power, and that equality would require a radical reordering of society.

rape   a culturally contested term referring to sexual violation. The legal definition in the United States today is: "penetration, no matter how slight, of the vagina or anus with any body part or object, or oral penetration by a sex organ of another person, without the consent of the victim" (FBI, 2012).

rape culture   an interlocking network of beliefs, attitudes, and behaviors that condone and encourage rape.

rape free societies   societies in which the incidence of rape is extremely low.

rape prone societies   societies in which rape is common.

replacement level   the total fertility rate at which a population's size is stable; in healthy societies the replacement level is about 2.1 children per women. See **total fertility rate**.

reproductive work   work that keeps a family going from day to day and generation to generation, including bearing and raising children, cooking and cleaning, etc. Similar but not identical to **care work**, typically contrasted with **productive work**.

reserve army of labor   a term used in Marxist theory for unemployed people (often women) who can be hired and fired at will by capitalists and can be paid lower wages than people (often men) with more stable employment.

rewarded femininity or **code femininity**   the most rewarded form of femininity in a society.

Roe v. Wade   the 1973 Supreme Court decision that legalized abortion before the third trimester.

schema   networks of information that enable the brain to process some inputs more easily than others.

second demographic transition   a period of change during which family structures become more diverse and cohabitation, divorce, and childbearing outside marriage become acceptable, all driven by an underlying belief that family life should be emotionally satisfying.

second shift   family-based **care work** done by someone, usually a mother, who also has paid employment.

self-help justice   justice that depends on retaliating personally for wrongs done to you or your family or associates, in the absence of government authorities that can be trusted to provide safety and justice.

separate spheres   the ideology that men and women have different natures, naturally engage in different activities, and appropriately segregate themselves into different aspects of a society.

service economy   an economy based primarily on people selling their time and skills, rather than physical objects, to other people. Many service economies are also **knowledge-based economies**.

sex   the reproductive biology we're born with; the organs, genetics, hormones, and secondary sex characteristics that enable new human beings to be born. Sociologists use "sex" to distinguish between females and males, while "**gender**" distinguishes between feminine and masculine.

sex negativity   the ideology, common in patrilineal societies, that sex is degrading and dangerous, especially for women.

sex work any sexual activity that is performed in exchange for money, food, clothing, drugs, or other material rewards. See also **prostitution**.

sexual alliance politics using sexual relationships as a medium of exchange to create or strengthen social, economic, or political ties between families.

sexual assault includes both **rape** and **sexual battery**.

sexual battery nonconsensual sexualized touching that does not include penetration, such as forced kissing or groping a breast or other body part.

sexual cultures how different societies think about sexuality, the values and norms they promote, and the behaviors they encourage, discourage, require, or prohibit.

sexual harassment unwanted sexualized conduct intended to make the recipient uncomfortable; some people use the term to refer only to verbal expressions, while others include **sexual battery**.

sexuality actions and experiences related to reproduction and eroticism.

shame being degraded or humiliated in the eyes of others.

Sheppard-Towner Act a 1921 federal law that established maternal and child health centers throughout the United States, which were de-funded in 1929.

social capital resources created by group membership and personal connections that help people solve problems and achieve their goals.

social institutions patterns of behavior that persist over the generations, embody many rules and assumptions, and govern a network of activities.

social learning theories theories that argue that children learn gender from other people, in most cases starting with their parents.

social order the ability of a society to provide housing, schools, clean water, medical care, safe streets, the rule of law, and a basic level of predictability for all its people.

social status one's rank vis-à-vis other people.

socialist feminists people who believe that both capitalism and patriarchy lead to gender inequality and that equality will require ending both economic and cultural sources of women's subordination.

socialization the process through which children (and adults) learn and internalize social roles that enable them to become competent participants in their societies.

society a human community.

sociological imagination the capacity to link personal problems to larger social issues.

Sportsworld highly gender-segregated athletic institutions in which elite male athletes have little contact with women other than cheerleaders.

stereotype a simplified image or belief about a social group that is commonly used to categorize and imagine other people, or oneself.

stereotype threat the impaired performance on a task that can result from feeling at risk of confirming a negative stereotype about a social group to which one belongs.

survival sex sex work performed to enable the worker and/or the worker's family to survive.

temperance literally moderation; historically a movement to prohibit the sale or consumption of alcohol.

theory a way of thinking that identifies, explains, and predicts patterns in a wide range of observations.

Title IX a 1972 federal law that prohibited gender discrimination in any educational program that receives federal assistance.

total fertility rate the statistically average number of children that would be born to each woman in a society given the fertility patterns at a given point in time. It is calculated using the age-specific fertility rates at that time and the assumption that all women will survive past their reproductive years.

traditionalization the tendency of couples in previously more egalitarian marriages to adopt more traditional gender patterns after the birth of a child.

trans men or **FTM** people who identify as men after being assigned female at birth.

trans women or **MTF** people who identify as women after being assigned male at birth.

transgendered or **trans** referring to people who identify as a gender that does not match the sex they were assigned at birth.

virgin/whore dichotomy the division of women into "good women" and "bad women" frequently made in patrilineal societies.

wage gap the difference in average income between different groups, for example by gender or race.

REFERENCES

16 and Pregnant. 2014. Full Cast and Crew. Available online at www.imdb.com/title/tt1454730/full credits

Abou El Fadl, Khaled. 2005. *The Great Theft: Wrestling Islam from the Extremists.* New York: HarperCollins.

Abu-Lughod, Lila. 2010. "The Active Social Life of 'Muslim Women's Rights': A Plea for Ethnography, Not Polemic, with Cases from Egypt and Palestine." *Journal of Middle East Women's Studies* 6(1): 1–45.

Acemoglu, Daron and James A. Robinson. 2012. *Why Nations Fail: The Origins of Power, Prosperity, and Poverty.* New York: Crown Business.

Acker, Joan. 1990. "Hierarchies, Jobs, Bodies: A Theory of Gendered Organizations." *Gender & Society* 4: 139–158.

Acker, Joan. 1998. "The Future of 'Gender & Organizations': Connections and Boundaries." *Gender, Work & Organizations* 5: 195–206.

Adams, David Wallace. 1995. *Education for Extinction: American Indians and the Boarding School Experience, 1875–1926.* Lawrence: University Press of Kansas.

Addams, Jane. 1910. *Twenty Years at Hull House with Autobiographical Notes.* New York: Macmillan.

Administration on Aging. 2011. "A Profile of Older Americans: 2011." Available online at www.aoa.gov/Aging_Statistics/Profile/2011/docs/2011profile.pdf

Adut, Ari. 2008. *On Scandal: Moral Disturbances in Society, Politics, and Art.* New York: Cambridge University Press.

Afifi-Soweid, R.A., M.B. Najem Kteily, and Mona Shediac-Rizkallah. 2002. "Preoccupation with Weight and Disordered Eating Behaviors of Entering Students at a University in Lebanon." *International Journal of Eating Disorders* 32(1): 52–57.

Agot, Kawango E., Ann Vander Stoep, Melissa Tracy, Billy A. Obare, Elizabeth A. Bukusi, Jeckoniah O. Ndinya-Achola, Stephen Moses, and Noel S. Weiss. 2010. "Widow Inheritance and HIV Prevalence in Bondo District, Kenya: Baseline Results from a Prospective Cohort Study." *PLoS ONE* 5(11). doi:10.1371/journal.pone.0014028

Ahmed, Kabir and Sukanta Sarker. 2013. *Contraceptives and Condoms for Family Planning and STI/HIV Prevention.* New York: UNFPA.

Ahmed, Leila. 1992. *Women and Gender in Islam.* New Haven, CT: Yale University Press.

Ahmed, Leila. 1999. *A Border Passage: From Cairo to America – A Woman's Journey.* New York: Penguin.

Ahmed, Leila. 2011. *A Quiet Revolution: The Veil's Resurgence, from the Middle East to America.* New Haven, CT: Yale University Press.

Aitchison, Cara. 2006. *Sport and Gender Identities: Masculinities, Femininities, and Sexualities.* New York: Routledge.

Alami, Aida. 2013. "Gender Inequality in Morocco Continues, Despite Amendments to Family Law." *New York Times*, March 17.

Alexander, Michelle. 2010. *The New Jim Crow: Mass Incarceration in the Age of Colorblindness.* New York: The New Press.

Ali, Kecia. 2006. *Sexual Ethics and Islam: Feminist Reflections on Qur'an, Hadith, and Jurisprudence*. New York: Oneworld.

Ali, Nujood, Delphine Minoui, and Linda Coverdale. 2010. *I Am Nujood, Age 10 and Divorced*. New York: Broadway Books.

Ali-Karamali, Sumbul. 2008. *The Muslim Next Door: The Qur'an, the Media, and that Veil Thing*. Ashland, OR: White Cloud Press.

Allen, Paula Gunn. 1986. *The Sacred Hoop: Recovering the Feminine in American Indian Traditions*. Boston: Beacon Press.

Alon, Sigal and Yitchak Haberfeld. 2007. "Labor Force Attachment and the Evolving Wage Gap between White, Black, and Hispanic Young Women." *Work and Occupations* 34: 369–398.

Alonso-Villar, Olga and Coral del Rio. 2013. "The Occupational Segregation of Black Women in the United States: A Look at its Evolution from 1940 to 2010." Working Paper 2013–304. Society for the Study of Economic Inequality.

Altman, Dennis. 2001. *Global Sex*. Chicago: University of Chicago Press.

Alvi-Aziz, Hayat. 2008. "A Progress Report on Women's Education in Post-Taliban Afghanistan." *International Journal of Lifelong Education* 27: 169–178.

Amadiume, Ifi. 1987. *Male Daughters, Female Husbands: Gender and Sex in an African Society*. London: Zed Books.

American Psychological Association. 2013. "Violence in the Media – Psychologists Study TV and Video Game Violence for Potential Harmful Effects." Available online at www.apa.org/research/action/protect.aspx

American Society for Aesthetic Plastic Surgery. 2012. "Cosmetic Surgery National Data Bank Statistics 2012." Available online at www.surgery.org/sites/default/files/ASAPS-2012-Stats.pdf

Amnesty International. 1999. "'Not Part of My Sentence': Violations of the Human Rights of Women in Custody." Available online at www.amnesty.org/en/library/asset/AMR51/019/1999/en/7588269a-e33d-11dd-808b-bfd8d459a3de/amr510191999en.pdf

Amott, Theresa and Julie Mattaei. 1999. *Race, Gender, and Work: A Multi-Cultural Economic History of Women in the United States*. Cambridge: South End Press.

Anderlini, Sanam Naraghi. 2007. *Women Building Peace: What They Do, Why It Matters*. Boulder, CO: Lynne Rienner Publishers.

Anderson, Chris. 2005. *The Long Tail: Why the Future of Business is Selling Less of More*. New York: Hyperion.

Anderson, Eric. 2005. *In the Game: Gay Athletes and the Cult of Masculinity*. Albany: State University of New York Press.

Anderson, James D. 1988. *The Education of Blacks in the South, 1860–1935*. Chapel Hill: University of North Carolina Press.

Ansary, Tamim. 2002. *West of Kabul, East of New York: An Afghan American Story*. New York: Farrar, Straus, and Giroux.

Ansary, Tamim. 2009. *Destiny Disrupted: A History of the World Through Islamic Eyes*. New York: Public Affairs.

Aoki, Kenichi. 2002. "Sexual Selection as a Cause of Human Skin Colour Variation: Darwin's Hypothesis Revisted." *Annals of Human Biology* 29(6) 589–608.

Arendt, Hannah. 1951. *The Origins of Totalitarianism*. New York: Schocken Books.

Armstrong, Elizabeth and Laura Hamilton. 2013. *Paying for the Party: How College Maintains Inequality*. Cambridge, MA: Harvard University Press.

Armstrong, Elizabeth, Laura Hamilton, and Paula England. 2010. "Is Hooking Up Bad for Women?" *Contexts* 9: 22–29.

Armstrong, Karen. 1993. *A History of God*. New York: Knopf.

Armstrong, Karen. 2006. *Muhammad: A Prophet for Our Times*. New York: HarperCollins.

Armstrong, Karen. 2009. *The Case for God*. Waterville, ME: Thorndike Press.

Armstrong, Karen. 2014. *Fields of Blood: Religion and the History of Violence*. New York: Knopf.

Armstrong, Sally. 2013. *Uprising: A New Age is Dawning for Every Mother's Daughter*. New York: St. Martin's Press.

Ashraf' Malik Muhammad, Muhammad Aslam Adeeb, Akhtar Ali, Aijaz Ahmed Gujjar, Hassan Danial Aslam, and Muhammad Farooq Asif. 2011. "Community School Partnership in Nonformal Basic Education: Targets and Successes in Pakistan." *International Journal of Academic Research* 3: 297–302.

Aslan, Reza. 2005. *No god but God: The Origins, Evolution, and Future of Islam.* New York: Random House.

Associated Press. 2012. "A Triumph for Women from Qatar, Saudi Arabia and Brunei." *New York Times,* August 3.

Association for Library Service to Children. 2014. "Caldecott Medal and Honor Books, 1928–Present." Available online at www.ala.org/alsc/awardsgrants/bookmedia/caldecottmedal/caldecotthonors/caldecottmedal

Attic Paper, 1929. "McClelland Barclay Woman with Borzoi Dog." Available online at www.atticpaper.com/proddetail.php?prod=1929-body-by-fisher-ad-woman-borzoi

Austin, S. Bryn, Najat J. Ziyadeh, Sara Forman, Lisa A. Prokop, Anne Keliher, and Douglas Jacobs. 2008. "Screening High School Students for Eating Disorders: Results of a National Initiative." *Preventing Chronic Disease* 5(4). Available online at www.cdc.gov/pcd/issues/2008/oct/07_0164.htm

Ayikukwei, R., D. Ngare, J. Sidle, D. Ayuku, J. Baliddawa, and J. Greene. 2008. "HIV/AIDS and Cultural Practices in Western Kenya: The Impact of Sexual Cleansing Rituals on Sexual Behaviours." *Culture, Health, and Sexuality* 10(6): 587–599.

Aziz, Fahima. 2009. "Trends in Labor Force Participation Rates by Gender and Race." Available online at http://notizie.unimo.it/campusfile/file/atevt/file27790.pdf

Babcock, Linda and Sara Laschever. 2007. *Women Don't Ask: The High Cost of Avoiding Negotiation – and Positive Strategies for Change.* New York: Bantam.

Baker, Aryn and Ali Safi. 2008. "The Girl Gap." *Time,* January 17.

Baker, Carrie N. 2008. *The Women's Movement Against Sexual Harassment.* New York: Cambridge University Press.

Baker, Kelly J. 2011. *Gospel According to the Klan: The KKK's Appeal to Protestant America, 1915–1930.* Lawrence: University of Kansas Press.

Baker, Paula. 1991. *The Moral Frameworks of Public Life: Gender, Politics, and the State in Rural New York, 1870–1930.* New York: Oxford University Press.

Baldez, Lisa. 2010. "Foreword." In Javier Corrales and Mario Pecheny (eds.) *The Politics of Sexuality in Latin America.* Pittsburgh, PA: University of Pittsburgh Press, pp. ix–xiv.

Banaji, Mahzarin and Anthony Greenwald. 2013. *Blindspot: Hidden Biases of Good People.* New York: Delacorte Press.

Banerjee, Abhijit V. and Esther Duflo. 2011. *Poor Economics: A Radical Rethinking of the Way to Fight Global Poverty.* New York: Public Affairs.

Banerjee, Neela. 2006. "Woman Is Named Episcopal Leader." *New York Times,* June 19.

Banet-Weisner, Sarah. 2007. *Kids Rule! Nickelodeon and Consumer Citizenship.* Durham, NC: Duke University Press.

Banks, Adelle M. 2013. "Some Seventh-Day Adventists Forge Ahead on Women Clergy." *Religion News Service,* December 3. Available online at www.religionnews.com/2013/12/03/seventh-day-adventists-forge-ahead-women-clergy/

Banks, Adelle M. 2014. "Cracks in the 'Stained-Glass Ceiling': Women Reach Prominent Pulpits." *Religion News Service,* August 29. Available online at www.religionnews.com/2014/08/29/cracks-stained-glass-ceiling-women-reach-prominent-pulpits/

Barash, David P. 2013. "Costa Rica's Peace Dividend: How Abolishing the Military Paid Off." *Los Angeles Times,* December 15.

Barker, G., J.M. Contreras, B. Heilman, A.K. Singh, R.K. Verma, and M. Nascimento. 2011. *Evolving Men: Initial Results from the International Men and Gender Equality Survey (IMAGES).* Washington, DC: International Center for Research on Women (ICRW)/Rio de Janeiro: Instituto Promundo.

Barker-Benfield, Ben. 1972. "The Spermatic Economy: A Nineteenth Century View of Sexuality." *Feminist Studies* 1(1): 383–389.

Barr, Andrew. 1999. *Drink: A Social History of America.* New York: Carroll & Graf.

Barry, Ellen. 2013. "Policing Village Moral Codes as Women Stream to India's Cities." *New York Times,* September 19. Available online at www.nytimes.com/2013/10/20/world/asia/policing-village-moral-codes-as-women-stream-to-indias-cities.html?pagewanted=1

Barry, Ellen and Betwa Sharma. 2013. "Many Doubt Death Sentences Will Stem India's Sexual Violence." *New York Times,* September 13. Available online at www.nytimes.com/2013/09/14/world/asia/4-sentenced-to-death-in-rape-case-that-riveted-india.html?pagewanted=1

Bartko, W.T. and J.S. Eccles. 2003. "Adolescent Participation in Structured and Unstructured Activities: A Person-oriented Analysis." *Journal of Youth and Adolescence* 32: 233–241.

Basow, Susan. 2004. "The Hidden Curriculum: Gender in the Classroom." In Michele Antoinette Paludi (ed.) *Praeger Guide to the Psychology of Gender.* Westport, CT: Praeger, pp. 117–131.

Basu, Alaka Malwade. 2002. "Why Does Education Lead to Lower Fertility? A Critical Review of Some of the Possibilities." *World Development* 30(10): 1779–1790.

Bateup, Helen S., Alan Booth, Elizabeth A. Shirtcliff, and Douglas A. Granger. 2002. "Testosterone, Cortisol, and Women's Competition." *Evolution and Human Behavior* 23(3): 181–192.

Bauer, John, Wang Feng, Nancy E. Riley, and Zhao Xiaohua. 1992. "Gender Inequality in Urban China, Education and Employment." *Modern China* 18: 333–370.

Bayoumi, Moustafa. 2008. *How Does It Feel to Be a Problem? Being Young and Arab in America.* New York: Penguin Press.

BBC News. 1999. "TV Brings Eating Disorders to Fiji." Available online at http://news.bbc.co.uk/2/hi/health/347637.stm

Beam, Cris. 2007. *Transparent: Love, Family, and Living the T with Transgender Teenagers.* Boston: Harcourt.

Bearak, Barry. 2007. "Education in Afghanistan: A Harrowing Choice." *New York Times*, July 9. Available online at www.nytimes.com/2007/07/09/world/asia/09iht-afghan.4.6571860.html?pagewanted=all

Beck, Allen J., Marcus Berzofsky, Rachel Caspar, and Christopher Krebs. 2013a. *Sexual Victimization in Prisons and Jails Reported by Inmates, 2011–12.* Washington, DC: Bureau of Justice Statistics.

Beck, Allen J., David Cantor, John Hartge, and Tim Smith. 2013b. *Sexual Victimization in Juvenile Facilities Reported by Youth, 2012.* Washington, DC: Bureau of Justice Statistics.

Beck, Susan Abrams. 2001. "Acting as Women: The Effects and Limitations of Gender in Local Governance." in Susan J. Carroll (ed.) *The Impact of Women in Public Office.* Bloomington: Indiana University Press, pp. 49–67.

Becker, Anne. 1995. *Body, Self and Society: The View from Fiji.* Philadelphia: University of Pennsylvania Press.

Becker, Anne. 2004. "Television, Disordered Eating, and Young Women in Fiji: Negotiating Body Image and Identity During Rapid Social Change." *Culture, Medicine, and Psychiatry* 28: 534–559.

Becker, Gary S., William H.J. Hubbard, and Kevin M. Murphy. 2010. "Explaining the Worldwide Boom in Higher Education of Women." *Journal of Human Capital* 4(3): 203–241.

Belenky, Mary Field, Blythe McVicker Clinchy, Nancy Rule Goldberger, and Jill Mattuck Tarule. 1986. *Women's Ways of Knowing: The Development of Self, Voice, and Mind.* New York: Basic Books.

Bellesiles, Michael A. 2012. *A People's History of the U.S. Military.* New York: The New Press.

Bem, Sandra. 1981. "Gender Schema Theory: A Cognitive Account of Sex Typing." *Psychological Review* 88: 354–364.

Bem, Sandra. 1995. "Dismantling the Gender Polarization and Compulsory Heterosexuality: Should We Turn the Volume Up or Down?" *The Journal of Sex Research* 32: 329–334.

Bem, Sandra 1998. *An Unconventional Family.* New Haven, CT: Yale University Press.

Bemelmans, L. 1954. *Madeline's Rescue.* New York: Viking Press.

Benard, Stephen and Shelley J. Correll. 2010. "Normative Discrimination and the Motherhood Penalty." *Gender & Society.* 24: 616–646.

Bender, Thomas. 1993. *Intellect and Public Life: Essays on the Social History of Academic Intellectuals in the United States.* Baltimore, MD: Johns Hopkins University Press.

Benedict, Helen. 2009. *The Lonely Soldier: The Private War of Women Serving in Iraq.* Boston: Beacon Press.

Benedict, Jeff. 2004. *Out of Bounds: Inside the NBA's Culture of Rape, Violence, and Crime.* New York: Harper Press.

Bennhold, Katrin. 2010. "In Sweden, Men Can Have It All." *New York Times*, June 9.

Bennhold, Katrin. 2011. "Women Nudged Out of the German Workforce." *New York Times*, June 28.

Benson, Michael L., John Wooldredge, Amy B. Thistlethwaite, and Greer Litton Fox. 2004. "Domestic Violence Is Confounded with Community Context." *Social Problems* 51(3): 326–342.

Benson, Susan Porter. 1988. *Counter Cultures: Saleswomen, Managers and Customers in American Department Stores, 1890 to 1940*. Champaign: University of Illinois Press.

Berger, Joseph. 2013a. "Modesty in Ultra-Orthodox Brooklyn Is Enforced by Secret Squads." *New York Times*, January 29. Available online at www.nytimes.com/2013/01/30/nyregion/shadowy-squads-enforce-modesty-in-hasidic-brooklyn.html

Berger, Joseph. 2013b. "Out of Enclaves, a Pressure to Accommodate Traditions." *New York Times*, August 21. Available online at www.nytimes.com/2013/08/22/nyregion/hasidic-jews-turn-up-pressure-on-city-to-accommodate-their-traditions.html

Bhattacharya, Shilpo. 2012. "The Desire for Whiteness: Can Law and Economics Explain It?" *Columbia Journal of Race and Law* 2(1): 117–147.

Bhattacharyya, Gargi. 2008. *Dangerous Brown Men: Exploiting Sex, Violence, and Feminism in the War on Terror*. New York: Zed Books.

Bianchi, Suzanne M., John P. Robinson, and Melissa A. Milkie. 2006. *Changing Rhythms of American Family Life*. New York: Russell Sage.

Bianchi, Suzanne M., Liana C. Sayer, Melissa A. Milkie, John P. Robinson. 2012. "Housework: Who Did, Does or Will Do It, and How Much Does It Matter?" *Social Forces* 91: 55–63.

Billboard. 2011. Longbored-Surfer Charts. Available online at http://longboredsurfer.com/charts/2010.php

BJS (Bureau of Justice Statistics). 2013. "Data Collection: National Crime Victimization Survey (NCVS)" Available online at www.bjs.gov/index.cfm?ty=dc detail&iid=245#Questionnaires

BJS. 2014a. "Rates of Violent Victimizations by Household Income and Sex, 2010 2012." Generated using the NCVS Victimization Analysis Tool available online at www.bjs.gov/index.cfm?ty=nvat

BJS. 2014b. "Rates of Violent Victimizations by Race/Hispanic Origin-Expanded Categories and Sex, 2010–2012." Generated using the NCVS Victimization Analysis Tool Available online at www.bjs.gov/index.cfm?ty=nvat

Black, Jeremy. 2011. *A Brief History of Slavery*. Philadelphia, PA: Running Press.

Black, M.C., K.C. Basile, M.J. Breiding, S.G. Smith, M.L. Walters, M.T. Merrick, J. Chen, and M.R. Stevens. 2011. *The National Intimate Partner and Sexual Violence Survey (NISVS): Summary Report*. Atlanta, GA: Centers for Disease Control and Prevention.

Blackmon, Douglas A. 2008. *Slavery by Another Name: The Re-Enslavement of Black Americans from the Civil War to World War II*. New York: Doubleday.

Blau, Francine, Peter Brummond, and Albert Liu. 2012. "Trends in Occupational Segregation by Gender 1970–2009: Adjusting for the Impact of Changes in the Occupational Coding System." *Demography, Springer* 50(2): 471–492.

Bleier, Ruth. 1984. *Science and Gender: A Critique of Biology and Its Theories on Women*. New York: Pergamon.

BLS (Bureau of Labor Statistics). 2012. "Report 1038: Highlights of Women's Earnings in 2011." Available online at www.bls.gov/cps/cpswom2011.pdf

BLS. 2013a. Database. Available online at http://data.bls.gov/pdq/SurveyOutputServlet;jsessionid=CFA BC8F003C051D1F4E26391082EFA97.tc_instance8

BLS. 2013b. "Civilian Labor Force Participation Rates by Age, Sex, Race, and Ethnicity." Available online at www.bls.gov/emp/ep_table_303.htm

BLS. 2013c. "Employed Persons by Detailed Occupation, Sex, Race, and Hispanic or Latino Ethnicity." Available online at www.bls.gov/cps/cpsaat11.pdf

BLS. 2014a. "Employed Persons by Occupation, Race, Hispanic or Latino Ethnicity, and Sex." Available online at www.bls.gov/cps/cpsaat10.pdf

BLS. 2014b. "Table 6. Employment Status of Mother with Own Child Under 3 Years Old by Single Year of Age of Youngest Child and Marital Status, 2012–2013 Annual Averages." Available online at www.bls.gov/news.release/famee.t06.htm

BLS. 2014c. "Women in the Labor Force: A Databook." Available online at www.bls.gov/cps/wlf-databook-2013.pdf

Blue, Laura. 2008. "Why do Women Live Longer than Men?" *Time*, August 6. Available online at www.time.com/time/health/article/0,8599,1827162,00.html

Blumberg, Rae Lesser. 1984. "Toward a General Theory of Gender Stratification." *Sociological Theory* 2: 23–101.

Blumberg, Rae Lesser. 2004. "Extending Lenski's Schema to Hold Up Both Halves of the Sky – A Theory-guided Way of Conceptualizing Agrarian

Societies that Illuminates a Puzzle about Gender Stratification." *Sociological Theory* 22(2): 278–291.

Blumberg, Rae Lesser, and Robert Winch. 1972. "Societal Complexity and Familial Complexity: Evidence for the Curvilinear Hypothesis." *American Journal of Sociology* 77: 898–920.

Bolding, Joshua. 2012. "Women of Faith: Female Clergy are Shaping American Religion from the Pulpit." *Deseret News*, April 12.

Bongaarts, John. 2013. "The Implementation of Preferences for Male Offspring." *Population and Development Review* 39(2): 185–208.

Bonilla-Silva, Eduardo. 2013. *Racism without Racists: Color-Blind Racism and the Persistence of Racial Inequality in America*, 4th edn. Lanham, MD: Rowman & Littlefield.

Boswell, John. 1980. *Christianity, Social Tolerance, and Homosexuality*. Chicago: University of Chicago Press.

Bounds Littlefield, Marci. 2008. "The Media as a System of Racialization: Exploring Images of African American Women and the New Racism." *American Behavioral Scientist* 51: 675–685.

Bownes, I.T. and E.C. O'Gorman. 1991. "Assailants' Sexual Dysfunction During Rape Reported by Their Victims." *Medicine, Science, and the Law* 31(4): 322–328.

Boylan, Jennifer Finney. 2003. *She's Not There: A Life in Two Genders*. Sydney: Bantam.

Bradsher, Keith. 2013. "After Bangladesh, Seeking New Sources." *New York Times*, May 15.

Branch, John. 2011. "Confronting an Enduring Taboo." *New York Times*, April 7. Available online at www.nytimes.com/2011/04/08/sports/08outsports. html?pagewanted=all&_r=0

Branch, John. 2014. "N.F.L. Prospect Michael Sam Proudly Says What Teammates Knew: He's Gay." *New York Times*, Feb. 9. Available online at www.nytimes.com/2014/02/10/sports/michael-sam-college-football-star-says-he-is-gay-ahead-of-nfl-draft.html

Braslow, Laura, Janet C. Gornick, Kristin Smith, Nancy Folbre, and Harriet B. Presser. 2012. "Who's Minding Their Kids? U.S. Child Care Workers' Child Care Arrangements: An Assessment Using the SIPP." Presented at the Population Association of America. May 3–5. Available online at http://paa2012.princeton.edu/abstracts/120870

Braude, Ann. 1993. "The Perils of Passivity: Women's Leadership in Spiritualism and Christian Science." In Catherine Wessinger (ed.) *Women's Leadership in Marginal Religions: Explorations Outside the Mainstream*. Urbana, University of Illinois Press, pp. 55–67.

Breiding, M.J., J. Chen, and M.C. Black. 2014. *Intimate Partner Violence in the United States – 2010*. Atlanta, GA: Centers for Disease Control and Prevention.

Brill, Stephanie A. and Rachel Pepper. 2008. *The Transgender Child: A Handbook for Families and Professionals*. Berkeley, CA: Cleis Press.

Bristow, Michael. 2009. "Chinese Delegate Has 'No Power.'" *BBC News*, March 4. Available online at http://news.bbc.co.uk/2/hi/asia-pacific/7922720.stm

British Embassy. 2006. "Pancake Day (Shrove Tuesday) in the UK." Available online at http://web.archive.org/web/20070223204148/www.britainusa.com/sections/articles_show_nt1.asp?d=0&i=60062&L1=0&L2=0&a=41276

Brodie, Janet Farrell. 1994. *Contraception and Abortion in 19th-Century America*. Ithaca, NY: Cornell University Press.

Brooks, Deborah Jordan and Benjamin A. Valentino. 2011. "A War of One's Own: Understanding the Gender Gap in Support for War." *Public Opinion Quarterly* 75(2): 270–286. Available online at http://poq.oxfordjournals.org/content/75/2/270.short

Brown, Alyssa. 2012. "In U.S., Gender Gap in Personal Weight Worries Narrows." *Gallup Well-Being*, July 20. Available online at www.gallup.com/poll/155903/Gender-Gap-Personal-Weight-Worries-Narrows.aspx

Brown, Gordon. 2014. "Child Marriage Could Become Law in Iraq this Week, but It's a Global Scourge." *The Guardian*, April 29.

Brown, Kathleen M. 1996. *Good Wives, Nasty Wenches, and Anxious Patriarchs: Gender, Race, and Power in Colonial Virginia*. Chapel Hill: University of North Carolina Press.

Brown, M. 1954. *Cinderella, or the Little Glass Slipper*. New York: Scribner Press.

Brownmiller, Susan. 1975. *Against Our Will: Men, Women, and Rape*. New York: Simon & Schuster.

Bruce, Philip Alexander. 1907. *Economic History of Virginia in the Seventeenth Century*, vol. II. New York: Macmillan.

Bruckner, T. and R. Catalano. 2007. "The Sex Ratio and Age-Specific Male Mortality: Evidence for Culling in Utero." *American Journal of Human Biology* 19(6): 763–773.

Bruckner, Tim A., Ralph Catalano, and Jennifer Ahern. 2010. "Male Fetal Loss in the U.S. Following the Terrorist Attacks of September 11, 2001." *BMC Public Health* 10: 273.

Brumberg, Joan Jacobs. 1988. *Fasting Girls: The Emergence of Anorexia Nervosa as a Modern Disease.* Cambridge, MA: Harvard University Press.

Bunch, Charlotte, 1975. *Lesbianism and the Women's Movement.* Baltimore, MD: Diana Press.

Burke, Jason. 2013. "Delhi Rape: How India's Other Half Lives." *The Guardian,* September 10. Available online at www.theguardian.com/world/2013/sep/10/delhi-gang-rape-india-women

Burke, Jason and Manoj Chaurasia. 2014. "Lynching of Boy Underlines How the Curse of Caste Still Blights India." *The Guardian,* October 19. Available online at www.theguardian.com/world/2014/oct/19/lynching-boy-underlines-curse-caste-still-blights-india

Burke, Mary C., ed. 2013. *Human Trafficking: Interdisciplinary Perspectives.* New York: Routledge.

Burnet, Jennie. 2008. "Gender Balance and the Meanings of Women in Governance in Post-Genocide Rwanda." *African Affairs* 107(428): 361–386. Available online at http://afraf.oxfordjournals.org/content/107/428/361.short

Burnet, Jennie. 2012. "Women's Empowerment and Cultural Change in Rwanda." In Susan Franceschet, Mona Lena Krook, and Jennifer Piscopo (eds.) *The Impact of Quotas on Women's Descriptive, Substantive, and Symbolic Representation.* New York: Oxford University Press, pp. 190–207.

Burnham, Linda and Nik Theodore. 2012. *Home Economics: The Invisible and Unregulated World of Domestic Work.* New York: National Domestic Workers Alliance. Available online at www.domesticworkers.org/sites/default/files/HomeEconomicsEnglish.pdf

Butler, Judith. 1990. *Gender Trouble: Feminism and the Subversion of Identity.* New York: Routledge.

Butler, Sara. 2007. *The Catholic Priesthood and Women: A Guide to the Teaching of the Church.* Chicago: Hillenbrand Books.

Butterfield, Fox. 2002. "Study Finds Big Increase in Black Men as Inmates Since 1980." *New York Times,* August 28.

Cahn, Susan. 1995. *Coming on Strong: Gender and Sexuality in Twentieth-Century Women's Sport.* Cambridge, MA: Harvard University Press.

Calasanti, Toni and Neal King. 2005. "Firming the Floppy Penis: Age, Class and Gender Relations in the Lives of Old Men." *Men & Masculinities* 8: 3–23.

Caliendo, Stephen M. 2014. *Inequality in America: Race, Poverty, and Fulfilling Democracy's Promise.* Boulder, CO: Westview Press.

Campbell, Anne. 1993. *Men, Women, and Aggression.* New York: Basic Books.

Campbell, Sister Simone. 2014. *A Nun on the Bus: How All of Us Can Create Hope, Change, and Community.* San Francisco: HarperOne.

Cantor, Muriel and Joel Cantor. 1992. *Prime-Time Television: Content and Control.* Newbury Park, CA: Sage.

CARA (Center for Applied Research in the Apostolate). 2014. "Frequently Requested Church Statistics." Available online at http://cara.georgetown.edu/CARAServices/requestedchurchstats.html

Carbone, June and Naomi Cahn. 2014. *Marriage Markets: How Inequality Is Remaking the American Family.* New York: Oxford University Press.

Carnes, Mark C. 1989. *Secret Ritual and Manhood in Victorian America.* New Haven: Yale University Press.

Carnevale, Anthony P., Jeff Strohl, and Michelle Melton. 2011. "What's It Worth? The Economic Value of College Majors." Washington, DC: Georgetown University. Available online at http://cew.georgetown.edu/whatsitworth

Carr, Lois Green and Lorena S. Walsh. 1983. "The Planter's Wife: The Experience of White Women in Seventeenth-Century Maryland." In Stanley N. Katz and John M. Murrin (eds.) *Colonial America: Essays in Politics and Social Development.* New York: Knopf, pp. 94–122.

Carr, Lois Green and Lorena S. Walsh. 1988. "Economic Diversification and Labor Organization in the Chesapeake, 1650–1820." In Stephen Innes (ed.) *Work and Labor in Early America.* Chapel Hill: University of North Carolina Press, pp. 144–188.

Carrillo, Héctor. 2002. *The Night Is Young: Sexuality in Mexico in the Time of AIDS*. Chicago: University of Chicago Press.

Carrillo, Héctor. 2013. "How Latin Culture Got More Gay." *New York Times*, May 17.

Carroll, Susan J. 2001. "Representing Women: Women State Legislators as Agents of Policy-Related Changes." In Susan J. Carroll (ed.) *The Impact of Women in Public Office*. Bloomington: Indiana University Press, pp. 3–21.

Carter, Jimmy. 2014. *A Call to Action: Women, Religion, Violence, and Power*. New York: Simon & Schuster.

Catalano, Shannon, Erica Smith, Howard Snyder, and Michael Rand. 2009. "Female Victims of Violence." Washington, DC: Bureau of Justice Statistics.

Catalyst. 2014a. "Statistical Overview of Women in the Workplace." Available online at www.catalyst.org/knowledge/statistical-overview-women-workplace

Catalyst. 2014b. "Women in U.S. Management and Labor Force." Available online at www.catalyst.org/knowledge/women-us-management-and-labor-force

CAWP (Rutgers Center for American Women and Politics). 2012. "The Gender Gap: Attitudes on Policy Issues." Available online at www.cawp.rutgers.edu/fast_facts/voters/documents/GG_Issues Attitudes-2012.pdf

CBO (Congressional Budget Office). 2011. "A Description of the Immigrant Population: An Update." Washington, DC: Congressional Budget Office. Available online at www.cbo.gov/sites/default/files/cbofiles/ftpdocs/121xx/doc12168/06-02-foreign-bornpopulation.pdf

CDC (Centers for Disease Control, National Center for Health Statistics). 2001. "Births to Teenagers in the United States, 1940–2000." *National Vital Statistics Report* 49(10). Available online at www.cdc.gov/nchs/data/nvsr/nvsr49/nvsr49_10.pdf

CDC. 2011. "CDC Health Disparities and Inequalities Report – United States, 2011." *MMWR* 60 (Supplement). Available online at www.cdc.gov/mmwr/pdf/other/su6001.pdf

CDC. 2012a. "Health, United States, 2012, Death Rates." Available online at www.cdc.gov/nchs/hus/american.htm#deaths

CDC. 2012b. "Birth: Final Data for 2010." *National Vital Statistics Report* 61(1). Available online at www.cdc.gov/nchs/data/nvsr/nvsr61/nvsr61_01.pdf

CDC. 2012c. "Suicide: Facts at a Glance." Available online at www.cdc.gov/violenceprevention/pdf/suicide-datasheet-a.pdf

CDC. 2013a. "Births: Final Data for 2011." *National Vital Statistics Report* 62(1). Available online at www.cdc.gov/nchs/data/nvsr/nvsr62/nvsr62_01.pdf

CDC. 2013b. *HIV Surveillance Report, 2011*. Available online at www.cdc.gov/hiv/pdf/statistics_2011_HIV_Surveillance_Report_vol_23.pdf

CDPH (California Department of Public Health). 2011. *The California Pregnancy-Associated Mortality Review: Report from 2002 and 2003 Maternal Death Reviews*. Sacramento: Maternal Child and Adolescent Health Division. Available online at www.cdph.ca.gov/data/statistics/Documents/MO-CA-PAMR-MaternalDeathReview-2002-03.pdf

Center for Responsive Politics. 2013a. "Donor Demographics: Gender." Available online at www.opensecrets.org/bigpicture/donordemographics.php?cycle=2012&filter=G

Center for Responsive Politics. 2013b. "Sex, Money & Politics." Available online at www.opensecrets.org/news/reports/gender.php#men

Centre for the Study of Violence and Reconciliation. 2009. *Why Does South Africa Have Such High Rates of Violent Crime? Supplement to the 2nd Report on the Violent Nature of Crime in South Africa*. Johannesburg: CSVR.

Cha, Youngjoo and Kim Weeden. 2014. "Overwork and the Slow Convergence in the Gender Gap in Wages." *American Sociological Review*. doi: 10.1177/0003122414528936.

Chandrashekar, Vaishnavi and Shivam Vij. 2013. "India's 'Gender Gap' Exposed." *Christian Science Monitor*, January 28.

Chateauvert, Melinda. 2013. *Sex Workers Unite: A History of the Movement from Stonewall to Slut Walk*. Boston: Beacon Press.

Chattopadhyay, Raghabendra and Esther Duflo. 2004. "Women as Policy Makers: Evidence from a Randomized Policy Experiment in India." *Econometrica* 72(5): 1409–1443.

Chauncey, George. 1994. *Gay New York: Gender, Urban Culture, and the Making of the Gay Male World, 1890–1940*. New York: Basic Books.

Chen, Li-Ju. 2010. "Do Gender Quotas Influence Women's Representation and Policies?" *The Euro-*

pean Journal of Comparative Economics 7(1): 13–60. Available online at http://eaces.liuc.it/18242979 201001/182429792010070102.pdf

Cherlin, Andrew. 2009. *The Marriage-Go-Round*. New York: Knopf.

Chesebrough, David B., ed. 1991. *"God Ordained this War": Sermons on the Sectional Crisis, 1830–1865*. Columbia: University of South Carolina Press.

Child Care Aware. 2013. *Parents and the High Cost of Child Care 2013 Report*. Arlington, VA: Child Care Aware.

Childs, Sarah and Mona Lena Krook. 2008. "Critical Mass Theory and Women's Political Representation." *Political Studies* 56: 725–736.

Chiroro, P., G. Bohner, G.T. Viki, and C.I. Jarvis. 2004. "Rape Myth Acceptance and Rape Proclivity: Expected Dominance Versus Expected Arousal as Mediators in Acquaintance-Rape Situations." *Journal of Interpersonal Violence* 19(4): 427–442.

Chodorow, Nancy. 1978. *The Reproduction of Mothering: Psychoanalysis and the Sociology of Gender*. Berkeley: University of California Press.

Chong, Alberto and Eliana La Ferrara. 2009. "Television and Divorce: Evidence from Brazilian Novelas." *Journal of European Economic Association: Papers and Proceedings* 7: 458–468.

Chowdhury, Anis. 2009. "Microfinance as a Poverty Reduction Tool – A Critical Assessment." New York: United Nations Department of Economic and Social Affairs. Available online at www.un.org/esa/desa/papers/2009/wp89_2009.pdf

Christakis, Nicholas A. and James H. Fowler. 2009. *Connected: How Your Friends' Friends' Friends Affect Everything You Feel, Think, and Do*. New York: Back Bay Books.

Chuku, Gloria. 2005. *Igbo Women and Economic Transformation in Southeastern Nigeria, 1900–1960*. New York: Routledge.

CIA. 2014a. "Gini Index." Available online at https://www.cia.gov/library/publications/the-world-factbook/rankorder/2172rank.html

CIA. 2014b. "The World Factbook." Available online at https://www.cia.gov/library/publications/the-world-factbook/

CICLSAL (Congregation for Institutes of Consecrated Life and Societies of Apostolic Life). 2014. "Final Report on the Apostolic Visitation of Institutes of Women Religious in the United States of America, 16.12.2014." Available online at http://press.vatican.va/content/salastampa/en/bollettino/pubblico/2014/12/16/0963/02078.html

Cinderella. 1950. [Film] United States: Walt Disney Productions.

Citron, Danielle Keats. 2014. *Hate Crimes in Cyberspace*. Cambridge, MA: Harvard University Press.

Clarey, Christopher. 2012. "Top Two Winning Nations Can't Help Being Rivals." *New York Times*, August 11. Available online at www.nytimes.com/2012/08/12/sports/olympics/us-and-china-developing-olympic-medal-rivalry.html?pagewanted=all&_r=0

Clarissa Explains It All. 1991–1994. [TV Sitcom] Orlando, FL: Universal Studios.

Clark, Roger. 2007. "From Margin to Margin? Females and Minorities in Newbery and Caldecott Medal-Winning and Honor Books for Children." *International Journal of Sociology of the Family* 33: 264–283.

Clark, Roger, Jeffrey Allard, and Timothy Mahoney. 2004. "How Much of the Sky? Women in American High School History Textbooks from the 1960s, 1980s and 1990s." *Social Education* 6(1): 57–62.

Clark, Roger, Monica Almeida, Tara Gurka, and Lisa Middleton. 2003. "Engendering Tots with Caldecotts: An Updated Update." In Emily Stier Adler and Roger Clark (eds.) *How It's Done: An Invitation to Social Research,*. Belmont, CA: Wadsworth, pp. 379–385.

Clark, Roger, Kieran Ayton, and Nicole Frechette. 2005a. "Women of the World, Re-write! Women in American World History High School Textbooks from the 1960s, 1980s, and 1990s." *Social Education* 69(1): 41–45.

Clark, Roger, Ashley Folgo, and Jane Pichette. 2005b. "Have There Now Been Any Great Women Artists?" *Art Education* 58: 6–13.

Clark, Roger, Julie Kessler, and Allyssa Coon. 2013. "Women and Girls Last: Female Visibility in Children's Picture Books by While, Black, Latino and Gay-Sympathetic Authors." *International Review of Modern Sociology* 39: 111–131.

Clark, Roger, Rachel Lennon, and Leanna Morris. 1993. "Of Caldecotts and Kings: Gendered Images in Recent American Children's Picture Books by Black and non-Black Illustrators." *Gender & Society* 5: 227–245.

Clark, Roger, Joel McCoy and Pamela Keller. 2008. "Teach Your Children Well: Reading Lessons to and About Black and White Adolescent Girls from Black and White Women Authors." *International Review of Modern Sociology* 34: 211–227.

Classen, C.C., O.G. Palesh, and R. Aggarwal. 2005. "Sexual Revictimization: A Review of the Empirical Literaure." *Trauma, Violence, and Abuse* 6(2): 103–129.

Clay-Warner, J. and C.H. Burt. 2005. "Rape Reporting After Reforms: Have Times Really Changed?" *Violence Against Women* 11(2): 150–176.

Cleves, Charity Hope. 2014. *Charity and Sylvia: A Same-Sex Marriage in Early America*. New York: Oxford University Press.

Coale, Ansley. 1973. "Demographic Transition." *International Population Conference*. Liège, IUSSP.

Cobble, Dorothy Sue, ed. 2007. *The Sex of Class: Women Transforming American Labor*. Ithaca, NY: ILR Press.

Cobble, Dorothy Sue, Linda Gordon, and Astrid Henry. 2014. *Feminism Unfinished: A Short, Surprising History of American Women's Movements*. New York: Liveright.

Cohen, Jon. 2013. "Gay Marriage Support Hits New High in Post-ABC Poll." *The Washington Post*, March 18.

Cohen, Patricia Cline. 1998. *The Murder of Helen Jewett*. New York: Vintage.

Cohen, Peter. 2004. "The Gender Division of Labor: 'Keeping House' and the Occupational Segregation of Labor in the United States." *Gender & Society* 18: 239–252.

Coleman, Isobel. 2010. *Paradise Beneath Her Feet: How Women Are Transforming the Middle East*. New York: Random House.

Colgate, Meika Loe. 2004. "Sex and the Senior Woman: Pleasure and Danger in the Viagra Era." *Sexualities* 7: 303–326.

Collier-Thomas, Bettye. 2010. *Jesus, Jobs, and Justice: African American Women and Religion*. New York: Knopf.

Collins, Gail. 2011. *When Everything Changed: The Amazing Journey of American Women from 1960 to the Present*. New York: Basic Books.

Collins, Jane L. and Victoria Mayer. 2010. *Both Hands Tied: Welfare Reform and the Race to the Bottom of the Low-Wage Labor Market*. Chicago: University of Chicago Press.

Collins, Patricia Hill. 1990. *Black Feminist Thought: Knowledge, Consciousness and the Politics of Empowerment*. Boston: Unwin Hyman.

Collins, Randall, Janet Saltzman Chafetz, Rae Lesser Blumberg, Scott Coltrane, and Jonathan Turner. 1993. "Toward an Integrated Theory of Gender Stratification." *Sociological Perspectives* 36: 185–216.

Coltrane, Scott. 2004. "Elite Careers and Family Commitment: It's Still about Gender." *Annals of the American Academy of Political and Social Science* 596: 214–220.

Common Sense Media. 2013. *Zero to Eight: Children's Media Use in America 2013*. San Francisco: Common Sense Media.

Congregation for the Doctrine of the Faith. 2012. "Doctrinal Assessment of the Leadership Conference of Women Religious." Available online at www.vatican.va/roman_curia/congregations/cfaith/documents/rc_con_cfaith_doc_20120418_assessment-lcwr_en.html

"Constitution of the Republic of South Africa." 1996. Available online at www.gov.za/documents/constitution/1996/a108-96.pdf

Cookson, Peter W. 2013. *Class Rules: Exposing Inequality in American High Schools*. New York: Teachers College Press.

Coontz, Stephanie. 1992. *The Way We Never Were: American Families and the Nostalgia Trap*. New York: Basic Books.

Coontz, Stephanie. 2005. *Marriage, A History: How Love Conquered Marriage*. New York: Viking.

Coontz, Stephanie. 2011. *A Strange Stirring: The Feminine Mystique and American Women at the Dawn of the 1960s*. New York: Basic Books.

Coontz, Stephanie. 2012. "The Myth of Male Decline." *New York Times*, September 29.

Cooper, David, Mary Gable, and Algernon Austin. 2012. "The Public Sector Jobs Crisis: Women and African Americans Hit Hardest by Job Losses in State and Local Governments." Washington, DC: Economic Policy Institute. Available online at www.epi.org/publication/bp339-public-sector-jobs-crisis/

Cooper, Marianne. 2014. *Cut Adrift: Families in Insecure Times*. Berkeley: University of California Press.

Corbett, Christianne and Catherine Hill. 2012. "Graduating to a Pay Gap: The Earnings of Women and Men One Year After College Graduation." Washington, DC: AAUW.

Corrales, Javier and Mario Pecheny, eds. 2010. *The Politics of Sexuality in Latin America*. Pittsburgh, PA: University of Pittsburgh Press.

Correll, Joshua, Bernadette Park, Charles Judd, and Bernd Wittenbrink. 2002. "The Police Officer's Dilemma: Using Ethnicity to Disambiguate Potentially Threatening Individuals." *Journal of Personality and Social Psychology* 83: 1314–1329.

Correll, Shelley J. 2013. "Minimizing the Motherhood Penalty." *Gender & Work Research Symposium*. Cambridge, MA: Harvard College. Available online at www.hbs.edu/faculty/conferences/2013-w50-research-symposium/Documents/correll.pdf

Correll, Shelley J., Stephen Benard, and In Paik. 2007. "Getting a Job: Is There a Motherhood Penalty?" *American Journal of Sociology* 112: 1297–1338.

Cott, Nancy F. 1977. *The Bonds of Womanhood: "Woman's Sphere" in New England, 1780–1835*. New Haven, CT: Yale University Press.

Cott, Nancy F. 1978. "Passionlessness: An Interpretation of Victorian Sexual Ideology, 1790–1850." *Signs* 4(2): 219–236.

Cott, Nancy F. 1987. *The Grounding of Modern Feminism*. Yale: Harvard University Press.

Courtwright, David T. 1996. *Violent Land: Single Men and Social Disorder from the Frontier to the Inner City*. Cambridge, MA: Harvard University Press.

Covert, Bryce. 2012. "Have We Gone from a Mancession to a Shecovery? Not Quite." *The Nation*, March 12. Available online at www.thenation.com/blog/166742/have-we-gone-mancession-shecovery-not-quite#

Cowan, Ruth Schwartz. 1983. *More Work for Mother: The Ironies of Household Technology from the Open Hearth to the Microwave*. New York: Basic Books.

Cowell, Alan. 2014. "Uganda's President Signs Antigay Bill." *New York Times*, February 24.

Craig, P., V. Halavatau, E. Comino, and I. Caterson. 1999. "Perception of Body Size in the Tongan Community: Differences from and Similarities to an Australian Sample." *International Journal of Obesity* 23: 123–130.

Crawford, James. 1999. *Bilingual Education: History, Politics, Theory, and Practice*, 4th edn. Los Angeles: Bilingual Educational Services.

Crenshaw, Kimberlé W. 1991. "Mapping the Margins: Intersectionality, Identity Politics, and Violence Against Women of Color." *Stanford Law Review* 43: 1241–1299.

Crenshaw, Kimberlé W. 2012. "From Private Violence to Mass Incarceration: Thinking Intersectionally about Women, Race, and Social Control." *UCLA Law Review* 59: 1418–1472.

Crittendon, Ann. 2010. *The Price of Motherhood: Why the Most Important Job in the World Is Still the Least Valued*, 2nd edn. New York: Holt.

Crosnoe, R. 2002. "Academic and Health-Related Trajectories in Adolescence: The Intersection of Gender and Athletics." *Journal of Health and Social Behavior* 43: 317–335.

Cross, Gary. 1997. *Kid's Stuff: Toys and the Changing World of American Childhood*. Cambridge, MA: Harvard University Press.

Crowther, Nigel. 2007. *Sports in Ancient Time*. Westport, CT: Greenwood Publishing Group.

D'Agati, Philip. 2013. *The Cold War and the 1984 Olympic Games: A Soviet-American Surrogate War*. New York: Palgrave Macmillan.

Dahlerup, Drude. 2006. *Women, Quotas, and Politics*. London: Routledge.

Dally, Ann. 1991. *Women Under the Knife: A History of Surgery*. Minneapolis, MN: Castle Books.

Dangerfield, Whitney. 2012. "Before and After Title IX; Women in Sports." *New York Times*, June 6. Available online at www.nytimes.com/interactive/2012/06/17/opinion/sunday/sundayreview-title ix-timeline.html

Daniels, Elizabeth. 2009. "Sex Objects, Athletes, and Sexy Athletes: How Media Representations of Women Athletes Can Impact Adolescent Girls and College Women." *Journal of Adolescent Research* 24: 399–422.

Danziger, Sheldon H. 2013. "The Mismeasure of Poverty." *New York Times*, September 18.

Dao, James. 2013. "In Debate Over Military Sexual Assault, Men are Overlooked Victims." *New York Times*, June 23.

Dargis, Mahohla. 2014. "In Hollywood, It's a Men's, Men's, Men's World." *New York Times*, December 24.

Davenport, Coral. 2014. "Pentagon Signals Security Risks of Climate Change." *New York Times,* October 13.

Davey, Monica. 2014. "Detroit and Retirees Reach Deal in Bankruptcy Case." *New York Times*, April 25.

Davis, Harold E. 1977. "The Scissors Thesis, or Frustrated Expectations as a Cause of The Revolution in Georgia." *The Georgia Historical Quarterly* 61(3): 246–257.

Dawood, N.J. 1990. *The Koran: With a Parallel Arabic Text.* New York: Penguin.

De Brauw, Alan, Daniel O. Gilligan, John Hoddinott, and Shalini Roy. 2012. "The Impact of Bolsa Família on Women's Decision-Making Power." *Social Science Research Network.* February 3. Available online at http://papers.ssrn.com/sol3/papers.cfm?abstract_id=1999073

De la Dehesa, Rafael. 2010. "Global Communities and Hybrid Cultures: Early Gay and Lesbian Electoral Activism in Brazil and Mexico." In Javier Corrales and Mario Pecheny (eds.) *The Politics of Sexuality in Latin America.* Pittsburgh, PA: University of Pittsburgh Press, pp. 175–196.

Delaney, Tim and Tim Madigan. 2009. *The Sociology of Sports: An Introduction.* Jefferson, NC: McFarland & Co.

D'Emilio, John. 1983. *Sexual Politics, Sexual Communities: The Making of a Homosexual Minority in the United States, 1940–1970.* Chicago: University of Chicago Press.

D'Emilio, John. 1992. *Making Trouble: Essays on Gay History, Politics, and the University.* New York: Routledge.

D'Emilio, John and Estelle Freedman. 1988. *Intimate Matters: A History of Sexuality in America.* Chicago: University of Chicago Press.

Demos, John. 2000. "The Tried and True: Native American Women Confronting Colonization." In Nancy F. Cott (ed.) *No Small Courage: A History of Women in the United States.* New York: Oxford University Press, pp. 3–50.

DeParle, Jason. 2011. "Domestic Workers Convention May Be Landmark." *New York Times*, October 8.

DeParle, Jason and Sabrina Tavernise. 2012. "For Women Under 30, Most Births Occur Outside Marriage." *New York Times*, February 17. Available online at www.nytimes.com/2012/02/18/us/for-women-under-30-most-births-occur-outside-marriage.html?pagewanted=1

Department of Health and Human Services. 2011. "Updated Illinois Rape Myth Acceptance Scale (IRMA)." Available online at www.hhs.gov/ash/oah/oah-initiatives/paf/508-assets/conf-2011-herman-irma.pdf

Derounian-Stodola, Kathryn, ed. 1998. *Women's Indian Captivity Narratives.* New York: Penguin.

De Schutter, Olivier. 2013. "Gender and the Right to Food: Executive Summary." United Nations. Available online at www.srfood.org/images/stories/pdf/otherdocuments/20130304_gender_execsummary_en.pdf

Desmond, Roger and Anna Danilewicz. 2010. "Women are On, But not In, the News: Gender Roles in Local Television News." *Sex Roles* 62: 822–829.

Deutsch, Sarah. 1987. *No Separate Refuge: Culture, Class, and Gender on an Anglo-Hispanic Frontier in the American Southwest, 1880–1940.* New York: Oxford University Press.

Devlin, Claire and Robert Elgie. 2008. "The Effect of Increased Women's Representation in Parliament: The Case of Rwanda." *Parliamentary Affairs* 61(2): 237–254. Available online at ttp://pa.oxfordjournals.org/content/61/2/237.full

Dew, Jeffrey and Bradford Wilcox. 2011. "If Momma Ain't Happy: Explaining Declines in Marital Satisfaction Among New Mothers." *Journal of Marriage and Family* 73: 1–12.

Dhruvarajan, Vanaja. 1989. *Hindu Women and the Power of Ideology.* Westport, CT: Praeger.

Dillon, Sam. 1997. "How to Scandalize a Politician: Bare a Love Affair." *New York Times*, January 22.

DoD (Department of Defense). 2013. "2012 Demographics: Profile of the Military Community." Available online at www.militaryonesource.mil/12038/MOS/Reports/2012_Demographics_Report.pdf

DoD. 2014a. "Provisional Metrics on Sexual Assault Fiscal Year 2014." Available online at www.sapr.mil/public/docs/reports/FY14_POTUS/FY14_DoD_Report_to_POTUS_Appendix_B.pdf

DoD. 2014b. "Report to the President of the United States on Sexual Assault Prevention and Response." Available online at www.sapr.mil/public/docs/reports/FY14_POTUS/FY14_DoD_Report_to_POTUS_SAPRO_Report.pdf

Douglas, Ann. 1977. *The Feminization of American Culture.* New York: Knopf.

Downs, Edward and Stacy Smith. 2010. "Keeping Abreast of Hypersexuality: A Video Game Character Content Analysis." *Sex Roles* 62: 721–733.

Doyne, Shannon, Holly Epstein Ojalvo, and Katherine Schulten. 2011. "100 Years Later: Examining the Impact of the Triangle Shirtwaist Factory Fire." *New York Times*, March 25.

Draper, Robert. 2014. "In the Company of Men: Why Is It So Hard to Prosecute Sexual Assaults in the Military?" *New York Times Magazine*, November 30.

Draper, Sharon. 2006. *Copper Sun.* New York: Atheneum Books for Young Readers.

Duberman, Martin. 1989. "'Writhing Bedfellows' in Antebellum South Carolina: Historical Interpretation and the Politics of Evidence." In Martin Duberman, Martha Vicinus, and George Chauncey, Jr. (eds.) *Hidden from History: Reclaiming the Gay and Lesbian Past.* New York: Penguin, pp. 153–168.

Dublin, Thomas. 1999. "Women, Work and Family: The View from the United States." *Journal of Women's History* 11(3): 17–21.

Duggan, Maeve. 2013. "It's a Woman's (Social Media) World." Pew Research Center. September 12. Available online at www.pewresearch.org/fact-tank/2013/09/12/its-a-womans-social-media-world/

Duroch, F., M. McRae, and R. Grais. 2011. "Description and Consequences of Sexual Violence in Ituri Province, Democratic Republic of Congo." *BMC International Health and Human Rights* 11(5).

Dworkin, Andrea. 1978. *Right-Wing Women.* New York: Perigee Books.

Dworkin, Andrea. 1987. *Intercourse.* New York: Free Press.

Dwyer, Rachel, Randy Hodson, and Laura McCloud. 2013. "Gender, Debt, and Dropping Out of College." *Gender & Society* 27(1): 30–55.

Eckholm, Erik. 2013. "A Pill Available in Mexico Is a Texas Option for Abortion." *New York Times*, July 13.

Economist. 2007. "Marriage in America: The Frayed Knot." May 24. Available online at www.economist.com/node/9218127

Economist. 2009a. "Bartered Brides: A Cruel Trade Across Vietnam's Border with China." March 12.

Economist. 2009b. "China's Predicament: Getting Old Before Getting Rich." June 25. Available online at www.economist.com/node/13888069

Economist. 2009c. "Hard Times: The Trouble with Pornography." September.

Economist. 2009d. "Go Forth and Multiply a Lot Less: Fertility and Living Standards." October 29. Available online at www.economist.com/node/14743589

Economist. 2010. "The Worldwide War on Baby Girls." March 4.

Economist. 2012a. "One Dishonourable Step Backwards: Indian Women." May 11.

Economist. 2012b. "For Richer, For Poorer." October 13.

Economist. 2012c. "The Path Through the Fields: Bangladesh and Development." November 3.

Economist. 2012d. "Preventing AIDS: A Drug Called Money." February 15.

Economist. 2013a. "Naked Ambition: Banning the Sex Industry." April 20.

Economist. 2013b. "Autumn of the Patriarchs." June 1.

Economist. 2013c. "Not Always With Us: Poverty." June 1.

Economist. 2013d. "Fifty Shades of Pink." July 6.

Economist. 2013e. "The Marriage Gap." December 14. Available online at www.economist.com/news/united-states/21591624-republicans-should-worry-unmarried-women-shun-them-marriage-gap

Economist. 2013f. "Suffer the Little Children." May 30. Available online at www.economist.com/blogs/graphicdetail/2013/05/daily-chart-19

Economist. 2014a. "Sex, Lies, and Statistics: The Economics of Prostitution." March 22.

Economist. 2014b. "Holding Back Half the Nation: Japanese Women and Work." March 29.

Economist. 2014c. "Paying for the Grey: Pensions and Retirement." April 5.

Economist. 2014d. "Is College Worth It?" April 5.

Economist. 2014e. "The Return of the Stay-at-Home Mother: Women, Work, and Children." April 19.

Economist. 2014f. "Ending Apartheid: The Rural-Urban Divide." April 19.

Economist. 2014g. "The Glass Precipice: Why Female Bosses Fail More Often Than Male Ones." May 3.

Economist. 2014h. "Back from the Edge." June 28. Available online at www.economist.com/news/china/21605942-first-two-articles-chinas-suicide-rate-looks-effect-urbanisation-back

Economist. 2014i. "The Final Frontier: Sanitation in India." July 19.

Economist. 2014j. "Poverty in Asia." August 30.

Economist. 2014k. "The Gay Divide." October 11.

Economist. 2014l. "To Have and to Hold: Slavery in Islam." October 18.

Economist. 2014m. "Ranking the Rankings: Performance Indices." November 8.

Economist. 2014n. "A Nordic Mystery." November 15.

Economist. 2014o. "Home Truths: Domestic Violence." December 6.

Economist. 2014p. "Professors as Judges." December 6.

Edin, Kathryn and Maria Kefalas. 2011. *Promises I Can Keep: Why Poor Women Put Motherhood Before Marriage*, 2nd edn. Berkeley: University of California Press.

Edin, Kathryn and Timothy J. Nelson. 2013. *Doing the Best I Can: Fatherhood in the Inner City*. Berkeley: University of California Press.

Ehrenreich, Barbara. 1983. *Hearts of Men: American Dreams and the Flight from Commitment*. New York: Anchor Books.

Eide, E.R. and N. Ronan. 2001. "Is Participation in High School Athletics an Investment or a Consumption Good?" *Economics of Education Review* 20: 431–442.

Eisenstein, Zillah R. 1979. *Capitalist Patriarchy and the Case for Socialist Feminism*. New York: Monthly Review Press.

Eisler, Riane. 1987. *The Chalice and the Blade*. San Francisco: Harper & Row.

El Feki, Shereen. 2013. *Sex and the Citadel: Intimate Life in a Changing Arab World*. New York: Pantheon.

Elliott, Diana B., Kristy Krivickas, Matthew W. Brault, and Rose M. Kreider. 2012. "Historical Marriage Trends from 1890–2010: A Focus on Race Differences." United States Census Bureau. Presented at the Population Association of America, May 3–5.

Available online at www.census.gov/hhes/socdemo/marriage/data/acs/ElliottetalPAA2012presentation.pdf

Elmendorf, Douglas W. 2013. "A Description of the Immigrant Population: An Update" Washington, DC: Congressional Budget Office. Available online at www.cbo.gov/sites/default/files/cbofiles/attachments/44134_Description_of_Immigrant_Population.pdf

eMarketer. 2014. "Mobile Continues to Steal Share of US Adults' Daily Time Spent With Media." Available online at www.emarketer.com/Article/Mobile-Continues-Steal-Share-of-US-Adults-Daily-Time-Spent-with-Media/1010782

Ember, Melvin and Carol Ember. 1971. "The Conditions Favoring Matrilocal vs. Patrilocal Residence." *American Anthropologist* 73: 571–594.

Emery, Michael and Edwin Emery. 1988. *The Press and America: An Interpretive History of the Mass Media*, 6th edn. Englewood Cliffs, NJ: Prentice Hall.

Engels, Friedrich. 1884 (1942). *Origin of the Family, Private Property, and the State*, trans. Alick West. Available online at www.marxists.org/archive/marx/works/download/pdf/origin_family.pdf

Enloe, Cynthia. 2000. *Maneuvers: The International Politics of Militarizing Women's Lives*. Berkeley: University of California Press.

Enloe, Cynthia. 2007. *Globalization and Militarism: Feminists Make the Link*. New York: Rowman & Littlefield.

Enloe, Cynthia. 2013. *Seriously! Investigating Crashes and Crises as If Women Mattered*. Berkeley: University of California Press.

Enloe, Cynthia. 2014. *Bananas, Beaches, and Bases: Making Feminist Sense of International Politics*, 2nd edn. Berkeley: University of California Press.

Entertainment Software Assocation. 2013. "2013 Essential Facts about the Computer and Video Game Industry." Available online at www.theesa.com/facts/pdfs/ESA_EF_2013.pdf

Entmacher, Joan, Abby Lane, Katherine Gallagher Robbins, and Julie Voghtman. 2012. "Insecure and Unequal: Poverty and Income Among Women and Families, 2000–2011." National Women's Law Center. Available online at www.nwlc.org/sites/default/files/pdfs/nwlc_2012_povertyreport.pdf

Epstein, Barbara Leslie. 1981. *The Politics of Domesticity: Women, Evangelicalism, and Temperance in*

Nineteenth-Century America. Middletown, CT: Wesleyan University Press.

Erickson-Schroth, Laura, ed. 2014. *Trans Bodies, Trans Selves: A Resource for the Transgender Community.* New York: Oxford University Press.

Eschbach, Karl, Glenn V. Ostir, Kushang V. Patel, Kyriakos S. Markides, and James S. Goodwin. 2004. "Neighborhood Context and Mortality Among Older Mexican Americans: Is There a Barrio Advantage?" *American Journal of Public Health* 94(10): 1807–1812.

Esposito, John L. and Dalia Mogahed. 2007. *Who Speaks for Islam? What a Billion Muslims Really Think.* New York: Gallup Press.

Estes, Steve. 2005. *I Am a Man! Race, Manhood, and the Civil Rights Movement.* Chapel Hill: University of North Carolina Press.

Esteve, Albert, Ron Lesthaeghe, and Antion Lopez-Gay. 2012. "The Latin American Cohabitation Boom, 1970–2007." *Population Development Review* 38: 55–81.

Faderman, Lillian. 1981. *Surpassing the Love of Men: Romantic Friendship and Love between Women from the Renaissance to the Present.* New York: William Morrow.

Fahim, Kareem. 2012. "Harassers of Women in Cairo Now Face Wrath of Vigilantes," *New York Times*, November 5. Available online at www.nytimes.com/2012/11/06/world/middleeast/egyptian-vigilantes-crack-down-on-abuse-of-women.html?pagewanted=all&_r=0

Fairclough, Adam. 2001. *Teaching Equality: Black Schools in the Age of Jim Crow.* Athens, GA: University of Georgia Press.

Faleiro, Sonia. 2014. "An Attack on Love." *New York Times*, November 2.

Faludi, Susan. 2006. *Backlash: The Undeclared War Against American Women.* New York: Broadway Books.

Faludi, Susan. 2007. *The Terror Dream: Myth and Misogyny in an Insecure America.* New York: Picador.

FAO (Food and Agriculture Organization of the United Nations). 2009. "Bridging the Gap: FAO's Programme for Gender Equality in Agriculture and Human Development." Rome: FAO. Available online at www.fao.org/3/a-i1243e/

Farr, Rachel H. and Charlotte Patterson. J. 2013. "Coparenting Among Lesbian, Gay, and Heterosexual Couples: Associations With Adopted Children's Outcomes." *Child Development* 84: 1226–1240.

Farr, Rachel H., Stephen L. Forssell, and Charlotte J. Patterson. 2010. "Parenting and Child Development in Adoptive Families: Does Parental Sexual Orientation Matter?" *Applied Developmental Science* 14(3): 164–178.

Fausto-Sterling, Anne. 2000. *Sexing the Body: Gender Politics and the Construction of Sexuality.* New York: Basic Books.

FBI. 2010. "Murder Victims by Race and Sex, 2010." Available online at www.fbi.gov/about-us/cjis/ucr/crime-in-the-u.s/2010/crime-in-the-u.s.-2010/tables/10shrtbl01.xls

FBI. 2012. "UCR Program Changes Definition of Rape." Available online at www.fbi.gov/about-us/cjis/cjis-link/march-2012/ucr-program-changes-definition-of-rape

FBI. 2013. "Table 43." Available online at www.fbi.gov/about-us/cjis/ucr/crime-in-the-u.s/2012/crime-in-the-u.s.-2012/tables/43tabledatadecoverviewpdf

Federal Register. 2013. "2013 Poverty Guidelines for the 48 Contiguous States and the District of Columbia" (January 24, 78 FR 5182, p. 5183). Department of Health and Human Services. Available online at https://federalregister.gov/a/2013-01422

Feldman, Noah. 2008. *The Rise and Fall of the Islamic State.* Princeton, NJ: Princeton University Press.

Ferguson, Kathy. 1984. *The Feminist Case Against Bureaucracy.* Philadelphia, PA: Temple University Press.

Fiedler, Maureen E. 2010. *Breaking Through the Stained Glass Ceiling: Women Religious Leaders in Their Own Words.* New York: Seabury Books.

Fincher, Leta Hong. 2014. *Leftover Women: The Resurgence of Gender Inequality in China.* London: Zed Books.

Finer, Lawrence B. 2007. "Trends in Premarital Sex in the United States, 1954–2003." *Public Health Reports* 122: 73–78.

Finer, Lawrence B. and Mia R. Zolna. 2011. "Unintended Pregnancy in the United States: Incidence and Disparities, 2006." *Contraception* 84(5): 478–485.

Fiorenza, Elisabeth Schüssler. 1979. "Word, Spirit, and Power: Women in Early Christian Communities." In Rosemary Ruether and Eleanor McLaughlin (eds.) *Women of Spirit: Female Leadership in the Jewish and Christian Traditions*. New York: Simon & Schuster, pp. 29–70.

Fiorenza, Elisabeth Schüssler. 1984. *Bread Not Stone: The Challenge of Feminist Biblical Interpretation*. Boston: Beacon Press.

Fiorenza, Elisabeth Schüssler. 1988. *In Memory of Her: A Feminist Theological Reconstruction of Christian Origins*. New York: Crossroad.

Fischer, David Hackett. 1989. *Albion's Seed: Four British Folkways in America*. New York: Oxford University Press.

Fish, Eric. 2013. "Eating Bitterness: Hardship and Opportunity for Rural Women in China." *The Atlantic*, May 17. Available online at www.theatlantic.com/china/archive/2013/05/eating-bitterness-hardship-and-opportunity-for-rural-women-in-china/275978/

Fish, M. Steven. 2011. *Are Muslims Distinctive? A Look at the Evidence*. New York: Oxford.

Fiske, David, Clifford W. Brown Jr., and Rachel Seligman. 2013. *Solomon Northup: The Complete Story of the Author of Twelve Years a Slave*. Westport, CT: Praeger.

Fiszbein, Ariel and Norbert Schady. 2009. "Conditional Cash Transfers." Washington, DC: The World Bank. Available online at http://siteresources.worldbank.org/INTCCT/Resources/5757608-1234228266004/PRR-CCT_web_noembargo.pdf

Flintan, Fiona. 2008. "Women's Empowerment in Pastoral Societies." WISP. Available online at http://cmsdata.iucn.org/downloads/gender_study_english_1.pdf

Flippen, Chenoa A. 2014. "Intersectionality at Work: Determinants of Labor Supply Among Immigrant Latinas." *Gender & Society* 28: 404–434. Available online at http://ftp.iza.org/dp6490.pdf

Fontanella-Khan, Amana. 2014. "India's Feudal Rapists." *New York Times*, June 4.

Forbes, Anna and Sara Elspeth Patterson. 2014. "The Evidence Is in: Decriminalizing Sex Work Is Critical." *RH Reality Check*, August 13.

Ford, Kathryn, Bridget Nolan, and Chris Evans. 1990. "Cultural Factors in Eating Disorders: A Study of Body Shape Preferences of Arab Students." *Journal of Psychoanalytic Research* 34: 501–607.

Forster, Stacy. 2009. "Number of Women in State Legislature Declining," *Journal Sentinel*. January 10. Available online at www.jsonline.com/news/state politics/37396194.html

Fortunato, Leanna, Amy M. Young, Carol J. Boyd, and Courtney E. Fons. 2010. "Hook-Up Sexual Experiences and Problem Behaviors among Adolescents," *Journal of Child & Adolescent Substance Abuse*, 19: 261–278.

Foucault, Michel. 1978. *The History of Sexuality, Volume I: An Introduction*. New York: Random House.

Fox-Genovese, Elizabeth. 1988. *Within the Plantation Household: Black and White Women of the Old South*. Chapel Hill: University of North Carolina Press.

Franklin, Ruth. 2011. "A Literary Glass Ceiling?" *The New Republic*, February 7.

Franzini, L., J.C. Ribble, and A.M. Keddie. 2001. "Understanding the Hispanic Paradox." *Ethnicity and Disease* 11(3): 496–518.

Freedman, Estelle. 2013. *Redefining Rape: Sexual Violence in the Era of Suffrage and Segregation*. Cambridge, MA: Harvard University Press.

Freedman, Samuel G. 2014. "A Generational Divide Worn on Their Heads." *New York Times*, April 18.

Freitas, Donna. 2013. *The End of Sex: How Hookup Culture Is Leaving a Generation Unhappy, Sexually Unfulfilled, and Confused About Intimacy*. New York: Basic Books.

Friedan, Betty. 1963. *The Feminine Mystique*. New York: Norton.

Friedman, Benjamin M. 2005. *The Moral Consequences of Economic Growth*. New York: Vintage Books.

Friedman, Elisabeth Jay. 2010. "Lesbians in (Cyber) Space: The Politics of the Internet in Latin American On- and Off-Line Communities." In Javier Corrales and Mario Pecheny (eds.) *The Politics of Sexuality in Latin America*. Pittsburgh, PA: University of Pittsburgh Press, pp. 312–333.

Friedman, Thomas L. 2005. *The World Is Flat: A Brief History of the Twenty-First Century*. New York: Farrar, Straus, and Giroux.

Friedman, Thomas L. 2014. "WikiLeaks, Drought, and Syria." *New York Times*, January 21.

Fry, Richard and D'Vera Cohn. 2010. "Women, Men, and the New Economics of Marriage." Pew Research Center. Available online at http://pew socialtrends.org/files/2010/11/new-economics-of-marriage.pdf

Fukuyama, Francis. 2014. *Political Order and Political Decay: From the Industrial Revolution to the Globalization of Democracy*. New York: Farrar, Straus, and Giroux.

Fuller, Linda K., ed. 2009. *Sexual Sports Rhetoric: Historical and Media Contexts of Violence*. New York: Peter Lang.

Gallup. 2010. "Education Trumps Gender in Predicting Support for Abortion." April 28. Available online at www.gallup.com/poll/127559/Education-Trumps-Gender-Predicting-Support-Abortion.aspx

Gallup. 2012a. "After the Arab Uprisings: Women on Rights, Religion, and Rebuilding." Washington, DC: Gallup. Available online at www.gallup.com/poll/155306/arab-uprisings-women-rights-religion-rebuilding.aspx

Gallup. 2012b. "U.S. Presidential Election Center." Available online at www.gallup.com/poll/154559/US-Presidential-Election-Center.aspx

Garcia-Moreno, Claudia, Henrica A.F.M. Jansen, Mary Ellsberg, Lori Heise, and Charlotte Watts. 2005. "WHO Multi-Country Study on Women's Health and Domestic Violence against Women." Geneva: World Health Organization. Available online at www.who.int/gender/violence/who_multicountry_study/en

Gates, Gary J. 2011. "Family Formation and Raising Children Among Same-Sex Couples." *National Council on Family Relations*. FF51. Available online at https://escholarship.org/uc/item/5pq1q8d7

Gates, Gary J. 2013. "LGBT Parenting in the United States." Los Angeles: The Williams Institute. Available online at http://williamsinstitute.law.ucla.edu/wp-content/uploads/LGBT-Parenting.pdf

Gates, Gary J. and Frank Newport. 2012. "Special Report: 3.4% of U.S. Adults Identify as LGBT." Gallup Poll, October 18. Available online at www.gallup.com/poll/158066/special-report-adults-identify-lgbt.aspx

Gates, Gary J. and Frank Newport. 2013. "LGBT Percentage Highest in D.C., Lowest in North Dakota." Gallup Politics, February 15. Available online at www.gallup.com/poll/160517/lgbt-percentage-highest-lowest-north-dakota.aspx

Gautier, Mary L., Paul M. Perl, and Stephen J. Fichter. 2012. *Same Call, Different Men: The Evolution of the Priesthood Since Vatican II*. Collegeville, MN: Liturgical Press.

Gendell, Murray. 2008. "Older Workers: Increasing Their Labor Force Participation and Hours of Work." *Monthly Labor Review*, January: 41–54. Available online at www.bls.gov/opub/mlr/2008/01/art3full.pdf

General Social Survey. 2012. "Survey Documentation and Analysis." Available online at http://sda.berkeley.edu/archive.htm

Gettleman, Jeffrey. 2010. "Americans' Role Seen in Uganda Anti-Gay Push." *New York Times*, January 3.

Gettleman, Jeffrey. 2011. "Congo Study Sets Estimate for Rapes Much Higher." *New York Times*, May 11.

Getz, Trevor R. and Heather Streets-Salter. 2011. *Modern Imperialism and Colonialism: A Global Perspective*. Boston: Prentice Hall.

Ghandnoosh, Nazgol. 2014. *Race and Punishment: Racial Perceptions of Crime and Support for Punitive Policies*. Washington, DC: The Sentencing Project.

Giddings, Paula J. 2007. *Where and When I Enter: The Impact of Black Women on Race and Sex in America*, 2nd edn. New York: William Morrow.

Gilkes, Cheryl Townsent. 2000. *If It Wasn't for the Women . . . : Black Women's Experience and Womanist Culture in Church and Community*. Maryknoll, NY: Orbis Books.

Gill, Rosalind. 2007. *Gender and the Media*. Cambridge: Polity Press.

Gilligan, Carol. 1982. *In a Different Voice: Psychological Theory and Women's Development*. Cambridge, MA: Harvard University Press.

Gilligan, James. 2001. *Preventing Violence*. New York: Thames & Hudson.

Gilmore, Glenda. 1996. *Gender and Jim Crow: Women and the Politics of White Supremacy in North Carolina, 1896–1920*. Chapel Hill: University of North Carolina Press.

Gimbutas, Marija. 1982. *The Goddesses and Gods of Old Europe*. Berkeley: University of California Press.

Giovanni, Nikki and Bryan Collier. 2005. *Rosa*. New York: Square Fish.

Glauber, Rebecca. 2008. "Race and Gender in Families at Work: The Fatherhood Wage Premium." *Gender & Society* 22: 8–30.

Glenn, Evelyn Nakano. 2008. "Yearning for Lightness: Transnational Circuits in the Marketing and Consumption of Skin Lighteners." *Gender & Society* 22(3): 281–302.

Glenn, Evelyn Nakano, ed. 2009. *Shades of Difference: Why Skin Color Matters*. Palo Alto, CA: Stanford University Press.

Global Commission on HIV and the Law. 2012. "Risks, Rights, & Health." New York: United Nations Development Program. Available online at www.undp.org/content/dam/undp/library/HIV-AIDS/Governance%20of%20HIV%20Responses/Commissions%20report%20final-EN.pdf

Glynn, Sarah Jane, Jane Farrell, and Nancy Wu. 2013. "The Importance of Preschool and Child Care for Working Mothers." Center for American Progress. Available online at www.americanprogress.org/wp-content/uploads/2013/05/ChildCareBrief-copy.pdf

Goffman, Ervin. 1959. *The Presentation of Self in Everyday Life*. New York: Doubleday.

Goffman, Ervin. 1979. *Gender Advertisements*. New York: Harper & Row.

Goldberg, Abbie E. 2010. *Lesbian and Gay Parents and Their Children: Research on the Family Life Cycle*. Washington, DC: American Psychological Association.

Goldberg, Gertrude Schaffner. 2009. *Poor Women in Rich Countries: The Feminization of Poverty*. New York: Oxford University Press.

Goldin, Claudia, Lawrence F. Katz, and Ilyana Kuziemko. 2006. "The Homecoming of American College Women: The Reversal of the College Gender Gap." *Journal of Economic Perspectives* 20(4): 133–156.

Goldman, Karla. 2014. "Reform Judaism in the United States." *Women's Jewish Archive Encyclopedia*. Available online at http://jwa.org/encyclopedia/article/reform-judaism-in-united-states

Goldstein, Joshua S. 2001. *War and Gender*. New York: Cambridge University Press.

Goode, Erica. 1999. "Study Finds TV Alters Fiji Girls' View of Body." *New York Times*, May 20. Available online at www.nytimes.com/1999/05/20/world/study-finds-tv-alters-fiji-girls-view-of-body.html

Goodwin, Robin and T. Emelyanova. 1995. "The Perestroika of the Family: Gender and Occupational Differences in Family Values in Modern-Day Russia." *Sex Roles* 32: 337–351.

Götz, M., O. Hofmann, H.-B. Brosius, C. Carter, K. Chan, S.H. Donald, J. Fisherkeller, M. Frenette, T. Kolbjørnsen, D. Lemish, K. Lustyik, D.C. McMillin, J.H. Walma van der Molen, N. Pecora, J. Prinsloo, M. Pestaj, P. Ramos Rivero, A.-H. Mereilles Reis, F. Saeys, S. Scherr, and H. Zhang. 2008. "Gender in Children's Television Worldwide." *Televizion* 21/2008/E. Available online at www.br-online.de/jugend/izi/english/publication/televizion/21_2008_E/goetz%20et%20al_engl.pdf

Graff, E.J. 1999. *What Is Marriage For?* Boston: Beacon Press.

Graham, Ruth. 2014. "Broke, But Not Deadbeat." *New York Times*, December 7.

Grant, Melissa Gira. 2014. "The Price of a Sex-Slave Rescue Fantasy." *New York Times*, May 29. Available online at www.nytimes.com/2014/05/30/opinion/the-price-of-a-sex-slave-rescue-fantasy.html?module=Search&mabReward=relbias%3As%2C%7B%221%22%3A%22RI%3A11%22%7D

Griego, Tina. 2014. "The Simple Policy that Led America's Biggest Drop in Teen Birth Rates." *The Washington Post*, August 20.

Griffin, Pat. 1998. *Strong Women, Deep Closets: Lesbians and Homophobia in Sport*. Champaign, IL: Human Kinetics.

Griffin, Susan. 1978. *Woman and Nature: The Roaring Inside Her*. New York: Harper & Row.

Griffin, Susan. 1981. *Pornography and Silence*. New York: Harper & Row.

Griffith, Jon. 2010. "Sports in Shackles: The Athletic and Recreational Habits of Slaves on Southern Plantations." *Voces Novae: Chapman University Historical Review* 2(1). Available online at http://journals.chapman.edu/ojs/index.php/VocesNovae/article/view/55/229

Gulley, Frank. 2014. "Commentary: United Methodism and the Ordination of Women." Available online at www.umc.org/what-we-believe/commentary-united-methodism-and-the-ordination-of-women

Gustin, E.W. 1909. *Election Day!* [cartoon]. Washington, DC: Library of Congress Prints and Photographs Division.

Guttmacher Institute. 2013a. "Facts on Americans Teens' Sexual and Reproductive Health." Available online at www.guttmacher.org/pubs/FB-ATSRH.html

Guttmacher Institute. 2013b. "Fact Sheet: Unintended Pregnancy in the United States." Available online at www.guttmacher.org/pubs/FB-Unintended-Pregnancy-US.html

Guttmacher Institute. 2014a. "Fact Sheet: Contraceptive Use in the United States." Available online at www.guttmacher.org/pubs/fb_contr_use.html

Guttmacher Institute. 2014b. "Fact Sheet: Induced Abortion in the United States." Available online at www.guttmacher.org/pubs/fb_induced_abortion.html

Guttmann, Allen. 1991. *Women's Sports: A History*. New York: Columbia University Press.

Haaga, John. 2000. "High Death Rate among Russian Men Predates Soviet Union's Demise." Washington, DC: Population Reference Bureau. Available online at www.prb.org/Articles/2000/HighDeathRateAmongRussianMenPredatesSovietUnionsDemise.aspx

Haidt, Jonathan. 2012. *The Righteous Mind: Why Good People are Divided by Politics and Religion*. New York: Pantheon.

Hallett, Stephanie. 2013. "Changing Your Last Name: Survey Reveals How Americans Feel about Women, Men Changing their Names." *Huff Post*, April 14. Available online at www.huffingtonpost.com/2013/04/14/changing-your-last-name_n_3073125.html

Hallward-Driemeier, Mary, Tazeen Hasan, and Ancz Bogdana Rusu. 2013a. *Women's Legal Rights over 50 Years: Progress, Stagnation, or Regression?* Washington, DC: The World Bank.

Hallward-Driemeier, Mary, Tazeen Hasan, and Ancz Bogdana Rusu. 2013b. *Women's Legal Rights over 50 Years: What Is the Impact of Reform?* Washington, DC: The World Bank.

Hamid, Mohammad. 2012. "Afghan Schoolgirls Poisoned in Anti-Education Attack." *Thompson Reuters*, April 17.

Hammer, Julaine. 2012. *American Muslim Women, Religious Authority, and Activism: More than a Prayer*. Austin: University of Texas Press.

Hampton, Robert L., Ricardo Carrillo, and Joan Kim. 2005. "Domestic Violence in African American Communities." In Natalie J. Sokoloff with Christina Pratt (ed.) *Domestic Violence at the Margins: Readings on Race, Class, Gender, and Culture*. New Brunswick, NJ: Rutgers University Press, pp. 127–141.

Hannum, Emily, Peggy Kong, and Yuping Zhang. 2009. "Family Sources of Educational Gender Inequality in Rural China: A Critical Assessment." *International Journal of Educational Development* 29: 474–486.

Hansen, Karen V. and Ilene J. Philipson, eds. 1990. *Women, Class, and the Feminist Imagination: A Socialist-Feminist Reader*. Philadelphia, PA: Temple University Press.

Hanushek, Eric. 2008. "Schooling, Gender Equity, and Economic Outcomes." In Mercy Tembon and Lucia Fort (eds.) *Girls' Education in the 21st Century: Gender Equality, Empowerment, and Economic Growth*. Washington, DC: The World Bank, pp. 23–40.

HarassMap. 2014. Available online at http://harassmap.org/en/

Hargreaves, Jennifer. 2002. "The Victorian Cult of the Family and the Early Years of Female Sport." In Sheila Scraton and Anne Flintoff (eds.) *Gender and Sport: A Reader*. London: Routledge, pp. 53–65.

Harper, C.C., M. Blum, H.T. de Bocanegra, P.D. Darney, J.J. Speidel, M. Policar, and E.A. Drey. 2008. "Challenges in Translating Evidence to Practice: The Provision of Intrauterine Contraception." *Obstetrics and Gynecology* 111(6): 1359–1369.

Harris, Gardiner. 2013a. "For Rape Victims in India, Police Are Often Part of the Problem." *New York Times*, January 22. Available online at www.nytimes.com/2013/01/23/world/asia/for-rape-victims-in-india-police-are-often-part-of-the-problem.html?pagewanted=all

Harris, Gardiner. 2013b. "India's Supreme Court Restores an 1861 Law Banning Gay Sex." *New York Times*, December 11.

Harris, Gardiner. 2014a. "Rape Ruled Out in Case of 2 Indian Girls." *New York Times*, November 28.

Harris, Gardiner. 2014b. "'Superbugs' Kill India's Babies and Pose an Overseas Threat." *New York Times*, December 4.

Harris-Perry, Melissa V. 2011. *Sister Citizen: Shame, Stereotypes, and Black Women in America*. New Haven, CT: Yale University Press.

Hart, Carl. 2013. *High Price: A Neuroscientist's Journey of Self-Discovery that Challenges Everything You Know About Drugs and Society*. New York: HarperCollins.

Hart, Timothy C. 2003. "Violent Victimization of College Students." Washington, DC: Bureau of Justice Statistics.

Hartman, Heidi. 1979. "The Unhappy Marriage of Marxism and Feminism: Towards a More Progressive Union." *Capital & Class* 3: 1–30.

Hartmann, Douglas. 2008. "High School Sports Participation and Educational Attainment: Recognizing, Assessing, and Utilizing the Relationship." LA84 Foundation. Available online at http://library.la84.org/3ce/HighSchoolSportsParticipation.pdf

Hartmann-Tews, Ilse and Getrud Pfister. 2003. "Women's Inclusion in Sport: International and Comparative Findings." In Ilse Hartmann-Tews and Gertrud Pfister (eds.) *Sport and Women: Social Issues in International Perspective*. London: Routledge, pp. 266–280.

Hartzell, E., M.S. Frazer, K. Wertz, and M. Davis. 2009. *The State of Transgender California: Results from the 2008 California Transgender Economic Health Survey*. San Francisco, CA: Transgender Law Center.

Hattery, Angela J. 2010. "Feminist Theory and the Study of Sport: An Illustration from Title IX." In Earl Smith (ed.) *Sociology of Sport and Social Theory*. Champaign, IL: Human Kinetics, pp. 97–113.

Hawes Publications. 2014. *New York Times Best Sellers List*. Available online at www.hawes.com/pastlist.htm

Hawkins, Billy. 2010. *The New Plantation: Black Athletes, College Sports, and Predominantly White NCAA Institutions*. New York: Palgrave Macmillian.

Hawthorne, Fran. 2012. "In Pursuit of the Female Philanthropists." *New York Times*, November 8. Available online at www.nytimes.com/2012/11/09/giving/groups-work-on-attracting-women-philanthropists.html?pagewanted=1&_r=0

Headland, Thomas N. and Janet D. Headland. 1997. "Limitation of Human Rights, Land Exclusion, and Tribal Extinction: The Agta Negritos of the Philippines." *Human Organization* 56: 79–90.

Henderson, Keith. 1985. "School Boards Losing Trustee Tradition, Gaining More Women." *Christian Science Monitor*, June 10. Available online at www.csmonitor.com/1985/0610/dboard2.html

Henry, Astrid. 2004. *Not My Mother's Sister: Generational Conflict and Third-Wave Feminism*. Bloomington: Indiana University Press.

Herbert, T. Walter. 2002. *Sexual Violence and American Manhood*. Cambridge, MA: Harvard University Press.

Hess, Amanda. 2014. "Why Women Aren't Welcome on the Internet." *Pacific Standard*, January 6. Available online at www.psmag.com/navigation/health-and-behavior/women-arent-welcome-internet-72170/

Hess, Cynthia, Ariane Hegewisch, Youngmin Yi, and Claudia Williams. 2013. "The Status of Women in North Carolina." Washington, DC: Institute for Women's Policy Research.

Hetey, Rebecca C. and Jennifer L. Eberhardt. 2014. "Racial Disparities in Incarceration Increase Acceptance of Punitive Policies." *Psychological Science*, August 5.

Heyrman, Christine Leigh. 1997. *Southern Cross: The Beginnings of the Bible Belt*. New York: Knopf.

Heyward, Carter. 1989. *Touching Our Strength: The Erotic As Power and the Love of God*. San Francisco: Harper & Row.

Hickey, Walt. 2014. "The Dollar-and-Cents Case Against Hollywood's Exclusion of Women." *FiveThirtyEight*, April 1. Available online at http://fivethirtyeight.com/features/the-dollar-and-cents-case-against-hollywoods-exclusion-of-women/

Hidayatullah, Aysha A. 2014. *Feminist Edges of the Qur'an*. New York: Oxford University Press.

Higgenbotham, Evelyn Brooks. 1993. *Righteous Discontent: The Women's Movement in the Black Baptist Church, 1880–1920*. Cambridge, MA: Harvard University Press.

Hitchman, Sara C. and Geoffrey T. Fong. 2011. "Gender Empowerment and Female-to-Male Smoking Prevalence Ratios." *Bulletin of the World Health Organization* 89: 195–202. Available online at www.who.int/bulletin/volumes/89/3/10-079905/en/

Hobbs, Allyson. 2014. *A Chosen Exile: A History of Racial Passing in American Life*. Cambridge, MA: Harvard University Press.

Hochschild, Adam. 1998. *King Leopold's Ghost: A Story of Greed, Terror, and Heroism in Colonial Africa*. Boston: Houghton Mifflin.

Hochschild, Arlie Russell, with Anne Machung. 1989. *The Second Shift: Working Parents and the Revolution at Home*. New York: Penguin.

Hodges, Melissa J. and Michelle J. Budig. 2010. "Who Gets the Daddy Bonus? Organizational Hegemonic Masculinity and the Impact of Fatherhood on Earnings." *Gender & Society* 24(6): 717–745.

Hodgson, Dorothy L. 1999. "Pastoralism, Patriarchy, and History: Changing Gender Relations Among Maasai in Tanganyika, 1890–1940." *The Journal of African History* 40(1): 41–65.

Hodgson, Dorothy L. 2001. *Once Intrepid Warriors: Gender, Ethnicity, and The Cultural Politics of Maasai Development*. Bloomington: Indiana University Press.

Hoebel, E. Adamson. 1960. *The Cheyennes: Indians of the Great Plains*. New York: Harcourt Brace.

Hoffert, Sylvia. 2003. *A History of Gender in America: Essays, Documents, and Articles*. Upper Saddle River, NJ: Prentice Hall.

Högberg, Ulf. 2004. "The Decline in Maternal Mortality in Sweden: The Role of Community Midwifery." *American Journal of Public Health* 94: 1312–1320.

Holland, Dorothy C. and Margaret A. Eisenhart. 1990. *Educated in Romance: Women, Achievement, and College Culture*. Chicago: University of Chicago Press.

Hondagneu-Sotelo, Pierrette and Ernestine Avila. 2005. "'I'm Here, but I'm There.' The Meanings of Latina Transnational Motherhood." In Maxine Baca Zinn, Pierrette Hondagneu-Sotelo, and Michael Messner (eds.) *Gender Through the Prism of Difference*, 3rd edn. New York: Oxford University Press, pp. 308–322.

Hong, Fan. 2003. "Women's Sport in the People's Republic of China: Body, Politics and the Unfinished Revolution." In Ilse Hartmann-Tews and Gertrud Pfister (eds.) *Sport and Women: Social Issues in International Perspective*. London: Routledge, pp. 224–237.

hooks, bell. 1981. *Ain't I a Woman: Black Women and Feminism*. Boston: South End Press.

hooks, bell. 1984. *Feminist Theory from Margin to Center*. Boston: South End Press.

hooks, bell. 1989. *Talking Back: Thinking Feminist, Thinking Black*. Boston: South End Press.

hooks, bell. 2004. *We Real Cool: Black Men and Masculinity*. New York: Routledge.

Horowitz, Helen Lefkowitz. 1987. *Campus Life: Undergraduate Cultures from the End of the Eighteenth Century to the Present*. Chicago: University of Chicago Press.

Horowitz, Helen Lefkowitz. 2002. *Rereading Sex: Battles Over Sexual Knowledge and Suppression in Nineteenth-Century America*. New York: Knopf.

Huber, Joan. 2007. *On the Origins of Gender Inequality*. Boulder, CO: Paradigm Publisher.

Hudson, J.I., E. Hiripi, H.G. Pope Jr., and R.C. Kessler. 2007. "The Prevalence and Correlates of Eating Disorders in the National Comorbidity Survey Replication." *Biological Psychiatry* 61(3): 345–358.

Hudson, Valerie M., Bonnie Ballif-Spanvill, Mary Caprioli, and Chad F. Emmett. 2012. *Sex and World Peace*. New York: Columbia University Press.

Hudson, Valerie M. and Andrea M. den Boer. 2004. *Bare Branches: The Security Implications of Asia's Surplus Male Population*. Cambridge, MA: MIT Press.

Humphrey, Stephen E. and Arnold S. Kahn. 2000. "Fraternities, Athletic Teams, and Rape: Importance of Identification with a Risky Group." *Journal of Interpersonal Violence* 15(12): 1313–1322.

Hunt, J. and Kasynathan, N. 2002. "Reflections on Microfinance and Women's Empowerment." *Development Bulletin* 57: 71–75.

Hunt, Mary E. and Diann L. Neu. 2014. *New Feminist Christianity: Many Voices, Many Views*. Woodstock, VT: SkyLight Paths.

Hvistendahl, Mara. 2011. *Unnatural Selection: Choosing Boys Over Girls, and the Consequences of a World Full of Men*. New York: Public Affairs.

Hymowitz, Kay, W. Bradford Wilcox, and Kelleen Kaye. 2013. "The New Unmarried Moms." *The Wall Street Journal*, March 15. Available online at http://online.wsj.com/article/SB100014241278873 23826704578356494206134184.html

ILO (International Labor Organization). 2012. "21 Million People Are Now Victims of Forced Labour, ILO Says." Available online at www.ilo.org/global/about-the-ilo/newsroom/news/WCMS_181961/lang—it/index.htm.

IMDB. 2014. "Frozen Release Info." Available online at www.imdb.com/title/tt2294629/releaseinfo?ref_=tt_ql_9

Immigration Policy Center. 2010. "Immigrant Women in the United States: A Portrait of Demographic Diversity." Available online at www.immigration

policy.org/sites/default/files/docs/Immigrant_Women_in_the_US_-_A_Portrait_of_Diversity_062810.pdf

Insight. 2010. "Lifting as We Climb: Women of Color, Wealth, and America's Future." Available online at www.insightcced.org/uploads/CRWG/LiftingAsWeClimb-WomenWealth-Report-InsightCenter-Spring2010.pdf

International Olympic Committee (IOC). 2013. "Factsheet: Women in the Olympic Movement. Update 2013." Available online at www.olympic.org/Documents/Reference_documents_Factsheets/Women_in_Olympic_Movement.pdf

Inter-Parliamentary Union. 2014. "Women in National Parliaments." Available online at www.ipu.org/wmn-e/classif.htm

IPPF. 2008. "First Trimester Abortion Guidelines and Protocols: Surgical and Medical Procedures." Available online at www.ippf.org/resource/First-Trimester-Abortion-Guidelines-and-Protocols

Ireland, Corydon. 2009. "Fijian Girls Succumb to Western Dysmorphia." *Harvard Gazette*, March 19. Available online at http://news.harvard.edu/gazette/story/2009/03/fijian-girls-succumb-to-western-dysmorphia/

Irving, Debby. 2014. *Waking Up White and Finding Myself in the Story of Race*. Cambridge, MA: Elephant Room Press.

Irwin, Neil. 2014. "How Are American Families Doing? A Guided Tour of Our Financial Well-Being." *New York Times*, September 8.

Jackson, Derrick Z. 2014. "18th Annual Graduation Gap Bowl." *Boston Globe*, January 7.

Jacobson, David. 2013. *Of Virgins and Martyrs: Women and Sexuality in Global Conflict*. Baltimore, MD: Johns Hopkins University Press.

Jeffrey, Julie Roy. 1998. *The Great Silent Army of Abolitionist Women in the Antislavery Movement*. Chapel Hill: University of North Carolina Press.

Jeffreys, Sheila. 2014. *Gender Hurts: A Feminist Analysis of the Politics of Transgenderism*. New York: Routledge.

Jensen, Robert and Emily Oster. 2007. "The Power of TV: Cable Television and Women's Status in India." NBER Working Paper No. 13305. Available online at www.nber.org/papers/w13305.pdf?new_window=1

Jewkes, Rachel, Lisa Vetten, Ruxana Jina, Nicola Christofides, Romi Sigsworth, and Lizle Loots. 2012. "What We Know – And What We Don't: Single and Multiple Perpetrator Rape in South Africa." *Crime Quarterly* 41: 11–19.

Jhally, Sut. 1984. "The Spectacle of Accumulation: Material and Cultural Factors in the Evolution of the Sports/Media Complex." *Insurgent Sociologist* 12(3): 41–57.

Joint United Nations Programme on HIV/AIDS. 2010. "Neonatal and Child Male Circumcision: A Global Review." Geneva: UNAIDS.

Jones, Jo and William Mosher. 2013. "Fathers' Involvement with Their Children: United States, 2006–2010." *National Health Statistics Report, 71*. Atlanta: Centers for Disease Control and Prevention.

Jones, Nikki. 2009. *Between Good and Ghetto: African American Girls and Inner-City Violence*. New Brunswick, NJ: Rutgers University Press.

Jones, Nikki. 2010. "'It's About Being a Survivor . . .': African American Girls, Gender, and the Context of Inner City Violence." In Meda Chesney-Lind and Nikki Jones (eds.) *Fighting for Girls: New Perspectives on Gender and Violence*. Albany: State University of New York Press, pp. 203–218.

Jones, Rachel K. and Joerg Dreweke. 2011. *Countering Conventional Wisdom: New Evidence on Religion and Contraceptive Use*. New York: Guttmacher Institute.

Jones, Rachel K. and Megan L. Kavanaugh. 2011. "Changes in Abortion Rates Between 2000 and 2008 and Lifetime Incidence of Abortion." *Obstetrics and Gynecology* 117(6): 1358–1366.

Jones, Rachel K., Lori Frohwirth, and Ann M. Moore. 2013. "More than Poverty: Disruptive Events Among Women Having Abortions in the USA." *Journal of Family Planning and Reproductive Health Care* 39(1): 36–43.

Jutel, Annemarie. 2010. "Framing Disease: The Example of Female Hypoactive Sexual Desire Disorder." *Social Science and Medicine* 70: 1084–1090.

Kahlenberg, Susan and Michelle Hein. 2010. "Progression on Nickelodeon? Gender-Role Stereotypes in Toy Commercials." *Sex Roles* 62: 830–847.

Kalish, Rachel and Michael Kimmel. 2011. "Hooking Up: Hot Hetero Sex or the New Numb Normative?" *Australian Feminist Studies* 26: 137–151.

Kann, Laura, Emily O'Malley Olsen, Tim McManus, Steve Kinchen, David Chyen, William A. Harris, and Howell Weschsler. 2011. "Sexual Identity, Sex of Sexual Contacts, and Health-Risk Behaviors Among Students in Grades 9–12." *Morbidity and Mortality Weekly Report*, June 6. Available online at www.cdc.gov/mmwr/preview/mmwrhtml/ss60e0606a1.htm?s_cid=ss60e0606a1_w

Kantor, Jodi. 2014. "Working Anything but 9 to 5." *New York Times*, August 13.

Karcher, Carolyn L. 1994. *The First Woman in the Republic: A Cultural Biography of Lydia Maria Child.* Durham, NC: Duke University Press.

Karim, Jamillah. 2009. *American Muslim Women: Negotiating Race, Class, and Gender within the Ummah.* New York: New York University.

Karkazis, Katrina. 2008. *Fixing Sex: Intersex, Medical Authority, and Lived Experience.* Durham, NC: Duke University Press.

Kathlene, Lyn. 2001. "Words that Matter: Women's Voice and Institutional Bias in Public Policy Formation." In Susan J. Carroll (ed.) *The Impact of Women in Public Office.* Bloomington: Indiana University Press, pp. 22–48.

Katz, Jackson. 1999. *Tough Guise: Violence, Media and the Crisis in Masculinity* [DVD]. Media Education Foundation.

Katz, Jonathan Ned. 1983. *Gay/Lesbian Almanac.* New York: Harper & Row.

Kaufman, Robert. 2002. "Assessing Alternative Perspectives on Race and Sex Employment Segregation." *American Sociological Review* 67: 547–572.

Kay, Katty and Claire Shipman. 2014a. *The Confidence Code: The Science and Art of Self-Assurance – What Women Should Know.* New York: Harper Business.

Kay, Katty, and Claire Shipman. 2014b. "The Confidence Gap." *The Atlantic* 313(4): 56–66.

Kearney, Melissa and Phillip Levine. 2014. "Media Influences on Social Outcomes: The Impact of MTV's *16 and Pregnant* on Teen Childbearing." NBER Working Paper 19795. Available online at www.nber.org/papers/w19795.pdf

Kellstedt, Paul M., David A.M. Peterson, and Mark D. Ramirez. 2010. "The Macro Politics of a Gender Gap." *Public Opinion Quarterly* 74(3): 477–498. Available online at http://poq.oxfordjournals.org/content/74/3/477.abstract

Kennedy, Bruce, Ichiro Kawachi, and Elizabeth Brainerd. 1998. "The Role of Social Capital in the Russian Mortality Crisis." *World Development* 11: 2029–2043.

Kenschaft, Lori. 2005. *Reinventing Marriage: The Love and Work of Alice Freeman Palmer and George Herbert Palmer.* Urbana: University of Illinois Press.

Kerber, Linda. 1997. *Toward an Intellectual History of Women.* Chapel Hill: University of North Carolina Press.

Kerber, Linda. 1998. *No Constitutional Right to Be Ladies.* New York: Hill and Wang.

Kessler-Harris, Alice. 1993. *Women Have Always Worked: A Historical Overview.* New York: The Feminist Press at CUNY.

Kessler-Harris, Alice. 2003. *Out to Work: A History of Wage-Earning Women in the United States*, 1st edn. 1982. New York: Oxford University Press.

Khadaroo, Stacy Teicher. 2013. "School Discipline: In Search of an Even Hand." *Christian Science Monitor*, March 31.

Khadaroo, Stacy Teicher. 2014. "Young Men Say 'No' to Sexual Violence." *Christian Science Monitor Weekly*, November 10.

Khandker, Shahidur R. 2005. "Microfinance and Poverty: Evidence Using Panel Data from Bangladesh." *World Bank Economic Review* 19(2): 263–286.

Khandker, Shahidur R. and Hussain A. Samad. 2014. "Dynamic Effects of Microcredit in Bangladesh." World Bank Policy Research Working Paper No. 6821. Available online at http://papers.ssrn.com/sol3/papers.cfm?abstract_id=2417519

Kierman, Jacob Alex, Kelly Daley, and Alyssa Pozniak. 2013. "Family and Medical Leave in 2012: Technical Report." Available online at www.dol.gov/asp/evaluation/fmla/FMLATechnicalReport.pdf

Kilbourne, Jean. 2010. *Killing Us Softly 4: Advertising Images of Women* [DVD]. Available online at www.mediaed.org/cgi-bin/commerce.cgi?preadd=action&key=241

Kimmel, Michael. 1994. "Masculinity as Homophobia: Fear, Shame and Silence in the Construction of Gender Identity." In H. Brod and M. Kaufman (eds.) *Theorizing Masculinities.* London: Sage, pp. 119–141.

Kimmel, Michael. 2006. *Manhood in America: A Cultural History*. New York: Oxford University Press.

Kimmel, Michael. 2013. *Angry White Men: American Masculinity at the End of an Era*. New York: Nation Books.

King, Deborah. 1988. "Multiple Jeopardy, Multiple Consciousness: The Context of a Black Feminist Ideology." *Signs* 14: 42–72.

King World. 2004. "King World Renewals for 'The Oprah Winfrey Show' Through 2010–2011 Season Reach 80% of the Country." Available online at www.thefutoncritic.com/news/2004/11/11/king-world-renewals-for-the-oprah-winfrey-show-through-2010-2011-season-reach-80-percent-of-the-country—17239/20041111kingworld01/

Kirjike, Nonuo, Toshihiko Nagata, Kumiko Sirata, and Naoki Yamamoto. 1998. "Are Young Women in Japan at High Risk for Eating Disorders? Decreased BMI in Young Females from 1960 to 1995." *Psychiatry and Clinical Neurosciences* 52: 279–281.

Kirk, Gwyn and Margo Okazawa-Rey. 2012. *Women's Lives: Multicultural Perspectives*, 6th edn. Boston: McGraw-Hill.

Kirk, Jackie. 2008. "Addressing Gender Disparities in Education in Contexts of Crisis, Postcrisis, and State Fragility." In Mercy Tembon and Lucia Fort (eds.) *Girls' Education in the 21st Century: Gender Equality, Empowerment, and Economic Growth*. Washington, DC: The World Bank, pp. 153–180.

Kirkwood, Thomas. 2010. "Why Women Live Longer: Stress Alone Does Not Explain the Longevity Gap." *Scientific American*, October 1. Available online at www.scientificamerican.com/article.cfm?id=why-women-live-longer

Knefel, Molly. 2013. "The School-to-Prison Pipeline: A Nationwide Problem for Equal Rights." *Rolling Stone*, November 7.

Kohlberg, Lawrence A. 1966. "Cognitive-Developmental Analysis of Children's Sex-Role Concepts and Attitudes." In Eleanor E. Maccoby (ed.) *The Development of Sex Differences*. Stanford, CA: Stanford University Press, pp. 82–172.

Koofi, Fawzia, with Nadine Ghouri. 2012. *The Favored Daughter: One Woman's Fight to Lead Afghanistan into the Future*. New York: Palgrave Macmillan.

Korieh, Chima. 2001. "The Invisible Farmer? Women, Gender, And Colonial Agricultural Policy in the Igbo Region of Nigeria, c. 1913–1954." *African Economic History* 29: 117–192.

Kraditor, Aileen S. 1969. *Means and Ends in American Abolitionism: Garrison and His Critics on Strategy and Tactics, 1834–1950*. New York: Pantheon.

Krakauer, Jon. 2015. *Missoula: Rape and the Justice System in a College Town*. New York: Doubleday.

Kramer, Andrew E. 2013. "Russia Passes Bill Targeting Some Discussions of Sexuality." *New York Times*, June 11. Available online at www.nytimes.com/2013/06/12/world/europe/russia-passes-bill-targeting-some-discussions-of-homosexuality.html?_r=0

Krebs, Christopher P., Christine H. Lindquist, Tara D. Warner, Bonnie S. Fisher, and Sandra L. Martin. 2007. "The Campus Sexual Assault (CSA) Study." Washington, DC: National Institute of Justice. Available online at https://ncjrs.gov/pdffiles1/nij/grants/221153.pdf

Kristof, Nicholas D. 2010. "Another Pill that Could Cause a Revolution." *New York Times*, July 31.

Kristof, Nicholas D. 2012. "A Veteran's Death, the Nation's Shame." *New York Times*, April 14. Available online at www.nytimes.com/2012/04/15/opinion/sunday/kristof-a-veterans-death-the-nations-shame.html

Kristof, Nicholas D. and Sheryl WuDunn. 2009. *Half the Sky: Turning Oppression into Opportunity for Women Worldwide*. New York: Knopf.

Kron, Josh. 2012. "Resentment Towards the West Bolsters Uganda's New Anti-Gay Bill." *New York Times*, February 28. Available online at www.nytimes.com/2012/02/29/world/africa/ugandan-lawmakers-push-anti-homosexuality-bill-again.html?pagewanted=all&_r=0

Kun, Karen E. 1998. "Vaginal Drying Agents and HIV Transmission." *International Family Planning Perspectives* 24(2). Available online at www.guttmacher.org/pubs/journals/2409398.html

Kutchinsky, B. 1991. "Pornography and Rape: Theory and Practice? Evidence from Crime Data in Four Countries Where Pornography Is Easily Available." *International Journal of Law and Psychiatry* 14(1–2): 47–64.

Kvam, Kristen E., Linda S. Schearing, and Valarie H. Ziegler, eds. 2009. *Eve and Adam: Jewish, Christian, and Muslim Readings on Genesis and Gender*. Bloomington: Indiana University Press.

Kyle, Donald. 2007. *Sport and Spectacle in the Ancient World*. Oxford: Blackwell.

Lacey, Marc. 2008. "A Lifestyle Distinct: The Muxe of Mexico." *New York Times*, December 6.

La Ferrara, Eliana, Alberto Chong and Suzanne Duryea. 2012. "Soap Operas and Fertility: Evidence from Brazil." *American Economic Journal: Applied Economics* 4: 1–31.

LaFraniere, Sharon. 2005. "An African Cleansing Rite that Now Can Kill." *New York Times*, May 12.

Lamanna, Mary Ann and Agnes Riedmann. 2009. *Marriages and Families: Making Choices in a Diverse Society*. Belmont, CA: Thomas Higher Education.

Landivar, Liana. 2013. "Labor Force Participation Among Asian, Black, Hispanic, and White Mothers in 20 Occupations." In Marla H. Kohlman, Dana B. Krieg, and Bette J. Dickerson (eds.) *Notions of Family: Intersectional Perspectives*. Bingley, UK: Emerald Group Publishing, pp. 263–286.

Landry, Bart. 2000. *Black Working Wives: Pioneers of the American Family Revolution*. Berkeley, CA: University of California Press.

Lane J., A.R. Gover, and S. Dahod. 2009. "Fear of Violent Crime among Men and Women on Campus: The Impact of Perceived Risk and Fear of Sexual Assault." *Violence and Victims* 24(2): 172–192.

Langelan, Martha J. 1993. *Back Off: How to Confront and Stop Sexual Harassment and Harassers*. New York: Simon & Schuster.

Lapchick, Richard. 2010. "The Racial and Gender Report Card: College Sport. The Institute for Diversity and Ethics in Sports." Available online at www.tide sport.org/RGRC/2010/2010_College_RGRC_FINAL.pdf

Lapchick, Richard, Juan Dominguez, Leslie Martinez, and Stephens Rogers. 2014a. "The 2014 Racial and Gender Report Card: Major League Baseball." Available online at www.tidesport.org/MLB%20RGRC%202014%20Revised.pdf

Lapchick, Richard, Drew Donovan, Erika Loomer, and Leslie Martinez. 2014b. "The 2014 Racial and Gender Report Card: National Basketball Association." Available online at www.tidesport.org/The%202014%20NFL%20Racial%20and%20Gender%20Report%20Card.pdf

Lapchick, Richard, Drew Donovan, Stephens Rogers, and April Johnson. 2014c. "The 2014 Racial and Gender Report Card: National Football League." Available online at www.tidesport.org/The%202014%20NFL%20Racial%20and%20Gender%20Report%20Card.pdf

LaPlante, Eve. 2005. *American Jezebel: The Uncommon Life of Anne Hutchinson, the Woman Who Defied the Puritans*. San Francisco: HarperOne.

Laqueur, Thomas. 1990. *Making Sex: Body and Gender from the Greeks to Freud*. Cambridge, MA: Harvard University Press.

Laqueur, Thomas. 2003. *Solitary Sex: A Cultural History of Masturbation*. New York: Zone Books.

Lareau, Annette. 2003. *Unequal Childhoods: Class, Race, and Family Life*. Berkeley: University of California Press.

Larrick, Nancy, 1965. "The All-White World of Children's Books." *Saturday Review* 48 (September 11): 63–65, 84–85.

Larson, Christina. 2013. "China's Female Factory Workers Face Widespread Sexual Harrassment." *Business Week*, December 10.

Larson, John Lauritz. 2001. *Internal Improvement: National Public Works and the Promise of Popular Government in the Early United States*. Chapel Hill: University of North Carolina Press.

Lawless, Jennifer L. and Richard L. Fox. 2012. *Men Rule: The Continued Under-Representation of Women in U.S. Politics*. Washington, DC: Women & Politics Institute.

Lawless, Jennifer L. and Richard L. Fox. 2013. *Girls Just Wanna Not Run: The Gender Gap in Young Americans' Political Ambition*. Washington, DC: Women & Politics Institute.

Lederer, Laura, ed. 1980. *Take Back the Night: Women on Pornography*. New York: Harper Perennial.

Lee, Cynthia. 2008. "The Gay Panic Defense." *UC Davis Law Review*. Available online at http://papers.ssrn.com/sol3/papers.cfm?abstract_id=1141875

Lee, Moon, Stacey Hust, and Lingling Zhang. 2011. "Effects of Violence Against Women in Popular Crime Dramas on Viewers' Attitudes Related to Sexual Violence." *Mass Communication and Society* 14: 25–44.

Lee, Richard and Irven DeVore. 1968. *Man the Hunter*. Chicago: Aldine.

Lefkowitz, Bernard. 1997. *Our Guys*. New York: Vintage.

Leistikow, Nicole. 2008. "Indian Women Criticize 'Fair and Lovely' Ideal." *WeNews*, April 28. Available online at http://womensenews.org/story/the-world/030428/indian-women-criticize-fair-and-lovely-ideal#.VBiIDy5dUi4

Lemmon, Gayle Tzemach. 2011. *The Dressmaker of Khair Khana*. New York: HarperCollins.

Lenhart, Amanda. 2007. "Cyberbullying and Online Teens." Pew Internet & American Life Project, June 27. Available online at www.pewinternet.org/files/old-media//Files/Reports/2007/PIP%20Cyberbullying%20Memo.pdf.pdf

Lenski, Gerhard. 1966. *Power and Privilege: A Theory of Social Stratification*. New York: McGraw-Hill.

Leondar-Wright, Betsy. 2014. *Missing Class: How Seeing Class Cultures Can Strengthen Social Movement Groups*. Ithaca, NY: Cornell University Press.

Lepore, Jill. 2013. *A Book of Ages: The Life and Opinions of Jane Franklin*. New York: Vintage Books.

Lerman, Robert I. 2002. "Marriage and the Economic Well-Being of Families with Children: A Review of the Literature." Urban Institute. Available online at www.urban.org/UploadedPDF/410541_LitReview.pdf

Lerner, Gerda. 1971. *The Grimké Sisters from South Carolina: Pioneers for Women's Rights and Abolition*. New York: Schocken.

Lerner, Gerda. 1986. *The Invention of Patriarchy*. New York: Oxford University Press.

Leslie, Julia, ed. 1991. *Roles and Rituals for Hindu Women*. Teaneck, NJ: Farleigh Dickinson University Press.

Lester, David, John F. Gunn III, and Paul Quinnett, eds. 2014. *Suicide in Men: How Men Differ from Women in Expressing Their Distress*. Springfield, IL: Charles C. Thomas Publishers.

Lesthaeghe, Ron. 1995. "The Second Demographic Transition in Western Countries: An Interpretation." In K. Mason and A.-M. Jensen (eds.) *Gender and Family Change in Industrialized Countries*. Oxford: Clarendon Press, pp. 17–62.

Levine, Rhonda. 2010. "Social and Cultural Capital: Race, School Attainment, and the Role of High School Sports." In Earl Smith (ed.) *Sociology of Sport and Social Theory*. Champaign, IL: Human Kinetics Publishers, pp. 115–128.

Lévi-Strauss, Claude. 1969. *The Elementary Structures of Kinship*, trans. James Harle Bell, John Richard von Sturmer, and Rodney Needham. Boston: Beacon Press.

Levy, Abe. 2003. "Black Baptist Church Ordains Four Women." *The Wichita Eagle*, February 15. Available online at http://m.semissourian.com/story/101726.html

Lewis, Helen. 2012. "Game Theory: Making Room for Women." *New York Times ArtBeat*, December 25. Available online at http://artsbeat.blogs.nytimes.com/2012/12/25/game-theory-making-room-for-the-women/?module=Search&mabReward=relbias%3Aw%2C%7B%221%22%3A%22RI%3A11%22%7D

Li, Eric P.H., Hyun Jeong Min, Russell W. Belk, Junko Kimura, and Shalini Bahl. 2008. "Skin Lightening and Beauty in Four Asian Cultures." *Advances in Consumer Research* 35: 444–449.

Library of Congress. 1915. "Marching for Women's Suffrage, New York City." [photo]. Available online at www.bawhp.org/

Lin, Ann Chih and David R. Harris, eds. 2010. *The Colors of Poverty: Why Racial and Ethnic Disparities Persist*. New York: Russell Sage Foundation.

Lincoln, Anne E. and Michael P. Allen. 2004. "Double Jeopardy in Hollywood: Age and Gender in the Careers of Film Actors, 1926–1999." *Sociological Forum* 19: 611–631.

Lindow, Megan. 2009. South Africa's Rape Crisis: 1 in 4 Men Say They've Done It. *Time*, June 20. Available online at www.time.com/time/world/article/0,8599,1906000,00.html

Lipka, Michael. 2014. "Controversy Over New Israeli Law Highlights Growing Ultra-Orthodox Population." Pew Research Center, March 13. Available online at www.pewresearch.org/fact-tank/2014/03/13/controversy-over-new-israeli-law-highlights-growing-ultra-orthodox-population/

Lisak, David and Paul M. Miller. 2002. "Repeat Rape and Multiple Offending Among Undetected Rapists." *Violence and Victims* 17(1): 73–84.

Lisak, David and Susan Roth. 1990. "Motives and Psychodynamics of Self-Reported, Unincarcerated Rapists." *American Journal of Orthpsychiatry* 60(2): 268–280.

Livingston, Gretchen. 2013. "The Rise of Single Fathers." Pew Research Social & Demographic Trends, July 2. Available online at www.pewsocialtrends.org/2013/07/02/the-rise-of-single-fathers/

Llewelyn-Davies, Melissa. 1981. "Women, Warriors, and Patriarchs." In Sherry Ortner and Harriet Whitehead (eds.) *Sexual Meanings: The Cultural Construction of Gender and Sexuality*. Cambridge: Cambridge University Press, pp. 330–358.

Locke, Benjamin D. and James R. Mahalik. 2005. "Examining Masculinity Norms, Problem Drinking, and Athletic Involvement as Predictors of Sexual Aggression in College Men." *Journal of Counseling Psychology* 52(3): 279–283.

Lockheed, Marianne. 2008. "The Double Disadvantage of Gender and Social Exclusion in Education." In Mercy Tembon and Lucia Fort (eds.) *Girls' Education in the 21st Century: Gender Equality, Empowerment, and Economic Growth*. Washington, DC: The World Bank, pp. 115–126.

Lopez, Nancy. 2003. *Hopeful Girls, Troubled Boys: Race and Gender Disparity in Urban Education*. New York: Routledge.

Lorber, Judith. 2011. *Gender Inequality: Feminist Theories and Politics*. Los Angeles: Roxbury.

Lorde, Audre. 1984. *Sister Outsider: Essays and Speeches*. Trumansburg, NY: Crossing Press.

Lui, Meizhu, Barbara Robles, Betsy Leondar-Wright, Rose Brewer, and Rebecca Adamson. 2006. *The Color of Wealth: The Story Behind the U.S. Racial Divide*. New York: New Press.

Lupton, Ben. 2006. "Explaining Men's Entry into Female-Concentrated Occupations: Issues of Masculinity and Social Class." *Gender, Work and Organization* 13: 103–128.

Lutz, Gene M., Disa L. Cornish, Melvin E. Gonnerman, Jr., Margaret Ralston, and Phyllis Baker. 2009. "Impacts of Participation in High School Extra-curricular Activities on Early Adult Life Experiences: A Study of Iowa Graduates." Des Moines: Iowa Girls' High School Athletic Union.

Lystra, Karen. 1989. *Searching the Heart: Women, Men, and Romantic Love in Nineteenth-Century America*. New York: Oxford University Press.

Maccoby, Eleanor and Carol Jacklin. 1974. *The Psychology of Sex Differences*. Stanford, CA: Stanford University Press.

MacKinnon, Catharine A. 1987. *Feminism Unmodified: Discourses on Life and Law*. Cambridge, MA: Harvard University Press.

Macy, Gary. 2007. *The Hidden History of Women's Ordination: Female Clergy in the Medieval West*. New York: Oxford University Press.

Macy, Gary, William T. Diewig, and Phyllis Zagano. 2012. *Women Deacons: Past, Present, Future*. Mahwah, NJ: Paulist Press.

Mager, John and James Helgeson. 2011. "Fifty Years of Advertising Images: Some Changing Perspective on Role Portrayals Along with Enduring Consistencies." *Sex Roles* 64: 238–252.

Malkin, Elisabeth. 2010. "Gay Marriage Puts Mexico City at Center of Debate." *New York Times*, February 6.

Manjoo, Rashida. 2014. "Report of the Special Rapporteur on Violence against Women, Its Causes and Consequences, Rashida Manjoo: Mission to India." New York: United Nations.

Mannathoko, Changu. 2008. "Promoting Education Quality through Gender-Friendly Schools." In Mercy Tembon and Lucia Fort (eds.) *Girls' Education in the 21st Century: Gender Equality, Empowerment, and Economic Growth*. Washington, DC: The World Bank, pp. 127–142.

Marchand, Roland. 1985. *Advertising the American Dream: Making Way for Modernity, 1920–1940*. Berkeley: University of California Press.

Marcotte, Amanda. 2014. "How 'Pick-Up Artist' Philosophy and Its More Misogynist Backlash Shaped Mind of Alleged Killer Elliot Rodger." *The American Prospect*, May 25.

Margolis, Eric. 2001. *The Hidden Curriculum in Higher Education*. New York: Routledge.

Markoe, Lauren. 2012. "Poll: Catholics Don't See Contraception Mandate as Threat to Religious Freedom." Public Religion Research Institute, March 15. Available online at http://public religion.org/newsroom/2012/03/poll-catholics-dont-see-contraception-mandate-as-threat-to-religious-freedom/

Marshall, Megan. 2005. *The Peabody Sisters: Three Women Who Ignited American Romanticism*. Boston: Houghton Mifflin.

Marshall, Megan. 2013. *Margaret Fuller: A New American Life*. Boston: Houghton Mifflin.

Marshall, Tom, 2014. "Text to Text: Bangladesh Factory Safety and the Triangle Shirtwaist Fire." *New York Times Learning Network*, April 8. Available online at http://learning.blogs.nytimes.com/2014/04/08/text-to-text-bangladesh-factory-safety-and-the-triangle-shirtwaist-fire/?_r=0

Martey, Rosa Mikeal, Jennifer Stomer-Galley, Jaime Banks, Jingsi Wu, and Mia Consalvo. 2014. "The Strategic Female: Gender-Switching and Player Behavior in Online Games." *Information, Communication, and Society* 17(3): 286–300.

Martin, Joyce A., Brady E. Hamilton, Michelle J.K. Osterman, Sally C. Curtin, and T.J. Matthews. 2013. "Births: Final Data for 2012." *National Vital Statistics Reports* 62(9).

Martinez, G., C.E. Copen, and J.C. Abma. 2011. "Teenagers in the United States: Sexual Activity, Contraceptive Use, and Childbearing, 2006–2010 National Survey of Family Growth." *Vital Health Statistics* 23(31). Available online at www.cdc.gov/nchs/data/series/sr_23/sr23_031.pdf

Martinez, Gladys, Kimberly Daniels, and Anjani Chandra. 2012. "Fertility of Men and Women Aged 15–44 Years in the United States: National Survey of Family Growth, 2006–2010." *National Health Statistics Report*. 51. Available online at www.cdc.gov/nchs/data/nhsr/nhsr051.pdf

Marx, Karl. 1867 (1884). *Capital: A Critique of Political Economy*, English edition. Available online at http://synagonism.net/book/economy/marx.1887-1867.capital-i.html

Masci, David. 2014. "The Divide Over Ordaining Women." Pew Research Center, September 9. Available online at www.pewresearch.org/fact-tank/2014/09/09/the-divide-over-ordaining-women/

Masood, Salman. 2006. "Pakistan Moves Toward Altering Rape Law." *New York Times*, November 16.

Matthews, Michael F. 2013. "The Untold Story of Military Sexual Assault." *New York Times*, November 25.

Mattson, Ingrid. 2008. *The Story of the Qur'an: Its History and Place in Muslim Life*. Oxford: Blackwell Publishing.

Mattu, Ayesha and Nur Maznavi, eds. 2014. *Salaam, Love: American Muslim Men on Love, Sex, and Intimacy*. Boston: Beacon Press.

Matulef, Jeffrey. 2013. "The Video Game Industry's Gender Wage Gap Is Worse Than You Think." Available online at Eurogamer.net. www.eurogamer.net/articles/2013-04-04-the-video-game-industrys-gender-wage-gap-is-worse-than-you-think

May, Elaine Tyler. 1980. *Great Expectations: Marriage and Divorce in Post-Victorian America*. Chicago: University of Chicago Press.

McAfee, Ward M. 1998. *Religion, Race, and Reconstruction: The Public Schools in the Politics of the 1870s*. Albany: State University of New York Press.

McAnally, Tom. 2014. "Commentary: Why Do United Methodists Ordain Women When the Bible Specifically Prohibits It?" Available online at www.umc.org/what-we-believe/commentary-why-do-united-methodists-ordain-women-when-the-bible-specificall

McCabe, Janice, Emily Fairchild, Liz Grauerholz, Bernice Pescosolido, and Daniel Tope. 2011. "Gender in Twentieth-Century Children's Books: Patterns of Disparity in Titles and Central Characters." *Gender & Society* 25: 197–226.

McCandless, Amy Thompson. 1999. *The Past in the Present: Women's Higher Education in the Twentieth-Century American South*. Tuscaloosa: The University of Alabama Press.

McCandless, David. 2012. InformationIsBeautiful.net. Available online at www.informationisbeautiful.net/visualizations/chicks-rule/

McCann, Joy. 2013. "Electoral Quotas for Women: An International Overview." Canberra: Parliament of Australia.

McCarthy, Justin. 2014. "Same Sex Marriage Support Reaches New High at 55%." Gallup Poll, May 21. Available online at www.gallup.com/poll/169640/sex-marriage-support-reaches-new-high.aspx

McCully E.A. 1992. *Mirette on the High Wire*. New York: G.P. Putnam's Sons.

McDevitt, Patrick. 2004. *May the Best Man Win: Masculinity and Nationalism in Great Britain and the Empire 1880–1935*. New York: Palgrave Macmillan.

McDougall, Dan. 2009. "When I Hear of Girls Working in London Who Swallow Acid, I Know It Could Have Been Me." *The Guardian*, May 23. Available online at www.theguardian.com/world/2009/may/24/domestic-workers-abuse-violence

McFague, Sallie. 1987. *Models of God: Theology for an Ecological, Nuclear Age*. Philadelphia: Fortress.

McGuire, Danielle L. 2010. *At the Dark End of the Street: Black Women, Rape, and Resistance – a New History of the Civil Rights Movement from Rosa Parks to the Rise of Black Power*. New York: Knopf.

McKee, Martin and Vladimir Shkolnikov. 2001. "Understanding the Toll of Premature Death Among Men in Eastern Europe." *British Medical Journal* 323: 1051–1055.

McKinley, James C. 1994. "Marathon and Ceremony Bring Gay Games to Close." *New York Times*, June 26. Available online at www.nytimes.com/1994/06/26/nyregion/marathon-and-ceremony-bring-gay-games-to-close.html?module=Search&mabReward=relbias%3Ar%2C%7B%221%22%3A%22RI%3A6%22%7D

McKinnon, Catharine. 1982. "Marxism, Method, and the Feminism, State: An Agenda for Theory." *Signs* 7: 514–544.

McMahon, Sarah and G. Lawrence Farmer. 2011. "An Updated Measure for Assessing Subtle Rape Myths." *Social Work Research* 35(2): 71–81.

McMillan, Sally G. 2015. *Lucy Stone: A Life*. New York: Oxford University Press.

McNeil, Donald G., Jr. 2011. "Broad Racial Disparities Seen in Americans' Ills." *New York Times*, January 13. Available online at www.nytimes.com/2011/01/14/health/14cdc.html

McNeill, Maggie. 2014. "Lies, Damned Lies, and Sex Work Statistics." *The Washington Post*, March 27. Available online at www.washingtonpost.com/news/the-watch/wp/2014/03/27/lies-damned-lies-and-sex-work-statistics/

McPherson, Miller, Lynn Smith-Lovin, and Matthew E. Brashears. 2006. "Social Isolation in America: Changes in Core Discussion Networks over Two Decades." *American Sociological Review* 71(3): 353–375.

McWhorter S.K., V.A. Stander, L.L. Merrill, C.J. Thomsen, and J.S. Milner. 2009. "Reports of Rape Reperpetration by Newly Enlisted Male Navy Personnel." *Violence and Victims* 24(2): 204–218.

Meena, Ruth. 2003. "The Politics of Quotas in Tanzania." Presented at The Implementation of Quotas: African Experiences, Pretoria, South Africa, November 11–12. Available online at http://static.quotaproject.org/fr/CS/CS_Tanzania_Meena_27_7_2004.pdf

Meloy, Michelle L., and Susan L. Miller. 2011. *The Victimization of Women: Law, Policies, and Politics*. New York: Oxford University Press.

Mendes, Elizabeth and Kykey McGeeney. 2012. "Women's Health Trails Men's Most in Former Soviet Union." Gallup World, July 9. Available online at www.gallup.com/poll/155558/Women-Health-Trails-Men-Former-Soviet-Union.aspx

Merchant, Carolyn. 1980. *The Death of Nature: Women, Ecology, and the Scientific Revolution*. San Francisco: Harper & Row.

Messner, Michael. 2007a. "Sports and Male Domination: The Female Athlete as Contested Ideological Terrain." In Michael Messner and Raewyn Connell (eds.) *Out of Play: Critical Essays on Gender and Sports*. Albany: State University of New York, pp. 31–46.

Messner, Michael. 2007b. "Masculinities and Athletic Careers." In Michael Messner and Raewyn Connell (eds.) *Out of Play: Critical Essays on Gender and Sports*. Albany: State University of New York, pp. 47–60.

Messner, Michael. 2007c. "Studying Up on Sex." In Michael Messner and Raewyn Connell (eds.) *Out of Play: Critical Essays on Gender and Sports*. Albany: State University of New York, pp. 71–90.

Messner, Michael, Michelle Dunbar, and Darnell Hunt. 2007. "The Televised Manhood Formula." In Michael Messner and Raewyn Connell (eds.) *Out of Play: Critical Essays on Gender and Sports*. Albany: State University of New York, pp. 139–154.

Messner, Michael, Margaret Duncan, and Catherine Cooky. 2003. "Silence, Sports Bras, and Wrestling Porn." *Journal of Sport & Social Issues* 27: 38–51.

Meyer, Jaimie P., Sandra A. Springer, and Frederick L. Altice. 2011. "Substance Abuse, Violence, and HIV in Women: A Literature Review of the Syndemic." *Journal of Women's Health* 20(7): 991–1006.

Milkie, Melissa. 2002. "Contested Images of Femininity: An Analysis of Cultural Gatekeepers' Struggles with the 'Real Girl' Critique." *Gender & Society* 16: 839–859.

Miller, Claire Cain. 2014a. "Can Family Leaves Be Too Generous? It Seems So." *New York Times*, August 9.

Miller, Claire Cain. 2014b. "The Leave Seldom Taken." *New York Times*, November 9.

Miller, Claire Cain. 2014c. "How Social Media Stifles Debate." *New York Times*, August 26.

Miller, Claire Cain and Liz Alderman. 2014. "Why U.S. Women are Leaving Jobs Behind." *New York Times*, December 12.

Miller, Kathleen E., Merrill J. Melnick, Grace M. Barnes, Michael P. Farrell, and Don Sabo. 2005. "Untangling the Links among Athletic Achievement, Gender, Race, and Adolescent Academic Outcomes." *Sociology of Sport Journal* 22(2): 178–193.

Miller, Kathleen E., Merrill J. Melnick, Michael P. Farrell, Donald F. Sabo, and Grace M. Barnes. 2006. "Jocks, Gender, Binge Drinking, and Adolescent Violence." *Journal of Interpersonal Violence* 21(1): 105–120.

Mills, C. Wright. 1959. *The Sociological Imagination*. New York: Oxford University Press.

Mincy, Ronald B., Monique Jethwani, and Serena Klempin. 2015. *Failing Our Fathers: Confronting the Crisis of Economically Vulnerable Nonresident Fathers*. New York: Oxford University Press.

Mintz, Beth and Daniel Krymkowski. 2010–2011. "The Intersection of Race/Ethnicity and Gender in

Occupational Segregation." *International Journal of Sociology* 40: 31–58.

Moghadam, Valentine M., Suzanne Franzway, and Mary Margaret Fonow. 2011. *Making Globalization Work for Women: The Role of Social Rights and Trade Union Leadership*. Albany: State University of New York Press.

Mohr, James C. 1978. *Abortion in America: The Origins and Evolution of National Policy*. New York: Oxford University Press.

Molina, John. 2005. "The History of Women's Basketball." Available online at www.womensbasketballmuseum.com/

Monk-Turner, Elizabeth, Mary Heiserman, Crystle Johnson, Vanity Cotton, and Manny Jackson. 2010. "The Portrayal of Racial Minorities on Prime Time Television: A Replication of the Mastro and Greenberg Study a Decade Later." *Studies in Popular Culture* 32: 102–113.

Moore, David W. 2002. "Gender Gap Varies on Support for War." Available online at www.gallup.com/poll/7243/gender-gap-varies-support-war.aspx

Moorhead, Joanna. 2006. "Different Planets." *The Guardian*, October 2. Available online at www.guardian.co.uk/lifeandstyle/2006/oct/03/healthandwellbeing.health

Moraga, Cherrie and Gloria Anzaldua. 1984. *This Bridge Called My Back: Writings by Radical Women of Color*. New York: Kitchen Table: Woman of Color Press.

Morgan, Edmund. 1975. *American Slavery, American Freedom: The Ordeal of Colonial Virginia*. New York: W.W. Norton.

Morgen, Sandra, Joan Acker, and Jill Weight. 2009. *Stretched Thin: Poor Families, Welfare Work, and Welfare Reform*. Ithaca, NY: Cornell University Press.

Morris, Benjamin. 2014. "The Rate of Domestic Violence Arrests Among NFL Players." *FiveThirtyEight*, July 31. Available online at http://fivethirtyeight.com/datalab/the-rate-of-domestic-violence-arrests-among-nfl-players/

Morris, Edward W. 2012. *Learning the Hard Way: Masculinity, Place, and the Gender Gap in Education*. New Brunswick, NJ: Rutgers University Press.

Morton, Nelle. 1985. *The Journey is Home*. Boston: Beacon Press.

Moss-Racusin, Corinne A., John F. Dovido, Victoria L. Brescoll, March J. Graham, and Jo Handelsman.

2012. "Science Faculty's Subtle Gender Biases Favor Male Students," *Proceedings of the National Academy of Sciences* 109(41):16474–16479. Available online at www.pnas.org/content/109/41/16474

Mott, Frank Luther. 1947. *Golden Multitudes: The Story of Best Sellers in the United States*. New York: MacMillan.

Mueller, Christina. 2007. "Racing to a Degree: High School Sports Help Girls Earn College Diplomas." *U.S. News & World Report*, August 8. Available online at http://christinamueller.files.wordpress.com/2010/08/mueller_story.pdf

Mufti, Shahan. 2013. *The Faithful Scribe: A Story of Islam, Pakistan, Family, and War*. New York: Other Press.

Mugisha, Frank. 2011. "Gay and Vilified in Uganda." *New York Times*, December 23.

Muhammad, Khalil Gibran. 2010. *The Condemnation of Blackness: Race, Crime, and the Making of Modern Urban America*. Cambridge, MA: Harvard University Press.

Müller-Baden, Emanuel. 1904. *Bibliothek des allgemeinen und prakischen Wissens, Bd. 2*. Berlin: Deutsches Verlaghaus Bong & Co. Available online at http://en.wikipedia.org/wiki/Thing_(assembly)#mediaviewer/File:Germanische-ratsversammlung_1-1250x715.jpg

Mundy, Liza. 2013. "The Gay Guide to Wedded Bliss." *The Atlantic*, June. Available online at www.theatlantic.com/magazine/archive/2013/06/the-gay-guide-to-wedded-bliss/309317/

Murdock, George Peter. 1949. *Social Structure*. Oxford: MacMillan.

Murnen, Sarah K. and Marla H. Kohlman. 2007. "Athletic Participation, Fraternity Membership, and Sexual Aggression Among College Men: A Meta-Analytic Review." *Sex Roles* 57:145–157.

Murray, Charles. 1984. *Losing Ground: American Social Policy, 1950–1980*. New York: Basic Books.

Murray, Charles. 2012. *Coming Apart: The State of White America*. New York: Crown Forum.

Murray, C.J.L., S.C. Kulkarni, C. Michaud, N. Tomijima, M.T. Bulzacchelli, T.J. Iandiorio, and M. Ezzati. 2006. "Eight Americas: Investigating Mortality Disparities across Races, Counties, and Race-Counties in the United States." *PLOS Medicine* 3(9): e260.

Murray, Stephen O. 2010. "Mexico." In Javier Corrales and Mario Pecheny (eds.) *The Politics of Sexuality in Latin America*. Pittsburgh: University of Pittsburgh Press, pp. 60–65.

Nanda, Priya, Abhishek Gautam, Ravi Verma, Aarushi Khanna, Nizamuddin Kham, Dhanashri Brahme, Shobhana Boyle, and Sanjay Kumar. 2014. *Study on Masculinity, Intimate Partner Violence, and Son Preference in India*. New Delhi: International Center for Research on Women.

Nanda, Serena. 1990. *Neither Man Nor Woman: The Hijras of India*. Belmont, CA: Wadsworth.

Nanda, Serena. 2014. *Gender Diversity: Crosscultural Variations*, 2nd edn. Long Grove, IL: Waveland Press.

Naples, Nancy A. and Manisha Desai, eds. 2002. *Women's Activism and Globalization: Linking Local Struggles and Global Politics*. New York: Routledge.

Nasaden, Premilla. 2011. *Rethinking the Welfare Rights Movement*. New York: Routledge.

National Archives 1908. "Lincoln Cotton Mills, Evansville, Ind. Girls at Weaving Machines; Warpers." Available online at http://research.archives.gov/description/523100

National Committee on Pay Equity. 2013. "The Wage Gap over Time: In Real Dollars, Women See a Continuing Gap." Available online at www.pay-equity.org/info-time.html

National Congregations Study. 2012. Available online at www.thearda.com/ncs/frequencies.asp

National Vital Statistics System. 2014. "National Marriage and Divorce Rate Trends." Available online at www.cdc.gov/nchs/nvss/marriage_divorce_tables.htm

NCAA. 2011. "NCAA Inclusion of Transgender Student-Athletes." Available online at www.ncaa.org/sites/default/files/Transgender_Handbook_2011_Final.pdf

NCAVP (National Coalition of Anti-Violence Programs). 2014. *Lesbian, Gay, Bisexual, Transgender, Queer, and HIV-Affected Hate Violence in 2013*. New York: NCAVP.

NCES (National Center for Education Statistics). 2013a. "Table 104.20." Available online at http://nces.ed.gov/programs/digest/d13/tables/dt13_104.20.asp

NCES. 2013b. "Table 318.10." Available online at http://nces.ed.gov/programs/digest/d13/tables/dt13_318.10.asp

NCES. 2014. "Table 303.70" Available online at http://nces.ed.gov/programs/digest/d13/tables/dt13_303.70.asp

NCHS (National Center for Health Statistics). 1973. *100 Years of Marriage and Divorce Statistics, United States, 1867–1967*. Washington, DC: Department of Health, Education, and Welfare.

NCHS. 1991. *Monthly Vital Statistics Report* Vol. 39 (1, 2, Suppl. 2). Washington, DC: Department of Health and Human Services.

NCHS. 2013. *Health, United States, 2012: With Special Feature on Emergency Care*. Hyattsville, MD: National Center for Health Statistics.

Ness, E. 1966. *Sam, Bangs & Moonshine*. New York: Holt.

Newport, Frank. 2012a. "Americans, Including Catholics, Say Birth Control is Morally OK." Gallup Politics, May 22. Available online at www.gallup.com/poll/154799/Americans-Including-Catholics-Say-Birth-Control-Morally.aspx

Newport, Frank. 2012b. "Seven in 10 Americans Are Very or Moderately Religious." Gallup Politics, December 4. Available online at www.gallup.com/poll/159050/seven-americans-moderately-religious.aspx

Newport, Frank and Igor Himelfarb. 2013. "In U.S., Record-High Say Gay, Lesbian Relations Morally OK." Gallup Poll. Available online at www.gallup.com/poll/162689/record-high-say-gay-lesbian-relations-morally.aspx

New York Times. 2000. "Southern Baptist Convention Passes Resolution Opposing Women as Pastors." *New York Times*, June 15. Available online at www.nytimes.com/2000/06/15/us/southern-baptist-convention-passes-resolution-opposing-women-as-pastors.html

New York Times Editorial Board. 2014. "Transgender Rights in India." *New York Times*, April 15. Available online at www.nytimes.com/2014/04/26/opinion/transgender-rights-in-india.html

Nhan, Doris. 2012. "U.S. Women, Title IX Win Big in Olympics." *National Journal*, August 13. Available online at www.nationaljournal.com/thenextamerica/education/u-s-women-title-ix-win-big-in-olympics-20120813

Ní Aoláin, Fionnuala, Dina Francesca Haynes, and Naomi Cahn. 2011. *On the Frontlines: Gender, War, and the Post-Conflict Process*. New York: Oxford University Press.

Nichols, John. 2001. "Women in Sports: Images from the Late Middle Ages." Available online at http://srufaculty.sru.edu/john.nichols/research/womensport.htm

Niebuhr, Reinhold. 1932. *Moral Man and Immoral Society: A Study in Ethics and Politics*. New York: Scribner.

Nielsen. 2012. "Advertising & Audiences, Part 2: By Demographic." Available online at www.nielsen.com/content/dam/corporate/us/en/reports-downloads/2012-Reports/nielsen-advertising-audiences-report-spring-2012.pdf

NIH (National Institutes of Health). 2014. "Inclusion of Women and Minorities in Clinical Research." Available online at http://orwh.od.nih.gov/research/inclusion/background.asp

Noah, Timothy. 2012. *The Great Divergence: America's Growing Inequality Crisis and What We Can Do About It*. New York: Bloomsbury.

Noble, Laurie Carter. 2001. "Olympia Brown." *Dictionary of Unitarian & Universalist Biography*. Available online at http://uudb.org/articles/olympiabrown.html

North, Anna. 2014. "Why A Video Game Critic Was Forced to Flee Her Home." *New York Times OpTalk*, August 29. Available online at http://op-talk.blogs.nytimes.com/2014/08/29/why-a-video-game-critic-was-forced-to-flee-her-home/?module=Search&mabReward=relbias%3Aw%2C%7B%221%22%3A%22RI%3A11%22%7D

Norton, Mary Beth. 1996. *Founding Mothers and Fathers: Gendered Power and the Forming of American Society*. New York: Knopf.

Norwood, Kimberly Jade. 2013. *Color Matters: Skin Tone Bias and the Myth of a Postracial America*. New York: Routledge.

Noss, Amanda. 2012. "Household Income for States: 2010 and 2011." Washington DC: Census Bureau. Available online at www.census.gov/prod/2012pubs/acsbr11-02.pdf

Nossiter, Adam. 2014. "Nigerian Islamist Leader Threatens to Sell Kidnapped Girls." *New York Times*, May 5.

Notestein, Fred. 1953. "Economic Problems of Population Change." *Proceedings of the Eighth International Conference of Agriculture*. London, Oxford University Press.

Novak, Michael. 1993. "Women, Ordination, and Angels." *First Things*, April. Available online at www.firstthings.com/article/1993/04/002-women-ordination-and-angels

NPR. 2014. "Cartoonist Alison Bechdel Awarded MacArthur Fellowship." September 19. Available online at www.npr.org/2014/09/19/349756552/cartoonist-alison-bechdel-awarded-macarthur-fellowship

Nussbaum, Martha. 2012. "Ignore the Stigma of Prostitution and Focus on Need." *New York Times*, April 19.

Nyhan, Brendan. 2014. "Bill Cosby's Sudden Fall, Explained Sociologically." *New York Times*, November 20. www.nytimes.com/2014/11/21/upshot/bill-cosbys-sudden-fall-explained-sociologically.html?module=Search&mabReward=relbias%3Ar%2C%7B%221%22%3A%22RI%3A11%22%7D&_r=0&abt=0002&abg=1

Oakes, James. 1982. *The Ruling Race: A History of American Slaveholders*. New York: Vintage Books.

OBOS (Our Bodies Our Selves). 2014. "History." Available online at www.ourbodiesourselves.org/history/

OECD (Organisation for Economic Co-operation and Development). 2011. "Doing Better for Families" Available online at www.oecd.org/social/soc/doingbetterforfamilies.htm

OECD. 2012. "PF2.1: Key Characteristics of Parental Leave Systems." Available online at www.oecd.org/els/soc/PF2.1_Parental_leave_systems%20-%20updated%20%2018_July_2012.pdf

OECD. 2014a. "OECD Family Database." Available online at www.oecd.org/els/family/database.htm

OECD. 2014b. "Infant Mortality: Deaths per 1000 Live Births." Available online at www.oecd-ilibrary.org/social-issues-migration-health/infant-mortality_20758480-table9

OHCHR (Office of the United Nations High Commissioner for Human Rights). 2013. "Ratification of the Convention on the Elimination of All Forms of Discrimination Against Women, January 2013." Available online at www.ohchr.org/Documents/Issues/HRIndicators/Ratification//Status_CEDAW.pdf

OHCHR, UNAIDS, UNDP, UNECA, UNESCO, UNFPA, UNHCR, UNICEF, UNIFEM, and WHO. 2008. "Eliminating Female Genital Mutilation: An Interagency Statement." Geneva: World Health Organization.

Okewo, Alexis. 2014. "Freedom Fighter: A Slaving Society and an Abolitionist's Crusade." *New Yorker*, September 8.

Okonjo, Kamene. 1976. "The Dual-Sex Political System in Operation: Igbo Women and Community Politics in Mid-Western Nigeria." In Nancy Hafkin and Edna Bay (eds.) *Women in Africa: Studies in Social and Economic Change*. Palo Alto, CA: Stanford University Press, pp. 45–89.

Olumide, Y.M., A.O. Akinkugbe, D. Altraide, T. Mohammad, N. Ahamefule, S. Ayanlowo, C. Onyekonwu, and N. Essen. 2008. "Complications of Chronic Use of Skin Lightening Cosmetics." *International Journal of Dermatology* 47(4): 344–353.

O'Mahony, Jennifer. 2012. "London 2012 Olympics: Saudi Arabian Judo Athlete to Compete in Hijab." *The Telegraph*, July 31. Available online at www.telegraph.co.uk/sport/olympics/news/9441707/London-2012-Olympics-Saudi-Arabian-judo-athlete-will-compete-in-hijab.html

Orbach, Susie. 1986. *Hunger Strike: The Anorectic's Struggle as a Metaphor for Our Age*. New York: Norton.

Orlech, Annelise. 2005. *Storming Caesar's Palace: How Black Mothers Fought Their Own War on Poverty*. Boston: Beacon Press.

Osgood, Kelsey. 2013. *How to Disappear Completely: On Modern Anorexia*. New York: Overlook.

O'Sullivan, Rory, Konrad Mugglestone, and Tom Allison. 2014. *Closing the Race Gap: Alleviating Young African American Unemployment Through Education*. Washington, DC: Young Invisibles.

Owens, Gary M. 2008. "Gender Differences in Health Care Expenditures, Resource Utilization, and Quality of Care." *Journal of Managed Care and Specialty Pharmacy* 14(3, Suppl): 2–6.

Oxendine, Joseph. 1988. *American Indian Sports Heritage*. Lincoln: University of Nebraska Press.

Pager, Devah and Hana Shepherd. 2008. "The Sociology of Discrimination: Racial Discrimination in Employment, Housing, Credit, and Consumer Markets." *Annual Review of Sociology* 34: 181–209.

Paglia, Camille. 1990. *Sexual Personae: Art and Decadence from Nefertiti to Emily Dickinson*. New Haven, CT: Yale University Press.

Parameswaran, R., and Cardoza, K. 2009. "Melanin on the Margins: Advertising and the Cultural Politics of Fair/Light/White Beauty in India." *Journalism & Communication Monographs* 11: 213–274.

Park, Hirho and Susan Willhauck. 2013. *Breaking Through the Stained Glass Ceiling: Women Pastoring Large Churches*. Nashville: The United Methodist Church.

Parker, Rebecca. 2008. *Saving Paradise: How Christianity Traded Love of This World for Crucifixion and Empire*. Boston: Beacon Press.

Parker-Pope, Tara. 2009. "What Are Friends For? A Longer Life." *New York Times*, April 20.

Parker-Pope, Tara. 2011. "An Older Generation Falls Prey to Eating Disorders." *New York Times Blog*, March 28. Available online at http://well.blogs.nytimes.com/2011/03/28/an-older-generation-falls-prey-to-eating-disorders/?_r=0

Parrot, Andrea, and Nina Cummings. 2006. *Forsaken Females: The Global Brutalization of Women*. Lanham, MD: Rowman & Littlefield.

Parsons, Talcott, 1942. "Age and Sex in the Social Structure of the United States." *American Sociological Review* 7: 604–616.

Parsons, Talcott. 1954. *Essays in Sociological Theory*. New York: Free Press.

Patel, Reena. 2006. "Working the Night Shift: Gender and the Global Economy." *ACME: An International E-Journal for Critical Geographies* 5(1): 9–27.

Patrinos, Harry. 2008. "Returns to Education: The Gender Perspective." In Mercy Tembon and Lucia Fort (eds.) *Girls' Education in the 21st Century: Gender Equality, Empowerment, and Economic Growth*. Washington, DC: The World Bank, pp. 53–66.

Patten, Eileen, and Kim Parker. 2011. "Women in the U.S. Military: Growing Share, Distinctive Profile." Pew Social and Demographic Trends. Available online at www.pewsocialtrends.org/files/2011/12/women-in-the-military.pdf

Patterson, James T. 1996. *Grand Expectations: The United States, 1945–1974*. New York: Oxford University Press.

Patterson, Orlando. 1982. *Slavery and Social Death: A Comparative Study*. Cambridge, MA: Harvard University Press.

Patterson, Orlando. 1999. *Rituals of Blood: Consequences of Slavery in Two American Centuries*. New York: Basic Civitas Books.

Patterson, Orlando. 2015. *The Cultural Matrix: Understanding Black Youth*. Cambridge, MA: Harvard University Press.

Paxton, Pamela Marie, and Melanie M. Hughes. 2007. *Women, Politics, and Power: A Global Perspective.* Thousand Oaks, CA: Pine Forge Press.

PayScale. 2014. "2013 College Education ROI Rankings: Does a Degree Always Pay Off?" Available online at www.payscale.com/college-education-value-2013

Pearce, Diana. 1978. "The Feminization of Poverty: Women, Work, and Welfare." *Urban and Social Change Review* 11: 28–36.

Pearlman, Deborah N., Sally Zierler, Annie Gjelsvik, and Wendy Verhoer-Oftedahl. 2003. "Neighborhood Environment, Racial Position, and Risk of Police-Reported Domestic Violence: A Contextual Analysis." *Public Health Reports* 118: 44–58.

Peiss, Kathy. 1986. *Cheap Amusements: Working Women and Leisure in Turn-of-the-Century New York.* Philadelphia, PA: Temple University Press.

Pekkarinen, Tuomas. 2011. "Gender Differences in Education." Presented at the Nordic Economic Policy Review Conference in Oslo, October 24. Available online at http://ftp.iza.org/dp6390.pdf

Penn, Michael L. and Rahel Nardos. 2003. *Overcoming Violence Against Women and Girls: The International Campaign to Eradicate a Worldwide Problem.* New York: Rowman & Littlefield.

Pennington, Bill, and Steve Eder. 2014. "In Domestic Violence Cases, N.F.L. has a History of Lenience." *New York Times*, September 19.

Peralta, Eyder. 2012. "Photo: The First Woman to Enter the Boston Marathon." NPR. Available online at www.npr.org/blogs/thetwo-way/2012/04/02/1498 76890/photo-the-first-woman-to-enter-the-boston-marathon

Perdue, Theda. 1998. *Cherokee Women.* Lincoln: University of Nebraska Press.

Pew Charitable Trusts. 2010. *Collateral Costs: Incarceration's Effect on Economic Mobility.* Washington, DC: Pew Charitable Trusts.

Pew Forum. 2008a. "U.S. Religious Landscape Survey, Religious Affiliation: Diverse and Dynamic." Available online at http://religions.pewforum.org/pdf/report-religious-landscape-study-full.pdf

Pew Forum. 2008b. "U.S. Religious Landscape Survey, Religious Beliefs and Practices: Diverse and Politically Relevant." Available online at http://religions.pewforum.org/pdf/report2-religious-landscape-study-full.pdf

Pew Forum. 2008c. "U.S. Religious Landscape Survey: Summary of Key Findings." Available online at http://religions.pewforum.org/pdf/report2 religious-landscape-study-key-findings.pdf

Pew Forum. 2012a. "The Global Religious Landscape." Available online at www.pewforum.org/files/2014/01/global-religion-full.pdf

Pew Forum. 2012b. "'Nones' on the Rise: One-in-Five Adults Have No Religious Affiliation." Available online at www.pewforum.org/files/2012/10/Nones OnTheRise-full.pdf

Pew Forum. 2013a. "Public Opinion on Abortion Slideshow." Available online at http://features.pew forum.org/abortion-slideshow/index.php

Pew Forum. 2013b. "The World's Muslims: Religion, Politics and Society." Available online at www.pewforum.org/files/2013/04/worlds-muslims-religion-politics-society-full-report.pdf

Pew Research Center. 2010. "Gender Equality Universally Embraced, but Inequalities Acknowledged." July 1. Available online at www.pewglobal.org/2010/07/01/gender-equality/

Pew Research Center. 2011a. "Employment of Clergy." March 31. Available online at www.pewforum.org/2011/03/31/churches-in-court3/

Pew Research Center, 2011b. "Muslim Americans: No Signs of Growth in Alienation or Support for Extremism." Washington, DC: Pew Research Center. Available online at http://www.pew research.org/daily-number/muslim-americans-no-signs-of-growth-in-alienation-or-support-for-extremism/

Pew Research Center. 2013a. "Growing Support for Gay Marriage: Changed Minds and Changing Demographics." March 20. Available online at www.people-press.org/2013/03/20/growing-support-for-gay-marriage-changed-minds-and-changing-demographics/

Pew Research Center. 2013b. "On Pay Gap, Millennial Women Near Parity – For Now." December 11. Available online at www.pewsocialtrends.org/files/2013/12/gender-and-work_final.pdf

Pew Research Center. 2013c. "Why Own a Gun? Protection Is Now Top Reason." March 12. Available online at www.people-press.org/files/legacy-pdf/03-12-13%20Gun%20Ownership%20Release.pdf

Pew Research Center. 2013d. "A Portrait of Jewish Americans: Overview." Available online at www.

pewforum.org/files/2013/10/jewish-american-full-report-for-web.pdf

Pew Research Global Attitudes Project. 2013. "The Global Divide on Homosexuality." June 4. Available online at www.pewglobal.org/2013/06/04/the-global-divide-on-homosexuality/

Pharr, Suzanne. 1988. *Homophobia: A Weapon of Sexism.* Little Rock, AR: Chardon Press.

Phillips, Michael, Xianyun Li, and Yanping Zhang. 2002. "Suicide Rates in China, 1995–99." *The Lancet* 359: 835–840.

Piazza, Jo. 2014. *If Nuns Ruled the World: Ten Sisters on a Mission.* New York: Open Road Media.

Pickup, Francine, ed., with Suzanne Williams and Caroline Sweetman. 2001. *Ending Violence Against Women: A Challenge for Development and Humanitarian Work.* Oxford: Oxfam Publishing.

Piketty, Thomas. 2014. *Capital in the Twenty-First Century.* Cambridge, MA: Harvard University Press.

Pincus, Jane. 2005. "The Travels of Our Bodies, Ourselves." *New England Journal of Public Policy* 20(2): Article 9.

Pinker, Steven. 2011. *The Better Angels of Our Nature: Why Violence Has Declined.* New York: Viking.

Planty, Michael, Lynn Langton, Christopher Krebs, Marcus Bezofsky, and Hope Smiley-McDonald. 2013. "Female Victims of Sexual Violence, 1994–2010." U.S. Department of Justice. Available online at www.bjs.gov/content/pub/pdf/fvsv9410.pdf

Plaskow, Judith. 1979. *Sex, Sin, and Grace: Women's Experiences and the Theologies of Reinhold Nieburh and Paul Tillich.* Lanham, MD: University Press of America.

Plaskow, Judith. 1991. *Standing Again at Sinai: Judaism from a Feminist Perspective.* San Francisco: Harper One.

Pleck, Elizabeth. 2004. *Domestic Tyranny: The Making of American Social Policy Against Family Violence from Colonial Times to the Present.* Bloomington: University of Illinois Press.

Polgreen, Lydia and Vikas Bajaj. 2010. "India Microcredit Faces Collapse from Defaults." *New York Times*, November 17.

Pope Francis. 2014. "Broaden the Space for Women in the Church." Available online at www.catholicculture.org/culture/library/view.cfm?recnum=10447

Population Reference Bureau. 2000. "Is Education the Best Contraceptive?" Washington, DC: Population Reference Bureau. Available online at www.prb.org/pdf/IsEducat-Contracept_Eng.pdf

Potts, Malcolm, and Thomas Hayden. 2008. *Sex and War: How Biology Explains Warfare and Terrorism and Offers a Path to a Safer World.* Dallas: BenBella Books.

Potts, Monica. 2013. "What's Killing Poor White Women?" *The American Prospect*, September.

Potuchek, Jean. 1997. *Who Supports the Family? Gender and Breadwinning in Dual-Earner Marriages.* Stanford, CA: Stanford University Press.

Powell, Shaun. 2007. *Souled Out? How Blacks Are Willing and Losing in Sports.* Champaign, IL: Human Kinetics.

Powell, Tunette. 2014. "My Son Has Been Suspended Five Times. He's 3." *The Washington Post*, July 24.

Primitive Methodist Church. 2014. "Chapter Four of the Discipline." Available online at www.primitivemethodistchurch.org/chapter4.html

Provost, Claire. 2012. "Anti-Prostitution Pledge in US AIDS Funding 'Damaging' HIV Response." *The Guardian*, July 24. Available online at www.theguardian.com/global-development/2012/jul/24/prostitution-us-aids-funding-sex

Pulitzer Prizes. 2013. "Prize Winners and Finalists by Category." Available online at www.pulitzer.org/bycat

Putnam, Robert D. 2000. *Bowling Alone: The Collapse and Revival of American Community.* New York: Simon & Schuster.

Putnam, Robert D. and David E. Campbell. 2010. *American Grace: How Religion Divides and Unites Us.* New York: Simon and Schuster.

Pyke, Karen D. 1996. "Class-Based Masculinities: The Interdependence of Gender, Class, and Interpersonal Power." *Gender & Society* 10(5): 527–549.

QuotaProject. 2014. Available online at www.quotaproject.org/uid/search.cfm#

Rabin, Roni Caryn. 2012. "Men Struggle for Rape Awareness." *New York Times*, January 23.

Rabin, Roni Caryn. 2014. "Labs Are Told to Start Including a Neglected Variable: Females." *New York Times*, May 14.

Rable, George C. 1984. *But There Was No Peace: The Role of Violence in the Politics of Reconstruction.* Atlanta: University of Georgia Press.

Radway, Janice. 1984. *Reading the Romance: Women, Patriarchy, and Popular Literature*. Chapel Hill: The University of North Carolina Press.

Raine, Adrian. 2014. *The Anatomy of Violence: The Biological Roots of Crime*. New York: Vintage Books.

Rainie, Lee. 2013. "Cell Phone Ownership Hits 91% of Adults." Pew Research Center, June 6. Available online at www.pewresearch.org/fact-tank/2013/06/06/cell-phone-ownership-hits-91-of-adults/

Ramadan, Tariq. 2007. *In the Footsteps of the Prophet: Lessons from the Life of Muhammad*. New York: Oxford University Press.

Ramey, Garey and Valerie A. Ramey. 2010. "The Rug Rat Race." *Brookings Papers on Economic Activity* 41(1): 129–199. Available online at www.nber.org/papers/w15284

Rand, Michael R., James P. Lynch, and David Cantor. 1997. "Criminal Victimization, 1973–95." U.S. Department of Justice. Available online at http://bjs.gov/content/pub/pdf/Cv73_95.pdf

Rastogi, Mudita and Paul Therly. 2006. "Dowry and its Link to Violence against Women in India." *Trauma Violence Abuse* 7: 66–77.

Rauf, Imam Faisal Abdul. 2005. *What's Right with Islam: A New Vision for Muslims and the West*. New York: HarperCollins.

Rawe, Kathryn. 2012. *A Life Free from Hunger: Tackling Child Malnutrition*. London: Save the Children.

Ray, Julie. 2014. "Worldwide, More Men Than Women Have Full-Time Work." Gallup, October 17. Available online at www.gallup.com/poll/178637/worldwide-men-women-full-time-work.aspx

Reagan, Leslie. 1997. *When Abortion Was a Crime: Women, Medicine, and Law in the United States, 1867–1973*. Berkeley: University of California Press.

Real, Terrence. 1997. *I Don't Want to Talk About It: Overcoming the Secret Legacy of Male Depression*. New York: Scribner.

Reid, Lori. 2002. "Occupational Segregation, Human Capital, and Motherhood: Black Women's Higher Exit Rates from Full-Time Employment." *Gender & Society* 16: 728–747.

Reinhard, Wolfgang. 2011. *A Short History of Colonialism*. New York: Manchester University Press/Palgrave Macmillan.

Reis, Elizabeth. 2009. *Bodies in Doubt: An American History of Intersex*. Baltimore: Johns Hopkins University Press.

Rennison, Callie Marie. 2014. "Privilege, Among Rape Victims: Who Suffers Most from Rape and Sexual Assault in America?" *New York Times*, December 21. Available online at www.nytimes.com/2014/12/22/opinion/who-suffers-most-from-rape-and-sexual-assault-in-america.html?module=Search&mab Reward=relbias%3Ar%2C%7B%221%22%3A%22 RI%3A6%22%7D

Renzetti, Claire M. and Vivian M. Larkin. 2011. "Economic Stress and Domestic Violence." Harrisburg, PA: National Resource Center on Domestic Violence. Available online at www.vawnet.org/applied-research-papers/print-document.php?doc_id=2187

Rich, Adrienne. 1980. "Compulsory Heterosexuality and Lesbian Existence." *Signs: Journal of Women in Culture and Society* 5(4): 531–660.

Rideout, V., U. Foehr, and D. Roberts. 2010. *Generation M2 Media in the Lives of 8- to 18-Year-Olds*. Menlo Park, CA: Kaiser Foundation Family.

Ring, Jennifer. 2009. *Stolen Bases: Why American Girls Don't Play Baseball*. Chicago: University of Illinois Press.

Ringrose, Jessica and Katarina Erikson Barajas. 2011. "Gendered Risks and Opportunities? Exploring Teen Girls' Digitized Sexual Identities in Postfeminist Media Contexts." *International Journal of Media and Cultural Politics* 7: 121–138.

Rios, Victor M. 2011. *Punished: Policing the Lives of Black and Latino Boys*. New York: New York University Press.

Ripley, Amanda. 2013. "The Case Against High-School Sports." *The Atlantic*, September 18. Available online at www.theatlantic.com/magazine/archive/2013/10/the-case-against-high-school-sports/309447/

Rivadeneyra, Rocío. 2011. "Gender and Race Portrayals on Spanish-Language Television." *Sex Roles* 65: 208–222.

Rivers, Caryl, and Rosalind C. Barnett. 2013. *The New Soft War on Women: How the Myth of Female Ascendance is Hurting Women, Men – and Our Economy*. New York: Penguin.

Roberts, Dorothy E. 2012. "Prison, Foster Care, and the Systemic Punishment of Black Mothers." *UCLA Law Review* 59: 1474–1501.

Robertson, Campbell. 2012. "82 Seconds, Long Enough for History." *New York Times*, August 3.

Rogers, F. Halsey and Emiliana Vegas. 2009. "No More Cutting Class? Reducing Teacher Absence and Providing Incentives for Performance." Washington, D.C.: The World Bank. Available online at www-wds.worldbank.org/servlet/WDSContentServer/WDSP/IB/2009/02/26/000158349_20090226142341/Rendered/PDF/WPS4847.pdf

Roman Catholic Womenpriests. 2014. "About RCWP." Available online at http://romancatholicwomenpriests.org/

Romance Writers of America. 2013. "Romance Industry Sales." Available online at www.rwa.org/p/cm/ld/fid=580

Roscoe, Will. 2000. *Changing Ones: Third and Fourth Genders in Native North America*. New York: Palgrave Macmillan.

Rosen, Ruth. 2006. *The World Split Open: How the Modern Women's Movement Changed America*. New York: Penguin.

Rosenberg, Charles F. 1973. "Sexuality, Class, and Role in Nineteenth-Century America." *American Quarterly* 25: 131–153.

Rosin, Hanna. 2009. "The Case Against Breast-Feeding." *The Atlantic*, April.

Rosin, Hanna. 2012. *The End of Men and the Rise of Women*. New York: Riverhead Books.

Rothman, Ellen K. 1984. *Hands and Hearts: A History of Courtship in America*. New York: Basic Books.

Rotundo, E. Anthony. 1993. *American Manhood: Transformations in Masculinity from the Revolution to the Modern Era*. New York: Basic Books.

Roy, Nilanjana S. 2010. "Fighting for Safe Passage on Indian Streets." *New York Times*, August 3.

Rubenfeld, Jed. 2014. "Mishandling Rape." *New York Times*, November 16.

Rubin, Gayle. 1975. "The Traffic in Women: Notes on the 'Political Economy' of Sex." In Rayna Reiter (ed.) *Toward an Anthropology of Women*. New York: Monthly Review Press, pp. 157–209.

Rubin, Gayle. 1984. "Thinking Sex: Notes for a Radical Theory of the Politics of Sexuality." In Carole S. Vance (ed.) *Pleasure and Danger: Exploring Female Sexuality*. New York: Routledge & Kegan Paul, pp. 267–319.

Ruddick, Sara. 1989. *Maternal Thinking: Towards a Politics of Peace*. New York: Ballantine.

Rudoren, Jodi. 2013a. "Looking to Israel for Clues on Women in Combat." *New York Times*, January 25.

Rudoren, Jodi. 2013b. "Standoff at Western Wall Over Praying by Women." *New York Times*, May 10. Available online at www.nytimes.com/2013/05/11/world/middleeast/3-ultra-orthodox-men-arrested-in-western-wall-standoff.html

Ruether, Rosemary Radford. 1983. *Sexism and God-Talk: Toward a Feminist Theology*. Boston: Beacon Press.

Russ, Joanna. 1983. *How to Suppress Women's Writing*. Austin: University of Texas Press.

Russell-Cole, Kathy, Midge Wilson, and Ronald E. Hall. 2013. *The Color Complex: The Politics of Skin Color in a New Millennium*. New York: Anchor.

Ryan, Camille L. and Julie Siebens. 2012. "Educational Attainment in the United States: 2009." United States Census Bureau. Available online at www.census.gov/prod/2012pubs/p20-566.pdf

Ryan, Michelle K. and S. Alexander Haslam. 2005. "The Glass Cliff: Evidence that Women are Over-Represented in Precarious Leadership Positions." *British Journal of Management* 16(2): 81–90.

Sabo, D., M.J. Melnick, and B. Vanfossen. 1989. *The Women's Sports Foundation Report: Minorities in Sports*. New York: Women's Sports Foundation.

Sadker, David, Myra Sadker, and Karen R. Zittleman. 2009. *Still Failing at Fairness: How Gender Bias Cheats Girls and Boys in School and What We Can Do About It*. New York: Scribner.

Saenz, Victor and Luis Ponjuan. 2009. "The Vanishing Latino Male in Higher Education." *Journal of Hispanic Higher Education* 8: 54–89.

Said, Edward W. 1978. *Orientalism*. New York: Vintage.

Said, Sammy. 2012. "Serena Williams Net Worth." Available online at www.therichest.com/celebnetworth/athletes/tennis/serena-williams-net-worth/

Sanday, Peggy Reeves. 1981a. *Female Power and Male Dominance: On the Origins of Sexual Inequality*. Cambridge: Cambridge University Press.

Sanday, Peggy Reeves. 1981b. "The Socio-Cultural Context of Rape: A Cross-Cultural Study." *Journal of Social Issues* 37(4): 5–27.

Sanday, Peggy Reeves. 2003. *Women at the Center: Life in a Modern Matriarchy*. Ithaca, NY: Cornell University Press.

Sanderson, David and Fiona Wilson. 2014. "It's No Wonder Boys Aren't Reading – The Children's Book Market Is Run by Women." *London Times*, April 19.

Sandler, K.S. 2004. "A Kid's Gotta Do What a Kid's Gotta Do: Branding the Nickelodeon Experience."

In H. Hendershot (ed.), *Nickelodeon Nation*. New York: New York University Press, pp. 45–68.

Sankaran, Lavanya. 2013a. "Caste Is Not Past." *New York Times*, June 15. Available online at www.nytimes.com/2013/06/16/opinion/sunday/caste-is-not-past.html

Sankaran, Lavanya. 2013b. "The Good Men of India." *New York Times*, October 19. Available online at www.nytimes.com/2013/10/20/opinion/sunday/the-good-men-of-india.html

Sapolsky, Robert M. 1994. *Why Zebras Don't Get Ulcers*. New York: Henry Holt.

Sapolsky, Robert. 1998. *The Trouble with Testosterone: And Other Essays on the Biology of the Human Predicament*. New York: Scribner.

Sarkeesian, Anita. 2013. "Damsel in Distress: Part 1 – Tropes vs Women in Video Games." Available online at www.youtube.com/watch?v=X6p5AZp7r_Q

Sarkeesian, Anita. 2014. "Women as Background Decoration: Part 1 – Tropes vs Women in Video Games." Available online at www.youtube.com/watch?v=4ZPSrwedvsg

Savage, Charlie. 2012. "U.S. to Expand Its Definition of Rape in Statistics." *New York Times*, January 6.

Sawhill, Isabel V. 2014. *Generation Unbound: Drifting into Sex and Parenthood without Marriage*. Washington, DC: Brookings Institution Press.

Sax, Leonard. 2007. *Boys Adrift*. New York: Basic Books.

Sayer, Liana C., Paula England, Paul Allison, and Nicole Kangas. 2011. "She Left, He Left: How Employment and Satisfaction Affect Men's and Women's Decisions to Leave Marriages." *American Journal of Sociology* 116(6): 1982–2018.

Schilt, Kristen. 2011. *Just One of the Guys? Transgender Men and the Persistence of Gender Inequality*. Chicago: University of Chicago Press.

Schilt, Kristen and Matthew Wiswall. 2008. "Before and After: Gender Transitions, Human Capital, and Workplace Experiences." *The B.E. Journal of Economic Analysis & Policy* 8(1): 1–28.

Schneir, Miriam. 1994. *Feminism in Our Time: The Essential Writings, World War II to the Present*. New York: Vintage.

Schooler, D. and E.A. Daniels. 2014. "'I am Not a Skinny Toothpick and Proud of It': Latina Adolescents' Ethnic Identity and Responses to Mainstream Media Images." *Body Image* 11(1): 11–18.

Schultz, Jaime. 2005. "Reading the Catsuit: Serena Williams and the Production of Blackness at the 2002 U.S. Open." *Journal of Sport & Social Issues* 29: 338–357.

Schultz, Jaime. 2014. *Qualifying Times: Points of Change in U.S. Women's Sport*. Urbana: University of Illinois Press.

Schwartz, Mary Ann and Barbara M. Scott. 2013. *Marriages and Families: Diversity and Change*. Boston, MA: Pearson.

Scott, Janny. 2005. "Life at the Top in America Isn't Just Better, It's Longer." *New York Times*, May 16. Available online at www.nytimes.com/2005/05/16/national/class/HEALTH-FINAL.html?pagewanted=all

Seabrook, Jeffrey. 2001. *Travels in the Skin Trade: Tourism and the Sex Industry*. London: Pluto.

Seager, Joni. 2009. *The Penguin Atlas of Women in the World*, 4th edn. New York: Penguin Group.

Searcey, Dionne. 2014. "For Women in Midlife, Career Gains Slip Away." *New York Times*, June 23.

Sears, Hal. 1977. *The Sex Radicals: Free Love in High Victorian America*. Lawrence: Regents Press of Kansas.

Secura, Gina M., Jenifer E. Allsworth, Tessa Madden, Jennifer L. Mullersman, and Jeffrey F. Peiper. 2010. "The Contraceptive CHOICE Project: Reducing Barriers to Long-Acting Reversible Contraception." *American Journal of Obstetrics and Gynecology* 203(2): 115.e1–115.e7.

Sedgwick, Eve Kosofsky. 1990. *Epistemology of the Closet*. Berkeley: University of California Press.

Sells, Michael. 1999. *Approaching the Qur'an: The Early Revelations*. Ashland, OR: White Cloud Press.

Seneca Falls Declaration of Sentiments. 1848. Available online at www.fordham.edu/halsall/mod/seneca falls.asp

Sennett, Richard and Jonathan Cobb. 1972. *The Hidden Injuries of Class*. New York: Knopf.

Sentencing Project. 2012. "Incarcerated Women Fact Sheet." Available online at www.sentencingproject.org/doc/publications/cc_Incarcerated_Women_Fact sheet_Dec2012final.pdf

Sentencing Project. 2014. "Fact Sheet: Trend in U.S. Corrections." Available online at http://sentencing project.org/doc/publications/inc_Trends_in_Corrections_Fact_sheet.pdf

Shadid, Humaira Awais with Kelly Horan. 2014. *Devotion and Defiance: My Journey in Love, Faith and Politics*. New York: Norton.

Shilts, Randy. 2007. *And the Band Played On: Politics, People, and the AIDS Epidemic*, rev. edn. New York: St. Martin's Griffin.

Shkolnikov, Vladimir M. and France Meslé. 2010. "The Russian Epidemiological Crisis as Mirrored by Mortality Trends." Rand Corporation. Available online at www.rand.org/pubs/conf_proceedings/CF124/cf124.chap4.html

Shroff, Aliza, Charles Lewin, and Dina Roth. 2004. "Body Image and Eating Disorders in India: Media and Interpersonal Influences." *International Journal of Eating Disorders* 35: 198–203.

Simpson, Ruth. 2004. "Masculinity at Work: The Experiences of Men in Female Dominated Occupations." *Work, Employment & Society* 18: 349–368.

Simri, Uriel. 1983. *A Concise World History of Women's Sports*. Jerusalem: Wingate Institute for Physical Education & Sport.

Singh, Rajiv. 2013. "Fairness Creams' Segment Slows Down: Has the Nation Overcome Its Dark Skin Complex?" *Economic Times*, August 18. Available online at http://articles.economictimes.indiatimes.com/2013-08-18/news/41421066_1_fairness-cream-fairness-products-skin-colour

Singh, S., G. Sedgh, and R. Hussain. 2012. "Unintended Pregnancy: Worldwide Levels, Trends, and Outcomes." *Studies in Family Planning* 41(4): 241–250.

Skloot, Rebecca. 2010. *The Immortal Life of Henrietta Lacks*. New York: Crown.

Skocpol, Theda. 1992. *Protecting Soldiers and Mothers: The Political Origins of Social Policy in the United States*. Cambridge, MA: Harvard University Press.

Skocpol, Theda and Vanessa Williamson. 2012. *The Tea Party and the Remaking of Republican Conservatism*. New York: Oxford University Press.

Sleeping Beauty. 1959. [Film] United States: Walt Disney Productions.

Smith, Barbara, ed. 1983. *Home Girls: A Black Feminist Anthology*. New York: Kitchen Table: Woman of Color Press.

Smith, Christine A. 2013. *Beyond the Stained Glass Ceiling: Equipping and Encouraging Female Pastors*. King of Prussia, PA: Judson Press.

Smith, Earl. 2005. *Race, Sport, and the American Dream*. Boulder, CO: Lynne Rienner.

Smith, Earl and Benny Cooper. 2010. "Race, Class, and Gender Theory: Violence Against Women in the Institution of Sport." In Earl Smith (ed.) *Sociology of Sport and Social Theory*. Champaign, IL: Human Kinetics, pp. 129–142.

Smith, Stacy L. and Choueiti, Marc. 2011. *Gender Disparity on Screen and Behind the Camera in Family Films: The Executive Report*. Los Angeles: Geena Davis Institute for Gender and Media.

Smith, Stacy, Marc Choueiti, Ashley Prescott, and Katherine Pieper. 2013. *Gender Roles & Occupations: A Look at Character Attributes and Job-Related Aspirations in Film and Television*. Los Angeles, CA: Geena Davis Institute for Gender and Media.

Smith, Susan Lynn. 1995. *Sick and Tired of Being Sick and Tired: Black Women's Health Activism in America, 1890–1950*. Philadelphia: University of Pennsylvania Press.

Smith-Rosenberg, Carroll. 1985. *Disorderly Conduct: Visions of Gender in Victorian America*. New York: Oxford University Press.

Snow White and the Seven Dwarfs. 1937. [Film] United States: Walt Disney Productions.

Sokoloff, Natalie J., ed., with Christina Pratt. 2005. *Domestic Violence at the Margins: Readings on Race, Class, Gender, and Culture*. New Brunswick: Rutgers University Press.

Solinger, Rickie. 1992. *Wake Up Little Susie: Single Pregnancy and Race Before* Roe v. Wade. New York: Routledge.

Solomon, Barbara Miller. 1985. *In the Company of Educated Women*. New Haven, CT: Yale University Press.

Sommer, Allison Kaplan. 2014. "Petition Asks El Al to Get Tough on Ultra-Orthodox 'Bullying and Harassing' of Female Passengers." *Haaretz*, October 3. Available online at www.haaretz.com/news/diplomacy-defense/.premium-1.618140

Song, Shige. 2012. "Does Famine Influence Sex Ratio at Birth? Evidence from the 1959–1961 Great Leap Forward Famine in China." *Proceedings of Biological Sciences* 279(1739): 2883–2890.

Sontag, Deborah and Lizette Alvarez. 2008. "Iraq Veterans Leave a Trail of Death and Heartbreak in U.S." *New York Times*, January 13. Available online at www.nytimes.com/2008/01/13/world/americas/13iht-vets.1.9171147.html?pagewanted=all

Southern Baptist Convention. 2000. "The Baptist Faith and Message." Available online at www.sbc.net/bfm2000/bfm2000.asp

Sparks, Sarah D. 2014. "Women's Voices Lacking on School Boards." *Education Week*, August 26. Available online at www.edweek.org/ew/articles/2014/08/27/02schoolboard.h34.html

Spitzer B., K. Henderson, and M. Zivian. 1999. "A Comparison of Population and Media Body Sizes for American and Canadian Women." *Sex Roles* 70: 545–565.

Spivak, Gayatri Chakravorty. 1988. "Can the Subaltern Speak?" In Cary Nelson and Lawrence Grossberg (eds.) *Marxism and the Interpretation of Culture*. Urbana: University of Illinois Press, pp. 271–313.

Spivey, Nigel. 2004. *The Ancient Olympics: A History*. New York: Oxford University Press.

Springer, Kristin and Dawne Mouzon. 2011. "'Macho Men' and Preventive Health Care: Implications for Older Men in Different Social Classes." *Journal of Health and Social Behavior* 52(2): 212–227.

Springer, Shira. 2014. "Why Do Fans Ignore Women's Pro Sports?" *Globe Magazine*, September 28.

Staats, Cheryl. 2014. *State of the Science: Implicit Bias Review 2014*. Columbus, OH: Kirwan Institute.

Stack, Carol B. 1974. *All Our Kin: Strategies for Survival in a Black Community*. San Francisco: Harper & Row.

Stage, Sarah, and Virginia B. Vincenti, eds. 1997. *Rethinking Home Economics: Women and the History of a Profession*. Ithaca: Cornell University Press.

Stansell, Christine. 1982. *City of Women: Sex and Class in New York, 1789–1860*. Champaign: University of Illinois Press.

Starhawk. 1982. *Dreaming the Dark: Magic, Sex, and Politics*. Boston, MA: Beacon Press.

Steele, Claude. 2010. *Whistling Vivaldi and Other Clues to How Stereotypes Affect Us*. New York: W.W. Norton & Company.

Steele, David. 2002. "Adding Insult to Injury: Most Pro Football Players Face a Future of Disability and Pain." *San Francisco Chronicle*, September 1. Available online at www.sfgate.com/health/article/Adding-Insult-to-Injury-Most-pro-football2775786.php#page-1

Steinfels, Peter. 1990. "Idyllic Theory of Goddesses Creates Storm." *New York Times*, February 1.

Steinhauer, Jennifer. 2013. "Reports of Military Sexual Assault Rise Sharply." *New York Times*, November 7.

Stevenson, Betsey. 2007. "Title IX and the Evolution of High School Sports." Available online at http://ideas.repec.org/p/ces/ceswps/_2159.html

Stevenson, Betsey and Adam Isen. 2010. "Who's Getting Married? Education and Marriage Today and in the Past: A Briefing Paper Prepared for the Council on Contemporary Families." January 26. Available online at www.contemporaryfamilies.org/images/stories/homepage/orange_border/ccf012510.pdf

Stevenson, Bryan. 2014. *Just Mercy: A Story of Justice and Redemption*. New York: Spiegal and Grau.

Stewart, Bruce. 1995. "American Football." Available online at http://wesclark.com/rrr/yank_fb.html

Stone, Merlin. 1976. *When God Was a Woman*. New York: Harcourt, Brace, Jovanovich.

Stowe, H.B. 1852. *Uncle Tom's Cabin; or Life Among The Lowly*. Boston, MA: Jon P. Jewett & Co.

Strain, Christopher B. 2010. *Reload: Rethinking Violence in American Life*. Nashville, TN: Vanderbilt University Press.

Strasser, Susan. 1982. *Never Done: A History of American Housework*. New York: Pantheon.

Stuber, Jenny M. 2011. *Inside the College Gates: How Class and Culture Matter in Higher Education*. Lanham, MD: Lexington Books.

Study of the Secretary-General. 2006. *Ending Violence Against Women: From Words to Action*. New York: United Nations.

Suellentrop, Chris. 2014. "Can Video Games Survive?" *New York Times*, October 26.

Sugrue, Thomas. 1996. *The Origins of the Urban Crisis: Race and Inequality in Postwar Detroit*. Princeton, NJ: Princeton University Press.

Sussman, Robert Wald. 2014. *The Myth of Race: The Troubling Persistence of an Unscientific Idea*. Cambridge, MA: Harvard University Press.

Swidler, Leonard. 2007. *Jesus Was a Feminist: What the Gospels Reveal about His Revolutionary Perspective*. Lanham, MD: Sheed & Ward.

Symons, Caroline. 2010. *The Gay Games: A History*. New York: Routledge

Sysomos. 2010. "Inside Blog Demographics." Available online at https://www.sysomos.com/reports/bloggers/

Tabuchi, Hiroko. 2013. "Desperate Hunt for Day Care in Japan." *New York Times*, February 26.

Talavage, Thomas, Eric Nauman, Evan Breedlove, Umit Yoruk, Anne Dye, Katherine Morigaki, Henry Feuer, and Larry Leverenz. 2013. "Functionally-Detected Cognitive Impairment in High School Football Players Without Clinically-Diagnosed Concussion." *Journal of Neurotrauma* 31(4): 327–338. Available online at http://online.liebertpub.com/doi/pdf/10.1089/neu.2010.1512

Tannenbaum, Leora. 1999. *Slut! Growing Up Female with a Bad Reputation*. New York: Seven Stories Press.

Tavernise, Sabrina. 2011. "Adoptions by Gay Couples Rise, Despite Barriers." *New York Times*, June 13. Available online at www.nytimes.com/2011/06/14/us/14adoption.html?pagewanted=all&_r=0

Tavernise, Sabrina. 2012. "Life Spans Shrink for Least-Educated Whites in the U.S." *New York Times*, September 20. Available online at www.nytimes.com/2012/09/21/us/life-expectancy-for-less-educated-whites-in-us-is-shrinking.html?pagewanted=all&_r=0

Tavernise, Sabrina. 2013. "Caesarean Deliveries Vary Widely, Study Finds." *New York Times*, March 4.

Taylor, Alan. 2001. *American Colonies*. New York: Penguin.

Taylor, Kate. 2013. "Sex on Campus: She Can Play That Game, Too." *New York Times*, July 12. Available online at www.nytimes.com/2013/07/14/fashion/sex-on-campus-she-can-play-that-game-too.html?_r=0

Teetzel, Sarah. 2011. "Rules and Reform: Eligibility, Gender Differences, and the Olympic Games." *Sports in Society* 14: 386–398.

Tembon, Mercy. 2008. "Overview." In Mercy Tembon and Lucia Fort (eds.) *Girls' Education in the 21st Century: Gender Equality, Empowerment, and Economic Growth*. Washington, DC: The World Bank, pp. 3–22.

Tetrault, Lisa. 2014. *The Myth of Seneca Falls: Memory and the Women's Suffrage Movement, 1848–1898*. Chapel Hill: University of North Carolina Press.

Thackston, W.M., trans. 2002. *The Baburnama: Memoirs of Babur, Prince and Emperor*. New York: Modern Library.

Thakur, Sunita. 2008. "India's Acid Victims Demand Justice," *BBC News*, April 9. Available online at http://news.bbc.co.uk/2/hi/south_asia/7270568.stm

Thaler, Richard H. 2013. "Breadwinning Wives and Nervous Husbands." *New York Times*, June 1. Available online at www.nytimes.com/2013/06/02/business/breadwinner-wives-and-nervous-husbands.html?pagewanted=all

Thappa, Devinder Mohan and Munisamy Malathi. 2004. "Skin Color Matters in India." *Pigment International* 1(1): 2–4. Available online at www.readcube.com/articles/10.4103/2349-5847.135419

Thomas, Sue, and Susan Welch. 2001. "The Impact of Women in State Legislatures: Numerical and Organizational Strength" In Susan J. Carroll (ed.) *The Impact of Women in Public Office*. Bloomington: Indiana University Press, pp. 166–181.

Thompson, Maxine and Verna Keith. 2001. "The Blacker the Berry: Gender, Skin Tone, Self-Esteem and Self-Efficacy." *Gender & Society* 15: 336–357.

Thompson, Roger. 1986. *Sex in Middlesex: Popular Mores in a Massachusetts County, 1649–1699*. Amherst: University of Massachusetts Press.

Thompson, Shona. 2003. "Women and Sport in New Zealand." In Ilse Hartmann-Tews and Gertrud Pfister (eds.) *Sport and Women: Social Issues in International Perspective*. London: Routledge, pp. 252–265.

Tick, Edward. 2005. *War and the Soul: Healing Our Nation's Veterans from Post-Traumatic Stress Disorder*. Wheaton, IL: Quest Books.

Tiggemann, M. and B. McGill. 2004. "The Role of Social Comparison in the Effect of Magazine Advertisements on Women's Mood and Body Dissatisfaction." *Journal of Social & Clinical Psychology* 23: 23–44.

Tiggemann, M., and A. Slater. 2004. "Thin Ideals in Music Television: A Source of Social Comparison and Body Dissatisfaction." *International Journal of Eating Disorders* 35: 48–58.

Tiku, Nitasha. 2014. "How to Get Girls into Coding." *New York Times*, May 31.

Timmons, Heather and Sruthi Gottipati. 2012. "Indian Women March: 'That Girl Could Have Been Any One of Us'," *New York Times*, December 30. Available online at www.nytimes.com/2012/12/31/world/asia/rape-incites-women-to-fight-culture-in-india.html?pagewanted=1&_r=0&ref=world

Tolbert, Caroline J. and Gertrude A. Steurnagel. 2001. "Women Lawmakers, State Mandates, and Women's Health." *Women and Politics* 22(2): 1–39.

Tompkins, Jane P. 1985. *Sensational Designs: The Cultural Work of American Fiction, 1790–1860.* New York: Oxford University Press.

Toosi, Mitra. 2002. "A Century of Change: The U.S. Labor Force, 1950–2050." *Monthly Labor Review,* May: 15–28.

Torregrosa, Luisita Lopez. 2012. "Latin America Opens Up to Equality." *New York Times,* May 1. Available online at www.nytimes.com/2012/05/02/world/americas/02iht-letter02.html?_r=0

Trible, Phyllis. 1984. *Texts of Terror: Literary-Feminist Readings of Biblical Narratives.* Minneapolis, MN: Fortress Press.

True, Jacqui. 2012. *The Political Economy of Violence Against Women.* New York: Oxford University Press.

Truman, Jennifer, Lynn Langton, and Michael Planty. 2013. "Criminal Victimization, 2012." Washington, DC: U.S. Department of Justice. Available online at www.bjs.gov/content/pub/pdf/cv12.pdf

Trussell, J., N. Henry, F. Hassan, A. Prezioso, A. Law, and A. Filonenko. 2013. "Burden of Unintended Pregnancy in the United States: Potential Savings with Increased Use of Long-Acting Reversible Contraception." *Contraception* 87(2): 154–161.

Tsui, Ming. 2007. "Gender and Mathematics Achievement in China and the United States." *Gender Issues* 24: 1–20.

Tsui, Ming and Lynne Rich. 2002. "The Only Child and Educational Opportunity for Girls in Urban China." *Gender & Society* 16: 74–92.

Tuana, Nancy, ed. 1989. *Feminism and Science.* Bloomington: Indiana University Press.

Turner, Jacob. 2011. "Sex and the Spectacle of Music Videos: An Examination of the Portrayal of Race and Sexuality in Music Videos." *Sex Roles* 64: 173–191.

Tyack, David and Elisabeth Hansot. 1992. *Learning Together: A History of Coeducation in the Public Schools.* New York: Russell Sage Foundation.

Ulrich, Laurel Thatcher. 1982. *Good Wives: Image and Reality in the Lives of Women in Northern New England, 1650–1750.* New York: Knopf.

Ulrich, Laurel Thatcher. 1990. *A Midwife's Tale: The Life of Martha Ballard, Based on Her Diary, 1785–1812.* New York: Knopf.

UNAIDS. 2012. "UNAIDS Report on the Global AIDS Epidemic." Available online at www.unaids.org/en/media/unaids/contentassets/documents/epidemiology/2012/gr2012/20121120_UNAIDS_Global_Report_2012_with_annexes_en.pdf

UNDP (United Nations Development Programme). 2013a. "Table 4: Gender Inequality Index." Available online at http://hdr.undp.org/en/content/gender-inequality-index-gii

UNDP. 2013b. "Citizen Security with a Human Face: Evidence and Proposals for Latin America." New York: UNDP.

UNDP. 2014. "Gender Inequality Index." Available online at http://hdr.undp.org/en/data

UNECE Statistical Database. n.d. Available online at http://w3.unece.org/pxweb/dialog/varval.asp?ma=003_GEWEEmplSectSPN_r&path=../database/STAT/30-GE/03-WorkAndeconomy/&lang=1&ti=Employment+by+public+and+private+sector%2C+sex

UNESCO. 2010. "Adult and Youth Literacy: Global Trends in Gender Parity." Available online at www.uis.unesco.org/FactSheets/Documents/Fact_Sheet_2010_Lit_EN.pdf

UNESCO. 2011. "UNESCO and Education." Available online at http://unesdoc.unesco.org/images/0021/002127/212715e.pdf

UNFPA. 2012. "Maternal Health Thematic Fund: Annual Report 2012." New York: UNFPA.

UNICEF. 2011. "Regional Overview for the Middle East and North Africa: MENA Gender Equality Profile." Available online at www.unicef.org/gender/files/REGIONAL-Gender-Equality-Profile-2011.pdf

UNICEF. 2013. "Female Genital Mutilation/Cutting." Available online at www.unicef.org/media/files/FGCM_Lo_res.pdf

UNICEF. 2014. "India: Nutrition." Available online at www.unicef.org/india/children_2356.htm

Uniform Crime Reporting Statistics. 2013. Available online at www.ucrdatatool.gov/

United Nations. 2000. "United Nations Millennium Declaration." September 18. Available online at www.unmillenniumproject.org/documents/ares552e.pdf

United Nations. 2013. "World Contraceptive Patterns, 2013." Available online at www.un.org/en/development/desa/population/publications/pdf/family/worldContraceptivePatternsWallChart2013.pdf

United Nations. 2014a. "The Millennium Development Goals Report, 2014." New York: United Nations.

Available online at www.undp.org/content/dam/undp/library/MDG/english/UNDP%20MDG%20Report%202014%20EN%20Final.pdf

United Nations. 2014b. "We Can End Poverty: Millennium Development Goals and Beyond 2015." Available online at www.un.org/millenniumgoals/

United Nations Population Division (UNPD). 2013. "Total Fertility." Available online at http://esa.un.org/unpd/wpp/Excel-Data/fertility.htm

United Nations Population Division (UNPD). 2013. "World Fertility Patterns 2013." Available at http://www.u.org/en/development/desa/population/publications/fertility/fertility-patterns-2013.shtml

United Nations Statistical Division. 2011. "Divorces and Crude Divorce Rates." Available online at http://unstats.un.org/unsd/demographic/sconcerns/mar/mar2.htm

Univision. 2014. "Voice of the People." Available online at www.univision.com/interactivos/openpage/2014-02-06/la-voz-del-pueblo-matriz-1

UN News Centre. 2013. "Deputy UN Chief Calls for Urgent Action to Tackle Global Sanitation Crisis." March 21. Available online at www.un.org/apps/news/story.asp?NewsID=44452#.VBh1Gi5dUi4

UN News Centre. 2014. "Some 437,000 People Murdered Worldwide in 2012, UN Crime Agency Reports." April 10. Available online at www.un.org/apps/news/story.asp?NewsID=47544#.U_YWnbxdUi5

UN Treaty Collection. 2013. "Convention on the Elimination of All Forms of Discrimination Against Women." Available online at https://treaties.un.org/Pages/ViewDetails.aspx?src=TREATY&mtdsg_no=IV-8&chapter=4&lang=en#17

USADA (United States Anti-Doping Agency). 2012. "True Sport: What We Stand to Lose in Our Obsession to Win." Available online at www.truesport.org/library/documents/about/true_sport_report/True-Sport-Report.pdf

USAID. 2012. "Gender Equality and Female Empowerment Policy." Available online at www.usaid.gov/sites/default/files/documents/1870/GenderEquality Policy.pdf

U.S. Bureau of the Census. 1975. *Historical Statistics of the United States*. Washington, DC.

U.S. Census Bureau. 2012a. "Annual Estimates of the Resident Population." Available online at www.census.gov/popest/data/national/asrh/2012/index.html

U.S. Census Bureau. 2012b. "Table 695. Money Income of Families – Number and Distribution by Race and Hispanic Origin" Available online at www.census.gov/compendia/statab/2012/tables/12s0695.pdf

U.S. Census Bureau. 2012c. "Table 713. People Below Poverty Level by Selected Characteristics: 2009." Available online at www.census.gov/compendia/statab/2012/tables/12s0713.pdf

U.S. Census Bureau. 2012d. "Table 59. Households, Families, Subfamilies, and Married Couples: 1980 to 2010." Available online at www.census.gov/compendia/statab/2012/tables/12s0059.pdf

U.S. Census Bureau. 2013a. "Educational Attainment in the United States: 2012 – Detailed Tables." Available online at www.census.gov/hhes/socdemo/education/data/cps/2012/tables.html

U.S. Census Bureau. 2013b. "People in Poverty by Selected Characteristics: 2011 and 2012." Available online at www.census.gov/hhes/www/poverty/data/incpovhlth/2012/table3.pdf

U.S. Census Bureau. 2013c. "Table 1. Educational Attainment of the Population 18 Years and Over, by Age, Sex, Race, and Hispanic Origin: 2013." Available online at www.census.gov/hhes/socdemo/education/data/cps/2013/tables.html

U.S. Census Bureau. 2013d. "Voting and Registration." Available online at www.census.gov/hhes/www/socdemo/voting/publications/historical/index.html

U.S. Census Bureau. 2014a. "Annual Estimates of the Resident Population by Sex, Race, and Hispanic Origin for the United States, States, and Counties: April 1, 2010 to July 1, 2013." Available online at http://factfinder.census.gov/faces/tableservices/jsf/pages/productview.xhtml?src=bkmk

U.S. Census Bureau. 2014b. "Educational Attainment in the United States: 2012 – Detailed Tables." Available online at www.census.gov/hhes/socdemo/education/data/cps/2012/tables.html

U.S. Census Bureau. 2014c. "Table 599. Employment Status of Women by Marital Status and Presence and Age of Children." Available online at www.census.gov/compendia/statab/cats/labor_force_employment_earnings.html

U.S. Census Bureau. 2014d. "Table P-2. Race and Hispanic Origin of People by Median Income and Sex." Available online at www.census.gov/hhes/www/income/data/historical/people/

U.S. Census Bureau. 2014e. "QuickFacts" Available online at http://quickfacts.census.gov/qfd/states/00000.html

U.S. Department of Agriculture. 2013. "Household Food Security in the United States in 2012." September. Available online at www.ers.usda.gov/publications/err-economic-research-report/err155.aspx#.U3S6xOCE7ww

U.S. Department of State. 2012. "Pakistan 2012 Human Rights Report." Available online at www.state.gov/documents/organization/204621.pdf

U.S. Department of State. 2013. "Trafficking in Persons Report." Available online at www.state.gov/documents/organization/210737.pdf

Valocchi, Stephen. 2005. "Not Yet Queer Enough: The Lessons of Queer Theory for the Sociology of Gender and Sexuality." *Gender & Society* 19: 750–770.

Van Creveld, Martin. 2008. *The Culture of War*. New York: Random House.

Van Syckle, Katie. 2014. "The Tiny Police Department in Southern Oregon that Plans to End Campus Rape." *New York Magazine*: The Cut, November 9. Available online at http://nymag.com/thecut/2014/11/can-this-police-department-help-end-campus-rape.html

Velasquez-Manoff, Moises. 2013. "Status and Stress." *New York Times*, July 27.

Vennum, Thomas. 1994. *American Indian Lacrosse: Little Brother of War*. Baltimore: Johns Hopkins University Press.

VIDA. 2011. "The Count 2010." May 16. Available online at www.vidaweb.org/the-count-2010/

Volpp, Leti. 2005. "Feminism versus Multiculturalism." In Natalie J. Sokoloff with Christina Pratt (eds.) *Domestic Violence at the Margins: Readings on Race, Class, Gender, and Culture*. New Brunswick, NJ: Rutgers University Press, pp. 39–49.

Wade, Lisa. 2013. "American Men's Hidden Crisis: They Need More Friends!" *Salon*, December 7. Available online at www.salon.com/2013/12/08/american_mens_hidden_crisis_they_need_more_friends/

Wadud, Amina. 1999. *Qur'an and Woman: Rereading the Sacred Text from a Woman's Perspective*. New York: Oxford University Press.

Wadud, Amina. 2006. *Inside the Gender Jihad: Women's Reform in Islam*. Oxford: OneWorld.

Wagner, Sally Roesch. 2001. *Sisters in Spirit: The Iroquois Influence on Early American Feminists*. Summertown, TN: Native Voices.

Walker, Alice. 1983a. *The Color Purple*. New York: Washington Square Books.

Walker, Alice. 1983b. *In Search of Our Mothers' Gardens: Womanist Prose*. San Diego, CA: Harcourt, Brace, Jovanovich.

Walker, Rebecca, ed. 1995. *To Be Real: Telling the Truth and Changing the Face of Feminism*. New York: Anchor.

Walk Free Foundation. 2014. *The Global Slavery Index 2014*. Available online at http://d3mj66ag90b5fy.cloudfront.net/wp-content/uploads/2014/11/Global_Slavery_Index_2014_final_lowres.pdf

Wallace, Michele. 1978. *Black Macho and the Myth of the Superwoman*. New York: The Dial Press.

Wallis, Cara. 2011. "Performing Gender: A Content Analysis of Gender Display in Music Videos." *Sex Roles* 64: 160–172.

Wallis, Jim. 2005. *God's Politics: Why the Right Gets It Wrong and the Left Doesn't Get It*. San Francisco: HarperCollins.

Walsh, Declan. 2014. "Taliban Besiege Pakistan School, Leaving 145 Dead." *New York Times*, December 17.

Walters, Mikel L., Jieru Chen, and Matthew J. Breiding. 2013. "The National Intimate Partner and Sexual Violence Survey (NISVS): 2010 Findings on Victimization by Sexual Orientation." Atlanta, GA: Centers for Disease Control and Prevention. Available online at www.cdc.gov/violenceprevention/pdf/nisvs_sofindings.pdf

Waltman, Max. 2012. "Criminalize Only the Buying of Sex." *New York Times*, April 20. Available online at www.nytimes.com/roomfordebate/2012/04/19/is-legalized-prostitution-safer/criminalize-buying-not-selling-sex

Walton, Dawnie. 2013. "ESSENCE's Images Study: Bonus Insights." *Essence*, October 7. Available online at www.essence.com/2013/10/07/essence-images-study-bonus-insights

Walvin, James. 2005. *Atlas of Slavery*. New York: Routledge.

Wang, Shirley Koshin. 2010. "Violence and HIV/AIDS: Violence against Women and Girls as a Cause and Consequence of HIV/AIDS." *Duke Journal of Gender Law and Policy* 17: 313–332.

Wang, Wendy, Kim Parker, and Paul Taylor. 2013. "Breadwinner Moms." Pew Social and Demographic Trends. Available online at www.pewsocialtrends.org/2013/05/29/breadwinner-moms/

Warner, Judith. 2005. *Perfect Madness: Motherhood in the Age of Anxiety*. New York: Riverhead Books.

Warren, Elizabeth and Amelia Warren Tyagi. 2003. *The Two-Income Trap: Why Middle-Class Parents Are Going Broke*. New York: Basic Books.

Washington, Harriet A. 2007. *Medical Apartheid: The Dark History of Medical Experimentation on Black Americans from Colonial Times to the Present*. New York: Doubleday.

Wax, Emily. 2005. "Virginity Becomes a Commodity in Uganda's War Against AIDS." *Post*, October 7, p. A01.

Waylen, Georgina. 2007. *Engendering Transitions: Women's Mobilization, Institutions, and Gender Outcomes*. New York: Oxford University Press.

Weatherford, Carole Boston, and Kadir Nelson. 2006. *Moses: When Harriet Tubman Led Her People To Freedom*. New York: Hyperion Books.

Webb, Stephen Saunders. 1984. *1676: The End of American Independence* New York: Knopf.

WEF (World Economic Forum). 2012. "The Global Gender Gap Report 2012." Geneva: World Economic Forum.

WEF. 2013. "The Global Gender Gap Report 2013." Geneva: World Economic Forum.

WEF. 2014. "The Global Gender Gap Report 2014." Geneva: World Economic Forum.

Weitzman, Lenore, Deborah Eifler, Elizabeth Hokado, and Catherine Ross. 1972. "Sex-Role Socialization in Picture Books for Preschool Children." *American Journal of Sociology* 77: 1125–1150.

Welborne, Bozena. 2010. "An A for Cosmetics and a C for Substance: Assessing Gender Quotas in the Middle East and North Africa." APSA 2010 Annual Meeting Paper. Available online at http://ssrn.com/abstract=1642733

Welchman, Lynn and Sara Hossain, eds. 2005. *"Honour": Crimes, Paradigms, and Violence Against Women*. New York: Zed Books.

West, Candace and Don Zimmerman. 1987. "Doing Gender." *Gender & Society* 1: 125–151.

Western, Bruce. 2006. *Punishment and Inequality in America*. New York: Russell Sage.

Wetzstein, Cheryl. 2013. "Supreme Court Strikes Down Obama-Backed 'Prostitution Pledge' in AIDS Funding." *Washington Times*, June 20.

White, Deborah Gray. 1998. *Too Heavy a Load: Black Women in Defense of Themselves, 1894–1994*. New York: Norton.

White, Evelyn C., ed. 1990. *The Black Women's Health Book: Speaking for Ourselves*. Seattle, WA: Seal Press.

White, Kevin. 1993. *The First Sexual Revolution: The Emergence of Male Heterosexuality in Modern America*. New York: New York University Press.

White House Task Force to Protect Students from Sexual Assault. 2014. "Not Alone." Available online at www.whitehouse.gov/sites/default/files/docs/report_0.pdf

WHO (World Health Organization). 2004. "Gender and Mental Health Research." Available online at www.who.int/gender/documents/en/mentalhealthlow.pdf

WHO. 2005. "Violence Against Sex Workers and HIV Prevention." Available online at www.who.int/gender/documents/sexworkers.pdf

WHO. 2011a. "Global HIV/AIDS Response. Epidemic update and health progress towards Universal Access." Progress report 2011. Available online at www.unaids.org/en/media/unaids/contentassets/documents/unaidspublication/2011/20111130_ua_report_en.pdf

WHO. 2011b. "Unsafe Abortion." Geneva: World Health Organization. Available online at http://www.whqlibdoc.who.int/publications/2011/9789241501118_eng.pdf

WHO. 2012. "Prevention and Treatment of HIV and Other Sexually Transmitted Infections for Sex Workers in Low- and Middle-Income Countries: Policy Brief." Available online at http://apps.who.int/iris/bitstream/10665/77744/1/WHO_HIV_2012.19_eng.pdf?ua=1

WHO. 2013. "Life Expectancy by Country." Available online at http://apps.who.int/gho/data/node.main.688?lang=en

WHO. 2014a. "Estimated Deaths ('000) by Cause, Sex, and WHO Member State, 2012." Available online at www.who.int/healthinfo/global_burden_disease/estimates/en/index1.html

WHO. 2014b. "Gender and Women's Mental Health." Available online at www.who.int/mental_health/prevention/genderwomen/en/

WHO. 2014c. "Global Status Report on Alcohol and Health, 2014." Available online at www.who.int/substance_abuse/publications/global_alcohol_report/msb_gsr_2014_1.pdf

WHO, UNICEF, UNFPA, and The World Bank. 2012. "Trends in Maternal Mortality: 1990 to 2010." Available online at www.unfpa.org/webdav/site/global/shared/documents/publications/2012/Trends_in_maternal_mortality_A4-1.pdf

Wilchins, Riki Anne. 2004. *Queer Theory, Gender Theory: An Instant Primer*. Los Angeles: Alyson Books.

Wildsmith, Elizabeth, Nicole R. Steward-Streng, and Jennifer Manlove. 2011. "Childbearing Outside of Marriage: Estimates and Trends in the United States." Washington, DC: Child Trends. Available online at www.childtrends.org/wp-content/uploads/2013/02/Child_Trends-2011_11_01_RB_Nonmarital CB.pdf

Wilkerson, Isabel. 2010. *The Warmth of Other Suns: The Epic Story of America's Great Migration*. New York: Vintage Books.

Wilkinson, Richard, and Kate Pickett. 2009. *The Spirit Level: Why Greater Equality Makes Societies Stronger*. New York: Bloomsbury Press.

Williams, C.L. 1992. "The Glass Escalator: Hidden Advantages for Men in the 'Female Professions.'" *Social Problems* 39: 253–267.

Williams, Walter L. 1986. *The Spirit and the Flesh: Sexual Diversity in American Indian Culture*. Boston: Beacon Press.

Williamson, Joel. 1986. *A Rage for Order: Black-White Relations in the American South since Emancipation*. New York: Oxford University Press.

Wilson, William Julius. 1996. *When Work Disappears: The World of the New Urban Poor*. New York: Knopf.

Wingfield, A.H. 2009. "Racializing the Glass Escalator: Reconsidering Men's Experiences with Women's Work." *Gender & Society* 23: 5–26.

Winner, Brooke, Jeffrey Peipert, Qiuhong Zhao, Christina Buckel, Tessa Madden, Jenifer E. Allsworth, and Gina M. Secura. 2012. "Effectiveness of Long-Acting Reversible Contraception." *New England Journal of Medicine* 366: 1998–2007.

Wittberg, Patricia. 2012. "A Lost Generation?" *America: The National Catholic Review*, February 20. Available online at http://americamagazine.org/node/150414

WMC (Women's Media Center). 2014. "The Status of Women in the U.S. Media 2014." Available online at http://wmc.3cdn.net/2e85f9517dc2bf164e_htm62xgan.pdf

Wolf, Naomi. 1992. *The Beauty Myth*. New York: Knopf Doubleday.

Women's Campaign Forum. 2007. "Vote With Your Purse." Available online at www.wcffoundation.org/assets/documents/wcff-vote-with-your-purse-2007.pdf

World Bank. 2011a. *Gender Equality and Development*. Washington, DC: World Bank.

World Bank. 2011b. "Reproductive Health at a Glance: Nigeria." Available online at www-wds.worldbank.org/external/default/WDSContentServer/WDSP/IB/2011/07/28/000333038_20110728005114/Rendered/PDF/629440BRIEF0Ni0BOX0361514B00PUBLIC0.pdf

World Bank. 2012. "Life Expectancy at Birth, Male" and "Life Expectancy at Birth, Female." Available online at http://search.worldbank.org/data?qterm=life+expectancy+gender&language=&format=

World Bank. 2013a. "GDP Per Capita." Available online at http://data.worldbank.org/indicator/NY.GDP.PCAP.CD

World Bank. 2013b. "Women, Business, and the Law 2014." Washington, DC: World Bank. Available online at http://wbl.worldbank.org/u/media/FPDKM/WBL/Documents/Reports/2014/Women-Business-and-the-Law-2014-FullReport.pdf

World Bank. 2014. "Fertility Rate, Total (Births per Woman)" Available online at http://data.worldbank.org/indicator/SP.DYN.TFRT.IN

World Bank Data. 2014. "School Enrollment, Secondary (% Gross)." Available online at http://data.worldbank.org/indicator/SE.SEC.ENRR

"Worldwide Guide to Women in Leadership." 2014. Available online at www.guide2womenleaders.com/

Wright, Robin. 2011. *Rock the Casbah: Rage and Rebellion Across the Islamic World*. New York: Simon & Schuster.

Yacoobi, Sakena. 2008. "Building a Better Future for Afghanistan through Female Education." In Mercy Tembon and Lucia Fort (eds.) *Girls' Education in the 21st Century: Gender Equality, Empowerment, and Economic Growth*. Washington, DC: The World Bank, pp. 181–200.

Yang, Bong-Min. 2001. "The National Pension Scheme of the Republic of Korea." Washington, DC: World Bank Institute.

Yellin, Emily. 2005. *Our Mothers' War: American Women At Home and at the Front During World War II*. New York: Free Press.

YouGov. 2013. "Has 'Feminist' Become a Dirty Word?" May 1. Available online at http://today.yougov.com/news/2013/05/01/has-feminist-become-dirty-word/

Young, Cathy. 2014. "Feminist Face-Off." *Boston Globe*, September 2.

Young, Louise M. 1989. *In the Public Interest: The League of Women Voters, 1920–1970*. New York: Greenwood Press.

Yousafzai, Malala with Christina Lamb. 2014. *I Am Malala: The Girl Who Stood Up for Education and Was Shot by the Taliban*. New York: Little, Brown & Company.

Zagano, Phyllis. 2012. "A Woman on the Altar: Can the Church Ordain Women Deacons?" *U.S. Catholic* 77(1): 18–21. Available online at www.uscatholic.org/church/2011/11/woman-altar-can-church-ordain-women-deacons

Zagarri, Rosemarie. 2015. *A Woman's Dilemma: Mercy Otis Warren and the American Revolution*, 2nd edn. Malden, MA: Wiley-Blackwell.

Zarrett, Nicole, K. Fay, Y. Li, J. Carrano, E. Phelps, and R.M. Lerner. 2009. "More than Child's Play: Variable- and Pattern-Centered Approaches for Examining Effects of Sports Participation on Youth Development." *Developmental Psychology* 45: 368–382.

Zhou, Jinghao. 2003. "Keys to Women's Liberation in China: An Historical Overview." *Journal of International Women's Studies* 5: 67–77.

Zikmund, Barbara Brown. 2003. "UCC Celebrates an Anniversary: 150 Years of Women Clergy." *UCNews*, September. Available online at www.ucc.org/ucnews/sep03/ucc-celebrates-an.html

Zimmerman, Jonathan. 2014. "Sexual Assault on Campus and the Curse of the Hookup Culture." *Los Angeles Times*, May 7.

Zinser, Lynn. 2008. "Phone Call from China Transformed '84 Games." *New York Times*, July 14. Available online at www.nytimes.com/2008/07/14/sports/olympics/14olympics.html?pagewanted=1&mabReward=relbias:r,{&_r=1%221%22:%22RI:6%

INDEX

Figures and photos are indicated by *italic* page numbers; boxes and tables by **bold** numbers.